WASHINGTON
TERRITORY

WASHINGTON TERRITORY

ROBERT E. FICKEN

WSU PRESS

Washington State University Press
Pullman, Washington

Washington State University Press
PO Box 645910
Pullman, Washington 99164-5910
Phone: 800-354-7360
Fax: 509-335-8568
E-mail: wsupress@wsu.edu
Web site: www.wsu.edu/wsupress

Library of Congress Cataloging-in-Publication Data

Ficken, Robert E.
  Washington Territory / Robert E. Ficken.
    p. cm.
  Includes bibliographical references (p.   ) and index.
  ISBN 0-87422-249-4 (alk. paper)
    1. Washington (State)—History—To 1889. I. Title.

F891 .F496 2002
979.7'03—dc21   2002003120

Front cover: Oregon Steam Navigation Co. Engine No. 1 of the Middle Cascades railway, and
a map of early Washington—the territorial boundaries at the time included what is now
Idaho and parts of western Montana and Wyoming.

Back cover: Territorial Governor Isaac I. Stevens, and a view of the Hudson's Bay Co.'s
Ft. Vancouver and the U.S. Army's Vancouver Barracks.

Table of Contents

For
Matthew,
as he commences on the path
of young adulthood

Acknowledgments

The author is obliged to a number of institutions and individuals for vital assistance in the writing of this book. Much of the primary research was carried out in the various departments of the University of Washington Library in Seattle. Important documentation also came from the libraries of Washington State University and the University of Oregon, from the Washington State and Eastern Washington State historical societies and from the Oregon Historical Society. In Olympia, the Washington State Archives and the Washington State Library provided materials of relevance to the territorial period. The Seattle Federal Records Center was of particular importance for documents relating to the history of Indian-white relations in Washington Territory. The Minnesota Historical Society facilitated usage of the records of the Northern Pacific Railway and the Tacoma Public Library did the same in the case of the Tacoma Land Company.

Ed Nolan of the Washington State Historical Society kindly loaned microfilm copies of the W. Milnor Roberts, Henry Villard and Jay Cooke papers. Among archivists, Richard Berner and Karyl Winn of the University of Washington and Joyce Justice of the Federal Records Center have, in particular, been of primary importance in the preparation of this and earlier historical efforts. The influence of Robert E. Burke remains constant. The Washington State Historical Society, the Washington State University Library and the Issaquah Historical Society provided excellent assistance in the assembly of illustrations. At Washington State University Press, Keith Petersen encouraged the project in its early stages and Glen Lindeman did an outstanding job in seeing it through to completion.

Matthew Ficken, who graduates from high school in June 2002, provided continual and extraordinarily patient assistance in computer-related areas. Lorraine, the author's companion in the positive and negative adventures of life, supplied, as in the past, the necessary though oft-overlooked inspiration for the book's conception and completion.

Introduction

C REATED IN 1853, Washington Territory expired, after a political life of thirty-six years, upon admission to the Union in 1889. Only five of the western territories created after 1850, Alaska and Hawaii included, languished longer in dependent status. On average, the territorial existence for all nineteen post-1850 states spanned twenty-seven years. Limited to the thirteen admissions prior to 1890, the figure declines sharply to eighteen years. Only the Dakotas, at thirty-one years, came close to matching the Washington figure. The five longer-lived entities on the complete list, moreover, were the product of peculiar circumstances, social, political and/or geographical. Utah was denied statehood due to the presumed eccentricities of its Mormon population. The Hispanic Southwest, Arizona and New Mexico, appeared ineligible, at least to Anglo-Americans, because of what the *Seattle Post-Intelligencer* termed "the foreign character" of a society "largely composed of Spaniards and half-breeds."[1] Alaska and Hawaii were too distant from the rest of the country, the former with too few people and the latter with too many Asians and Polynesians.

In many respects, Washington's long territorial servitude was entirely undeserved. Despite a relatively small settler population base, Puget Sound at an early date supplied lumber to California and the nations and colonies of the Pacific Rim. Eastern Washington emerged in the 1870s as a major producer of grain, supplying wheat and flour to regional mines and, via shipment through Portland, distant markets from San Francisco to Liverpool. Washington featured industrial development and commercial agriculture and was economically deserving, at the least, long before the year of admission, 1889.

Why, then, did Washington remain a territory for thirty-six years, while neighboring Oregon passed from territorial status in 1848 to admission in 1859? Historians often point to the partisan difficulties experienced by a Republican territory seeking admission during an era in which at least the presidency or one or the other houses of Congress was in Democratic hands. Moreover, deliberate standards, focusing on population and other supposedly objective criteria, prevailed to a greater extent in the later nineteenth century than in the earlier period when Oregon, Nevada and Colorado were admitted. Although the politically mechanistic argument cannot be ignored, other factors were also of consequence to the course of events, or non-events. Contemporary observers, for one thing, were less convinced than hindsight analysts of Washington's ironclad Republicanism. The territory, after all, elected a *Democratic* congressional delegate in 1884 and 1886.[2]

What really mattered was the lack of faith in Washington exhibited over many years by territorial residents themselves. Washington was not, in fact, politically viable. The complete lack of communications over the Cascades prevented unity, in politics and in economics. As the result of geography and lack of transportation, Washington was as much of a special, or peculiar case as Utah or New Mexico. For decades, Puget Sound, the focal point of western Washington, was, from the ownership and marketing patterns of the lumber industry, a virtual San Francisco hinterland. Eastern Washington, meanwhile, depended on the Columbia River, the downstream route to Portland, for supplies and markets. The region west of the Cascades was, for all practical purposes, an extension of California. The region east of the Cascades was a satellite of Oregon. Reflecting the contrasting focal points, movements for division of the territory were a regular facet of public affairs. So, too, was the ongoing rivalry between Portland and the several Puget Sound ports for control of the interior trade and commercial dominance of the Pacific Northwest.[3]

The key factor making Washington eligible for statehood was completion of the Northern Pacific Railroad over the Cascades to Commencement Bay on Puget Sound. The immigration of large numbers of people from the East instantly became possible, as did the selling of lumber and wheat on a west-to-east basis. Directly linking Spokane—or Spokane Falls to use the correct name of the times—with Tacoma, the Palouse and the Coeur d'Alene with the Sound and the Strait of Juan de Fuca, the railroad broke the Columbia River monopoly on cross-regional trade, fatally undermining Portland's economic leadership of the Pacific Northwest. The advantage in a long struggle for mastery shifted dramatically from Portland to Puget Sound, from fresh water to salt water.

Economics—lumber and wheat and railroading—and the relation between commercial progress and environment provide the main subject matter for Washington Territory history and the principal linkage between that history and post-1889 developments. Just as politically aware individuals made inevitable comparisons to the American Revolution and George III, settlers in general complained of monopolies and outsider domination. The Hudson's Bay Company, target of missionaries, pioneers, and Governor Isaac Stevens, was only the first in a series of "foreign" evil corporate entities. The great early sawmills, built in the interest of gold rush California, were, complained a Puget Sound newspaper, "controlled by irresponsible SHARPERS and SPECULATORS, resident in...San Francisco." The Oregon Steam Navigation Company, and its successor the Oregon Railway & Navigation Company, supposedly condemned Washington settlers to excessive passenger and freight rates and the dictation of Portland. Another firm carrying the discordant name of the rival state, the Oregon

Improvement Company, focused its designs upon Puget Sound. And the greatest corporate entity of all, the Northern Pacific Railroad, provoked a legion of critics on both sides of the Cascades.[4]

On the secondary field of political affairs, Washington experienced the same unhappy developments as other places west of the Mississippi. The major offices were invariably filled by outsiders, appointed by distant administrations according to the cynical dictates of the spoils system.[5] Elected locally, the congressional delegate and territorial legislators exercised little real authority. Preoccupied with the business of everyday life, most settlers ignored politics. The earliest proposals for admission to the Union were widely ignored. Barely half the electorate approved an abortive state constitution in 1878. Only the railroad-related demographic and economic growth of the 1880s made Washington a truly united commonwealth and persuaded the populace to endorse admission by a meaningful margin.

The history of Washington Territory, Elisha Ferry noted in his inaugural address as the state's first elected governor, "remains to be written."[6] Although modern scholars have produced worthy biographies and specialized studies, the relevant chapters of H.H. Bancroft's 1890 all-in-one-volume history of Washington, Montana, and Idaho remain, for all their imperfections and biases, the closest approximation of a decent overall treatment. Researching and writing the present book, the author learned at difficult first-hand why earlier writers failed to undertake, much less complete, such a study. On the one hand, an enormous amount of documentary material was available. On the other, large gaps in the evidentiary record could only be filled through hard, long-term digging.

Begun in some innocence of the difficulty of the task commenced, this history of Washington Territory was finished in the manner of a marathon, in exhausted satisfaction of a work decently, if imperfectly, accomplished.

Robert E. Ficken
Issaquah, Washington

Arthur A. Denny. *Washington State Historical Society, Tacoma*

Chapter One

The Best Portion of Oregon

I have no kind of doubt but that the best portion of Oregon lies north of the Columbia.—William Strong[1]

FLOWING FROM A THICK-MUSCLED shoulder of Mount Rainier, the Cowlitz meets the great River of the West at a waterlogged point five dozen miles above the sea. Arguably the most important Columbia tributary below the Willamette, the Cowlitz River failed to impress nineteenth-century visitors. Navigation, by canoe, was limited to less than forty tortuous miles. During the greater part of the year, a settler diarist noted, the stream was "rather shallow and muddy." Travelers suffered from "blood-sucking mosquitoes" and complained of the "gloomy" surroundings. Biting insects and dreary scenery aside, the Cowlitz was the vital corridor, the extended portage, connecting southern and northern Oregon.[2]

Recognizing the corridor's strategic importance, Hudson's Bay Company traders and supply parties used the old "common Indian road" between the Columbia and Puget Sound. Organizing the Puget's Sound Agricultural Company, the firm placed prairie tracts near the head of canoe navigation on the Cowlitz and, on the southern Sound, at Fort Nisqually under the auspices of this subsidiary operation. Cowlitz Farm was "a respectable show," the U.S. naval explorer Charles Wilkes reported in 1841, featuring a thousand tidily cultivated acres, grist and sawmills, a dairy plant and the "large well hewed log house" occupied by the resident superintendent. Retired trappers, Indian laborers and overland immigrants, imported by the company in a settlement experiment predating the Oregon Trail, tended to the various chores of the place. The farm and Nisqually gave the British a solid demographic head start beyond the Columbia, pending resolution of the ancient and periodically contentious Oregon boundary question. English subjects outnumbered Yankees by a ten-to-one margin and the Hudson's Bay Company held the principal means of communication.[3]

Opening their own overland wagon trail in 1843, Americans escaped depression and uncertainty at home in favor of productive farms and better times in the distant Oregon Country. That year and in succeeding travel seasons, most immigrants went to the broad and fertile valley of the Willamette, heeding authoritative accounts warning settlers away from the land north of the Columbia. The dark region on the far side of the river, Thomas J. Farnham wrote on the basis of an 1839 Pacific Northwest tour, was "of little value except for its timber." The vast forests of towering fir and cedar, Farnham advised, were "so heavy and so matted with branches, as to require the arm of a Hercules to clear a farm…in an ordinary lifetime." Methodist missionary Gustavus Hines considered the enormous evergreen trees reliable indicators of inferior soil. "There are but few places," he confided to church friends in the East, "…where any thing can be raised."[4]

For a time, the Columbia, from old Fort Vancouver to Astoria's befogged environs, was the unofficial mile-wide boundary of American settlement. Englishman John R. Jackson, a butcher by trade, established the first claim beyond the river, several miles from Cowlitz Landing, in 1844. Little known to history, Jackson was widely respected by contemporaries, "one of northern Oregon's most energetic, enterprising and substantial citizens" and master of "the best farm on the route…to Olympia." Close behind, Americans took land along the lower Cowlitz in the neighborhood of Monticello, the "little skittering town" two miles above the stream's mouth. Exposed to regular flooding—the place was washed away altogether in 1867—Monticello enjoyed brief fame as the poorly sited seat of government for Lewis County, one of the two original Oregon Territory counties north of the Columbia.[5]

On the basis of intelligence from these cross-Columbia pioneers, thoughtful observers questioned the earlier reports critical of northern Oregon. "North of the Columbia, particularly in the vicinity of Puget's Sound," the Oregon City *Oregon Spectator* proclaimed, "the country, susceptible of settlement, is much more extensive, and the soil much better than before represented." Rumors of rich coal deposits, supposedly confirmed by testing of samples sent to California, contributed to the developing positive image of a previously maligned region. John Jackson provided further verification, writing that "the prairie land" bordering Puget Sound was "nowhere excelled, in those qualities which are peculiarly adapted to the great growth, and rare perfection of vegetables."[6]

Michael Simmons, James McAllister, David Kindred, Gabriel Jones and George Bush, a black man supposedly prevented from claiming land south of the Columbia by racist Oregonians, settled, with their wives and children, on Puget Sound in November 1845. After consulting the traders at Fort Nisqually, the Americans founded New Market, or Tumwater, on the Deschutes River. The falls site commanded, according to an early homesteader, "one of the best mill-streams I have ever seen falling about 75 feet in about 300 yards" before flowing to nearby tidewater. As advance scout and leader of the first families, the Kentucky-born Simmons merited, from personal friends and later historians, "the appellation of the Puget's Sound pioneer."[7]

Under orders from John McLoughlin, the chief factor at Vancouver, Fort Nisqually provided all manner of assistance to the Simmons party and to subsequent American arrivals by the Cowlitz trail. The New Market families received, noted a February 1846 entry in the post journal, "a bullock each" and "small supplies of coffee[,] sugar and molasses." Thereafter, a settler recalled, the English "allowed us anything we wanted out of the store that we could live on," taking shingles in partial repayment of the debt owed the establishment. When Simmons built a sawmill at the falls, Hudson's Bay donated the machinery and agreed to purchase his output. Although sales of rough lumber in Hawaii and California "glutted" those markets, as Nisqually trader William F. Tolmie complained, the relationship continued. Settler gratitude, especially with the 1846 boundary accord giving Oregon south of the 49th parallel to the United States, compensated, in terms of good will, for losses recorded in stiff-paged British account ledgers.[8]

Relying, for lack of an alternative, upon Hudson's Bay Company charity, settlers continued moving north through the Cowlitz corridor. Travel upstream from Monticello was by Indian canoe, with an out-of-doors overnight stay required. At the head of navigation, travelers with cash to spare rented horses for the final stage of the journey. By 1850, transportation was organized on an efficient basis. Edward Warbass, the owner of mercantile houses at Monticello and Cowlitz Landing, which he renamed, in a moment of infelicitous self-promotion, Warbassport, had "Battaux and Canoes running constantly." The proprietors of the "greatly improved" Cowlitz Hotel offered "saddle horses…at all times upon reasonable terms" and maintained a relay station for the exchange of tired mounts.[9]

American immigrants arrived "daily in good numbers to have 'a look at the Country,'" William F. Tolmie recorded in his official Fort Nisqually journal in the spring of 1847. Expanding upon the original settlement nucleus, newcomers took claims in close proximity to the English post. The Hudson's Bay Company protested the founding of Steilacoom, in particular, as a trespass upon its land, protected by the Anglo-American boundary agreement. When a U.S. citizen was killed after being caught in a crossfire between quarreling Indians at the fort, a regular Army garrison was established in 1849. "Steilacoom received the preference," Tolmie reported of this initial federal government presence on the Sound, "on account of the number of buildings already erected there."[10]

Poorly sited New Market was soon eclipsed as the center of American life on Puget Sound. "A Lowell in miniature" so far as industrial power was concerned, the Deschutes River falls were, unfortunately, two miles from practical ocean shipping. Locating what appeared to be a much better site for commercial development, Edmund Sylvester and Levi Smith founded Olympia on nearby Budd Inlet. "Right handy" for loading ships, Sylvester claimed, Olympia also turned out to be ill chosen. Tidal fluctuation in the constricted southern Sound was, to say the least, dramatic; there was a twenty-two foot differential between highest and lowest stages of the year. "Almost one half" the settlement was "subject to overflow" at normal high tide, local promoters admitted. Vessels anchored three-quarters of a mile offshore to avoid grounding at the ebb. For the moment, however, Olympia's position at the end of the overland route from the Columbia made it the focus of immigration and the leading choice for capital of a territorial government established in northern Oregon.[11]

Despite the early attractions of New Market, Steilacoom, and Olympia, the American presence in North Oregon—by 1850 the region's commonly used name—was modest, in both overall and relative terms. Contemporary estimates placed the non-Indian population at one thousand, divided between the right bank of the Columbia and the southernmost Sound. The U.S. share, according to longtime settler and jurist William Strong, "would not exceed 150 men, women and children." Official 1850 census figures affirmed that only 87 of the 192 adult Clark County residents had been born in the United States. For Lewis County, which covered both the Cowlitz corridor and Puget Sound, the ratio of American nativity, while slightly higher, was still a mere 157 out of 313 adults. As a practical matter, North Oregon remained, to a considerable extent, English territory.[12]

The American minority had two basic grievances, communications and foreign monopoly. Dependence upon "the miserable, aboriginal method of transportation from Monticello to Warbassport" retarded settlement north of the Columbia. White males supposedly refused to entrust wives, children and freight to Indians and their frail craft. As a result, Puget Sounders complained, "hundreds" of families opted to "remain in the Willamette Valley." Flooding, from heavy rain or sudden snowmelt, often closed the Cowlitz corridor. At such times, the normally sluggish stream turned "wild as a cataract." If North Oregon were ever to attain even an approximation of its potential, the region's friends insisted, a wagon road must be opened to the Sound and shallow draft steamers put into service on the Cowlitz.[13]

Future prospects also depended upon expelling the Hudson's Bay Company from North Oregon. Despite the considerable assistance extended them, John McLoughlin complained, immigrants were ungrateful and, indeed, "strongly prejudiced against us." Memories of the Revolution and the War of 1812, kept alive by the fulminations of expansionist politicians, explained, in part, the anti-English feeling. Neither the Anglo-American boundary agreement nor the creation of Oregon Territory in 1848, moreover, had any apparent impact upon the firm's economic predominance. "Business will of course go on as usual," Hudson's Bay officials privately noted, thanks to the treaty protection south of the 49th parallel. "Almost the whole direct foreign trade of the Territory is in their hands," Astoria customs clerk George Gibbs pointed out in reporting that the enterprise generated over $300,000 a year in "aggregate product." Between the demise of the fur trade and the firm's refusal to purchase made-in-Oregon goods, Gibbs and other critics asserted, "the proceeds of sales…are transmitted to England, where the stockholders reside, and create an annual drain of specie hence." The managers at Vancouver, Nisqually, and the other posts replicated, in foul undemocratic mode, "the manner of the absentee landlords of Ireland."[14]

Greedy foreigners appeared intent upon monopolizing Oregon's land, as well as its commerce. The English argued that the treaty guarantee covered all tracts claimed by the Hudson's Bay Company and the Puget's Sound Agricultural Company, including 167,000 acres tributary to Fort Nisqually. Outraged Americans insisted that protection extended only to acreage actually in use as of 1846. Supposedly relying upon "falsehoods and misrepresentations," the British appropriated land where "no human had molested one stick of nature's growth." Adding to the frustration of settlers, the United States declined, pending diplomatic negotiations, to survey areas within the Hudson's Bay claim. Attempting to evict "squatters" between the Nisqually and Puyallup rivers, company agents had no means of enforcing the private edict against settlement. Taking advantage of this weakness, "lawless" Americans stole stock and goods from Fort Nisqually and Cowlitz Farm.[15]

Without the slightest indication of embarrassment, American settlers formally castigated the Hudson's Bay Company. Assembled in November 1848 under the chairmanship of Michael Simmons, the citizens of New Market denounced the "misrepresentation and fraud" practiced by employees of a "monarchical government." Nisqually factor Tolmie, claimed resolutions adopted at the public meeting, sent "Spanish cattle known to be but little more domesticated than the…buffalo" upon the grazing tracts of U.S. citizens, sold shoddy made-in-England merchandise at inflated rates and "refused to furnish…sheep, at any price." Exhibiting similar indecent deliberation, the Oregon legislature accused the Hudson's Bay Company, in an 1849 memorial to Congress, of deliberately and maliciously retarding settlement beyond the Columbia.[16] North and south of the river, steady demographic change, in the form of an increasing American population, was counted upon as the most effective means of destroying an alien economic organism.

Approving the Oregon Donation Act in 1850, Congress incidentally set the northern portion of the territory on the road to independent political status. Secured by congressional delegate Samuel Thurston, the statute, as subsequently amended, granted 320 acres—640 acres if the recipient was married—to eligible adult white males establishing residence prior to 1856. Free and abundant acreage, unburdened by debt or disputation, was hard to resist, even in the contemporary context of the California gold rush. "Oregon is filling up with settlers beyond all former calculation," a federal official advised. Although the Donation Act was of greatest significance south of the Columbia, settlement north of the river advanced at an impressive rate. Many of the individuals and families bound for Puget Sound traversed "the great thoroughfare," as Michael Simmons insisted upon calling the traditional Cowlitz route. Increasing numbers, particularly those with machinery and other bulky goods, took a roundabout alternative, by sea out of the mouth of the Columbia. A careful 1853 census recorded 3,965 non-Indian inhabitants of North Oregon, slightly more than half on the Sound.[17]

Expecting the Donation Act to encourage the expansion of agriculture, Samuel Thurston instructed friends at home to inform arriving Americans that "I have got them all a farm." The principal result, particularly on Puget Sound, was instead the founding of towns by individuals intent upon marketing real estate and selling goods. "Nearly every man in Oregon has a *City* of his own," one settler joked of this all too evident tendency. The discovery of gold in California and the frenzied rush to the Sierra Nevada from all corners of the globe provided the driving force behind urbanization. San Francisco, a visiting Army officer named U. S. Grant wrote of the once-sleepy Mexican port, was "the wonder of the world." Boomtowns closer to the mining districts offered equally wondrous moneymaking opportunities. The demand for lumber sent prices soaring to between $300 and $500 per thousand feet. "Every body...on the coast," a merchant recalled of the resultant timber production malady, contracted "the saw mill fever."[18]

Nine hundred miles of deep Pacific Ocean, swept by wild storms and roiled by treacherous currents, lay between Puget Sound and the golden bay of San Francisco. The Columbia River, though, was the only point closer to California remotely suitable for resolution of the milling fever. Documented in horrifying detail since the explorations of George Vancouver, the hazards at the mouth of the Columbia produced wide-awake nightmares among timber-mad mercantilists. Widely noted, the summary account written by Charles Wilkes was, alone, sufficiently graphic to scare investors away from the river:

> Mere description can give little idea of the terrors of the bar of the Columbia: all who have seen it have spoken of the wildness of the scene, and the incessant roar of the waters, representing it as one of the most fearful sights that can possibly meet the eye of the sailor. The difficulty of its channel, the distance of the leading sailing markers, their uncertainty to one unacquainted with them, the want of knowledge of the strength and direction of the currents, with the necessity of approaching close to unseen dangers, the transition from clear to turbid water, all cause doubt and mistrust.

According to other first-hand reports, stalwart sea captains fortified themselves with "deep quaffs of brandy," ministers of the gospel fell to trembling knees in devout prayer and ordinary passengers "seemed hardly to dare to breathe till…over the bar."[19]

Oregonians insisted that even the expert commentaries of Vancouver and Wilkes greatly exaggerated the danger. The Columbia's defenders accused "interested parties" of spreading "prejudicial" nonsense, defaming "our noble river" in the face of contrary truth. "That this river like many others has sand bars in its wide mouth *is true*," the *Oregon Spectator* commented, "but that such a river, in such a country, now does and always will afford a channel sufficiently broad and deep for the safe entrance of the largest vessels…*is equally true*." Charted by government surveyors in 1850, a newfound passage over the bar was "straight & wide" and "deep enough for all purposes of…trade." The Cape Disappointment lighthouse, the dozen "iron can buoys" recently anchored in the Columbia's mouth, and experienced bar pilots insured troublefree, even carefree, crossings.[20]

Puget Sound possessed an enormous natural advantage over the river. Few persons truly believed in the Columbia's safety and fewer, still, contested the superiority of the Sound. North Oregon's first newspaper, the Olympia *Columbian*, focused upon the contrast from the commencement of publication in September 1852. Bemused by the periodic discovery of improved bar crossings, editor Thornton McElroy noted that on the Sound "there is no such thing as a 'north channel' which can only be entered semi-sometimes, or a 'south channel' whose eccentric vagaries are such as to require watching over-night to know where to find it in the morning." Nor must vessel masters pay expensive pilotage fees. According to popular gossip, moreover, the intrepid Columbia River pilots were "more generally found in Astoria than outside the bar," waiting in saloons, whiskey in hand, until ships were safely inside the entrance before taking up their duties.[21]

Free of shoals and blessed with numerous deep-water anchorages, Puget Sound was, in the *Columbian*'s view, "one continuous harbor throughout its entire length." Contrary winds encountered when rounding Cape Flattery at the entrance to the Strait of Juan de Fuca were the closest approximation to navigation hazard between the open sea and Olympia. Sailing into the Sound for the first time in January 1850, Isaac Ebey had "no pilot aboard, nor any person who had been along the waters before and yet we had no difficulty." Fourteen to eighteen hundred miles of shoreline—contemporary observers failed to determine an agreed-upon figure—afforded more outlets for commerce, a visitor noted, than "possessed by any other region of equal area in the world." In the nearest thing to a criticism, the Sound ranked behind San Francisco Bay as merely "the second best Harbor on the Western shore of America."[22]

Ease of navigation was but one of two breathtaking features making the estuary a "lumber-men's paradise." The Sound, a visiting journalist exclaimed, "is skirted on either side, throughout its length and breadth, with...valuable timbered land, all of which is easy of access to the shore." Another impressed traveler reported seeing "dark, dense forests...in every direction." In mighty evergreen fact, the region west of the Cascades was overgrown with the heaviest continuous stand of trees in North America. Perusing published estimates of thirty-five to over a hundred thousand feet to the acre, experts conceded the impossibility of making an accurate calculation of the amount of timber bordering Puget Sound. One thing beyond doubt, however, was the perfect suitability of Douglas fir, growing strong and tall to the water's edge, for heavy construction purposes.[23]

"The vast amount of timber that will be consumed in California...," Isaac Ebey wrote from Puget Sound in February 1850, "will make this a very desirable location for those who want to make money." Intending to build industrial communities, would-be moneymakers came by sea from Portland and from San Francisco. Francis Pettygrove, Loren Hastings and their associates founded Port Townsend, at the entrance to the Sound, in the winter of 1852. The settlement, a booster recalled, was deliberately situated "right in the angle formed by the Straits of Fuca and Admiralty Inlet...where vessels inward bound with a fair wind, must generally stop...as the wind...usually dies out here." Loading timber and piling upon California-bound ships, the founders, Pettygrove claimed, secured a "considerable profit."[24]

Later in 1852, Henry Roeder, a German-born sea captain, and R. W. Peabody settled at the mouth of Whatcom Creek on Bellingham Bay. Planning to export lumber to San Francisco, the partners failed to take into consideration the irregular flow of the creek, their source of power, and the regular low tides, which left Whatcom stranded a half-mile from deep water. Vessels could not tie up at the Roeder-Peabody mill. Passengers had to wade, or be carried, ashore over vast mudflats. The plant ran only intermittently, then burned to the ground. Edmund Fitzhugh's coal mine at Sehome, the one place on the bay where tidal conditions accommodated navigation, emerged as the mainstay of the Bellingham economy. Fitzhugh, a Virginia attorney and gold rush migrant to San Francisco, discovered the first lumps in the tangled roots of a fallen Douglas fir. Importing machinery and workers from California, he shipped an inaugural cargo south in 1853 and soon claimed to be earning $27,000 a year from the operation.[25]

Halfway between Port Townsend and Olympia, Arthur Denny and party established a settlement at Alki Point on Elliott Bay in late 1851, naming their beachfront cabins, in a burst of grandiloquent optimism, New York. In February 1852, most of the inhabitants relocated to the inner bay, where winds and currents were better suited to loading timber cargoes, and founded Seattle near the mouth of the Duwamish River. That October, Henry Yesler built the first Puget Sound steam-powered sawmill on a waterfront tract set aside for the purpose. Although the facility was an invaluable economic focal point and the only structure worthy of note, Yesler lacked the resources and the business sense to properly exploit the lumber trade. Seattle was "not much of a town," as a visitor wrote, with, in the most charitable self-promoting estimate, barely a hundred residents.[26]

Of all the lumber-oriented towns, Steilacoom enjoyed the most success. Arriving in 1852, sea-going merchant Lafayette Balch revived the existing "squatter" community. His sawmill, cargo vessels and San Francisco sales yard gave Steilacoom the early lead in the coasting trade. At $13,000 per quarter, the Army payroll supplied an additional economic stimulus. Outsiders belittled Steilacoom as an over-promoted "*claim* in the Fir Timber," but the evidence of genuine progress was difficult to ignore. Visiting in 1853, Ezra Meeker discovered that "everything was new, with an air of business bustle." Seven ships lay at anchor, unloading or taking on cargo, and "the descent of timber on the rollways sounded like thunder." After inspecting Seattle and other points, Meeker decided, on the basis of "the greater activities that we saw there than anywhere else on the waters of the Sound," to settle in Steilacoom.[27]

Maintaining position as the largest Puget Sound community, with four hundred inhabitants in 1853, Olympia was at the end of the line for seaborne commercial traffic. The long wharf constructed over the Budd Inlet flats only partially alleviated the problem of inconvenient tides. In February 1851, however, Olympia was named port-of-entry for North Oregon, thereby becoming a center of government. The dozen substantial dwellings, the five saloons and the bowling alley within municipal limits, one newcomer observed, made Olympia "a fast place." The town cast more votes in territorial elections, boasted Michael Simmons, who had relocated from New Market, "than all the balance of the Sound together."[28]

California gold had an undeniable impact upon North Oregon. "The shipping interest on the Sound is steadily improving," the *Columbian* advised in late 1852, "and we hear of vessels at almost every convenient point along its entire length awaiting for cargoes, in the shape of sawed lumber, square timber and piles." Fifteen sawmills, all but Henry Yesler's powered by water, ran constantly, when not out of mechanical order. Another half dozen were currently under construction. Reporting that Puget Sound handled "more shipping [sic] in proportion to our numbers than any portion of Oregon," customs collector Isaac Ebey listed fifty ships as regularly involved in the timbering trade. Taking advantage of prevailing labor shortages, a traditional new country problem exacerbated by the availability of free land under the Donation Act, settlers wielding axes and saws secured what an old-timer called "plethoric purses." One pioneer received $75 a month cutting piles for Lafayette Balch. Another immigrant remembered $100 as the standard monthly pay. Steilacoom mill hands, experienced or not, refused to work for less than $20 a day.[29]

North Oregon, Isaac Ebey predicted on the basis of performance to date, "will be the 'Commercial State' in time." In 1853, San Francisco capitalists made substantial advances toward confirming Ebey's prognostication. William Sayward built the Port Ludlow mill near Port Townsend. George Meigs went into business at Port Madison on Bainbridge Island. William Renton commenced his regional career with a plant on Elliott Bay. Pope & Talbot's Puget Mill Company subsidiary constructed the Sound's largest manufacturing complex at Port Gamble, or Teekalet, a narrow Kitsap Peninsula inlet. The newcomers were New England merchants lately relocated to gold rush California, from families long-experienced in the handling of lumber and ships. Heavily financed and possessing both vessels and distant sales outlets, they differed from earlier mill owners of the Yesler type. Able to efficiently exploit natural resources and markets, foreign and domestic, the Yankees created a regionally distinctive manufactory. In 1860, southern Oregon had four times as many sawmills as the territory north of the Columbia. The northerners, though, produced twice the lumber, employed double the number of workers and represented a greater rate of investment.[30]

Dwarfing the competition in size and in profit, the New Englanders also produced a major shift in the geography of Puget Sound lumbering. Yesler, Balch and the other pioneers were located, for the most part, in existing settlements on the eastern shore. The new industrialists went to the westside, particularly to the tree-covered Kitsap Peninsula, which became, on a per capita basis, the wealthiest section of the Sound. The San Francisco-owned mill towns were "little kingdoms" and "principalities." The sole purpose was the production of lumber and only persons contributing to that goal secured resident status. According to local humorists, no doctors, lawyers or professionally trained individuals of any kind, excepting "half a dozen gamblers," lived in Kitsap County. Isolated from conventional settled places, timber port proprietors monopolized trade with employees through company stores and illegally logged the public domain.[31]

Lumbering dominated the economic life, directly and indirectly, of North Oregon. The other noteworthy commercial enterprise, oystering, also developed in response to California markets. North of the Columbia's mouth, the hardpacked sand of the Long Beach Peninsula shielded Shoalwater Bay from the sea. Stable and deep, the harbor entrance was the safest on the coast between San Francisco and the Sound. On the inside, however, shoals deposited by the Willapa River and other streams revealed themselves upon the retreat of the tide, giving the estuary its off-putting name. Writing of Shoalwater Bay in his 1857 memoir *The Northwest Coast*, James G. Swan complained that would-be investors and settlers, spoiled by Puget Sound, exhibited undue prejudice: "those who never before saw salt water till they crossed the plains, are doubtful of the utility of a bay where twice in twenty-four hours they can see the bottom."[32]

Ignored by early traders and captains, Shoalwater Bay's vast shellfish beds had been exploited for ages by local Indians. California merchants experienced in the Atlantic coast oyster trade noted that the harbor was close enough to San Francisco to avoid significant losses from spoilage en route. By 1850, a determined and often inebriated white and Indian harvester colony was ensconced on the beach. "Each oysterman has a bed," James Swan reported, "which is marked by stakes driven into the flats, and can be reached at any time, either by foot at low water, or in boats at high tide." The insatiable gold rush demand for luxury items, foodstuffs included, made for frenzied activity and subprofits. In 1853 alone, four schooners—one vessel, the *Maryland*, made a half dozen roundtrip voyages during the year—carried twenty thousand bushels of oysters, worth $129,000. The business, a visitor to aptly named Oysterville reported in understated fashion, was "no mean thing."[33]

Puget Sound "is beginning to awaken," Governor John Gaines exclaimed in his 1852 annual message to Oregon's legislative assembly. Fully aware of their achievements to date and of their prospects, Sound country pioneers readied a declaration of independence. Geography and economic progress made a new territory north of the Columbia both desirable and inevitable. "Northern Oregon," the Olympia *Columbian* pointed out, ". . . embraces an area sufficient for the formation of a state as large as Ohio, Indiana or Kentucky." Overcoming poor transportation and indifferent government, settlers had made enormous strides. "Many claims have been taken on the Sound," the *Columbian* proudly broadcast, "and much of the public domain has been reclaimed from the wild and slumbering lethargy, to subserve the cause of civilization on the Pacific."[34]

A new territory was just compensation for indignities long endured. "Neither time nor room would answer our purpose in one article," said Olympia's indignant newspaper, "to set forth all the grievances which northern Oregon has been compelled to submit to." The southerners "have us under the foot and wish to roll us in the dust," an angry reader agreed. Although Congress appropriated funds for all of Oregon, the money was spent only south of the Columbia. The Sound was denied protection against the Indians and extension of the government surveys. Dispatching a memorial to Washington requesting construction of a road across the Cascades, the territorial assembly, which had only two northern members, specified that the route be via Mount Hood, not Mount Rainier. The creation of new counties—Pacific in 1851 and Thurston, Pierce, King and Jefferson in 1852—apparently exhausted the legislature's interest in North Oregon. According to the *Columbian*, the only practical solution was "A LEGAL DIVORCE FROM THE SOUTH."[35]

Olympia's Fourth of July festivities in 1851 featured a visit from the officers and crew of the sloop-of-war *Falmouth*, a reading of the Declaration of

Independence by Hugh Goldsborough, Michael Simmons's business partner, and, one celebrant noted, "a hearty enjoyment of the creature-comforts." One of the many liquor-flowing toasts commended "the future State of 'Columbia,' North of the Columbia River." Addressing the crowd on the "wants of that portion of Oregon Territory north of the Columbia," attorney John Chapman provoked a general and semi-alcoholic discussion of regional problems. By unanimous vote, those still able to stand and deliver upon their convictions approved a resolution calling for a convention to examine "the propriety of an early appeal to Congress for a division of the Territory." Three days later, the superior court session regularly held at John Jackson's Cowlitz corridor farm was transformed into an organizational meeting for the convention. Together, noted Isaac Ebey, these developments were "the incipient steps nort[h] of the Columbia River for a new Territory."[36]

North Oregon became, for Ebey and his colleagues, the Columbia Territory. When formally organized, they expected, the new territory would be bounded on the south and on the east by the great stream. "Does it not seem," asked a leading advocate of division, "that nature destined the Columbia river to be the dividing line between two…powerful States?" Dictated by geography, the proposed boundary reflected separate Oregon Country spheres. "The relative positions of the two divisions of Oregon," the Olympia *Columbian* affirmed, "forbid that the *southern* portion should ever seek the waters of the Sound in the pursuit of its maritime affairs, or that the commerce of the *northern* section could ever find a channel in the waters of the Columbia." Outright ignorance also influenced the thinking on boundaries. Aside from Francis Chenoweth, a New York-born lawyer who explored the "magnifficent [sic] plains" of the Yakima Valley in 1851, few settlers possessed informed knowledge of conditions east of the Cascades. Columbia Territory supporters believed, incorrectly, that an eastern line along the river "would include within our jurisdiction the beautiful and fertile valley of the Walla-walla."[37]

Pursuant to the July arrangements, the Columbia Territory convention convened in Warbassport on August 29, 1851. The twenty-four delegates represented, in the main, the Cowlitz corridor, with only Steilacoom's Thomas Chambers attending from north of Olympia. Most were farmers, the principal exceptions being attorney John Chapman, Lewis County Sheriff A. J. Simmons and Doctor David Maynard, a recent arrival from the states. Rather than debate the key issue at hand, the convention resolved that "reasons too well known to require repetition" justified separation from Oregon. Leaving the actual petition to Congress to a three person drafting committee, the members focused, during two days of marginally rational deliberation, upon matters of secondary or premature significance. Presupposing rapid and favorable congressional action upon Columbia Territory, a dozen new counties were organized west of the Cascades.

Over-optimistic delegates also voted to reconvene in May 1852 on behalf of Columbia's admission to statehood.[38]

Writing on behalf of Michael Simmons and F. S. Balch, who opted out of the assignment, John Chapman crafted the Columbia Territory congressional memorial. "Government and order is contemplated for the convenience and benefit of the people," the would-be Jefferson of the Far Northwest pointed out in a series of less-than-graceful statements. "The inhabitants North of the Columbia River," said Chapman, "receive no benefit…whatever from the Territorial Government of Oregon." Due to the concentration of public services south of the river, "it costs more for a citizen in the North…to travel to a clerk's office, or to reach a District Judge than it does for a man to travel from St[.] Lewis [sic] Missouri to Boston…and back." Reflecting contemporary prejudice, much of the document actually amounted to a diatribe against the Hudson's Bay Company. The "British Trading Post," supposedly, "never pretended to carry on an agricultural pursuit," yet it now claimed legal possession of "one of the finest portions of the Country at the very head of 'Pugets Sound.'" Those Americans "willing to incur the displeasure of a large monied institution" must, Chapman complained, proceed in the risk-all manner of "an Army storming a Castle."[39]

Possibly misapprehending the petition as a declaration of independence from British corporate monopoly, rather than from Oregonian political tyranny, Congress ignored the memorial. Fortified by population growth and economic expansion on Puget Sound, pro-division forces remained active. "There are not half a dozen intelligent citizens between Whidby's Island and the Cowlitz river," the *Columbian* claimed with more certainty than good grammar, "who does not only see the propriety and necessity of a separate territorial government, but who are not, also, strongly…in favor of a speedy accomplishment of that object." By the fall of 1852, conditions appeared suitable for another concerted effort. Noting, in mid-October, that "quite a number of the most…influential citizens of northern Oregon" would soon be attending court at John Jackson's homestead, the *Columbian* called upon the attorneys, litigants and hangers-on there assembled to arrange a second territorial convention.[40]

In contrast to the disorganized 1851 session, the meeting was designed in advance to produce a definitive result. Because support for the new territory was strongest on the Sound and weakest on the Columbia, where homesteaders oriented themselves toward Portland and the Willamette Valley, planners assigned the convention to Monticello. "Living, as they do, on the boundary line between the two divisions of Oregon," the *Columbian* noted of river settlers, ". . . it is but natural to suppose that their sympathies are pretty equally divided between the north and the south." If Olympia or some other Puget Sound point had been selected, lukewarm Columbians, subjected to extra inconvenience and expense on behalf of a debatable cause, "would probably have entirely failed in giving their attendance." A sympathetic committee drafted all resolutions beforehand

and called upon local citizens to select delegates committed to creating Columbia Territory. Pressed by the organizers, Cowlitz River mercantile interests agreed to discount the cost of travel to and from Monticello.[41]

On November 25, 1852, forty-four individuals convened in the Lewis County "court room," an ornate assembly place at least when compared to the Warbassport storehouse used in 1851. The delegates manifested a more urban tone than evident the previous year. Engineer Hugh Goldsborough joined Michael Simmons from Olympia. Attorney Frank Clark replaced farmer Thomas Chambers as Steilacoom's representative. Loren Hastings attended on behalf of Port Townsend. Seattle sent Arthur Denny, David Maynard and G. N. McConaha. Given the advance planning, a single day sufficed for the completion of business. "The only question as to a division of this Territory," keynote speaker Quincy Brooks pronounced, "are questions of time and manner: when shall the division be made, and…how shall the dividing line run?" Both queries, Brooks responded on behalf of the convention, had obvious answers: "our wants demand the immediate organization of the 'Territory of Columbia,' and…the Columbia river should be the southern and eastern boundary line."[42]

Addressing the public, pro-territory forces predicted rapid congressional approval of the Monticello memorial. Privately, Columbia's friends reminded one another to be patient, as no response, positive or negative, would be forthcoming until at least 1854. However, to widespread astonishment, as Isaac Ebey informed his brother in May 1853, "the organization took place sooner by one year than we expected." Sentiment south, rather than north, of the Columbia mattered in the end. Political observers considered Oregon Territory, as presently constituted, too large for a proper state and recommended a substantial reduction in size as a necessary prelude to admission. Delegate Joseph Lane, homespun hero of the Mexican War and Oregon's Democratic party leader, agreed. Intent upon becoming a United States senator at the earliest possible date, Lane sacrificed North Oregon, and considerable acreage east of the Cascades, on behalf of personal ambition.[43]

Introduced by Lane in December 1852, legislation creating Columbia Territory was already under consideration. "Oregon is too large for one…State," the delegate noted in explaining himself to supporters in the Willamette Valley. Although the late-arriving Monticello petition was mentioned in debate, the territorial assembly's pro-division memorial, asserting that the two sections were "in a great degree distinct communities, with different interests," provided Lane with vital south-of-the-river support. Discussing the proposal, House members decided that the name should be changed to Washington, avoiding confusion with the District of Columbia. The reasoning defied comprehension, Washington being no improvement in this respect, but the honor extended the first president of the United States enhanced the prospects for approval.[44]

Suitably amended, Joseph Lane's handiwork passed the House of Representatives on February 8, 1853. "The most striking feature in the Bill," the *Columbian* observed upon receiving the news five weeks later, "is the name which is given to our Territory." Despite the patriotic nature of the substitution, Washington "met with some distaste among many of our citizens." A new territorial government north of the river was, of course, far better than no division at all. Olympia residents therefore waited, Isaac Ebey wrote, "on the tip-toe" for senatorial action in the final days of the congressional session. The Senate approved creation of Washington Territory on March 2, 1853, a day prior to adjournment. President Millard Fillmore, concluding his term in the executive mansion, immediately signed the act of Congress.[45]

Learning of Washington Territory's creation on April 25, Olympians fired a ragged hundred-gun salute from locally available muskets, rifles and pistols. A single negative note marred the celebration, fear that the region had exchanged "our poor dependency upon the cold charities of Oregon" for direct subservience to a distant federal government. Under "the ancient system of territorial organization," the *Columbian* pointed out, officials must be appointed from afar, rather than elected under a form of self-governance. Colonial methods appropriate for impoverished or remote societies were "wholly foreign…to the wants, the absolute necessities, of a people whose home is upon the…shores of a vast ocean, whitened with the sails of the richest…traffic known to the commercial world." Self-interest required, in the *Columbian*'s view, that "every trace of proconsulary" be quickly "eradicated" and that "the closest approximation to the sovereignty of a State" be attained at the earliest opportunity. The newspaper awaited the arrival of Washington's first governor in the manner of "a bride who looks anxiously for the coming of the groom." Already, however, a struggle between localized and outside control—the driving force in the political life of the western territories—portended an uncertain betrothal.[46]

Washington Territory had both a different name and substantially larger limits than expected. Instead of following the Columbia upstream to the English possessions on the east, the original boundary left the river at the 46th parallel, running direct to the Rocky Mountains. Upon Oregon's admission to the Union in 1859, expanded territorial bounds embraced modern Washington and Idaho, plus Montana and Wyoming west of the Continental Divide. The borders made no sense, except in light of Oregon's eagerness to shed acreage in the interest of becoming a state. The land east of the Cascades was, in any event, only nominally part of Washington. Like water flowing downhill in accordance with the physical laws of gravity, communication and trade followed the Columbia River, making the eastern section of the new territory Oregonian, regardless of mapmakers and politicians.[47]

Intent upon retaining effectual control of the region beyond the mountains, Portland merchants improved upon nature's linkage with the interior. Oregon's first river steamer, the *Columbia*, went into service in 1850. Within a year, eleven boats served local waters. The luxurious *Lot Whitcomb*, pride of Captain John Ainsworth, ran on a regular schedule between the Willamette and the Cascades, the head of navigation on the lower Columbia. "The price of passage is low, the fare and accommodations…excellent," travelers reported of "the pleasure trip" up and down river. Additional transportation improvements, including a portage railroad at the Cascades and a steamboat to run between that obstruction and The Dalles, were planned. Lobbying commenced, also, for construction of locks and canals by the federal government, the definitive means of removing obstacles to the flow of commerce.[48]

Efforts on the Sound to circumvent Portland were frequent, fervent and entirely unsuccessful. "We have all for some time," Hugh Goldsborough wrote to southern Oregon friends, "felt the want of a more direct route…to Puget Sound, than the present round about way down the Columbia river…and up the Cowlitz." The "greatest obstacle" confronting North Oregon, the *Columbian* pronounced, was the struggle "attendant upon gaining admission within its borders." The lack of a road across the Cascades giving travelers the option of turning off the overland trail in the Walla Walla Valley direct for the Sound, forced the entire annual migration down "the wretched trail heading into [the] Willamette valley." Once there and subject to Oregonian "misrepresentations," few immigrants had the funds or the stamina left to undertake a further journey via the Cowlitz.[49]

Despite wholesale lack of geographical knowledge and engineering expertise, Puget Sound settlers insisted that crossing the Cascades entailed no great risk to life or property. "A route can be surveyed almost any where through them," the *Columbian* observed in reducing mountains to molehill status. Planners need only choose from among "hundreds of gaps and openings." Amateur mountaineers reported seeing "several passes at intervals" in the course of a failed climb of Mount Rainier. Claiming to know the perfect route, fur trade veteran Robert Lansdale offered to reveal the location in return for a handsome finder's fee.[50]

Olympia citizens, organized by Michael Simmons, raised $1,500 for a wagon road in 1850. The "strong party of active young men" sent into the mountains failed, however, to construct anything of temporary, much less permanent, value. Promoting a "private enterprise" toll route over the Cascades in 1851, Isaac Ebey made no recorded headway. That summer, the Warbassport convention petitioned Congress for a road between the Sound and the Walla Walla Valley. "The distance is shorter from Pugets Sound to Wallawalla than from Wallawallah [sic] to Fort Vancouver," the delegates contended, "and…it is more difficult to travel from…Fort Vancouver to Pugets Sound than from Walla Walla to the Sound." Oregon's legislative assembly endorsed the plan, in its own congressional memorial, submitted in early 1853.[51]

North Oregon's most influential friend, Joseph Lane, secured construction funds for a military road between Fort Walla Walla, the old Hudson's Bay Company post on the Columbia, and Steilacoom. The project was assigned to Captain George McClellan, the engineer charged with finding passes through the Cascades for the 1853 northern transcontinental railroad survey led by Isaac Stevens, Washington's first governor. Determined to "get an emigrant road through this fall," the governor instructed McClellan to "carefully advise with the prominent citizens of the Territory"—Michael Simmons and Isaac Ebey were specifically mentioned—"…in reference to the best location." To insure completion in time for the migration, and to stay within the appropriation, the track must "of necessity, be very rough." Stevens therefore directed the captain to employ only "experienced road men…who will not cut down a tree or use a spade, unless absolutely necessary."[52]

Convinced that "the realization of our greatest hopes depend upon the construction of the road," Olympia residents declined to wait for Captain McClellan. "Viewers" laid out a route following the Naches Pass Indian trail. Laborers set to work on both sides of the mountains, clearing the road toward the summit. Finally arriving in June, McClellan made his sole contribution, granting a contract providing, in effect, government reimbursement of the money already expended. As the result of local initiative, the road opened in time to accommodate the 1853 migration. Forty-six settlers, pioneers who would otherwise have been lost to the Willamette Valley, crossed the Cascades via Naches Pass, with eleven wagons and sixty-two head of cattle. The tally, small for the present, appeared to be a preview of greater cross-mountain travel in future seasons, especially in view of expected improvements to the route.[53]

An enormous and imperfectly known domain fell within Washington Territory's political limits, from foggy Pacific Ocean beaches to sky-high, granite Rocky Mountain peaks. In terms of actual American occupation, however, Washington was relatively constricted. Other than a few retired Hudson's Bay men and their Indian families, no bona fide settlers resided east of the Cascades; it was an inhospitable region of aridity best left, in the opinion of most contemporary students, to the exclusive possession of resident Indian tribes. On the west side, settlement was concentrated along major watercourses, Puget Sound and the Columbia River. Indians monopolized the long seacoast north of the Shoalwater Bay oyster camps, past Grays Harbor and around Cape Flattery to near Port Townsend. Beneath the Chinook jargon word "Alki," the territorial seal featured a log cabin, an immigrant wagon and a growing city upon a great harbor, capturing the essence of an infant Washington that was, in dank tideflat truth, little more than the rain country about the Sound.[54]

Brigadier General Isaac I. Stevens depicted in a stylized Civil War era lithograph. *Washington State Historical Society, Tacoma*

Chapter Two

A Grand Element of National Strength

This territory must be settled and developed as a grand element of national strength.—Isaac I. Stevens[1]

ON MARCH 17, 1853, Major Isaac Ingalls Stevens accepted appointment as governor of Washington Territory, exchanging a promising military career for the peculiar hazards of political conflict. Stevens often made an unappealing first impression—he was short, given to drink, at least according to rumor, and habitually dressed in what one settler called the "rough" attire of a "backwoodsman"—but invariably imposed himself upon others through intellect and personality. After graduating first in the West Point class of 1839 and serving with distinction in the Mexican War, the Massachusetts native was posted to the Coast Survey in Washington City. The assignment allowed ample time and opportunity for cultivation of relationships with the nation's leading politicians, including Franklin Pierce, the fellow New England Democrat elected president in 1852. As governor, Stevens intended to lead Washington to statehood, advancing himself in the process. Although contemporary critics made fun of him as a "Man of Destiny," a pint-sized personification of aggressive Young America, the characterization perfectly fit his chosen role in the world of public affairs.[2]

Stevens was, as an admirer noted, "all energy" and therefore unwilling to restrict himself to the common duties of a mere territorial governorship. President Pierce also appointed him superintendent of Indian affairs for Washington Territory, a logical extra responsibility since the making of treaties, east and west of the Cascades, was an obvious, and long-delayed, public necessity. Assuming a third vital assignment, the governor surveyed, while on the way west, the northernmost of four possible transcontinental railroad routes under consideration by the War Department. "I can best promote the Interests of the Territory," he explained, "by...making the necessary surveys to determine the practicability, cost and time of constructing a Rail Road...to Puget Sound."[3]

Formal inauguration of the territorial government was necessarily postponed until Stevens arrived overland from the Mississippi River. "We wish the Territory could be instantly organized," the Olympia *Columbian* observed in June 1853, "but the prospect of a Railroad...from the States to Puget Sound...more than satisfies us for the delay." Calling upon advocates of the northern and the extreme southern routes to unite against "the gluttony" of California, the *Columbian* recommended that "the sagacious south" support the Stevens-surveyed option in return for northern endorsement, "after another acquisition of Mexican territory," of a second transcontinental line, between New Orleans and Mazatlan on the Pacific. "Our fortunate position, [and] splendid harbor for...fleets upon fleets," the newspaper boasted, "will bring to us the road, and its attendant advantages, to make Washington what its great name signifies it should be, the 'Star of Empire' that westward came."[4]

Carrying the Star of Empire in his trail-stained saddlebags, Isaac Stevens reached Olympia in late November 1853. Before returning to the East to collect his family, "the long looked for Governor" established an enduring reputation for hard work and politically astute behavior. He selected the polling places and the date, January 30, 1854, for the first territorial election. On a fast-paced trip to northern points, Stevens inspected potential railroad terminals, met native leaders and conferred, in Victoria, with his English counterpart, James Douglas. Taking advantage of the Indian superintendency patronage, he appointed Michael Simmons and other new friends to government service, creating a personal political organization. The governor also participated in the arrangements under which the *Pioneer and Democrat* succeeded the *Columbian* as Olympia's newspaper and became his journalistic mouthpiece. Demonstrating a deft expedient hand, Stevens aggressively took the settler side of the argument over Hudson's Bay Company claims, to the extent of prohibiting British trade with Washington Territory Indians as of July 1, 1854.[5]

Railroading remained the governor's principal concern. Wasting no time in reporting upon his survey, Stevens dispatched a preliminary draft to the War Department in mid-December. The expedition, he asserted, established "the entire practicability of a railroad route" by the northern line. George McClellan's "fine summer's work" had "thoroughly developed" the topography of the Cascade Range, including the location and nature of Snoqualmie and other "practicable mountain passes." The first individual to seriously think of Washington Territory on an east-to-west basis, Stevens claimed to have unlocked the potential of the interior Northwest. The most unappealing portion of eastern Washington, the coulee-pierced basin bordering the upper Columbia, still contained "farming land enough" to justify "the occupation of the whole country by stock raisers." Recommending the early construction of locks and canals, the governor foresaw a Columbia River opened to steamboat navigation as far upstream as Kettle Falls, close to the international border.[6]

So far as Puget Sound residents were concerned, selection of the Stevens route as the one best suited to construction of a transcontinental railroad was inevitable. The official response in Washington City, however, was more dismissive than approving in nature. Individuals familiar with the governor's personal ambitions, friends included, discounted his findings as exaggerated and self-serving. McClellan had actually made only a cursory examination of the mountains, calling into question all positive observations regarding the passes of the Cascades. Secretary of War Jefferson Davis, whose personal agenda embraced a determination to build first by the southern route, issued a negative, if equally suspect, assessment, further reducing the prospects of congressional action favorable to the Sound.[7]

The Pacific railroad remained the goal of goals on Puget Sound, the quickest means of overcoming the region's isolation and developing its resources. With undiluted enthusiasm, Isaac Stevens advocated construction over the remainder of his gubernatorial term and while serving as delegate to Congress. The legislative assembly chartered Washington's own short-lived Northern Pacific Railroad Company, with Stevens as president, in 1857. Gold discoveries periodically renewed interest in rail connections with the Mississippi River. The *Pioneer and Democrat* regularly reprinted favorable articles from eastern newspapers and railroad journals. Washington Territory representatives attended transportation conventions in California and in the East, keeping the transcontinental dream alive.[8]

"His patronage is great and his power," territorial jurist Edward Lander observed of Isaac Stevens in 1856. Power and patronage were, in turn, products of ambition and the Indian superintendency jobs and contracts. Stevens was an atypically strong governor in an inherently weak and insignificant political system, rather than a representative figure or model for subsequent behavior. A full dozen appointees succeeded him in the executive chair. Few manifested abnormal energy. From Fayette McMullin to Miles Moore, no governor exercised control over the official spoils at the disposal of the federal Indian department.[9]

Some five hundred individuals, local postmasters included, eventually labored on the federal payroll in Washington Territory. Enshrined since the Age of Jackson, near-immortal appointive dictates subjected all, from the governor to the lowliest employee on the most forgotten Indian reservation, to removal upon a change of presidential administrations. Because Washington had a single non-voting congressional delegate and cast no electoral votes, the likelihood of a local resident being appointed to a major position was minimal. Instead, outsiders—from states where patronage might truly reward past loyalty and influence future partisan contests—filled the important offices. Presidents Franklin Pierce and James Buchanan, for instance, placated the South by naming, as the second and third territorial governors, Virginia's Fayette McMullin and Kentucky's Richard Gholson. Elwood Evans, though a bona fide Puget Sound pioneer, sought the governorship in 1861 as favorite son of his home state, Pennsylvania. Following Oregon's admission to statehood, south-of-the-Columbia politicians controlled a number of Washington jobs, particularly those involving residence in towns close to the border.[10]

Ability and honesty counted, if at all, as secondary factors in securing and retaining federal office. Seattle attorney John McGilvra, himself originally an outsider patronage recipient, described Washington as "a sort of Botany Bay" for "broken down political hacks." The observation applied even to the territorial judiciary. Although some supreme court appointees, like Harvard graduate Edward Lander, possessed appropriate credentials, most were representative products of the regular qualifications-bedamned selection process. Victor Monroe, one of the original 1853 jurists, was a notorious alcoholic incapable, most days, of performing even routine paperwork. Isaac Stevens secured the appointment of Edmund Fitzhugh in 1858, despite the embarrassing, though hardly disqualifying, fact that the Bellingham Bay coal mine owner was under indictment for murder. Judge Charles Darwin compiled Washington's first collected laws in 1868, but was better known for engaging in a notorious affair with his Port Townsend landlady, the wife of the collector of customs.[11]

Formal organizational charts, placing the chief executive at the top, encouraged misleading views of territorial government. Isaac Stevens excepted, occupants of the office had more prestige than genuine stature. Until 1864, the governor lacked authority to veto acts of the legislature. He exercised no statutory control over the other executive branch members, the secretary, the federal attorney and the United States marshal. The governor's patronage was limited, traditionally, to commissioning notaries public, awarding an annual university scholarship, and occasional selection of institutional caretakers and exhibition delegates. In 1874, Congress made the auditor, the treasurer and other officials—previously elected by the assembly—gubernatorial appointees. Finally reckoned "a potent political factor," the governor thereafter disposed, at most, of three dozen jobs. The pardoning power was, in the meantime, more often a source of aggravation and scandal than of meaningful influence. Widely maligned during the 1870s as a "pardon broker," Elisha Ferry was nearly dismissed from office after freeing a convicted murderer, the son of a partisan ally.[12]

Contemporary observers discounted the practical importance of Washington's governorship. Expressing a common view, Elwood Evans believed the superintendency of Indian affairs the "best, most lucrative and...from its patronage" the "most *influential* position" in the territory. Reflecting upon the many employees to be hired and fired, one superintendent, James Nesmith, wrote that "Gen[eral] Jackson...never had a greater, or more varied crowd...about his back door, or back-side, begging for the spoils of office." Contracts for reservation supplies and annuities—Nesmith spent "about a half a million of dollars in the last eight months" of 1858—provided numerous opportunities for personal profit and political advantage. When the federal government combined the Washington and Oregon superintendencies in the interest of efficient management, alarmed politicians of both territories immediately protested. Current and prospective crises in relations with the tribes actually justified, they maintained, three Indian superintendencies, with attendant jobs and funding, in the Pacific Northwest.[13]

A rival assessment held the customs house, moved to Port Townsend in 1854, "the best office in the Territory." In addition to salary, the position paid "fees and emoluments" upon duties collected and illegal goods seized and included both a personal dwelling and the right to employ a family member as clerk. Reporting that a "light-fingered" thief had lifted $150 from his "pantaloons pocket" while he slept in the office, Isaac Ebey incidentally revealed that the task required substantially less than wide-awake attention. Estimating his annual earnings at a conservative $3,500, Ebey farmed a claim and pursued various business and political interests while on the federal payroll. With foreign trade increasing, the collectorship was said to be "worth between $5000 & $6000…per annum" by the mid-1860s.[14]

Upon initial reflection, the territorial secretary appeared to have entirely non-remunerative responsibilities. Charles Mason, the original holder of the position, rented office space and looked after the public records. Detailing his duties on behalf of the legislature, Henry McGill gave the job a clerical aspect:

> Two days before the opening of the Session…I placed upon the desk of each member, in both Halls, one inkstand, sand box, wafer box, wafer stamp, pens and pen holders, and a small supply of stationery; and immediately upon the organization of the House I delivered into the charge of each of the chief clerks…a sufficiency of letter, fools cap and note paper, official and letter envelopes, paper cutters, pencils, pens, pen holders, India rubber erasers, tape, twine, sand, wafers & blotting and packing paper.

The secretary, however, also disbursed funds appropriated by Congress for assembly salaries and expenses. He became acting governor, without additional pay, in the absence of the chief executive, a frequent happenstance. Mason served in that capacity from April through November 1854 and again between May and December 1855. Substituting for Richard Gholson, who returned to Kentucky in 1860 to organize that state's secession movement, Henry McGill filled the post for such a lengthy period that "acting" was finally dropped from his title in popular usage.[15]

Would-be publishers of the assembly journals and statutes, a job worth $10,000 a year by 1860, were supposedly "as plentiful as huckleberries in summer." Citing the general welfare, Charles Mason ignored orders to send the inaugural 1854 works east for printing. Delay must be avoided, he explained, so that Washington residents "might have some idea of what laws were in force." The Democratic-controlled legislature selected the *Pioneer and Democrat* territorial printer, continuing to do so through 1861. The result, though highly profitable to the newspaper and to the party, was anything but a public service. Paper shortages prevented publication of the initial laws until late 1855, establishing a pattern in which the statutes of one assembly session appeared in print only after the convening of the next meeting of the body. "Before the people have become acquainted with what the law is," Elwood Evans pointed out, "...a succeeding Legislature, modifies it by amendments."[16]

Secretarial involvement with the printing took a new unwholesome turn during the Civil War. Again in control of the legislature after a single session in the minority, the Democrats announced plans in 1863 to use funds supplied by a Republican Congress to finance an opposition paper in the territory. Citing instructions from the Treasury Department and a debatable legal argument invalidating the assembly election method used since 1854, Elwood Evans, a recent Lincoln appointee, claimed the right to personally select the printer. Republicans rejoiced momentarily, the *Seattle Gazette* exclaiming that the secretary had saved "the public treasury from being plundered by the enemies of the country." No wartime patriot, Evans was actually interested in enhancing the power of his office and in securing personal profit. To the consternation of true-blue party colleagues, the coveted contract went to the veteran Democratic editor, Thornton McElroy, the public face in a printing business partly owned by Evans.[17]

Regardless of partisan affiliation or personal philosophy, settlers viewed federal officeholders with contempt. "There is perhaps no more serious cause for complaint among the people," a Steilacoom newspaper reflected in December 1860, "...than the importation of strangers to exercise Executive authority." Appointees were worse than mere "strangers to the wants and interests" of the territory: "Very often they are found utterly incompetent...sometimes they prove to be imbeciles or fools, and sometimes arrant knaves." While defending Democratic incumbents against such accusations, the *Pioneer and Democrat* agreed "upon principle" that "the control of affairs" ought to be "placed more directly in the hands of our people." One writer suggested that all federal officials be required to reside and work in British Victoria, where they "could enjoy the fumes of the best tobacco and get drunk on the best whisky" without harming honest American citizens. Democrats on the one hand and Whigs in the process of becoming Republicans on the other featured a common element in their party platforms, the plank opposed to the "exporting to this Territory [of] any more talent in the shape of officers."[18]

Busy, indeed over-busy, clearing farms and building towns, settlers left local elective politics to a relatively small class of attorneys, merchants and outright charlatans, for whom the general welfare was invariably a foreign concept. Under the caucus, or convention, system of selecting candidates, the political process was easily and repeatedly manipulated, for good or for ill, by self-selected and self-interested individuals. In 1854, Democratic leaders promoted territorial unity by nominating river resident Columbia Lancaster for Congress. Different priorities in 1855, when a delegate was chosen for the full two-year term, required that Lancaster be dropped, against his wishes, from the ticket. Governor Stevens, currently preoccupied with Indian treaty making, intended to run for the congressional seat in 1857, an ambition that might be threatened should the incumbent become entrenched. Controlling the convention, the Stevens forces stage-managed a shift to J. Patton Anderson, who planned to return to his Mississippi home and had no intention of ever coming back to the Pacific Northwest.[19]

A common congressional campaign theme reflected both general hostility toward federal officials and a lack of meaningful territorial issues. Contrasting his candidacy with that of Democrat Anderson, Whig William Strong ran in 1855 as a genuine Northwesterner: "His family are among us—he lives upon the claim which his residence has secured to him." Unable to refute the charges of advance absenteeism levied against their man, Anderson supporters reminded voters that Strong himself originally came to the region as an appointed judge and had, as a typical outsider, engaged "in acts of arrogance, assumption and neglect, whilst a member of the bench." William H. Wallace was an authentic Washingtonian, whether losing in 1859 or winning in 1861. The "proprietor of a considerable section of the town of Steilacoom" in the former year, he was in the latter "a *bona fide* citizen" depending "upon his own efforts for a living." Democratic opponents Isaac Stevens and Selucious Garfielde, on the other hand, arrived in the territory "with commissions in their pockets, to enjoy…the benefits of easy official positions," dining in elegant perpetuity "at the Government crib."[20]

Significant tendencies manifested themselves in the election returns, particularly the basic north-south territorial division. Although Anderson easily defeated Strong in 1855, carrying ten of the fifteen counties, the Democrat and the Whig ran virtually even on the Sound. Solid margins on the river and along the Cowlitz corridor solidified Anderson's victory. Despite a substantial increase in total returns, the same pattern prevailed later in the decade. Partially assisted by a suspect 193-1 count east of the Cascades, Isaac Stevens rolled to a landslide triumph over William Wallace in 1859, with 61 percent of the vote. The Republican led on Puget Sound, however, by a substantial margin outside the former governor's Olympia stronghold. In contrast, three of every four Columbia River voters and two out of three on the Cowlitz supported Stevens. Despite an overall impressive win, Democrats had reason for concern, as the relatively greater rate of population growth on the Sound suggested that the partisan advantage was bound eventually to swing in favor of the newly organizing Republicans.[21]

Partly the result of closed nominations and uninspiring candidates, the general public disinterest in the congressional campaigns also reflected the nonvoting delegate's lack of influence in the nation's capital. All that could be done to generate support for measures of regional benefit, advised Samuel Thurston, Oregon's first representative in Congress, was to "be…a hale fellow with the members of all sides…so that when a vote is wanted, a majority can be procured." By his own account, Columbia Lancaster "had but little ground to stand on" among House colleagues and found "it…difficult thing to cause the departments…to comprehend our wants." Even the energetic and well-connected Isaac Stevens—"the best working man that I ever knew" in Joseph Lane's opinion—experienced frustration during his two congressional terms. Constituents in immediate need of federal assistance invariably failed to appreciate the constraints upon apparently do-nothing delegates. In 1861, for instance, unhappy Republicans sent a territorial map to William Wallace as a none-too-subtle reminder that he ought "to look after…our interests at Washington City."[22]

Concerning matters of territorial government, settlers looked with disdain upon the house of representatives and the council, the lower and upper houses of the assembly. Pointing out a fundamental weakness, one critic observed that the legislature was, by law, "unable to wield that political power incident to a similar body in a State." According to Treasury Department instructions, the only "binding" statutes were those "made in connexion with the acts of Congress." Federally appropriated funds, after all, "cannot be said to belong to the Territory absolutely" and therefore must be expended according to policies devised in the nation's capital. Citing the built-in lack of initiative, the shortage of money and the substantial time wasted upon election of clerks and printers, a contemporary student suggested that "this Territory would…be as well or even better off…if it had never had a legislature." Agreeing, at least in part, with this assessment, the assembly successfully petitioned Congress in 1866 to substitute biennial sessions, strictly limited to forty days, for the annual meetings previously held in Olympia.[23]

Yearly or otherwise, the house and the council rarely dealt with matters of genuine social or economic importance. Despite widespread criticism of the damage inflicted upon "the most sacred of contracts," most sessions featured the granting of divorces to influential petitioners, including, on one memorable occasion, Governor Fayette McMullin. When not engaged in "wholesale divorcing," the assembly tinkered with statutes already in effect, "picking…to pieces and putting together again" the territorial laws. Combined with the habitually slow work of the public printer, this habit "at once made it very difficult," a complainant noted, to understand "what was actually in force," as neither the citizenry nor the courts had any sure means of knowing whether laws had been "repealed or modified."[24]

One persistent issue dramatized the inability to act without regard to sectional, partisan or personal considerations. Under authority of the territorial organic act, Governor Stevens designated Olympia the provisional capital, a logical choice considering the town's size and location at the crossroads of land and water communication. In January 1855, the legislature formalized the selection and provided for construction of a temporary capitol building to accommodate its chambers and the territory's library. The decision, however, was by no means final. A future session might, under new political or demographic circumstances, amend the 1855 statute and transfer the capital to some other point.[25]

Appropriating $50,000 for permanent capitol and penitentiary buildings, Congress supplied construction plans, but left other decisions to local officials. The assembly reaffirmed the earlier choice of Olympia, assigned the prison to Vancouver on the Columbia and appointed commissioners to supervise work. Substituting for Richard Gholson, Acting Governor Henry McGill, a former assistant to President James Buchanan, served as disbursing agent for the federal fund. Upon receipt of the first installment in the summer of 1860, he immediately cleared the Olympia capitol site.[26]

Rejecting the penitentiary, Vancouver instead sought the capital, on the basis of superior, if hardly evident, urban and geographical advantages. Under pressure from Olympia property interests and himself committed to Budd Inlet, McGill moved ahead in preemptive fashion, dismissing a pro-Vancouver commission member and proceeding with construction. Ignoring the fact that work was well advanced, the legislature voted in December 1860 to move the capital to the Columbia River. Adding to the confusion, the assembly also provided for a territorial referendum on the location issue.[27]

Henry McGill, rather than legalistic or commonsensical argument, saved Olympia. Prior to the vote moving the capital to Vancouver, he had expended $3,000 on construction, money that would be wasted if the decision was allowed to stand. When the Treasury Department ordered an immediate halt to the work, the acting governor refused, claiming that superiors in Washington City surely had no intention of abrogating "contracts legally entered into by me." Excoriated on the Columbia River, Democrat McGill was the hero of the day from Olympia to Port Townsend, the best appointment "ever…made at Washington for our Territory" in the opinion of the Republican *Puget Sound Herald*.[28]

Olympia won the July 1861 capital referendum, leading Vancouver by a two-to-one margin. Although most assembly members convened in Olympia that fall, a significant minority, unwilling to accept the will of the voters, gathered on the Columbia. Before either body attempted to conduct business, the territorial supreme court reestablished Olympia as the legal capital, at least for the moment, on the basis of a technical flaw, the failure to include an enabling clause, in the 1860 removal act. The decision was hardly definitive, since the assembly could still move the capital, provided proper form was followed. McGill's defiant stand and the fiscal impact of the Civil War counted for more in determining the outcome. Finding "the Capital *de facto*" in Olympia upon his arrival in late 1861, new secretary L. Jay S. Turney bluntly informed angry Vancouverites that the status was final. Challenged militarily by slavery and disunion, he pointed out, the United States must not be asked "for a single dollar…not essentially necessary." Federal money had just "furnished," in the building completed under McGill's supervision, a "comfortable Capitol" and no funds were available "to rent another."[29]

Assessing and collecting territorial taxes, county government was, for settlers, the most important everyday component of the political system. The modest fiscal burden, however, generated neither intense scrutiny nor serious public debate. Much of the public service was covered free-of-charge by funds supplied from Washington City. In 1856, Cowlitz County residents paid, altogether, a mere $71. Elsewhere, the tax bill that year was $443 in Thurston County, $417 in Pierce County and $74 in King County. The counties exhibited their own brand of inefficiency and irresponsibility. Although a single mandated rate, four mills per dollar of property value, prevailed from the Pacific to the Rockies, actual liability varied, depending upon the whims of locally elected officials. "The same kind of land," one observer noted, "which in one county is assessed at…$15 an acre is assessed in the next county at…$2.50 and less." Absentee owners paid more than genuine inhabitants and the politically influential less than the regular citizen. According to an informed estimate, the failure to equalize assessments cost the territory a third of its potential annual revenue. Sloppy bookkeeping and the casual means of delivering receipts to Olympia produced additional loss and encouraged theft.[30]

Detailing the many natural wonders of Puget Sound, an early Washington historian in 1903 confessed that "it is difficult to speak in terms of moderation." Beginning with the initial letters sent home by new settlers, observations regarding the weather were certainly immoderate. The climate was "more healthy than that of C[alifornia]," at least "as warm as in Pennsylvania" and, indeed, "thoroughly English." Writing of "general" conditions during his first early winter weeks in Seattle, the Reverend David Blaine praised the "long clear mild days—with hardly a cloud visible" and temperatures "just cool enough to feel well with…[warm] clothing on." Nature's free-to-all health spa, Puget Sound was, said Blaine, "a pleasant country…for invalids."[31]

Then the rains came, in full driving force or in days-long drizzle. "Rain, rain, rain!" a Seattle newspaper lamented in the midst of one period of inclemency. Skies turned gray, roads disappeared into boot-sucking mud and high water prevented mail delivery. "All the people who came across the plains…last fall," the *Columbian's* Thornton McElroy wrote in 1853, "are heartily sick of it, and curse the hour they ever started to where there was no *winter*." Catherine Blaine, the wife of Seattle's disillusioned minister, concluded a litany of weather-related complaints with a sarcastic aside: "You would rightfully infer that we are not very comfortable."[32]

Immigrants expecting the future, regardless of the current Puget Sound emphasis upon lumbering, to be in agriculture also experienced tribulation. "At least one million acres…contiguous to salt water," Hugh Goldsborough assured prospective settlers in 1852, contained soil rich enough to "readily produce from twenty-five to thirty bushels of wheat…without any manure and with but one plowing." Judge Francis Chenoweth compared open tracts adjacent to the Sound to "the 'bottom' lands of the Mississippi." As for heavily timbered acreage, "about one third," according to another confident prognostication, ". . . will make No. 1 farms when cleared." Early returns from the southern Sound apparently confirmed the view that the region was, in all essentials, a farming country. Demand for flour in Olympia and Steilacoom was met entirely by imports from San Francisco in 1852. Three years later, local wheat, ground at the falls of the Deschutes River, satisfied the needs of both communities. All that was needed to make Puget Sound a vast farming country was hard work. "It takes time to get the land subdued and the wilde [sic] nature out of it," a Whidbey Island settler explained in 1853. "When that is accomplished we can increase our crops to a very large amount and…make the cultivation of the soil a very profitabal [sic] business."[33]

Most would-be farmers, especially those planning "to plow furrows a mile long," grasped reality upon first seeing the forest. The labor and cost required to clear land slowed development, even when fire was used to simplify timber felling. Staggered by the "thick tangle" of forested cover along the lower Puyallup River, Ezra Meeker estimated that he would need thirteen years to completely clear a quarter section. When timber was removed, moreover, the soil generally proved inferior in quality. "The land immediately on the Sound and for about twenty miles back is gravelly," Thornton McElroy reported from Olympia. After an 1854 visit, Treasury Department agent J. Ross Browne dismissed Puget Sound as "a good country for coarse lumber and nothing more," the "agricultural prospects" ranking "far below those of Oregon or California."[34]

Acreage directly upon the Sound might be worked to a certain extent once the timber was gone, but the sites best suited to agriculture were on fresh water. Seven major rivers entered Puget Sound: the Nooksack, Skagit, Stillaguamish, Snohomish, Duwamish, Puyallup and Nisqually. Deposited by floods, rich soil was ready for plowing. "An idea of its productiveness," one condescending writer asserted of the Puyallup, "may be found from the fact of the Indians having grown 700 bushels of potatoes to the acre, and this in their crude mode of cultivation, without the benefit of the intelligence and experience of the whites." On the Skagit, the largest stream, pioneers discovered "the most desirable tracts on the Sound" on "bottoms averaging from three to ten miles wide."[35]

Theoretically, at least, the rivers were navigable, a positive feature in a time when travel and communication depended upon watercourses. Under prevailing conditions, however, canoes were the only craft suitable for use. Massive timber jams—trees and snags washed downstream by floods and left tangled together above and beneath the surface—blocked the streams. A series of huge drifts constricted the Skagit, covering a mile-and-a-half in combined length. Three jams, each at least a hundred yards long, plugged the lower Stillaguamish. Entering the Puyallup in 1853, Ezra Meeker was soon face-to-face with a "solid drift of monster trees and logs, extending from bank to bank up the river." Rising and falling with the flow of the tides in the Sound, the "rafts" precluded commercial development and diverted water onto adjacent lands.[36]

Pioneers attempting to open the richest tracts of all, downstream from the jams on the grass-covered tidal sections, experienced another form of frustration. The half dozen outlets of the Skagit, for instance, drained twenty thousand acres of flats and marsh. Floods dropped off new layers of soil, but higher stages of the tide overflowed the acreage. Extensive damage resulted when heavy rainfall or snowmelt coincided with abnormally high tidal flows. The first whites at the mouth of the Snohomish River named their precarious settlement, appropriately enough, New Holland. Costly reclamation work was a necessary preliminary to sustained utilization.[37]

Log jams and tidal conditions prevented meaningful development of agriculture west of the Cascades. According to an 1861 account, Washington Territory farmers produced only "one tenth of what is necessary for home consumption." Urban settlers spent $200,000 a year importing beef and dairy products from Oregon. Port Townsend residents alone consumed "on an average three beeves in two days." Flourmills ran on a semi-steady basis only by shipping wheat north from San Francisco. The expectation that demand in the lumber ports would stimulate local agricultural output failed to take into consideration the fact that mill companies purchased supplies in California, providing cargoes for their vessels on the run up the coast.[38]

Dependence upon outside sources of food, combined with increased immigration, had predictable economic consequences. Noting that the number of cattle on the Sound held steady between 1850 and 1853, "while the inhabitants have more than trebeled [sic]," Isaac Ebey informed a distant relative that "hence...a great many persons in the Country are destitute of Cattle." Further inflated by draft animal requirements in the logging camps, oxen currently sold at $300 a yoke. "In making your preparations for a trip to this Country," Ebey advised his brother Winfield, "you would do well to remember...[to] transfer every species of property you have into Cattle." Other pioneers recommended that "putting money in stock" was "as good an investment as can be made."[39]

Writing in January 1853, Olympia newspaper editor Thornton McElroy blamed the settler influx of the previous fall for a prevailing circumstance: "provisions are very scarce and very high;—in fact there is scarcely any thing to eat in the country." Flour cost thirty dollars per hundred pounds, meat—"and it is very *lean* beef at that"—sixteen cents a pound and butter a dollar a pound. In Seattle, the Reverend David Blaine paid "a dollar per dozzen [sic]" for eggs. Attempting, in common with other federal officials, to "eke out my pay," surveyor general James Tilton planted vegetables "on two sides and in the rear" of his Olympia home. High prices also applied to imported manufactured goods. Whidbey Island settler Nathaniel Hill bought a pair of boots for $5.25. Isaac Ebey reported paying a dollar for "good…woolen socks." Forewarned immigrants traveling to Puget Sound by sea bought as many household items as possible in "the City," the common pioneer designation for San Francisco.[40]

Settler diet reflected the failure to achieve self-sufficiency. A "hearty" Whidbey Island meal, Nathaniel Hill advised, consisted of "slapjacks," potatoes and coffee, accompanied by "a little…Rum with a cigar." Detailing the urban equivalent, Thornton McElroy wrote of living "principally on bread, butter, potatoes, oysters and clams." Local waters overflowed in marine resources, compensating in part for the shortfall in farm production. More than one diarist described killing fish "with sticks." Attorney Daniel Bigelow recalled that "a dozen clams could be taken up at one shovel full." Although some whites fished for themselves, most relied upon Indian suppliers, taking advantage of the low prices relative to other commodities. Captain William C. Talbot, founder of the Puget Mill Company town, reported from Port Gamble that "we live on [fish] nearly all togather [sic]." On behalf of its employees, the firm purchased six dozen salmon a day, paying "in trade equal to about from 6 to 17 [cents] cash each."[41]

Puget Sound was, James Swan wrote, a watery "mine of wealth," waiting to be opened by astute fisheries capitalists. The whaling and halibut grounds off Cape Flattery, currently the preserve of the Makah Indians, drew particular attention from prospective investors. The Sound, moreover, had its own extensive shellfish resources—one newspaper reported "immense beds four or five feet thick" near Olympia—ready for Shoalwater-style exploitation. Salmon and oysters sold at high prices in San Francisco and ought to have attracted, other factors being favorable, interest to the region. Territorial leaders urged eastern fishing concerns to "send a colony to locate on the Strait of Fuca," without success. The mileage to California, of no consequence for a commodity like lumber, figured heavily into calculations regarding perishable products. "The vessels are so long going from the fishing grounds to San Francisco," Swan lamented, "that the fish become hard, and…dried up." Capitalists refused to take the risk. Subsistence-oriented Indians, the only source of labor, declined, in any event, to produce more of a surplus than necessary to secure manufactured items in trade.[42]

By default, Puget Sound developed, not as an agrarian commonwealth or as a fishing colony, but, in an oft-used expression, as "the great lumber market of the Pacific Coast." A higher percentage of Washingtonians depended upon this industry for support than was the case in any other western state or territory. Nine of every ten vessels sailing north from the Golden Gate, in one estimate, headed for the Sound, to load at the milling ports. Due to regular market fluctuations in California, the larger sawmills soon entered the overseas trade, supplementing their original coasting business. Washington Territory lumber was sold in Honolulu, in South America and across the Pacific in Australia and China. "A person desirous of going to almost any foreign port," the *Pioneer and Democrat* noted, "would scarcely ever be delayed an unreasonable length of time in finding a vessel on which to obtain a passage." Except for cattle and potatoes sent to Victoria, and Bellingham Bay coal shipped to San Francisco, timber was the only item of consequence exported from Puget Sound.[43]

Owned by Pope & Talbot, a San Francisco partnership of "downright Yankees," the Puget Mill Company was Washington Territory's first major American-owned corporate enterprise. "We do about as much business as all the rest of the Sound," Andrew Pope privately boasted in the early months at Port Gamble. Solidifying this initial advantage, Pope and his associates invested profits in additional production capacity and in shipping. Taking particular pains to control the important Honolulu market, the company sold lumber where prices were highest. Puget sent approximately half its annual cut overseas, while competitors relied largely upon California. "The mill is kept running constantly, day and night," the *Pioneer and Democrat* observed of the result. Calling Port Gamble the "Bangor of the Pacific," a visiting journalist reported that "as usual, a fleet of vessels were loading for different ports in the Pacific."[44]

Logging activities were carried on close to the shoreline and as near the sawmills as practical circumstances allowed. The mills ran twenty-four hours a day, when dictated by demand, with even the resident partners doffing frock coats and rolling-up sleeves to join in the physical labor. Built on tideflat wharves, the crowded plants had no room for storage, so lumber was loaded direct from the saws upon waiting vessels. The beacon-like smoke from burning slabs helped shipmasters navigate the Sound. Sparks thrown off by high-speed machinery or flames from an oil lamp threatened, at any moment, to ignite disastrous fires in the combustible material common to all millsites. In 1864, for instance, the Port Madison sawmill burnt in a matter of minutes, at an uninsured loss of $200,000 to owner George Meigs.[45]

Despite lacking the potential for serious population growth, the lumber ports were the most impressive settlements on Puget Sound. Semi-civilized little bits of New England, the towns reflected Yankee origins. "Every thing seems so comfortable, and on such a liberal scale," a frequent visitor to several of the communities observed. The ports had schools and rudimentary hospitals, institutions rarely found elsewhere on the Sound. Even a truly isolated place like Seabeck, the Hood Canal headquarters of the Washington Mill Company, boasted of its church, schoolhouse, library, hotel, bandstand and baseball field. Cookhouses served the best food in the territory, encouraging experienced hands to remain on the payroll.[46]

Residents of donation claims or conventional towns on the eastern shore of Puget Sound had no reason to feel better off. Farmers and urban dwellers worked as hard as logging hands and mill employees. Clearing the land, even in small

amounts, involved arduous and sustained toil. "I am almost used up in my arms
[,] shoulders and breast," confessed Michael Luark, a homesteader on the
southern Sound. Labor, skilled and unskilled, was in short supply, compelling
townspeople to bear heavy burdens. "I am completely wore out by constant attention to business…," Thornton McElroy of the Olympia *Columbian* wrote
home in the fall of 1853. "I have had to be Editor, Publisher, Compositor, *Devil*
and all hands, besides having the financial affairs to attend to, which is almost
three men's work."[47]

Compared to the mill ports, regular towns held little, if any, appeal. Although considered "the civilized part of the Sound," Olympia had more stumps
than buildings. Catherine Blaine noted that Seattle in 1854 "had but one street
built on and that but thinly" and that "the sides and middle" of this muddy thoroughfare were "all alike stumpy." Horses, cattle and hogs wandered about un-
tended. Amenities were more notable by their absence than by their presence.
Outside the lumber company towns, Puget Sound had three schools in 1853, all
private institutions in Olympia. By 1860, schooling was available in Pierce
County and at Port Townsend. Public education failed in Seattle, however, when
the schoolmaster abandoned his duties to prospect for gold. Except for the occasional traveling minstrel show, urban residents enjoyed few formal outlets for
recreation. In a rare instance of creative response to the public demand for
amusements, local officials opened a bordello in the otherwise underutilized
Pierce County jail.[48]

Immigrants went without all manner of things taken for granted back home.
Housing was scarce, expensive and poorly constructed. Few households possessed factory-made furniture or carpets, the affluent and the poor alike using
do-it-yourself tables, chairs and beds. Postage stamps were unavailable and assorted "ten cent pieces, & shillings" composed a makeshift coinage. In the absence of banks, financing was difficult to arrange. Thornton McElroy, William
Winlock Miller and others with cash to spare—not to mention corrupt government appointees with access to public deposits—operated backdoor banks, loaning money at rates of three to four percent a month. Federal employees suffered,
in particular, frequent delays in the receipt of salaries forcing them to live on borrowed funds, paying interest to the likes of McElroy and Miller.[49]

Building wooden houses close together and burning fires in small rooms,
town residents exposed themselves to danger. Tending his Olympia domicile,
James Tilton "caused all the shavings and *debris* incident to a new building to be
collected…and burnt," placed the stove upon "a flooring of bricks" and used "no
light except that of sperm candles." Most settlers allowed brush and other flam-
mable material to pile up outside their dwellings. Many used lumber in the construction of fireplaces and chimneys. Pinchpenny taxpayers rejected proposals
for hook and ladder companies and sand and water buckets, even though such
elementary schemes would have qualified property owners for insurance.

Warning of the common hazard facing Puget Sound settlements, the *Pioneer and Democrat* pointed out that "a fire, fairly under way, with a favorable wind for its ravages would sweep the town from one end to the other and consume almost every house within its limits."[50]

Detailing another unhappy facet of territorial society, the *Puget Sound Herald* reported in 1859 that "the proportion of white men to white women here is almost twenty to one." The news was more observation than revelation, for the sexual imbalance was impossible to avoid. Bachelors "likely to remain so unless there is a large importation of women" occupied the Cowlitz corridor claims, Michael Luark noticed in the course of an 1853 tour. Thornton McElroy recalled that "there was but *two* ladies in town" when he first settled in Olympia. Single women married quickly. Males, out of necessity, cooked, washed and sewed for themselves. Washington, moreover, was apparently bound to remain an overwhelmingly masculine territory. "There are hundreds of single men here well able to go to the States and 'woo and wed,'" Judge Francis Chenoweth pointed out, "but to leave their business would be ruinous." In the best-known of several attempts to import brides from the Atlantic coast, Asa Mercer brought three dozen "belles" to Seattle in 1866.[51]

Out of practicality, Indians and newcomers intermingled, producing another common and troublesome feature of Puget Sound life. Usable land was narrowly confined between the Cascades and tidewater, covered with heavy stands of timber and intersected by numerous flood-prone rivers. Immigrants opened farms and founded towns in places already utilized, at least for portions of the year, by Indians. Native peoples were also key factors in the early territorial economy, trading salmon and shellfish, working on claims and in the mills and providing transportation services. Dogfish oil, used by the lumber industry as a lubricant, came exclusively from tribal suppliers. White men took native wives-of-convenience, thereby qualifying for the additional 320 acres allowed Donation Act claimants with spouses. Indian prostitutes satisfied sexual needs, at least for clients able to pay the established Puget Sound rate, four dollars per assignation. Settlers acknowledged their dependence by mastering the Chinook jargon, with the help of newspaper-published dictionaries. The reason was clear, wrote one journalist: "all immigrants and new settlers are more or less under the necessity of employing Indian service."[52]

Most whites believed that reliance upon the Indians was fundamentally harmful to economic and social progress. "They are a thieving, pilfering, slothful, disgusting dirty set," Hugh Goldsborough summed up a widely endorsed point of view, "and these inborn propensities make them troublesome and destructive of one's evenness of temper." At Port Townsend, as in other settlements, the "unsightly...smoky, filthy huts of the savages" occupied "valuable property...needed for building purposes." Rural settlers complained of Indians loitering about in a threatening manner, especially when pioneer husbands were away on business. In country or in town, natives supposedly responded to decent treatment with shameless ingratitude. "You may feed them all they can eat & give them all [the clothing] they can put on to day," stated David Blaine, "& to morrow they will come back & ask for more." Blamed for the sexual promiscuity of "degraded" whites, Indians further offended "the eyes of decency" by doffing their clothes in hot weather. After an up-close examination of naked men on a Seattle beach, Catherine Blaine reported that "their skins seem as tough as horse hide, and they know as little of shame as the beasts of the field."[53]

All settlers, urban and rural alike, lived in profound isolation. Thousands of miles of mountain and prairie or blue ocean separated the Far Northwest from old homes, relatives and friends. The United States post office was partially to blame. Aware of the high probability of loss en route, Treasury Department agent J. Ross Browne mailed copies of an important report from Salem, Astoria and Olympia in the summer of 1854, hoping that at least one would somehow get through to Washington City. Within the region, mail from the Willamette Valley usually reached Puget Sound in three weeks, "coming," James Tilton explained, "on Horse back part of the way, by Steamer part, on the Cowlitz River by Canoe manned by Indians, & part of the way by ox teams through the mud the rest of the distance." Until 1858, the only direct letters between the Sound and the outside world were carried informally by passengers and crewmembers aboard lumber company schooners.[54]

The weekly Pacific Mail steamer from San Francisco to Portland deposited Puget Sound letters on the Oregon side of the Columbia, opposite the mouth of the Cowlitz River. Should the vessel's arrival be delayed until after the departure of the northbound postal canoe, Governor Isaac Stevens pointed out, "the people of Washington Territory are kept without their Mail for ten days, it being all the time at the village of Rainier." Rain and snow often closed the Cowlitz to all traffic. "It has frequently happened," Stevens wrote from the Sound, "that the inhabitants of this part of the country have been kept six weeks without a mail...when it has reached the Columbia River in three days from its leaving San Francisco." At such times, quipped the *Pioneer and Democrat*, "the President's [Annual] Message will be...read by the subjects of the Czar, about as soon as the people of this portion of the Pacific will be permitted to give it a perusal."[55]

Service was no better on Puget Sound, where the only road, opened in 1852, ran from Tumwater to nearby Olympia. Communication north of the territorial capital was by water and, under the best of conditions, haphazard. "The entire want of any steam vessels upon these waters," Governor Stevens reported in early 1854, "renders travel...a matter of great inconvenience & delay & of some danger; as the only conveyance is by means of canoes." A semi-regular canoe route, for passengers and mail, connected Olympia and Seattle. Otherwise, people depended upon informal arrangements with local Indians. The native-operated transportation system was the subject of endless white complaint. Indians supposedly had "no idea of the value of time," an infuriating trait bound to result in delayed departures, missed business appointments and lost moneymaking opportunities. They refused to venture out in threatening weather and could never be fully trusted with life and property. When territorial council member G. N. McConaha drowned en route to Seattle in May 1854, suspicion immediately centered upon his Indian paddlers, even though the victim, a notorious drunkard, most likely overturned the canoe in an alcoholic fit.[56]

Going into business on the Olympia-Victoria run in September 1854, with stops at intermediate settlements, the *Major Tompkins* inaugurated the steamboating era on Puget Sound. Mail and passenger service declined "from bad to worse" in the opinion of most inhabitants. Keeping to no posted schedule, according to one complainant, the steamers hurried "in and out of way-ports as if the devil or a sheriff was always after them." Awakened in the middle of the night, travelers raced to the landing "in their stockings and night-caps" rather than risk being left behind. Letters mailed in Seattle for Hood Canal were delivered two weeks later in Seabeck, thirty-five miles away by direct line. The shortage of licensed engineers and experienced pilots supposedly made travel more, rather than less, hazardous, a view supported by frequent breakdowns and occasional sinkings. The *Major Tompkins* was wrecked off Vancouver Island in 1855. Another boat, the *Traveler*, went down near Port Gamble in 1858, with only an officer and two deck hands saved. Bribery—territorial delegate William Wallace received $500 from the winning bidder in 1861—influenced the awarding of the annual Puget Sound postal contract, with negative consequences for efficiency and safety.[57]

Listing the many unwholesome aspects of life on Puget Sound—the rain, the poor housing, the Indians, the lack of mail—Catherine Blaine delivered a telling observation: "I do not know of a single person that would have come if they had known the true state of things here." Settlers, another early Seattle resident recalled, "had to experience many hardships…and to endure long years of isolation and privation." Standards common to everyday life in the states collapsed under the strain of bad weather and loneliness. "The early associations of frontier life," Clarence Bagley remembered in looking back from the turn-of-the-century, were "essentially bad." Males "drank, gambled, [and] ran with women" and females, though often willing to put up a moral front, behaved no better in private.[58]

Pioneers endured in the expectation of someday enriching themselves through urban and territorial growth. Those possessing Donation Act acreage could hardly avoid wealth, as in the case of Thomas Chambers, whose Steilacoom claim was worth over five thousand dollars by 1853. Persons paying for land expected to "double" their money "in two years." Speculation was a universal preoccupation. Confident that Seattle would become the Puget Sound terminus of a transcontinental railroad, the Reverend David Blaine acquired four prime lots and abandoned himself to the enthusiastic mantra of a new and true religion, real estate. "We shall try to secure two more," he advised relatives, "and if we had money I should consider it a profitable investment to purchase...while they can be had so cheaply."[59] Materialism was paramount and, among other unwholesome developments, the Indians stood little chance of avoiding an ignoble fate.

Charles H. Mason. *Washington State Historical Society, Tacoma*

Chapter Three

Respect and Consideration

We venture the assertion with confidence, that the rights of the Indians...have commanded more respect and consideration...than has been accorded to any Indians since the march of civilization crossed the Allegheny mountains.
—Olympia *Pioneer and Democrat*[1]

FROM ITS EARLIEST DAYS, the United States of America made every effort to treat Indians according to high legal and moral precepts. Citing the alleged superiority of Euroamerican culture, policymakers had no trouble justifying the acquisition of tribal lands and resources desired by settlers. At the same time, federal authorities were determined to protect native peoples against complete dispossession and outright physical extinction. Assimilation—"civilization" in the favored term of the time—was the ultimate goal. By 1850, the reservation, carefully bordered and with sufficient land for eventual conversion into individually owned plots, emerged as the training ground for implementation of government policy. Transferred from the War Department to the new Department of the Interior in 1849, the Office of Indian Affairs struggled, with the best intentions possible, to remake Native Americans.[2]

Peace in the West depended, in theory, upon extinguishing native possessory rights before the arrival of settlers. Overland wagon migration to Oregon began in 1843, however, three years prior to abrogation of the Joint Occupation Agreement and extension of American sovereignty south of the 49th parallel. Congress waited until 1848 to create Oregon Territory. The territorial government formally commenced business in the spring of 1849. "It is unfortunately too true," the regionally experienced Army officer Benjamin Alvord recalled of the resulting confusion, "that the whole early settlement of this Country...was in utter neglect of the Indian title."[3]

Samuel Thurston's Donation Act allowed settlers, as a concerned federal official pointed out, to legally claim land "owned and occupied by a people that the Government has always acknowledged to be the bona fide and rightful owners of the soil." Thurston had also secured a companion measure authorizing treaties west of the Cascades. Controlled by Democrats, the Senate refused to ratify agreements concluded by Whig commissioners in the Willamette Valley, on the lower Columbia River and along the southern Oregon coast. Nothing further was done, either side of the Columbia, to address the impending crisis created by the donation legislation. When Isaac Stevens took up his governorship in late 1853, the Indians held rightful title to Washington Territory.[4]

From personal observation and informed sources, Governor Stevens calculated that "the whole number of Indians in Washington Territory" was precisely 14,059, or four times the settler population. Unlike the immigrants, who concentrated west of the Cascades, the natives resided in roughly equal numbers on both sides of the mountains. Federal agent Edward Starling reported that the Puget Sound tribes had lately "become more restless and consequently more troublesome" regarding the failure to receive payment for land taken under the Donation Act. In a related problem—local courts refused to enforce the federal law prohibiting importation of alcohol into country still legally in Indian possession—an out-of-control, hundred-proof torrent engulfed western Washington. The Indians were "rather disposed to be saucy" when inebriated, noted Starling's successor, Michael Simmons, "twitting the whites with having *stolen* their land without any intention of ever paying for it." Whiskey was at the root of violence on the Strait of Juan de Fuca and on Whidbey Island in the winter of 1854.[5]

Despite such localized encounters, few observers expected the Puget Sound Indians to mount large-scale organized resistance. The local people were divided into numerous small tribes and bands, poorly armed and inclined, when not provoked, to peaceful pursuits. Trouble was more likely to come from the direction of British and Russian territory. Northern Indians paid regular visits to the Sound, to trade, work in the sawmills and make mischief. Traveling in enormous ocean-going canoes, some a hundred feet long, the northerners frightened isolated settlers and indigenous villagers. "Propelled by 50 or 60 paddles, provided with large arm chests, abundantly supplied & constantly in order," Captain George Stoneman reported from the Army garrison at Fort Steilacoom, "a fleet of these boats is truly formidable."[6]

In April 1854, white men charged, upon more-than-sufficient evidence, with the "wanton & unprovoked murder" of a visiting Northern Indian were acquitted by an Olympia jury. This sorry episode provided the rationale for a retaliatory attack. The isolated settlers on Bellingham Bay made the ideal target. Raiders descended on the bay in late May, killing two Americans and burning several cabins before paddling off to Vancouver Island. Hurrying to the scene from Steilacoom, soldiers were unequipped to mount a waterborne pursuit. The Hudson's Bay Company confessed that it was unable to restrain the nominal subjects of the British crown. Informed of the bloodshed while on an extended visit to the East, Isaac Stevens recommended that "presents" be distributed to the Northern Indians, the "only course," in his opinion, likely to prevent further humiliating "depredations" against Bellingham Bay.[7]

Violence also appeared likely east of the Cascades, even though there were no American settlers and the government maintained, at most, sporadic contact with the tribes. The Yakama, the Cayuse, the Walla Walla and the Nez Perce, the Indians in possession of country most likely to eventually interest whites, were well mounted, well armed and skilled in the arts of war. "They are exceedingly fearful of being dispossessed of their lands," wrote Benjamin Alvord, currently in command at Fort Dalles, "but are likely to remain at peace with the Americans unless…forcible settlements of their country should be attempted." Attempting to prevent a collision, the Army prohibited the settlement of eastern Oregon and Washington in the summer of 1853.[8]

Convinced that they had a perfect right to file claims east of the Cascades, settlers ignored Benjamin Alvord's widely published proclamation. Whites intended to take land upriver from The Dalles, "not only without the consent of the Indians," a federal official reported in late 1853, "but in the face of their strong remonstrance." Determined to open mineral resources to exploitation and the "inexhaustible grass" of the Walla Walla Valley to stock interests and farmers, Isaac Stevens contributed to the growing tension. As an inducement to homesteading, the governor demanded extension of the General Land Office surveys across the mountains. "I consider its speedy settlement so desirable," he wrote of eastern Washington, "that all impediments should be removed."[9]

Treaty making, the definitive means of removing impediments, was finally approved by Congress in August 1854. Actual work north of the Columbia was delayed until December, when Governor Stevens returned from a prolonged visit to the Atlantic coast. Determined to make up for lost time, he vowed to "accomplish the whole business, extinguishing the Indian Title to every acre of land in the Territory" prior to arrival of the fall wagon trains in 1855. Together with commissioners appointed to assist him on Puget Sound, the governor studied the so-called "Omaha treaties," recent assimilation-oriented agreements reflecting, according to Commissioner of Indian Affairs George Manypenny, "the policy of the Government." Harvard-trained lawyer George Gibbs assumed the task of drafting a standard Washington Territory treaty based upon these documents.[10]

Provided with the "Omaha" model and personally in favor of assimilation, Stevens was hardly a free agent in dealing with the tribes. His one significant addition to the framework supplied by Commissioner Manypenny became, with the passage of time, the most widely quoted provision of the Washington treaties: "The right of taking fish, at all usual and accustomed grounds and stations, is further secured to said Indians in common with all citizens of the Territory." Though much debated in a later era, the governor's intent was perfectly clear. Because assimilation was considered to be a lengthy process, requiring at least a generation of reservation education and experience, the Indians must feed themselves by traditional means until completion of the anticipated transformation to agriculture. "It was…thought necessary to allow them to fish at all accustomed places," Stevens and his commissioners concluded, "since this would not in any manner interfere with the rights of citizens and was necessary for the Indians to obtain a subsistence."[11]

Between Christmas Day and the end of January, Governor Stevens concluded the treaties of Medicine Creek, Point Elliott, Point No Point and Neah Bay, establishing nine tidewater reservations. "The councils were conducted & the Treaties concluded," he informed Commissioner Manypenny, "in all fairness, justice and honor." Expecting timely Senate ratification, the governor ordered agent Michael Simmons to prepare for relocation "in July, August & September," opening ceded land to immigrants arriving in the fall of 1855. In the rush to administer self-congratulation, Stevens failed to comprehend, much less appreciate, significant differences of Indian opinion. The agreements left the daily and seasonal routine of tidewater villages relatively undisturbed. Indians living away from saltwater, however, expressed unhappiness over giving up their homes and diversified subsistence habits. Some tribes, like the Nooksack on the northern Sound, failed to attend the councils, but were expected to voluntarily move to the reservations as if they had been actual signatories.[12]

An over-confident Stevens had already sent personal secretary James Doty across the Cascades to prepare for the much-anticipated Walla Walla council. Although various native leaders expressed opposition to the proposed land cession, Doty informed the governor that he would experience "little difficulty" coming to terms with the tribes. Attended by five thousand Indians and lasting from May 29 through June 11, 1855, the council was a moving and colorful affair. The rain-punctuated conference was also highly contentious, upsetting to most of the individuals present. Kamiakin of the Yakamas clarified his bitterness regarding the entire process. The Nez Perce head chief Lawyer declared his intention to sign, but Looking Glass, a tribal rival, spoke emotionally against the concept of selling land. In private meetings, Stevens used his persuasive skills to secure formal agreement to the treaties. Three large agencies resulted: the 5,100 square mile Nez Perce reservation in southeastern Washington and northwestern Oregon, the 1,200 square mile Yakama reservation between the Cascades and the Columbia River and the 800 square mile Umatilla reservation, entirely within Oregon Territory.[13]

Escorted by Nez Perce warriors, Stevens rode east upon the conclusion of the proceedings, intent upon clearing the northern railroad line in meetings with the Flathead and the Blackfoot. Convinced that "we are succeeding grandly with our Indian business thus far," the governor equated marks on sheets of paper with genuine acceptance of the treaties and had no idea of the ill feeling left behind. His subordinates, meanwhile, irresponsibly tested the willingness of the Indians to accept whites into eastern Washington. Although the Walla Walla treaties took effect only upon Senate ratification, the Olympia *Pioneer and Democrat*, editorial organ of the territorial Democracy, proclaimed in late June that "the land ceded is now open for settlement." By the end of the year, homesteaders occupied fifty claims in the Walla Walla Valley.[14]

Warning Governor Stevens, via long-riding messengers, of the "very uneasy state" of Indian opinion, George Gibbs informed his political patron of a second potentially negative development, the discovery of gold in northeastern Washington's Colville Valley. The first reports of the find reached the settlements in early July. "Real, yellow, glittering gold…has been brought in, in large quantities," the Steilacoom *Puget Sound Courier* announced. "A great many persons" intended to "leave immediately…for this new Ophir of the Pacific." With the existence of California-style wealth taken for granted, the only real question was which route to take, from The Dalles north or from the Sound, over the Naches road or Snoqualmie Pass.[15]

"Gold hunters" departed for Colville "almost daily." By late summer, advised Acting Governor Charles Mason, Olympia was "quite deserted." Curtailing production at Port Gamble because of lost hands, the Puget Mill Company joined other employers in advancing wages, vainly attempting to recruit from a rapidly shrinking worker supply. Returning in mid-September from a personal inspection, congressional delegate J. Patton Anderson reported "plenty of gold over an extent of country near one hundred miles square but too scattering to be profitably collected by the implements" then available. Anderson's assertion that the true value of the diggings could be determined only by "one year of thorough prospecting" with "the aid of power machinery" ought to have been sobering news. Two hundred miners nonetheless determined to winter in the Colville Valley, braving snow and frozen streams in the semi-mindless quest for riches.[16]

Far away at Fort Benton on the Missouri River, Governor Stevens, better attuned to "the gold excitement" than to the implications of his treaties, expressed grave "apprehension" over developments east of the Cascades. From the Sound or from The Dalles, the trails to Colville converged in the Yakima Valley. Ignoring the dangerous consequences of such behavior, some goldseekers engaged in various acts of depredation, molesting women and stealing horses. The inevitable result, wrote a concerned J. Patton Anderson, was "disaffection and hostility… this side of the mines." Young men of the Yakama nation retaliated upon actual transgressors and innocent travelers. "Straggling parties of miners," Acting Governor Mason advised at summer's end, "have been cut off…to the extent so far as we can judge of some twelve or fifteen.[17]

Rumors of impending war east of the Cascades troubled the authorities. Regular troops left Steilacoom and The Dalles at the end of September, to converge upon the Yakima Valley and, by a demonstration of strength, discourage further violence. Unaware of these military movements, Isaac Stevens instructed eastern Washington Indian agent Andrew J. Bolon to quell the disturbances. Bolon himself was killed, however, when waylaid on September 23. The agent's death horrified settlers, especially because of erroneous claims that the murder had been ordered by Yakama tribal leaders. Major Granville Haller's battle-inexperienced and poorly outfitted command, the southern component of the Army's campaign, collided with a superior force on October 6. Suffering five fatalities and enduring a grim two-day standoff, the major withdrew, on Indian sufferance, to The Dalles. Together, the Bolon murder and Haller's retreat opened the Yakama War of 1855–1856.[18]

Americans living directly upon tidewater discounted the possibility of violence west of the mountains. Settlers living on inland claims attempted, however, without success, to warn territorial leaders of the discontent among Indians in their vicinity. Reports that the Sound tribes had formed a "league" with the Yakamas caused a brief panic in mid-September. Homesteaders returned to their farms when an Army patrol failed to find any sign of hostile movements. On October 28, however, Indians killed eight whites in the White River Valley. Shocked by the "massacre," terrified pioneers from Monticello on the Columbia to Bellingham Bay took shelter in hastily built blockhouses. "Those who, a short time before insisted that the Indians were all friendly," wrote Seattle's Arthur Denny, "…now declare[d] most vehemently that all were hostile, and must all be treated as enemies." The close relations between the river-dwelling Nisquallies and the Yakamas, facilitated by convenient passes in the Cascades, convinced most whites that a region-wide anti-American conspiracy had come into bloody existence.[19]

Washington Territory was poorly equipped to conduct a war on a single front, much less on two fronts. Governor Stevens returned to the Sound only in January and even then he was on the defensive, from partisan accusations that the miserable conflict was "Stevens' War." In the early months, at least, direction of the war effort fell to Acting Governor Charles Mason and to surveyor general James Tilton, neither of exhibited capacity as strategist or popular leader. The territory's inability to pay freight charges caused a San Francisco merchant to withhold shipment of a much-needed consignment of muskets, rifles and ammunition, which exacerbated an already serious weapons shortage. Men were also in short supply, compelling the reliance east of the Cascades upon Oregon volunteers. Until its credit was exhausted in the spring of 1856, Washington Territory relied on the Puget Mill Company and the Hudson's Bay Company for supplies, purchased in anticipation of Congress appropriating funds to retire the debt.[20]

Fortunately for the territory, the Indians declined to seriously test the questionable American war-making capacity. East of the Cascades, seven hundred regulars and Oregon volunteers marched to the Yakima Valley in late October.

Aside from one minor clash, the Yakamas withdrew ahead of the advancing column. The expedition returned to The Dalles unchallenged, after rounding up horses, destroying food supplies and, for prejudicial good measure, sacking the Catholic Ahtanum mission. Still eager for blood, Oregon's aggressive Governor George Curry next sent his volunteers to the Walla Walla Valley. Abandoning all notions of intelligent, not to mention decent, conduct, the Oregonians unnecessarily widened the conflict, attacking the previously neutral Walla Wallas and brutally murdering their leader, Peopeomoxmox.[21]

West of the Cascades, where the hostile Indian force barely numbered two hundred warriors, the "war" was limited to occasional skirmishes. Expecting to "drive the enemy thro the passes of the Cascades," as "General" James Tilton ordered a hapless subordinate, Washington Territory floundered into a belated recognition of climatic and topographical obstacles. Regulars and volunteers ventured from Steilacoom to the White River on two occasions in November, only to withdraw when confronted by heavy rain and muddy trails. Giving up altogether after a sniper killed the popular Lieutenant William Slaughter, the Army went on the defensive for the winter, satisfied with erecting protective outposts around the settlements.[22]

Attempting to restore settler spirits upon his return to Olympia in January 1856, Governor Stevens demanded a more aggressive approach. "The war shall be prosecuted until the last hostile Indian is exterminated," he vowed in an address to capital residents. In particular, the Army ought to immediately launch a winter campaign against the Yakamas, restoring communications with Colville and removing the threat to overland immigration. Rejecting this unwanted advice, regular officers blamed Stevens himself for at least the Yakama War and accused Oregon and Washington of exaggerating the danger in order to run up grossly inflated bills for congressional reimbursement. From his California headquarters, General John Wool informed Stevens that he would take the field only in the spring, when the grass was up and the passes opened by the melting of the snow. This highly unpopular, if perfectly rational, decision accounted for an unusual expansion, in the public mind, of the conflict, at least east of the Cascades. "In short," pronounced the *Pioneer and Democrat*, "it is a war of Gen. Wool and the Indians against the...inhabitants of this portion of the Pacific coast."[23]

Cooperation between the regulars and the volunteers prevailed, henceforth, only west of the mountains. Engaging in their first offensive action since White River, Indians fired into Seattle in late January. They inflicted a single fatality before withdrawing unscathed under bombardment from a naval vessel anchored in Elliott Bay. In the aftermath of this "Battle of Seattle," Colonel Silas Casey set regulars, territorial recruits, and native allies to work extending roads and bridges toward the White River. Flushed out by this methodical intrusion, the enemy attacked construction parties on the first and again on the tenth of March. Driven off on both occasions, the Indians crossed the mountains to sanctuary with the Yakamas. The Puget Sound war was suddenly at an end.[24]

Most whites expected the conflict to resume momentarily, possibly by an outbreak on the part of previously uninvolved groups. Adding to the unrelieved tension, revenge-minded settlers murdered Indians. Blamed by his political opponents for the treaties, then for the war and now for an uncertain peace, Governor Stevens gave way to sustained emotionalism. Beset, in his own words, by "cliques, combinations and sinister influences," he interpreted disagreement as disloyalty and equated personal opposition with outright treason. Despite the lack of credible evidence for the charge, the governor had confined mixed-blood homesteaders to Fort Nisqually for allegedly supporting the Indian cause. After the March fighting, seven of the accused individuals attempted to return home, only to be arrested by territorial volunteers. Outflanking attempts to secure release of the prisoners, Stevens declared martial law in Pierce County on April 3.[25]

Vainly attempting to hold a hearing on the matter in Steilacoom, Judge Edward Lander was briefly detained on May 7. Moving to Olympia, Lander ordered the prisoners set free and, when this edict was ignored, threatened the governor with a contempt citation. Hastily responding, Stevens proclaimed martial law in Thurston County and arrested his judicial antagonist a second time. In the face of hostile public opinion and a renewed attempt to convene court in Steilacoom, the governor backed down, revoking his orders on May 25. "There was no manner of necessity for Martial Law," reflected Judge Francis Chenoweth in a succinct contemporary assessment. "As far as I could see the Indians were conquered at the time." Stevens claimed, weakly, that his election to Congress in 1857 was an after-the-fact endorsement. The reality, though, was that he had dealt himself a self-inflicted political wound of sufficient severity that full recovery was problematical.[26]

While Stevens struggled with the martial law fiasco, the eastern Washington war petered out, with no definitive conclusion in battle or on council ground. In April 1856, Colonel George Wright marched to the Yakima Valley, went into camp on the swollen Naches River and commenced talks with the Indians, encamped on the opposite bank. Horrified at the prospect of peace without chastisement of the enemy, the only means, in his view, of removing the Indian obstacle to settlement, the governor attempted to provoke an open confrontation. At his orders, Colonel Benjamin Shaw led territorial volunteers across the Cascades in June, to strike the Yakamas in the flank. When the Indians scattered, Shaw pushed on to the southeast rather than join Wright in difficult pursuit. In mid-July, he finally drew blood, attacking a defenseless column of old men, women and children south of the Oregon line.[27]

Attempting to capitalize upon Washington Territory's inglorious military triumph, Governor Stevens convened a second Walla Walla council. When intemperate demands angered many of the Indians present, he had to be "rescued" by the Army. Suitably humiliated by the latter experience, the governor was "mortified" to learn that Colonel Wright, who had finally settled Yakama matters in bloodless fashion, intended to pacify the Walla Walla Valley in no-shots-fired style. Expressing the views of most whites, Stevens denounced the regulars for "a surrender to…hostile Indians, unprecedented in our history." Talking instead of fighting, out of apparent cowardice, Wright had "degrade [d] our flag" and "disgraced his service." Compounding the insult with genuine injury, the Army promised to secure abrogation of the Walla Walla treaties and prohibited settlers from returning to eastern Washington. For the territory, the ban on settlement signified the practical loss of the war. So long as powerful and untamed tribes remained in control beyond the Cascades, Americans would be restricted to the narrow and second class land between Puget Sound and the slopes of the mountains.[28]

The conflict came to an inconclusive and unhappy close in 1856 with numerous questions unanswered. Honoring the "rights and usages of war," the Army refused to turn Indians over for punishment by the civil authorities. Isaac Stevens countered that the wanted Indians were lawbreakers, rather than prisoners of war, and must not be set free. The Nisqually Leschi, the governor's most prominent opponent on the Sound, had "committed acts of atrocity under circumstances of peculiar treachery and bloodthirstiness almost beyond example." With many whites bent upon revenge, the Indians would fall victim to brutal reprisal if released. Confirming the relevance of this practical concern, Leschi's brother Queimuth was murdered while under guard in the governor's Olympia office. Although their identities were widely known, the killers escaped prosecution. Stevens expressed more outrage over the killing taking place "in the Executive office" than with the crime itself.[29]

Leschi himself met a prolonged and undeserved fate, as the victim of one governor's ambition and another's cowardice. Formally pursuing the Nisqually leader in the courts, Stevens fortified a politically important argument blaming the Indians, not his treaties, for the war. Captured in November, Leschi promptly went on trial for the murder of a territorial volunteer. The evidence was "far from conclusive," one of the governor's associates privately conceded, and the trial ended in a hung jury, the outcome a sure indication of the flimsy nature of the case. In March 1857, however, a second trial produced the desired conviction. Tribal representatives attended the proceedings as special territorial guests. Through detailed interpretation, Stevens reported, the "justice of the law" was conveyed to his native invitees.[30]

Elected to Congress in 1857, Stevens left Leschi's execution to the new governor, Fayette McMullin, a former Virginia congressman and continuing public advocate of slavery. A prestigious defense team, including most of the officers at Fort Steilacoom, organized on behalf of the condemned man following the second trial. Aided by Hudson's Bay Company factor William F. Tolmie, Lieutenant August Kautz exposed perjured testimony and determined the identity and whereabouts of the actual killer. Meeting with Leschi's defenders on January 16, 1858, McMullin examined the evidence and left all present with the clear impression that he would soon issue a pardon. Before he could act, McMullin received a petition signed by hundreds of Puget Sounders, threatening him with bodily harm, at the least, should Leschi be "respited." Willing to let an innocent man hang rather than face down a mob, the governor immediately denounced clemency as "a gross violation of Justice." Attending an anti-Leschi "indignation" meeting, he "participated somewhat," by his own account, "in the excitement of the occasion and indulged in some very strong language of censure upon…the officers of the garrison." Once the sentence was carried out, on February 19, McMullin demanded that the War Department recall Colonel Silas Casey and the other regulars for daring to interfere with law and order in Washington Territory.[31]

Adding to Governor McMullin's burdens, the Northern Indians persisted in their intimidating visits to Puget Sound. Northerner threats to "kill every Boston they can lay their hands on" resulted in construction of Army posts on Bellingham Bay and at Port Townsend. The United States Navy took action, as well, launching a successful amphibious assault on an encampment near Port Gamble in November 1856. In the spring of 1857, however, canoe sightings sent whites fleeing to blockhouses in Whatcom, Sehome and other points. The Northern Indians carried out their most daring raid in August, murdering Isaac Ebey before returning to British territory with the well-known Whidbey Island pioneer's head as a grisly trophy.[32]

Taking office in the midst of the panic over Ebey's murder, Fayette McMullin vowed to punish the killers. In a burst of aggressive energy, he inspected the crime scene, consoled the victim's relatives and visited Victoria for consultation. "Many of the people are collected in block houses for safety," the governor reported, "while others…are preparing to leave the territory altogether." As in the past, McMullin soon learned, nothing positive could be done, either to apprehend suspect individuals or to prevent future attacks. Upon the return of good weather in the spring of 1858, he posited a deadly prospect: "our unprotected northern settlements will be continually liable to the incursions of those numerous & formidable savages…whilst we have not a single arm of offence with which we can…reach & chastize them."[33]

On a more positive note, the various Indian alarms resulted in construction of Washington's first road system. Demands for improved transportation predated the creation of a separate government in North Oregon. At congressional hearings and in meetings at the War Department, territorial delegate Columbia Lancaster argued the case for military roads, roads that would also benefit civilian travelers. In particular, Lancaster wanted Vancouver linked with The Dalles, "so that we can get to the east side of the Cascade mountains in winter," and also he wanted the Columbia River connected with Puget Sound, "so that the people of Oregon can join with the people of our Territory and concentrate at any point in either Territory at an hours notice." Appropriating funds for the two projects in February 1855, Congress assigned the work to a new Army agency, the Pacific Coast Office of Military Roads.[34]

George Horatio Derby, the eccentric engineering lieutenant assigned to Oregon and Washington, personally supervised construction of "a good road across the Portage" at the Cascades in 1856. Together with steamboat service below and above that point, the project "certainly fulfil[led]," in his view, "all the conditions of a Military Road." Despite assorted difficulties, including squabbles over the exact route and contractor problems, Monticello and Puget Sound were connected in various stages of work carried out between 1857 and 1861. New undertakings authorized by Congress linked Olympia with Seattle and the latter, albeit only by a trail suitable for pack animals, with Whatcom. Although water continued to be the preferred means of transportation, land travel along the eastern shore of the Sound became feasible for the first time.[35]

Insufficient funding and unrealistic planning, unfortunately, generated inferior results. "Derby's road," one officer wrote of the Cascades portage route a few months after its completion, "has proved an entire failure—all the deep cutting having washed away, down the river." The Cowlitz corridor road was a permanent improvement-of-sorts. Daily Olympia-Monticello stage service commenced in January 1861, covering the eighty-eight miles in twenty-eight hours, with eleven intervening stops. "The annihilation of time and distance," a duly impressed commentator proclaimed, "seems incomprehensible." The experience exhausted, rather than exhilarated, most travelers. Crowded into open coaches, passengers were covered in dust in summer and splattered with mud in the winter rainy season. Bouncing "over roots of great trees, and into [the] hollows between them," the stages followed little more than "a path cut through the dense forest." Repair crews fell behind in the work of removing fallen timber and repairing flood-damaged bridges, forcing weary ticketholders to endure long delays.[36]

A major new development focused attention upon communications with Bellingham Bay. "Much excitement exists on Vancouver's Island," the *Pioneer and Democrat* announced in early March 1858, "in consequence of the alleged discovery of rich gold deposites [sic]…in the British possessions." The Hudson's Bay Company had already acquired a hundred pounds of dust from Indians working isolated Fraser River bars. Back from a quick exploratory trip, Whatcom's R. W. Peabody reported the first miners on the scene earning five to six dollars a day, in spite of high water. "The question is settled beyond a doubt," said Peabody, "that gold can be found in as large quantities as ever found in California." The best prospects appeared to be on the Fraser upstream from Fort Hope to the mouth of Thompson's River. Signs of gold were evident, though, all along the international border, "south as well as north, crossing the 49th parallel at various points."[37]

"Gold," a Puget Sound homesteader wrote in the third week of April, "is all the talk here." At the first news of the strike, Sehome coal miners departed for the Fraser. Most of the garrison at Fort Bellingham deserted. Mill and logging camp hands and lumber ship crews soon followed, curtailing timber production and exports. The initial contingent from California, aboard three steamers packed well beyond legal limit with eight hundred men and a few women, entered Victoria harbor at the end of the month. According to the best contemporary estimates, by early summer thirty thousand miners were on hand, most having arrived by sea from San Francisco.[38]

Although the Fraser River was in British territory, the rush was primarily a matter of Americans attempting to reach the mines through U.S. points-of-entry. Shoals obstructed the Fraser and troublesome Hudson's Bay Company officials patrolled the stream. Navigation, except for traffic carried in canoes, terminated at Fort Hope, a hundred miles from the sea and "many hard miles" short of the main diggings. The "iron bound coast" north of the Fraser offered neither safe landing places nor shortcuts to the interior. Bellingham Bay, on the other hand, was the closest port with relatively direct access to the mining country. Going ashore at Whatcom, properly outfitted goldseekers could traverse the intervening prairie along the 49th parallel.[39]

Miners gathered at Bellingham Bay, waiting for low water on the Fraser and the opening of the road across the border. "Whatcom had all the appearance of San Francisco in 1848," one detainee noted of the sudden urban boom, "houses going up in every direction, on lots, streets, alleys, and water flats." The eight frame dwellings counted in May became a hundred by the first of July. Most arrivals simply set up tents along the beach. "All the worst characters of the coast" assembled in Whatcom, claimed a would-be prospector. Gambling was carried on "in every saloon, restaurant, and accessible place." Together with the standard varieties of immorality, from softest to hardest core, games of chance and no-chance made the community, in a horrified onlooker's opinion, "as much like the city of Sodom of old as ever a town could well become in this advanced day of the world."[40]

Remaking Whatcom into a sodden Barbary Coast of the North, the gold excitement affected the entire Puget Sound basin. "The news of extensive mines, "the *Pioneer and Democrat* pointed out, "…came upon us at a time when the country was not prepared for this state of things." With provisions in short supply and the prospect of obtaining mining implements "entirely out of the question," prices mounted to unprecedented levels. Shipping disappeared from the central and southern Sound, vessel owners concentrating on the needs of Whatcom, Victoria and Port Townsend. Animosity toward the Hudson's Bay Company was rekindled, on account of what Isaac Stevens described as "the enormity and absolute illegality" of the firm's attempt to regulate affairs on the British side of the 49th parallel. New interest, meanwhile, was sparked in the northern transcontinental railroad, a project bound to aid exploitation of the mines.[41]

Completed in August, the Nooksack-Fraser wagon road opened unimpeded access to the mining country, guaranteeing a prime local object, the "growth and prosperity of Whatcom." The gold rush, however, was already well on the way to a retreat. A thousand disappointed miners, reported as "highly disgusted," returned to California in July alone, most without ever advancing inland from Bellingham Bay. Those actually reaching the diggings, at Texas Bar, Santa Clara Bar and other remote places, also suffered disappointment. "It is true that gold has been found everywhere," reported John Nugent, a special American State Department agent, "but, for the most part, diffused in such small quantities as not to reward the labor of digging for it." The odds, Nugent calculated, worked against the individual prospector, for "in the whole region there are not eligible placers more than enough to give remunerative employment to about fifteen hundred miners."[42]

Even though there was less gold than advertised, the collapse was more a failure of logistics than of prospecting enthusiasm. Provisions were scarce and not easily transported to the isolated camps. Food was costly to begin with and by fall, a miner recalled, "there was none to be bought at any price." Beginning in late August, canoes carrying Fraser River refugees, men without the means for a ticket to San Francisco, landed in the Puget Sound settlements on virtually a daily basis. "They had a truly poverty-stricken appearance," the Steilacoom *Herald* noted of one party, "some being shoeless, others hatless, and all more or less ragged."[43] Briefly the territory's largest community, Whatcom became Washington's first ghost town, occupied by bewildered tideflat diehards. On the Sound in general, the sudden availability of non-Indian workers, from the ranks of distressed prospectors, compensated for falling prices and real estate values. Misbehavior on the part of individuals traveling to and from the Fraser, on the other hand, helped bring on a resumption of warfare.

Washington Territory, as a working political entity in 1858, extended only as far as the margins of the Columbia Basin. The Army maintained posts in the Yakima and Walla Walla valleys. Snow, however, isolated Fort Simcoe from the outside world during the winter. On account of the prohibitive cost of imported feed, the Fort Walla Walla horses were sent to The Dalles for the cold weather months, immobilizing the garrison. The territorial Indian superintendency assigned agents to the Yakamas and Nez Perce, but unfriendly tribal elements forced the officials to reside, out of harm's way, at The Dalles and at Walla Walla, far from the reservations to be established under the still-unratified treaties.[44]

An uneasy truce prevailed east of the Cascades. Except for those bands trading with Fort Simcoe, agent Richard Lansdale reported from The Dalles, "the great body of the [Yakama] nation have no desire for intercourse of any kind with the whites." Pressed upon the War Department by a determined Isaac Stevens, continued demands for the arrest of Indians accused of murder added to the tension. Planning for the Mullan Road, to link Fort Walla Walla with Fort Benton on the Missouri River, antagonized the Palouse, the Spokane and the Coeur d'Alene, previously neutral tribes. In accord with past military attempts to protect the Indians and preserve the peace, General Newman Clarke, the new Army commander on the Pacific coast, reaffirmed the ban on settlement upriver from The Dalles.[45]

Gold again provided the opportunity for whites and Indians to engage in violence. Driven by the profits of isolated wartime miners, a renewed rush to Colville commenced in 1857. The usual nasty encounters ensued on the trails and at the mines. The Fraser River excitement sent an even larger number of goldseekers into the region east of the Cascades. The likely consequences of the "recent discoveries of Gold Fields" compelled a reluctant Army to prepare for war. Attempting to forestall hostilities by a demonstration of superior military force, Lieutenant Colonel Edward Steptoe marched from Fort Walla Walla with 164 men on May 6, 1858, expecting to visit Colville and quell the disturbances.[46]

Ten days out, Steptoe's ill-conceived expedition encountered a thousand Palouse, Spokane and Coeur d'Alene warriors south of the Spokane River. Seriously outnumbered and equipped with inferior weapons, the colonel sensibly ordered a withdrawal. The retreat quickly degenerated into a near-rout. Seven whites were killed before the command regrouped atop a ridge, ready for a last-stand. Covered by darkness, the soldiers again retreated, however, crossing the Snake River and reaching Fort Walla Walla on May 22. Humiliating the Army, the "Steptoe Disaster" marked the long anticipated renewal of war in eastern Washington.[47]

Settlers and their political representatives saw the Disaster in positive terms, as sure to provoke the Army into a more aggressive stance. Steptoe's folly "made a great impression here," Isaac Stevens wrote from the halls of Congress, discrediting "the temporizing measures of the military" and the notion that violence in the Pacific Northwest was the fault of the treaties, rather than Indian mendacity. Disregarding the danger, miners briefly persisted in attempts to reach the Fraser and Colville. On June 20, however, the Yakama Owhi attacked a party of goldseekers on the Wenatchee River, sending the terrified whites into several days of wild flight. Sheltering at Simcoe, The Dalles, and Walla Walla, thwarted prospectors demanded that the Army reopen the trails and end, permanently, the threat to the gathering of wealth.[48]

Beset by angry miners and determined to avenge Steptoe, Colonel George Wright, once again in field command east of the Cascades, imposed stiff terms upon a vanquished foe. Marching north from Fort Simcoe, Major Robert

Garnett captured and executed ten persons accused of crimes against whites. Operating from Fort Walla Walla and equipped with new long-range rifles, Wright's main column engaged the Palouse, the Spokane and the Coeur d'Alene in early September. Official casualty figures for the "battles" of Four Lakes and Spokane Plains, sixty dead Indians and a single wounded soldier, reflected the colonel's superior weaponry.[49]

Accepting the Indian surrender, Wright administered a draconian punishment of the sort long-demanded by white civilians. Although the Walla Walla agreements remained unratified, and in any event applied to only a portion of the people involved in the 1858 conflict, the Olympia *Pioneer and Democrat* insisted that the hostile tribes be "taught to respect their treaties, and to cease their depredations." The colonel ordered a thousand Indian horses killed, effectively ending the capacity of the Palouse and their allies to make mobile war. After military trial, seventeen Indians, including the surviving murderers of Andrew Bolon, were hanged. The executions and the destruction of stock, rather than the fighting, justified Wright's succinct description of his campaign as a "march...of destruction."[50]

Other actions added to the Army's newfound popularity. Established in late 1858 as an independent military command, the Department of Oregon placed the security interests of the Pacific Northwest on equal footing with those of California. General William S. Harney, assigned to the department after years of fighting the Sioux and the Cheyenne on the Great Plains, intended to settle all questions, east and west of the Cascades. An unanticipated crisis in the summer of 1859 provided him with the opportunity to improve defenses against the Northern Indians. San Juan Island, the westernmost of the picturesque San Juan chain, was closer to Victoria than to the Washington Territory mainland. Possession was in peaceful and apparently eternal dispute between the United States and Great Britain, the former claiming Haro Strait and the latter Rosario Strait as the boundary. Two dozen Americans and a small number of Hudson's Bay Company employees coexisted in relative harmony, the only difficulty arising from attempts by Whatcom County to collect taxes from all concerned. On June 15, however, a company hog was killed, producing the international incident locally known as the Pig War. Regulars from Fort Bellingham, under Captain George Pickett, and British troops landed on San Juan. Naval vessels of both nations cruised offshore, protecting the landing parties and the rival claims to sovereignty.[51]

In keeping with Harney's aggressive reputation, a boundary dispute became the pretext for a counterstroke against the Northern Indians. So near Victoria, San Juan Island was, the general pointed out, "the most suitable point from which to observe and prevent the Northern Indians from visiting our settlements to the south of it." Operating from an advanced base, a Navy steamer would, presumably, have little problem heading off canoes bound for the Sound.

Washington Territory public opinion endorsed the concept. Pickett's landing was "a very judicious step," claimed the *Puget Sound Herald,* sure to eventually halt "predatory incursions" from Vancouver Island. In the process, the Anglophobic Olympia *Pioneer and Democrat* exclaimed, Harney had foiled a "diabolical scheme" of the Hudson's Bay Company for "the planting of British Colonies upon American soil."[52]

Washington City, unfortunately, was far away and little concerned over the Indian threat. In the nation's capital, General Harney appeared to be risking war over a side of Canadian bacon. Blaming the general for an unnecessary Anglo-American quarrel, President James Buchanan recalled him from the Pacific Northwest. Initiating talks for peaceful resolution of the dispute, the State Department rebuked Richard Gholson for encouraging Puget Sound tribes, in his single notable act as Washington's governor, to attack the northerners, whenever and wherever encountered. Finally established in 1872—by then, American population growth had virtually eliminated the Northern Indian danger—under international arbitration, the Vancouver Island-Washington Territory boundary followed Haro Strait, leaving the disputed island a U.S. possession. The San Juan imbroglio also served as a symbolic final stand for another longtime nemesis, the Hudson's Bay Company. A special commission awarded the firm and the Puget's Sound Agricultural Company $650,000 in total compensation for property and claims south of the 49th parallel.[53]

Military activism produced results east, as well as west, of the Cascades. Ignoring a protest from the Indian Office, the Army revoked the settlement ban after Wright's victory, opening the way, at last, for genuine expansion of Washington Territory. Senate ratification of the Stevens treaties, in 1859, removed a last legal obstacle to claimtaking. According to newspaper reports, two thousand whites, intent upon exploiting the rich grasslands near Fort Walla Walla, planned to take advantage of the opportunities now available in eastern Washington.[54]

By one informed account, forty thousand head of cattle roamed the range east of the mountains within a year of treaty ratification. Originally three log shanties catering to the garrison of the nearby Army post, Walla Walla became, in a matter of months, the largest inland Northwest settlement. A visitor reported fifty frame buildings in place, with two restaurants, a hotel and several saloons in active business. The cattle trade and the military profession were masculine endeavors, so white women were rare and Sunday was the rowdiest day of the week, with substantially more gambling and drinking than preaching and reflection.[55]

Centered upon fast-growing Walla Walla, the settlement of eastern Washington set in motion a fundamental shift in the territorial axis. In 1853, the American population was divided into roughly equal Puget Sound and Columbia River components. By 1860, one in six non-Indian residents lived east of the Cascades. Walla Walla County ranked third among the territory's nineteen counties. While the Sound held position, with 46 percent of the white inhabitants, the river country lost badly, with barely a quarter of the end-of-decade population.[56] Firmly established and bound, assuming continuation of present trends, to be accentuated, Washington's prime internal rivalry was now on an east-west line across the Cascades, supplanting the old north-south Cowlitz corridor fault.

Oregon's admission to the Union in 1859 generated serious discussion of the benefits Washington Territory might gain from a similar achievement. Upon superficial analysis, the 1860 federal census affirmed that statehood was no idle ambition. According to the Vancouver *Chronicle*, the 11,578 Washingtonians represented an "increase…at the rate of 864.75 *per centum*" over the 1850 North Oregon figure. Should "this progressive movement… continue to the same degree," the *Chronicle* asserted in a widely reprinted prediction, statehood was guaranteed before 1870. The problem with such optimistic forecasts was that Washington remained sparsely populated, particularly after the addition of southern Idaho, with less than one-tenth of a white person per square mile, a fraction of the rate in Oregon.[57] Indians, moreover, still outnumbered settlers, a factor likely to discourage favorable action on the part of Congress. Washington was, in wide-open spaces reality, a long way from membership in the assemblage of states.

John C. Ainsworth. *Oregon Historical Society, Portland (OrHi 8353 #23)*

Chapter Four

The Real Condition of Affairs

Having spent the last three weeks upon said (Nez Perce) Reservation I have seen the real condition of affairs there… The lands of the Indians, even in some instances their little farms are being taken from them, their stock is being stolen, intoxicating Liquor is being sold and given to them without measure, and in one instance at least one of their number was shot down in cold blood… Their condition is indeed wretched and they are almost in despair.—John J. McGilvra[1]

GOLD DISCOVERIES in the wild Fraser River canyons encouraged the plausible, and pleasant, belief that precious metals might be uncovered elsewhere in the Pacific Northwest. Colonel Wright's campaign, followed by Senate ratification of the Stevens treaties, cleared the way for thorough investigation of inviting valleys east of the Cascades. Prospectors worked the border-straddling Similkameen River and the Wenatchee, flowing cold from snow-laden Cascade peaks to the Columbia. "That the entire region from Fort Simcoe up to and beyond the 49th parallel…abounds in extensive deposits of gold," the Steilacoom *Puget Sound Herald* proclaimed, "we have too much evidence before us to doubt for an instant."[2]

In the spring of 1860, reports of gold upon the Nez Perce reservation shifted attention to the eastern reaches of Washington Territory. From his Fort Walla Walla headquarters, federal agent Andrew J. Cain "labored to mold public opinion properly in regard to a proper observance of the laws" forbidding trespass upon treaty-protected Indian land. Flaunting the prohibition, Elias Pierce led a prospecting party up the Clearwater River, finally unearthing "the pay dirt strata" in September. "I am satisfied that gold discoveries have been made…" Cain soon reported, "and that no longer period than next spring will elapse before miners will be pouring into the country from all quarters." Taking the field to expel Pierce, soldiers from Fort Walla Walla turned back on account of heavy snow. Several dozen whites, organized as the Oro Fino Mining District, remained on the Clearwater over the winter.[3]

Ordering, in "clear[,] explicit and reiterated" terms, the removal of the miners, Superintendent of Indian Affairs Edward Geary privately conceded that attempts to protect the reservation were futile. With hundreds of goldseekers already en route, he advised as spring opened in 1861, "it is no longer possible to resist the tide of adventurers setting toward this new attraction." By the first of June, three thousand prospectors worked likely places in the Clearwater Valley. In newly established Lewiston, at the river's mouth, lots sold for $800 and up, despite the scarcity of timber for building purposes. There was not wood enough in the vicinity, wrote a recent arrival, "to boil a coffee pot." Upstream, Oro Fino had three restaurants, sixteen general stores, eighteen saloons, two bankers, four doctors and "fortunately," one correspondent noted, "…no lawyers yet." Attempting to prevent bloodshed, Superintendent Geary persuaded the Nez Perce to cede the original diggings, in return for a military post, Fort Lapwai, to guard the remainder of their country.[4]

Nez Perce gold diverted regional attention from the year's great national developments, secession and civil war. Happy Olympia Republicans had greeted Abraham Lincoln's victory the previous November with a hundred-gun salute and a whiskey-fueled parade, "ringing bells, blowing horns, and attesting their joy in every conceivable manner." Otherwise, debate over the nation's fate was limited to the brief 1861 campaign for congressional delegate. Politically compromised by his involvement with the Southern half of the split-Democratic presidential ticket, Isaac Stevens decided against an attempt at a third term. Republican strategists put forth their nominee, Steilacoom's William H. Wallace, as the candidate of the Union and denounced the official Democratic standard-bearer, Selucious Garfielde, as a Confederate supporter. Heralded by Wallace as a referendum on the war, the July election provided, at best, a lukewarm endorsement of the North. To be sure, the Republican won easily. The credit was due, however, to the split in opposition ranks produced when Edward Lander entered the race as an honest Democrat alternative to the ethically challenged Garfielde. Wallace led by a large margin in western Washington, but secured barely a quarter of the vote east of the Cascades.[5]

Despite the war, the Democrats developed on the far side of the mountains a new electoral base with considerable potential, in light of ongoing gold discoveries and population growth, for expansion. Federal offices, however, were filled according to national, rather than local, trends. Lincoln's inauguration in March 1861 produced a wholesale political upheaval, the first in Washington's history. "Astonished" that his loyalty to the Union had been "called in question in the public prints," Isaac Stevens returned to the military wearing bright general's stars and intent upon securing military glory. Displaced from customary duties, most leaders of the territorial Democracy set patriotism above politics, at least for the duration. Outgoing Surveyor General James Tilton, an open and unapologetic slaveholder during his years on the Sound, took a public oath of allegiance to the North. Valiant Selucious Garfielde, the one notable exception, sat out the war in British Columbia, attempting to renounce his American citizenship in the interest of developing a north-of-the-border legal practice.[6]

New Republican appointees took office in the midst of an expanding crisis east of the Cascades. The original attempt at holding the mining boom along the line of the Clearwater, one official noted, was "like attempting to restrain the whirlwind." Moving south in the summer of 1861, prospectors made major discoveries in the Salmon River country, inside and outside the Nez Perce boundary. Serving the two thousand persons holding claims in its narrow tributary gulches, Florence, the newest boomtown, was supposedly "better built...than Lewiston." Merchants out to profit from the congenital thirstiness of miners "established their whisky shops on every road and trail," a high-ranking Indian department officer reported after a trip to Fort Lapwai, "at the crossing of every river and creek and at almost every spring." Claiming that the task was impossible, General Benjamin Alvord, now commanding all military forces in the Pacific Northwest, made no attempt to remove trespassers from "a reservation as large as the State of New York." Even George McClellan's vaunted Army of the Potomac, Alvord claimed, would fail if sent west to protect the Indians.[7]

More whites than Nez Perce resided upon a reservation legally off-limits to non-Indians. Pure disaster for the Nez Perce, the gold rush was celebrated elsewhere in the Pacific Northwest as a near-miraculous development. At the time of the original strike, wheat and flour sold in the upper country at prices five to six times above prevailing rates in the Willamette Valley. Subsequent requirements for food and implements made for even greater profit margins. "Any article of groceries was from $1 up to $2.50 a pound," a prospector wrote from Florence in July 1862, "and for several weeks the demand could hardly be supplied even at that, in such numbers had the people flocked into the place." Situated on the trail between Wallula, the head of regular navigation, and Lewiston, Walla Walla prospered immediately as the "Sacramento of the Upper Columbia," the inland point of distribution for goods needed in the diggings.[8]

Local merchants sent $50,000 worth of freight to the Salmon River alone during a single week in December 1861. Walla Walla quickly became more than a transshipment center for food and manufactured items shipped upstream from Portland. The rolling grass-covered hills west of town and north in the direction of the Touchet River made Walla Walla the Willamette Valley, as well as the Sacramento, of the mines. All but five thousand of the thirty thousand cattle in the vicinity perished in the harsh winter of 1862, stimulating the shift from grazing to farming. By 1864, four thousand acres were planted in wheat, "the only grain crop," according to the *Walla Walla Statesman*, "that finds a ready cash market at a remunerating price." In 1865, seven thousand barrels of locally ground flour went by packtrain to the mining camps.[9]

Catering to soldiers and itinerant miners, Walla Walla was originally a half-way-to-Hell town, with saloons and gambling dens "as common as 'blackberries in bear time.'" After several gunfights, a philosophical resident observed that

"considering the number of idlers and loafers, the amount of crime is not great."
Respectable Walla Wallans gradually overcame the community's anything-goes
reputation. By mid-1862, enough children were present to warrant a public
school. Opened in 1863, a regular cemetery replaced the previously used Boot
Hill burial ground, where horses and cattle disturbed unmarked graves. In place
of the pioneer makeshift jail, a facility so insecure that imprisonment was voluntary, town leaders built an escape-proof house of incarceration. The first brick
buildings east of The Dalles reflected the prosperity of a local economy based
upon freighting and an expanding agricultural hinterland. No later than 1863,
remote Walla Walla was the largest and wealthiest urban area in Washington Territory.[10]

A commercial artery flowing in gold, the Columbia River linked Portland,
the San Francisco of the Northwest, to Walla Walla and the mines. Organized in
1860, the Oregon Steam Navigation Company consolidated existing water-
oriented operations on the lower, middle and upper Columbia. The O.S.N. followed a basic principle enunciated by one of the partners, Simeon G. Reed: "if
the business is there to warrant a Steamboat in runing [sic], and the river can be
navigated we will see that it is done, for it is *our interest to do so*." Like the
Hudson's Bay Company of old, the firm provided the best service possible, invested heavily in improvements and treated competitors with nothing-personal
ruthlessness. In 1862, the O.S.N. constructed light draft steamers able to run
from The Dalles to Lewiston on the Snake in the high water period between
mid-April and the first of August.[11]

He and his associates, said Captain John Ainsworth, the most dynamic of
the partners, were "good Generals," able to grasp the strategic importance of the
navigation obstructions at the Cascades and The Dalles. "We could see,"
Ainsworth recalled, "that the O.S.N. Co. must control the portages, or the portages *must* control and swallow up the company." In 1862, the firm constructed
a railroad at the Cascades, following the Washington Territory bank. Another rail
line soon covered the thirteen-and-a-half miles between The Dalles and the
mouth of the Deschutes River on the Oregon side. The result, Ainsworth
pointed out, was definitive: "The O.S.N. Co[mpany] was now master of the
river."[12]

Possessing the keys to the Columbia River, the Oregon Steam Navigation
Company generated tremendous earnings. Passengers bound for Walla Walla
and the mines traveled in speed and comfort, relative to previous modes of regional transportation. Inevitably, the O.S.N. became the latest target of anti-
monopoly sentiment in the Pacific Northwest, an American-owned successor to
the Hudson's Bay Company. Determined, as a Lewiston newspaper observed, to
"do the largest business with the least risk to their steamers," the firm ignored
towns and settlers "who cannot return to them the highest profits." During an
early rate war, the *Walla Walla Statesman* urged "merchants and shippers of the

upper country" to "patronize the opposition line." No one doubted, after all, that "the Navigation Company would come back immediately to their old style of exorbitant rates if they were allowed to break down the opposition."[13]

Abraham Lincoln's most controversial territorial appointee assumed the task of protecting the Nez Perce reservation from miners and corporate enterprise. Restoring the separate Pacific Northwest Indian superintendencies, the Lincoln administration cultivated Democratic support for the war by naming opposition party member Benjamin F. Kendall, an active figure in local business and governmental affairs since arriving with the Stevens railroad survey expedition, to the Washington position. Kendall possessed an "excellent character," the pro-administration *Puget Sound Herald* proclaimed and was "not a party man at all." Patronage-minded Republicans were nonetheless outraged. "It is truly an appointment '*not fit to be made*,'" one partisan newspaper complained. Recently elected congressional delegate William H. Wallace made Kendall's removal, sooner rather than later, his number one priority.[14]

Ignoring his early critics, Kendall set about reforming the administration of Indian affairs. Visiting the Nez Perce reservation, he found the employees busy, when not consorting with " female Indian companions," wasting government funds upon construction of buildings "hardly fit for human habitation." The Yakama agency, headquartered at Fort Simcoe, also merited overhaul. Teaching supervisor James Wilbur, a well-known Methodist missionary bent upon eradicating Catholicism among the Indians, had "usurped" the authority of agent A. A. Bancroft, his incompetent nominal superior. Dismissing Wilbur—and, for good measure, his wife and nephew—from government employment, Kendall claimed the right to personally hire and fire reservation personnel, west and east of the Cascades.[15]

The superintendent thereby ran afoul of Doctor Anson Henry, Washington's most outlandish Republican. Organizing Oregon for old Illinois friend Abraham Lincoln in 1860, Henry relied upon federal surveying contracts north of the Columbia for support. Threatened with prosecution for fraud, he was instead appointed, following the inauguration, territorial surveyor general. Taking full advantage of this reversal in fortune, the doctor sent employees into remote mountain ranges and valleys, seeking gold and silver deposits for personal investment. Criticized for ignoring areas already settled, he promised the commissioner of the General Land Office "an interest" in all mines discovered. Henry had a single, and highly effective, line of defense against accusations of corruption: "President Lincoln has known me intimately for near thirty years, having lived in the same village with him for some twenty years of that time." Even party colleagues condemned the doctor as a "leech" and a "cunning old fox." The loyalty of his sole journalistic defender, the Olympia *Washington Standard*, was secured and maintained by placing editor John Miller Murphy on the federal payroll.[16]

Henry expected, as Lincoln's dear neighbor, to control all federal appointments in the territory, an ambition thwarted by Kendall's declaration of personal responsibility for the Indian service positions. "He not only refused every man I had suggested to him," the surveyor general fumed, "but removed the very men I had urged him to retain." Attempting to conceal what was, in reality, a dispute over patronage, Henry accused Kendall of "wantonly outraging the religious element of the whole country" by dismissing James Wilbur. In replacing the "kind & benevolent" missionary with an alcoholic, atheistic and adulterous fellow Democrat, the superintendent clarified "his contempt for every thing holy." Deliberately stirring up the politically influential Methodist church element, the doctor all but guaranteed that his antagonist's tenure would be short and miserable.[17]

Rejecting advice from friends to be more conciliatory, Kendall declared that the mere thought of Anson Henry defending religion ought to horrify all genuine Christians. The doctor's inspired brief on behalf of "praying men" provided the Lincoln administration with a rationale for restoration of the superintendency to Republican control. Decided upon in January 1862, Kendall's removal was officially announced in April. His successor was Calvin Hale, an Olympia merchant whose questionable business and political reputation failed to deter territorial party stalwarts from submitting an enthusiastic endorsement. Hale promptly restored the Reverend Wilbur to the Yakama reservation, who, now promoted to agent, was determined more than ever to persecute Catholic Indians in the name of Methodism.[18]

Vowing to "return...the favor" by exposing Anson Henry's "chequered career" to a suitably disgusted public, Kendall acquired an Olympia newspaper, the *Overland Press*, as his personal outlet. Months of increasingly venomous journalistic debate—the subsidized *Washington Standard* represented the surveyor general—culminated in violence and bitter murder. Brandishing a cane, Horace Howe, one of Henry's associates, attempted to publicly beat Kendall in late December 1862. Drawing a pistol, the latter fired four times, slightly wounding his attacker. Howe returned to the chase in early January, this time shooting Kendall dead in cold blood. A grand jury indicted the killer for manslaughter, but the Thurston County prosecutor refused to proceed on anything less than a factually appropriate first degree murder charge.[19]

Nothing was done, during Benjamin Kendall's brief unhappy tour of office, to ameliorate the Nez Perce crisis. Confirming the near-universal belief that the entire region between the Cascades and the Rocky Mountains was "one big gold field," the prospecting mania spread far beyond the reservation in 1862. Gold was discovered in the Boise River basin, producing, the *Walla Walla Statesman* observed as twenty-five thousand persons hurried to southern Idaho, "another mining excitement equalizing any that have yet taken place." Miners also opened the rugged eastern Oregon canyons of the John Day and Powder rivers. In northeastern Washington, valuable deposits were found in the countryside about Pend Oreille and Coeur d'Alene lakes and, on both sides of the international border, along the Kootenai River. Chinese immigrants worked Big Bend bars on the upper Columbia River, where lack of wood restricted prospectors to panning.[20]

Major new discoveries produced shifts in regional transportation patterns. Opening for business two dozen miles below Wallula, Umatilla was the Columbia River terminus for a direct trail to eastern Oregon and southern Idaho mining centers. Keeping "pace with the times," as one observer noted, the O.S.N. built steamers to navigate Pend Oreille Lake, the Snake above Hells Canyon and the Columbia north of Kettle Falls. Rather than surrender even a portion of the trade, Walla Walla merchants blazed their own road to the Grand Ronde Valley, linking up with the Umatilla-Boise route. Previously little more than a "sand heap," Wallula was outfitted with urban amenities, enhancing its stature in relation to the downstream competition. First proposed by Captain John Mullan in 1862, a railroad between Walla Walla and Wallula drew considerable interest among local business concerns as the logical means of thwarting outside challenge.[21]

Although failing to secure funding for its railroad project, Walla Walla survived the competition with Umatilla. "Other towns may be built up faster and thrive better for a short time," the *Statesman* proclaimed, "but Walla Walla…will outlive them all." The center of a fast-growing agricultural district, the community moved well beyond the mine-supply stage of development. Half buried in riverside dunes, Umatilla, in contrast, lacked real long-term prospects. Regardless of the inconvenience, packers serving Boise preferred to operate out of Walla Walla, where they could obtain food and feed at the lowest prices. Further solidifying its position, the town became the interior hub of Ben Holladay's Portland-Salt Lake coach line in 1864, handling the nine-passenger wagons linking the Pacific Northwest with the central overland stage route.[22]

In the midst of the latest gold rushes, the government finally addressed the Indian relations issue. Unable to protect the Nez Perce against trespass, Congress decided in 1862 to take the land trespassed-upon from the tribe. The task of substantially reducing the reservation was assigned to three undistinguished commissioners: Calvin Hale, William Rector of the Oregon superintendency and Lapwai agent Charles Hutchins. Rector was the only one to show up for the scheduled council. Claiming sole responsibility for Nez Perce affairs, Hale refused to cooperate with his Oregonian counterpart. Charged with corruption, Hutchins had been suspended from office. Over the winter, new agent J. W. Anderson prepared the way, as best he could, for a rescheduled council. "It will be a hard matter," he reported after a series of tense meetings with tribal leaders, "to make them believe the government will fulfill the stipulations of a new treaty more faithfully than it carried out the provisions of the old." Using the delay to good personal advantage, Calvin Hale secured complete control of a reconstituted commission, with Charles Hutchins, somehow restored to the public payroll, as principal assistant.[23]

Accompanied by an exhausted retinue of third class Olympia politicians, Superintendent Hale reached Lapwai in May 1863, there to confront, eventually, two thousand unhappy Indians. The government's no-compromise stance, plus tribal unwillingness to openly break with the Americans, nonetheless produced an apparent comprehensive agreement. The treaty, Hale proudly informed the Indian Office, relinquished "about 9/10 of the former Reservation" to the United States, at a bargain sales price of $265,000. In miserable truth, the document was the product of ignorance and greed. Only those Indians under the influence of Lawyer, the head chief, actually signed the treaty. Bands residing outside the reduced reservation refused, insisting, quite properly from the perspective of Nez Perce culture and history, that the others had no right to sell their homes. There was absolutely no basis for the astonishing claim of Charles Hutchins that the council "to a considerable extent quieted the apprehensions" of the entire Nez Perce nation.[24]

An enormous Indian reservation embracing parts of three modern states was, under Calvin Hale's treaty, cut back to a much smaller tract between the Clearwater and Salmon rivers in north-central Idaho. Gold, the prime agent responsible for the reduction in Nez Perce acreage, also contributed to a significant downsizing of Washington Territory. Good reasons, apparent to even distant observers, existed for a change in boundaries. "The time has come," the San Francisco *Alta California* stated in the spring of 1862, "when…Washington Territory should be divided, and a new territory organized out of the district east of the Cascade Mountains." Washington was larger than California and twice the size of New England, the *Alta* pointed out, and split into "two districts which are entirely dissimilar in all their resources and wants." The western region featured "the finest navigable inland waters, and the most valuable forests…in the world." The eastside was the "bare, barren and rocky" domain of the prospector and the cattleman.[25]

In accordance with the same logic, the Portland *Oregonian* expressed the conviction that "Washington Territory will soon be divided" along the crest of the Cascades, the new eastside territorial regime adopting "the beautiful name of Idaho." Walla Walla, the obvious choice for capital of the interior Northwest, supported the concept. Olympia, the *Statesman* asserted in a series of commentaries, had "humbugged and victimized" eastern Washington to such an extent that the residents opposed "any further affiliation with…clam-eating politicians." Despite the recent eastward population shift, Puget Sound opposed meaningful reapportionment of the legislature. The Sound also thwarted creation of a second judicial district east of the Cascades, forcing the single sitting judge to travel, as that trail-weary individual complained, a circuit of "more than 500 miles" via "S. Boat, wagon stage, on horseback and on foot."[26]

Puget Sound residents found such arguments entirely unconvincing. There was, in actuality, said the *Washington Standard* in a line of reasoning followed by other tidewater papers, a "substantial amity of interest between the Sound and Walla Walla regions." The former had lumber and the latter farm produce. One was the obvious market of the other. A division at the summit of the Cascades, moreover, "would reduce our area too much," keeping the westside remnant of Washington Territory "out of the Union for many years to come." Olympia, in particular, faced a serious threat. The territorial capital had been chosen in the pre-gold rush years of the north-to-south Washington. Now, however, it languished on the periphery of an east-west relationship, with the prospect of losing the capital, division or no division, to a more centrally located community.[27]

Offering its own variant of division, Puget Sound would follow a line described by the *Standard* as "extending north from the north-east corner of Oregon" to the 49th parallel. Under this proposal, Washington lost the Clearwater, Salmon and Boise districts, the most heavily populated section of the territory when transient miners were included in the tally, but retained the rich Walla Walla Valley. Olympia stood a better chance of remaining the capital with the boundaries thus reduced. Congressional delegate William H. Wallace and Surveyor General Anson Henry were transplanted Illinois friends of Lincoln upon the Sound. The Olympian point-of-view therefore held the advantage in the nation's capital. On March 4, 1863, President Lincoln signed legislation creating Idaho Territory, a gargantuan larger-than-Texas commonwealth encompassing modern Idaho and Montana, with part of Wyoming on the side. A victory for Puget Sound and a defeat for Walla Walla, the crucial western boundary ran due north from the mouth of the Clearwater to the international border.[28]

Fomented in Walla Walla, agitation persisted for another territorial reshuffle. The natural community of interests between northern Idaho and eastern Washington was reinforced when the capital was transferred from Lewiston to Boise. Panhandle residents unfortunate enough to have business in Boise traveled by way of a "tedious and difficult" mountain trail, the only direct means of communication. Washington east of the Cascades was equally isolated with respect to Olympia. A union of the two sections was a common sense response to prevailing geographical circumstances. First proposed in 1864, the realignment gathered widespread support. After all, the *Walla Walla Statesman* affirmed, the interior Northwest was "rich and growing" and had nothing to gain from further association with the "half dead carcase [sic] of Puget Sound."[29]

Viewed from the Pacific Northwest, the Civil War was noteworthy for the gold strikes in the upper Columbia drainage, discoveries altering Indian-white relationships and reorienting old territorial boundaries. Far from the wartime battlefronts, the region was still influenced by the great national bloodletting. The Lincoln administration naturally conceived the sole United States military mission to be destruction of the Confederacy. Washington Territory settlers, however, were more concerned with Indians than with Rebels. Rumored outbreaks, from Grays Harbor on the coast to Lewiston on the Clearwater, plus the continuing Northern Indian menace, explained the parochial objection to decisions made in the interest of preserving the Union. Territorial opinion condemned the recall, after Fort Sumter, of regular Army troops for service in the eastern theaters of war. "A more inopportune time could not have been chosen for this change," complained the *Puget Sound Herald*, "it being well known to everybody…that the Indians are preparing for a renewal of hostilities."[30]

Responding to protests from the Pacific Northwest, the War Department eventually authorized recruitment of Washington and Oregon volunteers to occupy the forts abandoned by departing regulars. Despite substantial enlistment bounties, appeals to patriotism and heavy recruiting in California, the ranks were never filled to anything like official capacity. "Until the mining fever subsides," the *Walla Walla Statesman* pointed out in explaining the local disinterest, "few men will be found here willing to direct their attention to the service of 'Uncle Sam.'" An exceptionally high desertion rate reflected a tendency of Californians to sign up only for free transportation up the coast to the diggings.[31]

Declining to rush, or even slowly walk, to the colors, Washington settlers demonstrated a basic aversion to sacrifice on behalf of the Northern cause. Diverting revenue to the military effort, the Treasury Department deliberately met government civil obligations at an even more dilatory pace than in peacetime. Unpaid employees and creditors, Anson Henry reported in late 1861, were compelled to either "borrow money at the rate of two & a half per cent a month" or to sell their vouchers to "money brokers" for "Seventy Five or Eighty cents on the dollar." Vexed by the prolonged non-receipt of his legislative pay, Seattle Republican Arthur Denny complained that "we have been robbed by the Government at the very time we were working like slaves for it." Adding to the consternation, Congress reduced federal salaries and, among other politically unwelcome economizing gestures, slashed the maximum contract payments allowed General Land Office surveyors.[32]

Although the conflict was virtually a foreign enterprise in its military aspects, Washington residents paid the same war taxes imposed upon directly involved Americans. Methods adopted by regional revenue code administrators led to widespread complaint about "incomprehensible requirements" and "mutton-headed officials." The Treasury Department also resorted to printing legal tender notes unbacked by either gold or silver. "Greenbacks" quickly became "the universal topic of conversation," as the Olympia *Washington Standard* quipped in early 1863. "It is as natural for a man to ask the price of 'greenbacks' when he meets you on the streets as it is for him to inquire of your health or that of your family." Pressed downward by Union military reverses, paper currency market values fell to as little as fifty cents on the dollar.[33]

Efforts to counteract the greenbacks, though occasionally ingenious, invariably failed. The Nez Perce demanded, unsuccessfully, that treaty money due them be paid in gold. Although difficult to legally enforce, personal loan agreements often required repayment in "coin." The Oregon Steam Navigation Company established special "legal tender rates" for passengers and shippers paying with greenbacks. The legislature narrowly defeated "debtor" and "special contract" measures mandating acceptance of the deflated notes at face value or mandating the use of specie in honoring financial obligations. Printing press money attained acceptance only in the closing stages of the war, circulating at near par with Northern victory assured.[34]

Washingtonians supported preservation of the Union, but disagreed with one another upon other wartime policies. "The question whether this war is to be prosecuted for the sole purpose of putting down the rebellion…," the *Walla Walla Statesman* observed in mid-1863, "or for the purpose of destroying slavery regardless of the consequences to the Union, is now the great issue of the day." Opposed, in common with most Democrats, to "amalgamation of the Caucasian and inferior colored races," the *Statesman* denounced the Emancipation Proclamation and the enlistment of black soldiers. Republicans, in contrast, applauded Lincoln's order freeing slaves in Confederate-controlled areas as the only "way to permanently end the rebellion."[35]

Issues mattered politically, however, only as occasionally useful partisan weapons. Political affairs focused, in war as in peace, upon the mundane concerns of seeking and retaining office. Already distinguished by the Kendall affair, Abraham Lincoln attained what a party newspaper termed "the acme of mediocrity," sending William Pickering of Illinois west as Washington's fourth governor. English-born and fussy, the new chief executive was inevitably dubbed "Old Pickwick" by local journalists. Early support of Lincoln's presidential ambition and subsequent campaigning on behalf of other Republicans had eventually brought him to the attention of the administration. Aside from extermination of those Indians failing to voluntarily withdraw from areas desired by settlers, he had one goal, the destruction of all enemies, real and imagined, without and especially within the ranks of the Republican party.[36]

"These are strange times," Arthur Denny observed in late 1863, "and some do very strange things indeed, in fact there seems to be comparatively…few men who can be trusted." Trusting only each other, for the moment, two of the strangest personages on the scene, Governor Pickering and Anson Henry, made war upon party foes. Customs collector Victor Smith, a follower of Secretary of the Treasury Salmon P. Chase, Lincoln's most likely challenger for the 1864 presidential nomination, was their initial mark. Already accused of embezzling funds, Smith made an inviting target.[37]

Unfulfilled by the standard varieties of corruption, Smith joined fellow federal appointees Hugh Goldsborough and John McGilvra in taking over a real estate venture at Port Angeles, on the Strait of Juan de Fuca midway between Cape Flattery and Admiralty Inlet. Renaming the place Cherbourg, Smith opened a store, commenced selling land and, in an 1862 move calculated to increase the value of his holdings, transferred the customs house from Port Townsend. Directly south of Victoria, a major Puget Sound export market, Port Angeles was an excellent harbor, sheltered by the Ediz Hook sandspit. Due to prevailing winds and currents, on the other hand, vessel masters preferred to use Port Townsend for much of the year, even on voyages to and from Vancouver Island.[38]

Except among his immediate business and political associates, Smith was condemned for crass venality, for using public funds, in wartime no less, to advance a private venture. Port Townsend residents hanged the collector in effigy and convened a special grand jury to indict him "for assault upon the people." Motivated, according to the town's current newspaper, the *North-West*, by the "disproportionate preponderance of his organ of acquisitiveness," Smith had "done more to create disaffection and promote disloyalty...than any twenty traitors in the South." Striking a blow at party factions opposed to a second Lincoln term, Governor Pickering appointed a special, and anything-but-objective, territorial commission to fully examine and publicize the case against Smith.[39]

Rivalries within the Lincoln administration and the appeals of territorial Republican leaders produced Smith's dismissal. Vowing to regain the collectorship, and to punish Pickering and Henry in the process of so doing, Smith traveled to Washington City in late 1863. His designs were frustrated, however, when Treasury Secretary Smith resigned from the cabinet. Grandiose Cherbourg, meanwhile, reverted to wilderness Port Angeles. Despite use of the customs house as a promotional device, land sales lagged well behind expectations, inflicting financial loss upon the developers. In December 1863, snow and ice in the nearby Olympic Mountains suddenly melted, washing most of the town, the federal building included, into the strait. "Fragments of houses, and hundreds of trees and stumps lie scattered about in every direction," the first newspaper correspondent on the scene reported, "and in some places they are piled one upon the other to the height of 30 feet."[40]

Before finishing off Victor Smith, Pickering and Henry turned upon another compromised Republican, territorial secretary L. Jay S. Turney, an alcoholic attorney from Illinois. Upon assuming the governorship in June 1862, Pickering supposedly discovered that Turney had taken once again to heavy drink, returning "like the Dog to his vomit, and like the sow to...wallowing in the mire." Of more serious import, politically, the secretary had attempted to award the annual public printing contract to Benjamin Kendall's Olympia newspaper, rewarding a new-made administration enemy and damaging loyal party journalists. "It was as vile on the part of Turney," charged the governor, never at a loss for vivid imagery, "as the treachery of the Traitor Judas." Dismissed at the end of 1862, Turney briefly and pathetically refused to vacate his official premises or to surrender the territory's seal and records.[41]

Olympians had no monopoly on the unenlightened conduct of territorial business. Opening its doors in 1861, the University of Washington occupied carefully landscaped grounds in Seattle. Topped with a belfry, the two story classroom structure was, claimed one architecturally inclined observer, "the best building in the Territory." A dwelling for the "Principal" and a boarding house able to accommodate three dozen persons graced the stump-bordered campus. The university, however, was something less than a genuine center of higher learning. Primary and secondary students also attended classes. Depending upon academic level, scholars paid $6 to $8 a quarter in tuition, plus $3 to $4 a week for room and board, laundry and firewood not included. The regimen focused on "the reading of the scriptures," supposedly "the only safe text book of morals." Strict regulations prohibited the student body from "frequenting" saloons and theaters and required observance of the Sabbath.[42]

Mandatory moral uplift for the students compensated, ironically, for the general lack of integrity exhibited by the school's founders. Federal law set aside two townships of public land in support of a territorial university. Actual ownership remained in government hands, official policy being, as proclaimed by the General Land Office, "merely to *reserve* and hold the *grant* in abeyance until the Territory shall have been admitted as a *State*, when a larger population under a State Constitution, will be the better able to judge of the wants of the people and subserve them in an educational point of view." Although this statement was a bit convoluted, the intent was perfectly clear to all interested parties. L. Jay S. Turney, serving as acting governor in 1861, pointed out that the university had no right to sell or otherwise dispose of the grant. Preparing anyway for a sale, U.W. officials admitted in advance to a violation of the law, in the expectation that some "future legalizing legislation" would retroactively validate their conduct.[43]

Specific and complimentary educational and economic necessities justified the law breaking. In the absence of a legislative appropriation, the university needed money to construct buildings. Anticipating the eventual termination of illegal logging on the public domain, the California-owned sawmills needed to acquire timberland. The solution to both problems was obvious, especially to lumbermen-regents Josiah Keller, Marshall Blinn and George Meigs. In April 1861, the Reverend Daniel Bagley, acting as university commissioner, announced that the grant was for sale, at $1.50 an acre, the proceeds to be used in erection of campus facilities. Surveyed and presently unclaimed land could be purchased anywhere within territorial limits, in parcels of at least 160 acres.[44]

Upon completion of business in 1863, sales amounted to 41,000 acres and receipts to $70,000. At least half the land sold went to lumber companies, the four largest Puget Sound sawmills alone purchasing 14,000 acres. The $30,000 left over after construction became an endowment fund. The incomprehensible nature of the financial arrangements and the eventual disappearance of records related to the transactions appeared to confirm contemporary suspicions that the University of Washington had been founded upon "gross extravagance if not downright fraud." A good deal of after-the-fact cleanup work was necessary. Accused of corruption by a reform board of regents, Daniel Bagley was exonerated by a legislative committee especially appointed to clear him of wrongdoing.[45]

U.S. attorney John McGilvra, meanwhile, urged the Lincoln administration and Congress to approve the sales, regardless of the circumstances. "Legally the Territory could not sell this land," McGilvra conceded. "But it has been done, and the land is now in the possession of purchasers who have paid...for it." The acreage in question, he asserted, was "mostly worthless except"—the exception was hardly of nominal importance—"for lumbering purposes." Validation of the transactions therefore did little real harm to the public interest. Accepting this dubious argument and ignoring the fact that all persons involved had been aware from the start of violating the law, the General Land Office concluded that repudiation of the university would impose "serious difficulties and embarrassments" upon "individuals who purchased these lands in good faith, and under the conviction the Territory had legally the power to dispose of them." In accordance with the G.L.O. finding, Congress amended the original university legislation in 1864, making the grant an outright gift, rather than a reservation of land.[46]

Public disgust with official misbehavior, in Olympia and Seattle, explained in part the continuing success of the opposition Democratic party at the electoral level of territorial politics. Either by clear majority or by adroit maneuvering, Democrats maintained control of the legislature for much of the war. The assembly defeated a pro-Union resolution in February 1862 and approved a similar measure the next session only when delegate William Wallace complained of his inability to secure federal funds for an apparently disloyal territory. Assuming the governorship of Idaho in 1863, Wallace opened a void successfully exploited by Democrat George Cole, the first political figure of note from eastern Washington.[47]

A New York native and 1850 migrant to Oregon, Cole opened a warehouse in Walla Walla during the early stages of the Clearwater River gold rush. Nominated for Congress in 1863, he mounted a determined campaign, taking the fight from the Democratic base east of the Cascades direct to Republicans on Puget Sound. Failing to explain how a Democrat could influence an administration of the opposition party, Cole promised, if elected, to secure removal of all federal officeholders in the territory. Supplementing this popular, if unrealistic, declaration, he executed a turn-the-tables move reminiscent of the three-way

1861 election, persuading former secretary L. Jay S. Turney to enter the race as an independent, vote-dividing Republican.[48]

Preoccupied with internal patronage matters, Republicans were determined to lose, no matter what damage it caused the administration. Official party nominee J. O. Raynor was so obscure that the *Washington Standard* could find no one in Olympia "who is acquainted with the candidate." Attacking Cole as pro-Southern and Turney as a turncoat drunkard, Republican leaders exhausted their intellectual faculties. Democratic strength east of the Cascades was decisive in the outcome. Securing two of every three tallies in eastern Washington—his Walla Walla County lead alone accounted for more than the margin of victory— Cole won 51 percent of the territory-wide three candidate vote. In the midst of the Civil War, Washington sent to Congress a genuine Copperhead delegate, opposed to the Emancipation Proclamation and to the "centralization of power" under Abraham Lincoln. For the duration, Republicans looked to William Wallace, representing Idaho in the nation's capital after his brief stint as governor, as their legitimate representative in Washington City.[49]

Serious efforts to unite Washington Territory and to establish overland communication with the United States began during the Civil War. Through the markets and fleets of the lumbering trade, the region west of the Cascades remained an economic appendage of San Francisco and the Pacific Rim. Idaho gold and the Oregon Steam Navigation Company tied eastern Washington, more than ever before, to Portland. Completed from California to Olympia and Seattle and on to the Fraser River in 1864, the telegraph represented a significant advance in contact with the outside world.[50] The principal focus, though, was on transportation—upon roads for the iron horse and for the horse-drawn wagon.

Lincoln's victory, followed by passage of the Pacific railroad bill, rekindled national and regional interest in the transcontinental railway. Chartered by Congress in 1864, the Northern Pacific Railroad had obvious importance for Washington Territory. To be completed by 1876, the congressionally authorized line ran west from Lake Superior to an unspecified Puget Sound terminus, with a branch following the Columbia River to Portland. The Central Pacific/Union Pacific combination to the south had a head start, but Washingtonians naively expected the northern route to be completed first, at substantial profit to the investors.[51]

There was no doubt, locally, of the Sound's superiority for railroad terminus purposes. "While Chicago...is destined to become the great central city of North America, and New York and Boston remain the great commercial depots upon the Atlantic seaboard," the *Washington Standard* proclaimed, "the commercial emporium of the Pacific is to be built at some point on Puget Sound." Competition for the terminal commenced at an early date. Seattle residents, just beginning to hope that their community might surge ahead of Olympia and Steilacoom to the first rank, acted as if the saltwater home of the Northern Pacific belonged, by natural right, to Elliott Bay. "We have," a self-convinced *Weekly Gazette* announced in mid-1864, "the best harbor…the only University, the finest waterworks, the biggest Union American flag, and…the most loyal people in Washington Territory."[52]

Rather than wait several years for the Northern Pacific to come all the way to them, some towns moved to attain railroad-related goals through their own relatively modest means. The Columbia, currently the commercial outlet of the Pacific Northwest, was closed by ice for weeks at a time in winter and, more particularly, obstructed year-round at its dreaded mouth. "The only effectual remedy for the dangers of this bar is a railroad from Puget Sound to the Columbia River," the Steilacoom *Herald* insisted. "When that is built…the mouth of the Columbia may be closed, for there will no longer be any need of it." The trade of eastern Washington, and of the Willamette Valley too, would flow to the sea at the Sound, the specific terminal point selected displacing Portland as the Northwestern metropolis. Organized in 1862, in anticipation of favorable congressional action on the Northern Pacific, the Puget Sound & Columbia River Railroad followed, as projected, either the Cowlitz corridor or a more direct line to Vancouver. Wartime money shortages and opposition from Oregon, unfortunately, frustrated efforts to start construction.[53]

Securing many of the same objectives at substantial reduction in expense, wagon roads were interim alternatives to rail lines. Tracing the necessarily convoluted methods of handling freight on the Columbia, the *Seattle Gazette* affirmed the need for a new approach:

> At present the only practicable mode of transportation is by the way of the Columbia River, by steamer, over the worst bar known to navigation, thence up the Columbia river to the mouth of the Willamette river, thence up the Willamette, to Portland, where a re-shipment takes place, thence back to, and up the Columbia river to the Cascades, where a portage of five miles requires two re-shipments, thence to the Dalles, where a portage of fifteen miles requires two more re-shipments, and thence, (when the water is not too low, or the river frozen up) to Wallula, where you re-ship it again and make a portage of thirty miles to Walla Walla…at a cost, from San Francisco, of one hundred dollars per ton.

If a good road were built between Puget Sound and Walla Walla, however, the commercial situation would change greatly for the better. In place of the three monthly steamers serving the Columbia, merchants could choose from among thirty-odd lumber company vessels sailing to the Sound. With a single transfer of goods required and the distance overland actually shorter than by water, promoters estimated a 20 percent savings in freight charges. Traversed en route, the Yakima Valley would be settled and developed in the process.[54]

Fund-raising drives failed to generate sufficient money to repair the old Naches Pass road, now blocked by fallen timber and other obstructions. Considerable doubt existed, anyway, as to whether the track originally blazed under George McClellan's loose supervision was the best crossing of the Cascades. "The dispute over routes," an Olympia newspaper observed, "and a sectional desire to have a certain route opened which shall come nearest certain towns or neighborhoods has been the main cause of delay in this matter." Professing neutrality as to which option was selected, Olympians insisted that Naches Pass, the alternative most beneficial to the southern Sound, merited superior ranking by objective criteria alone. Seattle residents countered that Snoqualmie Pass, due east of their community, was known to all informed persons as "the best, cheapest and shortest route on the Northern coast."[55]

Agreement upon the pass to be used was essential because construction of a "convenient and permanent road" depended upon federal government assistance. Even a united appeal was likely to fail, moreover, so long as Democrat George Cole represented Washington in a Republican Congress. Pending genuinely fair study and altered political circumstances, local communities attempted to start work, relying upon their own initiative. Convinced that opening Snoqualmie Pass would make Seattle "the emporium of Puget Sound," town inhabitants undertook a subscription drive in early 1865 to finance construction. A rival money-raising venture began in Olympia and Steilacoom on behalf of Naches Pass, dividing territorial resources and insuring that neither route would be available, any time soon, for travelers and freight companies.[56]

Lincoln's reelection in 1864 apparently guaranteed four more years of spoils-oriented politics in the Far Northwest. After many intraparty battles, Anson Henry and William Pickering had fallen out over the politically correct means of handling patronage. The ever flexible Henry welcomed defecting Democrats into the Republican ranks, at least when personally advantageous. The governor, however, opposed association with such allies of convenience. Traveling to the nation's capital in early 1865 to secure presidential support, both men found themselves engulfed in the crush of party leaders attending Lincoln's second inauguration. "Father Abraham is besieged by thousands of Pickerings and Henrys from all quarters of the country," the Democratic *Walla Walla Statesman* observed in a rare expression of sympathy for the president, "each particular office-seeker pressing his individual claims for place and spoils."[57]

Pickering pressed his particular claim in a late March meeting with the president. In subsequent recollections, "Old Pickwick" claimed that Lincoln promised to reappoint him, as well as his friends in the territory's federal establishment. Unfortunately, the chief executive departed for a fateful evening at the theater on April 14 before putting the pledge to paper. Presumably unaware of this potentially significant oversight, Washington's governor rushed to the assassination scene and accompanied Lincoln's body "deep in mud every step, to the

White House, and into his Bed room, where…I then gazed upon the plain, manly, honest face, I had both respected and loved from…1835 down to that sad, sad day." Closer to the Great Emancipator in death than in life, Pickering carefully informed the new president, Andrew Johnson, of his martyred predecessor's commitments in Washington Territory.[58]

Illinoisans to the end, Pickering and Henry saw their peculiar western political careers expire with Abraham Lincoln's death. Month after worrisome month passed with no official, or even unofficial, sign from President Johnson confirming Lincoln's promise. "I am beginning to fear," Pickering lamented in early 1866, "there has been some slip between the cup of reappointment and my lips."[59] The Civil War ended in profound disappointment for some prime Northwestern warriors. For Washington Territory, though, the war years had signal and enduring consequences. The discovery of gold resulted in the despoiling of the region's leading Indian tribe, the spread of settlement east of the Cascades and the final reordering of territorial boundaries.

U.S. Army artist Gustavus Sohon's eyewitness depiction of civilian packers watching infantry and cavalry engage the northern Indian alliance, Spokane Plains, September 5, 1858. *Washington State University Library, Pullman*

Selucious Garfielde, from Snowden, *History of Washington*, v. 4. *Washington State Historical Society, Tacoma*

Elisha P. Ferry, *Washington State University Library, Pullman (85-029)*

Judge Edward Lander—Governor Stevens' antagonist during the martial law fiasco. *Washington State Historical Society, Tacoma*

AUCTION!
SALE OF LOGS!

We will sell at Public Auction, to the
highest bidder, for United States Currency, a lot a

SAW LOGS

Seized on the part of the Government by Capt. B. B. Tuttle, Special Deputy, consisting of One Boom of

125,000 FEET,

More or less, at Camp of McGilvra Brothers, Little Skookum Inlet.

Sale will take place on

Saturday, Feb. 3d. 1872.

at 3 o'clock P. M., at the United States Land Office, at Olympia, Washington Territory.

J. P. CLARK, *Register.*
R. G. STUART, *Receiver.*

Olympia, W. T., Jan. 31st, 1872.

Olympia Transcript Print.

Public announcement, Olympia, 1872. *Washington State Historical Society, Tacoma (EPH B/979.7791/Au 22 Sa)*

THE
Chinese Must Go!

Mayor Weisbach

Has called a MASS MEETING for this (Saturday) evening at 7:30 o'clock

AT ALPHA OPERA HOUSE.

To consider the Chinese question.

TURN OUT.

Anti-Chinese proclamation, 1885. *Washington State Historical Society, Tacoma (EPH A/979.778031/W434)*

Early King County coal mine. *Issaquah Historical Society (91.7.16)*

Spokane Falls N.P.R.R. depot under construction, 1881. *Eastern Washington State Historical Society, Spokane (PJL 301 #4061)*

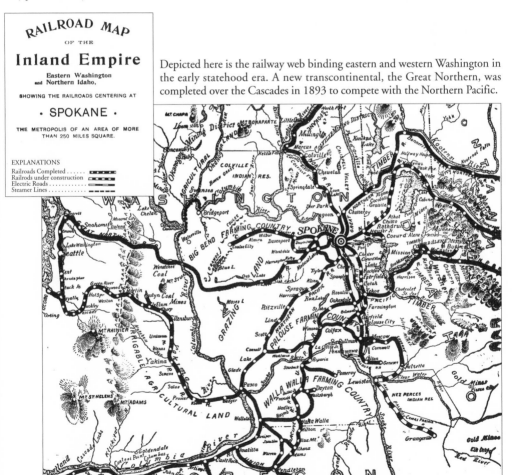

Depicted here is the railway web binding eastern and western Washington in the early statehood era. A new transcontinental, the Great Northern, was completed over the Cascades in 1893 to compete with the Northern Pacific.

Ainsworth, also known as Hades, at the Snake-Columbia confluence in 1884, shortly after completion of the N.P.R.R.'s Snake River bridge. *Washington State University Library (77-0045)*

The "Gold Spike" excursion at the Snake-Columbia ferry landing; Villard's moment of triumph before bankruptcy, 1883. *Washington State Historical Society, Tacoma (1996.40.45)*

"Headquarters building, terminus of N.P.R.R., Tacoma, W.T., Octr". 15th, 1888." *Washington State Historical Society, Tacoma (81.94.352)*

Sohon's drawing of Spokane Falls during Colonel Wright's campaign, 1858. *Washington State University Library, Pullman*

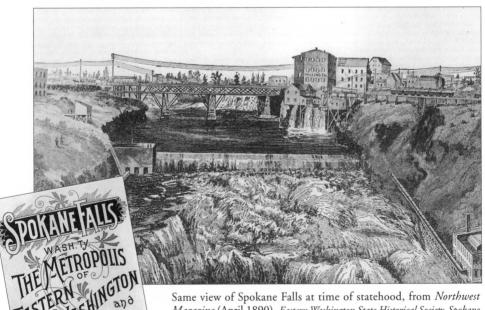

Same view of Spokane Falls at time of statehood, from *Northwest Magazine* (April 1890). *Eastern Washington State Historical Society, Spokane (L86-476)*

Boomtown literature. *Eastern Washington State Historical Society, Spokane*

Right: Composite view of early Seattle. *Washington State Historical Society, Tacoma (1995.10)*

Northern Pacific Railroad construction crew. *Washington State Historical Society, Tacoma (RR/NP CO2)*

Stampede Pass tunnel under construction. *Washington State Historical Society, Tacoma (RR/NP CO5)*

Nez Perces, ca. 1877. *Washington State University Library, Pullman (82-026)*

"Main Street and Harbour, Old Tacoma, W.T., 1888." *Washington State Historical Society, Tacoma (TAC/STR 14 to 1900)*

"Tacoma Mill, 1889." *Washington State Historical Society, Tacoma (81.94.363)*

"Farm residence of A. C. Dickinson," from Frank T. Gilbert, *Historic Sketches of Walla Walla, Whitman, Columbia and Garfield Counties* (1882).

Seattle after the 1889 fire, looking northeast from 1st and Jackson. *Washington State Historical Society, Tacoma (Asahel Curtis 6796)*

Chapter Five

The Tyre of the Pacific

Puget Sound, the great Mediterranean of the North-West, now has a known place on the map... Men of capital recognize the fact that here, upon this great inland sea, the Tyre of the Pacific is to be built, and hither the commercial eye is turning for its site. It will be found in the terminus of the great inter-oceanic railway, the Northern Pacific road, the rational, shortest and easiest connection between navigable waters. —Olympia *Washington Standard*[1]

MAJOR WASHINGTON POLITICAL CAREERS ended with the close of the Civil War. Languishing in lame-duck status, William Pickering waited in vain for appointment to a second gubernatorial term. Anson Henry literally went down with the ship, aboard the wrecked steamer *Brother Jonathan* off the California coast. Filling the vacuum, secondary antebellum figures emerged as the principal contenders for congressional delegate in 1865. The Republicans nominated Arthur Denny, founder of Seattle, veteran legislator and beneficiary of a pre-convention campaign orchestrated by the "six wise men," the federal officials still loyal to Governor Pickering. The Democrats countered with old Stevens hand James Tilton, currently the territory's treasurer.[2]

In typically breathless fashion, Pickering described Arthur Denny as "a *thoroughly loyal, intelligent, truthful, honest,* and *reliable man.*" Seattle's leading citizen was also, unfortunately, the dullest human being, alive or dead, in the territory. "Altogether," the *Walla Walla Statesman* reported after a Denny campaign appearance in eastern Washington, "the speaking was the most statue-like performance we ever witnessed." Devoid of emotional or intellectual appeal, the "dry as a fish" nominee turned the speaking chores over to paid surrogate Selucious Garfielde. A controversial pre-war figure on account of corruption in the Olympia land office, the onetime Democratic congressional candidate had spent the years since Fort Sumter in British Columbia. Safely recrossing the border in early 1865, Garfielde sought rehabilitation as a Republican, affirming a contemporary observation that "the phases in his political life are as changeable as the lines of the chameleon."[3]

Balancing a generally unwholesome reputation—the man was so depraved, said one critic, "that the flies blow him"—Garfielde was the region's greatest orator, in demand for speaking engagements from Puget Sound to San Francisco and so well-known that a sore throat was worthy of newspaper coverage. Blessed with "commanding figure" and "powerful voice," he convincingly debated any proposition or cause, pro and con. Garfielde's "versatility," one enemy admitted, "enables him to graduate from preaching to poker, and from Solon to Satyr, just as the tastes of his companions…may happen to dictate." Driven onto the Republican trail, Democrats sneered, by "a wondrous change" in "the spirit of his patriotism," he was the talking "packhorse" assigned to carry the mute Denny to victory.[4]

Garfielde made three dozen speeches on behalf of his employer. Speakers of both parties relied upon outlandish appeals to prejudice. Democrats contended, falsely, that the "radical" Denny favored elevation of "the black African…to a superior privileged equality" with whites, including the right to vote, and intended, if elected, to promote migration of "negro contrabands" to Washington Territory. Condemning James Tilton for this "Nigger on the brain" fixation, Republicans denied that their candidate supported black suffrage, no matter how limited in extent. The Democratic nominee was, instead, the true villain, "the willing tool of…fanatical destructionists" as former slaveholder, covert Rebel agent and post-war champion of the Lost Cause.[5]

Arthur Denny might just well have "walked alone over the course," the Olympia *Washington Standard* suggested in retrospect, dispensing with Garfielde's services. In the aftermath of Appomattox and Lincoln's assassination, Republican victory was all but guaranteed. Winning by a two-to-one margin, Denny carried seventeen of the territory's twenty counties, including eight from the 1863 George Cole column. Tilton drew barely a third of the once-Democratic vote in Clark County. On Puget Sound, sawmill-dominated Kitsap County favored Denny with an astonishing, and suspect, 98 percent of the ballots officially tabulated. Happy Republicans celebrated a better-late-than-never endorsement of the Union, erasing the "Cole-black stain" of 1863. Receiving a coveted bonus, Selucious Garfielde, an avid speculator in mineral-bearing lands, was soon appointed surveyor general, the perfect successor to the late and unlamented Anson Henry.[6]

≈≈≈

Transported from Seattle's stumpy hillsides to the fashionable confines of Washington City, Arthur Denny rewarded Garfielde, returned the Puget Sound customs house to Port Townsend and witnessed the tumultuous events of Reconstruction. President Andrew Johnson favored a relatively easy peace for the South, based upon abolition of slavery as the principal requirement. "Radical" Republicans in Congress demanded harsh treatment of the former Confederate states, amounting to military imposition of genuine social, political and economic change. Regardless of political affiliation, most Washington Territory residents supported the Johnson point of view. Abolition, the Democratic *Walla Walla Statesman* asserted, had "settled the negro question." Among Republican newspapers, the Olympia *Washington Standard* applauded "the wisdom of the President's plan of reconstruction" and warned against the "danger" of black suffrage. The *Pacific Tribune*, the self-appointed voice of territorial Radicalism, maintained that "the whole work of 'reconstruction'…consists in gathering up and setting in motion the old machinery of government as it existed in the seceding States before the war." There was, to be sure, bitter division between homegrown Radicals and Unionist Johnsonites. The argument, however, was primarily over patronage, with incumbent appointees favoring the administration and would-be officeholders endorsing the congressional opposition.[7]

Aggravating the patronage-related discord, former congressional delegate George Cole returned to the territory in January 1867, carrying a presidential commission as Unionist governor. Cole was greeted by a feeble cannon salute and recognized by the legislative assembly. William Pickering refused, however, to vacate the gubernatorial office. The impasse was broken only when the Senate, dominated by President Johnson's enemies, refused to confirm the nomination. New appointee Marshall F. Moore, an Iowa attorney, pre-war Democrat, and severely wounded veteran of Sherman's western campaigns, secured senatorial confirmation. Reaching Olympia, Moore found his official quarters stripped of furnishings and decoration, except for the besieged Pickering's stained bedstead, an apt symbol of territorial government.[8]

Reconstruction at least provided local politicians with vivid rhetorical devices. Nationally, Republicans waved the "bloody shirt," blaming all Democrats, fairly or not, for secession and the actions of the Confederacy. In Washington Territory, the party wielded a cynically altered off-the-rack variant, an unsoiled red-white-and-blue garment. Steilacoom attorney Frank Clark, the Democratic congressional candidate in 1867, was a surviving Monticello convention delegate and a genuine pioneer success story. Opposition propagandists transformed him into a "Hydra of Copperheadism" and an insult to "the patriot [Isaac] Stevens," Washington's sole battlefield casualty-of-note. The decisive factor in the campaign, however, was the selection of Wallula warehouseman Alvan Flanders, a transplanted Californian, as Republican nominee. Cutting, as expected, into the Democratic vote east of the Cascades, Flanders ran well enough in Walla Walla County to win territory-wide by a narrow margin.[9]

Focused on Walla Walla, the Flanders strategy reflected the continuation of a definitive trend: Republicans dominated west of the Cascades and Democrats, usually, on the east. Corruption was another ongoing facet of political life, as evident after the war as before. Government officials paid part of their salaries into party coffers, financing such activities as vote buying. The public printing remained an object of contention, since the funds supplied a partisan newspaper that "largely influenced," as Selucious Garfielde pointed out, "the politics of the Territory." Backcountry politicians "vote[d]...as many men as possible" in unsupervised polling places. Claiming that the Fourteenth Amendment authorized Indian suffrage, reservation agents assembled their charges on behalf of straight party tickets. Both parties imported illegal voters from British territory on the north and from Oregon on the south, a practice known as "colonizing." Democrats worried, for good reason, that Olympia-based Republican federal appointees "might manipulate the returns" in close contests. Edward Salomon, a Chicago resident sent west after being defeated for reelection to local office, became in 1871 the only governor in territorial history to be removed from office for legitimate cause, following exposure of his involvement in misuse of land office deposits.[10]

"The Cascade mountains constitute the dividing line between the timber and prairie regions of the territory," Selucious Garfielde informed an Atlantic coast lecture audience. "East of this range the country is principally open and covered with grass," he elaborated, while on the west "timber is the rule and prairie the exception." Pacific Northwest residents, of course, understood Washington's peculiar geographical situation, as well as the appropriate opportunities for profit, on one side or the other of the Cascades. "Puget Sound is *emphatically* a lumbering district," the Seattle promoter Asa Mercer wrote in an 1865 tract extolling the endless forest and the hazard-free inland sea. The great waterway "must be seen to be fully appreciated," observed Elisha Ferry, Garfielde's successor as surveyor general. "Not a shoal, nor sand bar, nor rock forming the slightest obstruction to navigation, is found between...the Straits and the head of the Sound."[11]

West of the Cascades, the relationship between trees and water produced the witticism that God, in dividing land from sea, must have forgotten Puget Sound. Despite highly favorable natural conditions, the timber industry failed to expand as expected during the Civil War and Reconstruction period. Three-fourths of the lumber produced in a typical year went to San Francisco. When demand dropped in California, the Sound felt the impact in the form of curtailed operations and unemployed workers. The Puget Mill Company erected a new plant at Port Gamble, becoming, by one estimation, a larger manufacturer "per annum than any other mill in the world." Washington firms as a whole, however, employed fewer hands in 1870 than in 1860 and recorded only a slight increase in overall output.[12]

Other features of the industry remained constant. "Any one whose ideas of lumbering establishments have been formed from the small mills of Oregon...," a visitor observed, "can have no true conception of the magnitude of those on Puget Sound." By substantial margins, regional manufacturers were larger, better financed and more export-oriented than competitors south of the Columbia. Maintaining their dominant position, the San Francisco mills turned out nine-tenths of Washington's lumber. Kitsap County held position as a center of afflu-ence, ranking third among the territory's counties—behind only Walla Walla and Thurston—in assessed property value, despite fewer than a thousand resi-dents. The lumber ports also continued to be the most cosmopolitan communi-ties on the Sound. Half their inhabitants were foreign-born, compared to a one-in-five rate for the territory as a whole. The percentage of young single men was a good deal higher, and of women significantly lower, than among the popula-tion-at-large.[13]

A new aspect of the business, the close relationship between lumbering and federal government policies, drew increasing notice. The major sawmill compa-nies acquired timbered acreage, but continued to freely log the public domain. Timber worth $40 million was, according to a subsequent investigation, stolen during the 1860s. Admitting that depredations might, at most, be "checked to some extent," law enforcement officials recognized the territory's economic de-pendence upon trespass and theft. Securing at least some return from a prime resource, the government adopted U.S. attorney John McGilvra's proposal that loggers pay a stumpage fee, initially 15 cents per thousand feet, for timber har-vested on federal land. Representing on average 50 cents a tree, the payment was a double bargain, for mill owners also indemnified themselves against prosecu-tion.[14]

Confirming the refrain that lumbering was the only industrial enterprise in Washington Territory, settlements without a major sawmill lagged far behind in the competition for economic supremacy. Whatcom had the only brick court-house in the territory and prime footage on a bay where "the royal navies of the world might safely glide," at least when the tide was high. The overbuilt gold rush era town was virtually deserted, however; consumed, as forlorn local boost-ers admitted, by "a tradition of failure" and beset with a delinquent tax list ap-propriate to "a city of some thirty or forty thousand inhabitants." Seattle counted upon its own superb harbor and proximity to Snoqualmie Pass for advancement to the first rank. The town remained dependent, though, on the uncertain per-formance of Henry Yesler's pioneer mill. Although Yesler expanded his opera-tion, filling in tideland with slabs and sawdust in the process, the often-idled plant was badly outclassed by California-owned competitors. Unimpressed visi-tors quickly discovered that Seattle was "a veritable mudhole" and unattractive. Sailors declined to go ashore on leave, "so unimportant was the town."[15]

Seattle and Bellingham Bay were saved by the realization that there were other means of making money west of the Cascades. Geological investigation uncovered "a grand coal field," extending from the northern end of the Cowlitz corridor to the close vicinity of the 49th parallel. The major veins, especially those accessible from tidewater, featured bituminous coal of average to superior quality, well-suited for urban lighting, heating and industrial purposes. "Competent engineers…," the *Washington Standard* reported in the fall of 1867, "speak of this coal as kindling quickly, burning freely and clean, emitting a strong heat, making little or no clinkers and leaving [only] about ten percent in ashes." In contrast to the sawmills, located in company towns along the western shore of Puget Sound, the best mining opportunities were near conventional settlements on the eastern bank.[16]

Edmund Fitzhugh returned to the South in 1861 and his pioneer Sehome mine passed into the control of the San Francisco-based Bellingham Bay Coal Company. Expending $100,000 on improvements, the new owners were, by the mid-1860s, the third or fourth largest supplier of the Bay Area market. Emulating the big sawmills, the firm made every effort to maximize efficiency and profits. Three company-owned vessels carried coal down the coast and passengers and freight north to the Sound. The Sehome general store outfitted employees, traded with settlers and Indians for skins and produce and became a major source of the potatoes consumed in California. Featuring spiffy billiard tables and racy adult reading material, the company saloon was acclaimed the territory's most sophisticated drinking establishment.[17]

Bellingham Bay produced, for several years, all the coal shipped from Washington Territory. The first extensive Seattle-area vein was discovered in 1863, in the green Cascade foothills of the Squak, or Issaquah, Valley. "The excitement…," a local newspaper noted of the initial find, "has reached such a pitch as to recall to the minds of old Californians the 'gold fevers' of that country." The boom was, as a matter of bombastic fact, "almost as prolific of *gas* as the coal itself is said to be." Promising deposits were located closer to town in 1864, near the southeastern shore of Lake Washington and along the Black River. A single field, all indications suggested, ran east from the lake as far as the Squak, broken only by the occasional ridge or low mountaintop. Designated Seattle coal, regardless of specific locale, the quality was "about 33 1/3 better than at Bellingham Bay."[18]

William Perkins opened the Seattle coal trade in early 1864, navigating a small barge up the Duwamish and Black rivers to Lake Washington and then to Lake Sammamish and Squak. At the end of a twenty-day voyage, he returned to Elliott Bay with a ten-ton cargo. The Coal Creek and the Lake Washington companies soon claimed the close-in lake mining tracts. Henry Yesler presided over the former concern and the latter included in its management such luminaries as Arthur Denny, Selucious Garfielde and the Reverend Daniel Bagley of university land-grant fame. Neither firm could afford anything beyond rudimentary exploitation, especially the expensive organization of transportation between the mines and the Seattle waterfront. In a fundamental problem for ambitious territorial business interests, capital was unavailable, except on prohibitive terms. Washington had no proper financial institutions, forcing borrowers to rely upon moneylenders, who charged interest as high as five percent a month. To advance beyond "the incipient stage," as Port Townsend observer James G. Swan pointed out, the Seattle mines must first be sold to outsiders.[19]

After prolonged and contentious negotiations, California interests purchased the Seattle coal properties in January 1870. Within a year of taking over, the new owners opened three veins and built both a railroad to Lake Washington and a second rail line connecting the lake with Elliott Bay. Chartered steamers, calling on a regularly scheduled basis, loaded at tidewater storage bunkers. The first coal exported from Seattle went to San Francisco in 1871, selling, the *Weekly Intelligencer* reported, "at the highest prices…as fast as it can be delivered." By mid-decade, the business exceeded one hundred thousand tons per annum.[20]

Energized by coal, Seattle's population expanded well beyond the 1,107 inhabitants officially recorded in the 1870 federal census. "This city, instead of being classed as one of the smaller towns upon the Sound…," the *Intelligencer* proudly announced, "now covers a greater area, contains more structures of different kinds, is the entrepot of a more extensive traffic and a larger business, has a greater influx of non-residents, and more actual residents, than any other place on this arm of the sea." Municipal government removed the last stumps and installed the first above-mud sidewalks. Further indicators of Seattle's new urban status included a permanent public school system—with three teachers—and a fire department.[21]

Though pressed by coal-powered Seattle, Walla Walla remained the territory's largest and wealthiest community. The Walla Walla Valley rivaled the deep timber-lined harbors of Puget Sound in both commercial opportunity and scenic charm. Looking down from a Blue Mountain vantagepoint in May 1868, a visiting Californian "felt like challenging the world to show a landscape that surpasses this in quiet rural beauty, at this bright spring time of the year." A network of streams resembling, when viewed from a high distance on a clear day, a vast liquid web accounted for the productivity. "They spread themselves in almost every direction," another California tourist, J. Ross Browne, wrote of the rivers and creeks, "not only in channels, but over and on top [of] the surface, constituting a most admirable system of self distributing natural irrigants." Built along Mill Creek, Walla Walla City itself illustrated the link between water and settlement east of the Cascades.[22]

Historically dependent upon trade with interior mining districts, Walla Walla altered its commercial relationships at the end of the Civil War. By 1865, the Clearwater and Salmon River mines, the closest and most-easily served diggings, accounted for barely a quarter of the upper Columbia country's gold output, the Boise River and southeastern Oregon increasing in relative importance. Regular stage and express service linked Walla Walla with southern Idaho. Local merchants claimed to offer the largest quantity of supplies at the lowest prices. Sacramento Valley competitors nonetheless secured and maintained a solid foothold, running packtrains, wagons and coaches to and from the mines. The Boise business was, moreover, a constant source of aggravation. Enterprising "swindlers" blocked the trails with tollgates, Idaho officials imposed special taxes upon visiting Washingtonians and returning packers attempted to pass inferior dust at full value in Walla Walla stores and saloons.[23]

Opened during the war, Montana's flourishing gold camps provided new opportunities for Walla Walla. "In the history of mining excitements," the *Statesman* announced in the spring of 1866, "we doubt whether there ever has been a rush equal to that now going on." The competitive equation was highly favorable, since the mines could be supplied only via the Columbia River, from Salt Lake City, or up the Missouri River from St. Louis. Walla Walla's single Pacific Northwest rival was the Oregon Steam Navigation Company's White Bluffs landing at Priest Rapids, the highest upstream point for commercial navigation on the Columbia. Travelers disembarking at White Bluffs and taking the slightly advantageous White Bluffs trail east actually were little closer to Montana than if landing at Wallula. White Bluffs was more irritant than serious competitor. Most of the trade flowed through Walla Walla—a half dozen packtrains departed each day during the summer season—and on to the mines over the Mullan Road, completed to Fort Benton in 1862.[24]

As the main mining excitement shifted from Idaho to Montana, Walla Walla prospered as a transshipment point, dispensing imported goods to the mines and funneling gold out to Portland. The enduring change, however, saw the town become at least as dependent upon wheat and flour as upon mineral wealth. Water and the best soil yet cultivated east of the Cascades accounted for the valley's exceptional fecundity. Farmers reported thirty bushels of wheat to the acre as the average yield and claimed fifty and more as the norm on the best acreage. "The wheat crop," the *Statesman* reported in April 1866, "promises to double that of any former year." The inability of local flouring mills to keep pace with a rate of production approaching, and then exceeding, a half million bushels annually was the only negative aspect of the upsurge. Downriver shipment to Portland mounted. Opening a new trade outlet, three thousand barrels of Walla Walla flour were sent to San Francisco in 1867. The first Atlantic coast consignment was shipped the following year. By 1870 at the latest, grain, not gold, was the Walla Walla mainstay.[25]

Local boosters pronounced Walla Walla the new and improved Willamette Valley of the Pacific Northwest. The climate was better and the growing season longer. Farmsteads were available at substantially lower prices. "Such land as can be had here for from two to five dollars per acre," wrote an eastern Washington student of comparative values, "is there worth from thirty to fifty dollars." Although Willamette wheat sold at a higher rate, greater yields east of the Cascades meant that inland farmers made more money, overall, at harvest. Publicizing these advantages and promoting settlement, Walla Walla interests organized agricultural expositions and immigrant aid societies, the first such promotional efforts in the territory.[26]

Necessary reliance upon the Oregon Steam Navigation Company was, in the view of Walla Walla's postwar newspaper, the *Union*, the "one great drawback that retards and dwarfs our growth." Expending large sums on improvements to service and still earning enormous profits, the Portland firm was, in many ways, the ideal capitalist enterprise. The *Yakima*—supposedly "the finest stern-wheel craft that ever kissed the waters"—and other modern steamers catered to a public demand for increased speed of travel. Confirming the contemporary observation that the O.S.N. was "not composed of boys who will kill the goose that lays the golden egg," the company followed a build-up-the-country policy with regard to passenger and freight charges. "The more I figure and look into it, the *lower* I am inclined to put our rates," Simeon G. Reed informed Captain John Ainsworth in early 1870. What counted, after all, was the volume of trade, the best means of covering expenses and circumventing possible competition. "I would rather see our Dalles Boat come in with 50 Pass. every day at $1.00 passage," said Reed, "than with *only* 5 at $10.00 passage."[27]

Up to a point, inland Northwest residents agreed that the company deserved praise. "Were it not for the O.S.N. Co.," a widely voiced refrain held, ". . . commerce would be carried on in indian canoes." Good works aside, the prevailing view was of a region at the mercy of a grasping Portland monopoly. Though safe and speedy, the steamers were often overcrowded and scheduled at inconvenient times. Merchants complained of the special storage charges assessed upon goods unloaded at Wallula. Boats ceased running, for weeks at a time, when winter ice formed in the Columbia or low water exposed hazardous rocks. Persons unable to postpone travel plans had to resort to the open-air Dalles stage, bundled in blankets and furs against the cold.[28]

Despite its self-styled ratemaking liberality, the O.S.N. supposedly imposed an onerous burden upon helpless communities. Even with periodic freight reductions taken into account, the *Walla Walla Union* insisted, charges remained "higher than on any other line, of the same distance, in the United States." The "greed and avarice" reflected in "extortionate" upriver rates opened the Montana and Idaho mines to competition from merchants utilizing cheaper supply routes. The major complaint rested upon the cost of downriver transportation. Wheat sold at $1.25 a bushel in San Francisco, two to three times the price in Walla Walla. Local farmers argued that the $6 per ton assessed by the O.S.N. between Wallula and Portland prevented them from "reap[ing] any of the advantages" inherent in this differential. With other expenses factored in, the cost of producing and shipping eastern Washington wheat to California worked out to a prohibitive $1.65 a bushel.[29]

In an additional grievance, the otherwise-efficient steamboat company failed to keep pace with the growing wheat output. Teamsters waited in line at Wallula in the fall of 1871 for twenty-four hours before unloading their wagons. Storage space was filled to and beyond capacity, grain piled up on the ground and hundreds of bushels remained unshipped, marooned on the riverbank, when the last boat of the season departed. "Every available house in Wallula," a chagrined Captain Ainsworth admitted, "is now fill'd with wheat, that will have to remain there 'till next May."[30]

Following the worthy principle that "God helps those who help themselves," Walla Wallans resuscitated the railroad to Wallula. The significant reduction in overall freight rates thereby attained—the current wagon rate was $6 a ton, the same as the O.S.N. charge to Portland—might just make local wheat competitive in California. A series of meetings resulted in organization of the Walla Walla and Columbia River Railroad Company, with physician-turned-banker Dorsey S. Baker the leading promoter. Advertised as an automatic route to riches for farmers and townspeople alike, the project attracted insufficient financial support. Envisioning increased traffic for its boats, the O.S.N. offered to invest $100,000, provided Walla Walla County guaranteed repayment of the $500,000 construction bill. A bond issue election was finally held in September 1871, but the voters defeated the Walla Walla and Columbia River. Led by the still enthusiastic Baker, the sponsors revised their plan, reducing estimated expenditures in anticipation of a second try at railroad-building.[31]

Cursed, as a lower Columbia River editorialist quipped, by O.S.N. charges "nearly *three times* the price of freight from Portland to China," Walla Walla prospered anyway. Stores and saloons opened seven days a week in damn-the-Sabbath fashion. A persistent housing shortage stimulated a continuing boom in the value of real estate. After the latest in a series of near-disastrous fires, on July 4, 1866, town residents approved a municipal waterworks and a fire department. Opening its doors that fall to fifty-five students, Whitman Seminary immediately became the territory's largest and most distinguished institution of higher learning, the only competition being Seattle's sorry university. The Excelsiors managed a run-happy 85-60 triumph in the inaugural contest of Washington's first baseball league.[32]

New settlers had no chance of locating farms anywhere near town, the naturally watered land having long since been claimed. In contemporary usage, however, the Walla Walla Valley and the county of the same name were coextensive, embracing all of Washington Territory east of the Columbia and south of the Snake River. Flowing from northeast to northwest of Walla Walla City, the Touchet River drained a fertile, if circumscribed, sub-region. Built alongside the Lewiston trail at the stream's upper forks in 1864, the M. S. Wait flourmill was the nucleus of a new settlement, originally named Delta. Within three years, Waitsburg had a hundred residents and, in addition to the pioneer milling establishment, a general store, hotel, restaurant, saloon and schoolhouse. Small numbers of homesteaders, meanwhile, took claims on tributaries of the Snake, including the Tucannon and the Alpowa.[33]

At twenty-eight thousand square miles "almost an empire within itself," Stevens County encompassed, at the end of the Civil War, everything north of the Snake and east of the Columbia. Originally named Spokane County by Colville Valley liquor dealers, northeastern Washington was home, at most, to four hundred settlers, miners and unemployed ruffians. Distance from markets and uncertain relations with the Indians kept most whites from crossing the Snake River, the demarcation line between relative comfort and wilderness. Pinckney City, the nominal seat-of-government, existed primarily to sell whiskey to soldiers from nearby Fort Colville and boasted a non-thriving population of thirty residents, divided equally into American, Indian and Chinese contingents.[34]

One section only of Stevens County had legitimate prospects. Ranging east from the Mullan Road to, and across, the Idaho line, the Palouse was already famed as a "vast scope of beautifully undulating and copiously fertile country." Preliminary investigation revealed an overall layer of nutritious soil "five to twelve feet in depth," the heaviest concentrations atop the rolling hills. Touring the region in 1869, W. Milnor Roberts of the Northern Pacific Railroad found that "grass grows every where," covering "all the hills and valleys without exception wherever we have come…and as far as the eye could see on either side." Crossing the Snake in what amounted, at the outset, to a slow extension of the Walla Walla settlement impulse, homesteaders took land along the initial tier of westward-flowing Palouse River tributaries. By 1871, two hundred Americans resided in the Union Flat Valley, a "large verdant" meadow blessed with "an endless supply of water." Initial per acre yields equaled the record of established eastern Washington farms. In the absence of a market, however, farmers fed the entire wheat crop to their hogs.[35]

A second eastern Washington settler front developed in the post-war years. Covering over a hundred miles from the Cascades in the northwest to the Columbia on the southeast, the Yakima Valley was, in reality, three major valleys. The uppermost section, the Kittitas, contained the headwaters of the Yakima River. Blessed with mountainside timber, good grass and streams, not to mention proximity to rumored gold deposits, Kittitas afforded the best opportunities for American settlement. Beneath the perfect shape of Mount Adams in the mid-valley, the Yakima skirted sage-covered wastes and was joined by important tributaries—the Wenas, the Naches and the Ahtanum—from the west. Below Union Gap, the Yakama Indian reservation was the principal feature of the third section, the Simcoe Valley. Basin-wide, the soil was "highly fertile and durable" according to a visiting California expert. Irrigation was a necessity, though, at least in the middle and lower valleys. The sparse forest cover in the latter regions also figured to retard the growth of an immigrant population.[36]

Strategically, the Yakima Valley was an east-of-the-Cascades version of the Cowlitz corridor. The most practical route of travel between the mountain passes and Walla Walla, it represented the key link in attempts to unite the territory. Continuing Indian war rumors, supposedly spread by Portlanders intent upon maintaining their hold on eastern Washington, scared off potential settlers in the early territorial era. The opportunities available to parties first on the scene nonetheless made the danger, even if real, a worthwhile risk. "The advantages of the Yakima country may be summed up in a few words," an early homesteader pointed out. "It has a good climate, rich soil, abundance of grass, is well watered and timbered, and in less than five years will have…railroads running through it."[37]

American settlement, from the direction of The Dalles, began in 1865. Some immigrants halted to open farms on the river-bordering benchlands of Klickitat County. Most continued on to the pine-covered Simcoe Mountains and Satus Pass. From an original base of fifteen families, the non-Indian population increased by a factor of six inside three years. Ahtanum Creek, flowing east to the Yakima River and draining, by local report, "some of the best land out of doors," was the initial focus of attention. Cattle, which could be driven to market, provided the pioneer economy mainstay. One resident of the "best stock range in the Territory" owned a thousand animals. Two other valley herds exceeded three hundred head apiece. Yakima City, at first an undersupplied general store at the mouth of the Ahtanum, became the county seat, there being no close approximation of urbanization in the region.[38]

Claimtaking in Kittitas stalled when the first settler had to be evacuated in the midst of a blizzard. Grazing interests from the lower Yakima Valley established themselves along several of the creeks in 1868, using these holdings for summer range and as staging areas for drives across Snoqualmie Pass. Twenty families crossed the pass from the Sound in 1871, settling near Ellensburgh, a townsite promoted by Seattle speculators. Between ninety and one hundred farmsteads, encompassing, according to newspaper stories, "about all the arable land there is on either side of the Yakima River," were opened that year. Settlers depended upon the long, rough and occasionally snowbound trail to The Dalles for supplies and postal services. A road to the upper Columbia at Priest Rapids, connecting with O.S.N. vessels, was widely discussed as a means of overcoming isolation. The definitive solution, though, was full activation of the Yakima corridor by a genuine system of cross-territory transportation.[39]

Waiting for the Northern Pacific to unite eastern and western Washington, tidewater residents briefly achieved the same objective through construction of the long-delayed Cascades wagon road. Unable to do business on the far side of the passes, the Sound country was supposedly "a half inanimate carcass, occasionally showing spasmodic symptoms of life." Once the natural cross-mountain corridor was properly exploited, the Seattle *Puget Sound Weekly* asserted, "lethargy" would give way to sustained prosperity, built in part upon expanding settlement of the Yakima Valley: "Can any sane person entertain the belief that supplies for that section would be received by way of the Dalles, with two or three hundred miles more of water carriage, nearly double the distance of land carriage, and the expense of rehandling…if there was a road from the Sound to the Yakima?"[40]

Olympia, Seattle's rival for western terminus of the road, agreed that the time had come to proceed with construction. Reconciliation of competing claims to superiority remained the sticking point. Funded by local subscriptions, an Olympia workcrew cleared away the worst obstructions on the Naches Pass route in the summer of 1865, allowing wagons to cross the mountains for the first time in over a decade. Pointing out the temporary nature of these repairs, Seattleites insisted that Snoqualmie was "a pass evidently designed for the use of man to improve as a thoroughfare." Indeed, the Cascades crossing behind their community was barely more than "a gap," with "but a single hill of any considerable size" to be traversed. Touring Snoqualmie Pass, Arthur Denny declared it, upon his honor as Washington's congressional delegate, by far the best choice.[41]

In 1866, Levi Farnsworth, a special commissioner appointed by the assembly to determine the recipient of a territorial construction subsidy, recommended, under highly suspicious circumstances, that Naches was "the most practicable of the two passes." Seattle secured the project after all, however, when Thurston and Pierce counties failed to supply the necessary local matching funds. Twenty five thousand dollars was expended upon construction during the outdoor working seasons of 1867 and 1868. The finished road ran east from Lake Washington, crossing Issaquah Creek before entering the foothills of the Cascades. On the opposite side of the summit, it terminated at an imperfectly designated point "in the open country of the Yakima Valley." Representing Washington Territory and King County, Henry Yesler, Arthur Denny and John McGilvra certified completion of the work to contract specifications.[42]

Seattle's Snoqualmie Pass road was, in slapdash reality, a case study in governmental incompetence. Because the contractor neglected to build along the shoreline of Lake Keechelus, east of the summit, persons with wagons had to cross that body of water on makeshift rafts. Within a year, travelers complained that the entire route was "nearly impassable" from fallen timber and "mud holes." Demanding additional support from the territory and pressing the federal government for money to extend the road to the Columbia, King County ignored maintenance concerns. The single county official demonstrating initiative did so by placing a personal tollgate across the right-of-way, extorting fees from passers-by. At most, the road encouraged settlement of the Kittitas country and provided improved conditions for cattle drives. The achievement of larger objectives depended, more than ever, upon railroads.[43]

"Rail road! Terminus! Lands! Corner Lots!" exclaimed Olympia businessman William Winlock Miller in December 1870. "Nothing but things of this kind are spoken of here now." Returning to Steilacoom at the conclusion of his career in Idaho politics, William H. Wallace found the Northern Pacific Railroad "the great topic" of the day on Puget Sound. Granted the odd-numbered sections of the public domain in forty-mile wide strips to either side of its track, the Northern Pacific was sure to have an enormous impact upon Washington. Through painstaking location of the main and branch lines, a Seattle newspaper noted, the company might, in theory, secure "one-half of all the lands" east and west of the Cascades. Upon actual construction, the railroad would secure title to over seven-and-a-half million acres, a fifth of the territory, most of this vast holding in the form of valuable timber and agricultural land.[44]

Despite some concern over the monopolization of acreage, Washingtonians welcomed the Northern Pacific as a belated manifestation of the wealth-generating transcontinental railway vision. To be sure, the N.P. was hardly the only option available to the territory. In December 1867, the Union Pacific proposed building a branch from its mainline to at least the Columbia River, providing "direct through railroad communication with all points east" at a cheaper, and more timely, rate of construction. Already at work connecting Portland and California by rail, the former "stagecoach king" Ben Holladay took control of the on-paper Puget Sound & Columbia River Railroad. Most people believed, however, that Washington needed and deserved an efficient transcontinental system, not some roundabout route, as in the case of the Union Pacific, across eastern Oregon and southern Idaho. Holladay's concept of an eventual north-south coastal linkage, from the Sound to San Francisco, appeared even more ramshackle in nature, calculated to benefit California rather than the Pacific Northwest.[45]

Newspapers, political parties and influential citizens extended support whenever the Northern Pacific requested "a little aid from Congress to…help along the railroad." Delays occasioned by early financial troubles and necessary realignment of stockholder interests justified, and allowed time for, major corporate decisions. Asserting control over N.P. policy, Jay Cooke, America's most prominent banker, focused the initial construction phase upon those portions of the line requiring the least expenditure. Through speedy progress on easily built, if geographically isolated, sections, Cooke reasoned, "we will be able to sell bonds rapidly enough…to unite them." Of particular relevance to the Pacific Northwest, the Northern Pacific would build, first, only as far as the mouth of the Snake River, relying on Oregon Steam Navigation Company vessels for downstream connection to the sea. In 1870, Congress authorized the shift of the mainline to the Columbia River, effectively postponing the expensive cross-mountain link to Puget Sound.[46]

Extensive survey work produced a general geographical framework for the railroad west of the Rockies. Topography and elemental engineering precepts resolved some key questions. High elevation, difficult passes and excessive gradients forced a looping detour along the Clark Fork to Pend Oreille Lake. "The selection," wrote engineer W. Milnor Roberts, "of the best direct practicable route between…two points previously established," the lake and the mouth of the Snake River, dictated that the Palouse be skirted in a northeast-to-southwest direction.[47] Other issues, tending more toward the subjective than the technical, were less easily settled. Should, for example, the true mainline, when finally constructed, follow the Columbia to Portland or, as originally mandated by Congress, cross the Cascades to Puget Sound? In the latter case, where would the terminus, the company's most valuable concession, be located?

Viewed from a regional perspective, the Northern Pacific saga was another chapter in the long rivalry between the Sound and Portland. Disputes over the relative railroading merits of inland sea and the River of the West animated dinnertime table talk and formal debate. The Columbia, Oregonians maintained, provided "the only feasible and reliable route through the Cascade range of mountains." Scoffing at "the ill conceived jealousy of our web-foot neighbors," Puget Sound residents detailed the many "insuperable" obstacles to navigation of the river, including ice, "wreck-making reefs" and the horrors of the bar. The Sound, in contrast, was "a broad and beautiful arm of the sea, full of harbors and bays, running inland 200 miles, almost to the Cascades." So-located, it was the "inevitable terminus" for all "systems of railroads, whether they come from the North, South, or East."[48]

John Ainsworth's rise to influence within N.P. executive ranks—retaining his O.S.N. position, the captain became western managing director for the transcontinental road in 1872—greatly troubled Puget Sound terminus advocates. The act of Congress relocating the mainline to Portland was, in comparison to this development, only momentarily disconcerting. Opinion held steady behind the conviction that the Northern Pacific must, sooner or later, come direct to tidewater in Washington Territory. "The primary object is to get a continuous line from Lake Superior to the Columbia," the Port Townsend *Message* explained with reference to the financial calculations behind the change in plan, "…and when that line is completed and in working condition, it will be extended to Puget Sound, just as the Central [Pacific] has passed by Sacramento and gone to San Francisco." In the short-term, moreover, a new congressional mandate and the prospective Ben Holladay challenge obligated the railroad to proceed immediately with a branch between the lower Columbia and the Sound.[49]

Preparing for construction of the Columbia River-Puget Sound branch, Jay Cooke announced that the road "may be carried along either side or both sides of the Sound, as far as may be desired, to any port or ports, which shall be selected." The company filed maps with the federal government covering all possible routes and destinations. In late 1871, the General Land Office withdrew the odd-numbered sections south of Steilacoom from private entry. A second withdrawal, covering the public domain north to the 49th parallel, followed in early 1872. Acreage covered by the orders was reserved for the Northern Pacific, to be gradually turned over as each twenty-five mile section of track was completed and certified by G.L.O. inspectors.[50]

Cooke's deliberately vague proclamation left all options open regarding the Puget Sound target. "There is not a single person, either in the company or out of it," the Port Townsend *Message* observed, "who knows the first thing about where the terminus will be." The contenders, and their respective merits and demerits, were, of course, perfectly obvious. Olympia still considered itself the leading community on the Sound, an opinion shared by few, if any, outsiders. The streets flooded at high tide and Budd Inlet remained an unsuitable anchorage. At Steilacoom, a lingering dispute over land claims compromised attempts to attract the Northern Pacific. The town's future lay, instead, in an institutional direction. The Grant administration selected nearby McNeil Island as the site for a federal prison. The Washington Territory asylum, previously located at Vancouver, Monticello and other temporary points, took up permanent quarters at Fort Steilacoom, abandoned by the military since the Civil War.[51]

Founded in 1868 by Portland speculators, Commencement City had a new name, Tacoma, and more-than-sufficient energy. The settlement consisted of a half dozen hastily erected buildings, clustered beneath a high bayside bluff. Reasoning that "a first class saw mill…will add fifty precent [sic] immediately to all our property here," the proprietors persuaded the Hanson and Ackerson lumbering interests to come north from San Francisco. Once in business, the mill ranked as the largest forest products manufacturer on the eastern shore of the Sound, a definite plus in the campaign for the Northern Pacific terminus. Any railroad official favoring an alternative to Tacoma would "on the same principle," claimed Morton Matthew McCarver, the spelling-challenged resident promoter, "recommend his imployers [sic] to take cownter feit [sic] for freights & passage instead of Gold & Silver."[52]

Rivals north of Commencement Bay had no intention of conceding Tacoma's superiority. Seattle had coal, Snoqualmie Pass, dozens of new shops, saloons and warehouses and a record of sustained postwar growth. Claiming that Bellingham Bay was better suited than Tacoma for purposes of navigation, Whatcom also sought the railroad. Implementing a municipal improvement plan, Port Townsend drained swamps, excavated hillsides, constructed an offshore bulkhead and installed a water plant to end reliance upon "salty sweepings." Such advances, townspeople figured, would entice the Northern Pacific to the western, instead of the eastern, shore of the Sound.[53]

Some, at least, of the attempts to promote previously undeveloped sites involved unscrupulous public officials. Surveyor general Selucious Garfielde tried to change the boundaries of the Nisqually Indian reservation in the interest of placing the terminus at the mouth of the Nisqually River. A resurvey of the Puyallup agency left the Commencement Bay tideflats, that portion of the waterfront best suited to commercial development, outside the treaty-described limits. Denying any connection with such endeavors, Jay Cooke pronounced "the Northern Pacific Company...the cleanest & most straight-forward corporation from the first letter of its charter all the way down that we have ever seen." Cooke's declaration aside, the railroad co-opted Washington Territory government on a regular basis. Following his election to Congress in 1869, Garfielde went on the firm's payroll, for services as lecturer, promotional pamphlet author and confidential Capitol Hill representative. Intent upon securing appointment as territorial governor, Elisha Ferry served the railroad "for the sake of 'auld lang syne.'" The Northern Pacific bought acreage at inflated prices from the chief judge of the supreme court and other officials. Every officeholder, regardless of party affiliation, received a pass.[54]

Cynicism was particularly notable in connection with the terminus question. "The concession of the *terminal city* is a big one," Cooke pointed out, "& worth a good many millions." Perfectly aware of this elemental facet of the railroading business, John W. Sprague, the executive in charge of Northern Pacific affairs in Washington Territory, stated that the winning, and presumably fortunate, community must donate "lands that will be increased in value a hundred or a thousand fold" by proximity to the terminus. Acreage "that will not be affected by the expenditures of this Co[mpany]," Sprague warned a delegation from one town, "will have little or no weight in fixing the point on the Sound" eventually selected.[55]

Local Puget Sound interests matched Cooke and his colleagues in the desire to secure profit from the railroad. "There never was a railway... projected into any country," the Seattle *Weekly Intelligencer* observed in the fall of 1870, "which occasioned so much speculation and anxiety as to its location and terminus as is the case with the Northern Pacific." Reporting from the Sound, a Portland journalist advised that "everybody seems really to have terminus on the brain." James G. Swan informed friends in San Francisco of the "wild prices...paid for beach lots, whose only value consists in the prospect that some day the Directors of some Railroad may pay a fabulous price for the privilege of locating a terminus there." Some speculators, like returned lumberman Marshall Blinn, covered their bets, purchasing land and laying-off "additions" at all contending points. Out of confidence or local patriotism, others focused on a single place.[56]

Although naysayers cautioned that "the end of the road will be designated...just where the interests of the road will demand it," most observers expected "liberal donations of land and money" to influence the decision. Olympia promised six thousand acres. Steilacoom proffered "a large portion of the present town site, and three-fourths of the adjacent lands, amounting in the aggregate to some ten thousand acres." The Tacoma development syndicate proposed giving Walla Walla orchardist Philip Ritz, an important N.P. stockholder, a quarter share "in all of our Inrtrests [sic] here." Whatcom residents formed the Bellingham Bay Land Association, intending to exchange "one-half" their pooled holdings for the terminus. Relying upon supposed confidential arrangements with railroad officials, Port Townsend offered to finance track laying along Hood Canal.[57]

Seattle alone refused to participate in the competition. "When the men who run this corporation," the *Intelligencer* commented in early 1871, "talk to people here about giving them millions of dollars worth of property to just tap this town…they presume upon a greater degree of stupidity than the people here are possessed with." The community fronted on the best harbor in the region and controlled access to Snoqualmie Pass, proven by recent explorations to have the most favorable grade and the least winter snow of all potential mountain crossings. Because the Northern Pacific was, out of obvious self-interest, sure to come to Seattle anyway, there was no need for local inducement. "That the company will avail themselves of this locality," the *Intelligencer* observed, "seems almost a foregone conclusion."[58]

Certain developments within Northern Pacific ranks shed light upon the matter. Early survey reports favored Seattle, as did a commission sent to the Pacific Northwest by Jay Cooke in 1869. Cooke privately expressed a desire to build to Bellingham Bay, incorporating the maximum amount of timber in the land grant. Insiders paid particular attention to the views of engineer W. Milnor Roberts, developed during the Cooke-financed tour and in the course of a detailed 1871 examination. Tacoma, Roberts found, was "not an attractive site for a city" because of its "bluffy" and "ill adapted" shoreline and the excessive depth of Commencement Bay. Whatcom and Seattle possessed the "only real harbors on the East side of the Sound." Of the two sites, he clearly preferred the former. "It is the *best* place I have seen…," Roberts advised of Whatcom, "so far as the water supply is concerned." The troublesome tidal problems could be circumvented by "building up or filling extensively on the mud flats." Whatcom Creek, moreover, was susceptible of sufficient exploitation to provide local industry with "a vast super-abundance" of power.[59]

In contrast to the public and private debate over the Puget Sound terminus, selection of the railroad's Columbia River starting point was relatively contention-free. Seeking a location suitable for both ocean-going vessels and eventual bridge construction, the Northern Pacific settled upon Kalama, at the mouth of the Lewis River. Documenting the resultant boom, a Portland newspaper reported that "the scenes about Kalama" rivaled "those of the most extensive

gold mining camp ever struck on the Pacific slope." Along with the railroad offices and shops, the town had, by the end of 1871, four hotels, three saloons, a
brewery and a "cheap John" discount store. Lots sold for $800 on average and at
substantially higher prices on streets above high water mark. Despite exposure to
flooding from the regular rise and fall of the Columbia, residents spoke, seriously, of becoming "the second city of the coast within the next three or four seasons," exceeded in wealth and influence only by San Francisco.[60]

The first section of track, twenty-five miles connecting the Lewis River with
the Cowlitz corridor, was completed in the fall of 1871. Preparing to assume title
to the initial stage of its western Washington land grant, the Northern Pacific
confronted a number of legal, political and financial problems. A complex early
dispute focused on disposition of private claims filed by in-the-know federal
employees between August 13, 1870, when the General Land Office withdrew
the odd-numbered sections from entry, and October 20, 1870, the date the
withdrawals were publicly announced in Washington Territory. Although John
Sprague "assured all who desired to go onto the Companys land to make farms
that they would be safe in doing so," a prolonged delay in setting the price for
farming acreage generated a near-crisis in public confidence. On another level of
concern, the N.P. experienced unexpected difficulty raising the money to keep
on schedule. The Franco-Prussian War and other crises upset European fiscal
markets. The demand for railroad bonds among American investors fell short of
original projections. Construction continued on the Puget Sound branch, but the
Pend Oreille division, linking the Snake River with northern Idaho, was indefinitely
postponed.[61]

Sooner or later, the railroad expected to capitalize upon the federal acreage
withdrawn from private entry. Care was taken, west of the Cascades, to lay track
through the most heavily timbered areas, since such land was worth $100 and
more per acre. Ongoing timber theft, unfortunately, meant that much of this
value was sure to be lost before the firm took actual possession. "I doubt if you
can realize," John Sprague advised Frederick Billings, the Northern Pacific partner in charge of policies relating to the grant, "the damage and loss our Company
is sustaining by the removal of Timber from Lands in reserve for us." Existing
statutes required prosecutors to supply legally exact locations for all acts of thiev-
ery, an impossible task in unsurveyed portions of the territory. Rather than station inspectors at the mills and in the logging camps, the General Land Office
relied upon a single easily corrupted agent for the entire Sound. Working on behalf of the lumber industry, congressional delegates made sure that only persons
friendly to the sawmills, like incumbent U.S. attorney Leander Holmes, secured
federal appointment.[62]

Intent upon protecting timber on tracts due for eventual inclusion in its
grant, the Northern Pacific assumed the responsibility neglected by government
authorities. "I propose," Sprague announced in May 1871, "to do all that can be

done…to stop trespassing on Govt. lands, on the Sound, for if they are not with-drawn now for the Company, they may be soon." N.P. attorney Hazard Stevens, the son of Washington Territory's first governor, secured appointment as a deputy U.S. marshal. Federal agent Benjamin Tuttle accepted a liberal fee to ac-tually carry out his assigned duty. Cruising Puget Sound and Hood Canal dur-ing the summer of 1871, Stevens and Tuttle seized illegally cut timber. Log-gers had no choice but to buy back the confiscated rafts at subsequent General Land Office auctions, since the alternative was bankruptcy via unpaid wages and other expenses. Appearing as private citizen rather than officer of the law, Stevens bid prices up to high levels before dropping out in favor of the logging camp operators.[63]

Private initiative succeeded where government negligence had failed. "The only way to deal with such cases…," Hazard Stevens wrote, "is to take the logs away to some point where they can be safely kept and not to let the loggers who cut them bid them in except at ruinous prices." The lesson was quickly and ef-fectively taught. Stevens reported in August 1871 that the seizures "have caused a feeling among loggers that they must leave, and keep off of, Govt. lands." The railroad's interest, however, was not so much in halting theft for the sake of halt-ing theft as in fighting illegality that would eventually cost it money. The North-ern Pacific had nothing to gain, and a good deal to lose, from putting the lum-ber industry out of business. "Now that we have pretty thoroughly broken up Timber stealing on the Sound and vicinity," John Sprague pointed out, "it is quite important that we arrange if possible to let parties cut Timber and pay 'stumpage.'"[64]

Stevens and Tuttle mounted new raiding parties when and where necessary, but Sprague's proposal became company policy. Henceforth, loggers paid stump-age fees previously due the government for logging the public domain to the Northern Pacific, a private business enterprise. The railroad soon found itself embroiled in a controversy over the highly dubious nature of this arrangement. Neither the General Land Office nor the Department of Justice authorized the practice. Federal prosecutors briefly charged John Sprague with fraud. Dismissed from the firm's service for, of all things, dishonesty, Hazard Stevens and Ben-jamin Tuttle became convenient scapegoats for their superiors. Outright theft was, to a considerable extent, halted. The immediate public benefit, though, was unclear and the reputation of the Northern Pacific for clumsy venality was en-hanced.[65]

Timber matters failed to divert attention from the supreme issue, the termi-nus. In an entirely unexpected development, the Northern Pacific announced in November 1871 that the Puget Sound branch would halt at Olympia. Proud lo-cal citizens anticipated such railroad-related advances as erection of a vast indus-trial complex at the falls of the Deschutes River and "a line of houses forming a continuous street all the way from Tumwater…to the terminal." Unfortunately, the N.P. soon announced that its decision in favor of Budd Inlet was only temporary in nature, a momentary pause prior to construction down the Sound. The announcement was unsettling, but growing realization that the company intended, in a complete reconsideration of priorities, to bypass Olympia truly devastated the community. The terminus was "gone to hell," William Winlock Miller lamented. "The whole thing is *dead, dead, dead.*" Brazenly facing down a threatened breach-of-contract lawsuit, railroad officials claimed that all arrangements had been "conditional and preliminary" in nature.[66]

Defeat for Olympia apparently reopened the region-wide terminal competition. "Where that point will be or when it will be definitely settled," observed William H. Wallace, "the Lord only knows and he wont tell." Rumors favored first one, and then another, town. "The terminus question seems to be interminable…," an eastern Washington editor quipped. By the winter of 1873 at the latest, however, certain developments suggested that the choice, engineering objections aside, was Tacoma. The Lake Superior and Puget Sound Land Company, jointly owned by the Northern Pacific and a "ring" of railroad stockholders, acquired extensive tracts adjacent to Commencement Bay. Captain John Ainsworth and Portland associate Simeon Reed organized their own company to exploit investment opportunities in and around Tacoma. The captain also took on the task, in association with Judge Richard Rice, of actually selecting the terminus on behalf of the N.P.[67]

Realizing, at literally the final moment, that Seattle's manifest advantages were of no account, town residents abandoned all scruples about groveling before corporations. "A very large number of acres of land, a great quantity of city lots, including a long water frontage, and very many outside tracts…together with a large sum of money have been bountifully offered to the N.P.R.R. Company," the *Intelligencer* reported in July 1873. A delegation led by Arthur Denny presented the total package, said to be worth over seven hundred thousand dollars, to Ainsworth and Rice at a hastily arranged conference. With "the fate of Seattle" in the balance, the *Intelligencer*, briefly reverting to complacent form, expressed confidence that "Tacoma can not compete with us."[68]

Tacoma easily triumphed over Seattle. Ratified by the Northern Pacific board of directors, John Ainsworth's self-interested decision favoring the community produced immediate jubilation on Commencement Bay. "The beach at that point," wrote William Winlock Miller after a hurried visit, "is litterally [sic] covered with adventurers going thither to make their fortunes." A newspaper correspondent reported the arrival of "streams of human life intent on finding business to do, claims to live on, land to buy and sell, [and] chances to speculate." Erected in a matter of hours, sixty wall tents served as "hotels, restaurants, saloons, provision and clothing stores, barber shops, shoe shops, land agencies, doctors' offices, churches and even brothels…ready to supply every want, good or bad, as soon as felt." Working from dawn to dusk, "choppers" felled the forest and cleared away underbrush, making room for the "City of the Future."[69]

Except among Tacoma's would-be profiteers, the decision was roundly condemned, on the basis that Ainsworth had selected the least worthy terminal in order to protect Portland. "The effects…will be," a Northern Pacific executive pointed out in an internal protest, "to relinquish the valuable Timber Lands in toto lying on Pugets Sound and also…valuable Coal fields east of Seattle." Jay Cooke privately bemoaned the loss of the most valuable portion of the grant west of the Cascades. Public reaction ranged from hostility to complete irrationality. "Every act of the Company in the future…," the Seattle *Intelligencer* exclaimed, "will continue to be watched with the keenest skepticism and suspicion." Seattle and Whatcom demanded the immediate opening of the odd-numbered sections north of Tacoma to settlement. Betrayed by the Northern Pacific, Elliott Bay interests announced plans for their own railroad to Walla Walla and points beyond.[70]

New troubles staggered the Northern Pacific in the immediate aftermath of Tacoma's selection. The sensational failure of Jay Cooke's banking house set in motion the Panic of 1873, the worst economic crisis yet experienced in American history. Unable to borrow money, the N.P. collapsed as a fiscally viable enterprise. Survival depended upon completion of the track to Tacoma, the only means of securing title to the townsite and the revenue from land sales on Commencement Bay. Advancing a substantial portion of his own fortune, the positive-thinking John Ainsworth—"I have seen dark days before, and therefore don't despair of living to see sunshine again"—accomplished the task. After Washington Territory refused to intervene militarily, the resourceful captain even compromised with a "mob," personally paying off construction workers who had gone on strike over nonpayment of wages.[71]

Driven on December 16, 1873, a final tarnished spike linked Tacoma with the Columbia River. There was little, if any, cause for celebration. West of the Rocky Mountains, the Northern Pacific Railroad consisted of the isolated Puget Sound branch. Public hostility to further assistance for the prostrate company suggested that this embarrassing state of affairs was likely to remain in effect for a lengthy period of time. Washington had a railroad, but it was a north-south line, an industrialized Cowlitz corridor, not the east-west connection needed for unification of the territory. With John Ainsworth in control, the branch was sure to be managed according to the interest of Portland-based outsiders. Awaiting the uncertain day of resumed construction, the northern and southern terminals languished. A visiting European journalist dismissed Tacoma as "not likely to become of much importance" and Kalama as "one of those places we sometimes fall upon in America, which, having had a brief prosperity, have suddenly collapsed."[72]

The Northern Pacific Railroad figured prominently in the concluding phase of Selucious Garfielde's shameless political career. After orating on behalf of Arthur Denny in 1865 and Alvan Flanders in 1867, Garfielde ran for Congress himself in 1869. Careful pre-convention organizing secured the Republican nomination, the only overt opposition coming from the politically inept Walla Wallan, Dorsey Baker. Unable to decide among a variety of contenders, the Democrats settled upon a compromise nominee, former Governor Marshall Moore. Party leaders reasoned, sensibly, that Moore's war record and upright character made a winning contrast with his opponent's well-known shortcomings.[73]

Candidate Garfielde was blamed, a supporter complained, for "every little shadow upon the political horizon." Concluding a survey of territorial affairs since 1853, the Olympia *Washington Standard* observed that "no man…has ever made a worse record or more disgraceful history." Garfielde was consistent only "in his rascality," said the *Walla Walla Statesman*, and, if elected, "infinitely more likely to make his mark in the gambling saloons…than he is on the legislation of the country." Republicans made no attempt to sanitize the record. Touring the territory on the party's behalf, Elwood Evans conceded that the nominee had loaned public funds for private profit while serving in the land office, but insisted that "it was perfectly natural for a man to use money deposited with him, in the expectation that he would be able to replace it when it became due." Admitting to past indiscretions, Garfielde excused himself, Lincoln-style, for having been "born in poverty" and educated "by the light of a pine knot fire, in a home too lowly even to afford candles."[74]

Distant and long-ago battles of the Civil War were refought one more time on the campaign fields. Although Marshall Moore had been awarded a general's stars for valor in combat and would die in 1870 from the lingering effects of severe battlefield injuries, Republicans accused him of unmanly and disloyal conduct. After purchasing "a place in the army…he was incompetent to fill," the Port Townsend *Message* claimed, the Democratic nominee had "trifled with the lives of the brave soldiers placed under his charge." Deep-down an enemy of the Northern cause, the former governor privately worshipped "the 'martyr Jeff Davis,' the 'hero Bob Lee,' [and] the assassin Wilkes Booth." Moore responded in patriotic kind, with at least some truth on his side. Delivering brief speeches, he confessed that unhealed wounds, suffered on behalf of the Union and the Lord, precluded lengthy oratory. Democrats portrayed Garfielde, the Civil War self-exile, as the real "traitor" and advocate of secession. Coming forth by the voluntary score, supposed eyewitnesses testified that, safe in British Columbia, he had rejoiced over Northern defeats and shed the only genuine tears of his entire miserable life at the news of Confederate losses.[75]

Garfielde won anyway, by a hold-your-nose margin of 149 votes out of 5,337 officially counted. Rejected by two of every three voters in Walla Walla County, he triumphed because of three-to-one support in Kitsap and Jefferson counties, where lumber industry influence was the major factor at the polls. Following the delegate-elect's rapid departure for Washington City, the present and former Republican officials who had covertly worked for Moore issued a declaration of anti-Garfielde principles. Signed by fifty "Bolters," including Governor Alvan Flanders, the "Manifesto" made a single notable fresh charge, that sawmill company money was responsible, as no untainted vote could ever be, for the election outcome. Waiting until after the votes were counted to publicly break with Garfielde, the Bolters resigned themselves to a preordained fate. Immediately upon reaching the nation's capital, Washington's new delegate went "systematically to work" on patronage matters, securing the removal of his enemies from office. Except for Flanders, who claimed to have voted for the entire Republican ticket—if true, he had doublecrossed his associates in the original doublecross of the party's nominee—the victims accepted dismissal without public complaint.[76]

Federal legislation providing for election of a territorial delegate in Washington in June 1870, and every two years thereafter, cut Garfielde's term in half, providing his foes with an early opportunity for revenge. Traveling east of the Cascades on behalf of the Bolters, the politically active lumberman Marshall Blinn attempted to arrange a formal union with Democrats. When this gambit failed, a three-way campaign for Congress ensued. James Mix, a Walla Walla attorney known for courtroom fisticuffs, was the Democratic nominee. Blinn ran as a well-financed independent. Although the race was projected as a "desperate battle," Mix had no support on Puget Sound and Blinn lacked appeal outside elite circles. Confounding his enemies, Garfielde won easily, carrying sixteen of the twenty-one counties.[77]

Safely elected to a full two years in office, Garfielde initiated the one memorable act of his congressional career—cheating the Indians of northeastern Washington out of their reservation. Established by a Grant administration executive order in March 1872, the Colville agency, bounded on the west by the Columbia and on the south by the Spokane River, included within its limits the best farming acreage in the area. Ignoring the fact that six of the eight assigned tribes already lived there, Garfielde claimed, on behalf of outraged whites, that the Indians considered the land unsuited to their needs. Accepting this falsehood, the president issued a new order, moving the reservation from the left to the inhospitable right bank of the Columbia. The sorry outcome was predictable: fearing starvation in a "barren country," most Indians refused to cross the river, attempting instead to maintain traditional homes in a region opened to settlement.[78]

Ugly betrayal of the Indians presumably increased Garfielde's popularity, at least among settlers in the Colville region. The first Washington delegate since Isaac Stevens to be reelected, he might have won again and again except for the changing requirements of the Northern Pacific. Initiated in 1871, the railroad's campaign against timber theft forced Garfielde to decide between the sawmills and the railroad, between old and new benefactors. Securing the removal of uncooperative federal officials, the company weakened the delegate's personal organization. Attempting to save U.S. attorney Leander Holmes, one of his prime cronies, Garfielde finally agreed to "defer largely" to Jay Cooke's "wishes" and accept the appointment of Samuel Wingard, a personal enemy. Behind-the-scenes disagreement also figured into the short territorial career of L. P. Beach, Elisha Ferry's successor as surveyor general.[79]

Intent upon protecting Puget Sound timber, the Northern Pacific turned on an ally unwilling to fully support an enterprise harmful to lumbermen. The railroad's "influence" in 1872 went instead to an "honest, industrious and…true friend," Olympia Democrat Obadiah B. McFadden. Born in Pennsylvania, McFadden had served as supreme court judge in both Oregon and Washington territories in the 1850s. A surviving Isaac Stevens follower and vocal wartime Unionist, he was well fortified against charges of disloyalty. "Old Mac" was also a skilled orator, close to Garfielde standards in the talents of professional persuasion. His audiences, a newspaper noted, "left the Hall with the firm belief that…there will be a marble capitol building erected in every county seat that wants one…[and] that the Northern Pacific Railroad will be compelled forthwith to build a branch road…to all the different point[s] on the Sound."[80]

Threatened by an able and well-financed opponent, Garfielde responded in brazen style. He was the personification of the Union, the Republican claimed, while Judge McFadden was a devoted friend of the Confederacy. Democratic orators supplemented the standard list of Garfielde transgressions with the imaginative new accusation that Washington's delegate intended to mount a filibustering expedition against Baja California. While McFadden campaigned vigorously on both sides of the Cascades, his supporters prepared to counter Republican dishonesty. "If they colonize," son-in-law William Winlock Miller warned of the importation of voters from Oregon and British Columbia, "let our friends colonize too." At a number of polling places, Indians attempting to cast Republican tickets turned away in the face of physical intimidation. McFadden was "certain to be elected," Miller pointed out, "if Garfielde's friends do not beat us by fraud at the polls."[81]

Unofficial returns, Miller advised Democratic associates in early November, indicated that "Selucious the Silver tongued is routed, horse, foot and dragoon." McFadden, in fact, won 55 percent of the vote, with nine counties shifting from the 1870 Republican column. Angered by his rejection, and especially by the role of the Northern Pacific in financing the opposition, Garfielde threatened to expose railroad corruption in the final weeks of the outgoing Congress. Fearing retribution, the company placed employee William McMicken's already arranged appointment as surveyor general on hold until completion of the defeated delegate's full term. Even loyal Garfielde Republican John Simms, the Indian agent at Colville, anticipated removal for a transgression no greater than being another McFadden son-in-law.[82]

To the surprise, and relief, of most observers, Garfielde renounced both vengeance and electoral politics. His subsequent life passed through a series of bitter disappointments, ending in tawdry humiliation. Securing a federal mail contract, the former delegate purchased a steamer for the San Francisco-Puget Sound run, only to have the vessel, and his investment, sink on the initial voyage. Attempting to establish a Washington City legal practice, Garfielde took on a complex, lengthy and ultimately losing case, all but bankrupting himself in the process. Depressed and deserted by his wife, he survived on the occasional patronage assignment from old colleagues in the Pacific Northwest. At the time of his death in 1883, the most flamboyant politician of the territorial era was proprietor of a sleazy Capitol Hill entertainment emporium—"ostensibly a cigar store" according to obituary notices—catering to the habits of congressmen.[83]

⚛⚛⚛

According to the 1870 federal census, exactly 37,432 human beings resided in Washington. In the most revealing aspect of the count, only 22,195 residents, 59 percent of the total, were white. Washington was a biracial commonwealth, particularly in comparison to its Pacific coast neighbors. With the confusing establishment of the Colville agency in 1872, every territorial Indian was assigned to one of fifteen reservations. A substantial portion of the native population, however, actually lived, seasonally or upon a permanent basis, outside these tracts. Treaty provisions authorized travel to customary places of subsistence, to fish, hunt and gather roots and berries. Two thousand persons belonging, by bureaucratic fiat, to the Pacific Northwest Indian superintendencies resided year-round on the banks of the Columbia and Snake rivers.[84]

Indians continued to play a vital, and often essential, role in territorial life. Makah tribal members supplied Puget Sound with halibut taken on the banks off Cape Flattery and with canoes obtained from Vancouver Island. Lummis sold timber to the Bellingham Bay Coal Company and made up most of the firm's labor force, below as well as above ground. Nez Perce farmers packed produce and dairy products into the mining camps. On "daily" visits to Walla Walla, native traders sold horses and buffalo robes to prospectors about to set out on the trails to the diggings.[85]

Settlers still generally regarded Indians as unwholesome, if often essential, nuisances. At Port Townsend, local tribespeople mingled uneasily with visiting native delegations from the Sound, the Strait of Juan de Fuca and Vancouver Island. Mixed together, traditional rivalries and rotgut whiskey—said by James G. Swan to be "a vile compound of alcohol, red pepper, tobacco, and coal oil"— generated frequent trouble and periodic threats of violence and arson. East of the mountains, all the tribes were held to account whenever an isolated miner or lone packer was assaulted. Direct action against offending Indians was occasionally taken, and regularly advocated, regardless of law or equity. Citing the fire danger, Port Townsend forcibly evicted local natives from their village. Predicting that only "milk-sop philanthropy…will protest," the *Walla Walla Statesman* endorsed the bounty placed on Paiute Indian scalps by south Idaho miners in 1866. Settlers in both eastern and western Washington demanded that the Army maintain expensive forts to deter attack by untrustworthy tribes and bands.[86]

Native residents composed a well-documented Washington minority. Federal census-takers, on the other hand, reported only 234 Chinese persons present in 1870, despite evidence of a much larger Asian population. Two hundred thousand Chinese, ninety percent men, migrated to the United States between 1849 and 1877. Most went to California, but a substantial number wound up in the Pacific Northwest. Actively promoting the importation of Asian laborers, the Oregon Steam Navigation Company offered special two-dollar "coolie" rates between Portland and Lewiston. The O.S.N. carried as many as two hundred individuals, crowded into out-of-the-way places with "all their worldly goods," on a single steamer. A typical *Walla Walla Statesman* account recorded the arrival from Wallula of "a little army of Chinamen" in August 1868: "They came in wagons, on horseback, and a foot, and really it seemed as though they would never stop coming."[87]

Four hundred Chinese miners worked the Columbia River bars above Priest Rapids in April 1865. By December, the figure was near one thousand. Another three hundred prospected the Kootenay River, just north of the border in British Columbia. Orofino, the original Clearwater boomtown, was, the Portland *Oregonian* reported, "given over to the Chinese" in 1865, an estimated eight hundred being on hand. Immigrants also found useful employment west of the Cascades. Four Chinese men commenced a commercial fishing venture on Elliott Bay in 1869. At Port Gamble, the Puget Mill Company employed sixty Asian laborers. A settler near the mouth of the Snohomish River reclaimed seventy acres of tideland with the aid of Chinese hired-hands.[88]

Like the Indians, the Chinese were both necessary workers and the targets of unwarranted abuse. "The objections to the Chinese are numerous…," the Seattle *Intelligencer* asserted in a comprehensive indictment. "They are ignorant, superstitious, sensualistic and brutal, as well as filthy, and often vicious and diseased, too." White residents of Walla Walla and Olympia blamed outbreaks of small pox and "pestilence" upon unsanitary Asian habits. When demolition of a Chinese laundry exposed a pool of "festering soap suds…from which emanated a smell that was almost overpowering," the *Walla Walla Union* demanded that "moon-eyed celestials" move wash houses to "less frequented streets." Seeking new ways to besmirch Selucious Garfielde's reputation, eastern Washington Democrats produced an outsized poster depicting the territorial delegate arm-in-arm "with a nigger on one side and a Chinaman on the other." Nativist newspapers encouraged whites to act vigilante-style outside the law whenever their interests conflicted with those of the newcomers.[89]

❧❧❧

"This Territory was organized in 1853," a Seattle journalist reminded his readers in 1864, "and is now the oldest Territorial Government in the United States." Neighboring Oregon had been a full-fledged member of the Union since 1859, but there was, as yet, little real enthusiasm north of the Columbia for Washington's elevation to similar status. Part of the explanation was economic in nature, for greatly increased local taxes would be required to support services freely provided under direct federal auspices. Republicans worried that Democrats would secure control of an elective state administration, and Democrats feared the same of Republicans. In Walla Walla, the Democratic *Statesman* dismissed statehood as "a doubtful proposition" and the Republican *Union* regarded any movement in the direction of admission as "premature" and "supremely ridiculous." Given the chance to express themselves directly on the issue, via proposals for a constitutional convention, the voters rejected a state of Washington in 1867, in 1869 and again in 1870.[90]

Uncertain boundaries reflected a widespread feeling that Washington was not, at present, properly constituted for statehood. Pressure mounted in Walla Walla and in Lewiston for the annexation of northern Idaho and creation of Nez Perce Territory east of the Cascades. Although Walla Walla County now held six of the thirty house seats and two of the nine council positions, its residents complained of their interests being sacrificed and their taxes expended for the benefit of Puget Sound. "A foregone conclusion" on the other side of the mountains, union with the Idaho panhandle was viewed with horror on the Sound. From the tidewater perspective, the annexation movement was "the first step in the grand conspiracy of the eastern against the western section." Even if a single territorial government was retained, the Olympia *Tribune* pointed out in January 1868, "the balance of power as well as population would be instantly transferred" and the capital lost to Walla Walla. Should Nez Perce Territory actually be created, economic development of Washington's remnant section, forever checked along the Cascade summit, immediately became an impossibility.[91]

Another proposal called for dividing both Oregon and Washington at the Cascades, the western portions of each forming a rearranged state and the eastern sections, at the outset, a new territory. "This agreement," the *Walla Walla Statesman* observed of the mutually beneficial consequences, "would secure…natural boundaries, and a population having an identity of interests." As in the case of annexing northern Idaho, opposition from Puget Sound thwarted ambitions east of the mountains. "None but the most short sighted territorians," one newspaper argued with respect to the idea of again becoming part of Oregon, "could allow themselves to take it up for the few immediate advantages it may appear to afford." Residence in a state was hardly worth the price of incorporation as an Oregonian satellite, with Portland in permanent control of the natural commercial outlet for the entire Pacific Northwest.[92] Frustrated for the moment, the drive for reformation of Washington's borders continued, testifying to the inherent elements of disunity within the territory and to the conviction that, absent the building of a true east-west railroad, political arrangements must sooner or later be altered to conform with geographical and economic relationships.

Noting the death of Michael Simmons, the original Puget Sounder, in November 1867, a local newspaper reflected upon the passing, in body and in spirit, of Washington's pioneer generation: "Those persons who have arrived in this Territory within the past five years have but a faint idea of the hardships, the perils, the trials and dangers, which were battled for, manfully withstood, and finally overcome, by the first settlers." Their successors stood now upon the uncertain threshold of a new age, an era to be opened fully upon completion of the transcontinental railroad. As a guide, a link between the pioneering times and the coming epoch, old admirers and recent immigrants alike looked to a rehabilitated Isaac Stevens, shot down in his military and political prime while leading the charge at Chantilly in 1862. Controversial at best in his lifetime, Stevens was reborn, among Democrats and Republicans, as a "gallant and devoted...patriot" on fatal Civil War battlegrounds. In 1868, the legislative assembly dedicated a monument to "the skillful and energetic engineer, the wise ruler, the great captain, [and] the honorable man." The governor's legend, legislators claimed, "will be ever green in our midst." The hero resided "in the shadowy Land of Spirits," the Port Townsend *Message* insisted, from where, "if Spiritualism be true," he audited "the doings of the present officials, and if need be, communicate[s] to them sound advice."[93] Bankruptcy halted the Northern Pacific, at least temporarily, and the territory suffered from disappointment and stagnation. Practical recommendations and stolid determination, no matter what the source, were dearly needed commodities.

Dorsey S. Baker. *Washington State University Library, Pullman (70-0085)*

Chapter Six

First Great Want of the People

The first great want of the people of Washington Territory, to-day, is facilities for transportation from the eastern extreme to the Sound, and that by some line controlled by themselves, and free from the curse of monopoly.—Seattle Weekly *Intelligencer*[1]

MAKING COMMENCEMENT BAY its western terminus and then going bank-rupt, the Northern Pacific Railroad outraged most Washington Territory residents. John Ainsworth and his parasitic associates had "made fools of a large portion of our people," William Winlock Miller wrote from Olympia. Throughout its entire sordid history, critics asserted, the N.P. had ignored the general welfare, trampling upon communities and individuals in the name of immediate monetary gain. "That corporation, which was once hailed as the greatest boon that could be conferred on our Territory," the Seattle *Intelligencer* observed, "has now come to be considered as only a gigantic curse which has the ability, the aim and the will to stifle and destroy all effective enterprise that does not contribute to its own advantage." With construction halted and a national depression in progress, immigration to the Pacific Northwest faltered. Real estate values collapsed in Olympia and slumped in Seattle. A number of Walla Walla Valley families abandoned eastern Washington for better prospects in a new southern California boomtown, Los Angeles.[2]

Finished only by extraordinary exertions on the part of Captain Ainsworth, the Kalama-Tacoma railroad was the one accomplishment, to date, of the Northern Pacific west of the Rockies. Daily trains hauled manufactured goods, produce and livestock between the Columbia and Puget Sound, at speeds up to forty miles an hour. Passengers, as opposed to horses and cattle, endured rough conditions. At all seasons, the scenery was limited to look-alike trees by the thousand, broken by the occasional rude pioneer clearing. Late summer forest fires filled the cars with smoke and ash. Traveling to the Sound in 1877, a fastidious tourist sat unhappily among "a Chinaman, an Indian half-breed, an ugly Flathead squaw, and a German immigrant family," offensive companions "strongly suggestive of the cosmopolitan character of the Northwest." Seen at regular intervals along the line, busy repair crews suggested that the railroad was either well maintained or subject to distressing accidents.[3]

The most powerful locomotive on the Puget Sound branch was named, appropriately, the *Ainsworth* in recognition of the venerable steamboat captain's role in building the line and in developing Commencement Bay as a Columbia River satellite. Retaining his post as regional managing director of the Northern Pacific, Ainsworth assumed the same position with the Tacoma Land Company, organized in September 1873. The latter firm's absentee president, Philadelphia financier Charles B. Wright, was also an important railroad official and stockholder. Such relationships facilitated transfers of real estate, securities and cash, as dictated by legal and financial considerations. The N.P. owned a controlling interest in the Tacoma Land Company. Persons associated with the transcontinental line held most of the remaining stock. For all practical purposes, the two concerns were one and the same, devoted to fully incorporating the Sound into Portland's economic machine.[4]

In an initial burst of high-class promotionalism, the Tacoma Land Company engaged landscape architect Frederick Law Olmsted to devise a town plan. The Panic of 1873, however, quickly ruined the expensive urban development scheme. A series of alarmed letters from Wright to Ainsworth detailed the depression's sudden impact: stock subscriptions fell far short of targeted goals and interest in Commencement Bay land dwindled. "Tacoma has given me more anxiety since the panic," said Wright, "than all other matters put together." Celebrating the impending failure of an upstart rival, Seattleites chortled that even John Ainsworth "could not make water run up hill."[5]

Portland's captain accomplished something akin to a gravity-defying feat. "The clasic [sic] 'I told you so'…," he wrote eastern associates, "has been shouted from one end of Puget Sound to the other," an unharmonious chorus of abuse that "has served to stir up the Adam within me, to put forth new efforts to the end, that life might be infused into the apparently dead carcass of the Tacoma Land Co[mpany]." Achieving an unlikely revival, Ainsworth overcame serious difficulties, not to mention peculiarities. To the chagrin of pre-terminus settlers, the railroad decided to build its own town on the bayfront. A mile and a half separated "old" from "new" Tacoma, a steam ferry providing the only means of communication between the two points. Downcast residents of the original Commencement Bay community reminded one journalistic observer of "the little dog watching the larger one gnaw the bone." Another visitor discovered that the "most important work…going on" was a gathering of three dozen people, assembled to watch two men execute an $8 stump removal contract. Somehow ignited into an eternal flame, sawdust and slabs floating in the bay adjacent to the Hanson and Ackerson mill represented the closest thing to a beacon of hope for old Tacomans.[6]

Development conditions at New Tacoma justified outsider descriptions of the infant town as an "absurdity," a "kite-flying expedition" and "the very last place on Puget Sound which any intelligent business man would select to invest his own money." The grade was so steep on the final three miles of track that engineers backed their trains downhill the entire distance. After much searching, surveyors located suitable anchorage for ocean-going vessels two miles offshore. "They have at last found bottom in Commencement Bay," outside newspapers sarcastically announced. "It is a remarkable fact," a bemused Oregonian wrote of this distinctive local navigation feature, "that…the question is not so much where to find water deep enough for ships to ride, but where to find it shallow enough for them to anchor." Clinging to the bluff above the station, the few houses resembled, according to one observer, "residence[s] among the mountaineous [sic] peaks of Switzerland."[7]

Gradual, if unspectacular, progress was nonetheless evident by the spring of 1874. Captain Ainsworth began construction of an imposing permanent depot on high ground. The Starr steamboat line, currently the dominant force in local waterborne transportation, agreed to make Commencement Bay its Puget Sound base. Chinese workers cleared trees and graded the first streets. Lots went on sale in April, at prices calculated to draw settlers from Seattle, Olympia and other competing points. Northern Pacific managers relocated from Kalama. The visiting Matthew P. Deady, the leading jurist of the Pacific Northwest, found Tacoma "a more eligible site than I expected after all I heard against it."[8]

Resuscitation of the Northern Pacific proceeded slowly, toward the realization of what one company official described as "a new deal." Joining other financially challenged railroading enterprises, the firm asked Congress for a federal guarantee of new bond issues. Although initial prospects appeared favorable, a for-the-record vote was eventually postponed until after the 1874 elections. "The word 'railroad,'" observed the *Walla Walla Union*, "was of itself almost enough to seal the fate of any bill that contained it." Meanwhile, time-consuming internal reorganization work culminated in the purchase of the Northern Pacific by a bondholder consortium headed by Frederick Billings in August 1875. With construction at a standstill throughout this uncertain period, barely five hundred miles of widely scattered track were in operating order between Lake Superior and Puget Sound.[9]

Territorial residents, New Tacomans obviously excepted, anticipated that one or more of several Northern Pacific alternatives would help them achieve long-delayed transportation objectives. The proposed Portland, Dalles & Salt Lake Railroad was a transcontinental, or at least a semi-transcontinental, line in its own right, if only on paper. By connecting Puget Sound and the Walla Walla Valley to the mainline, settlers could link up to the Union Pacific in Utah.

Unfortunately, the artless promoters, who had no plans to lay track themselves in the territory, called upon Congress for the eastern Washington portion of the N.P. grant, undercutting their initial appeal north of the Columbia. Acting in direct self-defense and indirectly on behalf of its Ainsworthian corporate cousin, the Oregon Steam Navigation Company built a portage railroad along the south bank of the Columbia at the Cascades, preempting the right-of-way, and cut freight rates to Umatilla and Wallula.[10]

When the Portland, Dalles & Salt Lake failed to register progress, so-called "people's" roads filled the vacuum. Following defeat of a local bond issue for a railroad to Wallula in 1871, Walla Walla promoter Dorsey Baker—"a man of remarkable energy...and bold[ness] in executing his plans" according to a contemporary admirer—went ahead anyway. Intent upon reducing expenditures wherever possible, Baker eliminated bridge crossings and switched from broad to narrow gauge. Wooden rails—fashioned from logs driven down the Yakima River—were covered with strap iron for some degree of durability and became a particularly ingenious, if definitely short-term, cost-cutting measure. Construction crews covered the sixteen miles between Wallula and the main ford of the Touchet River in the spring of 1874. Bemused observers dismissed the "little tram road" as "a perfect failure," however, on account of Baker's continuing inability to secure financial support.[11]

In return for finishing the line into Walla Walla, Baker needed a public subsidy. After considerable haggling, he eventually received one, including the land for a depot. Completed in October 1875, the railroad brought the era of the packer and the teamster to an end. Trains sped to and from Wallula in less than three hours, a third the time taken by hell-for-leather express riders. Although he soon replaced the fast-deteriorating wooden rails with iron, Baker's skinflint approach to construction and operation remained long in evidence. After a downpour, those portions of roadbed laid through alkaline soil took on, according to one weary traveler, "the condition of quicksand," forcing derailment-concerned customers to disembark and "foot it." Passengers rode in a single third-class conveyance "very little if any better than the ordinary box car." Walla Wallans debated whether the underpowered performance of the locomotives was caused by inferior equipment or by bad handling on the part of incompetent engineers and mechanics.[12]

Freight charges imposed by the Walla Walla & Columbia River Railroad confirmed that Baker was no better than a Portlander in taking advantage of a monopoly position. His $6 per ton wheat rate equaled the O.S.N. assessment for the run downstream from Wallula to the Willamette. Spoiling the great moment of regional economic liberation, the rail line afforded "no relief whatever," the *Statesman* noted in reporting the boycott mounted by angry farmers. The old wagon road had fallen into disrepair, limiting transportation alternatives and reducing the effectiveness of the anti-monopoly campaign. A standoff persisted until the spring of 1876, when Baker cut rates to a barely acceptable level. Arguments over freights, as well as accusations of preferential treatment, continued, however, to disturb relations between the company and Walla Walla residents.[13]

Detecting a genuine trend, the Portland *Oregonian* quipped in early 1874 that "railroads on paper" were "getting to be very plentiful" in Washington Territory. Badly, and repeatedly, mistreating Olympia, the Northern Pacific reneged on its original terminal promise, faced down a threatened lawsuit and refused, for several months, to return the deeds accepted in return for the aborted decision favoring the town. Thrice scorned, the community determined upon forging its own rail connection with the outside world, a feeder to nearby Tenino on the north-south Puget Sound branch. "Only fifteen miles of railroad," argued Hazard Stevens, the principal organizer of local development efforts, "...will restore Olympia's self-reliance." Once built, the Tenino road would supposedly encourage exploitation of tributary coal reserves, stimulate exports and, in the ultimate revenge, compel the Northern Pacific to relocate the Tacoma terminus, tearing up and shifting track from Commencement Bay to Budd Inlet.[14]

Stevens arranged in late 1873 for California railroading interests to build the Tenino line in return for a local subsidy and the acreage previously donated to the Northern Pacific. The arrangement collapsed, however, when town residents expressed serious opposition to the demands of outside capital. "The crisis of Olympia's destiny will come and pass," Stevens fretted, "and the die be cast against her while her people are wraggling over...'bonds.'" Founded on New Year's Eve 1873, the Olympia Railroad Union commenced a new effort at construction. Working with the O.R.U., congressional delegate O. B. McFadden secured federal legislation authorizing the use of Thurston County funds. At home, a subscription drive assembled cash and land from the territorial political establishment. Marshall Blinn represented anti-Garfielde Republican Bolters. Governor Elisha Ferry and Superintendent of Indian Affairs Robert H. Milroy led support among current federal appointees. Pioneer editor Thornton McElroy served as a reminder of the old pre-Civil War Democratic era. Organized by Ferry's wife, the feminine leaders of capital society volunteered their own distinctive form of assistance, offering to cook and do housework so that Chinese servants could be released for labor on the road to Tenino. County voters, meanwhile, approved a $75,000 bond issue for the project.[15]

A "combined action" of the entire community, the railroad was supposed to be built, as well as financed, by local hands. On the first in a series of April 1874 public work days, business activity ceased and three hundred men, led by a band and saluted by gunfire and ringing bells, marched into the woods to assist the regular Chinese crew. According to one eyewitness account, "judges, lawyers, clergymen [and] doctors" toiled "side by side, with as much earnestness as if their labors were for an individual purpose." Four miles of right-of-way were cleared and graded—ready for the laying of track. Progress stalled at this point, however, when storekeepers and professional persons declined to lend more than the symbolic hand initially exhibited. Olympia's three newspapers bemoaned the lack of local initiative and lamented that Dorsey Baker, a promoter of demonstrated organizing talent, lived in Walla Walla rather than on Puget Sound.[16]

Extensions granted by stockholding county officials kept the Tenino road alive on paper. In June 1877, the Thurston County Railroad Construction Company, organized under the auspices of Governor Ferry, took over from the Union. "A few stout-hearted citizens," announced John Miller Murphy of the *Washington Standard*, "have set the car of progress in motion, just where it stopped three years ago." Supplied with $15,000 from a bargain basement fundraising campaign, the firm completed the grade and somehow secured enough credit to procure rails and rolling stock. By the first of August 1878, the entire fifteen mile line was in working order, an achievement celebrated by firing an antique cannon mounted on the back of a very unfortunate mule. Carrying a full load of self-congratulating dignitaries, the inaugural train ran off the track, forcing the slightly injured and thoroughly embarrassed passengers to ride back to Olympia in wagons.[17]

Despite substantially greater financial resources, Seattle managed to only slightly exceed Olympia's mileage record. Responding to the 1873 Northern Pacific decision in favor of Tacoma, Elliott Bay transportation promoters organized the Seattle & Walla Walla Railroad Company, with Arthur Denny as president. "It is a life and death struggle for us," insisted editor David Higgins of the *Intelligencer*. Because of the locally self-evident fact that the "big city" of western Washington must develop "just at the point where the direct line over the Cascades struck the Sound," Seattleites expected to connect with one or more transcontinental lines, most likely in the vicinity of Walla Walla.[18]

Fortuitous developments in coal mining figured into the promotional calculations. Currently the fifth-ranking supplier of the San Francisco market, Seattle planned to improve upon this standing in the near future. Insurance problems reduced the English and Australian share of the trade, Vancouver Island exports were limited in quantity and flooding often shut down Monte Diablo, the principal California operation. The onetime Selucious Garfielde concern, now San Francisco-owned and renamed the Seattle Coal Company, increased production, shipping to Elliott Bay via railroad portage and Lakes Washington and Union. Newcastle, the firm's residential community, grew into a sooty landlocked boomtown, with four hundred inhabitants, schoolhouse, church, general store, saloon and other essential urban structures. Discoveries in the winter of 1874, meanwhile, unearthed what the *Puget Sound Dispatch* termed "literally a mountain of coal" at the south end of Lake Washington between the Cedar and Black rivers. Initially exploited by the Renton and the Talbot mines, the new veins added substance to the claim that Washington Territory, with Seattle the focus, was "the Pennsylvania of the Pacific."[19]

Moving fast at the outset, Denny and his colleagues engaged former Northern Pacific engineer Thomas Morris to prepare a detailed construction scheme. Unveiled in early 1874, the plan required an expenditure of $4.2 million, an astounding figure in comparison to the relatively small costs involved in the Dorsey Baker and Olympia projects. The line ran from Elliott Bay to the coal mines and then toward Snoqualmie Pass, where Morris envisioned "many rock cuts and high trestles...clinging to the side hills." East of the Cascades, the prospectus recommended crossing the Columbia at Priest Rapids and a linkage with the proposed Portland, Dalles & Salt Lake near Walla Walla. James Tilton, the onetime Democratic party stalwart, attorney James McNaught and Arthur Denny himself undertook lobbying missions to Washington City, seeking, among several forms of federal assistance, authorization for King and Walla Walla counties to subsidize construction.[20]

Overconfidence quickly gave way to frustration. The interior Northwest generally endorsed the project as offering a better means of shipping to and from tidewater. "It would be impossible," asserted the Dalles *Mountaineer*, "for the O.S.N. Company to compete with the Seattle route." In Walla Walla, however, Baker's Wallula line competed for support, financial and otherwise. Agents employed by John Ainsworth worked to discredit the cross-mountain railroad. The all-Seattle board of directors confirmed traditional eastern Washington suspicions of Puget Sound. Though sure to benefit from construction, settlers in the Yakima Valley had no money to contribute to the enterprise. Federal support was delayed and, when finally extended, it was both incomprehensible and unworkable in format.[21]

Retreating in the face of these obstacles, the Seattle & Walla Walla became, for the time being, another populist road. "The people of this city," the *Dispatch* reminded nay-sayers opposed to commencing work entirely with local resources, "are abundantly able to build fifteen miles of railroad without seriously embarrassing themselves." Helping things along, mill-owner Henry Yesler promised to build the first five miles, including the Elliott Bay trestlework. The Renton mine, presently dependent upon the Duwamish River for transportation, assumed responsibility for the section between the coaling operation and the stream. Copying Olympia, Seattle declared May 1, 1874, a public workday. The entire population, except for a boatload of hapless residents stranded by the falling tide, assembled at the mouth of the Duwamish. Several miles of riverbank were cleared and graded, ready for construction.[22]

This modestly impressive achievement was the high point of the original Seattle & Walla Walla effort. Responding to a rumor that they were about to be dismissed in a cost-cutting move, white crewmembers drove Chinese workers from the job in early June. Although the victims returned under armed guard, the "war on the Chinamen" persisted in the form of progress-inhibiting tension. Confirming his contemporary reputation as "an old man" who "has never yet learned the value…of keeping his word in a business transaction," Henry Yesler failed to undertake the tideflat trestle, leaving the railroad without connection to the Elliott Bay wharves. The continuing national depression precluded the raising of outside capital, forcing a suspension of construction once local resources were exhausted. At mid-decade, the homegrown Northern Pacific substitute consisted of only the three miles of track linking Renton to the Duwamish River.[23]

"Direct steam communication between…the eastern and western sections of this Territory" remained, as the *Intelligencer* pointed out, "a commercial necessity." Local coal producers, however, not distant wheat ranchers, were responsible for the resumption of work. The Renton mine needed a better means of shipment than that provided by the Duwamish and its tributaries, streams often running at below-navigable depth. "A last effort" drive to build as far as Renton began in the spring of 1876, financed by the coaling interests and by Arthur Denny and other traditional boosters. The vital Elliott Bay trestle was finally built—Seattleites used the works, which provided spectacular views of the Sound and the Olympic Mountains, for Sunday afternoon strolling—and trains soon ran on a regular schedule. Seattle Company planning for increased production at Newcastle, meanwhile, depended upon replacement of the present complex outlet via Lakes Washington and Union. Under an arrangement with the firm, the railroad was extended to Newcastle in 1878, making the total distance from saltwater twenty-one miles. Pending additional, and for the moment highly unlikely, funding agreements, Snoqualmie Pass, not to mention Walla Walla, remained a distant objective for Puget Sound transcontinental railroaders.[24]

Once constructed, either directly or through the coming together of independent segments, a railroad over the Cascades posed the ultimate threat to Portland and the Oregon Steam Navigation Company. Although the Northern Pacific was, for the moment, practically a regional subordinate of the O.S.N.—"a minnow," the *Walla Walla Union* quipped, "seems to have swallowed the great… whale"—sooner or later a revived, reformed and reoriented transcontinental line would challenge the steamboat monopoly. Preparing for an inevitable showdown, John Ainsworth and his associates petitioned the federal government for removal of "a few loose Boulders" from the Columbia River. East of Celilo Falls, at the entrance to The Dalles, the Columbia was often said to be "free," open to all with the enterprise to place vessels in service. In reality, a half dozen major navigation hazards, including John Day Rapids, Devil's Bend and the Lower and Upper Umatilla Rapids, intervened between the upstream portage railroad depot and Wallula. Ice formed each winter, ending travel until spring, except in those brief startling periods when warm Chinook winds from the coast melted snow, increased water levels and broke up nature's blockade. Walla Walla was isolated for as long as four months, the only mail coming overland from California and with New York newspapers more likely to arrive sooner than those published on the Sound.[25]

Despite its well-deserved reputation for shrewd management, the Oregon Steam Navigation Company was slow to adapt to changing river and trade conditions. The early-day mining traffic uppermost in mind, the firm designed vessels for prime use in spring and early summer, when stream flows were at the highest stage. The commercial emphasis had shifted, however, from an upriver focus on supplies and implements to a stress upon downstream wheat exports. The greatest demand for transportation now came in the fall, when water ran at a falling rate. Provided that great care was taken to avoid rocks, the Columbia was navigable in ice-free conditions. Because existing boats could be used on the Snake only from mid-April to the first of August, however, the annual harvest tributary to that river could not be shipped for months. In 1875, the O.S.N. finally began building steamers with hulls of sufficient length and width to allow for extreme shallow draft. The *Annie Faxon*, a flat-bottomed sternwheeler one hundred and sixty-five feet long and thirty-seven feet wide, with five feet in the hold, was the new standard of interior commerce.[26]

Pressed by the Oregon congressional delegation, the Corps of Engineers studied the rapids in the winter working seasons of 1869, 1870 and 1871. Most of the time and money devoted to the investigation was wasted. "Some of the bad places were not surveyed," a perplexed steamer captain complained, "while some of the worst rocks in those surveyed, do not appear on the charts." Ignoring expert local advice that the most dangerous obstruction was Homily Rapids, five miles above Wallula, uniformed engineers and their civilian assistants worked downstream at Umatilla, Devil's Bend and John Day. Citing the lack of express congressional authorization, the Army refused to make even preliminary studies of the Snake. Although the Corps concluded that prevailing commercial traffic failed to justify the expense involved, Congress ordered the agency to "improve" the Columbia River.[27]

Supposed to guarantee a year-round seven-foot depth between The Dalles and Wallula, the project called for meticulous calculation and arduous labor. The destruction of a single large boulder in John Day Rapids, for instance, required the drilling of 1,165 powder holes, each precisely four-and-a-half feet deep. The task had to be carried out in deep winter, the "season," Portland-based engineers advised, when "the river falls to the very lowest stage so that many rocks... become exposed above the surface of the water." Struggling to keep scows steady in ten-mile per-hour current, workers suffered from sustained exposure to the elements. Thirteen men were blown "to atoms," as an investigative report succinctly noted, in a pair of explosions. A supervising officer drowned when swept into a whirlpool.[28]

Opened in 1876, the seven foot navigation channel was neither a permanent "improvement" nor taken seriously by steamboat captains. Vessels still ran aground, and one actually sank, in places officially deemed safe. Army engineers confessed, after the fact, that calculations as to cubic yards removed and depth achieved were little more than estimates. The current and winter ice regularly deposited boulders of varying size, making for new and uncharted hazards. Rather than rely upon government reports, steamer masters maintained up-to-date wheelhouse logs, detailing the latest changes in river conditions. Captain Thomas Symons, the most experienced Army engineer on the Columbia, confidentially reported in 1891 that all navigation work east of The Dalles since 1869 had been "utterly worthless."[29]

For an expenditure in excess of $100,000, the Corps of Engineers enabled the Oregon Steam Navigation Company to run slightly larger boats for slightly longer periods of the year. Refining traditional love-hate emotions regarding Portland, upper country residents condemned the use of taxpayer money to assist a long-entrenched monopoly. The O.S.N. "does everything in first class style, and...there is not one fault that can be pointed out," a typical mid-decade editorial affirmed, "if, we except, the fact that...we are taxed too high for our freight." Whether in Oregon, Idaho or Washington Territory, similar language focused upon region-wide offense. The steamboat company owners "leisurely bleed the people of this country," the *Walla Walla Union* pronounced. "We are bottled up with very little hope that the cork will be pulled out any reasonable day," a Lewiston newspaper complained. According to a critic in The Dalles, the O.S.N. sapped "the very vitals of the country." A Walla Walla Valley editor compared the firm to "a great serpent...winding its cold blighting coils around the growing industries" of a struggling Northwest.[30]

Competition, argued those who would behead the great snake, was the real need of the upper Columbia, not the monopoly-facilitating efforts of the Corps of Engineers. For an idea of the benefits to be attained, advocates of a genuinely free river cited the example of Portland businessman Z. F. Moody. Running the aptly named *Teaser* between the Cascades and The Dalles in 1874 like "a swordfish fighting a whale," Moody compelled the leviathan O.S.N. to sharply reduce passenger and freight rates on the middle Columbia and eventually to buy his price-cutting boat. Walla Walla farmers, Lewiston merchants and other interested upriver parties called for placement of a locally owned steamer, even a sailing vessel, in service. The initial expenditure required would be comparatively small, as little as five thousand dollars in some estimates. The savings in the cost of shipping wheat to The Dalles would, in optimistic projections, more than repay the investment.[31]

As long as the Oregon Steam Navigation Company held The Dalles and the Cascades, competition and hazard-free transportation upstream were of little realistic account. "No amount of work...will relieve the interior of...thralldom,"

Thomas Symons asserted, "until means are found of carrying the products of the upper rivers past these great obstructions." Some O.S.N. critics advocated a public wagon road. Others proposed a free-to-all rail line between the eastern and western sides of the so-called "pass" of the Columbia. Directly or indirectly, however, the steamboat firm controlled the land needed for such undertakings, especially after the Cascades portage railroad was relocated from the north to the south bank. Anti-monopolists eventually argued for another form of river "improvement," a navigation canal at the Cascades.[32]

Responding this time to popular opinion, the Army moved against the strategic center of the O.S.N. monopoly. On the basis of detailed 1874 and 1875 studies, the Corps of Engineers proposed a canal exceeding seven thousand feet in length, with a pair of locks, along the Oregon side of the Cascades. The estimated cost, after refinements in the plan, was $1.7 million. Acting on behalf of the general welfare, military engineers actually inflicted no immediate harm upon the O.S.N. "Although one of the gates now closing the navigation of the river would thereby be opened," a board of senior engineers pointed out in endorsing the work of field personnel, "this company, without a canal at The Dalles, would still hold the keys of the other."[33]

Logic nonetheless dictated that a second expensive canal would someday be built, as otherwise the Cascades project would be without benefit. Expecting to eventually lose both keys, the O.S.N., ably assisted in the halls of government by Oregon congressional members, delayed the commencement of work until 1878. Contractor disputes, changes in plan and other embarrassing developments ensued and the project was not completed until 1896. Uncooperative with respect to the canal, the O.S.N. streamlined operations in areas where corporate welfare coincided with the public interest. Better-designed boats enabled prompt shipment of wheat tributary to the Columbia and improved service to the Snake River landings. Acquiring wharf property at Astoria, the company prepared for transit of wheat direct from the Cascades to ocean-going vessels at the river's mouth, ending the costly and time-consuming practice of shipping grain up the Willamette to Portland for transfer to downstream steamers.[34]

Eastern Washington's shift from a mining-oriented economy to an agricultural base was complete. Eighteen seventy-three was the last pre-railroading year, the final harvest season dependent entirely upon export by horse-drawn wagon. Dorsey Baker's thirty-something mile railroad allowed farmers to send wheat to the Columbia in more expeditious fashion, beating the ice and the close of navigation. California crop failures and European upheavals, diplomatic and military, generated an extended upswing in grain prices. Sales at 75 cents a bushel became commonplace and an advance to, and beyond, one dollar was widely anticipated. New machinery—the Walla Walla Valley's first steam thresher went into service in 1874—and better-than-average rainfall made possible a substantial increase in cultivated acreage and annual production figures above the million-bushel rate.[35]

Near-bonanza conditions in the wheat fields sparked an unprecedented wave of immigration. An Astoria newspaper recorded the standard query of passengers arriving at the mouth of the Columbia: "How far is it to Walla Walla?" Every steamer, stage and train "brings a greater or lesser number of strangers into our country," the *Walla Walla Union* advised in April 1875. Filings at the local land office increased from 421 in 1873 to 1,377 in 1877 and to 1,754 in 1878. Immigrants quickly discovered that there was "no chance for a man to get land" anywhere near Walla Walla City. Hay ranches were converted to wheat and poorly watered bench lands became farms. Most settlers went elsewhere in the greater valley. Drawing an imaginary line from the town north to the mouth of the Tucannon on the Snake River, a railroad investigator reported that "the land lying east of the line possesses a soil of great fertility capable of producing large crops." Two-thirds of the area between the Blue Mountains and the Snake was ideally suited for agriculture, featuring, an early homesteader happily wrote, "green grass in every direction." The Touchet and the Tucannon, and the latter's important tributary Pataha Creek, provided ample water for farming and for grinding wheat into flour.[36]

Founded in 1872 on the upper Touchet, sixteen miles south of the Snake River, Dayton was the leading urban byproduct of expanding wheat production. City-like amenities included flour and woolen mills, a brick-walled store, a flourishing hotel, two churches and a "well regulated brass band." Dayton was nonetheless an uncivilized place of materialist ambition enveloped in dust from never-ending winds. The school closed when residents refused to pay taxes. "Young hoodlums," the loutish offspring of prosperous farmers, loitered about and "soiled doves" occupied their own well-patronized quarter, separated from respectable folk by an appropriately festering ditch. Located, respectively, in 1877 and 1878, Pomeroy and Pataha City were in every respect—the good, the bad and the ugly—major rivals. Authorized by the territorial assembly in 1877, roads linked the young communities with one another, with Walla Walla and with steamer landings on the Snake.[37]

A farmer's life in the Walla Walla Valley, a San Francisco journalist claimed after visiting the old and the new settlements, "must be the perfection of that profession." Certain ongoing facets of the agricultural experience contributed, however, to a less-than-perfect reality for newly minted wheat cultivators. Dayton area producers exported by way of Grange City at the mouth of the Tucannon. Pomeroy and Pataha City utilized Texas Bar. The seasonal nature of O.S.N. traffic on the Snake was, therefore, a matter of common frustration. Individuals shipping through Walla Walla to Wallula experienced a different variety of aggravation, for Dorsey Baker's railroad was easily overstrained. The uncertain nature of deliveries to the Columbia encouraged Baker to manipulate rates, charging extra for priority treatment. The lack of surveys, meanwhile, led to an epidemic of claim jumping, producing at least one Wild West shootout in the streets of Dayton.[38]

To a much greater degree than in Walla Walla proper, the country settling up lacked timber for construction of buildings and fences. Farmers and towns-people traveled twenty miles and more to the Blue Mountains and there tres-passed upon federally owned forestland. Settlers logged in haphazard, as well as illegal, fashion, removing the best trees in the most convenient places and leav-ing behind the origins of an environmental disaster. "Through wasteful cutting and carelessness in the use of fire," the *Walla Walla Union* warned in late 1879, "the mountain sides have been denuded of timber, to such an extent, that we have floods in Winter and low water in Summer, to the great damage of the whole country." A partial solution to at least the problem of inconvenience was found by building flumes. A network of these expensive and breakdown-prone devices soon carried wood from the Blues to the principal settlements.[39]

Fast-developing local rivalries, accentuated by a Snake River, rather than a Walla Walla, orientation, produced political change in the recently settled areas. Over Walla Walla's protest, the legislature created Columbia County in 1875. Rapid growth—property values increased by two-thirds in a single year—placed Columbia at the economic and demographic forefront of the territory. Although residents argued that they had passed Walla Walla by fair count, Columbia offi-cially ranked third in population among Washington's counties in 1880, its much-reduced neighbor holding the overall lead. Dayton, meanwhile, be-came the sixth largest town, east and west of the Cascades.[40]

Resembling the gold rushes of earlier territorial times, the wheat explosion was uncontainable. Organized beyond the Snake, Whitman County added four hundred residents in the summer of 1876, a claim-seeking portent of the influx still to come north of the river. "Train after train of wagons are continually ar-riving," a settler soon reported from the Palouse. A correspondent traveling to Spokane Falls found the evening trailside crowded with the tents of "men, women and children fresh from the Western States and all delighted with the country." Another visitor, a merchant with substantial capital to invest, learned that he must become the "*bedfellow*" of strangers in order to secure above-the-floor accommodations for the night at filled-beyond-capacity lodging places. The new Colfax land office recorded a thousand filings between its opening in April 1878 and the following November. By 1880, Whitman was the territory's second most-populous county, leading Columbia across the Snake by five in-habitants.[41]

Wrinkled hills and all, the Palouse was, if anything, better suited to wheat cultivation than the Walla Walla Valley. "The black loam…is usually found to be from 8 to 10 feet deep," one newspaper reported. "It puts you in mind of the rich prairies of Illinois or Kansas," wrote John J. Browne, an attorney and merchant on the way to Spokane Falls. Besides possessing "a soil richer than any other portion of the Pacific coast," a railroad agent observed of the Palouse, "it enjoys…the advantage of being excellently watered, fine springs of pure water abounding every where." Actual residents were convinced that their adopted home was already the new Willamette Valley and bound to become the grain belt of America. The blackguard so densely evil as to utter the faintest criticism, asserted the Colfax *Gazette*, "would complain if he was in Paradise." "The Paluse [sic] is an excellent country," John Browne noted, "at any rate the people living here say so—and like 'Brutus and Cassius and the rest,' they are honorable people."[42]

Situated on a sluggish stretch of the Palouse River known as the "lake," Colfax—named, to the embarrassment of at least some residents, after Vice President Schuyler Colfax of Credit Mobilier fame—was the Walla Walla of the Palouse region. In addition to the regional postal and land offices, the town had two reputable hotels, one outfitted with "all modern improvements." Otherwise, the place offered the usual dreary features of interior Northwestern life: the streets were dirty, the school overcrowded when not closed by nonpayment of taxes and the male inhabitants prone to heavy drinking and regular attendance upon houses of prostitution. Reflecting upon the empty pews at church services, an offended Christian diarist described Colfax as "the strongest hole of infidelity I ever lived in." Carrying on a bizarre local tradition, young men bathed nude in public at the riverside. The strangest thing about Colfax, however, was its location beneath bluffs "nearly as high," to quote John Browne, "as the valley is wide," a constricted site bound to retard the expansion of population and business activity.[43]

Unhappiness with the slow pace of navigation work—demands for "improvement" of the Snake River dated back to the Civil War, but the Corps of Engineers waited until 1880 to make preliminary surveys—was only one component of a larger conviction that the United States Army was hostile to settlers east of the mountains. Since the apparent resolution of the Nez Perce reservation question in 1863, Washington Territory had experienced no major Indian-relations crisis. Eastern Oregon, in contrast, was troubled by years of fighting with Northern Paiute bands and, in the winter of 1873, by the Modoc War on the California border. Despite worries that the Modoc conflict might spark similar rebellions on one or both sides of the Cascades, Washington residents celebrated the long-term maintenance of peace. Troubling undercurrents suggested, however, that self-congratulation was really self-delusion. The off-reservation presence of substantial numbers of Indians, while entirely proper under the treaties, was bound to produce disturbance, especially in the context of rapidly increasing immigration. The Dreamer movement, predicting the eventual overthrow of the white newcomers, supplied an additional provocative element, particularly in light of reports that a thousand Indian warriors adhered to the teachings of Smohalla and lesser native prophets.[44]

Of particular importance, the 1863 Nez Perce treaty produced an inevitable, if long-delayed, clash. After selling the land of bands outside the reduced reservation, the head chief Lawyer opposed government plans to move those Indians upon the Lapwai agency. The treaty was not ratified until 1867, causing Nez Perce leaders to argue that it had been nullified by the passage of time. Visiting the nation's capital in 1868, Lawyer acceded to the accord in return for a promise that off-reservation Indians would be allowed to retain their traditional homes. The Nez Perce led in the 1870s by Chief Joseph maintained possession of winter quarters at the mouth of the Grande Ronde River in southeastern Washington and of summer fishing, hunting and grazing grounds in Oregon's Wallowa Valley. Other bands also remained in Washington Territory, along the Snake from above Lewiston to the Palouse River.[45]

Federal officials took no action to legally fortify the position of the off-reservation Nez Perce. "About one hundred white men," according to Lapwai agent John Monteith's report, moved stock into the Wallowa Valley in 1872, challenging Chief Joseph's right to the grass. Homesteaders and steamboat landing proprietors filed claims upon Snake River village sites. Complaining that the government was pro-Nez Perce, whites demanded the removal of the Indians. Conceding that the 1863 treaty was flawed, the Office of Indian Affairs tried, unsuccessfully, to establish a new reservation in the Wallowa country.[46]

Attempting, long after the fact, to right an obvious wrong, the hapless authorities antagonized white opinion east of the Cascades. Ignoring every pertinent fact, the *Walla Walla Union* denounced as "villainous" supposed attempts to "turn...settlers out of their homes" so that "a reservation already improved" might be handed over to Chief Joseph's "murdering, plundering, band of outlawed Indians." Bloodshed, at least, was apparently averted when General Oliver O. Howard ordered the off-reservation Nez Perce moved to Lapwai in 1877. The Oregon and Washington bands crossed to the Idaho side of the Snake River, ready to take up new unhappy homes. Murders committed by revenge-minded young men, however, transformed peaceful resolution of the dispute into an open and dramatic conflict, the Nez Perce War.[47]

With every strategic move and battlefield encounter during the summer and fall of 1877, the combatants moved further away from Washington Territory. The Nez Perce reputation for military prowess—"one Indian," the *Walla Walla Statesman* advised, "is equal to at least twenty soldiers"—explained an otherwise unjustifiable region-wide panic. Reports of the first hostilities arrived in Walla Walla "like a clap of thunder from a clear sky," interrupting public celebration of General Howard's short-lived pacification. Volunteers immediately assembled to guard the streets and a company of the better-armed residents set out for Lapwai to aid Howard and the federal troops. Dayton and Walla Walla pressed Governor Elisha Ferry for arms, ammunition and a territorial campaign of extermination. Sensibly concerned about being mistaken for hostiles, leaders of friendly and neutral Indian bands hastened to assure townspeople of their peaceful intentions.[48]

Veteran hands advised persons unfamiliar with the country to remain calm, ignore rumors and avoid antagonizing local Indians. False reports and counterproductive violence, after all, would retard economic development and play into the hands of Oregonians eager to divert settlers into areas south of the Walla Walla Valley. The *Union* recommended against retaliation when native men and women, on the way home from a camas-digging expedition, ransacked abandoned cabins north of the Snake: "A party of whites under similar circumstances would have been sorely tempted to act as did the Indians." Newspapers warned readers not to misinterpret the innocent movements of Indians taking up their normal summertime places of residence. Calm heads among the minority and fear on the part of the majority prevented the shedding of blood within territorial limits. The most negative aspect of the Nez Perce War for Walla Walla was a serious shortage of grain sacks, caused when the O.S.N. set aside civilian freight to make room for the highly profitable upstream shipment of troops and military supplies.[49]

Hard upon Chief Joseph's surrender in the fall of 1877, a new crisis arose east of the Cascades. All but ignored in the rush of wheat cultivators to Walla Walla and the Palouse, Yakima County experienced a 700 percent population increase during the 1870s, to 2,862 non-Indian residents. Much of this growth was in the upper Kittitas Valley, where gold discoveries on Swauk Creek and other watercourses brought prosperity to Ellensburgh. Although cattle raising remained the principal overall occupation, the opening of a brewery in Yakima City generated a demand for hops and made commercial agriculture a viable activity. The first irrigation ditches provided water for a rapid expansion of farming, pending the opening of outside markets by improvements in transportation. Urbanization kept pace with rural settlement, Yakima City claiming, in addition to a post office, courthouse, two schools and "a No. 1 race course," close to three hundred inhabitants.[50]

An Indian from outside the Yakima Valley supposedly threatened local progress. Citing the 1855 Walla Walla treaties, the government insisted that Chief Moses, leader of a band normally found roaming the Big Bend near the site of Wenatchee, move upon the Yakama reservation. Caught between cultures, the missionary-trained Moses enjoyed, among various materialistic delights, cash money, strong coffee and prime whiskey. He also opposed agency life, resisted settler encroachment and engaged in mildly provocative acts of resistance against federal authority. Although informed persons knew better, military and civilian leaders for some reason considered Moses a virtual Napoleon of the interior Northwest, ready, at the right moment, to lead a thousand warriors into desperate battle.[51]

Midway in the developing Moses story, Bannock Indians fled Idaho's Fort Hall reservation, riding west in the spring of 1878 to unite with the Northern Paiutes in the Oregon desert. At first, the threat to Washington Territory appeared to be highly, if not entirely, remote. Reporting the departure of soldiers for the front, which left only a military band to guard the upper Columbia, the *Walla Walla Statesman* joked that if Moses chose this opportune time to attack, "we must be compelled to...frighten our adversary into submission by unearthly noises." Disdain gave way to brief panic in June, however, when the Indians, followed by General Howard, turned north in the direction of the Blue Mountains. Walla Wallans feared encirclement by "red devils" and Yakama reservation employees fled across the Cascades. On Puget Sound, federal agents detected "spies and emissaries from the hostiles," attempting to persuade tidewater tribes to "go on the war path." The Army finally caught up with the Bannocks and the Paiutes in the second week of July, however, just below the Washington border. Aided by Umatilla and Warm Springs Indian recruits, Howard administered a sound and permanent defeat.[52]

Within weeks, Chief Moses was accused, falsely, of complicity in the murder of homesteaders near the mouth of the Yakima River. A locally mounted and stealthily conducted posse arrested Moses—the feared war chieftain was asleep in his blankets when seized—three days before Christmas. Under cover of the special holiday celebrations, James Wilbur, the longtime Yakama agent, rescued the captive from the authorities and placed him in protective custody on the reservation. County deputies besieged the agency until March 1879, when Moses departed, at federal invitation, for the nation's capital. The mission resulted in the creation of a home for his people—the Columbia, or Moses, reservation—located north of Lake Chelan and west of the Okanogan River. Developments thereafter were material, rather than martial, in nature. Preferring to reside on the Colville agency, Moses rarely ventured onto his personal domain, except to arrange such matters as the lease of grass to white stock interests. Gold discoveries and the machinations of speculators failed, therefore, to produce the trouble normally to be expected in such situations. In 1883, after another trip to Washington, Moses agreed to sell the tract.[53]

Eastern Washington experienced two major transformations during the 1870s. Powered by the wheat boom and the prospect of railroad construction, the settler population increased by a factor of five, to 31,316. Settlement, moreover, covered a greater geographical area: four of every five whites east of the Cascades lived in or near Walla Walla in 1870, compared to one-in-five a decade later. At the outset of the period, Indians roamed freely, occupying traditional haunts and pursuing customary activities, protected by the promises of an apparently honorable government. The newcomer demand for land, together with generally unwarranted fear of off-reservation native groups and leaders, forced an end to this way of life. Except in the northeastern reaches of the territory, the Indians were swamped by an immigrant tide. Symbolizing the fate of a people, Moses and Chief Joseph, who returned to the Pacific Northwest in 1885, spent the remainder of their lives as internal exiles at isolated Nespelem on the Colville reservation.[54]

In earlier times, Washington Territory amounted, so far as actual settlers were concerned, to little more than the region west of the Cascades. Recent developments fully altered a bygone equation, shifting the balance in favor of eastern Washington. By 1880, more than two-fifths of the non-Indian population resided beyond the mountains, compared to less than a third on Puget Sound. The east side had the three most heavily populated counties and five of the top seven. Urbanization was more pronounced on the Sound, but the interior claimed four of the nine largest towns: Walla Walla, Dayton, Goldendale in the Klickitat Valley and Colfax.[55]

Seattle, the lumber ports and possibly New Tacoma were the only western Washington places exhibiting economic initiative. Praising Olympia's well-graded thoroughfares and fine shade trees, visitors dismissed the "over-sanguine" townspeople as "a little slow in business matters" and, indeed, as prone to "old-fogyism." Nearby Steilacoom survived on the annual expenditures of the territorial asylum. With two hundred residents left, "no place in the world," claimed an observer straining for something positive to say about the place, was "better-fitted" for the stress-free accommodation of mental patients.[56]

The northern Sound also experienced asylum-like times. The pioneer Sehome mine closed in December 1877, completing the wreckage of the Bellingham Bay economy. The few remaining optimists pushed such unlikely projects as a federal navy yard—without substantial dredging, the vessels would have stuck in the mud at low tide—and creation of a "Central Park of the Pacific" along Whatcom Creek. Rather than rebuild the municipal bridge, which had collapsed, individuals with business to conduct in Whatcom made do with a conveniently fallen log. Port Townsend was another old place treated unkindly by the passage of time. A magazine writer's description of the town as "a quiet, pleasant abode for decent people" captured the prevailing malaise and deeply insulted residents conscious of the local historical reputation for hard-drinking and colorful characters. Across Admiralty Inlet, Whidbey Island, Puget Sound's original detached farm belt, also passed from youthful energy to aged debility. Houses and agricultural improvements, a traveling mainlander noted, had been erected "long enough ago to appear really venerable." By wide agreement, the island had the fewest saloons per capita, the least excitement and the worst postal service in the territory.[57]

Enchanted by the "clearness and stillness of the water and the luxuriance of the surrounding forest" while sailing Puget Sound in 1879, John Muir was reminded, more than anywhere else, of Lake Tahoe. Writers regularly extolled the "most remarkable sheet of water in the world" and the "most magnificent forests on the Continent." Unlike Muir, most took the superiority of pocketbook concerns for granted when recounting the wonders of the sea level Tahoe. "Probably no country in the world has the natural facilities for producing immense supplies of…timber of great size," wrote one among many journalists celebrating the transformation of scenery into sawmill profit.[58]

Timber industry experts debated whether Port Gamble or Port Ludlow, the latter recently purchased and remodeled by the Puget Mill Company, was the most efficient manufacturer on earth. A visitor to Port Blakely in late 1875 reported six vessels loading at the Bainbridge Island mill, "five on the way to it, and as many on the way from it." Forty to fifty ships, each making up to seven roundtrip voyages a year, were constantly employed in the shipment of forest products to California. Lumber cargoes also made up, in monetary value, the bulk of Puget Sound exports, enabling Washington Territory to maintain a substantial foreign trade balance. Only 37 of 261 active Washington industrial enterprises in 1880, sawmills accounted for three-fourths of the capital invested in territorial manufacturing and close to half the non-agricultural jobs. The camps and the milling ports paid the highest wages and able-bodied men in need of employment were "sure of a position."[59]

Despite strong evidence that lumbering was "carried on in a most thorough manner," the Washington Territory industry made no real progress during the 1870s. The failure of the Northern Pacific compelled continued reliance upon California and trans-oceanic markets. The only Puget Sound lumber sold east of the Cascades was the small amount shipped by rail from Tacoma to Kalama and up the Columbia aboard O.S.N. steamers. Overall production increased a mere 13 percent between 1870 and 1880. Washington actually dropped from the twenty-first to the twenty-sixth rank among the nation's timber-manufacturing states and territories. Although a slight addition to total employment was recorded, fewer individuals worked in the woods and in the mills in 1880 than in 1860. Payrolls fell by nearly half, reflecting wage reductions and temporary or permanent sawmill suspensions.[60]

Aside from disappointing performance, the decade was marked by growing concern over the waste of natural resources. Left behind in the woods, commercially undesirable trees and huge piles of debris provided the fuel for humid season conflagrations. "Not a summer passes," an Olympia newspaper noted in 1874, "but wild fires make sad havoc of…our forests." Enormous clouds of smoke enveloped Puget Sound for weeks at a time, interfering with navigation,

offending tourists and irritating residents. "We can see it and smell it," the Seattle *Intelligencer* complained of the miasma late one August, "and smell and see
but little else." Stymied by "the cloudy and smoky condition of the atmosphere,"
government surveyors were unable to calculate Seattle's exact longitude and lati-
tude. Concerned for both the economy and the public health, the territorial assembly took the first hesitant steps toward a corrective, approving legislation
making persons responsible for fires, by design or by accident, liable for damages
to property.[61]

Frequent assertions that the region needed "a greater variety of industries"
somewhat exaggerated the Sound country's reliance upon lumbering. Coaling,
of course, was an increasingly important activity, especially in Seattle. Shipbuild-
ing developed as a natural adjunct to lumber production. Puget Sound possessed, a newspaper pointed out, "timber unequalled for cheapness, strength,
elasticity and durability" and, in the several mill ports, "sites obviously adapted
for shipyards." Local firms turned out seven vessels in 1871 and four in 1873. As
the business expanded, the Port Ludlow yard alone built three schooners, a sloop
and a barkentine in 1876. Although San Francisco continued to lead the coast
in construction of ocean steamers, Port Madison on Bainbridge Island produced
more sailing craft than all Bay Area manufacturers combined. Washington Territory specialized, as well, in sea-going tugs and in light-draft steamboats designed for use on the rivers west of the Cascades.[62]

Since the time of Isaac Stevens, promoters had called for exploitation of
western Washington's abundant marine life. The difficulty remained the substantial spoilage on even relatively short voyages between the Northwest and San
Francisco. Market-oriented fishing became possible with the invention of a
means for airtight canning. California interests opened the first lower Columbia
River cannery in 1866. The subsequent growth of the industry was close to gold
rush proportions. Seven plants operated on the river in 1873, seventeen in 1875
and "not less than thirty"—including eleven on the Washington Territory
bank—in 1877. Beginning at a point forty miles above Astoria, a visitor reported, "there is scarcely a cove or place of shelter that it not occupied by what
in local parlance is termed a 'cannary' [sic]." At mid-decade, annual production
approximated a half-million cases, each containing forty-eight one-pound
cans.[63]

Regardless of ownership or specific location, canneries followed the same
procedures. "Literally it may be said," a visiting journalist observed, "that the
Chinamen do the dirty work, whilst the more pleasant parts of the business are
reserved for white men." The latter spent the night on the river, two to a boat.
The former processed fish, assembly-line fashion, slicing, washing and packing
salmon into colorfully labeled containers. On a normal shift, two dozen Chinese
workers turned out as many as fifteen thousand cans.[64]

Efficiency had consequences for the environment. "If the Columbia river cannaries [sic] keep at work," a Washington Territory newspaper warned, "it will not be long until salmon will be quite scarce." The trade, friends of the industry agreed, was sure "to decline as rapidly as it has grown up" unless federal and local authorities took prompt action to "regulate and sustain" the taking of salmon. The recently created United States Fish Commission recommended the building of hatcheries on the Columbia. Congress, joined by the legislatures of Oregon and Washington, approved protective measures, including mandated fishing seasons. Scientists promoted fish ladder devices, in the expectation that "thousands of salmon" would be saved from killing themselves "by striking on the rocks" in attempting to ascend the river's many rapids.[65]

Concern intensified in 1877 when the industry, despite ten new canneries, recorded an overall 25 percent decline in spring Chinook production. "Some there are who deem the scarcity of fish…a mere accident…," reported the Seattle *Intelligencer.* "But the more intelligent ones are satisfied that it will take at least three years of respite to bring the fisheries back to their old lucrative condition." Facing up to the likelihood of at least a short-term curtailment, factory owners shifted attention to Washington's unspoiled waters. River interests opened two Grays Harbor canneries, complete with Chinese workers. On Puget Sound, attention focused on Mukilteo, the location of Puget Sound fishing experiments dating back to the Civil War. Salmon, though smaller than those taken on the Columbia—the average fish filled three cans, compared to a river rate of at least eighteen—swam past the site in apparently inexhaustible numbers, bound for the Skagit and other streams. The two canneries commencing business in 1877 duplicated existing methods, including the use of labels claiming that the cans contained Columbia River salmon. Hoping to avoid, by preemptive measures, the problems associated with over-fishing, promoters called for extension of the federal Fish Commission mandate to the Sound and other forms of governmental assistance.[66]

Farming was another long-dreamt-of-ambition in western Washington. "Thousands of acres of excellent lands are lying idle," one champion of rain country agriculture noted in expressing a common regret. Some observers complained that negative accounts unfairly maligned local opportunities. Others noted that experienced immigrants preferred to go east of the Cascades, leaving Puget Sound to "a class…of men who know nothing about farming." Shortcomings related to transportation posed the main obstacle to development. The territory had no proper roads north of Seattle. One resident pointed out that with rivers as "the only high-ways," the canoe was "the *buggy* of the early settler." In their natural state, the major watercourses frustrated would-be homesteaders. Tidal flow and seasonal flooding inundated the lowest sections. Tortuous channels and enormous timber jams impeded navigation.[67]

Reclamation of the tidelands came first, the effort focusing on acreage in the vicinity of LaConner, a village on the east bank of Swinomish Slough in the Skagit River delta. Numerous tidal channels criss-crossed a tract seven miles long by three miles wide. The soil was extremely rich from centuries of alluvial deposits, but also, an early report confided, "completely saturated with salt water, at least once a day." Dike construction, an expensive trial-and-error process, began in 1871. "Many mistakes were made and much money uselessly wasted," a close observer recalled, before a suitable engineering scheme was devised and actual drainage commenced. Ten thousand acres were eventually reclaimed and planted in oats, barley and wheat. By 1879, exports to California exceeded the hundred-thousand ton mark, making the local boast that "the average yield…is sufficient to astonish one used to the most fertile Iowa prairies" a pardonable exaggeration.[68]

Work also began on the rivers. After an 1874 survey, the Corps of Engineers recommended that the federal government remove the jams on the Skagit, the premier tributary of Puget Sound. Something of a mini-land boom followed—previously, fifteen white persons, in two families, resided above the great rafts—in anticipation of favorable congressional action. When Congress appropriated less than a thousand dollars for the task, disappointed homesteaders directly assumed the responsibility. Claims that the blockages were "as permanent as the forests," the "accumulation of ages" and even the product of "Noah's flood" suggested the magnitude of the job. Organizing the Skagit River Jam Removal Company in early 1876, settlers sold salvaged timber to sawmills and piled debris to be floated out to the Sound in the spring. Similar volunteer efforts commenced on the other navigable streams.[69]

Despite registering a significant advance over the record of previous years, Puget Sound agriculture made only a modest impression upon persons used to eastern Washington standards. Local homesteaders insisted upon cultivating wheat, the crop most easily exported, even though damage-inflicting rain and other climatic challenges were hardly conducive to bountiful harvests. Hops alone attained genuine commercial importance. By 1880, Puyallup Valley growers, blessed with ideal soil conditions, had over a thousand acres in production. Prices fluctuated from year to year and shipping problems occasionally arose, but long-term gross earnings averaged eighteen cents a pound per annum, well above the ten cents going to combined expenses. "No other kind of farming pays so well," a contemporary study of the Sound economy concluded.[70]

Increasing agricultural exports, particularly in the form of hops, and general population growth encouraged notable improvements in external and internal communication. The Pacific Mail Steam Ship Company instituted regular five-times-a-month service between San Francisco and the Sound in the mid-1870s. No longer dependent upon the unscheduled sailings and less-than-posh accommodations of lumber company schooners, settlers boasted of being better served than Oregonians forced to come and go by the navigation-disadvantaged Columbia River. First-class sea voyages were by no means hazard-free, however, a harsh fact of saltwater life confirmed by the sensational loss of the *Pacific* in November 1875. Soon after departing Victoria in listing condition, the *Pacific* collided with the steamer *Orpheus* in the Strait of Juan de Fuca. The latter sailed on, a second ship refused to render assistance to the sinking vessel and a third, happening upon the wreckage, declined to search for survivors. The customs service boat stationed at Port Townsend might have steamed to the rescue, had not federal employees appropriated it for a private fishing trip to the Skagit River. All but two of the 238 persons aboard the *Pacific* perished, most, clad in life-jackets, from prolonged exposure to cold water.[71]

Within the confines of Puget Sound, steamboat service also increased in availability, if not in quality. Fare wars and frequent races between publicity-minded captains reflected the substantial number of vessels, at least three dozen according to an authoritative count, in regular service. Frequent sailings allowed Whatcom and Tacoma publishers to print their newspapers in Olympia. On the other hand, bizarre scheduling decisions and adverse natural conditions often made travel inconvenient and dangerous. Persons bound from Bellingham Bay to the Skagit River first had to go to Seattle, then change to a northbound steamer. The LaConner-Port Townsend run also involved a roundabout side voyage via Elliott Bay. If dredged and straightened, Swinomish Slough provided a direct weather-protected inside passage for craft sailing between the inner Sound and points close to the 49th parallel. Absent such improvements, the slough was a treacherous option, forcing all traffic, large and small, to the west of Whidbey Island, fully exposed to the strong winds and currents at the entrance to Admiralty Inlet.[72]

Serving as the hub for most steamer routes and handling virtually all of Washington's exported coal, Seattle made striking progress. The town maintained a three-to-one population advantage over Tacoma, new and old combined, and by 1880 had 3,533 officially tabulated residents, only fifty-five behind Walla Walla. Genuine achievement enhanced what had previously been little more than a vain San Francisco-of-the-rainy-north image. Opened in 1873, the community hospital—"the best...ever established in the Territory"—handled a hundred cases in a typical year, one third involving "paying patients." Commencing business in 1874, the municipal gas company provided energy for public and domestic lighting purposes. A visionary plan was developed, though not yet implemented, to bring water from the distant Cedar River in the Cascade foothills. The major streets were graded and raised above the tide. Snoqualmie Falls, east of the city, became the first and most sublime tourist attraction of the Puget Sound country. Still struggling, the University of Washington increased enrollment to seventy-two college level men and women, a three-fold enhancement of the student body. The fact that Seattle had more Chinese than Indian inhabitants—though hardly regarded by many as a change for the better—at least signaled the happy end of the frontier era.[73]

Upon its financial reorganization in 1875, the Northern Pacific prepared to resume active operations. Regular visits to the territory by top railroad executives confirmed the local wisdom that the transcontinental route was "too important to be abandoned, and the land subsidy too great to be lost." Under prevailing political and economic circumstances, however, caution governed the behavior of management. The N.P. still intended to secure assistance from the federal government before restarting construction. No-strings-attached congressional support was stymied, however, by the continuing unpopularity of railroads and by mutually destructive machinations on the part of rival transportation systems. Although O. B. McFadden's "election to Congress," a Northern Pacific official complained, "was a pretty expensive operation to us," Washington's representative refused to exercise the modest influence available to a territorial delegate on behalf of his controversial benefactors.[74]

The railroad might have gone ahead anyway, relying on the proceeds from land sales to finance track laying and purchase rolling stock. The problem with this pay-as-you-go approach was that the mandated deadline for completing the mainline, July 4, 1877, under most readings of the law, was fast approaching. According to complex legal arguments, the real cutoff point was in 1879 or 1880 and reversion of the odd-numbered sections to the public domain required explicit action by Congress. Under the most optimistic scenario, however, the Northern Pacific could not be finished even by 1880, a prognosis sure to deter investors from loaning funds on the collateral of land.[75]

Popular opinion, in general, supported the firm's reorganized management in asking Congress to extend the deadline, provided work was promptly resumed, existing disputes over claims resolved and a $2.50 per acre rate for land sales instituted. More sensitive than in the past to public relations concerns, the Northern Pacific adopted the $2.50 figure, with liberal credit terms, for agricultural acreage and abandoned its previous hard-nosed attitude toward settlers claiming prior possession of odd-numbered sections. The Portland, Dalles & Salt Lake and the Seattle & Walla Walla railroads, ventures expecting to secure substantial portions of a forfeited land grant, were harder to sidetrack. "We propose to contest every inch of ground with them," wrote attorney John McGilvra in expressing Seattle's attitude toward extending the N.P. time limit. Expressed with emotional force by new congressional delegate Orange Jacobs, a stockholder in the Seattle & Walla Walla, the Elliott Bay position was well voiced on Capitol Hill.[76]

Longtime Puget Sound-Columbia River enmities further complicated the extension question. Portlanders demanded that any new legislation specifically require construction of the mainline down the stream's southern bank, insuring that the road remain "an Oregon enterprise." Washingtonians insisted that the Northern Pacific be ordered to build across the Cascades, fulfilling the original Civil War era design. "The talk about the Columbia being 'the natural highway to the sea' is all humbug," argued the *Walla Walla Statesman*. Any railroad following the river worked to the advantage of Oregon, tightening a long-applied stranglehold. A direct connection to Puget Sound, on the other hand, opened a cheaper and more efficient outlet and encouraged, as an added bonus, territorial unification. Once instituted, the mutually profitable exchange of grain for lumber and coal would transform the Cascades from impenetrable north-south barrier to essential east-west linkage.[77]

Returning, after a two-year retirement, to an active managerial role in 1877, John Ainsworth was a well-placed asset in Portland's effort to once and for all capture the Northern Pacific. Upon assuming the railroad presidency in 1878, Frederick Billings was celebrated in Washington Territory as a counterweight to the captain. More dynamic than his predecessor, Charles Wright, Billings was also better informed regarding Pacific coast affairs. Less reliant on Ainsworth, he favored "the route over the Mountains" instead of "the route down the River." The new president sent surveying parties into the passes, but postponed a final official decision, citing the need to resolve both the extension controversy and division within company ranks. "It is better," Billings reasoned, "to delay a little, and have all hands agree that we are starting right."[78]

Northern Pacific executives dithered, Congress withheld timely aid and the one optimistic note came from an unlikely place, Commencement Bay. Major deposits of coal were discovered in the upper Puyallup Valley, twenty-eight miles from Tacoma, in the fall of 1874. Six hundred workers, two-thirds Chinese, completed a railroad to Wilkeson in 1877. On the bayfront, a long wharf led to deep water, enabling the loading of seagoing vessels direct from rail cars at all stages of the tide. Initial sales to San Francisco were disappointing, the disposition of "surface" and "gangway" coal arousing customer concern over quality. The Wilkeson track, on the other hand, intersected with the Northern Pacific, allowing overland shipment to the Columbia River via the Puget Sound branch. Now controlled by Henry Villard, the old Ben Holladay railroading and steamboat interests ranked high among the early purchases.[79]

Puyallup coal had a Seattle-like impact upon Tacoma. "The recent excitement," a news story from Commencement Bay recorded soon after the first cargo was exported, "...has had the effect of quickening sales of real estate, of filling up the empty houses, and of giving cheer to the people." Visitors noted a boom in the marketing of town lots. The Northern Pacific built car and machine shops and other support facilities, providing, the *Tacoma Herald* pointed out, "the greatest evidence of permanency ever erected in this portion of country." Trailing far behind Seattle, Tacoma, old and new together, still claimed over a thousand permanent residents by 1880, a firm foundation for future growth.[80]

According to a newspaper observation, Wilkeson was "the peg upon which the Northern Pacific Railroad has hung its hat." Needing a broader corporate support mechanism, company management decided to lay new track without advance congressional assistance. "The great enterprise starts again," Frederick Billings announced in December 1878, "and this time…never to stop til completion." The focus west of the Rockies was on the long-postponed Pend Oreille division, linking the mouth of the Snake River with Pend Oreille Lake in northern Idaho. With applications for the right to purchase four hundred thousand acres in the Palouse already in hand, the firm expected to secure handsome returns once work was well-advanced, from selling the odd-numbered sections turned over by the government.[81]

Construction began in April 1879, starting, a half-mile north of the Snake, at the most Godawful community ever opened to human habitation in the Pacific Northwest. Residents, demonstrating a fine appreciation for the natural surroundings, named the place Hades. Apparently intending the gesture to be complimentary, the railroad supplied a more genteel official name, Ainsworth. The townsite was "a bleak dreary waste," Army engineer Thomas Symons noted in the prelude to a more detailed condemnation:

> Ainsworth is one of the most uncomfortable, abominable places in America to live in. You can scan the horizon in vain for a tree or anything resembling one. The heat through the summer is excessive, and high winds prevail and blow the sands about and into everything. By the glare of the sun and the flying sands, one's eyes are in a constant state of winking, blinking, and torment, if nothing more serious results.

The N.P. erected temporary offices and other work-related structures, but wasted no time on such obviously superfluous tasks as naming streets.[82]

Eager to get as far from Hades as possible, crews proceeded at optimum speed, laying track at a pace of up to three-quarters of a mile per day. Only two wells, both over a hundred feet deep, were found near the initial section of track, so water was a major and constant concern. In the absence of local forest cover, the Northern Pacific tapped the distant headwaters of the Yakima River for timber. The most dramatic log drives in Washington history took place east, rather than west, of the Cascades. One hundred men spent three months carefully guiding the initial consignment, ten million feet, in early 1880. The irregular depth of water in the Yakima was by no means the only complication. Federal authorities, strictly interpreting the law allowing railroads to freely remove timber from public land for "contiguous" construction purposes, charged the company and its logging contractor, by coincidence territorial surveyor general William McMicken, with trespass. A prolonged legal dispute over cutting in the upper Yakima drainage threatened the roadbuilding timetable.[83]

Running northeast along the fringes of the Palouse direct to Spokane Falls, the Pend Oreille division opened a new region to settlement. "The entire country which we traversed," a visitor from Portland reported in the spring of 1880, "is covered with rich bunch and wool grass." The railroad-bisected section, another observer noted, was "a paradise for cattle." While "only occasional patches of tillable land" had thus far been located, the perceptive immigrant could expect to find "large areas…of the richest quality and sufficiently level for the use of all farm machinery." Philip Ritz, formerly of the Walla Walla Valley, demonstrated by early experiment that the better tracts could produce forty to fifty bushels of wheat to the acre. Pushing the sale of land, the Northern Pacific distributed promotional literature and offered discount rates for farmers, their stock and equipment. Small towns—Ritzville, Sprague and Cheney—went into business along the right-of-way, providing market outlets for local settlers and for isolated portions of the Palouse.[84]

Originally located by James Glover in 1873, Spokan, or Spokane, Falls was not, strictly speaking, a railroad town. The Northern Pacific was more involved, regionally, in Cheney, sixteen miles to the southwest, and in Sprague, the division headquarters. More so than any other place east of the mountains, however, Spokane had the potential to become a true center of industry. Lake Coeur d'Alene, across the Idaho line, was surrounded by vast stands of timber and controlled access to rumored millions in mineral wealth. The Spokane River, flowing from the lake, poured over a series of basaltic ledges at the townsite. Asserting that "neither pen nor pencil can adequately describe them," newcomer John Browne wrote a vivid account of the falls:

> See the great waters as they leap and jump and beat themselves into angry foam white as the driven snow, and then whirl and jump and leap again. Down over the rocks splashing and foaming the waters come with a might[,] power and force, heaving and swelling and thundering until earth and air and everything seems one moving, heaving, thundering, frothing, angry mass bent on destruction!

Dropping nearly two hundred feet in a stretch of less than a thousand feet, the river generated sufficient power to "drive more machinery than could be placed along a mile of its banks" according to a correspondent for the Portland *Oregonian*. "Travel the wide West over," another contemporary writer claimed, "and one cannot find a more desirable or favorable location at which to establish extensive…mills."[85]

"Beautiful and picturesque beyond description," as John Browne rhapsodized, the falls attracted more manufacturers and merchants than scenery-sensitive nature enthusiasts. Browne himself opened a mercantile establishment, with Anthony Cannon as partner, in April 1878. Supposedly "running over with persons who have gone there to make fortunes," Spokane had over three hundred residents by 1880. Settlers crossed the river to the north bank on a recently constructed bridge. A flume diverted water to several flouring mills and to the Pioneer sawmill, built to supply the advancing Northern Pacific with heavy-duty lumber. Amenities included a brewery, three top-of-the-line hotels and thirteen well-stocked general stores, the latter selling, a clerk noted, "everything that you can think of not excepting Whiskey & Cigars and Milwaukie [sic] bottled Beer." The creation of Spokane County left the remnant portion of Stevens County so lacking in people and resources that even the most ardent supporter of the move admitted to feelings of guilt.[86]

Eastern Washington's most promising town was situated in Indian Country. Refusing, for good reason, to move to the sterile Colville reservation, the Spokanes and the Coeur d'Alenes were fully exposed to land-hungry arriving settlers. At a council of the region's tribes, Governor Elisha Ferry and General Oliver O. Howard failed to secure voluntary acceptance of the immigrants. Painted and armed Indians visited Spokane in large numbers and on a regular basis, a merchant reported, buying "lots of stuff" and paying in "gold for what they get." The same storekeeper never went "to bed at night without my Henry Rifle within reach." Aggravating an already tense situation, the Northern Pacific forcibly evicted native occupants off the odd-numbered land grant sections.[87]

Built for money, the Pend Oreille division ran, for the moment, from nowhere to nowhere. To truly make an impact, the Northern Pacific needed both an outlet to the sea and a network of feeders linking the grain-producing countryside with a completed mainline. Once again confirming its reputation for meaning "business every hour out of the twenty-four," the Oregon Steam Navigation Company, not the N.P., first met the challenge. "As a matter of self protection," founding partner Robert Thompson urged, with John Ainsworth in agreement, that the O.S.N. must construct "roads running out from the river to the head of the agricultural vallies [sic]…as fast as our means will permit." Because the Cascades canal was bound to lead eventually to a similar navigation improvement at The Dalles, the firm would need to also lay track along the Columbia, preserving its regional transportation monopoly by a strategic shift from water to land. Unfortunately, the company charter and Oregon law prohibited the O.S.N. from building or owning railroads.[88]

Circumnavigating the statutory obstacles, the O.S.N. merged with the Henry Villard interests in June 1879, forming the Oregon Railway & Navigation Company. Arranged in a series of meetings between Ainsworth and Villard, the $6 million deal was widely reported as "the largest business transaction that has ever taken place on this coast." The combined O.R. & N. holdings included two hundred miles of railroad, thirty river steamers, four ocean-going vessels, four hundred miles of telegraph line and assorted urban and rural properties on both sides of the Cascades. In a related move of near-equal significance, Villard organized the Oregon Improvement Company, a corporate entity empowered, among a wide variety of activities, to build railroads and to buy, sell and develop real estate. One hundred thousand acres in the Palouse, previously acquired by the promoter and his associates, passed into O.I.C. ownership.[89]

Henry Villard, the aggressive president of the O.R. & N., immediately became the dominant business leader of the Pacific Northwest, exercising more influence over the development of Washington Territory than any other individual. Once a Civil War correspondent, the German-born Villard had capitalized upon connections in New York and among investors in his homeland to acquire control of the railroading and steamboat concerns originally developed by Ben Holladay. His alliance with the O.S.N. was entirely a matter of grudging mutual self-interest. Officials of the older company privately considered him "a smart Swiss Jew" and an operator "inclined to be somewhat sharp, not to say unscrupulous." Ainsworth worried that Villard was too dependent upon borrowed money and prone, from excess ambition, to undermine relations with the captain's other corporate connection, the Northern Pacific. "Too bad, too bad," Frederick Billings had already written in regard to his unhappiness "that the O.S.N. Co[mpany] is to pass into other hands."[90]

Surveying for a standard gauge railroad covering the hundred and ten miles between The Dalles and Wallula began in the fall of 1879, with construction scheduled for completion in time to handle the 1880 harvest. "The worst part of the Columbia river, for the purposes of navigation is avoided," the *Walla Walla Union* pointed out in reporting the prospective impact of this first major O.R. & N. step. Released from dependence on the steamers as far as The Dalles, wheat producers anticipated shipping greater amounts of grain at reduced cost, generating increased profits. By early winter, Villard had eight hundred laborers at work, grading the right-of-way and building bridges across the Deschutes and the John Day rivers, major Oregon tributaries of the Columbia. Steel rails and rolling stock, including seven locomotives, two hundred freight cars and five "first-class passenger cars," were en route from England to Portland, "loaded in clipper ships."[91]

While the O.R. & N. moved upstream, the Walla Walla & Columbia River Railroad—"a very long way of spelling Dr. Baker" according to one observer—altered direction. The line had originally been something of an underpowered joke—mounted daredevils literally rode around the moving trains to the cheers of passengers. The regional wheat boom, however, produced a four-fold increase in grain and flour shipments between 1875 and 1879. Mounting revenues allowed Baker to purchase better equipment and improve service. In 1879, he began construction of a narrow gauge branch from Walla Walla south into Oregon, planning to follow with an extension on to the Columbia at Umatilla. Upon completion of the project, steamers would be able to avoid the rapids intervening between the latter point and Wallula.[92]

When purchased by the O.R. & N., Dorsey Baker's evolving railroad system became the starting point for Villard's interior feeder network. The new owner immediately commenced work on branches between Walla Walla and the Snake River, one to Grange City at the mouth of the Tucannon and the other to Texas

Ferry. A crossing of the Snake above the worst navigation obstacles was contemplated, if possible prior to the 1881 harvest, allowing Palouse farmers to ship wheat by rail. The time required to reach Portland from Columbia and Whitman counties, presently ninety-six hours in high water periods, was reduced to twenty-four. "Had such a prediction been made four years ago," a local newspaper remarked in November 1880, "the man making it would have been branded as an idiot."[93]

Confidential negotiations between the O.R. & N. and the Northern Pacific for a *de facto* regional merger were facilitated by the many individuals holding large blocks of stock in both concerns. Frederick Billings agreed to build from Ainsworth to a linkup with Villard's operation at Wallula, an undertaking completed in December 1880. Although personally committed to a crossing "over the mountains to Puget Sound," Billings also agreed to joint N.P.-O.R. & N. financing of further construction down the Columbia from The Dalles to Portland, the firms to share equally all revenues west of Wallula. Villard thereby increased the freight-carrying capacity of the river route and again diverted the Northern Pacific, at least temporarily, from the direct line to the Sound.[94]

Though he was long-gone to a low reward, Selucious Garfielde's legacy remained in the form of Washington's highest political officials, all originally appointed with the blessing of the former congressional delegate. Elevated from the surveyor generalship in 1872, Elisha P. Ferry became the only two-term governor in Washington Territory history. His qualifications, if minimal, were well suited to the times, having served many years as an Illinois attorney and occasionally as a pre-Civil War host to a circuit riding bar colleague, Abraham Lincoln. An "entertaining and courteous gentleman," he was a local model of the current Illinoisan president, Ulysses S. Grant. Partially concealed behind the finely tailored facade of a corporate lawyer and amateur constitutional scholar, Ferry was also Garfielde's appropriate successor as the leader of Olympia-based officeholders. Assailed for issuing too many dubious pardons, he suffered periodic embarrassment when the beneficiaries of lenience committed new crimes. His administration of territorial contracts generated controversy, as in the case of the agreement under which close associate Hill Harmon assumed mismanagement of the Steilacoom asylum. Accusing Ferry of misappropriating funds while a wartime military attorney, federal auditors withheld his salary to recover the missing money.[95]

Governor Ferry, the *Walla Walla Statesman* noted, was literally and figuratively "a small man." This fact of biological and political life meant that his demonstrably inferior associates merited "animalcule" status. General Robert H. Milroy, who was briefly charged with treason after failing to impede Lee's 1863 invasion of the North, begged President Grant, as a fellow Union Army veteran, for appointment as territorial superintendent of Indian affairs. Suspended from office under official accusation of fraud, Milroy appealed to his reputation as "a Christian and a patriot," winning reinstatement after investigators found that he was merely incompetent. When the superintendency system was abolished in 1874, leaving the general "out of business...and in debt," he utilized a similar plea to obtain a new position as Indian agent, first on Puget Sound and then with the Yakamas east of the Cascades. Asked to resign by the Democratic Cleveland administration in 1885, Republican Milroy responded with the principled stoicism of a long-term spoils beneficiary, vowing to resist as long as his dismissal was "based on any charge of official *delinquency*." Should the demand be motivated by "political grounds only," however, "it will be speedily complied with."[96]

Territorial secretary Henry G. Struve also had an undistinguished military record, having deserted from the Army after enlisting as a young German immigrant prior to the Civil War. Admitting to this embarrassing transgression in 1874, he retained office and avoided prison thanks to a hastily issued presidential pardon. Republicans insisted, without shame, that Struve, "like any youth of education and spirit," had properly run away from "the dog's life of a common soldier in the barracks." Democrats chortled over the secretary's wisdom in avoiding service with the Navy, since "at sea the opportunities to *desert* are limited." In addition to the secretaryship, the brave politico held a variety of supposedly responsible positions, including county prosecutor, university regent and mayor of Seattle. Eventually resigning from government, Struve became the territory's leading specialist in the art of bribing legislators on behalf of corporate clients.[97]

Learning that the Illinois patronage quota was filled, quick-thinking Chicago lawyer and Washington supreme court aspirant Roger S. Greene secured appointment by claiming to be a Wisconsin resident. Friends, to say nothing of enemies, considered him "a religious crank" bound, by terminal foot-in-mouth habit, to "say or do a thing in the wrong way, at the wrong place or at the wrong time." Citing, for authority, a personal relationship with the Holy Spirit, Greene imposed harsher sentences upon prostitutes than upon violent criminals. "I would rather before him take my chances...on one of the high orders of felonies," said Elwood Evans, "than for buying a drink on a Sunday." Supported by the equally sanctimonious Governor Ferry, Greene had no biblical scruples about making money. He solicited funds for the "Gospel Ship," a trading vessel built, according to the false claim of its confidence-artist owners, to carry the word of God to coastal Indians. Correctly anticipating that the Northern Pacific would buy him out at a generous profit, Greene purchased, on the basis of inside information, acreage scheduled for inclusion in the land grant. Most local attorneys expressed disgust, but solid political credentials in the East kept Greene on the job for sixteen years, the longest-serving, and strangest, jurist in territorial history.[98]

Only the pre-existing bottom-of-the-barrel stature of the officeholding class kept federal appointees from descending even lower in public esteem. The veteran job seeker Elwood Evans, scoffed the *Walla Walla Statesman*, was "willing to take anything from a foreign mission to the President's old clothes." As a genuine Washingtonian, Evans at least deserved to be distinguished from the "carpet baggers" dispatched to the Pacific Northwest by an uncaring government. "Any dung-hill…is supposed to be good enough to 'import' from 'the States,'" an eastern Washington newspaper complained of a policy that placed the territory on the same footing as the defeated Southern Confederacy. Proposals for local election of the governor and other territorial officials, though unlikely to secure congressional approval, were among the few political ideas of the time to generate popular appeal.[99]

Voting already for congressional representative, Washington residents had little reason to care about the candidates or the results. Individual delegates reflected the apathy of a settler population unconcerned with political affairs. O. B. McFadden collapsed during the first session of the Congress elected in 1872 and, when able to return to the Sound, took to his deathbed. A New York-born and Michigan-raised Oregon politician, Orange Jacobs served briefly on the territorial supreme court before his nomination in 1874. Jacobs, a public lecturer on such old bromide subjects as "God helps them who help themselves," looked after himself by investing in, and fronting for, the Seattle & Walla Walla Railroad. Thomas Brents, or Brentz in the German spelling favored by some contemporaries, was another controversial Oregonian. A county clerk in that state, he invalidated enough Democratic votes to win election to the legislature, a fraud so blatant that fellow Republicans expelled him from the assembly. Remade as a Walla Walla lawyer, the "little pimp" was suspended from the bar after a public brouhaha with Judge Joseph Lewis. First sent to Congress in 1878, Brents repeatedly manifested what the *Statesman* saw as his single talent, the ability to make "himself the laughing stock." Benefiting from the territory's increasing Republican orientation, he won reelection in 1880 and 1882, on both occasions defeating Seattle attorney Thomas Burke, a candidate given to mystifying campaign orations on Greek and Roman philosophy.[100]

Politically aware Washingtonians agreed that admission to the Union, on the merits and regardless of partisan considerations, was long overdue. "We have already passed nearly 23 years in a state of…vassalage," a Seattle newspaper reminded its readers in 1875, "and to continue so much longer would naturally suggest a suspicion in the minds of the people that we were destined always to continue so." Without positive action in the nation's capital, another editorialist lamented, Washington was "liable to remain a territory for all time to come." The pioneer, especially, "ought to have realized all the advantages under a Territorial form of government by this time if any exists," a third journalist observed. Making their case, statehood advocates pointed out that Washington was responsible for a fourth of the grain harvested in the eight western territories and, with busy Morman Utah excluded from the calculation, half the industrial output.[101]

Rather than concede Washington's self-evident right to admission, Congress supposedly acted as if the Pacific Northwest was unworthy of consideration. "So far as assistance for the development of our Territory is concerned," a leading newspaper complained in early 1875, "we might as well look to the government of Japan for it, as from that at Washington [City]." The language of complaint was similar on both sides of the mountains, but there was considerable regional division as the best cure for the territorial malady. Traditional animosities, accentuated by recent demographic change, and the conviction that statehood was unlikely any time soon, accounted for growing sentiment east of the Cascades in favor of separation from Puget Sound. Natural "boundaries" united eastern Washington and northern Idaho, argued those favoring amalgamation of the two sections. "Insurmountable barriers," on the other hand, isolated both from their present-day capitals. Travel in the one case to Olympia and in the other to Boise, claimed an advocate of political rearrangement, was "almost like undertaking a journey around the world." In Walla Walla, the Republican *Union* and the Democratic *Statesman* insisted that "nine out of every ten voters" west and east of the boundary line favored annexation of the panhandle and formation of a new government.[102]

Given the trends then current in population and economic development, Puget Sound was headed, at best, toward permanent minority status in an enlarged territory. In the case of an actual division, the Sound, circumscribed in residents and space, could attain statehood only by reunion with Oregon. The most practicable means of at least partially circumventing separatist ambitions beyond the mountains was to secure admission to the Union as soon as possible. Achievement of this objective was no easy task, considering the contrary feelings of eastsiders and general public disinterest. Provided an opportunity to express themselves one way or the other on the subject in 1870, fewer than a thousand voters, territory-wide, had, as required, scribbled the words "For Convention" on their general election ballots.[103]

Careful advance planning appeared necessary to secure a pro-statehood petition to Congress. Some pundits expected Governor Ferry to brazenly declare a regular session of the Republican-controlled legislature the proper forum for drafting a constitution. Adopting a more indirect approach, the assembly authorized an April 1878 election of delegates, one from each of the territory's nine council and three judicial districts, plus three more on an at-large basis. These fifteen individuals, with a sixteenth representing northern Idaho, were to meet in Walla Walla, a location selected to encourage support east of the Cascades. The document there produced was to be presented to the voters at the regular 1878 election, to be rejected or approved for transmission to the nation's capital.[104]

Estimated at somewhere between one-fifth and one-half of the eligible electorate, turnout at the April election reflected the persistence of popular indifference toward statehood. The Republicans secured an eight-to-seven margin among the delegates chosen by those persons bothering to vote. Collectively, the convention members claimed legitimate standing for relative probity. The best known, or the least obscure, were Alex Abernethy, a pioneer Columbia River millowner and current Northern Pacific land agent, and Edward Eldridge, the longtime and increasingly lonely Bellingham Bay booster. Benjamin F. Dennison, former supreme court chief judge and victim of Garfielde's 1869 patronage purge, possessed the closest approximation of legal talent. Alonzo Leland of the *Lewiston Teller*, representing northern Idaho, was the nearest thing to a man of letters.[105]

Assembling in Walla Walla on June 11, 1878, the delegates conferred for forty working days, with time off for Sundays, the Fourth of July and an excursion, courtesy of the Oregon Steam Navigation Company, to Lewiston. No press representative from west of the mountains attended. Preoccupied with the dramatic events of the Bannock War and the ongoing troubles associated with Chief Moses, local newspapers provided scant coverage. In lieu of an official journal, the members contracted with the *Walla Walla Union*, an opponent of statehood, for "a synopsis of the proceedings." Judging from this somewhat irregular record, two issues preoccupied the delegates. A prolonged argument centered on whether or not Idaho's Leland had the right to cast a legal vote. The seventh daily session was devoted to respectful consideration of woman suffrage, in the form of a memorial personally presented by the redoubtable Abigail Scott Duniway. Upon the departure of Duniway and her supporters among the "ladies of Walla Walla and vicinity," female voting was, to the surprise of no one present, summarily rejected by a ten-to-four tally against.[106]

Signed by all delegates, Alonzo Leland included, on July 27, the constitution of the state of Washington would "require a life time to read" according to the *Walla Walla Statesman*. Citizens lacked the leisure and the literary erudition "to wade through the sea of words" and ought to be immediately supplied, the paper suggested, with a plain English summary "not to exceed 100 octavo pages" in length. Ill-natured kidding aside, the constitution was, in dead prose fact, an overlong, tedious document, cluttered with unnecessary detail in an attempt to restrict, by advance stroke, the powers of the new state government.[107]

Reduced to essentials, three provisions, each one reflecting the constitutional convention's true purpose, mattered. The first article, on boundaries, included Idaho north of the 45th parallel in the state. Once past this verbiage, designed to appeal to eastsiders, the document preserved the political power, even in an enlarged Washington, of west-of-the-Cascades residents and interests. Article fourteen, section two made Olympia virtually the permanent seat of government, to be replaced only in the unlikely event of an alternative receiving "a majority of all the votes cast" in a statewide election. Apportioning the original legislature, the constitution gave western Washington an advantage of six-to-three in the senate and twenty-to-twelve in the house. A body so composed was unlikely to reapportion itself in a manner detrimental to tidewater welfare.

The constitution was approved by an apparent two-to-one margin at the polls in November, with substantial support east and west of the Cascades. Properly understood, however, the referendum actually produced a narrow and sectionally based endorsement. Individuals wrote "for" or "against" on their ballots, with a majority of the total vote cast for congressional delegate required to pass the constitution. Since favorable tallies alone truly counted, there was a large fall-off in participation in areas opposed to statehood. One-fourth of the congressional voters registered no opinion, pro or con. The document was actually endorsed by only 51 percent of the electorate. Other than new immigrants and heavily Republican Whitman County, two-thirds of the eastern Washington voting population rejected statehood, either directly or by declining to state an opinion. On Puget Sound, in contrast, two of every three persons casting a ballot for Congress expressly endorsed the constitution. Setting aside Pierce County, the sole tidewater county in the negative column, the proposed state of Washington received an astounding 96 percent approval rating on the Sound.[108]

Washington Territory was divided, rather than united, upon the question of statehood. Longtime, often bitter, points of contention remained paramount, setting westerners against easterners, Republicans against Democrats, and Portland influence against the challenge of Puget Sound. Admission, the *Walla Walla Union* pointed out, was "premature." Armed with a sectional-endorsed constitution, delegate Thomas Brents moved forward anyway with legislation for a state of Washington, the Idaho panhandle included. An obnoxious partisan Republican in a Democratic Congress and a living dictionary definition of the word nonentity, Brents was without influence in the nation's capital. When he failed to draw serious attention to the cause, pro-statehood newspapers complained of unfair opposition party treatment. Western territories with fewer people and resources had, after all, been admitted with relative ease in the past.[109] What counted, however, was the evident division of Washington into rival sections—one looking to Oregon and the other to California and the ports of the Pacific—separated by lack of communications, with no common interest presently in view. For all its lumber and coal and wheat and railroad promotionalism, Washington, as territory or unlikely state, was a fundamentally misconceived political body.

Henry Villard. *Washington State University Library, Pullman (84-015)*

Chapter Seven

Great Auxiliary Meteors

Railroads, the great auxiliary meteors of modern commerce, civilization and prosperity, are reaching out over our Territory in all directions.
—Thomas H. Brents[1]

NORTHERN PACIFIC TRAINS crossed the mouth of the Snake River on the *Frederick Billings*, the largest and most powerful ferry in northwestern waters, fresh or salt. Rolled gently aboard—"not a sleeper disturbed, not a dream broken," one passenger noted—eight cars at a time were transferred between the southern and northern bank. Engineers paused, briefly if possible, for water at Ainsworth, a hellish place lately gone to ruin. Abandoning the seat of newly incorporated Franklin County, the better class of gamblers, saloonkeepers and prostitutes had followed the construction gangs and the payrolls up the Pend Oreille division line. Left-behind practitioners of the pleasure trades preserved, as best they could, the dark civic reputation of better days and happier nights. "This town," a visiting Spokane Falls newspaperman observed in June 1881, "can boast of...the largest number of bad men and women, and the greatest amount of sin, dust and general disagreeableness, of any place of its size on the coast." Respectable folk, though few in number, resorted, upon fully exasperated occasion, to vigilante justice, with no enduring impact upon local morals. "We entered Ainsworth in the evening with a regret," one through ticket holder recalled. "We left it in the morning without any."[2]

Beyond Ainsworth, the N.P. mainline bisected a sagebrush-covered waste best appreciated, said a frequent traveler, as a "Nevada desert." As closely as local conditions allowed, the route followed a straight line, deviating only to take advantage of convenient coulees. Timetables took into account stops for water at Eight, Twenty, Forty-eight and Sixty-seven Mile Wells. Filled to capacity by windmill-powered pumps, the huge wooden tanks were the only human-built structures on the sweat-stained eighty-four mile passage to Ritzville, the first semi-civilized station on the Pend Oreille division. The dreary journey was undertaken only for genuinely serious concerns of business or personal emergency. The "finest dust," wrote the Reverend George Atkinson, a regular customer and champion of the new transportation line, "...fills the air and the cars and the clothing, the food, one's ears and nostrils, and skin."[3]

In addition to being an ordained man of the cloth, the Reverend Atkinson was a self-taught climate and soils expert and, at least to contemporary admirers, "one of the most distinguished...writers on the resources of the Northwest." En route to Spokane Falls in 1881, he overheard a fellow passenger express the definitive Washington Territory lament: "We have fought for railroads. Now we must fight against them."

Convinced that the complaint betrayed total ignorance as to the many benefits provided by the Northern Pacific, Atkinson pointed out that the average settler now traveled to and from home in a single day, at a cost of a few dollars. "The business opportunities are over one hundred per cent. more," he calculated, "and the personal...comfort probably over one hundred per cent. more in favor of the railroads instead of against them." The N.P., moreover, deserved credit for the economic boom currently under way in the Columbia Basin. "A man's farm...slow at $6 or even $4 per acre," the minister exclaimed, "is now quick at $12 or $8 per acre and it will...steadily advance to double its present value." Expressed with Biblical certainty, the argument failed to persuade naysayers, who remained convinced that the same corporations responsible for progress also retarded, in various ways and at specific places, the general growth and development of Washington Territory.[4]

By 1880, Washington had, despite recent Northern Pacific efforts, less than three hundred miles of railway, half the figure for Idaho and Oregon and one-tenth the mileage claimed by California. Motivated by short-term fiscal stringency and lingering transcontinental ambition, the Seattle & Walla Walla Railroad intended to substantially augment this modest record. Expecting to refinance their obligations—a $100,000 payment to the Newcastle coal mine fell due in the summer of 1880—and resume construction toward Snoqualmie Pass, Arthur Denny and his associates turned to Wall Street. The Seattleites employed as their bond salesman a sharply dressed and socially refined Puget Sound newcomer, Watson C. Squire. A member by convenient marriage of the Remington firearms family, Squire was a wealthy international traveler and a modest power in New York Republican politics. Providing his flashy representative with a power of attorney, Denny remained ignorant of one character-revealing fact. Though on the Sound to invest in real estate, Squire was also on the run from charges of embezzlement brought by his in-laws.[5]

Seattle's naive railroaders also failed to appreciate the cunning of Henry Villard, president of the Oregon Railway & Navigation Company. Completing the Walla Walla Valley feeder lines planned by Dorsey Baker and pushing construction up and down the Columbia, Villard needed Newcastle as a source of coal for his steamers and trains. "The *R[.]R[.] is the key to the purchase of the mine,*" Thomas R. Tannatt, his local agent, reported from Elliott Bay. In terms of larger transportation strategy, Villard also knew that a working railroad across the Cascades would inevitably divert trade from the downriver route to Portland.[6]

In July 1880, Watson Squire informed his employers of a stunning, and entirely unexpected, development. Instead of negotiating a bond sale, he had sold the Seattle & Walla Walla outright to Henry Villard for $360,000. Meeting in emergency session, the directors immediately dismissed Squire, without the $25,000 fee previously promised. Near bankruptcy and without alternative funding options, the Denny group nonetheless accepted the arrangement. Through a separate $750,000 transaction, Villard also acquired the holdings of the Seattle Coal Company, Newcastle included.[7] The railroad and mining properties became administrative responsibilities of his affiliated corporate entity, the Oregon Improvement Company. Already paramount in eastern Washington and at Tacoma, Portland now controlled the principal economic activities centering upon Elliott Bay.

Examining Villard's recent purchases, Olympia editor John Miller Murphy warned that "Portland is to be the hub around which Puget Sound is to be made to revolve." Hardly reconciled to being a Willamette Valley hinterland, Washingtonians on both sides of the Cascades demanded an alternative means of shipment. Specifically, the Northern Pacific must finally build the long-promised cross-mountain railroad, direct from the upper Columbia River to the Commencement Bay waterfront. "Our natural outlet is Puget Sound," asserted Francis Cook of the *Spokan Times*, a publisher with first-hand experience in both eastern and western Washington. Avoiding frequent transfers and navigation hazards, a cost-effective road to the Sound allowed grain producers to retain a larger portion of their earnings and reordered traditional commercial connections. "When that work is finished," editors throughout the region agreed, "the death knell of Portland will have been sounded."[8]

The Northern Pacific appeared ready, as of early 1881, to actually begin construction. Overall, Lake Superior to the coast, the company had 942 miles of track laid, 247 miles underway and 970 miles yet to be located. To finance completion of the job, Frederick Billings secured $40 million in new loans. John Ainsworth's final, and irrevocable, retirement from active involvement in business removed a strong personal check upon the N.P. president's ambitions. In the first six months of the year, railroad managers stockpiled a quarter million ties at Tacoma. Seven vessels, loaded with iron, locomotives and rolling stock, sailed from Atlantic coast ports for Puget Sound. Addressing Olympia merchants, Governor William Newell announced, as a personal pledge from Billings, "that work would unquestionably commence on each side of the Cascade mountains."[9]

Preparations for construction brought fully to life the ultimate commercial threat to Portland and to the O.R. & N. Henry Villard's response was a grandiose version of the competition-eliminating strategy recently used against the Seattle & Walla Walla. Managing a subsequently famous "blind pool," funds secured from longtime associates, he acquired close to a majority interest in the Northern Pacific during the winter of 1881. The "daring venture," so described by a St. Paul newspaper, produced an immediate coast-to-coast sensation when revealed to the public in February. Nationally and regionally, the rationale appeared to be perfectly forthright and entirely cynical. Villard had moved against the N.P., Alonzo Leland of the *Lewiston Teller* astutely pointed out, "after he found he could not induce the management…to terminate their road west of Ainsworth." Followers of the Wall Street quotations grasped the meaning within days, as O.R. & N. stock mounted in value from $130 to $185 a share.[10]

On close to a unanimous note, the prospective change in N.P. administration outraged Washingtonians. Newspapers printed analyses of Villard's moves within funereal black borders. "Half of the best lands…have been donated to an enterprise which promised us a road direct to Puget Sound," the *Spokan Times* complained in predicting that this pledge would be dishonored should a change in management take place. "That Mr. Villard is desirous of delaying, for years, the construction of the N.P.R.R. over the Cascades," the *Walla Walla Union* advised, "is evident." Puget Sound residents "hoped and prayed," according to John Miller Murphy, that the O.R. & N. president "would not succeed in making the project for a great national highway the tail to his Portland kite."[11]

Pacific Northwest newspaper readers avidly followed the "war to the knife" in New York. The "reports of one day," the *Walla Walla Union* commented as Frederick Billings mounted an unexpectedly strong counterattack, "are contradicted the next." By early summer, though, the likely outcome appeared obvious. Beset by legal threat and physical infirmity and convinced that a late-coming Villard endorsement of the cross-mountain road was sincere, Billings signaled his readiness to surrender. While "the company should do nothing that will put its route over the Cascade range in danger of being taken away," he maintained, there was, after all, no need to "hurry in its construction." In late May, Billings sold most, if not all, of his stock to the "blind pool." Villard's election to the Northern Pacific presidency in September officially completed a stunning revolution in management. Washingtonians reconciled themselves to a new reality. "Villard is boss…," a Walla Walla Valley editor reflected. "We are in his power, and it is hardly worth while to kick against the man who holds the key to the only outlet for our country."[12]

Villard instantly became what another newspaper called the "one-man power" of the Pacific Northwest. In addition to the N.P. and the O.R. & N., he presided over the Oregon & Transcontinental Company, incorporated in June 1881 as an institutionalized successor to the "blind pool" mechanism. "Sort of a company within a company," the O. & T. funded construction of feeder lines and held the majority interest in both railroads. Villard thereby consolidated management and fortified himself against the sort of stockholder challenge that had befallen Billings. The O. & T. was a "master stroke of…financial genius," said a contemporary student of American business, providing "the delicate machinery by which all may be operated as parts of a greater system." Another "Villard"—Wall Street's informal designation for the several concerns—the Oregon Improvement Company, served as "hand-maid," developing land and mineral resources and running, where convenient, trains and steamers. For detailed information as to the value of his holdings, present and prospective, Villard established the Northern Transcontinental Survey, an ambitiously mounted and lavishly financed scientific exploration of western America.[13]

Except among a few eccentric journalists, Henry Villard was, for obvious reasons of local economic necessity, transformed overnight into Washington's first citizen. Newspapers published fawning accounts of the great man's "Napoleonic" genius and "Herculean" labors. Though of average height, in early middle age and portly enough to fit contemporary mogul standards, he possessed "a constitution of iron" and was "more thoroughly informed as to this whole country than any man in it." Unassuming in demeanor, eloquent in barely accented English, devoted to his children and even indifferent to money, Villard was "one man in a million." "It is Villard done this, and Villard done that, and Villard is going to do something else," one editor quipped of the attention expended upon the railroad baron. Playing to his role in the headlines, Villard adopted the selfless demeanor of a prime regional philanthropist. When the University of Washington, for instance, threatened to close its doors forever, he saved the cash-poor institution with a $4,000 grant.[14]

On tour with an expensive entourage of investors and demanding European nobles—one English lord insisted upon a private railroad car—Villard was deliberately accorded the sort of treatment normally reserved for the president of the United States. The N.P. chief executive had more to give, and more to withhold, than any government official, no matter how exalted. "It is not too much to say," a Seattle newspaper noted on the eve of one semi-royal visitation, "that impressions of our city and its surrounding resources will have a direct and important effect upon our immediate future." When the Northern Pacific decided against building into Walla Walla, crestfallen residents blamed a local hotel owner for providing Villard with inferior accommodations.[15]

Neglectful hotelkeeping aside, Walla Wallans actually did their best to entertain the distinguished guest. In April 1883, twelve hundred people and a military band greeted Villard, marching from the depot to the courthouse, where the N.P. president delivered an oration from the judge's bench. The people of Spokane Falls decorated the business district, including all six floors of the largest flourmill, and waited for hours beside the tracks for the delayed arrival of

Villard's special train. Planning for a September 1883 visit, the Seattle city council appropriated $3,000 to clean streets and fetid alleyways. Private citizens erected a pavilion on the university campus and purchased souvenirs to be given the visitors. The donated food, including five oxen, ten sheep, five hundred barrels of clams and a hundred pounds of coffee, appeared sufficient to stuff thousands of persons beyond the point of duly-impressed stupefaction.[16]

From long personal habit, Villard spoke bluntly—the onetime Civil War correspondent was widely conceded to be "frankness personified"—regarding the railways and the Pacific Northwest. Denouncing all forms of "prejudice against corporations," he insisted that monopoly was good. Advancing a "bold theory," Villard contended that the public benefited, to an even greater extent than the investor did, from centralized capital. Only the Northern Pacific and the O.R. & N., jointly managed under the Oregon & Transcontinental, could borrow enough money to build nationwide, or even regional, transportation projects in advance of revenue-producing settlement. "The fact that I represent…a great concentrated power," Villard informed a Seattle audience in April 1883, was the primary reason for "the material development that you see here and everywhere else on Puget Sound."[17]

Villard's "great desideratum" mandated completion of the N.P. mainline "just as fast as it can be done." The 1873 bankruptcy was, in his view, caused by "the folly of Jay Cooke in attempting to build the road in detached sections." Unable to run trains direct from Lake Superior to the coast, Cooke failed, inevitably, to generate the earnings needed to pay off loans and finance new construction. "The Northern Pacific must be built…on through business at first," Villard proclaimed. A completed transcontinental railroad, as here conceived, included the already existing connection with the O.R. & N. at Wallula. West of the Cascades, Villard intended, for the time being, to build between Portland and Kalama and between Tacoma and Seattle.[18]

Although pro-Cascade branch public opinion on the Sound was, to a considerable extent, mollified, Villard's strategy had negative consequences for Washington Territory. The paramount need to focus spending upon the mainline rationalized the abandonment of plans devised by Billings for commencement of work on the mountain crossing. Denying any intention of "trying to make the tail wag the dog," Villard nonetheless managed the Northern Pacific so as to fortify the O.R. & N. and the region's traditional business center. "There was a determined effort resolved upon by the former management…," he explained in an October 1881 Portland speech, "to disregard the Columbia River, to disregard the great commerce of this city, and to make direct for Puget Sound." The new regime had different ideas: "I mean that Portland will always remain the…emporium of the Northwest." To be sure, the necessity of building across the Cascades remained a long-range reality, as the only means of preempting competition. Portland capitalists, though, ought to take advantage of the delay by placing mercantile establishments and warehouses on the inland sea. "Take possession of [the] Puget Sound towns," Villard advised, "or such of them as are best adapted to shipping grain or other products of the country."[19]

Direct in action and speech, Villard hurried construction forward, applying a formula of five dollars in expenditure for each dollar of current revenue. The first Northern Pacific passenger train entered Spokane Falls on June 15, 1881, at 7:14 in the evening. South of the Snake, completion of the O.R. & N. Dalles-Wallula river railroad preceded Villard's takeover of the N.P. The impact upon regional travel was startling. "If a man has business in Portland…," *Walla Walla Union* editor P. B. Johnson wrote in the summer of 1881, "he puts on a clean collar, thrusts a tooth brush in his pocket, kisses the wife…and entering the sleeping-car at the depot, goes to bed…and wakes the next morning at The Dalles in time to take the seven-o'clock boat." Downstream and back, sixty hours sufficed for completion of a mercantile trip to western Oregon. The only hazard came from sand, drifting across the tracks and threatening derailment.[20]

Begun early in the Billings-Villard struggle, the O.R. & N. line between The Dalles and Portland was a construction nightmare. "No other railroad in the United States," one observer noted, "presents in forty-six continuous miles…like engineering difficulties." Running just above high water mark, the grade was "a succession of curves," without a mile of straight track anywhere on the route. Four thousand workers spent more than a year excavating the road by hand—there was too little space for horses or machinery—"over, in, and through basalt cliffs soaring directly out of the Columbia." The gorge was finally opened to through railroading in June 1882. The remainder of the line into Portland was completed by October. Another new era opened, eastbound passengers boarding on the Willamette at breakfast and disembarking fourteen hours later in Walla Walla in time for a late supper. The O.R. & N. removed the last regularly scheduled steamers from the Columbia, sending some vessels to the "Boneyard" and running the best craft through the rapids at high water for service elsewhere in the Pacific Northwest.[21]

Upriver from Portland, the interior was well on the way, one writer noted, to "being honeycombed" with rail lines. Accelerating an ongoing process, Henry Villard intended, said a Spokane newspaper, to "supply every valley in Eastern Washington with a railroad." The O.R. & N. switched from narrow to standard gauge track in the Walla Walla Valley, facilitating direct traffic to and from western Oregon. The firm also pushed its valley feeders to completion, laying rails to Dayton and to Grange City and Texas Rapids by early 1882. Despite the steep grade out of the Snake River canyon, plus the danger of colliding with cattle on the right-of-way, the railroad was yet another component of the regional transportation makeover. Henceforth, regular commercial boat traffic on the Snake was restricted to the stretch of river between Texas Ferry and Lewiston. Meanwhile, the O.R. & N. advanced south across the Oregon line, heading, according to present plans, toward Pendleton and Baker City.[22]

North of the Snake, the O.R. & N. originally contemplated an extension from Riparia, on the right bank opposite Grange City, to Colfax, connecting the Palouse with Walla Walla and Portland. Haggling among homesteaders intent upon profiting from sale of the right-of-way delayed construction. Concerned engineers, in any event, worried over the heavy grades encountered on the far side of the Snake. The practical union between the company and the Northern Pacific encouraged a change in plan. The reconceived railroad ran east from Palouse Junction on the N.P. mainline, with Colfax the immediate and the Idaho border the long-term objective. Partially completed by the summer of 1883, the Palouse branch drew intense scrutiny from interests concerned with commercial development east of the Cascades. Walla Walla, in particular, was threatened by the loss of direct access to the country beyond the river. "The round about connection via Wallula Junction, Ainsworth and the Palouse Branch," the *Union* complained, forced local merchants to undertake a "journey around three sides of a large parallelogram" and amounted to "a practical embargo on our trade in that direction."[23]

Villard moved forward west, as well as east, of the mountains. Upon completion of the Dalles-Cascades line, a thousand workers transferred from O.R. & N. employment to work on the Northern Pacific connection between Portland and the old Puget Sound branch. The route followed the Oregon bank of the Columbia, due to the shorter distance and the necessity of eventually building only one bridge—at a river crossing planned for a point two-and-a-half miles below Kalama. Finished in early 1883, the road united the two sections of Washington Territory, albeit, as one newspaper noted in stressing the arrangement's less-than-ideal nature, "by the round-about way of Portland." Passengers paid nine dollars to ride from the Willamette to Tacoma and back. For an additional sixty cents, through travelers sailed from Commencement Bay to Seattle aboard a Villard-owned steamer.[24]

Prior to the Watson Squire sale, Elliott Bay residents expected their home-made Seattle & Walla Walla to build across Snoqualmie Pass. Afterward, Seattle-ites convinced themselves that Henry Villard shared the faith in a crossing to eastern Washington. "It cannot be possible," the *Intelligencer* affirmed in August 1881, "that one or more lines of railroad will not be scaling the Cascade Mountains ere another twelvemonth has passed." Although the Seattle & Walla Walla was renamed the Columbia & Puget Sound, local boosters failed to appreciate the significance of the change. After all, Villard had "invested something like a million dollars here," a sum of money locally understood as a sure indicator of personal preference.[25]

Final selection of the N.P. terminus—termed "the celebrated Christmas present" by one journalist—remained an open question, at least outside New Tacoma. Broadcasting this cardinal tenet, Seattle belittled the pre-Villard management at every opportunity. "The railroad was made subservient...to the land company," its true welfare ruined to advance inner circle speculators. Seattle's claims, Tacoma papers responded, had "no greater substance than moonshine." Yes, the *Ledger* conceded, Villard's Elliott Bay investments were heavy. He was, however, merely "looking for profit, as other business men do, and could be counted upon to follow his own interests." Those interests dictated a continuing allegiance to Commencement Bay, the obvious focal point of N.P. developmental efforts. In a retirement interview, John Ainsworth pointed out that the railroad, as half-owner of the townsite, was "inseparably wedded to New Tacoma as against any other point." Agreeing with the captain, Northern Pacific managers correctly proclaimed that their firm had never spent a dollar in Seattle, since Villard's expenditures were made through the O. & T. and the Oregon Improvement Company.[26]

A friend to Seattle only to the extent that he sought full exploitation of the coal fields, Villard intended to both forestall competitors and postpone, as long as possible, the Cascade branch. Switching the Columbia & Puget Sound from narrow to standard gauge, the supposed community benefactor convinced townspeople that the line might still be extended across the mountains. Promising to build Seattle's second railroad, between Elliott Bay and Tacoma—provided property owners donated a waterfront right-of-way—Villard insisted that the project made an immediate direct eastern-western Washington connection unnecessary. Fortifying this contention, he promised Seattle the same passenger and freight rates charged Portland by the Northern Pacific.[27]

Several factors combined to produce the renewal of actual railroad work tributary to Elliott Bay. Concerned over declining coal quality at Newcastle, the Oregon Improvement Company promoted extension of the Columbia & Puget Sound from Renton at the south end of Lake Washington to veins in the Cedar and Green River valleys. P. B. Cornwall, the San Francisco owner of the defunct Bellingham Bay mine, intended to develop investments along the proposed route at Black Diamond. Ignoring ample evidence that the Columbia & Puget Sound was "merely…a local road for transportation of coal," Seattle citizens convinced themselves that the O.I.C. project provided another cross-Cascades option. Town residents pledged $150,000—Arthur Denny and Henry Yesler subscribed $10,000 apiece—in May 1883 to finance construction. With Cornwall's contribution also in hand, work began on twenty-six miles of track.[28]

Expecting to continue on beyond this point, local leaders organized the Seattle, Walla Walla & Baker City Railroad, a reformulated version of their old pet enterprise. Henry Yesler, Judge Thomas Burke, former territorial secretary Henry Struve and others in the management expected to eventually link up with the Union Pacific system in eastern Oregon. "This time," said Burke, "I think there will be no failure." Claiming, falsely, to have enough money committed to lay track "into the country east of the mountains," the firm promised to construct eighty miles in 1883 alone. For the moment, however, the project stalled upon a fundamental concern. If the Northern Pacific could not, at present, afford to construct its Cascade branch, what realistic hope did the Elliott Bay interests have of accomplishing the task? Once the N.P. crossed from eastern to western Washington, a locally managed rival would be at a considerable, and presumably fatal, competitive disadvantage. Bemused critics also pointed out that the proposed west-to-east line apparently contradicted Seattle's self-promoted claim of being the principal terminus for current north-south arrangements.[29]

Building only those roads that he wished to undertake, Henry Villard was, in carefully concealed truth, the principal enemy of the Seattle, Walla Walla & Baker City. Launched in August 1882, his Puget Sound Shore Railroad diverted local attention to the impending connection with Tacoma and Portland. The line ran from Black River Junction on the Newcastle coal road to Stuck Junction, a point seven-and-a-half miles away, by a new N.P. branch from the main Commencement Bay-Wilkeson route. Covering twenty-one miles, the project was, in railway slang, "a big little job" on account of the flood danger in a valley bottom drained by several streams. Altogether, five miles of trestle and four bridges were required. Through sustained work, the road was substantially completed and ready for traffic by the end of 1883.[30]

Constructed without company-owned linkages to tidewater on either the north or the south, the Puget Sound Shore nonetheless fortified local terminus claims. "It will…connect Seattle with the line of the Northern Pacific," asserted the *Seattle Post-Intelligencer*, a recent newspaper merger product immediately dubbed the *P-I*, "and will make this city the extreme northwest terminal point of the vast railroad system of the United States." The hilarity generated by such off-the-mark pronouncements was by no means restricted just to Tacoma. The Puget Sound Shore, many editors pointed out, was an Oregon & Transcontinental undertaking, with no actual N.P. involvement. By true right, Seattle was end-of-track only for the coal railroad, operated by another Villard creation, the Oregon Improvement Company. "We fear Seattle is inflated," the *Olympia Transcript* noted, "and if the bubble ever bursts, somebody will get hurt."[31]

◈◈◈◈◈

In one significant sense, transcontinental railroading made Washington Territory part of the American nation. To enhance the efficient scheduling of cross-country trains, railway companies divided the United States into the four standard time zones soon taken for granted in day-to-day life. The Northern Pacific officially instituted the system in the Pacific Northwest at noon on December 16, 1883. Most Oregon and Washington clocks, previously set in haphazard fashion according to local custom, were at that precise moment shifted ahead eleven minutes. This "remarkable revolution," the *Tacoma Ledger* observed, was "effected so suddenly and with so little public agitation that people scarcely realize as yet the boldness and the sweeping character of the innovation."[32]

Efficiency was hardly encouraged by reliance upon a transportation line following the Columbia River through Portland before reaching Puget Sound via the Cowlitz corridor. "The people of Washington Territory…," complained the *Seattle P-I* of a separation too-long endured, "are almost strangers." An immigrant from Indiana discovered that the principal territorial divisions might as well be "a thousand miles apart." Despite "reciprocal, complementary" interests in the exchange of lumber and coal for wheat and flour, western and eastern Washington were unable to properly exploit a common sense relationship. "We have a little trade between the two sections," a Yakima City newspaper stated in April 1883, "but it is carried on at enormous expense, and is not one-hundredth part what we would have were there direct communication." The only time he left Washington, reported Eugene Semple, the next-to-last territorial governor, was when traveling to and from the interior, official trips requiring an inconvenient detour through Oregon.[33]

Once again, the main opposition to a union of eastern and western Washington came from the Willamette metropolis. "As in the olden time 'all roads led to Rome,'" noted the Olympia *Courier*, "so in the latter days all roads terminated in Portland." Symbolically concentrating their power, the Villard companies maintained Pacific Northwest headquarters in the city. N.P. and O.R. & N. schedules forced through-travelers to spend a night in local hotels. Portlanders marketed Walla Walla wheat as Oregon grain, Washington lumber as Oregon pine, and Puget Sound fish as Columbia River salmon. The town's toll-assessing mercantile leaders, the *Walla Walla Union* suggested, ought to erect a towering monument to John Ainsworth for subverting the Northern Pacific to the service of Portland.[34]

Mounting a new campaign against Oregon, Washingtonians denounced the N.P.-O.R. & N. alliance as a vain attempt to "override the laws of nature." Enormous winter snowslides cut the Columbia gorge railroad in 1885, 1886 and 1888, halting all traffic between the interior and tidewater. The first and most serious blockade encompassed three weeks. One hundred seventy-five pitiful passengers, subsisting upon "oysters & other luxuries" foraged from the baggage, spent the duration in a snow-covered train west of The Dalles. The lesson, according to Spokane Falls editor Frank Dallam, one of the marooned unfortunates, was clear: "It shows the great necessity of other and better arranged communication with the ocean, and that cannot be secured until the completion of the Cascade division."[35]

A railroad across the mountains also outflanked that longtime obstacle, the Columbia River bar. In their eagerness to focus attention on the legendary obstruction, Oregonians complained, Washington newspapers equated the loss of a single small vessel to "the sinking of a whole fleet of men-of-war." "Every ship master who has crossed the Columbia bar," proclaimed the *Walla Walla Union*, "every ship owner who has suffered the delays incident to crossing that great obstacle…knows that he runs a greater risk of losing life and fortune…than he does in crossing any other bar in the world." Regular reports detailed the wintertime travails of steamers-by-the-dozen anchored inside the mouth "watching for a chance to slip out" and of vessels on the outside "beating about, weatherworn…awaiting a lulling of the tempest to cross in."[36]

In the succinct, albeit mathematically dubious, assessment of Governor William Newell, the Columbia was "frozen over four months of the year, dried up four months, fogged up four months and could hardly be navigated the rest of the year." Waiting for Villard to grasp the logic, if not the arithmetic, Seattle resurrected a Reconstruction era alternative, the Snoqualmie Pass road. The ill-maintained existing route had, in recent years, been utilized only by the annual cattle drive and occasional packer. Completed to Ellensburgh in 1884, the Snoqualmie Pass Trail and Wagon Road was, in comparison to its predecessor, a first class operation. Despite disappointing stock subscriptions and the lack of governmental aid, private investors built twenty-five bridges and fourteen relay stations, laid corduroy rails where appropriate and blasted a passage-way out of a cliff above Lake Keechelus. Travelers paid $2 for horse and rider, $3.50 per wagon and yoke of oxen and 50 cents a head for cattle. Until construction of the Cascade branch, the *P-I* announced, "this new road…will render the settlers…absolutely independent of the Oregon Railway and Navigation Company and the Northern Pacific Railroad."[37]

Trains, rather than wagons, of course had to cross the Cascades before any meaningful shift from the Columbia River became practicable. By far the most "eagerly watched" N.P. alternative, the Oregon Short Line, reflected Jay Gould's determination to provide the Union Pacific with a company-owned outlet to the sea. As of January 1883, the O.S.L. ran from Granger, Wyoming, on the U.P. mainline, to Pocatello, Idaho, a distance of over three hundred miles. A further two hundred miles was graded through the valley of the Snake to a point opposite Huntington, Oregon, at the mouth of the Burnt River. Field survey activities indicated, to most observers, a plan to continue construction across northeastern Oregon or down the Snake to Lewiston. The ultimate destination, Puget Sound, appeared self-evident to commentators not under the influence of Portland. "The Oregon Short Line…is heading straight for Seattle," the *P-I* broadcast, "and coming at a gait that will bring it into our limits certainly within two years." Whatcom, just beginning to prosper from agricultural settlement on the northern Sound, filed a strong counterclaim to the Gould terminus. Whatever the outcome, Washingtonians expected the Short Line to be first over the Cascades, firmly established as Villard's "great rival."[38]

Territorial residents celebrated a premature end-run around Portland. A January 1883 agreement between the Northern Pacific and the Union Pacific divided territory, pooled business at common points and, in the original published terms, established a Montana alliance between the N.P. and the Utah Northern, another U.P. subsidiary. Rumors that the accord required the Oregon

Short Line to halt construction after bridging the Snake at Huntington were confirmed in March. Already building southeast of Pendleton, the O.R. & N. continued past Baker to a union with the O.S.L. Interests desiring to ship to and from Puget Sound denounced Portland's second transcontinental line, opened to through traffic in December 1884. "Another great railroad conspiracy on Wall Street," the *Yakima Signal* charged, had caused the Short Line to be "'snuffed out'…by the Columbia river gang." The people of Washington Territory, the *Walla Walla Union* contended, were thereby "made the bond servants of the Northern Pacific…for years to come."[39]

Henry Villard, of course, placed little faith in the word of Jay Gould, a mogul on record as believing that "agreements between…companies are made to be broken." Gould, he fully expected, would resume construction at the earliest opportune moment, in the direction of Puget Sound, threatening the Northern Pacific with the loss of the best mountain crossings, a substantial portion of its land grant and the dominant position in regional trade. Checking a dangerous rival at the Snake, Villard activated the Cascade branch, or division, as a preemptive stroke against the Oregon Short Line. The project had the happy side-effect of actually benefiting Portland in the short-term, since the advancing tracks provided, at least until one of the passes was actually crossed, a much-improved Oregon outlet for the commercial needs of a growing Washington region.[40]

So far as most settlers of the early 1880s were concerned, the great valley of the Yakima River was largely stock-raising country. An expanding population east and west of the Cascades, not to mention the demands of railroad construction crews, made for generally high profits. Ranging between $15 and $22 a head, beef prices "as good as gold" made for wealthy, or at least near-wealthy, ranchers. Harsh weather, however, was a regular feature of life between the mountains and the Columbia, making the industry an unattractive long-term proposition. "The cattle are by no means as numerous on the range as they were previous to the hard winter of 1881," a newspaper reported of the 1883 roundup. "A circuit in which would then have been found as many as eighty thousand head does not now embrace as many as twenty thousand." Most observers agreed on the necessity for a shift to agriculture. The soil, from two to twenty feet deep in most locations, was good and the irrigation potential considerable. Provided with water, a Villard investigator advised, "almost the entire area…is adapted to almost any crop the climate will permit of being grown." The quarter million bushel 1880-grain harvest suggested the rate of return to be expected once farmers were in contact with outside markets.[41]

Writing from Yakima in March 1882, a settler summed up the central obstacle to regional development: "It is impossible to get the products of the country to a point where they will command money." The Dalles route, exploited to the utmost practicable extent, was difficult, expensive and frequently closed in winter. Running steamers to the foot of Priest Rapids, the O.R. & N. established a warehouse at "Grainville." Central valley producers, however, had to pay even higher freight charges to the landing. The new outlet was of practical value only to homesteaders in the Kittitas region. Opening a road to the river from Ellensburgh, local farmers complained over the irregular scheduling of boats. Few people mourned when a December 1883 windstorm blew Grainville into the Columbia.[42]

Anticipating the Northern Pacific, settlers entered the Yakima Valley in ever-increasing numbers. Excavation began for the Naches-Cowiche ditch west of the Yakima River and the Moxee development on the east, the largest irrigation projects yet undertaken. Growth was especially dramatic in the Kittitas section, among the well-watered foothills of the Teanaway River drainage. "Several thousand acres of agricultural lands have been located...during the present season," a correspondent reported in the summer of 1883. Villard's men discovered coal deposits near Cle Elum, east of Snoqualmie Pass and a few miles from the projected N.P. line. Ellensburgh, the principal supply point for prospectors and farmers, replaced Yakima City as the regional population center.[43]

Starting work, for apparently sound reasons, in the Yakima Valley—the first contract was let in the spring of 1883—Villard compromised his immediate personal prospects. Already, the cost of completing the mainline from Lake Superior to the Columbia River had soared to $39.6 million, double the estimate of 1880. The Cascade division, requiring an expensive tunnel, figured to absorb at least an additional $6 million. Privately, N.P. investors complained of accelerating debt, extravagant expenditures and one-man mismanagement. "It was impossible," Villard himself confessed, "to give each of the corporations that executive care called for in justice to the interests of their stockholders." Personally resolving disputes between the various interconnected firms, he was compelled to act "so to speak, on both sides," with obvious baneful consequences for sound decision-making. Beginning in late summer 1883, the "Villard" securities—previously considered "the safest...property listed on the New York Stock Exchange"—dropped in value, by a combined $20 million as of mid-October.[44]

Conceived as a grand celebration of transportation brilliance, the Northern Pacific "golden spike" ceremony became, instead, a dramatic, if momentarily concealed, manifestation of the company crisis. In a final exercise of fiscal grandiosity, Villard spent $600,000 hauling investors, celebrities-for-hire and minor dignitaries, Arthur Denny and a party of Seattleites included, to the western Montana site in September 1883. The route taken followed the Pend Oreille division from Ainsworth, a line constructed solely to get from Point A to Point B at the least possible expense. Missing the rich wheat-producing hills of the Palouse, just to the east, representatives of Atlantic coast and European financial houses saw only the dreariest landscape imaginable, creating negative impressions bound to be telling the next time Villard called for money. Hailing the inauguration of communications with the East, an Olympia newspaper compared "the formal opening of the Northern Pacific" to "the discovery of a new world."

Washingtonians rightly pointed out, however, that the transcontinental connection was far from truly completed. Ceremonial spikes and ostentatious gatherings aside, the road at present ended "in a sand-hill at Wallula," depending upon the O.R. & N. beyond that remote point.[45]

Returning from his scene of imperfect triumph, Villard was immediately challenged for control of the affiliated companies. Denying any concern "with regard to the magnitude of the floating debt," Charles B. Wright, president of the Tacoma Land Company and stockholder critic of the pro-Portland policy, demanded "the economical management of the road in the future." Villard emerged victorious from the initial board of directors confrontation. The Northern Pacific, however, desperately needed to borrow $20 million, a loan that required the approval of the Wright faction. Several weeks of intense negotiation culminated in mid-December with Villard's resignation from the Oregon & Transcontinental and the O.R. & N. Pleading exhaustion, he surrendered the N.P. presidency in the first week of January 1884. Declining to officially succeed Villard in office, Wright now held, through his own holdings and those of friends, the dominant position in the railroad.[46]

Unable, still, to fathom their erstwhile hero's motivations, Seattleites mourned the loss of a local benefactor. "Mr. Villard has…endeared himself to the people of this city," the *P-I* asserted in condemning the "wreckers and stock gamblers" responsible for his downfall. Elsewhere, territorial opinion took a contrary slant, fully expressed without fear of retribution from a defanged champion of outsider interests. Newspapers detailed Villard's supposed shortcomings and mistakes. Compelled, for two years and more, to restrain a sense of victimization, Tacomans were especially elated. Villard had "swallowed up" the Northern Pacific, claimed the *Tacoma News*, making it "an appendage to the Oregon traffic system." Newly vocal enemies east and west of the Cascades cited the dramatic upswing in "Villard" stock prices as confirmation of the after-the-fact accusations of arrogance, incompetence and favoritism.[47]

Henry Villard was "dead and buried," the *Tacoma Ledger* happily proclaimed, but the consequences of his demise were substantial. Pending final negotiation of the vital $20 million loan, Charles Wright instituted strict top-to-bottom economies. Construction projects, including the Cascade division, were immediately shut down. The normally bustling Tacoma railroad shops curtailed repair and maintenance work. The edict even extended, critics of false economizing gestures contended, to removal of lights from railway switches. The suspensions, Wright promised, were "only temporary," a truthful pledge providing modest solace to laborers discharged in mid-winter without advance notice or the means of sustaining their families.[48]

Disentangling Villard's companies one from another, the new regime faced "complications and embarrassments" in most, if not all, areas of operation. "There are said to be some places where it is a lucky child who knows his own father," the *Legder* reflected of the organizational mess left behind. "Surely, for the last two or three years he was a lucky employee…who knew which of half a dozen corporations he was working for." After financing regional O. & T. and Transcontinental Survey activities, the Oregon Improvement Company failed in attempts to collect reimbursement from those no-longer affiliated concerns. The O.I.C. had also been responsible for developing coal properties on Puget Sound. A bitter dispute with the Northern Pacific developed when the latter firm claimed possession of veins tributary to Commencement Bay. The N.P., meanwhile, charged Oregon Improvement $8,000 for unspecified services performed in the past by the transcontinental line. Pleading "the depressed condition of our business," the O.R. & N. refused to continue paying its allotted share of expenses incurred by the Northern Pacific immigration bureau. Unable to commence operations due to confusion over which of the companies was responsible for management, the recently completed Puget Sound Shore railway earned instant, and infamous, fame as the "Orphan Road."[49]

Judge Thomas Burke's initial announcement that "Villard's downfall has produced…no visible effect" upon Seattle was invalidated by the subsequent course of events. Within weeks, the Tacoma Land Company faction's victory was reflected in depressed real estate values and business activity on Elliott Bay. "People grasp their money very tightly now days," Burke reported in April 1884, "and are slow to buy property of any kind." Renewed interest, once the Puget Sound Shore proved a non-starter, in the Seattle, Walla Walla & Baker City project faltered upon the lack of funding for construction. With the $150,000 coal railroad subsidy due for collection in 1884, most subscribers declined to honor their pledges. John Howard, the San Francisco-based manager of the Oregon Improvement Company, was at first philosophical regarding his inability to collect: "They would gladly give me the money but most of them have overspeculated in real estate, and haven't it to put up." As the weeks passed, however, Howard was increasingly exasperated by the defaulters. "Very few of these people," he fumed of the Seattleites, "have done their whole duty." In defense of non-compliance, local leaders insisted that the O.I.C. had reneged upon undocumented promises to transform the coal line into a cross-mountain railroad.[50]

Looking toward "a radically different policy," Spokane Falls editor H. T. Cowley pointed out that, post-Villard, "the Northern Pacific will stand out more distinctly…and find its own way to the Sound, through the Cascade mountains." Across the territory, observers agreed that the N.P. was virtually "compelled" by new circumstances, namely separation from the O.R. & N., to build from eastern to western Washington. The line could never claim true transcontinental status, or be a consistently viable business, while dependent for access to tidewater upon a rival, and potentially unfriendly, concern. One last time, the terminal passion beset Puget Sound—"like Banquo's ghost," a humorist said, the ancient issue "will not down"—with Olympia joining Seattle, Whatcom and Port Townsend in extending welcome arms to the Northern Pacific.[51] The Tacoma Land Company ascendancy guaranteed, however, that the Cascade division would, in addition to being constructed in the shortest possible time, have the same destination determined upon eleven years earlier, Commencement Bay.

Selection of the superior mountain crossing was the crucial component in Cascade division construction planning. Snoqualmie Pass generally received top ranking in terms of lowest elevation and least snowfall, but was disqualified because of the historical and geographical connection with Seattle. The choice, instead, was between Stampede Pass, east of Tacoma, or Naches Pass to the southeast. The final determination, noted one analyst, was "a question mainly of expenditure." East and west of the mountains, the natural approach to Naches Pass followed a favorable grade. Construction of a long tunnel beneath Stampede Pass, on the other hand, allowed for a lower overall gradient by that route. Engineering and cost considerations, together calculated, produced a November 1882 verdict in favor of the Stampede Pass option.[52]

Shifting focus from Portland to Tacoma, Villard's successors intended to open the direct line at the earliest possible moment. New contracts, calling for simultaneous construction on both the east and the west sides of the mountains, were issued in February 1884. On the western portion of the route, the N.P. persuaded federal authorities, over protests from Seattle, to approve the Wilkeson coal road as the Cascade division mainline. Two dozen miles remained to be built, from Puyallup through the narrow gorge of the upper Green River. The work, though, was difficult, involving removal of extensive forest cover, erection of trestles and bridges and drilling of two tunnels.[53]

On the eastern side of Stampede Pass, one hundred and seventy-seven miles intervened between Pasco, the new railroad boomtown at the mouth of the Snake, and the summit. Except for rock cutting in the Yakima River canyon above the central valley, the route, wrote Eugene Smalley of the railroad-subsidized *Northwest* magazine, "was as easy to build across as a prairie." The main difficulties were certainly outside the technical engineering sphere. "The sage brush is very thick," an N.P. official reported, "and the weather is very hot and the water is very scarce." Overcoming thirst and perspiration, workers laid track as far as Ellensburgh, two-thirds of the way to the pass, by early 1885.[54]

Real estate developments preoccupied Northern Pacific management as work proceeded up the valley. The line necessarily passed through Yakima City, the longtime county seat and home to five hundred residents, at the mouth of Ahtanum Creek. Aside from the courthouse, the community's wooden buildings, including two schools and a bank, were considered "very inferior in character" by outsiders. The railroad briefly negotiated with the inhabitants, looking to the usual grant of substantial acreage and other material favors. When these efforts stalled, the N.P. dismissed the town as "badly located." Yakima, supposedly, was built upon swampy ground, subject to flooding and too close for comfort to the Yakima Indian reservation.[55]

Strangely, the same objections did not apply to the railroad's preferred choice, only three-and-a-half miles north near the juncture of the Naches and Yakima rivers. The firm owned over seven hundred acres at the site and expected the owners of the adjoining thousand acres to donate half their holdings. "The half interest they *retain*...," N.P. land department commissioner Charles Lamborn noted of the inducement represented by a new urban development, "will be rendered 10 times as valuable as the *whole* would otherwise have been." The board of directors officially founded North Yakima in November 1884. Public opinion, near and far, immediately denounced the unwarranted bypassing of Yakima City. "The grasping and overreaching nature of a great corporation was never better illustrated," charged a typical condemnatory editorial. Led by their good ministers, the reverends Flint and Dixon, Yakima residents filed a lawsuit and declared a boycott of those business establishments contemplating relocation.[56]

For a moment, Yakima's resistance encouraged visions of a repeat "story of St. Paul and Minneapolis...in that promising domain." The railroad, though, offered to pay the cost of moving buildings to the new site. Providing free lots and other favors to churches—Flint and Dixon quickly abandoned their principles—and key merchants, the N.P. undermined the opposition. Considerable care was taken, meanwhile, to lay out an attractive city. Extra-wide streets were planted with shade trees. A ditch from the Naches supplied water for irrigation and domestic consumption. Anticipating a long-term eastward shift in Washington's population base, railroad planners set aside acreage for a territorial or state capitol building and other governmental structures. "One thing is sure," a pleased executive commented, "North Yakima will be recognized before long as the handsomest town in Washington Territory, and a model town in almost every respect."[57]

Most of Yakima City moved to North Yakima in early 1885. Straining twenty-mule teams slowly hauled frame structures, cut into sections where necessary and placed upon rollers, across the prairie. The principal hotel "was taken without interruption of its...traffic," reported an astounded eyewitness. "Meals were cooked and all the work...discharged while the building was in motion, the boarders eating and sleeping in the building continuously." The town banker maintained regular business hours during the ten days required to shift his operation, vault and all, from the old to the new site. Forestalling any possibility of a reoccupation of rival developers, the railroad dismantled all remaining houses at the mouth of the Ahtanum. "It looks like a town struck by a clyclone [sic] that has carried the building[s] away," advised the resident N.P. agent, "and dropped a plank here and a plank there."[58]

Enriching the Northern Pacific, North Yakima was a real estate byproduct of the principal engineering matter at hand, getting the Cascade line over the mountains. The Stampede Pass tunnel, with an estimated $2.4 million pricetag, was both an expensive and a time-consuming project. "The work…will require in the neighborhood of two years," the *Tacoma Ledger* lamented, "during which time…you have over 200 miles of railroad…nearly if not quite productive, except [for] the last twenty-five miles." If this so-near-yet-so-far gap could be closed while the tunnel was under construction, the newspaper pointed out, "two wheat crops" might be shipped to "the sea-board," earning substantial profit and speeding unification of the territory. Devised by N.P. chief engineer Adna Anderson, the $300,000 solution ranked, according to one observer, with the Seven Wonders of the Ancient World and the Great Wall of China.[59]

Literally scaling a cliff, the Northern Pacific Switchback was akin, said an early passenger, to "climbing Jack's bean-stalk." The engineering problem—how to ascend, in under two miles, approximately eleven hundred feet above the tunnel's elevation—was, if mind teasing, at least straightforward. Anderson's workers cut five tiers into the mountainside, three west of the summit and two on the east, shoring up the hanging roadbeds with stone embankments. Once the system went into operation, crews attached "decapods"—the most powerful locomotives in the world weighing over a hundred tons apiece, with five drive wheels on each side—to the front and rear of a train. Upon reaching the initial switch, the engineer reversed course, after carefully inspecting brakes and other vital parts, backing to the next change-of-direction point. "Thus, in a zig-zag way…," as one travel account described the process, "gaining in height with every switch, until the summit is reached." The transit covered seven miles, all told, at an average speed of four miles an hour. Experienced from the plush comfort of a Pullman car, the Switchback was a nineteenth-century amusement park ride, with no extra charge to ticketholders. "Jules Verne's alleged trip to the moon," a Tacoman exulted, "or a tour among the clouds in a balloon is not more thrilling."[60]

On Wednesday, June 1, 1887, at two minutes past six in the evening, the last spike was driven on the Switchback, precisely seventy-eight miles east of Tacoma. "It was a strictly business proceeding," the *Ledger* recounted, in stark honest American contrast to the silly 1883 display orchestrated by Henry Villard in Montana. "There was no pomp," the paper's on-the-scene account reiterated, "no blare of trumpets, no glitter of gorgeous palace coaches, no imported aristocracy, no flowing of wine or great banquet, and no high-sounding speeches." Nothing, in fact, but the noble sweat of labor and the ringing sound of hammers striking upon hardened metal. The *Ledger* possibly exaggerated in hailing "the laying of the last rail on the summit of the Cascade mountains" as "the greatest event in the history…of the entire Pacific northwest." Regional transportation patterns, however, were immediately turned upside down. The N.P. mainline, entirely independent of the O.R. & N., ran henceforth up the Yakima Valley to and across Stampede Pass. Through passengers to and from Portland changed cars at Commencement Bay.[61]

Arriving in Tacoma at 7:15 P.M. on July 3, the first train from St. Paul ignited, one day early, an Independence Day "pageant of patriotism." Townspeople and visitors—six thousand individuals in the lowest crowd estimate—cheered from the hills as the thirteen cars came to a halt at the N.P. depot. Cannon roared, bells rang and, somewhat incongruously given the Fourth of July theatrics, a British warship anchored in the bay fired repeated salutes. Formed into five divisions, a parade advanced beneath "a forest of flags and cedar boughs" to a platform erected above the summer-sparkling waters of the Sound. Newspaper reports captured the essence, if not the exact words, of the remarks delivered by the assigned orators. "Now comes the Northern Pacific railway like another 'Mayflower,'" the *Ledger* pronounced, "bringing the germs of civilization in its path." America's railroad, "conquering the mountain barriers" at long, long last, was ready to transport "masses of mankind to the shores of the Pacific, where soon shall spring up marts of commerce as great as on the Atlantic slope."[62]

Work proceeded upon the definitive means of once and for all crossing the Cascades: the single-track Stampede Pass tunnel, at close to ten thousand feet the second-longest bored in the United States. On the east side, contractor Nelson Bennett's employees hauled heavy equipment, boilers and, for that matter, every supply item from the railhead over a planked trail and then, above the snowline, upon skids. An expensive flume diverted Mosquito Creek, a stream previously dropping in a waterfall directly across the spot selected for the tunnel opening. Shops, bunk and cook houses, and storage facilities were erected in a narrow canyon close by the project. The usual disreputable camp followers arrived, establishing their own private resort, "Tunnel City," a quarter of a mile away. Verminous saloons, brothels and eating places fronted upon a bottomless muddy street strewn with broken bottles, rotting garbage, and, given the consumer advantages of railroad connections, "oyster, sardine and fruit cans."[63]

One hundred and thirteen men, half in and half outside the tunnel, worked at a rate of sixteen feet per ten-hour shift toward an under-the-mountain union. A movable platform, the "go-devil," allowed workers to drill holes, blast rock and remove debris at maximum pace. "It was a novel and almost weird experience," wrote a visitor to the brightly illuminated site buried deep beneath Stampede Pass, "to suddenly emerge upon such a scenery of brilliance and activity…and I felt…much as Rip Van Winkle did, when, in the rocky fastnesses of the Catskills, he encountered the spirits of old Hendrick Hudson and his crew." Heavy timber-work, fixed in place with wedges, supported roof and walls to contract specifications of twenty-two feet in height and sixteen-and-a-half feet in width.[64]

"For the third time," the historian Murray Morgan observes in assessing the May 1888 opening of the Stampede Pass tunnel, "the Northern Pacific had been completed, this time for real." Until the installation of electric lights at the end of the year, passengers sat for nearly two miles "in Egyptian darkness." Otherwise, Washington Territory's long-frustrated railroad, directly connecting the Pacific Northwest with the East and Puget Sound with the great Columbia Basin, was at last fully in bright-as-noon operation. "There remains no obstacle to rapid and economical railway service," Eugene Smalley pointed out. The distance between St. Paul and Tacoma, 2,058 miles by the old O.R. & N. connection, was reduced to 1,941 miles, saving 117 miles on every through shipment. The same reduction applied to eastern Washington freight consigned to points beyond Pasco. The Yakima Valley, in particular, experienced a commercially quickening shift in transportation regime. People and goods bound from North Yakima to the Sound traveled 466 miles by way of Portland under the defunct system. The opposite direction trip via Stampede Pass covered a relatively insignificant 169 miles.[65]

Regardless of personal feelings and past controversies, Washingtonians agreed that the Northern Pacific represented "a monument to the inherent power of Henry Villard." The transcontinental road was bound to be finished someday, no matter which faction or individual ran the company. Sooner or later, no matter what the wishes of Portland, a railroad across the Cascades was sure to be constructed. These were truisms of geography and economics. The mainline was completed at the earliest conceivable date, however, because of the vision, energy and arrogance of a single human being. Villard's willingness to ignore manifest obstacles, to borrow money today in anticipation of the gains, or at least the loans, of tomorrow, provided Washington with a modern transportation network. By 1888, the territory had a thousand miles of track—slightly over six hundred owned by the N.P. system and slightly less than three hundred by the O.R. & N.—a four-fold increase in seven years.[66] Each and every mile facilitated new settlement, new economic development and new eligibility for membership in the American Union.

Eugene Semple. *Washington State University Library, Pullman (85-022)*

Chapter Eight

A Stalwart Young Empire

A stalwart young empire has outgrown the leading strings by which mother Portland has so long held us.—Walla Walla Statesman[1]

O N A BRIGHT JUNE DAY in 1885, Spokane area residents gathered at Waverly, a settlement twenty miles southeast of the Falls on Hangman, or Latah, Creek for the annual county picnic. The homesteaders in attendance dined upon roasted beef and sizzling venison, consumed hard and soft liquid refreshment by the gallon and played catch-as-catch-can baseball and roughhouse hide-and-seek. The main table sagged beneath the weight of a giant cake, the grand prize to be awarded the immigrants from the best-represented state or territory. Late in the afternoon, the judges called the roll, proceeding in alphabetical order. Amidst cheers and good-natured catcalls, Missouri, with seventy native men, women and children on hand, briefly surged to the lead, only to be surpassed by Oregon and its ninety sons and daughters. "But when Washington…was called," a young farm wife reported, "you aught [sic] to have seen the babies held up."[2] Winning by acclamation—the remaining contenders, Wisconsin and Wyoming, obviously had no chance—the infant Washingtonians represented, by their pastry-winning presence, a fundamental demographic fact. Most adults still came from somewhere else, from distant places thought of as home. Their children, in contrast, made up a rising generation born in a time of a rapidly increasing territorial population, forever linked to Washington towns and farms.

Confirming the lesson of Waverly's baked goods competition, Washington's population mounted from 75,000 in 1880 to 357,000 in 1890, an astounding 356 percent increase. Reversing wheat-induced trends of the preceding decade, a shift from east to west and from rural to urban got substantially under way. Seattle, Tacoma and Spokane became, and remained, the premier Washington towns. Walla Walla, for two decades the territorial leader, was by 1888 barely a fourth the size of Seattle. Together, the fast-growing cities on Elliott and Commencement bays had more residents than the combined total for the fifteen biggest communities, Spokane included, on the other side of the Cascades.[3]

Washingtonians boasted, more than ever before, of growth and development on every hand and in every direction. "We are in the enjoyment of an immigration of no mean character," the *Seattle Post-Intelligencer* reported in the spring of 1882. The seasonal settler influx, an eastern Washington newspaper advised later that year, was "without a precedent in the history of any country as difficult of access as this has been." Another observer pointed to a sure sign that a long-postponed future was, finally, on the verge of realization: "The necessity for any more lies being told…for the purpose of stimulating emigration has past [sic]."[4]

Building railroads up the Columbia and the Pend Oreille line to Spokane Falls and beyond, Henry Villard accelerated the pace of immigration. Northern Pacific agents distributed promotional pamphlets—over six hundred thousand copies in 1882 alone—in the East and in Europe and sold cut-rate rail and steamboat tickets. "Every steamer arriving in Portland brings hundreds of people looking for homes…," the Colfax *Gazette* noted, "and the trains…are daily crowded with men, women and children all eager to secure cheap and productive lands in this region." The N.P. dispatched new arrivals direct from Portland to Spokane, where local employees helped find claims, preferably on odd-numbered land grant sections. One way or another, people also made their way to Puget Sound. According to the *P-I*, "not less than one half…and sometimes nearly all" the passengers inbound from California transferred to the cars of the Sound branch at Kalama.[5]

"Thousands of men and women," moreover, waited in the East for final completion of the Northern Pacific, "that they may avoid the tedious and expensive journey by way of San Francisco." Driven in September 1883, Villard's official "golden" spike initiated a period of even greater company support for emigration to the Pacific Northwest. "They have established such low rates on 'emigrant movables,'" the *Walla Walla Union* pointed out, "that it has been possible for a farmer…to move with his family, his farm tools, his household goods, [and] his animals to Eastern Washington for a trifling outlay of money." A St. Paul-to-Spokane Falls ticket cost $42. Ten day layover allowances provided time for thorough investigations of the countryside.[6]

Most immigrants traveling under Northern Pacific auspices went to eastern Washington. Some settled in railroad-promoted communities like Sprague or Cheney. N.P. land policy focused, however, upon the marketing of farm tracts. "The greater the population adjacent to their road," a journalist observed of the firm's interest in building up the country, "the greater is their profits." Although some migrants complained of "pretty high priced" land, the $2.60 per acre originally charged was a reasonable figure. Beginning in 1883, sales were based upon assessed valuation, at a $4 minimum with easy credit terms. The company sold 340,000 acres between Ainsworth and Spokane Falls in 1881 and 145,000 in 1886, reflecting persistent newcomer interest in railroad acreage, regardless of the cost.[7]

According to one informed calculation, "not ten in a hundred of the male-settlers...would be in the country to-day were it not for the Northern Pacific railroad." Federal land, however, was an attractive alternative to acreage from the grant. The government charged $1.25 an acre under the preemption laws, with a six-month residency required. Homestead Act claimants paid nothing, but committed themselves to five years of continuous occupation prior to receipt of title. Although the General Land Office eventually doubled the preemption price on even-numbered sections within "the railway belt," immigrants enjoyed bargain terms. The more expensive tracts were clearly "worth more," due to proximity to transportation and towns. Together, the Colfax and Walla Walla land offices disposed of a half million acres in 1881 and again in 1883. Spokane-based G.L.O. employees transferred 196,000 acres from the public domain to private ownership in 1887 and another 273,000 acres in 1888.[8]

With substantial amounts of money at stake, the Northern Pacific exhibited great care in the administration of its landholdings. Corruption and indifference, on the other hand, allowed individuals to secure substantial public acreage at little or no cost. Reporting in detail from eastern Washington, a General Land Office investigator explained how "the doctor...the lawyer, merchant, editor, saloonkeeper and barber" obtained land courtesy of the federal government. Building "what is called a house, which frequently is 10 x 12 in size" and hiring "from five to ten acres...broken," the "settler" proved residence. At the conclusion of the mandatory waiting period, six months under preemption, the claimant took legal possession, with full title to a farm to be rented out or held for speculative purposes.[9]

Fraud, a readily comprehended means of acquiring land under late nineteenth century standards of private and public morality, had negative consequences for the region. "'There is something rotten in Denmark,'" an east-of-the-mountains observer noted, "and...our actual population is not being adequately augmented, in accordance with the lands filed upon." Thick federal registers and boards-and-nails speculator shacks created the erroneous impression of a filled-up country closed to opportunity-seeking newcomers. "Hardly one acre in fifty...is being put to any use," a Palouse booster complained, "yet the land hunter is sent away." Advising immigrants to recognize the wide-open-spaces reality and contest patently illegal claims, editors insisted that "the amount of good arable land" actually available was "almost beyond the comprehension of one who has not given the subject deep thought."[10]

Until completion of the N.P. branch, the N.P. and the O.R. & N. linked up south of the Snake at Wallula Junction. Passengers slept "as safe," according to an eastbound traveler, "as a letter in the mail-bag" while cars were transferred from one line to another. The Junction itself was little more than a drafty railroad hotel with attached drinking and eating salons. The humorist Bill Nye found "the abomination of desolation" assigned as his room for the night reeking of "plug tobacco and perspiration" and advised that travelers sleep out-of-doors in a snowbank. Although the edifice burned to the ground in January 1886, the Junction continued to demarcate the spheres of rival firms.[11]

During Henry Villard's tenure, the Northern Pacific operated north of the Snake River and the Oregon Railway & Navigation Company, the Palouse branch excepted, to the south. This division of territory remained in effect following the magnate's downfall in 1883. "The further development of each section," the *Walla Walla Union* complained of a continuing monopoly situation, "is made dependent upon the ideas of the managers…controlling its means of transportation." Except for connections between Dayton and Pomeroy and across the Blue Mountains to Pendleton, the O.R. & N. network was largely complete by 1881. Wheat growers above Riparia shipped their entire crop by steamer to that Snake River landing. Ongoing Corps of Engineers efforts kept a navigation channel open in high flow periods. As the water fell, however, so too did the river's grain-carrying capacity.[12]

Shippers allied, by distant corporate fiat, to the O.R. & N. found themselves at a distinct and increasing disadvantage to better-situated competitors. The charge for transporting wheat by river and rail to Portland, 39 cents a bushel in 1881, represented two-fifths of the entire freight cost between Lewiston and Liverpool. The company, moreover, failed to efficiently handle the mounting production from its captive territory. At the close of the 1881 season, over thirty thousand tons of grain remained unshipped at Walla Walla and other points. Informed sources reported a seventy-five thousand-ton surplus in 1884. A visitor to one of the Snake landings discovered "every place for storage…full and a large area of ground outside…also covered." Further expansion of regional output was discouraged. "The acreage harvested…," claimed Alonzo Leland, the veteran commentator on interior commercial matters, "is not one-tenth of what it would have been had the people been certain that they could get their grain to market."[13]

Because grain in bulk could not be easily, or safely, handled aboard river and ocean vessels, wheat consigned to the O.R. & N. had to be sacked. Aside from the necessary inconvenience, the sacks, costing eleven cents each, were a heavy expense. North-of-the-Snake producers, in contrast, quickly abandoned the practice once export via Puget Sound became feasible. Constructing elevators along its line, the Northern Pacific enabled ranchers to store grain in anticipation of higher prices. The shipper connected with the N.P. "is given the further great power," the *Walla Walla Union* pointed out, "of being able, if so disposed, to readily borrow money…on his crop, using the handy and reliable elevator receipts for security."[14]

Grain producers south of the Snake were shut out of the Puget Sound export trade, compounding their cost disadvantages. The Sound "is such a vast, safe, easily navigated harbor," the *Union* noted, "that ship owners will send their vessels to any of the many ports thereon for less freight than they will ask to go to

Portland." In illustration of the point, the wheat-carrying steamer *W. F. Babcock*, sailing from Commencement Bay in January 1887, paid $2,059 in port expenses. The cost out of the Columbia River would have been $6,075, including a thousand dollars for bar towage and five hundred dollars for pilots. "As a consequence," the monthly *West Shore* magazine observed, "wheat is worth more at Tacoma…than at Portland."[15]

Walla Wallans insisted that the Northern Pacific had deliberately located the Pend Oreille division by "the most northern and most circuitous of the possible routes" in order to perpetuate their economic dependence upon Portland. The obvious solution was an updated version of Dorsey Baker's pioneer rail link to the Columbia. "A railroad, independent of the O.R. & N. line and connecting with the Northern Pacific," the *Union* advised in understated fashion, "would prove of great value." Behind a less-than-inspiring motto, "On to Ainsworth," a campaign began in 1885 to secure financing for the project. Merchants and growers eventually contracted with promoter George W. Hunt for incorporation of their road in his farm-country Oregon & Washington Territory Railway. Completed in 1889, at the very end of the territorial period, the feeder cut Walla Walla's decades-long downriver connection.[16]

Transportation company policies accelerated an ongoing shift from Walla Walla to the breathtaking Palouse. "The surface of this country," a resident wrote of the unique region north of the Snake, "looks as if it had been…ruffled, tucked, puckered and puffed, with seven rows of flounces." The Palouse was "a land of hills and dales," another writer noted, "of wandering, crooked creeks, of torpid tortuous little rivers, that run here and there amid the highlands as though playing at hide-and-seek." Immigrants used to flat terrain were amazed to find that the uncountable hilltops were the most desirable locations, with the deepest soil, best water and least exposure to frost. The prime tracts hugged the Idaho border, in a twenty-five to thirty mile wide strip running almost to Spokane Falls. Painting their wagons with optimistic slogans, "Palouse or Bust" being the favorite, settlers crossed the Snake River in ever-mounting numbers. The homesteading opportunities were almost beyond calculation, especially if the greater region west of Colfax to the Pend Oreille division mainline was added to the equation. "Not more than one-tenth of the government lands…have been settled upon," a report from the scene advised, and the Northern Pacific held "about one and a-half million acres ready for sale."[17]

Gradually, the Palouse changed its market orientation from the Snake River to Spokane Falls. In the first years of settlement, lack of fiscal resources and disagreement among rival communities as to the best routes interfered with the construction of decent wagon roads. Mercantile interests at the Falls agreed, belatedly, to a strategic roadbuilding campaign. "What is greatly needed by this city," argued *Review* editor Frank Dallam in July 1884, "is a system of highways tapping the agricultural sections," particularly, in an obvious reference to the Palouse, "that magnificent farming land that has a name the length and breadth of the Territory." Financed, in part, by public taxation, the most important parts of the network were completed by the fall of 1885. Spokane emerged as a central transshipment point for eastern Washington grain. "Yesterday was an astonisher in the quantity of wheat delivered," the *Review* reported in early October. "There must have been upwards of two hundred teams in during the day, which…would give a grand total of 8000 bushels." Bad weather, though, reduced the utility of the roads, limiting, among other things, the extent to which farmers could load wagons.[18]

Spokane shared common interests with the Northern Pacific. "Whatever is done by the N.P.R.R.Co. to encourage the growth of Spokane Falls," a local newspaper, the *Times*, sensibly observed, "is but as bread cast upon the waters, to be gathered again in a…greatly increased measure." Reflecting this fundamental connection, the N.P. decided in the fall of 1885 to invest heavily in the construction of feeders. The Spokane & Palouse Railway included Charles Wright and Robert Harris of the transcontinental road and Spokaneites Anthony Cannon and Paul Mohr among the incorporators. Their plan was to build in a southeasterly direction toward the Idaho line—a substantial portion was completed during the 1886 construction season—and an eventual terminus at Moscow. Places served by the advancing S. & P. would, of course, transfer business from the Snake, the O.R. & N. and Portland to Spokane, the Northern Pacific and Puget Sound.[19]

Since Villard's downfall and the commencement of serious work on the Cascade branch, the strategically weakened Oregon Railway & Navigation Company had sought financial resuscitation through a lease of its assets to the N.P. or to the Union Pacific, parent of the Oregon Short Line. Amidst continuing negotiations—the O.R. & N. was absorbed into the U.P. system under an 1887 arrangement formalized in 1889—the Portland firm reacted in self-defense to Spokane's Palouse strike. Work resumed on the Palouse branch, which had stalled at Colfax under Villard. One line of track ran northeast in the direction of Farmington and a second southeast to Moscow. Bypassing Moscow, its original destination, the S. & P., in the meantime, built through Pullman before crossing into Idaho.[20] Still underway in 1889, the "war" for the Palouse supplied the countryside with a quickly assembled modern transportation network, further stimulating settlement and economic development.

West of Spokane Falls, a second satellite territory opened up, this time with only modest aid from railroading. The Big, or Great, Bend country was delineated on three sides by the Columbia River. Treeless and with limited water, the region repelled many would-be settlers. Overgrown in "exceedingly nutritious" bunch-grass, the generally level landscape nonetheless afforded "excellent range for large numbers of horses and cattle." The stupendous Grand Coulee, prehistoric product of geologic forces too enormous for laypersons of the time to rationally comprehend, divided the Big Bend into roughly equal sections. Studying the black walls and crumbled debris, one visitor saw in the "canyon" the "scenery of the moon." According to a classically inclined observer, Dante ought to have "included among the punishments of his Inferno that of being chained for all eternity to the rocks…in the fierce sunshine." Nomadic Indians and a few eccentric characters composed the entire population of this outback. "Wild Goose Bill" operated a ferry at the mouth of Foster Creek, a Columbia tributary draining a desolate subregion studded with weird volcanic pustules. "McIntee" the "Cattle King" ran a thousand head on the floor of the Grand Coulee, managing a cowboy empire from a windowless hut in the fashion of "the Calmuck Tartars."[21]

Settlement of the Big Bend began at a difficult-to-fathom pace. Returning from a spring 1881 tour, territorial surveyor general William McMicken reported homesteaders active "as far West as the Columbia, and also North…on Foster Creek." The number of survey stakes, he noted, was remarkable, considering that the smallest piece of wood must be "hauled from 15 to 20 miles in many places." Immigrants took twenty-five hundred acres of railroad land, and roughly the same of government acreage, in 1882. Every account from the scene in 1883 broadcast the news of "immigration pouring into the…country at a rate beyond all expectation." Grown with little rain, the initial crops were encouraging. On a negative, if hardly surprising, note, the Big Bend story also reflected the prevailing speculative philosophy of the time and place. After an 1882 visit, a Spokane journalist described the typical claimholder as a "non-resident, non-producing, non-tax paying, land-grabbing, law-evading, speculator waiting for the industrious settler to improve the land all around him and make his claim valuable."[22]

Considering the reality of things, waiting for someone else to actually demonstrate the country's potential was a sound decision. The boom-and-bust saga of Okanogan City, founded in 1883 as "the future great city of the Big Bend," illustrated a principal obstacle to successful development. The promoters constructed six buildings, planted shade trees and sold several lots before discovering, too late, that their water supply was unsuited to cost-efficient exploitation. Happening upon the derelict place in 1886, a party of thirsty journalists found the last holdout refusing to sell even a glass of the precious liquid, no matter what the offer. Transportation was as scarce as water. All supplies came by wagon from Spokane Falls, a nine-day round trip for settlers west of the Grand Coulee. Expecting federal navigation improvements on the Columbia above the Snake, investors sent the steamer *City of Ellensburgh* through Priest Rapids and Rock Island Rapids in 1888, only to see their useless vessel stranded at the mouth of the Wenatchee River when Congress refused to appropriate money for amelioration of the hazards.[23]

Immigrants sensibly preferred to settle close to existing railroad lines, locations offering ready-made access to outside markets and sources of supply. When completed, the Northern Pacific allowed Pacific Northwest residents to ship goods to and from the East. "Prices must come down and the modes of doing business, as well as the channels through which it is transacted, be changed," proclaimed the *Walla Walla Union*. The first direct eastern shipment to Yakima, a consignment of two thousand medium quality cigars, arrived in October 1883. Ritzville officials soon announced the importation of "made in Chicago" chairs for their pioneer schoolhouse. The main impact, though, was the opening of a new outlet for grain. Thirty carloads of Walla Walla Valley wheat were sent to Minneapolis in September 1883, commencing a potentially profitable trade. Prices in Liverpool were a penny or two less via Lake Superior than by San Francisco, but the eighteen-cent per-bushel saving on freight resulted in a substantial gain for growers. A serious shortage of rolling stock, unfortunately, prevented a wholesale shift from the traditional export route. Producers shipped a mere thirteen thousand tons over the Rockies between July 1885 and May 1886, compared to a quarter million tons of wheat and flour to Portland.[24]

Arguments over freight rates continued to focus on the cost of doing business with tidewater. Specific charges varied from time to time and from place to place. Eastern Washington residents believed in general, however, that the railroads discriminated in favor of Portland and treated certain inland points better than others. Citing economies of scale, the rail firms maintained lower schedules for long hauls than for short hauls. On a mile-for-mile basis, the *Walla Walla Union* complained, east-of-the Cascades shippers paid the O.R. & N. and the N.P. "a higher rate than is charged by any other reported road." On items from the East, moreover, the Northern Pacific assessed a tariff equal to the through fee to Portland plus the cost of reshipment from the Willamette River. Eastside mercantile interests were unable to fully exploit trade opportunities and consumers paid artificially high prices.[25]

The contrasting progress of eastern Washington's principal urban areas reflected the supposed advantages enjoyed by communities with favorable railroad connections. Still the territorial population leader in 1880, Walla Walla faded to fourth inside of three years. By 1890, the town, with 4,709 residents, was barely a tenth of Seattle's size. Lagging far behind in growth, Walla Walla possessed undeniable charm. Tall Lombardy pines, planted during the Civil War, provided comforting shade for wide streets. Thirty brick buildings, including a new courthouse touted as the best-designed structure on either side of the mountains, graced the central business district. Set upon large landscaped lots, wealthy residences accounted for Walla Walla's reputation as "a city of homes." Whitman College, the "Athens of the Northwest," added to a much-cultivated image of sophistication.[26]

Visiting in the hot weather months of 1882, the unimpressed Olympia editor John Miller Murphy reported that dust was the perfect symbol for what ailed Walla Walla. Rising "in a dense cloud at the passage of every vehicle," he wrote, "it penetrates every crevice and finds its way into rooms with doors and windows closed." Like Murphy's omnipresent grit, a sense of hubris afflicted the town.

Walla Wallans "seem to think," noted long-time observer Alonzo Leland, "that it is the hub of all the Northwest and that everything should, by right, center here." Although railroads were correctly perceived as a life-or-death matter, there was no need to proffer land, cash or other inducements to construction. "To read the Walla Walla papers," an Oregon editor quipped in April 1883, "one would suppose that the only thought or intention of Mr. Villard…is to comply with the wishes of the people of that city." Instead of actively encouraging a transcontinental line to come its way, Walla Walla elected anti-railroad politicians to the legislative assembly, there to argue for increased taxation, rate regulation and land grant forfeiture.[27]

Walla Walla residents failed to exercise civic responsibility. Defeating measures for parks and a modernized municipal waterworks, voters exhibited skinflint tendencies. Town leaders, Alonzo Leland pointed out, devised development schemes for exploitation by outside capital: "But if they will not invest a dollar themselves in the commencement of the work, but only solicit others to do so for their benefit…they will be likely to wait till they become dead ducks." Agreeing with this critique, a local editor explained that Walla Walla "had too many rich men, who were satisfied to get one and a half to two per cent a month by loaning their money, and were not willing to invest it in any industries that would develop the place."[28]

Going after something nobody else wanted, Walla Walla selected, in a lone initiative, the path of least challenge. Over the years, the territorial penitentiary had been assigned to a series of unwilling host communities. For lack of a willing alternative, the assembly finally engaged Thurston County sheriff William Billings to operate a prison at Seatco, southeast of Olympia near Tenino. In an arrangement conducive to exploitation and indecent treatment, Billings received seventy cents a day per inmate, plus the proceeds from hired-out labor. Poorly fed prisoners worked hard, cutting wood for the Northern Pacific. Until Governor William Newell ordered the irons removed at night and on Sundays, convicts wore shackles twenty-four hours a day. Exposure of the abuses created an opportunity for Walla Wallans to transform their city of homes into the home of the big house.[29]

Statesman editor Frank Parker, an active participant in the penitentiary movement, privately described the campaign as a "boodle business," undertaken to stimulate land values, provide employment and supply local farms with convict labor. "Times have been dull here," another principal noted in explaining the enthusiasm generated on behalf of an institution shunned by other towns. Organized by realtor and Republican activist F. W. Paine, prison advocates donated a building site and promised to meet construction and operation costs in excess of the funds provided by the territory. In December 1883, the assembly assigned a Walla Walla-dominated commission the task of selecting a permanent penitentiary site. Acting upon the panel's advice, legislators approved the Walla

Walla project in January 1886, appropriating $80,000 for construction. Work began immediately on the fortress-like edifice, featuring stone walls three feet thick and eighty-four two-person cells.[30]

With assignment of the first prisoner scheduled for the spring of 1887, artful last minute maneuvering saved the penitentiary. Eugene Semple, the incoming Democratic governor, opposed the project, particularly the proviso allowing private parties to make up deficiencies in public spending. In his final preemptive acts as territorial chief executive, Watson Squire appointed F. W. Paine superintendent, ordered relocation of the convicts presently at Seatco and supplied Walla Walla Republicans with enough signed blank employment commissions to insure that only party members would find work at the prison. Taking office on April 23, Semple promptly suspended his predecessor's orders, pending a personal investigation. Beset by angry Walla Wallans, Democrats included, the governor soon relented, allowing the prisoner transfer to go ahead. Loading the inmates aboard an underprovisioned special train on May 11, Paine delivered ninety-three hungry men two days later, after passing through Oregon without bothering to inform state authorities of his potentially dangerous cargo.[31]

Neither the governor nor the legislature thought to provide the penitentiary with operating funds or official rules and regulations. Initially honoring their pledge—the assembly eventually responded favorably to petitions for full restitution—Walla Wallans advanced $25,000 for food and black-and-white striped clothing. Superintendent Paine, the real-estate-agent-turned-unprofessional-penologist, and a new Walla Walla-controlled prison commission managed affairs without reference to Olympia. When not attending to patronage matters, administrators devoted their time to securing new territorial funds. Two-man cells could not be used as intended, Paine explained, since the prisoners had turned out to be "unfit associates for any other human beings." Responding to unsupported claims that the penitentiary was on the verge of being "over-run by the criminal classes," the legislature appropriated $173,000 for a second cellblock in 1888.[32]

Spokane Falls prospered in the years of Walla Walla's decline, despite claims from early-day rival Cheney that an Indian actually held legal title to the Spokane townsite. "Nature as Engineer and Architect," the residents enthused, had "performed her most perfect work" in northeast Washington. "As fine a stream of water as ever man laid eyes upon," the Spokane River formed the northern limits of the original business and homemaking center. Dropping, by the latest amateur calculation, 130 feet in 260 yards, the falls supplied a power source, claimed railroad writer Eugene Smalley, "more ample and convenient for use than that furnished Minneapolis by the Falls of St. Anthony." To the east, Idaho Territory's largely untapped Coeur d'Alene country featured mile-after-mile of virgin forests and mountain-upon-mountain of presumed mineral wealth. On the south, the Palouse, rapidly filling up, looked to Spokane as its marketing outlet.[33]

Townspeople and visitors alike remarked upon the phenomenal rate of growth. By 1883, the Falls, with a fulltime population of twelve hundred, ranked eighth in the territory. Washington's second most populous county, behind only King, Spokane County advanced to the number four position in assessed property value. The town features included four bridges, three churches, two private colleges—one Methodist, the other Catholic—a pair of "fine avenues," Riverside and Howard, and, under construction, a public library with shelves for six hundred volumes. Virtually a brand-new place, Spokane also presented the customary crudities. The best buildings were little more than unadorned wood frame structures. Overflowing outhouses offended the senses, visual and olfactory. Citizens used the falls as "a common receptacle," dumping garbage and "barn sweepings" into the municipal water supply. Saw and flour mill pollution ruined fishing opportunities.[34]

Although gold discoveries were, from time to time, of major historical significance, Washington was not an important mining center. Of the eight hundred million dollars in western precious metals output recorded in the ten years prior to 1881, barely a million was credited to Washington. Territorial mines produced $63,526 in 1883, one-tenth the figure for Oregon. Some interest focused, during the 1880s, on the Colville country north of Spokane. Reasoning that modest past results somehow foretold rich future returns, prospectors and speculators looked again to the valley of the Okanogan, on both sides of the 49th parallel.[35] As in the past, however, the finds of genuine worth took place outside the borders.

Evidence "in the shape of nuggets…as big as hazel nuts" confirmed longstanding rumors of gold in the Coeur d'Alene wilderness in September 1883. Miners made the initial discoveries on Eagle and Pritchard creeks, which were tributaries of the north fork of the Coeur d'Alene River and barely accessible by rough trails from Montana on the east and Washington on the west. Prospectors, reported one of the first individuals on the scene, "will have to pack their blankets, grub and whisky…and climb up the side of a mountain." Six thousand hardy, or at least foolhardy, wealth seekers made the trip prior to the onset of winter. Half that number stayed over on hastily staked claims, awaiting the arrival of spring and prime placer mining weather. Men and women crowded into the cabins and tents of Eagle City at the rate of a hundred new arrivals a day. The camp had twenty-five saloons—one operated by Wyatt Earp—a half dozen lodging houses and three restaurants, where pork and bean meals cost $2.50, fifty cents extra for eggs on the side. Lots changed hands for five thousand dollars and up, and a weeks-old issue of the Portland *Oregonian* sold for seventy-five cents.[36]

Stay-at-home critics warned the unwary against falling victim to another regional prospecting disappointment. "Better raise potatoes on Puget Sound…," an Olympia newspaper advised, "than own a salted gold mine a thousand miles away." Closer to hand, optimistic business interests set in motion rival strategies for control of the Coeur d'Alene. Heron, Belknap and other Montana settlements on the Northern Pacific mainline opened roads to the mines. Portland investors put steamers in service on Coeur d'Alene Lake and River, running from Coeur d'Alene City to Mission, thirty miles short of the main diggings. Forming the Coeur d'Alene Transportation Company, Spokane merchants blazed a wagon route to the lake, a line suitable for eventual conversion to rails.[37]

Initially, at least, distant naysayers proved to be the better forecasters. Upon the melting of the snow in 1884, miners, many penniless and without equipment, discovered that the gold was either buried deep in bedrock or stranded in high bars hundreds of feet above running water. Individual miners, therefore, had to give way to the corporations able to supply capital and machinery. A single *Spokane Falls Review* paragraph captured the complete boom-and-bust cycle:

> Hundreds of people, catching the fever, rushed into camp in the dead of winter, all anxious to get there first. Listening to no advice, blind to everything that would have opened their eyes…only bent upon picking up a fortune…men faced every difficulty without a thought of the future… The reaction was more sudden than the original excitement and these men displayed just as much anxiety to get out of the diggings as they had a few weeks before to get into them… Hundreds of men went in and came out again without seeing the ground, without sinking a pick, without so much as examining the country. The disheartened and disappointed crowd spread broadcast the statement that the mines were a fraud and a failure.

Valuable Eagle City lots became worthless within twenty-four hours. The Coeur d'Alene Transportation Company, Spokane's ticket to mine-related wealth, collapsed with its affairs "in such a tangle," one investor wrote, "as to puzzle a lawyer from…Philadelphia."[38]

Fortunately, shrewd and properly funded individuals remembered that the Coeur d'Alene was, as yet, only partially explored. "The much maligned" region, Frank Dallam of the *Review* promised, "will prove, in time, as rich in the precious metals as the far-famed country of the Montezumas." Miners moving further up the north fork installed the first stamp mill at Murray in late 1884. Attention, and renewed mania, shifted to the south fork of the Coeur d'Alene in 1885. Prospectors located, and named, the Bunker Hill and Sullivan mines on facing slopes of Milo Gulch. "The ore was of such high grade," noted the *Review*, "that it was acknowledged from the first to be one of the most remarkable discoveries known in mining history." Capital, for once, was readily available. Built on the canyon floor beneath the tunnels, a concentrator reduced silver-bearing rock before export to Helena over a hastily constructed N.P. branch. Spokane merchants diverted as much of the four million-dollar annual trade as possible to Washington Territory. Expanding upon existing transportation firms, Daniel C. Corbin installed an efficient Falls-oriented system in 1886. Taking over the lake and river steamers, he ran one railroad from Spokane to Coeur d'Alene City and another up the south fork to Wardner, the original boomtown in the vicinity of the Bunker Hill and Sullivan.[39]

Reaching out for both the Coeur d'Alene and the Palouse, Spokane became the metropolis of the interior Northwest. "The mines above here, and the great wheat region a few miles south…seem to predict a future for the place," a recent immigrant wrote home in April 1887. "The question of the railroad center of eastern Washington is settled," the *Review* announced. By 1889, Northern Pacific officials recorded a local population of nearly fifteen thousand, representing a ten-fold increase in six years and firm third-place standing in the territory. Certain unsavory habits served as persistent reminders of pioneer times. Residents continued to dump garbage in the river. Except for Riverside Avenue, the streets turned to "hog wallows" upon the slightest rainfall. Most observers, though, stressed such signs of progress as the elegant new brick and stone business buildings, the splendid urban estates in the "additions" opened by developers and the installation of street railways. Accustomed to thinking of themselves as occupants of "a second Minneapolis," Spokaneites now saw their community as a sort of all-in-one Twin Cities of the Pacific Northwest, combining at a single point transportation, trade, power and financing.[40]

Much of Spokane's reputation, and all of eastern Washington's for agricultural production, rested upon the grain trade. Blessed with unusually fertile soil and per-acre yields substantially above the national average, the Palouse and the Walla Walla Valley led the way as recognized centers of wheat cultivation. Annual reports extolling "the finest, largest and best crops" ever grown nonetheless obscured some revealing facts. Second among the western territories in bushels produced, Washington lagged far behind the leader, Dakota. Territorial farmers turned out six million bushels of wheat in 1882, two-thirds the Oregon figure and a seventh of the California. Acres cultivated for 1885 were, with westside farms factored in, slightly more than four hundred thousand for Washington, nearly nine hundred thousand for Oregon and close to three million for California. The most heavily cultivated county in the interior Northwest was Oregon's Umatilla. In true significance, pre-1889 agriculture east of the mountains had planted the regional seeds for an astonishing post-statehood harvest.[41]

West of the Cascades, certain geographic features retained their traditional force. "Every mariner…," a Tacoma newspaper advised, "knows that the navigation of Puget Sound is as easy and as safe as it is possible for any section of the treacherous main to be." Tourists compared the Sound to favorite lakes and Mediterranean scenic spots. Traveling "through many miles of woodland where nearly every tree was over 250 feet high," James Bryce pronounced the forested tracts bordering the great waterway "the finest which the United States possess." A magazine writer came away with "a confused impression of a limitless forest of great density, upon which the energy of man may be expended for centuries without any appreciable effect." Capturing the vital connection between timber and water while outward-bound on a California steamer in 1889, Rudyard Kipling wrote that the Sound "lay still as oil under our bows, and the wake of the screw broke up the unquivering reflection of pines…a mile away."[42]

Citing a recent upward trend in timber prices, a Port Townsend newspaper reported the return, in early 1882, of "the good old times in the lumber business on Puget Sound." Regular news stories covering the "active and strong demand for lumber" reflected near-sensational developments in Washington's great signature industry. Except during a brief mid-decade slump, sawmills ran full time, prospering as never before. Output mounted by a factor of seven between 1880 and 1890, passing the billion feet a year mark and attaining fifth place among the nation's lumber-producing states and territories. Annual sales increased, during the decade, at an even more impressive rate, from under two million dollars to over seventeen million dollars. Directly and indirectly, lumbering accounted for much of the economic growth leading to statehood.[43]

Writing an eastern acquaintance, Cyrus Walker, the longtime Puget Mill Company resident partner, noted that "the lumber market of the Sound," at present as in the past, "may be considered all countries and ports on the Pacific Ocean." Producers sent 284 cargoes to California in 1886, most through San Francisco Bay, and 166 to foreign purchasers. Australia took 64, Honolulu 27 and Valparaiso 24 of the exported shipments. Forest products made up nearly half the $1.7 million value of Washington's 1882 exports. Even with substantial amounts of wheat and flour added to an enlarged list of products, timber accounted for nearly a million dollars of the $3.6 million in goods shipped abroad in 1885. The sawmills made Puget Sound one of America's busiest commercial centers, with close to 2,800 vessels entering or clearing port during the year 1886 alone.[44]

Visiting Cyrus Walker's pioneer Port Gamble operation in 1883, a journalist described the organized violence of lumber production in near-poetic terms:

> The air was resonant with shrill saw-mill noises. Lurid smoke, like that from smelting works, poured up from the fires. The mill itself was a deafening, blinding, terrifying storm of machinery: saws by dozens, upright, horizontal, circular, whirring and whizzing on all sides; great logs, sixty, a hundred feet long, being hauled up, dripping, out of the water, three at a time, by fierce clanking chains, slid into grooves, turned, hung, drawn, and quartered, driven from one end of the building to the other like lightning—a whole tree slaughtered, made into planks, lathes, staves blocks, shavings and sawdust, in the twinkling of an eye.

The old San Francisco plants added capacity to meet rising demand. Pope & Talbot's Puget Mill Company, with facilities at Gamble, Ludlow and Utsalady, held position as the leading firm. Figures showing Blakely shipping nearly fourteen million feet in the first quarter of 1886, Tacoma thirteen million, Gamble eleven million and Ludlow seven million suggested the relative importance of the individual ports. Blakely vied for years with Tacoma's Hanson & Ackerson mill for recognition as the largest single producer. Rebuilt after an 1888 fire, William Renton's Bainbridge Island property finally claimed the undisputed title of world champion sawmill.[45]

In a major historical change, the western Washington economy shifted partway from a California to an eastern orientation. Henry Villard drove his debt-encrusted final spike at precisely the right industrial moment. The ongoing forest slaughter in Michigan, Wisconsin and Minnesota, states supplying a third of post-Civil War America's lumber, forced Great Lakes mill owners to find new sources of raw material. The Pacific Northwest, with abundant timber, higher yields and lower prices per acre, was the obvious relocation point. Traveling in speed and in comfort aboard the transcontinental railroad, lumbermen closely inspected Puget Sound. "The forest remains, for the most part, in virgin condition," one visitor reported. Despite thirty-odd years of earnest cutting, another advised, the San Francisco firms "have merely culled the trunks from the shore." From 1882 on, newcomers invested substantial amounts of money west of the Cascades. Selling eighty thousand acres and a Commencement Bay millsite to a consortium headed by Chauncey Griggs in May 1888, the N.P. placed the new face of regional industry squarely before the public eye. In operation by the following winter, the St. Paul & Tacoma Lumber Company made the City of Destiny the Sound's manufacturing hub.[46]

New eastern money also helped open a previously isolated region to exploitation. Flowing in a westerly direction, the Chehalis River, with its major tributaries the Wynooche and the Satsop, connected the Cowlitz corridor with the seacoast. The federal government removed snags from the stream in the early 1880s, allowing shallow draft steamers to reach Montesano, fifteen miles above the mouth, year-round and Chehalis, on the N.P., in high water periods. Settlers took up the best agricultural tracts. The problem, for commercial navigation, remained the stream's outlet, Grays Harbor. Booster assertions that the harbor "is, always has been, and always will be…the finest body of sheltered navigable water on the coast north of San Francisco" clashed with the actual state of things. At the entrance to the harbor, the principal channel across the bar shifted from year to year in position, configuration and depth. Over the dozen miles intervening between the Pacific and the Chehalis, vast shoals restricted, and at low tide often prevented, vessel movements. The installation of signal buoys was the only immediate result of a detailed Army engineer study of the hazards in 1881.[47]

Although serious navigation improvements were delayed, the Corps of Engineers study and the likelihood of early railroad construction produced a boom in Grays Harbor town and milling sites. George Emerson, the original harbor lumberman and the last major representative of the old San Francisco industry, arrived in 1881. As resident agent for Asa Mead Simpson, a still-active Gold Rush era proprietor of operations up and down the coast, Emerson acquired fifteen thousand acres of land and founded the North Western Lumber Company at Hoquiam. Great Lakes investors soon followed, concentrating their efforts at nearby Aberdeen. Attracted by the relatively low cost of doing business, Puget Sound mill owners joined in, jointly purchasing and enlarging the Cosmopolis plant in 1889. By then, Grays Harbor, the "Duluth of the Pacific," was firmly entrenched as Washington's number two lumber-producing region.[48]

Railroading finally came to Grays Harbor as a side effect of developments in western Washington lumbering. Historically, timber removal was restricted to areas close to the shoreline, one or two miles being the optimum hauling range for draft animals. With acreage easily accessible from tidewater logged-off, however, operators were forced to move inland and adopt expensive technology. During the 1880s, the steam donkey engine and the logging railroad became prime features of the Washington forest. By 1887, the territory's 107 miles of forest railroad—Oregon had only seven miles—ranked tenth in the nation, seventh in terms of carrying capacity. The St. Paul & Tacoma Lumber Company was the first major manufacturer in the region to secure its raw material entirely by rail.[49]

Construction of those roads of particular importance to Grays Harbor began in 1883, in isolated Mason County. Great Lakes investors based their Satsop Railroad at Shelton, on Big Skookum Bay. The Port Blakely Mill Company laid track from nearby Little Skookum, in the direction of twelve thousand prime acres belonging to the firm. Together, the dozen miles operated by the two concerns as of January 1887 shipped a half million feet of logs a day. Satsop and Blakely both intended to build on to Grays Harbor, establishing common carrier service between the coast and the sound. Much of the completed Port Blakely road was, in fact, incorporated after statehood into the Northern Pacific Grays Harbor branch, the line ultimately responsible for integrating the harbor into the Northwest economy.[50]

Lumbering, on Grays Harbor and elsewhere, was obviously the vital commercial activity in western Washington. "More people are engaged both directly and indirectly in it than in any other of our industries," the *Seattle P-I* pointed out in 1886, and "more capital is invested in it, and more money is put in circulation through it." The claim was so self-evident that activities of secondary importance drew relatively little attention. "Even native Washingtonians and the oldest settlers," a Tacoma newspaper observed, "are slow to believe that, valuable as the immense fir forests…undoubtedly are, there are other sources of wealth." Coal, produced at five King County and three Pierce County mines, was of substantially greater importance during the 1880s than in the previous decade. Puget Sound became the leading supplier of California, shipping a half million of the nearly two million tons imported by San Francisco in 1883 and 1884. Seattle and Tacoma sent over two hundred cargoes, valued at $1.6 million, to the Bay Area in 1886 alone. Among the western states and territories, Washington ranked second only to Wyoming in coaling activity.[51]

Experts considered the Puyallup Valley veins, thirty miles from Tacoma, "superior in quality," despite a tendency to run at odd angles. The original Wilkeson operation declined in importance, however, becoming better known for coke oven experimentation. Attention centered instead upon Carbonado, on the Carbon River three miles by rail from Wilkeson, a site opened by Northern Pacific stockholders in 1880. At Seattle, Oregon Improvement Company "assistant manager" John Howard, a Pennsylvania executive hired by Henry Villard to rationalize affairs on the Pacific coast, proclaimed a personal strategy: "the concern which can always have an assured supply of coal…to meet always the demand now existing and to be developed, with facilities to economically store and load coal…has the key to this situation both now and for the future." In a quick succession of efficiency-minded moves, he first acquired a fleet of colliers able to carry passengers and cargo, ending the firm's reliance upon chartered steamers. A revamped San Francisco wharf enabled the unloading of the largest ship afloat in under twenty-four hours. Expanding the former Seattle & Walla Walla Railroad Elliott Bay properties, Howard added enough bunker and general storage space for a thirty-six hour turn-around time.[52]

Howard believed that extension of the Columbia & Puget Sound road was "our salvation," even without the subsidy promised by Seattle. Newcastle remained an industry mainstay, with total San Francisco sales, by 1888, of over a million and a half tons. Quality, however, was an increasing problem. The main tunnel, now two miles long, required expensive hauls to the surface and was subject to fire and flood. A rival operator thought "slate and dirt…a better name" than coal for the Newcastle product. One third of the mine's raw material output, a journalist estimated, was, in profit-draining fact, waste: "in every direction…can be seen great masses of the smoldering trash…looming up higher than the roofs of the highest houses." Pushed by the aggressive Howard, the railway project opened superior O.I.C. veins at Franklin, the Green river terminus, and at the intervening Cedar Mountain and Black Diamond developments. Altogether, Elliott Bay coal shipments for 1885, just under two hundred thousand tons, represented a 40 percent increase over 1880. Based upon current and anticipated performance, King County claimed for itself the "Pennsylvania of the Pacific" title previously shared with Tacoma and Sehome.[53]

Something of a Puget Sound growth industry in the mid-1870s, fishing stalled a bit late in the decade. Overcoming momentary doubt as to the long-term viability of local runs, the Oregon-controlled Columbia River fishery soared, in the meantime, to new and truly incredible heights. Over six hundred thousand cases, representing approximately two million salmon, were turned out in 1883. Seventeen hundred boats supplied the forty canneries on the lower river. Thoughtful persons, however, recognized that an inevitable catastrophe lay partially concealed behind the superficially impressive statistics. Long-term trends confirmed that prices fell as output increased. Local government officials, particularly on the Washington bank, failed to enforce existing protective regulations. "The business...," critics and friends alike recognized, "needs systematizing...to avoid excessive competition, limit the production to demand and maintain fair prices." The only concrete action taken, though, was involuntary in nature, in the form of bankruptcies closing one in four canneries and reducing overall output to less than four hundred thousand cases by 1887.[54]

Attention turned again to the northern waters. "It is now certain," the *P-I* reported in August 1887, "that the supply...from the ordinary sources will fall far short of the demand and there will be a place in the market for all the Puget Sound fish that our canners can supply." Tacoma's two canners, in operation since 1883, expanded capacity. Packers opened plants on Elliott Bay and at Point Roberts, the remote four-mile-square peninsula dangling beneath the 49th parallel. Developments on the eve of statehood, however, served mainly to set the stage for turn-of-the-century expansion. A four-fold increase over 1880, the twenty-two thousand cases shipped from Puget Sound in 1888 were only a fraction of the sagging Columbia River tally.[55]

Fishing and coaling were, as a general rule, carried on in places close to one or the other of the Sound's rival urban centers. Merged by act of the legislative assembly in 1883, "old New Tacoma" and "older Tacoma" became the "new city of Tacoma, one and inseparable." The officially tabulated combined population, barely enough in 1880 to fill a dozen decent houses, reached 36,000 by 1890. After several days spent in the interesting company of "men who spit," Rudyard Kipling wrote at length of a community "smitten by a boom," with buildings grand and rude "thrown like a broken set of dominoes" over stump-riddled bluffs and a "raw...small of fresh saw-dust" in the air. Bolstered by deep water, the Northern Pacific, and a rate of growth more rapid than Seattle's, Tacoma appeared on the way to becoming the recognized metropolis of Puget Sound and the largest city north of San Francisco.[56]

"I never saw a lot of people more sanguine of the great future which is surely before them than these Tacomans," reported Frank Parker of the *Walla Walla Statesman* after an 1884 visit. "The whole place," another Walla Wallan agreed, "wears an inviting appearance of life, enterprise and faith in the future." In addition to grocery stores, saloons, hostelries and churches by the dozen, the city had a reputation for being "modern in almost all of its improvements." Gas and electric plants and the municipal waterworks were up-to-date in every operating respect. Street railways and a cable car system, the latter under construction at the end of the decade, provided residents with advanced forms of urban transportation. Built at a cost of $150,000 and dominating a perfectly manicured lawn, the luxurious Tacoma Hotel was considered by well-heeled travelers the most elegant, and expensive, establishment on the Pacific coast. The Northern Pacific, meanwhile, drafted ambitious plans for dredging navigable waterways out of the Puyallup River tideflats, opening ideal sites for industrial development.[57]

Tacoma's abiding weakness derived, ironically, from the source of its strength. The Northern Pacific and the Tacoma Land Company (T.L.C.) were by far the largest Pierce County property owners. Charles Wright's reputation as "the father and founder of Tacoma" was factually based. In addition to the railroad and the townsite firm, the Philadelphia investor presided over the concerns providing water, gas and electricity. The land company constructed the Tacoma Hotel, donated acreage for churches and parks and subsidized the *Ledger*, the establishment newspaper. Largely involved in just about every activity, Wright and his associates effectually checked competition from unaffiliated individuals and business concerns. Owning the waterfront, the N.P. and the T.L.C. made Tacoma "an inland city—or more properly, a seaport city cut off from the sea." No vessel could anchor and take aboard cargo, no municipal street could reach the central bayfront, without corporate consent. Denied the ability to exercise initiative, Tacomans insisted that the railroad provide them with better roads and other civic improvements, without delay and free of charge. As the population increased, the number of people actually working for the Northern Pacific declined in proportion and local issues took on a distinctive general welfare versus private interest coloration.[58]

Seattle, meanwhile, already possessed many of the features, positive and negative, that would eventually make it the singular urban area of the Pacific Northwest. Persons arriving by sea, still the most practical means of reaching the place, gazed upon what one traveler described as "a picture of entrancing loveliness" when entering Elliott Bay, especially at night. Illuminated by gas and electric lights, buildings and streets were "duplicated and extended in the clear and glassy waters of the harbor." Townspeople believed in what the *P-I* called "the spirit which is not content with 'well enough,' but which seeks to make the most of every opportunity." Privately excavated, the original Lake Washington canal was used mainly for towing logs to Lake Union at the city's backdoor. Seattle's population, though failing to match the Tacoma or Spokane rate of growth, increased from 3,553 in 1880 to 42,837 in 1890, well in advance of the overall territorial pace.[59]

Contrasting with the situation on Commencement Bay, the wealthiest Seattle property owners were individuals, not corporations. Virtually free of Northern Pacific-type influence, the dynamic community offered greater opportunities. Seattle "is on the dead run all the time," reported attorney Thomas Burke, who happily confessed to being "in speculations…up to my eyes." The famous "Seattle Spirit," though, was best represented in private business affairs, as suggested by some genuinely unsavory aspects of local life. Malfunctioning water and sewer systems failed to meet the needs of consumers and posed an ongoing danger to the public health. "The filth and drainage…oozing out from beneath the sidewalks…," wrote one resident, "made the air unwholesome and sickening." Partially filled in over the years with sawdust, slabs and dirt, the tideflats south of Yesler's mill wharf also challenged the senses. "This heap of rotting vegetable matter," a horrified visitor noted, "has become a festering mass of corruption emitting horrible odors and poisonous gases."[60]

A local pride and joy, the University of Washington also compromised the city's self-promoted reputation for progress. President A. J. Anderson resigned in 1882, assuming a more lucrative, and substantially more prestigious, position as head of Whitman College. University officials were condemned in all corners of the territory after securing modest financial support from the legislative assembly. The U.W. was a glorified "high school," critics charged, run "almost exclusively" by and for Seattle. Of the 137 students enrolled in 1880 and 1881, only 77 took college-level courses. Ten graduates were recorded between 1879 and 1881. When Governor Eugene Semple appointed a Tacoman to the board of regents in 1888, the new member's colleagues, Seattleites all, protested the infringement upon long-established parochial management. Administrators and professors simply ignored Semple's attempts to assert territorial control and to establish a federally funded agricultural experiment station on campus.[61]

Railroads, one area where Seattle's ambitions had always been thwarted, continued to be the municipal obsession. Local newspapers persisted in the fiction that the Puget Sound Shore line, intersecting with the Northern Pacific at Stuck River Junction, made Elliott Bay a transcontinental terminus, relegating Tacoma to the status of "a station." Shutdown in the post-Villard wreckage, the "Orphan Road" finally resumed operation in October 1885, after passing, unfortunately for Seattle, "into the hands of the enemy." Arranging the schedule so that farmers could do business in Tacoma and return home the same day, while those going to Seattle must stay overnight, the N.P. secured the Puyallup and the White River trade for Commencement Bay. Similar adroit scheduling required rail passengers from Portland to disembark at Tacoma and complete the journey to Elliott Bay by water.[62]

Seattle came closest to obtaining a real railroad at the very end of the territorial period. Two elements previously missing, intelligent local leadership and Eastern capital, accounted for a genuine advance in railroading. Daniel H. Gilman, a shrewd New Yorker recently dispatched to Puget Sound as a representative of Wall Street investors, devised, in the winter of 1884, "a scheme...for making a few millions" out of the Cascade foothills coal deposits at Squak. With Judge Thomas Burke as his principal associate, Gilman organized the Seattle, Lake Shore & Eastern Railroad Company. As originally projected, the line ran around the northern end of Lake Washington to Squak, with plans for an extension across Snoqualmie Pass as money and circumstances allowed. The first coal shipment to San Francisco was exported from the S.L.S. & E. dock in April 1888. According to over-enthusiastic *P-I* reportage, it was "the most notable event in the history of Seattle."[63]

By then, the basic plan had been altered to reflect a more grandiose vision. Track would still be laid as far as the Snoqualmie summit, so that the Scottish investor Peter Kirk might exploit iron deposits in the pass. The mainline, however, now ran north to the Snohomish River and a mountain crossing via an as-yet-to-be-determined pass. Connections with the Canadian Pacific at the 49th parallel were also contemplated. Aided by a Spokane subsidy, construction began from the Falls westbound toward the Columbia River. Insuring control of a prime bridge site, Judge Burke founded Wenatchee, the future apple capital of America. Too much, at least in retrospect, was attempted in too short a time at too many widely scattered places. Work on the overextended Seattle, Lake Shore & Eastern was suspended in the winter of 1889, pending new and unlikely Wall Street financial support. The completed portions of the several S.L.S. & E. segments nonetheless represented two hundred railroad miles, ten times the mileage previously achieved by hapless Elliott Bay transportation interests.[64]

Rapid population growth and the rise of cities generated increasing social tension in western and eastern Washington. Foreign-born persons—one of every five territorial residents as of 1880—appeared, in particular, to threaten traditional values and the stability of society. In the face of mounting demands for roads, schools and other amenities, taxpaying landowners complained of being outvoted and overburdened by shiftless newcomers. "At every election," the *Walla Walla Union* fulminated in October 1883, "opium fiends, bummers and strangers from all parts…are placed upon an equality and have as much to say as those who pay thousands of dollars in property taxes." Townspeople and rural dwellers alike bemoaned the evils supposedly perpetrated by "tramps" and "vagabonds," favored terms of the day for individuals refusing to work upon employer-mandated terms.[65]

Encouraged by negligent law enforcement agencies, crime apparently infested the territory. "The people…are so terrified," a Seattle newspaper claimed, "that they go to bed at night expecting to find their houses have been entered and robbed when they wake up in the morning." The lax punishments administered genuine criminals by Roger S. Greene, the jurist responsible for superior court functions on Puget Sound, supposedly encouraged lawbreaking and violence. "There has been too much religion and not enough law in this District," critics maintained in blaming the Bible-spouting Greene for the increasing number of vigilante episodes. Lynching three men accused of murder in January 1882, Seattle residents justified the action by explicit reference to the judge's supposed irresponsibility. In August 1883, Dayton citizens hanged James McPherson, a convicted murderer thought to be capable of avoiding execution through bribery of public officials. Cheney inhabitants, meanwhile, avoided the need for a formal trial by summarily dispatching the "red ravisher," an otherwise anonymous Indian suspected of assaulting a white woman.[66]

Public education was one of several widely favored methods of addressing the territory's social crisis. "It's much cheaper," an eastern Washington editor reminded his readers, "to build school houses than jails and…if we neglect the former, we will be forced to adopt the latter." In the past, territorial residents had paid scattershot attention to educational issues. Walla Walla held a well-deserved reputation for good schools. Colfax provided scholars with a decent building, but lacked money for employment of teachers or acquisition of textbooks. According to concerned citizens, Spokane Falls was "negligent" with regard to the "humiliating" state of local school conditions. Seattle's "Spirit" failed to extend to the educational sphere. "Children," an investigator reported in 1882, "were found in cramped, crowded, illy ventilated and poorly lighted rooms."[67]

Approved by the assembly in 1882, Washington's first "mandatory" attendance statute required towns and cities with more than three hundred eligible children to provide three months of free schooling per year. Local boards of education were authorized to levy taxes for construction and operation of necessary facilities. Though limited in practical application, the law generated considerable controversy. Property owners opposed paying for the education of non-taxpayers. Employers decried the likely impact on their child labor supply. Parents living upon the earnings of their offspring protested the imposition of discriminatory hardship. The initial campaigns were highly emotional affairs, with concern for the general welfare motivating one side and "ignorance, penuriousness and old fogyism…the other." Olympia voters rejected their first levy and approved subsequent proposals, in 1883 and 1885, only by narrow margins. Tacoma school districts voted down money requests, compelling directors to deal with classroom overcrowding by expelling students for whom there was no space.[68]

Prohibition also attracted support as a necessary social reform. "Our plan," a supporter observed of the dry movement, "is to make it a crime to drink to excess and intoxication, and to punish all who do so." The opposition was equally determined and, quite possibly, better fortified. Dollar and cent considerations complicated the debate. Imposing a $300 annual saloon license fee in 1877, the legislative assembly had intended to drive marginal operators out of business. Local governments across the territory, however, became dependent upon strong drink. Ellensburgh financed its entire municipal budget with licensing money. Whatcom County schools secured $10,000 a year from saloonkeepers. Tacoma took in over $15,000, allocating a third to educational expenses.[69]

Alcoholic indulgence had few public defenders, at least upon the specific liquid merits. Community leaders and business organizations nonetheless sided with whiskey when the legislature scheduled local option elections for June 1886. "There are two ways of treating the liquor question," the *Walla Walla*

Union pointed out in a typical expression of urban opinion, "the sentimental and the practical." Excepting the most naive prohibitionists, no one really believed that consumption of strong spirits could be totally, or even significantly, eradicated. "To attempt to absolutely and completely stop the manufacture and sale of whisky," said the *Union*, "is as impossible as it would be to attempt to stop the Columbia flowing over the falls at the Cascades." A genuine attempt at enforcement, much less continuation of local services currently paid for by license revenue, entailed a substantial increase in taxes. The inevitable result, in areas opting for prohibition, was commercial depression, with no corresponding social benefit.[70]

The balloting confirmed the division between practical and idealistic thinking. Rural areas, where saloons were already few and far between, voted in favor of banning alcohol. Dayton and Colfax, on the other hand, were the largest towns endorsing prohibition. Seattle, Tacoma and Spokane Falls all rejected the proposition by wide margins. Staid Walla Walla defeated the measure by a decisive 1,149 to 725 tally. "In these returns," a Commencement Bay newspaper correctly reflected, "we read most conclusively a strong feeling, even among temperance people, against relinquishing our hold upon the handsome revenue derived from the traffic for the dire uncertainty of being able to enforce prohibitory measures."[71]

Woman suffrage, another progressive nostrum, was supported by males and females alike. "If they can reform politics…," a rural editor advised, "then in God's name let them vote." Assuming that women desired to participate in the electoral process, the *Walla Walla Union* adopted a common-sensical point of view: "there is not, so far as we can see any strong reason for denying their request." On a more activist note, the *Tacoma News* considered the extension of voting rights a "triumph" in the eternal "battle" for "self-government." The movement, however, had as many determined enemies as committed friends. Opponents belittled suffrage advocates as "an odd looking lot" of "short-haired women and long-haired men." Judge Thomas Burke and other political sophisticates worried that such a radical step would offend Congress and "imperil our present chances of becoming a state."[72]

Votes for women were authorized by legislative fiat in 1883. In practice, suffrage hardly revolutionized the political system. "The avidity with which the better class of ladies…availed themselves of the benefits of the new law," equal rights advocates claimed, "completely exploded the old, threadbare argument" that females had no interest in voting. The feminine rate of participation, though, was even worse than that long-exhibited by men. Women cast fewer than two hundred of the eleven hundred tallies in unified Tacoma's initial mayoral election, one of the first ballot box opportunities under the statute. Although females made up 39 percent of the territorial population, they contributed only eight thousand of the forty-three thousand votes recorded for congressional delegate in 1884. Some commentators credited the 1886 local option victories to the extension of suffrage. Saloons, however, remained open almost everywhere in Washington. "Numbers of women," the *Walla Walla Union* pointed out, must have "voted 'the whisky ticket.'"[73]

Controversy arose in the courthouse, not at the polls. Ignoring legal arguments that the 1883 statute failed to authorize such service, Judge Roger Greene impaneled female jurors as a means of furthering his personal campaign against alcohol, gambling and houses of prostitution. "Virtuous women," the veteran attorney Elwood Evans, a prominent suffrage supporter, complained, "are adopted as the *foils* to make war on prostitutes and combat what is called the Social Evil." Some observers considered the practice an improvement, at least in the hearing of cases involving sexual assault. For the most part, however, husbands, brothers and fathers resisted having their "wives, sisters or daughters shut up in a jury room for hours or days." Fashionable ladies generally found the enforced association with liquor dealers and whorehouse "soiled doves" to be both onerous and offensive duty.[74]

Suffrage was, in any event, a short-lived experiment. Citing the lack of a legally proper title to the original bill, the territorial supreme court declared the measure unconstitutional in February 1887. Joined by Democratic leaders, voting rights advocates blamed a Republican "conspiracy" for the decision. One of the two majority jurists, though, was a Democrat and Greene, first named to the bench by U. S. Grant, filed the lone dissent. The legislature reinstituted woman suffrage in 1888, this time in properly written form. An obviously unsympathetic court again invalidated the law, claiming that a binding statute must first be authorized by Congress.[75]

According to the 1880 census, Washington was home to slightly over three thousand Chinese residents, almost equal to the surviving Indian population. Doubtless an undercount, this figure was soon augmented in difficult-to-ignore fashion by the demands of the regions' railroads. The Tacoma *Ledger* warned in early 1882 of "a vast army of Mongolians," apparently "congregating at Hongkong for the purpose of coming to the Pacific coast." Seventeen vessels, carrying as many as eight hundred laborers apiece, entered the Columbia River between April and July. Two-thirds of the twenty-seven hundred workers on the Pend Oreille division line were Chinese, employed at 85 cents a day compared to $2 for whites. Asians accounted for five hundred of the eight hundred employees carried on the O.R. & N. payroll in the Walla Walla Valley. The Dalles-Cascades and Portland-Kalama projects together engaged "thousands of Chinamen." Chinese recruits made up more than half the seventeen hundred strong N.P. construction crew assigned to Stampede Pass in 1887.[76]

Great Asian hordes, meanwhile, supposedly stood ready to illegally enter Washington Territory from British Columbia. Despite seaborne vigilante patrols mounted by the Orcas Island Anti-Chinese League, the many intricate channels of the San Juans were made to order for smuggling between Victoria and the mainland. A single government inspector was responsible for the entire border from the Cascade Range west to Cape Flattery. "It is therefore possible," a Tacoma journalist noted, "for scores and hundreds of Chinamen to come across the line…in broad daylight." Canadian officials refused to accept the return of illegal immigrants apprehended by U.S. authorities. Chinese awaiting deportation to their homeland made up two-thirds of the inmate population at the McNeil Island federal penitentiary.[77]

Chinese immigrants endured misunderstanding and mistreatment. "No laboring free man who has the least regard for health, cleanliness, comfort, or even decency…," congressional delegate Thomas Brents proclaimed in a widely circulated House address, "stands any show whatever in competition with these…Mongolian slaves." Walla Wallans blamed the Chinese for disease outbreaks, stagnant property values and, somewhat ironically, the inconvenience caused when laundries and restaurants closed during cultural festivals. Puget Sound newspapers accused Asian underworld figures of fomenting opium addiction among white persons. A brief, but emotional, controversy arose in Seattle when the budget-conscious city government hired a coolie contractor to repair streets. Continuing a long campaign of bigotry, the *P-I* demanded that the territorial assembly find some practical means of expelling all persons born in China from Washington.[78]

Most white residents, outright bigots included, conceded, however, that Chinese workers could not be dispensed with, on the railroads, in the mills or in the common activities of everyday life. "The simple fact is, they seem a necessary element in the make-up of our population," the *Walla Walla Union* noted:

> They are employed as cooks; they raise our vegetables and we eat them; they wash our clothes because we cannot do it ourselves; they saw our wood because they will do it cheaper than any one else; they are employed to do the menial work that no other person can be hired to do.

Even in Tacoma, a center of vocal nativist agitation, a newspaper admitted that "it is practically impossible at present to find white substitutes to perform" the "species of work" handled in the city's Asian laundries. "No Chinese, no canneries," the fishing industry on the Columbia and Puget Sound succinctly explained.[79]

Being single men for the most part with modest living expenses, the Chinese were able, and usually willing, to subsist upon reduced rates of compensation. Employers, of course, took full advantage of this circumstance. John Howard engaged Chinamen at eighty cents a day for the Oregon Improvement Company, "while decent white labor costs $1.80," thereby saving, at minimum, two thousand dollars a month. In an added bonus, Howard noted in 1885, "we have had on the whole better results from them…than we had from the white labor." The pay differential, though provocative, was unlikely to cause real outrage so long as jobs were plentiful for all concerned. The *Walla Walla Statesman* warned, however, that should the prevailing economic boom stall, "thousands of men will be thrown out of employment and…trouble will commence."[80]

Founded in 1869, the Knights of Labor, industrial America's initial national worker movement, first drew support in the Pacific Northwest because of factors other than wages. Pay was, in fact, high in comparison to other regions. The twelve-hour shift, six days a week, was, on the other hand, a standard and much-hated feature. Logging, lumbering and mining were inherently dangerous activities, with often-gruesome injury frequent, and accidental death not uncommon. Outside the major cities, conditions were primitive. Even a permanent camp like Newcastle consisted of little more than "rude cabins…built wherever room between the stumps could be found." Curtailing production to stimulate prices, management ignored the plight of laid-off workers.[81]

Unwilling to admit that industrial workers had legitimate grievances, middle class opinion generally condemned the Knights of Labor. Demands for reduced hours of work appeared downright sissified to farmers, men and women used to toiling from dawn to dusk "in order to secure a livelihood." Washington Territory had barely advanced beyond rude settlement status and the concept of employers and employees having fundamentally divergent interests clashed with the apparent equality of life and opportunity. "In Seattle…every man is a worker," a new daily paper, the *Times*, insisted. "The bank president was a hod carrier a few years ago, and the hod carrier of to-day may be a bank president a few years hence." Newspapers willing to concede labor's right to organize invariably denounced the one effective weapon in the union arsenal, the strike. "The restriction…as exercised by the strikers on the other workingmen," the *Tacoma Ledger* asserted, "is essentially unintelligible and inconsistent with all civilization, is emphatically wrong in principle…and has never been recognized, approved or contemplated by any law that was ever enacted this side of the dark ages."[82]

Taking place at roughly the same time, completion of several railroad projects and a short-term sawmill curtailment produced a sharp, albeit brief, economic downturn in the mid-1880s. The burden fell, supposedly, upon higher-paid white workers, allowing the Knights of Labor to broaden its appeal by playing to popular prejudice. The *Tacoma News*, in a common expression of editorial opinion, called for a racial approach to layoffs: "We say, and we say most emphatically…let Chinese laborers be discharged, and let worthy white citizens take their places." After all, said the *News*, "white labor is the first thing to be looked after and protected in a white man's country." Lurid accounts of baby stealing and specious "scientific" findings that the Chinese were not human beings added incendiary ingredients to the bigot's economic brew.[83]

On September 2, 1885, white coal miners in Rock Springs, Wyoming, attacked Asian co-workers, killing over two dozen persons. "The Chinese question," as Cyrus Walker wrote one of his partners, immediately became the "all absorbing topic all over the Sound." Considerable support was expressed for the murderers. "It is a hasty judgment that condemns only the rioting miners," the *Seattle Post-Intelligencer* observed in defense of violence carried out upon "the principle that self preservation is the first law of nature." The real villains were "the company which imported the Mongolians" and "the corrupt and incompetent officials who have allowed the stream of Asiatic immigrants to flow on." The railroad-subsidized *Northwest* magazine called Rock Springs "a warning to corporations seeking cheap labor."[84]

Violence broke out locally, near Issaquah, on September 7. The Wold family hop ranch had just replaced a mostly Indian crew with three dozen Chinese pickers. Five young white men, said to be members of "the best known...families in the valley," and two of the displaced Native Americans armed themselves and crept, well after dark, to within a few feet of the tents occupied by the sleeping workers. Firing ten to twenty rounds, the assailants killed three Chinese, including a victim shot in the back while answering the call of nature in nearby bushes. As the survivors fled to Seattle, the killers swaggered about town, expecting, one newspaper suggested, to be "presented with gold medals." Briefly condemned—"without doubt," the Olympia *Washington Standard* stated, "it was the most cowardly action in the criminal history of the Territory"—the murderers eventually went free when shameless King County juries acquitted the first two defendants on grounds of self-defense.[85]

Meanwhile, Knights of Labor members drove Asian employees from the Oregon Improvement Company's Newcastle and Franklin mines in the second week of September. Recognizing that the Chinese were only pawns in a larger dispute between capital and the union movement, manager John Howard vowed to "shut...down, until we feel that we are free to manage our property according to our own policy, and not at the dictation of a lot of demagogues and scum." Over the following weeks, Puget Sound was troubled, according to the *P-I*, by "unrest, disquiet and apprehension." After an anti-Chinese congress met in Seattle, Governor Watson Squire arranged a counter-demonstration by the "better class of citizens." Momentarily, property owner solidarity appeared triumphant, at least in Seattle. "Ninety-nine out of every hundred of our people," the *P-I* reported, "deprecate violence and are willing to abide by the laws."[86]

Tacomans refused to listen to their traditional railroad-affiliated leaders. Briefly attempting to defend the Chinese, John Sprague and other Northern Pacific managers retreated to their offices and mansions. "The set of men who have...been the arbiters of Tacoma's fate," corporate critics chortled, "have lost their grip on the direction of affairs." Only eight of the over two hundred special Pierce County deputies appointed to protect the Chinese reported for duty. On

November 3, municipal authorities assisted in a roundup of the entire Asian population. Two hundred persons were escorted to the outskirts of town and loaded, early the following morning, aboard an outbound train. Ignoring ample evidence of coercion, property destruction and stolen money, Tacoma residents insisted that the victims had been treated with compassion and had actually volunteered for expulsion. Recommending the extension of the "Tacoma Method" to other points on the Sound, the *Ledger* pointed out, logically, that "the way to get rid of the Chinese is to get rid of them."[87]

Although the same harsh truism applied to Seattle, a significantly different set of circumstances influenced the situation on Elliott Bay. Owning substantial real estate in the city, Governor Squire was bound to adopt a resolute stance, especially when backed-up by other community leaders. Squire's best chance to retain office under a Democratic administration, moreover, was to emulate President Grover Cleveland's opposition to organized labor. At his urging, the War Department dispatched troops to the Sound on November 7, first to Seattle and then to Commencement Bay. Acting upon intelligence supplied by the Northern Pacific, the military arrested the organizers of the expulsion movement in Tacoma. Conservative Seattleites credited the soldiers with forestalling an assault upon local Chinese residents. The regulars returned to their Vancouver barracks at mid-month, a crisis apparently weathered.[88]

Reduced to behind-the-scenes plotting over the holidays, the Seattle anti-Chinese movement reignited in late January, after the legislative assembly rejected bills prohibiting Asian employment and land and business ownership. Striking on February 7, the expulsion forces compelled 196 Chinese to immediately depart by steamer. One hundred and eighty-five individuals placed themselves under the protection of a Home Guard, previously recruited from among "law-abiding, law upholding, patriotic citizens." Following an exchange of gunfire, Governor Squire proclaimed martial law. The territorial militia occupied Seattle and a series of gubernatorial orders closed saloons, imposed a curfew and evicted "vagabonds" from the city. Convinced that local force was insufficient to put down "a state of active insurrection," Squire appealed to President Cleveland for federal intervention. Arriving on the 10th, soldiers supervised the arrest of twenty persons accused by the Home Guard of instigating trouble.[89]

Many observers, in and outside Seattle, accused the civil authorities, Watson Squire in particular, of greatly and deliberately exaggerating the magnitude of the crisis. General John Gibbon, the Civil War and Indian-fighting veteran in command of the military contingent sent to the city, "found every thing perfectly quiet and peaceful." "Prompt action" by the Home Guard, Gibbon advised, terminated "the notorious proceedings" prior to his arrival. Reports spread that the governor had called for federal troops in order to secure paying tenants for his vacant Seattle buildings. Responding that the rent charged the federal government was not "unreasonable" and that "damages" inflicted by the soldiers caused him to actually lose money, Squire mounted an unconvincing defense. Favorable coverage in eastern newspapers and magazines nonetheless made the governor a momentary hero on the Atlantic coast. Bolstered by heavy support from Seattle Democrats, who considered his removal "a public calamity" sure to "encourage the mob to renewed violence," Squire secured an additional year in office.[90]

There was nothing coincidental about the fact that Seattle and Tacoma, the centers of anti-Chinese agitation, were the points targeted by organized labor in its campaign against unchecked capital. The sudden return of prosperity created an unprecedented number of jobs—"never in the history of Puget Sound was labor so scarce," the *P-I* exclaimed in the summer of 1887—and all but eliminated the issue of low wage competition. The union question continued, however, to upset life west of the Cascades. As critics had warned, the expulsion of the Chinese led immediately to a successful Knights of Labor campaign for the ten-hour day in the timber camps and mills. Renewed and sustained disputes over wages and working conditions caused John Howard to despair that "the very heavens seem falling about our heads in the coal business." For two years, local politics in Seattle and Tacoma focused upon bitter campaign struggles between Loyal League tickets and ad hoc People's parties backed by labor. Alarmed property owners persuaded the legislature to enact a tough new militia law, providing, essentially, for a permanent anti-union territorial brigade. Employers, meanwhile, hired private detectives to infiltrate the Knights, gathering intelligence and sowing discord.[91]

Management had no intention of giving in to labor. The sawmill companies had resident partners in daily contact with employees and were sometimes amenable to reductions in hours or increases in pay, provided such gestures appeared to be voluntary. The coal mines, though, were railroad-owned or affiliated, with decisions made on the Atlantic coast. On behalf of his distant superiors, John Howard promised to "lock horns with this gang that proposes we should stand and deliver...our property to them." Operators reduced production, so that only loyal men need be hired for the remaining jobs. Sworn in by compliant federal officials, special U.S. deputy marshals guarded the works. In his part-time role as ranking officer of the territorial militia, the Oregon Improvement Company's attorney recommended that the government provide military protection. East of Snoqualmie Pass, the Northern Pacific imported strikebreakers and well-armed "detectives" for service at its Roslyn mine. On-the-scene managers denied store credit, and therefore food and supplies, to suspect workers, an effective means of forcing such individuals to depart.[92]

Something of a labor-management impasse developed under the regime of Eugene Semple, the Democrat appointed governor in April 1887. A Vancouver sawmill owner, the new occupant of the gubernatorial chair was a longtime critic of the Oregon Railway & Navigation Company and other corporations. Under the "lax administration" of his Olympia predecessors, he claimed, "the public

good was often subordinated to private...greed." Unlike Squire, whose philosophy of government was influenced by personal stockholdings, Semple did not
believe the territory was bound by some elemental law of economics to intervene
on behalf of—indeed at the behest of—employers. When the Oregon Improvement Company demanded that the militia be sent to Newcastle, he refused, declaring that while "it is proper for public officers to take precautions, in advance,
where reasonable apprehension of a disturbance exists...the apprehension must
have some foundation more substantial than the mere opinion...of a Coal
Co[mpany]." Personally investigating the Roslyn situation, the governor described the imported N.P. detectives as "an organized body of mercenaries" and
denounced the "invasion" of Washington by "armed men from other jurisdictions." Semple, to be sure, took no overt action supportive of labor. His honest
neutrality, though, was a major departure from practice. Management lost no
time in securing his removal. Although the territory's days were numbered, the
Republican Benjamin Harrison administration, inaugurated in March 1889,
promptly appointed Miles C. Moore, a safe-and-sound, business-certified Walla
Walla merchant, to the governorship.[93]

Politically, pre-Civil War trends continued to manifest themselves, the one notable change being a hardening of ancient grievances. Washington, according to
Seattle attorney John McGilvra, "had more politicians to the *square acre* than any
other part of Uncle Sams dominions." Most, unfortunately, were outsiders, "in-
terlopers" appointed by distant presidents for obscure partisan reasons of no relevance to the Pacific Northwest. Although the territory had surpassed neighboring Oregon in population, it remained in a "state of vassalage," administered
according to the same procedures "King George used to govern the American
colonies." Some appointees, Republican refugees from the post-Reconstruction
South, were historically genuine Carpetbaggers, rewarded by party leaders with
new lives and careers in the Far West. President Chester Arthur, for instance,
named George Turner, a youthful veteran of the federal bench in Alabama, to the
territorial supreme court in 1884. Generally considered an inferior jurist, Turner
was one of many examples cited in support of a plea from both sides of the Cascades: "Give us home talent."[94]

    To the very end, Washington's governors remained imported talents-of-sorts.
New Jersey's William Newell was the last to claim the invaluable Lincoln connection, based upon service as personal physician to the Illinoisan while the two
men served together in Congress in the 1840s. Although Seattle Republicans
endorsed Watson Squire, one of their own, for the position in 1884, the appointment was actually made according to the wishes of the New York party organization—the young state legislator Theodore Roosevelt was a signatory to the
nominating petition—and its premier member, President Arthur. Despite

operating a Vancouver sawmill, Eugene Semple was considered an Oregonian, on account of long experience in political and business affairs south of the Columbia. Affectionately known as a "mossback" though only in his mid-forties, Miles Moore became in March 1889 the first full-fledged territorial resident to serve as governor. On the scene in Walla Walla since the Nez Perce gold rush, Moore had spent, by far, more pre-appointment time in Washington than all of his predecessors combined.[95]

Few informed observers of territorial politics paid serious attention to the chief executives. "Governorships…," the *P-I* noted, "are positions of honor than of profit." The sorry state of the federal judiciary was of substantially greater consequence in the conduct of day-to-day affairs. Population and economic growth produced inevitable strains upon the legal system. "The business of this office," the King County attorney reported in January 1888, "has increased more than one hundred percent in the past four years." Even with a fourth member added to the bench, the courts were overwhelmed. Meeting in early 1889 from 8:30 in the morning until midnight, with brief intermissions for lunch and dinner, the supreme court disposed of sixty cases in twenty-two days. "At the end of the day," one jurist confessed, "I feel so worn out that when I have a letter to write, I generally have to do it…by the aid of a stenographer." Republicans and Democrats agreed that the problem was compounded by the appointment of inexperienced outsiders. "Here on Puget Sound," a Seattle lawyer wrote, "we need for Judges men who have been brought up on the seaboard, and understand commerce." Under long-established procedure, however, the positions continued to be filled by imports like the Reconstruction politico Turner and Frank Allyn, an Iowan dispatched to the coast in 1887 on the advice of his homestate congressional delegation.[96]

In a countervailing development, the profits to be made locally in private business ventures reduced the appeal of federal jobholding. Thomas Burke, attorney, real estate speculator, railroad promoter and two-time Democratic congressional candidate, "wouldn't cross the street to get the best office in the Territory." His appointment as chief justice in late 1888 was considered the greatest honor extended by the United States to a real Washingtonian. Burke, though, agreed to serve only on an interim basis, his resignation to be accepted no later than March the following year. "The position is one of honor and responsibility," he explained in a private letter, "but the salary is only $3,000. a year, and I can't afford to hold the office long at that rate."[97]

Population growth, and shifting demographic trends from east to west of the mountains, accentuated the most obvious fact about Washington politics. "The territory is strongly republican," the Colfax *Gazette* advised in July 1882, "and a nomination on the republican ticket insures an election." Once selected by the party convention, the candidate for delegate might just as well book passage for the nation's capital. "When any sort of a figure-head is safely strapped on the great Republican jackass," a veteran political observer wrote, "it has sufficient endurance and strength to carry the load, and even beat the time of blooded stock." How else explain the success of Thomas Brents, a three-term member of Congress so deficient in intellect and self-comprehension that he actually considered himself the Washingtonian best-qualifed for post-statehood service in the U.S. Senate. Majority party journals maintained a crocodile-teared deathwatch on the territorial Democracy, a moribund entity with neither financial support nor party-subsidized newspaper. From an objective standpoint, Republicans ought to have held every elective office, in city, town and country-side.[98]

Unbeatable in theory, the territory's dominant partisan organization was troubled by problems of the sort common to one party systems. The general low repute of officeholders inevitably reduced the popularity of those who had, for years, held most of the positions, appointive and elective. The close relationship between the Northern Pacific and Elisha Ferry, the party's great stalwart of the 1880s, linked Republicanism with the railroads in the public mind. Advocates of Washington's admission to the Union blamed the Republicans for the failure of statehood under the administrations of Rutherford Hayes, James Garfield and Chester Arthur. Assorted long-term quarrels undermined party unity. Ferry and his associates, for instance, worked hard to thwart the aspirations of recent federal appointees. Seattleites and Tacomans were, of course, constitutionally incapable of agreeing upon candidates, issues or the time of day. "Stupidity and neglect," one veteran politician warned, without apparent effect, was sure to erode, if not entirely undermine, the party's built-in territory-wide advantage.[99]

Taking advantage of circumstances, Democrats belied accusations that they were brain-dead relics of a bygone pre-Civil War America. Democratic leaders provided covert support, and declined to run candidates in counties where "independents" challenged the existing Republican order, a stratagem nearly resulting, on at least one occasion, in effectual control of the legislature. The party prospered in 1884 upon that rarest of all political developments, a genuinely divisive issue. For years, territorial opinion was virtually unanimous in opposing congressional revocation, in part or in whole, of the railroad land grants, as such action would delay, if not prevent, construction of the transcontinental line across the Cascades. Convinced that Henry Villard intended to make Elliott Bay his terminus, Seattleites were as adamant as Tacomans in condemning anything that might interfere with the project. Upon Villard's fall, however, the Elliott Bay perspective immediately changed to one advocating forfeiture. Once the Northern Pacific was sidetracked, the right-of-way would supposedly be open, and a federal subsidy available, for a locally sponsored cross-mountain connection. "No man need look for the support of the people of Western Washington…at the coming election," Judge Thomas Burke asserted in equating Seattle's interest with that of an entire region, "who is not a zealous[,] earnest and sincere advocate of the unconditional forfeiture of the land grant."[100]

Judge Burke's ideal 1884 pro-forfeiture candidate materialized in the form of a Democratic sojourner who never resided in the territory long enough to qualify as a voter. The son of a prominent Indiana senator, young Charles Voorhees came west to build a political career in an unlikely place, Colfax. Although he was not a professional actor, as opponents claimed in attempting to portray him as a proto-John Wilkes Booth, the legally trained newcomer was a dramatic orator, a "bellowing calf" given to denouncing the railroads in profanity-laced style. As if in deliberate counterpart, the Republicans nominated James Armstrong, a one-legged Civil War veteran, career patronage recipient and devoted public servant of the Northern Pacific interest. Reflecting the unusual excitement, the general growth of the territory and the temporary impact of woman suffrage, nearly 42,000 persons voted, more than double the 1882 turnout. The Voorhees victory margin, a mere 146 votes, depended entirely upon normally Republican King County, where he led by a three-to-one margin.[101]

Dispatched to the nation's capital, Seattle's man in the Palouse almost immediately ran low on luck. Committed to revocation of the land grant, a proposition regarded as disastrous everywhere else in the territory, Voorhees appeared both foolish and out-of-touch with his constituents. A substantially watered-down version of forfeiture, introduced by the Oregon congressional delegation as a diversionary pro-Northern Pacific stratagem, passed the Senate, only to fail in the House. The Democratic Congress ignored statehood, shifting the onus on that issue from the Republicans to Washington's ineffective boy delegate. President Cleveland left Watson Squire and other opposition holdovers in place for half his term, then sent outsiders to fill the major positions, preventing Voorhees from building a personal organization among quarrelsome Democrats on the happy common ground of jobholding.[102]

Written off as a manifestation of "insincerity, temporizing, hoodwinking, deceit and downright falsehood," Washington's leading non-resident politician apparently stood little chance of reelection in 1886. Inventive in crisis, Voorhees returned "home," in the aftermath of the Puget Sound disturbances, to combine his forfeiture line with an up-to-date diatribe against the Chinese presence in Washington Territory. Republican division again proved the key factor. Self-destructive party leaders, needing the King County vote to win, punished Seattle for voting Democratic in 1884 by sharply reducing its representation at the territorial convention. Winning in relative ease, Voorhees led principal challenger Charles Bradshaw by two thousand votes in a three-way race. By 1888, however, his once-fortunate career in the Pacific Northwest was clearly over. Completion of the Cascade division eliminated the land grant as a viable, even a make-believe, issue. The anti-Chinese movement had lost most, if not all, political force. Voorhees ran again because no one else was willing to head a losing ticket. The result confirmed that, contrary factors under control, Washington was intrinsically Republican. John Allen, the N.P. attorney east of the Cascades, demolished the incumbent, 26,281 to 18,910. Even King County turned upon its dry country champion, giving the victor three of every five votes.[103]

Neither the rejection of forfeiture nor the downfall of Voorhees altered Seattle's basic position on regional railroading. Northern Pacific promises, said Thomas Burke, amounted to what "the Indians would call *cultus wah wah* which, translated from the classical Chinook, means 'worthless, good for nothing talk.'" Washington residents, Seattleites included, nonetheless realized that the railroads had carried the territory to the verge of statehood. "They open up new tracts of land," an east-of-the-Cascades newspaper reminded those readers inclined to excessive criticism, "they give impetus to trade, they increase values, they stimulate industries, they develop commerce." The territorial "treasury" was well-stocked with lumber, coal and golden grain, advised a westside editor, "and all that is needed is men and women to pronounce the 'open sesame.'" Assisted by its corporate relations and competitors, the N.P. wielded the magic formula, opening markets and importing settlers by the score. "Here there is something for everyone to do," the *Ellensburgh Capital* observed of the result in early 1889, "the capitalist finds employment for his money, the laborer finds his muscles in demand, and the mechanic and artisan is ever in demand."[104]

Strangers for thirty years and more, western and eastern Washington came together upon the basis of fundamental commercial and political exchange. "Profitable development" for all, a Port Townsend journalist argued in 1881, depended upon "a total breaking down and obliteration of sectional lines." The shift from division to unity, though still incomplete, was the work of the railroad linking the Columbia Basin with Puget Sound. The Cascade railway erected what a Tacoma newspaper called "a bond between the people of the Territory." Legislators from the interior once needed weeks and a detour through Oregon to reach Olympia, but now made the trip in a single day. Separation along the crest of the Cascades, an enduring issue since the first miners went up the river to the diggings, lost force as a worthwhile vision. "If there is any animosity existing between the people on either side of the...mountains," the *Walla Walla Statesman* announced in abandoning a cherished proposal of the past, "it exists solely in the minds of a very few."[105] Created in 1853 by poorly informed distant decisionmakers, Washington was at last whole, thanks to the achievement of ancient transportation dreams.

Chapter Nine

Through Years Added to Years

*Many of those around me have looked forward to statehood through years
added to years until they almost despaired of the realization of their hopes.*
—Elisha P. Ferry[1]

A T MID-AFTERNOON ON Thursday, June 6, 1889, an overheated glue pot exploded in a Seattle woodworking shop, igniting shavings and other debris. Driven by a stealthy breeze, the flames quickly spread to nearby saloons and boarding houses. Emergency workers rushed to the scene, only to discover that the municipal water system, a relic from "the days of smaller things," was incapable of generating sufficient pressure to hose down upper stories. The authorities ordered buildings and then entire blocks blown up, opening breaks that failed, unfortunately, to retard the advancing fire. The conflagration died of its own accord, from lack of additional fuel, in early evening. The business district—over a hundred acres of offices, stores and dwellings—was gone, at an estimated loss of $15 million. Every waterfront mill, from Henry Yesler's pioneer enterprise to the modern Stetson & Post lumbering complex, had been destroyed. Depots, wharves and trestles belonging to the Puget Sound Shore and the Columbia & Puget Sound railroads lay in ruins.[2]

In immediate aftermath, the disaster became history's prime example of the "Seattle Spirit," the conviction that "enterprise and determination" governed the course of human affairs on Elliott Bay. "The fire had scarcely been extinguished," wrote Judge Thomas Burke, "before the rebuilding of the City…had been begun." Close to $40,000 in pledges funded a municipal relief fund. The homeless, the hungry and the city government took shelter in the armory, the most substantial surviving structure. "Already," the *Times* reported from makeshift quarters in a canvas tent, "the sound of the hammer and saw is heard." The opportunity provided by the disaster, Burke advised, encouraged community leaders to contemplate building a "new Seattle…in all respects vastly superior to the old."[3]

Sawmills and shingle plants, no longer the best usages for prime waterfront real estate, were relocated to Ballard, then an independent town north of Seattle's limits. Renewed emphasis was directed, across the bay, to residential and commercial development of West Seattle, a project recently undertaken by San Francisco capitalists.[4]

Paying particular attention to Seattle, the *Times* suggested that Washington Territory was "fated to be consumed by fire." Annual forest conflagrations were as much a part of late summer as humid days and uncomfortable nights. In the final territorial years, the focus shifted from timber to town as an unprecedented number of communities burned. Many observers detected a symbolic link between the destruction of old wooden buildings, on the one hand, and the advance, on the other, from backward political status toward statehood.[5]

Young Spokane first confronted disaster in the summer of 1880, when a blaze ignited by a careless smoker destroyed a block of shops. A January 1883 fire destroyed seven buildings. An August 1884 blaze, breaking out in the quarters of a "prostitute known as Georgie," left Main Street in ruins. The municipality afterward installed a high pressure pumping system connected to the falls, supposedly making the "town...entirely safe against any more large fires." That December, however, the year's fourth conflagration "left ugly cicatrixes on the face of our fair city." A popular restaurant, and the adjoining apartments, burned in March 1886. The California Hotel, Spokane's finest, went up in flames in May 1887. A September 1888 fire proved, beyond doubt, that the vaunted protective works were "inadequate" for a rapidly growing community. "The supply of water," a witness noted, "was so absurdly light, that one man could do, at the nozzle, the work formerly performed with difficulty by three men."[6]

Urban fire also struck west of the Cascades. A May 1882 kitchen blaze spread to and destroyed eighteen neighboring buildings in "one of the blackest days...ever seen" in Olympia. The Carlton House and the U.S. land office, the latter set afire by an improperly extinguished bureaucratic cheroot, burned in separate September 1883 Budd Inlet incidents. That November, flames originating in a Seattle brewery burned the King County courthouse. The last of three major 1884 Tacoma fires ravaged seventeen saloons, leaving a mere seven establishments to satisfy local drinking requirements.[7]

Admission's year, 1889, featured the most spectacular blazes. Barely a month after the Seattle disaster, flames burned two hundred buildings in Ellensburg, at a loss of $2 million to the aspirant for designation as state capital. "It was an ocean of flame," the local newspaper reported, "which raged in unabated fury and only stopped when there was nothing left to feed upon." On August 4, Spokane Falls endured the greatest conflagration of its history, past to present. Traced to a greasy restaurant near the N.P. depot, the fire swept over thirty blocks, leaving smoldering ruin in place of eastern Washington's commercial nexus. Reflecting upon the spirited and simultaneous reconstruction of three leading cities, the *Seattle Times* broadcast an optimistic territory-wide lesson: "What better evidence of the future of Washington could be given."[8]

Washington burned and so also did political opinion, at least regarding the slow advance toward membership in the Union. "We not only desire admission," the Port Townsend *Argus* asserted in late 1882, "but we are *entitled* to it." Insisting that the territory was "already ready for admission," the *Seattle P-I* pointed out that Washington had "population enough, wealth enough and resources enough." The commonwealth, according to a Spokane newspaper, "not only meets, but surpasses all the requirements of statehood." By mid-decade, at the latest, Washington had more residents than the states of Oregon, Nevada, Colorado and Delaware. Washingtonians nonetheless remained, said another journalist, in a "chrysalis condition," unable to "burst forth" in full possession of their rights as American citizens. "It is a burning shame and disgrace," a final editorial observer concluded.[9]

One question, the exact method by which Washington should enter the Union, provoked short-lived debate. Puget Sound favored moving ahead on the basis of the 1878 constitution. "The territory," argued the Olympia *Transcript*, "has already held a constitutional convention, framed a constitution…and been at a large expense for the same, and there is little reason in doing it all over again." Leaving, for all practical purposes, the capital and a majority of the legislative seats west of the Cascades, the draft governmental framework naturally appealed to tidewater residents. Republicans and Democrats east of the mountains insisted upon a new convention. "At no hour since the…constitution was framed, in 1878," the *Walla Walla Union* affirmed, "have we been willing to accept Statehood under the provisions of that document." With territorial unity a paramount necessity for admission, westsiders reluctantly abandoned their defense of the existing constitutional terms.[10]

Puget Sounders also endorsed a proposal long-favored on the far side of the Cascades, the addition of northern Idaho to Washington, before or at statehood. "We believe it," Port Townsend editor Allen Weir wrote of west-of-the-mountain views favoring annexation, "to be the feeling of nine-tenths of the…people." Panhandle residents certainly appeared to be adamant regarding the proposal. The present territorial boundary, Alonzo Leland pointed out, was only "an imaginary line." Unfortunately, southern Idaho, fortified by the territory's federal appointees, expressed equally determined opposition to realignment. When Congress approved legislation annexing the northern counties in 1887, President Grover Cleveland declined, under pressure from the southerners, to sign the measure.[11]

Even for the common good of statehood, other questions defied resolution. "Our people were not consulted in the naming of the Territory," the *P-I* reminded readers unfamiliar with Pacific Northwest history. Although no territory had ever been admitted under an altered name, widespread agreement on the need for a change was evident by 1880. In a fit of self-serving promotion,

Tacoma proffered the native word for the great Cascades peak, towering above the valley of the Puyallup. There was no rush, elsewhere, to acceptance of "Tacoma." Seattle countered with "Columbia," that old, though still-confusing, favorite from Warbassport and Monticello days. Some commentators called for adoption of one of the "many smooth and pretty Indian names" not associated with Commencement Bay. Others suggested that a historical figure be honored in place of Washington, with "Lincoln" and "Webster" put forward as qualified choices. The *Walla Walla Union* campaigned for "Whitman," after the Oregon Country missionary Marcus Whitman.[12]

In May 1888, the *P-I* asked readers to submit their preferred names for the future state. Most of the nearly seven hundred responses favored "Washington." Among those submitting a second choice, "Columbia" drew the greatest support. Territory-wide, the practical choice came down to "Washington" versus "Tacoma." Hostility toward Commencement Bay and the Northern Pacific, rather than any great regard for the current name, worked against change. Making the state an advertising device for one city, and its dominant corporation, an Olympia editor claimed, "would be an outrage" against the interests and moral well being of the general population. Another journalist would rather use a "latinized version of 'Shorty'" than follow the dictates of the railroad. More by default than by genuine preference, "Washington" survived the challenge.[13]

Olympia remained the capital for the same lack-of-an-acceptable-alternative reason. Eastern Washington demanded removal of the seat of government from "the extreme western border" to "some point in a more central part of the territory." Burdened by the geographic logic, defenders of the status quo had great difficulty making a rational case for their cause. "Every school child in the United States" supposedly knew Olympia from social studies memorization exercises, but the place was years removed from vitality. The newspapers condemned local residents for failing to support much-needed improvements, including a railroad to Grays Harbor and a new wharf to deep water. Between high prices and poor service, merchants lost the timber camp trade to down-Sound competitors. Comparing Olympia to Victoria, the very-British provincial center on Vancouver Island, a visiting reporter delivered an intentional insult. A "sabbath-like" atmosphere prevailed seven days a week and the townspeople exhibited neither "rush nor hurry nor bustle."[14]

Of the several contenders east of the Cascades for the honor to be stripped from Olympia, the obvious places had problems of their own. Walla Walla, public opinion on both sides of the mountains agreed, ought to be satisfied with its penitentiary. The geographical argument for relocation eliminated Spokane Falls, on the extreme eastern border. Specifically designed as Washington's future capital, North Yakima was the most eligible replacement. The town occupied a centrally located spot on the principal east-west transportation corridor. The Northern Pacific offered prime city center acreage and money for erection of buildings and moving the public records. Attempting to force relocation through the assembly prior to statehood, the N.P. aroused both anti-corporate sentiment and a politically significant alignment favorable to the current capital. Olympia, though unpopular and probably undeserving, enjoyed the united support of Puget Sound. Several eastside communities, on the other hand, furthered their own ambitions for the capital by opposing North Yakima.[15]

So long as the territory was denied admission, arguments over names and capital sites amounted to little more than parlor entertainment. Despite assistance from Governor William Newell, a New Jersey-based politician with better eastern connections, delegate Thomas Brents made no headway with statehood legislation. In 1884, the Democrats won the White House and both houses of Congress, reducing the already faint prospects of success. Territorial Democrats publicly supported membership in the Union. Privately, however, local party leaders warned President Grover Cleveland that a state of Washington would result in two Republican senators, one voting Republican congressman and three Republican electoral votes in the next presidential contest. For the moment, those Washingtonians aware of political realities set aside a cherished ambition. "The hope of...admission," a Seattle editor lamented, "...must now be regarded as extinct as the Dodo." An unamused eastside newspaper owner noted that "Alki," Chinook jargon for "bye and bye," had become, with the passage of years and the dashing of hopes, an unusually apt territorial motto.[16]

Political "considerations" and "machinations" worked against a united and deserving territory. Virtually impossible to breach in the past, the political door suddenly opened upon the national Republican victory in 1888. The Republican party was "the party of the West," the *P-I* exclaimed, and, as such, bound by justice and by self-interest to the cause of western statehood. The entryway, however, was still partially obstructed. President Benjamin Harrison would not be inaugurated until March 1889. The new Congress was not scheduled to meet in regular session until the following December. Although repudiated, the old Senate and House, Charles Voorhees included, and Grover Cleveland remained on the job through the post-election winter. "A Democratic majority, smarting under defeat," the *Walla Walla Union* pointed out, was unlikely to admit the eligible territories, since the additional electoral votes thereby handed the Republicans would "render the probabilities of the election of another Democratic President as few as are the chances of constructing a railroad to the moon."[17]

In expectation of Harrison calling a special session of Congress, local admission advocates busily organized themselves. "If statehood is worth having," the *P-I* reasoned, "it is worth asking for." A Spokane Falls mass meeting called for territory-wide county assemblies to meet on Washington's Birthday for the purpose of preparing statehood petitions. As a preliminary to these gatherings,

Spokane summoned a brief convention for Ellensburg in the first week of January. Local party committees and other interested bodies in urban areas on both sides of the mountains quickly selected representatives.[18]

Convening in Ellensburg on January 3, the one-day assembly was a Republican-dominated affair, chaired by Watson Squire, designed to make "the desires of a long-neglected people known to the powers that be." The standard arguments for admission, including a quarter-million-strong population of "intelligent and patriotic" Americans and "inexhaustible" supplies of timber, coal and wheat, were rehearsed in the resulting petition to Congress. Looking to the long haul, the delegates appointed a permanent committee to plan the Washington's Birthday celebrations and arranged for a follow-up convention to meet in North Yakima in May.[19]

Unexpected developments in Washington City made the work of Ellensburg superfluous. Early in the winter congressional session, the Senate, controlled by Republicans since the 1886 off-year elections, approved legislation admitting the Dakotas. Intent upon securing credit for an inevitable development, House Democratic leaders endorsed a more ambitious measure, covering North and South Dakota, Montana and Washington. "As the Republicans will soon be able to do whatever they choose," the *P-I* noted, "the Democrats would not be yielding much." Complaining of "duplicity" and "this tardy act of justice," statehood supporters nonetheless took "the shortest way to the desired end." Passed by Congress in February, the so-called "omnibus" bill was signed by President Cleveland on Washington's Birthday. The act authorized election of delegates in May, a constitutional convention in July and an October 1 vote on both the constitution and the principal state government offices.[20]

Genuine territory-wide approval of a constitution was more likely in 1889 than in 1878. The act of Congress required the governor and the chief judge of the supreme court to divide Washington into twenty-five districts of roughly equal population. Only two of the three delegates allotted from each district could be from the same party. The Republicans, firmly entrenched as the majority party, thereby secured control of the proceedings, but the Democrats were guaranteed a significant minority position. "Neither…," commented the *Spokane Falls Review*, "could reasonably ask more or less than to be represented according to its strength." Announced by Governor Miles Moore in late April, the districts corresponded, as close as practical circumstances allowed, to the total vote cast in the 1888 elections. King County secured ten seats, Pierce County six and Spokane County four, imparting in advance an urban orientation to the convention.[21]

The mid-May delegate elections produced anticipated results. The Republicans won forty-five seats, five less than the maximum possible, and the Democrats twenty-eight. Two independents were elected as the product of "fusion" campaigns on Puget Sound. The victors tended to be politically experienced and relatively youthful professionally trained persons. Twenty-one were practicing attorneys. Twenty-five of the seventy-one individuals supplying birthdates were under forty years of age. Eighteen had served in the territorial assembly. One, William Prosser, was a former member of Congress, from his home state of Tennessee. Overall, the 1889 delegates were more impressive than those sent to the 1878 convention. Seattle's John Hoyt, currently in charge of the Dexter Horton Bank, had come to Washington after stints as governor of Arizona and Idaho territories. With George Turner, representing Spokane Falls, Hoyt had also spent a term on the supreme court. John J. Browne was the richest inhabitant of Spokane. Physician-turned-wheat rancher N. G. Blalock owned a thousand acres near Walla Walla. Andrew West, a recent transplant from the Great Lakes, was the wealthiest lumberman on Grays Harbor.[22]

A month and a half intervened between the election and the convention, allowing time to address, and in some cases settle, certain troublesome issues. The challenge to Olympia presently mounted by North Yakima, Ellensburg and Pasco was sure to be "a disturbing element," should an attempt at resolution be made at the convention. Harmony among the delegates was preserved by a general agreement to submit the capital question to the voters in a separate ballot measure. Reasoning that an otherwise indifferent electorate might accept woman suffrage and prohibition as the price of admission, advocates of those pre-tested "reforms" sought to include them in the constitution. Worried that inclusion might actually endanger passage, convention planners "clear[ed] the way for a fair fight" via independent October 1 votes on suffrage and prohibition.[23]

Some issues were destined, no matter what, to preoccupy the convention in floor debate and committee rooms. Washington would inherit an empire upon admission. In addition to sections 16 and 36, or the equivalent, in every township donated for support of the schools, the federal government granted specific tracts to finance construction of a capitol and other public buildings. The total, a newspaper estimated, "well nigh reaches two millions of acres, and all…rapidly appreciating in value." School acreage could either be sold, at not less than $10 an acre, or leased for periods up to five years. Some analysts wanted to sell as rapidly as possible, stimulating settlement and, following Oregon's example, creating "a permanent…fund for the support of common schools." To others, the land was "the inheritance of the children," worthy of protection from "the vandalism of grasping corporations." Already, the per-acre value of the school sections averaged $75 across the territory, so the lease option had appeal as a means of preserving increased real estate valuations for public benefit.[24]

Opinion was even more divided over disposition of the tidelands. From the earliest days of settlement, the export-oriented Puget Sound economy impinged upon such tracts, since ships could be loaded and unloaded only at wharves extending out from the shore to deep water. The federal government retained title below the line of mean high tide. Private upland owners, however, had the right, under riparian doctrine, to build adjacent docks and other improvements. By the mid-1880s, facilities valued at a half million dollars were in place on Elliott Bay alone. The flats immediately southeast of Henry Yesler's sawmill were, to a considerable extent, filled in. "Streets have been extended through and over it," the *Seattle Times* reported of the "old slough" and structures of brick and wood "built on piles driven twenty feet down." At Tacoma, the Northern Pacific planned an ambitious development of the tidal areas at the mouth of the Puyallup River. Various Whatcom railroad schemes required exploitation of the "hard and solid...foundations" at the bottom of Bellingham Bay. Farmers also utilized tidal-flow places, most notably in the case of the thousands of diked and reclaimed acres in the Skagit River delta.[25]

Firstcomer shoreline owners denied later arrivals access to the waterfront. Tideland rivalries were, however, by no means limited to contests between early and recent settlers. The Oregon Improvement Company claimed to own part of Elliott Bay as heir to a legally questionable assembly grant to Arthur Denny's Seattle & Walla Walla Railroad in 1873. Citing, among assorted dubious pretexts, alleged rights as planters of oyster beds, "a swarm of salt water lunatics"—Judge Burke's reference to squatters—drove piling into the Seattle and Tacoma tideflats. "It seems to be the idea of a lot of grabbers...," the *P-I* reported, "that because title to the flats is not vested in individuals, they are legitimate plunder." Advocates of public port development argued that the cities should take control of the tidal sections, that future improvements might be in accordance with "harmonious" plans, rather than under the current "go-as-you-choose no-system." Despite the oft-heard contention that people on the far side of the Cascades knew "little, if anything" about such matters, eastsiders also insisted upon a voice in disposition of the tidelands, because of the inevitable impact on the means of exporting wheat.[26]

All parties expected the convention to resolve the conflicting claims. "Then is the time we must get in our work," John Howard advised in setting aside ample resources for "convincing arguments" on behalf of the Oregon Improvement Company. Congress specified the methods for dealing with school acreage, but said nothing about tidal tracts. Between existing federal law and the long-established "equal footing" doctrine, under which new states possessed the same rights as the old states, no one doubted that title to the tidelands passed to Washington upon admission. The debate focused on the next step. Waterfront interests wanted the constitution, Howard wrote, to give "owners of fast shore land a preference right to purchase the tide land in front of their holdings." Squatters hoped to administer "a rude awakening" to riparian claimants. A third position, well represented among the convention delegates, advocated continuing state ownership. "They are a rich inheritance," the *Tacoma News* observed of the tidal regions, and "should be carefully preserved...at least until such a time as they will command the highest price."[27]

Meeting in Olympia on July 4, two days short of a month since the great Seattle fire, delegates, interest group representatives and reporters exposed themselves to various midsummer discomforts. Between the convention and the territorial teachers' institute, convening in the capital under long-planned arrangement, accommodations and restaurant meals were at a premium. "The stranger arriving in Olympia now," a turned-away journalist lamented, "might be led to exclaim, with a slight improvement upon Richard III: 'A room! a room! my fortune for a room.'" Temperatures soared, on a daily basis, to ninety degrees and above, and noxious smoke from forest fires permeated the air, indoors and out. Sweaty cheek by dripping jowl, the delegates crowded into the small chamber normally used by the legislative assembly.[28]

Opening day featured a combined celebration of the Fourth of July and Washington's impending admission to the Union. A hundred flag-waving little girls, militia troops and two bands, one from Commencement Bay and the other provided by local Indians, marched behind a steam fire engine to the convention hall. Governor Miles Moore and, unaccountably, the mayor of Tacoma delivered brief remarks of welcome and advice from the house speaker's rostrum. John Hoyt's selection as presiding officer reflected divisions in Republican ranks and a victory of "anti-railroad" over "railroad" men, in other words of Seattleites over friends of the Northern Pacific.[29]

Under genuinely uncomfortable conditions, the delegates met, Sundays and the occasional Monday excepted, through August 23. In the first days, oratory-minded members pontificated upon pet nostrums. Critics, from Governor Moore to the smallest-circulation weekly newspaper, complained that the delegates were wasting time and money and "infring[ing] on the domain of the Legislator." The focus thereafter shifted from floor debate to closed sessions of the twenty-six standing committees, composed of self-nominated individuals willing to work, in secret, either on behalf of favored causes or against chosen enemies. Unable, as a result, to cover the real convention, reporters bemoaned "the attempt to do the business...*in camera*."[30]

Committees provided the ideal means to formally dispose of divisive issues. Woman suffrage and prohibition petitions were respectfully received and immediately sent behind closed doors, consigned to separate votes in October. The state capital question was handled in similar fashion, under ingenious committee language drafted by Thomas M. Reed, a longtime Budd Inlet partisan. Olympia remained the "temporary" seat of government until "a majority of all the votes cast" in a general election favored a specific "permanent" alternative, an unlikely prospect so long as more than two challengers were in the field.[31]

Most matters were resolved with a minimum of public rancor. Based on California's system, the judiciary article, providing for five supreme court justices, superior courts in each of the counties and continuous sessions, was generally considered a much-needed reform in the means of conducting legal business. Establishing an original legislative body of seventy house and thirty-five senate members and authorizing future increases, Article II, Section 2, addressed fears that a small legislature would be corrupted by special interests. Some observers complained of the $6,000 salary to be paid the lieutenant governor, an official with mostly ceremonial responsibilities, but the executive branch provisions otherwise generated little criticism.[32]

On a more controversial note, the convention rejected a majority report from the committee on corporations recommending inclusion of a railroad commission in the constitution. The document, as finally approved, retained strong anti-corporate language—"monopolies and trusts," for instance, "shall never be allowed"—but actual regulation of business was left to the legislature. After a good deal of discussion and disagreement, Article XVI authorized the sale of state lands at auction, provided winning bids at least equaled appraised valuation. No more than a quarter of the total state acreage, however, could be sold prior to January 1895 and no more than half before January 1905. Territorial experiences with railroad construction subsidies, and a current proposal for Walla Walla County bonds in aid of a new Northern Pacific project, made local government indebtedness an emotional issue. The delegates initially voted down a committee recommendation allowing such arrangements. Seattle representatives, otherwise happy to inflict a defeat upon the N.P., protested an outright ban as interference with plans for financing post-fire reconstruction on Elliott Bay. The result was a compromise constitutional provision allowing cities and counties to incur debt, with the approval of three-fifths of the electorate, up to 5 percent of assessed property value.[33]

Tidelands provided, as expected, Olympia's principal "monkey and parrot" show. The state of Washington asserted, in Article XVII, "ownership to the beds and shores of all navigable waters…up to and including the line of ordinary high tide." Concluding, on the eve of the convention, that their original goal, explicit recognition of their right to purchase adjacent tidal tracts, was beyond reach, shoreline interests pursued a revised agenda. The fallback position was, in the words of John Howard, one of "work[ing] for a deferment of the question," with the more easily influenced legislative branch to eventually decide among the sale, lease and public ownership alternatives. Elisha Ferry, Watson Squire and Cyrus Walker, who arrived from Port Gamble with five thousand dollars in cash to distribute among the delegates, joined in the exercise of corporate persuasion. Committee-devised language was accepted in one of the final floor votes. Article XV required appointment of a commission, "whose duty it shall be to locate and establish harbor lines in the navigable waters" adjacent to cities. Section 2, declaring that the legislature "shall provide laws for the leasing" of tracts between the lines so designated and high tide mark, supplied the means by which private industry expected to maintain effectual waterfront control.[34]

Signed by weary delegates in late August, the constitution was generally considered a "tolerably liberal," if imperfect, document. "There are some provisions which ought to have been left out," one editor remarked in a commonly expressed opinion, "and some principles which should have been included." Complaints included the failure to definitively resolve the tideland controversy, the lack of a railroad commission and the cost of the enlarged judicial system. No major voice of influence, however, called for rejection at the polls. Majority Republicans were unlikely to deny installation of their heavily favored slate of candidates for state office by voting against the constitution. Congress, moreover, had mandated that the convention reconvene in the event of defeat. "While there are several things in the Constitution which should be out, and several things out which should be in," the *Walla Walla Union* reflected of this practical consideration, "we deem it better to adopt it…than to defeat it and run the chance of having a better one formed by the men who constructed the present one."[35]

Virtually every observer of Washington politics agreed as to the likely outcome. "It is safe to predict," the *Spokane Falls Review* noted a month prior to the October 1 voting date, "that the constitution will be adopted by a large majority." Anticipating his elevation to the U.S. senate by the first state legislature, Watson Squire set to work distributing the federal patronage soon to be at his disposal. Except for occasional Republican accusations that the Democrats opposed statehood, the constitution was rarely mentioned, directly or indirectly, during the campaign. The race for state capital, with North Yakima and Ellensburg mounting heavily publicized campaigns against Olympia, was far more dramatic. Despite less-than-unanimous support for Budd Inlet on Puget Sound—Tacomans following the N.P. line, for instance, favored Yakima—the division of loyalties east of the Cascades made achievement of the necessary majority highly uncertain.[36]

Downed telegraph wires, from a series of intense rainstorms sweeping the territory in the final days of its legal existence, prevented the prompt counting of votes. The official tally was not released for two weeks, generating impatience rather than suspense. Washington voters endorsed the constitution by nearly a four-to-one margin. Only four of the thirty-four counties—Walla Walla, traditionally a center of sentiment for territorial division, Columbia and sparsely populated Franklin and Skamania—cast negative votes. Least popular in such areas of economic stagnation, statehood drew the heaviest support in dynamic locales. King, Pierce and Spokane counties favored the constitution and admission by overwhelming rates of approval. Local communities intent upon winning the capital also extended extraordinary support. Ninety-three percent of the electorate in Ellensburg's Kittitas County and 89 percent in Yakima County endorsed membership in the Union.[37]

Landslide results were also recorded in the other contests. Elisha Ferry became Washington's first elected governor, besting Democrat Eugene Semple with 58 percent of the vote. Republicans won thirty-four of the senate seats and sixty-three in the house, a legislative ratio so one-sided as to make the new state, at the outset, a one-party domain. Woman suffrage and prohibition went down by respective margins-against of two-to-one and three-to-two. Three small counties favored the ban on liquor and four supported electoral rights for women. Olympia finished first in the race for capital, with just over 25,000 votes, but fell far short of the majority required to permanently secure the seat of government. Nearly 28,000 combined, the North Yakima and Ellensburg tally suggested that, if one or the other had dropped out in favor of its regional rival, the political center of Washington would have shifted from west to east of the Cascades.[38]

Overnight squalls gave way to bright early winter sunshine as the government of the nation's forty-second state was formally installed on November 18, 1889. Sworn in that morning, the Republican legislature set impatiently to work. Just before noon, a parade assembled with Miles Moore, the outgoing caretaker executive, and Elisha Ferry, his elected successor, in the lead. National Guard infantry and cavalry detachments and whoop-it-up members of local fraternal organizations marched to the capitol building. Intent upon their duties, legislators briefly paused to witness the inauguration ceremony.

Prior to taking the oath of office at three-quarters after the hour, Ferry spoke for twenty-five minutes, to occasional applause from a crowd determined to properly celebrate a momentous occasion. Statehood, he asserted, was "the consummation of hopes long deferred, yet ever renewed." A Puget Sounder for nearly two decades, the governor deliberately ignored the past, in favor of predicting Washington's future: "With resources superior to those of any other equal area, with a population as enterprising as it is courageous, with a climate which commends itself to all who experience it, occupying a position at the gateway of the Oriental and Occidental commerce…there is no reason why the State of Washington should not…take rank among the most prominent States of the Union; nor why our people should not enjoy the peerless blessings of prosperity, health and happiness."[39]

Chapter Notes

Abbreviations

BL	Bancroft Library, University of California, Berkeley
C	*Columbia*
EWSHS	Eastern Washington State Historical Society
FRC	Federal Records Center, Seattle
IY	*Idaho Yesterdays*
MHS	Minnesota Historical Society
NA	National Archives
OHQ	*Oregon Historical Quarterly*
OHS	Oregon Historical Society
PHR	*Pacific Historical Review*
PNQ	*Pacific Northwest Quarterly*
UO	University of Oregon Library
UW	University of Washington Library
WAC	Western Americana Collection, Yale University Library
WHQ	*Washington Historical Quarterly*
WSA	Washington State Archives
WSHS	Washington State Historical Society
WSL	Washington State Library
WSU	Washington State University Library

Notes—Introduction

1. *Seattle Post-Intelligencer*, Dec. 15, 19, 1888. Territorial longevity figures derived from the tables in Ted Morgan, *A Shovel of Stars: The Making of the American West, 1800 to the Present* (New York: Simon & Schuster, 1995), 509–514.
2. For examples of the traditional partisanship contention, see Merle Wells, "The Long Wait for Statehood," *C*, 2(Fall 1989), 21–22; Keith A. Murray, "Statehood for Washington," *C*, 2(Winter 1989), 34–35. Howard Lamar notes that congressional Democrats believed Washington would adhere to their party. Howard R. Lamar, *Dakota Territory, 1861–1889: A Study of Frontier Politics* (New Haven: Yale University Press, 1956), 264–265.
3. On the extension of historic Oregon-Puget Sound rivalries into modern times, see Carl Abbott, "Regional City and Network City: Portland and Seattle in the Twentieth Century," *Western History Quarterly*, 23(Aug. 1992), 293–319.
4. Olympia *Washington Pioneer*, Dec. 10, 1853. On the widespread phenomenon of George III rhetoric, see Earl Pomeroy, *The Territories and the United States, 1861–1890: Studies in Colonial Administration* (Seattle: University of Washington Press ed., 1969, 1947), 103–104. The inability of locally based business interests to compete with outsiders is an ongoing theme of William L. Lang, *Confederacy of Ambition: William Winlock Miller and the Making of Washington Territory* (Seattle: University of Washington Press, 1996).
5. Earl Pomeroy estimates that barely a third of all western territorial positions were filled by genuine local residents. Pomeroy, *Territories and the United States*, 73–74.
6. *Walla Walla Union*, Nov. 23, 1889.

Notes—Chapter One
The Best Portion of Oregon

1. To Thomas Corwin, Oct. 17, 1850, Oregon and Washington Territorial Papers, House File, Records of the House of Representatives, RG 233, NA.
2. Michael F. Luark Diary, Sept. 3, 4, 1853, UW; Diary of a Journey from Fort Vancouver in 1835, 73–74, Private Papers of Sir James Douglas, BL; Theodore Winthrop to mother, July 23, 1853, in Theodore Winthrop, *The Canoe and the Saddle*, ed. John H. Williams (Tacoma: Priv. pub., 1913), 259–260. Also see John M. McClelland, Jr., *Cowlitz Corridor: Historical River Highway of the Pacific Northwest* (Longview: Longview Publishing Co., 1953) and Kent D. Richards, "A Good Serviceable Road: The Cowlitz Columbia River to Puget Sound Connection," *C*, 6(Winter 1992–1993), 6–11.
3. T. C. Elliott, ed., "Journal of John Work, November and December, 1824," *WHQ*, 3(July 1912), 227; Edmond S. Meany, *Diary of Wilkes in the Northwest* (Seattle: University of Washington Press, 1926), 26; Portland *Oregonian*, July 17, 1852; Joseph Schafer, "Documents Relative to Warre and Vavasour's Military Reconnoissance in Oregon, 1846–7," *OHQ*, 10(March 1909), 56. On Cowlitz Farm and Hudson's Bay colonization efforts, see James R. Gibson, *Farming the Frontier: The Agricultural Opening of the Oregon Country, 1786–1846* (Seattle: University of Washington Press, 1985), chaps. 4, 5.
4. Thomas J. Farnham, *Travels in the Great Western Prairies, the Aanahuac and Rocky Mountains, and in the Oregon Territory* (New York: Greeley & McElrath, 1843), 99; Gustavus Hines, *Oregon: Its History, Condition and Prospects* (Buffalo: Geo. H. Derby & Co., 1851), 340–341. Even the forest north of the Columbia appeared inferior. "In those parts I visited," Neil Howison of the U.S. Navy reported in 1846, "there was not a stick of timber suitable for ship-building." See "Report of Lieutenant Neil M. Howison on Oregon, 1846," *OHQ*, 14(March 1913), 49–50.
5. McClelland, *Cowlitz Corridor*, 12; Olympia *Columbian*, Dec. 25, 1852; Portland *Oregonian*, July 17, 1852; Luark Diary, Sept. 4, 28, 1853; Olympia *Daily Tribune*, Dec. 20, 1867; Seattle *Weekly Intelligencer*, Dec. 30, 1867.
6. Oregon City *Oregon Spectator*, Feb. 19, 1846; March 9, 23, May 18, Oct. 26, 1848.
7. Samuel Crockett and Jesse Ferguson accompanied the five families. George Waunch, another member of the Simmons party, settled just north of what is now Centralia. Herndon Smith, comp., *Centralia: The First Fifty Years, 1845–1900* (Centralia: Centralia American Revolution Bicentennial Committee, 1975, 1942), 62–63; Hubert Howe Bancroft, *History of Washington, Idaho, and Montana, 1845–1889* (San Francisco: The History Company, 1890), 1–4; Notes Copied From the Hudson's Bay Company Account Books at Fort Nisqually, 1833–1850, 16, UW; Antonio Rabbeson Reminiscences, 9–10, BL; "Edmund Sylvester's Narrative of the Founding of Olympia," *PNQ*, 36(Oct. 1945), 334; Luark Diary, Oct. 8, 1853; Portland *Oregonian*, July 17, 1852.
8. Notes Copied From the Hudson's Bay Company Account Books, 16–17, 19–22; Fort Nisqually Journal, Feb. 9, 1846, UW; Rabbeson Reminiscences, 10–11; Samuel Hancock, *The Narrative of Samuel Hancock, 1845–1860* (New York: Robert M. McBride & Company, 1927), 57–58; "Cowlitz Farm Journal," in Charles Miles and O. B. Sperlin, eds., *Building a State: Washington, 1889–1939* (Tacoma: Washington State Historical Society, 1940), 577, 579; "Sylvester's Narrative," 334–335. Tolmie quoted in Edmond S. Meany, "First American Settlement on Puget Sound," *WHQ*, 7(April 1916), 140–141.
9. T. F. McElroy to Sarah B. McElroy, Aug. 10, 1852, McElroy Family Papers, UW; Anna Maria Foxwell James to Elizabeth Foxwell, Nov. 14, 1852, James Family Papers, UW; Alfred Hall to Brother and Sister, Jan. 1, 1853, Alfred Hall Correspondence, BL; Portland *Oregonian*, July 10, 17; Nov. 20, 1852; Steilacoom *Puget Sound Herald*, Sept. 3, 1858. Also see McClelland, *Cowlitz Corridor*, 19–21.
10. Fort Nisqually Journal, March 29, 1847; May 1; Aug. 24, 1849; Bancroft, *History of Washington*, 5–8; William F. Tolmie to Thomas M. Chambers, Dec. 20, 1849, Thomas M. Chambers Papers, WSHS; Joseph Lane to P. F. Smith, June 8, 1849; J. S. Hatheway to W. T. Sherman, June 8, 1849, both Pacific Division Records, U.S. Army Continental Commands, RG 393, NA; to Lane, Sept. 11, 1849, Records of the Oregon Superintendency of Indian Affairs, 1845–1873, M2, NA.
11. Sylvester substituted Olympia for Schictwood, the local Indian name "signifying Bear _____" and therefore easily "converted into blackguard meaning." Steilacoom *Puget Sound Herald*, Jan. 6, 1860; "Sylvester's Narrative," 335, 338; Portland *Oregonian*, July 17, 1852; Olympia *Columbian*, Jan. 8, 1853; Olympia *Pioneer and Democrat*, July 22, 1854; Seattle *Weekly Intelligencer*, June 10, 1872; Luark Diary, Oct. 8, 1853.
12. Combining the two counties, 154 of 505 adults were natives of Canada or the British Isles. The thirty Hawaiians recorded in the 1850 census also reflected the long Hudson's Bay Company presence. Clinton A. Snowden, *History of Washington: The Rise and Progress of an American State* (New York: The Century History Company, 4 vols., 1909), 2:443; William Duncan Strong, ed., "Knickerbocker Views of the Oregon Country: Judge William Strong's Narrative," *OHQ*, 52(March 1951), 64–65; Mrs. John B. Moyer, comp., Statistics of the First Federal Census of Washington Territory, 1860, typescript in UW, 1–25.
13. Portland *Oregonian*, Jan. 29; March 26, 1853; Olympia *Columbian*, Oct. 9; Dec. 25, 1852; Jan. 15; Feb. 26, 1853; Oregon City *Oregon Spectator*, Sept. 5, 1850.

14. McLoughlin blamed the anti-company prejudice on Senator Thomas Hart Benton of Missouri. John McLoughlin to Captain John Gordon, Sept. 15, 1845, in Leslie M. Scott, ed., "Report of Lieutenant Peel on Oregon in 1845–6," *OHQ*, 29(March 1928), 58–59; Peter Skene Ogden and James Douglas to Tolmie, Nov. 4, 1846; Douglas to Tolmie, April 19, 1847, both in Fort Nisqually Journal; George Gibbs to A. Van Dusen, Sept. 4, 1852, Oregon and Washington Territorial Papers.

15. Memorial of the Legislative Assembly of Oregon, July 26, 1849, Oregon and Washington Territorial Papers; J. B. Chapman to Daniel Webster, Sept. 24, 1852; James Tilton to John Wilson, May 10, 1855, both Letters Received from the Surveyors General of Washington, 1854–1883, RG 49, NA; Olympia *Columbian*, April 9, 1853; George L. Whiting to Tilton, July 19, 1855, Letters Received from Commissioner, General Land Office, Bureau of Land Management Records, Series 88, RG 49, FRC; Fort Nisqually Journal, Nov. 4, 5, 7; Dec. 20, 1849; John E. Ballenden to Tolmie, Nov. 1, 1852, William F. Tolmie Papers, UW. A good summation of the legal issues is found in Hazard Stevens to J. W. Sprague, Dec. 19, 1871, Northern Pacific Railway Company Land Department Records, MHS.

16. Oregon City *Oregon Spectator*, Jan. 11, 1849; Memorial of the Legislative Assembly, July 26, 1849, Oregon and Washington Territorial Papers.

17. Thurston privately boasted of his successful opposition to "all attempts to strike out the word 'white' in our land bill." Although Donation Act land was free, settlers could reduce the four years of residency required to one by paying $1.50 an acre. Anson Dart to L. Lea, July 19, 1851, Correspondence of the Office of Indian Affairs, Letters Received, 1824–1881, M234, NA; Portland *Oregonian*, Dec. 20, 1851; Jan. 31; March 27, 1852; Michael T. Simmons to Lane, March 8, 1852, Joseph Lane Papers, OHS; Arthur A. Denny, *Pioneer Days on Puget Sound* (Seattle: C. B. Bagley Printer, 1888), 12; F. W. Pettygrove to Philip Foster, Jan. 15, 1852, F. W. Pettygrove Letters, Jefferson County Historical Society; Olympia *Washington Pioneer*, Dec. 17, 1853; Olympia *Columbian*, Aug. 6; Oct. 8, 29, 1853; Samuel R. Thurston to Wesley Shannon, June 22, 1850, Wesley Shannon Letters, OHS; James M. Berquist, "The Oregon Donation Act and the National Land Policy," *OHQ*, 58(March 1957), 17–35.

18. Thurston to Shannon, Nov. 16, 1850, Samuel R. Thurston Correspondence, WSL; Medorem Crawford to S. G. Crawford, Jan. 24, 1850, Medorem Crawford Papers, UO; U. S. Grant to Julia Dent Grant, Sept. 19, 1852, in John Y. Simon, ed., *The Papers of Ulysses S. Grant* (Carbondale: Southern Illinois University Press, 11 vols. to date, 1967–), 1:266; E. Colvile to J. H. Pelly, Dec. 8, 1849, in E. E. Rich, ed., *London Correspondence Inward from Eden Colvile, 1849–1852* (London: The Hudson's Bay Company Record Society, 1956), 13; John W. Caughey, ed., "Life in California in 1849 As Described in the 'Journal' of George F. Kent," *California Historical Society Quarterly*, 20(March 1941), 29; Henry Roeder Reminiscences, BL.

19. Edmond S. Meany, Jr., "The History of the Lumber Industry in the Pacific Northwest to 1917" (Ph.D. diss., Harvard University, 1935), 6–7; Charles Wilkes, *Narrative of the United States Exploring Expedition* (London: Ingram, Cooke, and Co., 2 vols., 1852), 2:176; Miss A. J. Allen, comp., *Ten Years in Oregon: Travels and Adventures of Doctor E. White and Lady West of the Rocky Mountains* (Ithaca: Andrus, Gauntlett & Co., 1850), 51; Charles Henry Carey, ed., "Diary of Reverend George Gary," *OHQ*, 24(Dec. 1923), 393; Caroline C. Leighton, *Life at Puget Sound* (Boston: Lee and Shepard, 1884), 45. In a further problem, contrary winds occasionally kept ships bar-bound for weeks. See Sir George Simpson, *Narrative of a Journey Round the World, During the Years 1841 and 1842* (London: Henry Colburn, 2 vols., 1847), 1:245–247. For a table of distances between San Francisco and various northern ports, see Olympia *Pioneer and Democrat*, March 14, 1856.

20. Portland *Oregonian*, April 12; July 12, 1851; Oregon City *Oregon Spectator*, Dec. 10, 1846; March 18, 1847; March 23, 1848; Oct. 4, 1849; Gibbs to Van Dusen, Sept. 4, 1852, Oregon and Washington Territorial Papers; Lewis A. McArthur, "The Pacific Coast Survey of 1849 and 1850," *OHQ*, 16(Sept. 1915), 258.

21. Ironically, the *Columbian* was originally owned by Thomas J. Dryer, the pro-Columbia River publisher of the Portland *Oregonian*. McElroy to S. McElroy, Aug. 10, 1852, McElroy Family Papers; Portland *Oregonian*, Jan. 31, 1852; Olympia *Columbian*, Sept. 11; Oct. 16, 1852; April 2; Sept. 17, 1853; W. A. Katz, "*The Columbian*: Washington Territory's First Newspaper," *OHQ*, 64(March 1963), 33–40; Strong to Corwin, Oct. 17, 1850, Oregon and Washington Territorial Papers; Port Townsend *Weekly Message*, Jan. 16, 1868.

22. Olympia *Columbian*, Jan. 8, 1853; Portland *Oregonian*, Sept. 18, 1852; A. S. Mercer, *Washington Territory: The Great Northwest, Her Material Resources, and Claims to Emigration* (Ithaca: L. C. Childs, 1865), 8; *Port Townsend Register*, April 18, 1860; "Business Broadside of 1853," *WHQ*, 20(July 1929), 231; C. L. Hooper to Watson C. Squire, Oct. 15, 1884, Watson C. Squire Papers, WSA; Isaac N. Ebey to Parents, Feb. 20, 1850; to Winfield S. Ebey, Sept. 28, 1853, Winfield S. Ebey Papers, UW; McArthur, "Pacific Coast Survey," 257; Henry J. Winser, *The Pacific Northwest* (New York: N.p., 1882), 12–13; Albert D. Richardson, *Beyond the Mississippi: From the Great River to the Great Ocean* (Hartford: American Publishing Company, 1867), 414–415.

23. Richardson, *Beyond the Mississippi*, 415; Portland *Oregonian*, July 17, 1852; C. M. Scammon, "Lumbering in Washington Territory," *Overland Monthly*, 5(July 1870), 55; "Business Broadside of 1853," 229; *Tenth Census of the United States*, Vol. IX, *Report on the Forests of North America* (Washington, D.C.: Government Printing Office, 1884), 573–575; Hugo Winkenwerder, "Forestry and Lumbering," in Howard T. Lewis and Stephen I. Miller, eds., *The Economic Resources of the Pacific Northwest* (Seattle: Lowman & Hanford Company, 1923), 209; Meany, "History of the Lumber Industry," 26–32.

24. "Villages spring up here in a few days," a newcomer to the Pacific Northwest noted. Ebey to Parents, Feb. 20, 1850, Ebey Papers; D. E. Blaine to Brother and friends, Nov. 22, 1853, Blaine Family Letters, UW; Bancroft,

History of Washington, 19–21; Ezra Meeker, *Pioneer Reminiscences of Puget Sound* (Seattle: Lowman & Hanford, 1905), 72; Immigration Aid Society, *Northwestern Washington, Its Soil, Climate, Productions and General Resources* (Port Townsend: Port Townsend *Argus*, 1880), 15; F. W. Pettygrove Reminiscences, 10–11, BL; Albert Briggs Reminiscences, 35, BL

25. Roeder Reminiscences, 8–12, 28–45; Edward Eldridge Reminiscences, 2–4, BL; Puget Sound Journal, May 11, 1871, W. Milnor Roberts Papers, Montana State University Library; Phoebe Goodell Judson, *A Pioneer's Search for an Ideal Home* (Lincoln: University of Nebraska Press, 1984, 1925), 198–199; Nathaniel D. Hill Diary, Jan. ? 1854, Jefferson County Historical Society; Bellingham *American Reveille*, May 19, 1918; Olympia *Columbian*, July 30, 1853; Olympia *Pioneer and Democrat*, May 13, 1854; March 5, 1858; James Alden to A. D. Bache, Nov. 3, 1855, in *Annual Report of the Superintendent of the Coast Survey, 1855*, 189.

26. Daniel B. Bigelow Diary, Jan. 25, 1852, WSHS; William Petit Trowbridge Journal, July 28, 1853, WSHS; Meeker, *Pioneer Reminiscences*, 65–66; Denny, *Pioneer Days*, 16–17, 21; Henry L. Yesler Reminiscences, 4, 7, BL; Pettygrove Reminiscences, 12; William S. Lewis, ed., "Reminiscences of Joseph H. Boyd, An Argonaut of 1857," *WHQ*, 15(Oct. 1924), 249; D. Blaine to ?, April 4, 1854, Blaine Family Letters; C. D. Boren to John and Sarah Denny, May 3, 1853, Arthur A. Denny Papers, WSHS. Also see John R. Finger, "A Study of Frontier Enterprise: Seattle's First Sawmill, 1853–1869," *Forest History*, 15(Jan. 1972), 24–31; Thomas W. Pohl, "Seattle, 1851–1861: A Frontier Community" (Ph.D. diss., University of Washington, 1970), 55–66, 70–83, 101–102, 131–134.

27. Balch's mercantile holdings exceeded in value the combined total for all other Steilacoom business establishments. Steilacoom *Puget Sound Herald*, April 9; Oct. 22, 1858; Dec. 11, 1862; Charles Prosch, *Reminiscences of Washington Territory* (Seattle: N.p., 1904), 7; Report on the Business Houses in Steilacoom, Oct. 1, 1859, William H. Wallace Papers, UW; Ebey to Lane, Jan. 23, 1852, Lane Papers; Trowbridge Journal, Aug. 9, 1853; Meeker, *Pioneer Reminiscences*, 52–53, 73–74.

28. Previously, vessels sailing between foreign ports and Puget Sound had to clear customs at Astoria on the Columbia River. Olympia *Pioneer and Democrat*, July 22, 1854; W. S. Hodge to Simpson P. Moses, March 21, 1851, Letters Sent by Secretary of Treasury to Collectors of Customs at Pacific Ports, M176, NA; Strong to Corwin, Oct. 17, 1850; Samuel R. Thurston, "The Reasons why Oregon Should be divided into three Collection Districts," n.d., both Oregon and Washington Territorial Papers; Ebey to Rebecca Ebey, June 8, 1851, Ebey Papers; Portland *Oregonian*, May 24, 1851; J. Ross Browne to James Guthrie, Sept. 4, 1854, Letters and Reports Received by the Secretary of the Treasury from Special Agents, 1854–1861, M177, NA; George Suckley to Brother, Dec. 24, 1853, George Suckley Letters, WAC; Simmons to Lane, June 22, 1852, Lane Papers.

29. Olympia *Columbian*, Nov. 6, 1852; March 26; July 9, 1853; Ebey to W. Ebey, May 2, 1852; Sept. 28, 1853, Ebey Papers; Prosch, *Reminiscences*, 13–14; Washington Pioneer Project, *Told by the Pioneers: Reminiscences of Pioneer Life in Washington* (Olympia: W.P.A., 3 vols., 1937–1939), 1:188; "Narrative of James Longmire: A Pioneer of 1853," *WHQ*, 23(April 1932), 140–141; Hancock, *Narrative*, 157–158; David Denny to J. Denny, March 2, 1853, Denny Papers.

30. As in the case of the Pope & Talbot-Puget Mill Company relationship, the other mills were also operated by local subsidiaries of San Francisco parent firms. Ebey to W. Ebey, April 20, 1853, Ebey Papers; Puget Mill Co. Agreement, Dec. 20, 1852, Josiah Keller Papers, WAC; Cloice R. Howd, "Development of Lumber Industry of West Coast," *Timberman*, 25(Aug. 1924), 194. Also see James N. Tattersall, "The Economic Development of the Pacific Northwest to 1910" (Ph.D. diss., University of Washington, 1960), 65–67. For a complete list of sawmills and their 1858 capacities, see Meany, "History of the Lumber Industry," 11.

31. In 1857, territorial tax collections were three times greater in Kitsap County than in King County. Statement of the Financial Condition of the Territory of Washington, copy in William P. Winans Papers, WSU; Iva L. Buchanan, "An Economic History of Kitsap County, Washington, to 1889" (Ph.D. diss., University of Washington, 1930), 2, 108–112, 133–139; Edith Sanderson Redfield, *Seattle Memories* (Boston: Lothrop, Lee & Shepard Co., 1930), 31; John S. Hittell, *The Commerce and Industries of the Pacific Coast* (San Francisco: A. L. Bancroft & Company, 2nd ed., 1882), 586; Edward Clayson, Sr., *Historical Narratives of Puget Sound: Hoods Canal, 1865–1885* (Seattle: R. L. Davis Printing Co., 1911), 11.

32. Robert A. Habersham to Thomas W. Symons, Oct. 10, 1890, in *Annual Report of the Chief of Engineers, 1890*, 3267; Charles Powell to Chief of Engineers, Jan. 30, 1882, Portland District Records, U.S. Army Corps of Engineers, RG 77, FRC; James G. Swan, *The Northwest Coast, or, Three Years' Residence in Washington Territory* (Seattle: University of Washington Press, 1972, 1857), 30; Olympia *Pioneer and Democrat*, Aug. 19, 1859. "Long Beach Peninsula" is a popular term; the U.S. Geological Survey actually identifes this area as the North Beach Peninsula.

33. Although Puget Sound had sufficient natural oyster beds to "supply a dozen such cities" as San Francisco, the extra sailing time precluded major commercial development. Olympia *Columbian*, Oct. 30, 1852; Steilacoom *Puget Sound Herald*, March 7, 1861; Swan, *Northwest Coast*, 59–63; Portland *Oregonian*, June 11, 1853; Report of the Commerce of Shoalwater Bay, n.d., Oregon and Washington Territorial Papers; *Port Townsend Register*, May 2, 1860.

34. Olympia *Columbian*, Sept. 25; Oct. 2, 1852; Jan. 29; Feb. 19; April 2, 1853.

35. Ibid., Sept. 18, 25; Oct. 2, 16, 30; Nov. 13, 1852; Jan. 29, 1853; Richard J. White to Lane, Feb. 1, 1852, Oregon and Washington Territorial Papers; Portland *Oregonian*, Jan. 8, 1853. For a list of Washington counties

and their dates of incorporation, see M. F. Maury to Secretary of Washington Territory, Feb. 13, 1861, Washington Territorial Documents, WSHS.

36. Oregon City *Oregon Statesman*, Aug. 5, 1851; Portland *Oregonian*, July 26, 1851; Oregon City *Oregon Spectator*, July 29; Aug. 19, 1851; Ebey to W. Ebey, July 20, 1851, Ebey Papers.

37. Pioneers knew of the agricultural potential of the Walla Walla Valley from the story of the Whitman Mission and from overland trail encounters with Indians in the Blue Mountains. Ebey to Lane, Jan. 23, 1852; F. A. Chenoweth to Lane, Oct. 28, 1851, both Lane Papers; Olympia *Columbian*, Nov. 20; Dec. 11, 1852; Portland *Oregonian*, July 12, 1851.

38. Conclusions regarding delegates are based on Moyer, comp., Statistics of the First Federal Census. David Maynard became one of the pioneers of Seattle, which was founded subsequent to the 1851 convention. Portland *Oregonian*, Sept. 20, 1851; Oregon City *Oregon Spectator*, Sept. 23, 1851. For further details, see John McClelland, Jr., "Almost Columbia, Triumphantly Washington," in David H. Stratton, ed., *Washington Comes of Age: The State in the National Experience* (Pullman: Washington State University Press, 1992), 54–55. Also see Edmond S. Meany, "The Cowlitz Convention: Inception of Washington Territory," *WHQ*, 13(Jan. 1922), 9.

39. A Petition to divide Oregon Territory, Aug. 1851, Oregon and Washington Territorial Papers. Also see McClelland, "Almost Columbia," 55–56.

40. Olympia *Columbian*, Oct. 23; Nov. 6, 1852.

41. Ibid., Oct. 23; Nov. 6, 13, 1852.

42. Only Michael Simmons, David Maynard, John Jackson and Seth Catlin attended both the 1851 and the 1852 conventions. Ibid., Dec. 4, 11, 1852. Also see McClelland, "Almost Columbia," 60–62; Kent D. Richards, *Isaac I. Stevens: Young Man in a Hurry* (Pullman: Washington State University Press, 1993, 1979), 153–154.

43. The Monticello convention adjourned with plans to reconvene in May 1853 for an aggressive final push to victory. Olympia *Columbian*, Dec. 4, 18, 1852; March 24, 1853; Ebey to W. Ebey, March 22; May 20; Sept. 28, 1853, Ebey Papers; Oregon City *Oregon Spectator*, Nov. 25, 1851. On Lane's interest in statehood, see James E. Hendrickson, *Joe Lane of Oregon: Machine Politics and the Sectional Crisis, 1849–1861* (New Haven: Yale University Press, 1967), 86–87.

44. In addition to the Columbia Territory memorial, an assembly suddenly willing to act on behalf of North Oregon approved road legislation, created three new counties and granted a divorce to David Maynard. Olympia *Columbian*, Jan. 22, 29; Feb. 12; March 12; April 9, 1853; McClelland, "Almost Columbia," 62–66; Terrence Cole, "The *Other* Washington: The Naming of Northern Oregon," *C*, 8(Fall 1994), 6–8. Also see Hendrickson, *Joe Lane of Oregon*, 59.

45. Olympia *Columbian*, April 16, 1853; Ebey to W. Ebey, April 20, 1853, Ebey Papers; McClelland, "Almost Columbia," 65–66. The complete text of the Washington Territory bill is in Portland *Oregonian*, May 7, 1853. For continuing complaints over the territory's name, see Olympia *Washington Standard*, Jan. 13, 1866.

46. Olympia *Columbian*, April 30; May 7; Oct. 22, 1853. Also see Kenneth N. Owens, "Pattern and Structure in Western Territorial Politics," *Western Historical Quarterly*, 1(Oct. 1970), 375–377.

47. Bisecting the countries of several important Indian tribes, including the Walla Walla and the Nez Perce, the 46th parallel boundary inadvertently created jurisdictional problems for Washington and Oregon. Isaac I. Stevens to Joel Palmer, Jan. 3, 1854, Records of the Washington Superintendency of Indian Affairs, 1853–1874, M5, NA.

48. Oregon City *Oregon Spectator*, Oct. 24, 1850; June 5, 19; Oct. 7, 1851; Sept. 2, 1853; Portland *Oregonian*, June 12, 1852. Also see Randall V. Mills, *Stern-Wheelers Up Columbia: A Century of Steamboating in the Oregon Country* (Palo Alto: Pacific Books, 1947), 15–21.

49. Oregon City *Oregon Spectator*, Sept. 5, 1850; H. A. Goldsborough to Lane, April 11, 1852, Lane Papers; Olympia *Columbian*, Sept. 11, 18, 25; Oct. 30, 1852.

50. Olympia *Columbian*, Sept. 18, 25; Oct. 9, 1852.

51. Oregon City *Oregon Spectator*, Sept. 5, 1850; Simmons, et al. to Lane, March 8, 1852; Simmons to Lane, March 8, 1852, internal evidence indicating that the letter was actually written in 1853, both Lane Papers; Petition for Military road north of the Columbia from Pugets Sound to Fort Walla Walla, n.d., Oregon and Washington Territorial Papers; Olympia *Columbian*, Jan. 22, 1853.

52. Olympia *Columbian*, March 5, 1853; Stevens to J. Patton Anderson, April 18, 1853; to George B. McClellan, April 5, 16, 1853, Isaac I. Stevens Papers, UW; Jefferson Davis to McClellan, May 9, 1853, George B. McClellan Correspondence, UW. The government ignored the likelihood that the road, by passing through their country, would antagonize the Yakama Indians. Benjamin Alvord to E. Townsend, June 5, 1853, Pacific Division Records.

53. Olympia *Columbian*, April 30; May 28; June 18; July 16, 23; Sept. 24; Oct. 15, 1853; Stevens to McClellan, April 26, 1853, Stevens Papers. The War Department was displeased with McClellan for taking such a minor role in construction of the road. W. Turrentine Jackson, *Wagon Roads West: A Study of Federal Road Surveys and Construction in the Trans-Mississippi West, 1846–1869* (New Haven: Yale University Press, 1964), 90–92.

54. Tilton to Wilson, Sept. 12, 14, 1855, Letters Received from the Surveyors General; Olympia *Pioneer and Democrat*, Feb. 25, 1854.

Notes—Chapter Two
A Grand Element of National Strength

1. Olympia *Washington Pioneer*, Dec. 24, 1853.
2. Noting the governor's initials, humorists dubbed him "Two-Eyed Stevens" and proclaimed "Glory to II of Oregon." Catherine Blaine to mother, Jan. 17, 1854, Blaine Family Letters, UW; James G. Swan, *The Northwest Coast, or, Three Years' Residence in Washington Territory* (Seattle: University of Washington Press, 1972, 1857), 341; H. D. Wallen to John Wool, Oct. 26, 1856, John Wool Papers, New York State Library; Edmund Fitzhugh to James G. Swan, July 22, 1860, James G. Swan Papers, University of British Columbia Library; Steilacoom *Puget Sound Herald*, Jan. 3, 1861; Olympia *Washington Standard*, May 11, 1861. For the governor's pre-1853 life and career, see Kent D. Richards, *Isaac I. Stevens: Young Man in a Hurry* (Pullman: Washington State University Press, 1993, 1979), chaps. 1–5.
3. Olympia *Washington Pioneer*, Jan. 14, 1854; Isaac I. Stevens to W. L. Marcy, March 22, 1853, Isaac I. Stevens Papers, UW; J. J. Abert to Jefferson Davis, March 26, 1853, Letters Sent to Secretary of War, Records of the Topographical Engineers, RG 77, NA; Davis to Stevens, April 8, 1853, Correspondence of the Office of Exploration and Surveys Concerning Isaac Stevens' Survey of a Northern Route for the Pacific R.R., 1853–61, RG 48, NA. Stevens reported to the State Department, to the Office of Indian Affairs in the Interior Department and to Secretary of War Jefferson Davis. Administration of the territories was transferred from State to the Department of the Interior in 1873. See Earl Pomeroy, *The Territories and the United States, 1861–1890: Studies in Colonial Administration* (Seattle: University of Washington Press. 1969, 1947), chaps. 2, 3.
4. The Minnesota legislature had already chartered a North Western Rail Road Company, to build from St. Paul to the Sound. Before setting out Stevens attended to some official matters, purchasing books for a Washington Territory library, helping Charles Mason secure the territorial secretaryship and ordering U.S. Marshal J. Patton Anderson to prepare a detailed census. Olympia *Columbian*, Feb. 19; May 14; June 4, 11; July 23, 30; Sept. 3, 1853; Portland *Oregonian*, Oct. 22, 1853; Stevens to J. Patton Anderson, April 18, 26, 1853, Stevens Papers, UW; to James Mason, May 20, 1853, Pierce and Buchanan Administration Appointment Files, NA; Richards, *Stevens*, 172–173.
5. Olympia *Washington Pioneer*, Dec. 3, 17, 24, 1853; Jan. 28, 1854; Olympia *Pioneer and Democrat*, June 17; July 8, 1854; Proclamation by the Governor of the Territory of Washington, n.d., Isaac I. Stevens Papers, WSA; W. F. Tolmie to Stevens, Dec. 27, 1853; Address to Citizens of Thurston County, Dec. 19, 1853; Stevens to Tolmie, Jan. ? 1854, all Stevens Papers, UW; to M. T. Simmons, March 22, 1854; to A. J. Bolon, March 23, 1854; to William H. Tappan, March 23, 1854, Records of the Washington Superintendency of Indian Affairs, 1853–1874, M5, NA; to Isaac N. Ebey, Dec. 13, 1853; to Peter Skene Ogden, Dec. 20, 1853, U.S. State Department, Washington Territorial Papers, NA; Thomas J. Dryer to T. F. McElroy, Sept. 26, 1853, McElroy Family Papers, UW. On the apocryphal story that Olympia residents failed to recognize Stevens, due to his uncouth appearance, see Richards, *Stevens*, xi.
6. Olympia *Washington Pioneer*, Dec. 17, 24, 1853; Stevens to H. W. Halleck, Jan. 2, 1854; to James Doty, Jan. 1, 1854, Stevens Papers, UW; *Reports of Explorations and Surveys…for a Railroad from the Mississippi River to the Pacific Ocean* (Washington, D.C.: Thomas H. Ford, 1860), 12:251–253, 255–257. Also see D. W. Meinig, *The Great Columbia Plain: A Historical Geography, 1805–1910* (Seattle: University of Washington Press, 1968), 193–198.
7. The War Department returned the original draft for correction of unreadable penmanship and defective maps and tables. Increasing tension between the North and the South prevented agreement upon any of the lines surveyed in the mid–1850s. Olympia *Pioneer and Democrat*, June 17, 1854; George Suckley to Rutsen Suckley, Dec. 9, 1853; to John, Jan. 28, 1854, George Suckley Letters, WAC; G. K. Warren to Emory, July 19, 1854, Correspondence Concerning Stevens' Survey; Philip Henry Overmeyer, "George B. McClellan and the Pacific Northwest," *PNQ*, 32(Jan. 1941), 3–60. Also see William H. Goetzmann, *Army Exploration in the American West, 1803–1861* (New Haven: Yale University Press, 1959), 301.
8. The related subject of regional railroading also drew interest. In 1854, the territorial assembly debated construction of lines connecting Puget Sound with the Columbia River and the Great Salt Lake. Charles M. Gates, ed., *Messages of the Governors of the Territory of Washington to the Legislative Assembly, 1854–1889* (Seattle: University of Washington Press, 1940), 46–47; Steilacoom *Puget Sound Herald*, July 23, 1858; Oct. 14, 1859; Stevens to President of the Railroad Convention, April 3, 1860, Stevens Papers, UW; to James O'Neal, Feb. 9, 1857, Northern Pacific Railway Company Land Department Records, MHS; Olympia *Pioneer and Democrat*, Feb. 25; Aug. 5, 1854; Oct. 18, 1858.
9. Stevens maintained that patronage was a source of weakness, since he must cause "heart burnings and discontents" among rejected jobseekers. Edward Lander to Anderson, Dec. 19, 1856; F. A. Chenoweth to J. Black, Dec. 26, 1857; Note of Hon. I. I. Stevens in relation to application of F. A. Chenoweth for reappt., n.d., all Records relating to the Appointment of Federal Judges and U.S. Attorneys and Marshals, Washington, 1853–1902, M198, NA.
10. Although the territorial governor was required by law to be a Washington resident, the consideration could be honored after, rather than at the time of, appointment. Shelton *Mason County Journal*, Jan. 21, 1887; Robert

H. Simmons, "The Transition of the Washington Executive from Territory to Statehood," *PNQ*, 55(April 1964), 76; H. H. Bancroft, *History of Washington, Idaho, and Montana, 1845–1889* (San Francisco: The History Company, 1890), 209, 211; Elwood Evans to J. W. Nesmith, July 19, 1861, U.S. State Department Appointment Papers, RG 59, NA; Whatcom *Bellingham Bay Mail*, Oct. 17, 1874.

11. Monroe attempted to conceal his alcoholism by delivering public lectures on the benefits of prohibition. The three supreme court judges spent much of their time on separate district court duty, with only brief joint sessions in Olympia. "The decisions of our Supreme Court since 1854," U.S. attorney John Allen reported in 1878, "would be contained in the compass of an ordinary volume." John J. McGilvra to the President, Dec. 16, 1886; John B. Allen to Charles Devens, Nov. 18, 1878; J. S. Clendenin to Davis, May 15, 1854; to Franklin Pierce, May 15, 1854; Stevens to Pierce, July 13, 1854; to Black, March 16, 1858; Alvan Flanders to Henry Stansbery, Dec. 5, 1867, all Records relating to the Appointment of Federal Judges; Olympia *Pioneer and Democrat*, April 1, 1854; May 25, 1859; Steilacoom *Puget Sound Herald*, April 1, 1859; Seattle *Weekly Intelligencer*, Jan. 13, 1868; Port Townsend *Weekly Message*, July 18; Sept. 25, 1867; June 25; July 16; Aug. 27, 1868. On the territory's lower court system, see John R. Wunder, *Inferior Courts, Superior Justice: A History of the Justices of the Peace on the Northwest Frontier, 1853–1889* (Westport: Greenwood Press, 1979).

12. Simmons, "Transition of the Washington Executive," 76–78; Anson G. Henry to William H. Wallace, Feb. 4, 1861, William H. Wallace Papers, UW; W. T. Weed to William Pickering, April 13, 1863, Manson F. Backus Collection, UW; J. Dillon to E. P. Ferry, Dec. 18, 1877, Elisha P. Ferry Papers, WSA; Giles Ford to E. S. Salomon and J. G. Sparks, Sept. 31, 1870; Salomon to W. P. Winans, Dec. 6, 1871, both Edward S. Salomon Papers, WSA; Democratic Party Circular, n.d., Eugene Semple Papers, UW; Leander Holmes to M. F. Moore, March 30, 1868, Marshall Moore Papers, WSA; Port Townsend *Weekly Argus*, Oct. 26, 1877; C. M. Bradshaw to Ferry, June 28, 1878, Elisha P. Ferry Papers, UW.

13. Evans to Wallace, Sept. 1, 1861, Wallace Papers; Nesmith to Matthew P. Deady, July 17, 1857; June 22, 1858, Matthew P. Deady Papers, OHS; Fayette McMullin to Jacob Thompson, March 22, 1858; Stevens to J. W. Denver, Jan. 10, 1859, both Correspondence of the Office of Indian Affairs, Letters Received, 1824–1881, M234, NA.

14. James Guthrie to Ebey, June 15, 17, 1854; W. S. Hodge to Simpson P. Moses, March 21, 1851, all Letters Sent by Secretary of Treasury to Collectors of Customs at Pacific Ports, M176, NA; Olympia *Pioneer and Democrat*, Aug. 5, 1854; T. J. McKenny to Hazard Stevens, Feb. 25, 1868, Hazard Stevens Correspondence, WSL; Ebey to W. S. Ebey, May 20, 1853, Winfield S. Ebey Papers, UW; Steilacoom *Puget Sound Courier*, Aug. 24, 1855. On early operations of the Puget Sound customs house, see William L. Lang, *Confederacy of Ambition: William Winlock Miller and the Making of Washington Territory* (Seattle: University of Washington Press, 1996), 28–47.

15. Responsibility for the federal funds subjected the secretary to a variety of onerous tasks and criticisms. Treasury Department drafts often arrived in amounts too large for local cashing, forcing trips to Portland and San Francisco or reliance upon potentially untrustworthy agents in those places. Charles Mason was reprimanded for constructing a plank sidewalk between Olympia lodging houses and the capitol building. A successor was chastised for excessive spending on candles. Elisha Whittlesey to C. H. Mason, Dec. 15, 1853, C. H. Mason Correspondence, WSL; Henry McGill to Henry Mills, Dec. 15, 1859; Evans to First Comptroller, April 8, 1863; to R. W. Taylor, June 7, 1865; Mason to Whittlesey, Nov. 24, 1854; Feb. 20, 1865; to Wm. Medill, July 15; Nov. 24, 1857, all Washington Territorial Papers, UW; to Adams & Co., Feb. 5, 1855, Stevens Papers, WSA; Guthrie to Mason, June 19, 1854, Washington Territorial Documents, WSHS; Olympia *Washington Standard*, Feb. 2, 1861; Olympia *Pioneer and Democrat*, March 1, 1861; Richard Gholson to Lewis Cass, Jan. 27, 1860; to Black, Feb. 14, 1861, State Department, Washington Territorial Papers.

16. Pending official publication of the statutes, the courts allowed newspaper accounts of legislative proceedings to be cited in legal argument. Mason to Whittlesey, Aug. 10; Nov. 17, 1854; Evans to First Comptroller, Oct. 31, 1863; to Taylor, Sept. 1, 1863, all Washington Territorial Papers, UW; McElroy to Mother, July 24, 1864, McElroy Family Papers; Olympia *Washington Standard*, Jan. 3, 1863; Oct. 15, 1864; John F. Darrow to J. M. Murphy, Sept. 25, 1860, John Miller Murphy Papers, WSL; Medill to Mason, Oct. 2, 1857; Whittlesey to Mason, Jan. 17, 1855, both Mason Correspondence; *Olympia Transcript*, Nov. 30, 1867; Olympia *Pioneer and Democrat*, April 14; Sept. 14, 1855; Steilacoom *Puget Sound Courier*, July 27, 1855.

17. Secretaries Henry McGill and L. Jay S. Turney had both claimed the privilege exercised by Evans, only to give in to legislative protest. Olympia *Pioneer and Democrat*, Feb. 29, 1856; Evans to First Comptroller, Oct. 31, 1863; to C. Crosby, Dec. 10, 1863, Washington Territorial Papers, UW; *Seattle Gazette*, Dec. 26, 1863; Olympia *Washington Standard*, Feb. 2, 1861; Dec. 12, 1863; Steilacoom *Puget Sound Herald*, Feb. 13, 1862; *Olympia Transcript*, Nov. 30; Dec. 7, 1867.

18. The final quotation is from the 1855 Whig platform. Olympia *Pioneer and Democrat*, June 2; Sept. 14, 1855; Steilacoom *Puget Sound Courier*, Aug. 24, 1855; Steilacoom *Puget Sound Herald*, Nov. 22, 1862; Port Townsend *Weekly Message*, Dec. 31, 1868. Also see Roland L. DeLorme, "Westward the Bureaucrats: Government Officials on the Washington and Arizona Frontier," *Arizona and the West*, 22(Autumn 1980), 223–236.

19. The delegate selected in January 1854 served only through the regular 1855 election. A delegate to the founding convention of the Confederacy and then a Southern general, Anderson died in 1872 without ever returning to Washington. Olympia *Pioneer and Democrat*, Feb. 4, 1854; May 12, 1855; Olympia *Washington Pioneer*, Dec. 17, 1853; Jan. 14, 1854; Columbia Lancaster to Swan, Dec. 29, 1854, Swan Papers; Steilacoom *Puget Sound Courier*, May 31; June 7, 1855; Steilacoom *Puget Sound Herald*, June 27, 1861; Olympia *Puget Sound*

Weekly Courier, Oct. 12, 1872. On Lancaster's career in Pacific Northwest politics, see Oregon City *Oregon Spectator*, Dec. 9, 1847; May 18, 1848; Feb. 27; Dec. 2, 1851; March 2, 1852; Mentor L. Williams, ed., "A Columbia Lancaster Letter About Oregon in 1847," *OHQ*, 50 (April 1949), 40–44.

20. Steilacoom *Puget Sound Courier*, May 19, 31, 1855; Olympia *Pioneer and Democrat*, May 19, 1855; Steilacoom *Puget Sound Herald*, June 24, 1859; June 27, 1861; Olympia *Washington Standard*, May 25; June 1, 1861.

21. The 1855 figure does not include the suspiciously unanimous 48-0 tally for Anderson east of the Cascades, a vote count reaching Olympia only after announcement of the official results. Subtracting the Walla Walla ballots, Stevens still had 58 percent of the vote in 1859. There was no apparent correlation between the 1855 congressional vote and the territorial prohibition referendum, defeated at the same election. Anderson won four of the five counties most in favor of prohibition and six of the nine most opposed. The population of Clark County increased by 45 percent between 1853 and 1860. Together, however, Thurston, Pierce and King counties grew by 65 percent. Olympia *Pioneer and Democrat*, Aug. 24, 31, 1855; Sept. 14, 1860; Steilacoom *Puget Sound Herald*, Sept. 7, 1855; Aug. 19, 1859; Olympia *Washington Pioneer*, Dec. 17, 1853. Also see Norman H. Clark, *The Dry Years: Prohibition and Social Change in Washington* (Seattle: University of Washington Press, rev. ed., 1988, 1965), 22–27.

22. Stevens wrote that "only a good deal of exertion and the daily visiting [of] the office" enabled him to secure timely dispatch of Indian department funds to Washington Territory. Samuel R. Thurston to Wesley Shannon, March 1; Aug. 17, 1850, Samuel R. Thurston Correspondence, WSL; Lancaster to Swan, et al., Sept. 29, 1854; Jan. 27, 1855, Swan Papers; Joseph Lane to W. W. Miller, Feb. 15, 1859, William Winlock Miller Collection, UW; Olympia *Pioneer and Democrat*, March 11, 1859; Port Townsend *North-West*, Nov. 23, 1861; Stevens to Nesmith, Dec. 2, 1857, Stevens Papers, UW.

23. Special legislative sessions required express congressional authorization. Seattle *Weekly Intelligencer*, June 13, 1870; Whittlesey to Mason, March 4, 1854, Mason Correspondence; *Seattle Gazette*, Jan. 9; Feb. 2; May 10, 1864; Evans to Taylor, Sept. 1, 1863, Washington Territorial Papers, UW; Bancroft, *History of Washington*, 267; *Walla Walla Statesman*, July 7, 1866; Seattle *Puget Sound Weekly*, Sept. 3, 1866; Port Townsend *Puget Sound Weekly Argus*, Oct. 12, 1877; O. H. Platt to Paul Strobach, Jan. 8, 1887, Watson C. Squire Papers, UW.

24. H. H. Bancroft claimed that McMullin's motive in accepting the governorship was the opportunity of obtaining a legislative divorce. Olympia *Washington Standard*, Dec. 22, 1860; Feb. 1, 1862; Steilacoom *Puget Sound Herald*, Jan. 23, 1862; Port Townsend *North-West*, Feb. 1, 1862; Bancroft, *History of Washington*, 209; *Port Townsend Register*, Feb. 22, 1862; Seattle *Weekly Intelligencer*, Sept. 25, 1875; Evans to Taylor, Sept. 1, 1863, Washington Territorial Papers, UW.

25. Olympia *Washington Standard*, Aug. 17, 1861; Olympia *Pioneer and Democrat*, Dec. 23, 1854; Jan. 13, 1855; Mason to Medill, July 16, 1857, Washington Territorial Papers, UW; *Port Townsend Register*, Dec. 19, 1860.

26. Olympia *Pioneer and Democrat*, Aug. 13, 1858; Feb. 10, 1860; Olympia *Washington Standard*, Aug. 17, 1861; Steilacoom *Puget Sound Herald*, July 27, 1860; McGill to Medill, July 7, 1860, Richard D. Gholson Papers, WSA. On McGill's connection with Buchanan, see Pickering to Abraham Lincoln, Jan. ? 1864, State Department Appointment Papers.

27. McGill charged that Columbia River interests intended to delay work until "the incessant rain of the winter season will have commenced," giving Vancouver extra time to mount its challenge. The legislature also assigned the territorial university to Seattle and moved the penitentiary to Port Townsend, like Vancouver an unwilling host to the institution. Olympia *Washington Standard*, Dec. 15, 1860; Aug. 13, 1861; *Port Townsend Register*, Dec. 19, 1860; Miller to Stevens, Nov. 28, 1860, Stevens Papers, UW; McGill to Geo. Gallagher, July 23; Aug. 4, 1860; to Medill, May 1, 1861, Henry McGill Papers, WSL; Olympia *Pioneer and Democrat*, Aug. 24; Dec. 21, 1860; Steilacoom *Puget Sound Herald*, Dec. 20, 1860; May 2; Nov. 4, 1861.

28. McGill ordered the territorial librarian, an official selected by the assembly, not to move books to Vancouver. McGill to Medill, Dec. 20, 1860; May 4, 1861; to Gay Hayden, Oct. 9, 1860, McGill Papers; Port Townsend *North-West*, Nov. 30, 1861; L. Jay S. Turney to A. J. Lawrence, Sept. 9, 1861; to Edward Bates, Sept. 17, 1861, Washington Territorial Papers, UW; Steilacoom *Puget Sound Herald*, Aug. 29, 1861; Olympia *Washington Standard*, Aug. 24, 1861.

29. Twenty-three communities received votes in the referendum, Steilacoom finishing third and Port Madison fourth. Olympia *Washington Standard*, Aug. 13; Dec. 14, 28, 1861; Steilacoom *Puget Sound Herald*, Dec. 12, 1861; Port Townsend *North-West*, Nov. 30, 1861; Turney to Paul K. Hubbs, Oct. 22, 1861; to Lawrence, Sept. 9, 1861, Washington Territorial Papers, UW.

30. Statement of the Financial Condition of the Territory of Washington, 4, 10, 12, 16, copy in William P. Winans Papers, WSU; LaConner *Puget Sound Mail*, Oct. 11, 1879; Whatcom *Bellingham Bay Mail*, July 28, 1877; Olympia *Pioneer and Democrat*, Sept. 14, 1860; *Walla Walla Union*, Oct. 18, 1879; P. J. Primrose to T. M. Reed, Aug. 9, 1879, Ferry Papers, WSA; L. B. Hastings Journal, Feb. 4, 1874, WSHS.

31. William F. Prosser, *A History of the Puget Sound Country* (New York: The Lewis Publishing Company, 2 vols., 1903), 1:9; Harriet Carleton Dyer to Brother, Jan. ? 1854, Harriet Carleton Dyer Correspondence, WSHS; Articles relative to affairs in the Pacific written by James G. Swan for the *Boston Transcript* in 1857, Stevens Papers, UW; Suckley to Mary Suckley, Dec. 30, 1854, in "Sidelights on the Stevens Railway Survey," *PNQ*, 36(July 1945), 246; I. J. Benjamin, *Three Years in America, 1859–1862*, trans. Charles Reznikoff (Philadelphia: The Jewish Publishing Society of America, 2 vols., 1956), 2:165; D. E. Blaine to Brother and friends, Nov. 22, 1853; to ?, April 4, 1854, Blaine Family Letters.

32. Seattle *Puget Sound Semi-Weekly*, April 16, 1866; McElroy to Sarah E. McElroy, Jan. 11; Dec. 4, 1853, McElroy Family Papers; C. Blaine to Mother, Jan. 17, 1854, Blaine Family Letters; David Denny to John Denny, March 2, 1853, Arthur A. Denny Papers, WSHS. On the cultural impact of precipitation, see Richard Maxwell Brown, "Rainfall and History: Perspectives on the Pacific Northwest," in G. Thomas Edwards and Carlos A. Schwantes, eds., *Experiences in a Promised Land: Essays in Pacific Northwest History* (Seattle: University of Washington Press, 1986), 13–27. For the settler experience with weather, see David Laskin, *Rains all the Time: A Connoisseur's History of Weather in the Pacific Northwest* (Seattle: Sasquatch Books, 1997), chapt. 3.

33. Portland *Oregonian*, Sept. 18, 1852; Port Townsend *North-West*, Aug. 30, 1860; Olympia *Washington Standard*, Feb. 15, 1862; Olympia *Pioneer and Democrat*, Aug. 17, 1855; Walter Crockett to Harvey Black, Oct. 15, 1853, Walter Crockett Letters, UW.

34. Praised as "the most extensive agricultural district on the Lower Sound," Whidbey Island was a partial exception. Even there, however, farm production fell below expectations. Harriet L. Inman, "The Drawbacks of Washington Territory," *Northwest Illustrated Monthly Magazine*, 5(April 1887), 53; J. M. Harrison, *Harrison's Guide and Resources of the Pacific Slope*, Part 1, *Embracing Washington Territory* (San Francisco: C. A. Murdock & Co., 2nd ed., 1876), 26–27; Ezra Meeker, *Pioneer Reminiscences of Puget Sound* (Seattle: Lowman & Hanford, 1905), 34–35; McElroy to S. McElroy, Aug. 10, 1852, McElroy Family Papers; Michael F. Luark Diary, May 2, 1854, UW; J. Ross Browne to Guthrie, Sept. 4, 1854, Letters and Reports Received by the Secretary of the Treasury from Special Agents, 1854–1861, M177, NA; Seattle *Puget Sound Semi-Weekly*, April 16, 1866; Whatcom *Bellingham Bay Mail*, April 23, 1875; Port Townsend *Puget Sound Weekly Argus*, Aug. 3, 1877; Richard White, *Land Use, Environment, and Social Change: The Shaping of Island County, Washington* (Seattle: University of Washington Press, 1980), chapt. 2.

35. Steilacoom *Puget Sound Herald*, May 20, 1859; Oct. 9, 1862; *Port Townsend Register*, Feb. 1, 1860; Olympia *Pioneer and Democrat*, Aug. 20, 1858; Chas. C. Terry to Philip Foster, Sept. 20, 1858, F. W. Pettygrove Letters, Jefferson County Historical Society; James Tilton to Thomas A. Hendricks, Feb. 24, 1858, Letters Received from the Surveyors General of Washington, 1854–1883, RG 49, NA.

36. *Port Townsend Register*, Feb. 1, 1860; Seattle *Weekly Intelligencer*, Feb. 26, 1872; Meeker, *Pioneer Reminiscences*, 60; Steilacoom *Puget Sound Herald*, Oct. 9, 1862; Whatcom *Bellingham Bay Mail*, June 6, 1874; Feb. 27, 1875.

37. High water occasionally altered the course of rivers, as in the case of a mid-nineteenth century flood that shifted the principal outlet of the Nooksack River from the Strait of Georgia to Bellingham Bay. Eldridge Morse Notebooks, 20:5–9, BL; Eugene Canfield to Swan, Jan. 22, 1885, Swan Papers; Olympia *Pioneer and Democrat*, Aug. 20, 1858; *Port Townsend Register*, Feb. 1, 1860; *Seattle Weekly Gazette*, Dec. 10, 1863; Seattle *Weekly Intelligencer*, Nov. 28, 1870; Feb. 26, 1872; Whatcom *Bellingham Bay Mail*, Dec. 20, 1873; April 10, 1875; July 21, 1877.

38. Despite the best efforts of the lumber companies to secure, northbound cargoes, many ships sailed to the Sound in ballast. *Port Townsend Register*, Feb. 6, 1861; Port Townsend *North-West*, Oct. 25, 1860; Olympia *Washington Standard*, Oct. 3, 1863; Steilacoom *Puget Sound Courier*, Sept. 21, 1855; Ezra Meeker, *Washington Territory West of the Cascade Mountains* (Olympia: Transcript Office, 1870), 19; Ernest Ingersoll, "From the Frazier to the Columbia," *Harper's New Monthly Magazine*, 68(April 1884), 715.

39. One fortunate settler reported buying a yoke of oxen for the bargain price of $150. Tilton to John Wilson, Sept. 12, 1855, Letters Received from the Surveyors General; McElroy to S. McElroy, Jan. 11, 1853, McElroy Family Papers; Ebey to W. Ebey, April 20; May 20, 1853, Ebey Papers; Nathaniel D. Hill Diary, Jan. 4, 1853, Jefferson County Historical Society; Dyer to Brother William, Jan. 16, 1853, Dyer Correspondence.

40. McElroy to S. McElroy, Jan. 11, 1853, McElroy Family Papers; D. Blaine to ?, April 4, 1854, Blaine Family Letters; William S. Lewis, ed., "Reminiscences of Delia B. Sheffield," *WHQ*, 15(Jan. 1924), 58–59; Tilton to Wilson, June 14, 1855, Letters Received from the Surveyors General; Hill Diary, March 17, 1853; Ebey to W. Ebey, Sept. 28, 1853, Ebey Papers; Dyer to Brother, Jan. ? 1864, Dyer Correspondence. On usage of "the City," see Donald H. Clark, "An Analysis of Forest Utilization as a Factor in Colonizing the Pacific Northwest and in Subsequent Population Transitions" (Ph.D. diss., University of Washington, 1952), 50.

41. Hill Diary, Dec. 5, 1852; April 18, 1853; McElroy to S. McElroy, April 3, 1853, McElroy Family Papers; Henry C. Mosely Diary, Nov. 23, 1853, WSHS; Daniel R. Bigelow Reminiscences, n.p., WSHS; Luark Diary, Oct. 23, 1853; W. C. Talbot to Charles Foster, Sept. 4, 1853, Josiah Keller Papers, WAC.

42. Fishing Commencement Bay on successive mornings in August 1853, two white men caught 2,350 "good large salmon." A modest start at commercial exploitation was made in 1863 at Mukilteo. Swan to William H. Seward, April 8, 1867; to Rufus Leighton, July 1, 1869, Swan Papers; Steilacoom *Puget Sound Herald*, May 13, 1859; March 7, 1861; Olympia *Columbian*, Jan. 15; Aug. 27; Sept. 10, 1853; Port Townsend *North-West*, Oct. 11, 1860; "Business Broadside of 1853," *WHQ*, 20(July 1929), 232; Olympia *Pioneer and Democrat*, March 5, 1858; Stevens to Grinnell & Co., Jan. 9, 1854, Stevens Papers, UW; Port Townsend *Weekly Message*, Jan. 9, 1868; *Seattle Gazette*, Dec. 10, 1863.

43. Puget Sound mills dominated the territorial lumber industry, producing 70.7 million feet in 1860, compared to 6.5 million feet on the Columbia River. *Annual Report of the Commissioner of the General Land Office, 1867*, 62; *1868*, 344; Mrs. A. H. H. Stuart, *Washington Territory: Its Soil, Climate, Productions and General Resources* (Olympia: *Washington Standard*, 1875), 11–13; Charles Stevens to Brother Levi, July 3, 1853, in R. Ruth Rockwood, ed., "Letters of Charles Stevens," *OHQ*, 37(Dec. 1936), 338; Steilacoom *Puget Sound Herald*, Jan. 3, 1861; Edmond S. Meany, Jr., "The History of the Lumber Industry in the Pacific Northwest to 1917" (Ph.D. diss., Harvard University, 1935), 105–110, 114–117, 121–122; Olympia *Pioneer and Democrat*, Dec. 27, 1857;

Nov. 23, 1860. On changing lumber trade patterns, see Thomas R. Cox, *Mills and Markets: A History of the Pacific Coast Lumber Industry to 1900* (Seattle: University of Washington Press, 1974), chapt. 5.

44. Steilacoom *Puget Sound Herald*, May 28, 1858; March 11, 1859; Olympia *Pioneer and Democrat*, Feb. 17, 1855; Feb. 27, 1857; Steilacoom *Puget Sound Courier*, July 20, 1855; *Port Townsend Register*, Jan. 18; Feb. 15, 1860; Port Townsend *North-West*, Jan. 17, 1861; Iva L. Buchanan, "Lumbering and Logging in the Puget Sound Region in Territorial Days," *PNQ*, 28(Jan. 1936), 38–39; Meany, "History of the Lumber Industry," 121. Andrew Pope quoted in Robert E. Ficken, *The Forested Land: A History of Lumbering in Western Washington* (Seattle: University of Washington Press, 1987), 29.

45. C. M. Scammon, "Lumbering in Washington Territory," *Overland Monthly*, 5(July 1870), 58–60; W. B. Seymore, "Port Orchard Fifty Years Ago," *WHQ*, 8(Oct. 1917), 259; J. Murphy, "Summer Ramblings in Washington Territory," *Appleton's Journal*, 3(Nov. 1877), 393; Port Townsend *North-West*, Oct. 18, 1860; Olympia *Washington Standard*, May 28, 1864.

46. Clark, "Analysis of Forest Utilization," 54–55; Caroline C. Leighton, *Life at Puget Sound* (Boston: Lee and Shepard, 1884), 25–26; Iva L. Buchanan, "An Economic History of Kitsap County, Washington, to 1889" (Ph.D. diss., University of Washington, 1930), 280, 283–284; Edward Clayson, Sr., *Historical Narratives of Puget Sound: Hoods Canal, 1865–1885* (Seattle: R. L. Davis Printing Co., 1911), 5; Port Townsend *North-West*, Sept. 20; Oct. 18, 1860; Henry L. Yesler Reminiscences, 13, BL.

47. Luark Diary, March 9, 1854; McElroy to S. McElroy, Sept. 4, 1853, McElroy Family Papers.

48. Olympia males raced horses on the town's federally funded plank sidewalk. Steilacoom sports enthusiasts chased chickens through the town, shooting the unfortunate creatures and, occasionally, innocent bystanders. Thomas W. Pohl, "Seattle, 1851–1861: A Frontier Community" (Ph.D. diss., University of Washington, 1970), 35; Samuel Bowles, *Across the Continent: A Summer's Journey to the Rocky Mountains, the Mormons, and the Pacific States, with Speaker Colfax* (Springfield: Samuel Bowles & Company, 1866), 200–201; C. Blaine to Seraphina, Aug. 4, 1854, Blaine Family Letters; *Seattle Weekly Gazette*, March 4, 1865; Olympia *Washington Standard*, July 3, 1869; Olympia *Columbian*, July 16, 1853; Steilacoom *Puget Sound Herald*, July 9, 1858; Nov. 27, 1859; Oct. 10, 1861; Dec. 12, 1863; Port Townsend *North-West*, Sept. 27, 1860; March 15, 1862; Olympia *Pioneer and Democrat*, Nov. 28, 1856; Bigelow Diary, Oct. 28, 1853.

49. Lewis, ed., "Reminiscences of Delia B. Sheffield," 58–59; Leighton, *Life at Puget Sound*, 25–26; D. Blaine to ?, April 4, 1854; to Father, June 21, 1854; to Parents, Dec. 6, 1853; C. Blaine to Mother, Jan. 17, 1854, all Blaine Family Letters; Tilton to Commissioner of General Land Office, Aug. 18, 1857; to Hendricks, July 20, 1858; to Wilson, June 14, 1855, Letters Received from the Surveyors General; McElroy to Mother, Jan. 6, 1861, McElroy Family Papers; Miller to Ladd & Tilton, May 8, 1870, Miller Family Papers, UW; Ebey to W. Ebey, Nov. 19, 1852, Ebey Papers.

50. Olympia came close to destruction by fire on three occasions in 1855. Tilton to Wilson, June 14, 1855, Letters Received from the Surveyors General; Olympia *Washington Standard*, Feb. 14, 1863; Olympia *Pioneer and Democrat*, March 10, 1855; Port Townsend *North-West*, March 29, 1862; Steilacoom *Puget Sound Herald*, April 8, 1859.

51. Steilacoom *Puget Sound Herald*, Aug. 26, 1859; March 2, 1860; Luark Diary, Sept. 15, 1853; McElroy to S. McElroy, Dec. 18, 1853, McElroy Family Papers; Bigelow Reminiscences, n.p.; Port Townsend *North-West*, Aug. 30, 1860. The best source on Asa Mercer's famous experiment is Roger Conant, *Mercer's Belles: The Journal of a Reporter*, ed. Lenna A. Deutsch (Pullman: Washington State University Press, 1992, 1960). Also see Arthur A. Denny to D. Bagley, Sept. 23; Nov. 23, 1865, Daniel Bagley Papers, UW.

52. Edmund Fitzhugh employed Indians to load vessels at the Bellingham Bay coal mine. Eben Weld to Martin Weld, Feb. 15, 1851, Martin Weld Letters, UW; Luark Diary, April 28, 30, 1854; D. Blaine to Parents, Dec. 6, 1853, Blaine Family Letters; S. Baxter to P. B. Cornwall, Dec. 13, 1875, Sehome Coal Company Records, Center for Pacific Northwest Studies, Western Washington University; Thomas F. Gedosch, "A Note on the Dogfish Oil Industry of Washington Territory," *PNQ*, 59(April 1968), 100–102; Olympia *Columbian*, Jan. 15, 1853. For an appreciation of the constricted nature of early Washington settlement, see Map 30 in James W. Scott and Roland L. DeLorme, *Historical Atlas of Washington* (Norman: University of Oklahoma Press, 1988).

53. Port Townsend residents blamed Indians for the town's rowdy reputation. Portland *Oregonian*, Sept. 18, 1852; *Port Townsend Register*, March 28, 1860; D. Blaine to ?, Feb. 5, 1855; to Mother, Aug. 4, 1854; C. Blaine to Seraphina, Aug. 4, 1854; to ?, Nov. 23, 1854, all Blaine Family Letters; James G. Swan Reminiscences, n.p., WSHS; Victor J. Farrar, ed., "Diary of Colonel and Mrs. I. N. Ebey," *WHQ*, 7(Oct. 1916), 321; 8(April 1917), 132–133, 135.

54. Browne to Guthrie, Sept. 4, 1854, Letters and Reports Received by the Secretary of the Treasury; Tilton to Wilson, May 18, 1855, Letters Received from the Surveyors General; C. Blaine to Seraphina, March 29, 1854; to ?, March 13, 1855, Blaine Family Letters. For complaints about the mail prior to the organization of Washington Territory, see Ebey to Lane, Jan. 23, 1852, Joseph Lane Papers, OHS.

55. Stevens to James Campbell, Dec. 6, 1853, Stevens Papers, UW; McElroy to S. McElroy, Jan. 11; Dec. 4, 1853, McElroy Family Papers; Olympia *Pioneer and Democrat*, Feb. 4, 1854.

56. *Olympia Transcript*, Jan. 4, 1868; Stevens to Commissioner of Indian Affairs, Feb. 10, 1854, Records of the Washington Superintendency of Indian Affairs; to Daniel Hazard, May 26, 1853; to Secretary of War, Feb. 20, 1854, Stevens Papers, UW; William Petit Trowbridge Journal, July 27, 1853, WSHS; Hill Diary, Nov. 28, 1852; C. Blaine to ?, May 8, 1854, Blaine Family Letters; Mosely Diary, May 4, 1854; Luark Diary, May 7, 1854.

57. Olympia *Pioneer and Democrat*, Oct. 7, 1854; Feb. 24, 1855; Port Townsend *Weekly Message*, Dec. 19, 1867; *Seattle Weekly Gazette*, Aug. 20, 1864; Seattle *Weekly Intelligencer*, Sept. 23, 1867; Jan. 4, 1869; Steilacoom *Puget Sound Herald*, March 12; April 2, 1858; Dec. 11, 1862; Seattle *Puget Sound Daily*, July 3, 1866; P. Keach to Wallace, Oct. 15, 1861, Wallace Papers; Hugh Goldsborough to Miller, Sept. 3; Nov. 30; Dec. 20, 1864; Sept. 25, 1865, Miller Family Papers.

58. C. Blaine to ?, May 8, 1854; D. Blaine to Father, June 21, 1854, both Blaine Family Letters; Clarence Bagley to Edward Huggins, April 10, 1903; Jan. 26, 1904, Clarence Bagley Papers, UW; McElroy to S. McElroy, April 3, 1853, McElroy Family Papers.

59. A. Benton Moses to Thomas M. Chambers, Nov. 1, 1853, Thomas M. Chambers Papers, WSHS; Dyer to Brother William, Jan. 16, 1863, Dyer Correspondence; D. Blaine to Brother Saron, Nov. 20, 1854, Blaine Family Letters. For similar speculative thoughts in Steilacoom, see Suckley to M. Suckley, Dec. 30, 1854, in "Sidelights on the Stevens Survey," 246.

Notes—Chapter Three
Respect and Consideration

1. April 11, 1856.

2. For post-1790 federal Indian legislation, see *Annual Report of the Commissioner of Indian Affairs, 1892*, 14–23. The best secondary sources on federal policy are Francis Paul Prucha, *American Indian Policy in the Formative Years: The Indian Trade and Intercourse Acts, 1790–1834* (Cambridge: Harvard University Press, 1962); Ronald N. Satz, *American Indian Policy in the Jacksonian Era* (Lincoln: University of Nebraska Press, 1975); Robert A. Trennert, Jr., *Alternative to Extinction: Federal Indian Policy and the Beginnings of the Reservation System, 1846–51* (Philadelphia: Temple University Press, 1975).

3. Benjamin Alvord to John J. McGilvra, Oct. 8, 1862, John J. McGilvra Papers, UW.

4. Anson Dart to L. Lea, July 19, 1851, Correspondence of the Office of Indian Affairs, Letters Received, 1824–1881, M234, NA; C. F. Coan, "The First Stage of the Federal Indian Policy in the Pacific Northwest, 1849–1852," *OHQ*, 22(March 1921), 54–56.

5. The Stevens population estimate was hardly definitive. An 1844 Hudson's Bay Company census of Puget Sound produced a figure less than half the governor's. In 1841, Captain Charles Wilkes reported a substantially different number. Isaac I. Stevens to James Doty, Jan. 1, 1854, Isaac I. Stevens Papers, UW; to George W. Manypenny, Sept. 16, 1854, in *Annual Report of the Commissioner of Indian Affairs, 1854*, 457–460; Dec. 26, 1853; to J. Mix Stanley, Jan. 2, 1854; to Charles H. Larnard, Dec. 19, 1853; Feb. 9, 1854; Edward A. Starling to Stevens, Dec. 4, 1853; Michael T. Simmons to Stevens, July 1, 1854; George Gibbs to Stevens, Feb. 7, 1854; to Geo. B. McClellan, April 23, 1854; Henry C. Wilson to Stevens, March 22, 1854; Gibbs, Notes of Expedition to secure murderers, n.d.; J. S. Smith to Stevens, March 5, 1854, all Records of the Washington Superintendency of Indian Affairs, 1853–1874, M5, NA; Walter Crockett to Harvey Black, Oct. 15, 1853, Walter Crockett Letters, UW; Alban W. Hoopes, *Indian Affairs and Their Administration: With Special Reference to the Far West, 1849–1860* (Philadelphia: University of Pennsylvania Press, 1932), 75–76.

6. DeL. Floyd-Jones to E. Townsend, Sept. 1, 1853; George Stoneman to Townsend, July 5, 1855, both Pacific Division Records, U.S. Army Continental Commands, RG 393, NA; W. T. Sayward to Stevens, April 24, 1856; Stevens to Manypenny, July 13, 1854, both Records of the Washington Superintendency of Indian Affairs; Steilacoom *Puget Sound Courier*, May 31, 1855.

7. Stevens to Manypenny, July 13; Aug. 15, 1854; Edmund C. Fitzhugh, et al. to C. H. Mason, May 30, 1854; Mason to Manypenny, July 1, 1854, all Records of the Washington Superintendency of Indian Affairs; James Douglas to William F. Tolmie, May 30, 1854, William F. Tolmie Papers, UW.

8. Alvord to Townsend, April 22, 24; July 17, 1853, Pacific Division Records; McClellan to Stevens, Aug. 22, 1853, Records of the Washington Superintendency of Indian Affairs; Olympia *Columbian*, May 28, 1853. For early efforts to deal with the interior tribes, see J. L. Parrish to Samuel R. Thurston, July 15, 1850, Samuel R. Thurston Papers, OHS.

9. Address to Citizens of Thurston County, Dec. 19, 1853, Stevens Papers, UW; Memorial to Congress, April 1854, Oregon and Washington Territorial Papers, House File, Records of the House of Representatives, RG 233, NA; Alvord to Townsend, July 17, 1853, Pacific Division Records; Joel Palmer to Manypenny, Dec. 20, 1853, Records of the Oregon Superintendency of Indian Affairs, 1845–1873, M2, NA; Stevens to John Wool, May 2, 1855, Isaac I. Stevens Papers, WAC; to Manypenny, Dec. 29, 1853, Records of the Washington Superintendency of Indian Affairs.

10. Manypenny to Palmer, Aug. 12, 1854; Charles E. Mix to Stevens, Aug. 30, 1854, both Correspondence of the Office of Indian Affairs, Letters Sent, 1824–1881, M21, NA; Francis Paul Prucha, ed., *Documents of United States Indian Policy* (Lincoln: University of Nebraska Press, 1975), 87–89; Olympia *Pioneer and Democrat*, Dec. 9, 1854; Stevens to Manypenny, Dec. 21, 1854; May 1, 1855; Treaty Council Proceedings, Dec. 7, 10, 1854, all Records of the Washington Superintendency of Indian Affairs. Also see *Annual Report of the Commissioner of Indian Affairs, 1854*, 213–214.

11. The fishing provision is quoted from the third article of the Medicine Creek treaty of 1854. Stevens may also have seen the language as a means of preempting opposition to the treaties. Stevens to Manypenny, Sept. 16, 1854, in *Annual Report of the Commissioner of Indian Affairs, 1854*, 455–456; Treaty Council Proceedings, Dec. 26, 1854; Samuel R. Ross to E. S. Parker, July 18, 1870, both Records of the Washington Superintendency of Indian Affairs.

12. The Point Elliott treaty set aside land at Tulalip for a central reservation, the expectation being that many, if not all, of the Puget Sound tribes would eventually be concentrated there. On another unanticipated front, the Steilacoom *Puget Sound Courier*, the territory's first opposition paper, lambasted the treaties as "shameless" and "disgraceful farces." Stevens to Manypenny, Feb. 23; May 11, 1856, Records of the Washington Superintendency of Indian Affairs; Edmond Mallet to E. A. Hayt, Oct. 29, 1878; R. H. Milroy to E. P. Smith, May 23, 1874, both Correspondence of the Office of Indian Affairs; Marian W. Smith, *The Puyallup-Nisqually* (New York: Columbia University Press, 1940), 12, 20–25; Simmons to James W. Nesmith, Dec. 31, 1857, Tulalip Agency Records, WSU; Steilacoom *Puget Sound Courier*, Aug. 24, 31; Nov. 23, 1855. For a shrewd appreciation of the Nooksack-Lummi situation on Bellingham Bay, see G. E. Pickett to W. W. Mackall, May 21, 1857, Fayette McMullin Papers, WSL. For detailed treatment of the Puget Sound councils, see Kent D. Richards, *Isaac I. Stevens: Young Man in a Hurry* (Pullman: Washington State University Press, 1993, 1979), 199–207. The governor's habit of ignoring significant tribal divisions was also evident in the case of the failed Chehalis River council of February 1855. See, for a firsthand account, James G. Swan, *The Northwest Coast, or, Three Years' Residence in Washington Territory* (Seattle: University of Washington Press, 1972, 1857), 338–352.

13. Stevens and Oregon Superintendent of Indian Affairs Joel Palmer served as co-commissioners, an arrangement dictated by the fact that many of the Indians present divided the year between the two jurisdictions. Doty to Stevens, March 4, 26; April 3, 1855; Stevens and Palmer to Manypenny, June 12, 1855; Stevens to Manypenny, June 14, 1855, all Records of the Washington Superintendency of Indian Affairs; James Doty Journal, April 1– 4; May 21, 25–27, 29, 1855, typescript in UW; Lawrence Kip Journal, May 25–27; June 1, 11, 1855, copy in Joseph H. Brown Papers, OHS. Also see Richards, *Stevens*, 215–226.

14. Delay at Walla Walla forced postponement of a council scheduled for the Spokane River. Stevens to Manypenny, June 14, 1855; to A. J. Bolon, Aug. 30, 1855, Records of the Washington Superintendency of Indian Affairs; to Simmons, July 17, 1855, Stevens Papers, UW; Palmer to Manypenny, Oct. 9, 25, 1855, Records of the Oregon Superintendency of Indian Affairs; T. J. Cram, "Topographical Memoir of the Department of the Pacific," House Ex. Doc. No. 114, 35th Cong., 2nd sess., 85–86; Olympia *Pioneer and Democrat*, June 29, 1855.

15. Gibbs to Stevens, Aug. 7, 1855, Records of the Washington Superintendency of Indian Affairs; Steilacoom *Puget Sound Courier*, June 21; July 5, 20, 27; Aug. 10, 17, 1855; Olympia *Pioneer and Democrat*, July 20; Aug. 3, 1855; Michael F. Luark Diary, July 3, 1855, UW.

16. Luark Diary, Aug. 11; Sept. 19; Oct. 14, 1855; David Blaine to Parents & Sisters, Aug. 6, 1855, Blaine Family Letters, UW; Mason to Gibbs, Sept. 14, 1855, Charles H. Mason Correspondence, WAC; Josiah Keller to Charles Foster, Aug. 5, 1855, Josiah Keller Papers, WAC; James Tilton to John Wilson, Sept. 12, 1855, Letters Received from the Surveyors General of Washington, 1854–1883, RG 49, NA; Olympia *Pioneer and Democrat*, Sept. 21, 28, 1855.

17. Stevens to Gibbs, Aug. 30, 1855, Stevens Papers, WAC; Luark Diary, Sept. 19, 1855; Olympia *Pioneer and Democrat*, Sept. 21, 1855; Mason to Stevens, Oct. 3, 1855, Records of the Washington Superintendency of Indian Affairs; to G. Rains, Sept. 22, 1855, to M. Maloney, Sept. 24, 1855, Records of the Washington Territory Volunteers, WSL.

18. Gibbs to Stevens, Aug. 7, 1855; Stevens to Manypenny, Aug. 30, 1855, both Records of the Washington Superintendency of Indian Affairs; to Gibbs, Aug. 30, 1855, Stevens Papers, WAC; Luark Diary, Sept. 19, 24–26, 30; Oct. 10, 1855; Olympia *Pioneer and Democrat*, Sept. 28; Oct. 12, 19, 1855; Steilacoom *Puget Sound Courier*, Sept. 28, 1855; R. R. Thompson to Palmer, Sept. 28, 1855; Palmer to Manypenny, Oct. 9, 1855, both Records of the Oregon Superintendency of Indian Affairs; Rains to Mason, Sept. 29, 1855; J. Cain to Mason, Oct. 9, 1855; Mason to W. C. Pease, Oct. 18, 1855, all Records of the Washington Territory Volunteers; Journal, Oct. 7, 1855, Granville O. Haller Papers, UW.

19. Blamed by settlers for the White River killings, the Nisqually leader Leschi, previously a respected figure among whites, was not a participant in the affair. D. Blaine to Parents, Jan. 24, 1855; to ?, Feb. 5, 1855, Blaine Family Letters; Simmons to Stevens, March 26, 1855, Records of the Washington Superintendency of Indian Affairs; A. Cox, et al. to Stevens, July 12, 1855, Records of the Washington Territory Volunteers; Steilacoom *Puget Sound Courier*, Aug. 31; Sept. 28; Oct. 12, 1855; Olympia *Pioneer and Democrat*, Sept. 28; Oct. 5, 1855; Mason to Gibbs, Sept. 14, 1855; to Wool, Oct. 20, 1855; to George L. Curry, Oct. 20, 1855, Mason Correspondence; Luark Diary, Oct. 2, 3, 5, 23, 1855; Samuel James to Thomas Foxwell, Feb. 12, 1856, James Family Papers, UW; John G. Parker, Jr. to G. Hays, April 5, 1856, McMicken Family Papers, UW; Fitzhugh to Fayette McMullin, Sept. 12, 1857, McMullin Papers, WSL; Arthur A. Denny, *Pioneer Days on Puget Sound* (Seattle: C. B. Bagley, Printer, 1888), 65; Abby J. Hanford Reminiscences, 5, BL; Edmond S. Meany, ed., "Van Ogle's Memory of Pioneer Days," *WHQ*, 8(Oct. 1922), 278–279; Tolmie to Stevens, April 26, 1856, Stevens Papers, WAC.

20. Despite the assistance rendered by the Hudson's Bay Company, settlers accused the firm of secretly encouraging the hostile Indians. Steilacoom *Puget Sound Courier*, Oct. 26; Nov. 23, 1855; Olympia *Pioneer and*

Democrat, Oct. 12, 26, 1855; Tilton to Thomas A. Hendricks, Nov. 2, 1855, Letters Received from the Surveyors General; to Douglas, Nov. 1, 1855; Douglas to Tilton, Nov. 6, 19, 1855, all in Clarence B. Bagley, ed., "Attitude of the Hudson's Bay Company during the Indian War of 1855–1856," *WHQ*, 8(Oct. 1917), 297–299; Curry to Thomas R. Cornelius, April 16, 1856, George L. Curry Letters, OHS; W. W. Miller to R. S. Robinson, Jan. 22; July 22, 1856, William Winlock Miller Letterbook, UW; H. A. Goldsborough to Gibbs, Jan. 4, 1856, George Gibbs Letters, WAC; H. W. Halleck to Stevens, April 1, 1856, Washington Territorial Documents, WSHS.

21. Curry to Mason, Oct. 25, 1855, Mason Correspondence; to Cornelius, Feb. 17, 1856, Curry Letters; Journal, Nov. 6–13, 15, 1855, Haller Papers; J. Orin Oliphant, "Journals of the Indian War of 1855–56," *WHQ*, 15(Jan. 1924), 14–15; Wamon C. Hembree, "Yakima Indian War Diary," *WHQ*, 16(Oct. 1925), 275277; Gibbs to Stevens, Jan. 27, 1856, Records of the Washington Superintendency of Indian Affairs.

22. Wool to Silas Casey, Feb. 12, 1856, John Wool Papers, New York State Library; Tilton to William H. Wallace, Oct. 31, 1855, William H. Wallace Papers, UW; C. Blaine to ?, Dec. 18, 1855, Blaine Family Letters; Fort Nisqually Journal, Oct. 30, 31; Nov. 1, 10, 28, 29; Dec. 8, 1855, UW; John Nugen to Gibbs, Dec. 21, 1855; Jan. 14, 1856, Gibbs Letters; Mason to Gibbs, Dec. 8, 1855, Mason Correspondence.

23. Olympia *Pioneer and Democrat*, Jan. 25; Feb. 15; June 20; Sept. 12, 1856; Portland *Oregonian*, Dec. 29, 1855; Jan. 5, 19; Aug. 30, 1856; Stevens to Manypenny, Dec. 22, 1855, Records of the Washington Superintendency of Indian Affairs; to E. O. Keyes, Jan. 20, 1856; to Curry, Feb. 17, 1856, Records of the Washington Territory Volunteers; to Wool Dec. 23, 1855; to George Wright, Jan. 30, 1856; Wool to Stevens, Feb. 12, 1856, all Stevens Papers, WAC; to L. Thomas, Dec. 18, 25, 1855; Jan. 19, 1856; to Winfield Scott, Feb. 19, 1856, Wool Papers; Henry C. Hodges to McClellan, June 12, 1856, George B. McClellan Correspondence, UW; M. McCarver to Joseph Lane, Feb. 27, 1856, Joseph Lane Papers, Indiana University Library; "Campaign of Maj. Gen. John E. Wool...Against the people and Authorities of Oregon and Washington," 1, 3, pamphlet in Elwood Evans Papers, WAC.

24. Keyes to Townsend, Jan. 30, 1856, Pacific Division Records; G. Gansevoort to James C. Dobbin, Jan. 31, 1856, Guert Gansevoort Letterbook, Library of Congress; Stevens to N. Hill, Feb. 17, 1856, Records of the Washington Superintendency of Indian Affairs; to E. Lander, Feb. 17, 1856; to John Sewell, Feb. 29, 1856; Hays to Stevens, March 2, 10, 15, 27; April 1, 1856, all Records of the Washington Territory Volunteers; Tilton to Hays, Feb. 20, 1856; Joseph A. White to Hays, March 15, 1856, both McMicken Family Papers; Casey to Stevens, March 7, 1856, Stevens Papers, WAC.

25. Casey to Mackall, Aug. 15, 1856, Pacific Division Records; Stevens to J. Cain, Nov. 14, 1856, Records of the Washington Superintendency of Indian Affairs; to Nesmith, July 25, 1857; to Tolmie, March 8, 1856; Goldsborough to Stevens, March 5, 1856, all Stevens Papers, UW; Fort Nisqually Journal, May 21–23, 1856; Tolmie to H. N. Peers, May 24, 1856, Tolmie Papers; D. Blaine to ?, June 20, 1856, Blaine Family Letters; S. Swartwout to Stevens, July 7, 1856, Records of the Washington Territory Volunteers; Steilacoom *Puget Sound Courier*, Jan. 4, 25, 1856; J. S. Smith to J. Black, Feb. 24, 1856, Feb. 24, 1858, Records relating to the Appointment of Federal Judges and U.S. Attorneys and Marshals, Washington, 1853–1902, M198, NA; Tilton to J. S. Hurd, Feb. 11, 1856, Clarence B. Bagley Collection, UW. For complete details, see Richards, *Stevens*, chapt. 11; Roy Lokken, "The Martial Law Controversy in Washington Territory, 1856," *PNQ*, 43(April 1952), 91–119.

26. Although rumors that he would be dismissed proved to be untrue, Stevens was censured by the Pierce administration. From his seat in Congress, a vindictive Stevens vetoed the reappointment of Lander and Chenoweth. Francis Chenoweth to McMullin, March 6, 1858, McMullin Papers, WSL; to Black, Dec. 26, 1857; Note of Hon. I. I. Stevens in relation to application of F. A. Chenoweth for reappt., n.d.; Smith to Black, Feb. 24, 1858; Stevens to Black, March 16; June 23, 29, 1858, all Records relating to the Appointment of Federal Judges; to Fitzhugh, May 18, 1856, Records of the Washington Superintendency of Indian Affairs; to S. A. Douglas, May 25, 1856, Stevens Papers, UW; to Lewis Cass, Jan. 3, 1857, U.S. State Department, Washington Territorial Papers, NA; J. Patton Anderson to Gibbs, July 18, 1856, Washington Territorial Documents; Townsend to Wool, July 16, 1856, Wool Papers.

27. Wright's expedition is best followed through his field reports, published in William N. Bischoff, S.J., "The Yakima Campaign of 1856," *Mid-America*, 31(July 1949), 170–208. The key sources for the volunteer campaign are Itinerary of the march of the Right Wing...under command of Lt. Col. Shaw, Stevens Papers, WAC; George C. Blankenship Diary, UW; and, for the story of the attack on the Indians, H. D. Wallen to Wool, Nov. 25, 1856, Wool Papers.

28. Stevens to B. F. Shaw, Aug. 2, 1856; to Swartwout, Aug. 31, 1856, Records of the Washington Territory Volunteers; to J. Cain, Nov. 14, 1856; to Manypenny, Aug. 18, 31, 1856, Records of the Washington Superintendency of Indian Affairs; Oct. 22, 1856(two letters of this date), Correspondence of the Office of Indian Affairs; to Lane, Oct. 22; Nov. 21, 1856, Lane Papers; to Edward Steptoe, Nov. 22, 1856, Stevens Papers, WAC; Portland *Oregonian*, Oct. 11, 25, 1856; Wright to Mackall, July 18; Oct. 31, 1856, Pacific Division Records; Wool to Thomas, Nov. 19, 1856, Wool Papers.

29. Wright to Mackall, July 25, 1856, Pacific Division Records; to Stevens, Oct. 4, 1856; Casey to Stevens, Oct. 20, 21; Nov. 2, 1856; Stevens to Wright, Oct. 4, 1856, all Stevens Papers, WAC; to Manypenny, Oct. 11, 21, 1856; to J. Cain, Aug. 20; Nov. 21, 1856; to S. S. Ford, Sr., Oct. 20, 1856; Ford to Stevens, Nov. 27, 1856, all Records of the Washington Superintendency of Indian Affairs; Charles M. Gates, ed., *Messages of the Governors*

of the Territory of Washington to the Legislative Assembly, 1854–1889 (Seattle: University of Washington Press, 1940), 39–40; Meany, ed., "Van Ogle's Memory," 280–281.

30. Stevens claimed that the Indians had been "plotting" the outbreak of hostilities "for at least two or three years." Stevens to Casey, Feb. 2, 1856; Stevens Papers, WAC; to Manypenny, Nov. 1, 1856; April 3, 1857; to Ford, Oct. 20, 1856; Wesley Gosnell to Stevens, March 31, 1857, all Records of the Washington Superintendency of Indian Affairs; Gates, ed., *Messages of the Governors*, 25.

31. August V. Kautz Journal, Dec. 21, 22, 24, 28–30, 1857; Jan. 4, 16, 20, 21, 1858, Library of Congress; Casey to Mackall, Jan. 21, 28, 1858, Pacific Division Records; Resolution of Indignation Meeting, Jan. 22, 1858, in *WHQ*, 5(Jan. 1914), 55–56; Butler P. Anderson to ?, May 4, 1858, in *WHQ*, 1(Jan. 1907), 59; McMullin to John B. Floyd, April 22, 1858; Fayette McMullin Papers, WSA; Steilacoom *Puget Sound Herald*, Oct. 22, 29, 1858.

32. Simmons to Stevens, April 4; May 1, 1857; Thomas J. Hanna to Simmons, Aug. 12, 1857; Fitzhugh to Stevens, Feb. 8, 15; March 28, Nov. 13, 1856, all Records of the Washington Superintendency of Indian Affairs; to McMullin, Sept. 12, 1857, McMullin Papers, WSL; Stevens to Manypenny, Dec. 5, 1856, Correspondence of the Office of Indian Affairs; Mason to Douglas, Aug. 26, 1857, in "Defending Puget Sound Against the Northern Indians," *PNQ*, 36(Jan. 1945), 71; to Officer Commanding the Pacific Division, Aug. 26, 1857, State Department, Washington Territorial Papers. Ebey's scalp was recovered in Victoria in 1860. His spirit supposedly revealed the head's location during an 1862 seance in an eastern Oregon mining camp. *Port Townsend Register*, Aug. 11, 1860; Harry N. M. Winton, ed., "The Powder River and John Day Mines in 1862; Diary of Winfield Scott Ebey," *PNQ*, 34(Jan. 1943), 77–78.

33. Seven Northern Indians taken hostage in Port Townsend to compel surrender of the killers promptly escaped. McMullin to Jacob Thompson, Oct. 22, 1857, Correspondence of the Office of Indian Affairs; to James Buchanan, Oct. 20, 1857, in *WHQ*, 1(Jan. 1907), 53; to W. S. Ebey, Oct. 9, 1857; to D. G. Farragut, June 18, 1858, McMullin Papers, WSL; to Stevens, March 24, 1858, Stevens Papers, UW; Simmons to Nesmith, Aug. 15, 26, 1857, Records of the Washington Superintendency of Indian Affairs; Douglas to Tolmie, Sept. 30, 1857, Tolmie Papers; Ebey to Wallace, Oct. 14, 1857, Wallace Papers.

34. Petition for Military Road north of the Columbia from Pugets Sound to Fort Walla Walla, n.d., Oregon and Washington Territorial Papers; Columbia Lancaster to James G. Swan, Dec. 29, 1854, James G. Swan Papers, University of British Columbia Library; W. Turrentine Jackson, *Wagon Roads West: A Study of Federal Road Surveys and Construction in the Trans-Mississippi West, 1846–1869* (New Haven: Yale University Press, 1964, 1952), 96.

35. Jefferson Davis to Hartman Bache, May 14, 1855; Report on the proposed Military Road from the Dalles…to Columbia Barracks, recd. April 18, 1856; Report on proposed Military Road from Columbia Barracks to Fort Steilacoom, n.d.; Bache to George H. Derby, May 6, 1855; to J. J. Abert, March 16; April 24, 1858; to G. H. Mendell, May 6, 1858; Gibbs to Derby, July ? 1856; G. H. Mendell to Bache, Oct. 26, 1856; Sept. 1, 1857; Jan. 16; April 20, 1858; to George Thom, Sept. 16, 1858; W. W. deLacy Report on Steilacoom to Bellingham Bay route, n. d.; Thom to Abert, April 1, 1859; to George W. Sloan, Aug. 13, 1859; Derby to Bache, Oct. 1; Nov. 1, 18; Dec. 5, 1855; April 4; May 19, 31; July 12, 23; Aug. 1, 1856, all Pacific Coast Office of Military Roads Records, RG 77, NA; to Gibbs, June 30, 1856, Washington Territorial Documents; J. C. Woodruff to Floyd, Jan. 17, 1859, Oregon and Washington Territorial Papers. For complete details on Washington Territory roadbuilding, see Jackson, *Wagon Roads West*, 96–106.

36. Wallen to Wool, Feb. 10, 1857, Wool Papers; Woodruff to Floyd, Jan. 17, 1859, Oregon and Washington Territorial Papers; Olympia *Washington Standard*, Nov. 23, 1860; Jan. 19, 1861; Steilacoom *Puget Sound Herald*, Jan. 24, 1861; Samuel Bowles, *Across the Continent: A Summer's Journey to the Rocky Mountains, the Mormons, and the Pacific States, with Speaker Colfax* (Springfield: Samuel Bowles & Company, 1866), 199–200; Albert D. Richardson, *Beyond the Mississippi: From the Great River to the Great Ocean* (Hartford: American Publishing Company, 1867), 411–412; Mrs. Frances Fuller Victor, *All Over Oregon and Washington* (San Francisco: John H. Carmany & Co., 1872), 230–231; James S. Lawson Reminiscences, 117, BL; Notes on Journey from Portland, Oregon, to Olympia, Washington, July 7, 1869, W. Milnor Roberts Papers, Montana State University Library.

37. Olympia *Pioneer and Democrat*, March 5, 12; April 9, 1858; Steilacoom *Puget Sound Herald*, April 2, 23, 1858; Archibald Campbell to Cass, July 4, 1858, Records relating to the First Northwest Boundary Survey Commission, 1853–69, NA.

38. A. J. Chambers to Thomas M. Chambers, April 22, 1858, Thomas M. Chambers Papers, WSHS; Olympia *Pioneer and Democrat*, March 12; April 30, 1858; Steilacoom *Puget Sound Herald*, March 26; April 9, 16, 23, 30, 1858; William J. Ballou Reminiscences, 3, BL; R. W. Walker to Cass, June 18, 1858; John Nugent to Cass, Jan. 8, 1859, both State Department, Washington Territorial Papers; Walter N. Sage, "The Gold Colony of British Columbia," *Canadian Historical Review*, 2(Dec. 1921), 340; Raymond E. Lindgren, "John Damon and the Fraser River Rush," *PHR*, 14(June 1945), 184; Jean Barman, *The West beyond the West: A History of British Columbia* (Toronto: University of Toronto Press, rev. ed., 1996), 62, 66.

39. Some prospectors took an all-land route to the gold country, along the eastern side of the Cascades north from The Dalles. Nugent to Cass, Jan. 8, 1859, State Department, Washington Territorial Papers; Steilacoom *Puget Sound Herald*, May 14, 21; June 11, 25; July 2, 16, 1858; Robert Frost, "Fraser River Gold Rush Adventures," *WHQ*, 22(July 1931), 203–204.

40. Olympia *Pioneer and Democrat*, May 7; July 30; Aug. 13, 1858; Steilacoom *Puget Sound Herald*, April 30; May 21, 28; June 4, 1858; Whatcom *Northern Light*, July 3, 1858; C. C. Gardiner, "To the Fraser River Mines in 1858," ed. Robie L. Reid, *British Columbia Historical Quarterly*, 1(Oct. 1937), 245; George F. G. Stanley, ed., *Mapping the Frontier: Charles Wilson's Diary of the Survey of the 49th Parallel, 1858–1862* (Toronto: Macmillan of Canada, 1970), 25; Lindgren, "Damon and the Fraser River Rush," 186; F. W. Howay, ed., "To the Fraser River: The Diary and Letters of Cyrus Olin Phillips, 1858–1859," *California Historical Society Quarterly*, 11(June 1932), 152.

41. Olympia *Pioneer and Democrat*, April 30; Oct. 1, 1858; Steilacoom *Puget Sound Herald*, April 16; June 18; Aug. 20, 27; Nov. 12, 1858; Stevens to Cass, July 21, 1858, Stevens Papers, UW; Walker to Cass, June 18, 1858; Nugent to Cass, Jan. 8, 1859, both State Department, Washington Territorial Papers.

42. Whatcom *Northern Light*, July 3; Aug. 21, 1858, the latter as reprinted in P. R. Jeffcoat, *Nooksack Tales and Trails* (Ferndale: Sedro-Woolley *Courier-Times*, 1949), 103; Olympia *Pioneer and Democrat*, July 30, 1858; Nugent to Cass, Jan. 8, 1859, State Department, Washington Territorial Papers.

43. Robert Frost, "Personal Recollections of an Overland Trip…to the Frazier River Mines in 1858," 6, typescript in UW; Barman, *West beyond the West*, 67–68; Steilacoom *Puget Sound Herald*, Aug. 20, 27; Oct. 1, 1858.

44. R. H. Lansdale to Nesmith, Feb. 13, 1858; William Craig to Stevens, Dec. 19, 1856; Jan. 5, 16; Feb. 16, 1857, all Records of the Washington Superintendency of Indian Affairs; James Wheeler, Jr. to O. H. P. Taylor, Nov. 9, 1857, Kate D. Taylor Papers, OHS.

45. Lansdale to Nesmith, Feb. 13; March 1, 1858, Records of the Washington Superintendency of Indian Affairs; Steptoe to Mackall, May 23, 29, 1858; Wright to Mackall, May 26, 1858; Newman S. Clarke to Cooper, June 1, 1858, all Letters Received by the Office of the Adjutant General, 1822–1860, M567, NA; Jack Dozier, "The Coeur d'Alene Indians in the War of 1858," *IY*, 5(Fall 1961), 23–24; Nesmith to Wright, June 17, 1857; to Mackall, Aug. 30, 1858, Records of the Oregon Superintendency of Indian Affairs.

46. James Barron to Wallace, April 7, 1856, Wallace Papers; Cain to Stevens, Dec. 13, 1856; Craig to Stevens, April 20, 1857, both Records of the Washington Superintendency of Indian Affairs; Clarke to Cooper, June 1, 1858; Steptoe to Mackall, April 17; May 2, 1858, all Letters Received by the Adjutant General, 1822–1860.

47. Steptoe to Mackall, May 23, 29, 1858, Letters Received by the Adjutant General, 1822–1860. For the best account of the Steptoe Disaster, see Robert Ignatius Burns, S.J., *The Jesuits and the Indian Wars of the Northwest* (New Haven: Yale University Press, 1966), chapt. 6.

48. Stevens to Nesmith, July 18, 1858, in J. Ronald Todd, ed., "Letters of Governor Isaac I. Stevens, 1857–1858," *PNQ*, 31(Oct. 1940), 444–445; Portland *Oregonian*, May 29, 1858; Steilacoom *Puget Sound Herald*, June 11; Aug. 13, 1858; Lansdale to Nesmith, June 30, 1858, Records of the Washington Superintendency of Indian Affairs; James Archer to mother, July 1, 17; Aug. 2, 1858, James Archer Letters, Maryland Historical Society; Frost, "Fraser River Gold Rush Adventures," 203–207.

49. All fatalities were inflicted in the first encounter, the Indians thereafter keeping beyond the range of the deadly rifles. Noting the at-a-distance nature of the fighting, some observers belittled the "heroism" of the Army. Robert Garnett to Mackall, July 17; Aug. 30, 1858, Pacific Division Records; Wright to Mackall, Sept. 2, 6, 1858, in John Mullan, "Topographical Memoir…of Colonel Wright's late Campaign against the Indians," Senate Ex. Doc. No. 32, 35th Cong., 2nd sess., 19–20, 22–24; Lawrence Kip, *Army Life on the Pacific: A Journal of the Expedition Against the Northern Indians* (New York: Redfield, 1859), 52, 56–59, 63–65; Nesmith to Mix, Sept. 30, 1858, Correspondence of the Office of Indian Affairs; to Lane, Sept. 30, 1858, Lane Papers. For a detailed history of the campaigns, see Burns, *Jesuits and the Indian Wars*, chapts. 7, 8.

50. Olympia *Pioneer and Democrat*, Oct. 22; Nov. 19, 1858; Wright to Mackall, Sept. 9, 15, 24, 1858, in Mullan, "Topographical Memoir," 26, 35, 55–56, 68–69; Kip, *Army Life*, 70–72, 75–76, 92, 101, 103–106; John C. Lawrence, "Pioneer Experiences," *WHQ*, 16(Oct. 1925), 263; John E. Smith, "A Pioneer of the Spokane Country," *WHQ*, 7(Oct. 1916), 270, 272.

51. Olympia *Pioneer and Democrat*, Nov. 19, 1858; Robert Carleton Clark, "Military History of Oregon, 1848–1859," *OHQ*, 36(March 1935), 52; W. S. Harney to Assistant Adjutant General, July 19, 1859, Department of Oregon Records, U.S. Army Continental Commands, RG 393, NA; Stevens to Douglas, May 12, 1855; McMullin to Cass, Nov. 3, 1857; Mason to Cass, Dec. 23, 1858; Nugent to Cass, Jan. 8, 1859, all State Department, Washington Territorial Papers. For full details on the San Juan affair, see Barry M. Gough, *The Royal Navy and the Northwest Coast of North America, 1810–1914: A Study of British Maritime Ascendency* (Vancouver: University of British Columbia Press, 1971), chapt. 7.

52. Harney to Cooper, Aug. 29, 1859; to Assistant Adjutant General, July 19, 1859; A. Pleasanton to Pickett, July 18, 1859; to Casey, July 18, 1859, all Department of Oregon Records; Steilacoom *Puget Sound Herald*, July 29; Aug. 5, 19, 1859; Olympia *Pioneer and Democrat*, Aug. 19, 1859; Mason to Cass, Dec. 23, 1858, State Department, Washington Territorial Papers.

53. Colonel George Wright, the new departmental commander, endorsed Harney's basic strategic concept. San Juan Island, said Wright, was "a good Post of observation," likely to deter waterborne movements of Indians from British territory. In another popular move, the Army stopped paying the annual $600 rent due the Hudson's Bay Company for use of the land at Fort Steilacoom. W. R. Drinkard to Harney, Sept. 3, 1859, in House Ex. Doc. No. 65, 36th Cong., 1st sess., 11; Steilacoom *Puget Sound Herald*, Oct. 28, 1859; Sept. 28, 1860; Wright to Thomas, July 28; Aug. 28; Sept. 20, 1860, Department of Oregon Records; Richard D. Gholson to Harney, Aug. 22, 1859; to Cass, Nov. 1, 1859; Cass to Gholson, Feb. 4, 1860, all Richard D. Gholson Papers, WSA;

Olympia *Pioneer and Democrat*, June 1, 1860; Port Townsend *North-West*, Sept. 13, 1860; Frank E. Ross, "The Retreat of the Hudson's Bay Company in the Pacific Northwest," *Canadian Historical Review*, 18(Sept. 1937), 279–280.

54. Pleasanton to Assistant Adjutant General, Dec. 7, 1858, Department of Oregon Records; Nesmith to Mix, Nov. 19, 1858; to Dennison, Nov. 24, 1858, Records of the Oregon Superintendency of Indian Affairs; Stevens to Nesmith, Jan. 4; April 22, 1859, Stevens Papers, UW; Steilacoom *Puget Sound Herald*, March 18, 1859. Also see J. Orin Oliphant, *On the Cattle Ranges of the Oregon Country* (Seattle: University of Washington Press, 1968), 81–82.

55. Olympia *Pioneer and Democrat*, Aug. 24, 1860; D. W. Meinig, *The Great Columbia Plain: A Historical Geography, 1805–1910* (Seattle: University of Washington Press, 1968), 201–204; Howard S. Brode, ed., "Diary of Dr. Augustus J. Thibido of the Northwest Exploring Expedition, 1859," *PNQ,* 31(July 1940), 342–343, 345.

56. Olympia *Washington Pioneer*, Dec. 17, 1853; Olympia *Pioneer and Democrat*, Sept. 14, 1860.

57. Steilacoom *Puget Sound Herald*, April 1, 1859; Sept. 19, 1861, reprinting from Vancouver *Chronicle*, Sept. 5, 1861; *Ninth Census* (Washington, D.C.: Government Printing Office, 1872), 1:595.

Notes—Chapter Four
The Real Condition of Affairs

1. To Thomas Cornelius, June 16, 1862, John J. McGilvra Papers, UW.

2. Steilacoom *Puget Sound Herald*, April 29, 1859; Feb. 24; June 6; Nov. 9, 1860; Olympia *Washington Standard*, Jan. 12; Feb. 2, 1861; Port Townsend *North-West*, June 13, 1861.

3. A. J. Cain to E. R. Geary, May 8, 18, 25; June 1; Aug. 28; Nov. 16, 27; Dec. 29, 1860, Records of the Washington Superintendency of Indian Affairs, 1853–1874, M5, NA; Geary to A. B. Greenwood, Nov. 27, 1860; to W. P. Dole, April 23, 1861, Records of the Oregon Superintendency of Indian Affairs, 1848–1873, M2, NA; Unident. newspaper clippings, H. H. Bancroft Scrapbook, 67, BL; Portland *Weekly Oregonian*, Dec. 22, 1860. Also see Leonard J. Arrington, *History of Idaho* (Moscow: University of Idaho Press, 2 vols., 1994), 1:183–184.

4. Geary to W. S. Harney, May 14, 1860; to Cain, Dec. 18, 1860, Records of the Washington Superintendency of Indian Affairs; to Dole, April 23, 1861, Records of the Oregon Superintendency of Indian Affairs; to A. S. Johnston, April 22, 1861, Department of the Pacific Records, Letters Received, 1861–1865, NA; Robert Newell to J. W. Nesmith, April 27; June 30, 1862, James W. Nesmith Papers, OHS; Sacramento *Daily Union*, May 14, 1862; Steilacoom *Puget Sound Herald*, Sept. 5. 1861; James W. Watt, "Experiences of a Packer in Washington Territory Mining Camps During the Sixties," *WHQ,* 19(July 1928), 207–208; George S. Wright to Geary, Dec. 22, 1860, Correspondence of the Office of Indian Affairs, Letters Received, 1824–1881, M234, NA; Portland *Weekly Oregonian*, April 20, 1861. For a sense of the excitement, see "News from the Nez Perce Mines," *IY,* 3(Winter 1959–1960), 19–29.

5. Olympia *Washington Standard*, Nov. 23, 1860; May 11, 18; June 1, 15, 22, 29, 1861; Isaac I. Stevens to Nesmith, May 22; June 19, 1861, Isaac I. Stevens Papers, UW; Port Townsend *North-West*, June 6, 13, 20, 27, 1861; Steilacoom *Puget Sound Herald*, June 27; Aug. 15, 1861. For detailed coverage of the campaign, see Robert W. Johannsen, *Frontier Politics and the Sectional Conflict: The Pacific Northwest on the Eve of the Civil War* (Seattle: University of Washington Press, 1955), 211–216.

6. Tilton's slave was seized by British authorities in Victoria in 1860. Stevens to Nesmith, May 22; June 19, 1861, Stevens Papers, UW; Olympia *Washington Standard*, Oct. 5, 26, 1861; June 5, 1869; Olympia *Pioneer and Democrat*, Sept. 28, 1860; James Tilton to Henry M. McGill, Sept. 30, 1860, in *WHQ,* 1(Oct. 1906), 71; McGill to Lewis Cass, Oct. 8, 1860, U.S. State Department, Washington Territorial Papers, NA; Port Townsend *North-West*, Oct. 4, 1860; Port Townsend *Weekly Message*, March 25, 1870.

7. Report, Jan. 2, 1862, Benjamin F. Kendall Papers, UW; San Francisco *Alta California*, Nov. 4, 1861; Steilacoom *Puget Sound Herald*, Nov. 7, 1861; Olympia *Washington Standard*, Nov. 16, 23, 1861; Portland *Weekly Oregonian*, July 12, 1862; C. H. Hale to Dole, Sept. 30, 1862, Records of the Washington Superintendency of Indian Affairs; James O'Neill to General Steele, June 23, 1866; to Geo. C. Hough, Jan. 14, 1867; Benjamin Alvord to Dole, Sept. 8, 1863, all Correspondence of the Office of Indian Affairs; to Assistant Adjutant General, Oct. 4, 15, 1862, Department of the Pacific Records; to Nesmith, Nov. 25, 1862, Nesmith Papers; "Grievances of the Nez Perce," *IY,* 4(Fall 1960), 6–7; G. Hays to McGill, Sept. 8, 1861, Henry M. McGill Papers, WSL. Also see "Fabulous Florence!" *IY,* 6(Summer 1962), 22–31.

8. James Mullany to Mary Mullany, Nov. 5, 1860, Mary Mullany Letters, OHS; Hays to B. F. Kendall, April 19, 1862, Benjamin F. Kendall Papers, OHS; Steilacoom *Puget Sound Herald*, March 27, 1862; Portland *Daily Oregonian*, July 26, 1862; *Walla Walla Statesman*, Dec. 10, 1861; Jan. 10; Feb. 1, 1862; Feb. 3, 1865.

9. *Walla Walla Statesman*, Dec. 10, 1861; Jan. 10, 25; Feb. 8, 22, 1862; Feb. 17; Nov. 10, 1865; Report on Washington and Idaho, 1879, Henry Villard Papers, Houghton Library, Harvard University; D. W. Meinig, *The Great Columbia Plain: A Historical Geography, 1805–1910* (Seattle: University of Washington Press, 1968), 223–225; Steilacoom *Puget Sound Herald*, March 27, 1862.

10. In separate 1862 incidents, homeless persons and troopers from the fort rioted in the streets, looting stores and beating merchants. Fire, from a faulty lamp in the quarters of "a Spanish courtezan," nearly destroyed Walla Walla in 1864. Portland *Weekly Oregonian*, Nov. 23, 1861; March 15, 22, 1862; *Walla Walla Statesman*, Jan. 10; March 15; April 19, 1862; April 25; May 30; Oct. 17, 1863; May 13, 1864; Dec. 15, 1865; C. S. Kingston, "The Northern Overland Route in 1867: Journal of Henry Lueg," *PNQ*, 41(July 1950), 251; A. S. Mercer, *Washington Territory: The Great Northwest, Her Material Resources, and Claims to Emigration* (Ithaca: L. C. Childs, 1965), 25; Statement of the Financial Condition of Washington Territory, 18, copy in William P. Winans Papers, WSU.

11. Robert Thompson, one of the O.S.N. founders, had inaugurated the steamboating era on the upper Columbia with the 1858 launching of the *Colonel Wright* at The Dalles. John Mullan to S. H. Long, Nov. 12, 1862, Records of the Topographical Engineers, Letters Received, RG 77, NA; John C. Ainsworth Reminiscences, 54–55, 77–82, OHS; Randall V. Mills, *Stern-Wheelers Up Columbia: A Century of Steamboating in the Oregon Country* (Palo Alto: Pacific Books, 1947), 41–43, 130–131; Dorothy O. Johansen, "The Oregon Steam Navigation Company: An Example of Capitalism on the Frontier," *PHR*, 10(June 1941), 179–181; S. G. Reed to George Hunter, July 29, 1876; to A. H. Gordon, Sept. 11, 1873, Simeon G. Reed Papers, Reed College Library; R. R. Thompson to D. F. Bradford, June 15, 1866, John C. Ainsworth Papers, UO; *Walla Walla Statesman*, June 1; Sept. 6; Nov. 8, 1862; March 21; July 4, 1863; Olympia *Washington Standard*, Sept. 13, 1862; July 4, 1863. For a contemporary tribute to the O.S.N. management, see Samuel Bowles, *Across the Continent: A Summer's Journey to the Rocky Mountains, the Mormons, and the Pacific States, with Speaker Colfax* (Springfield: Samuel Bowles & Company, 1866), 193–194.

12. Ainsworth Reminiscences, 86–87, 99; Portland *Weekly Oregonian*, June 14, 21, 1862; *Walla Walla Statesman*, Oct. 4, 1862; Thompson to Bradford, June 15, 1866, Ainsworth Papers. Also see Johansen, "Oregon Steam Navigation Company," 183–184; Mills, *Stern-Wheelers Up Columbia*, 68–72.

13. Simeon Reed reported company profits for July 1865 alone as slightly in excess of $110,000. By 1866, original partner Daniel Bradford realized $333,000 from his initial $37,500 investment. Reed to J. W. Ladd, Aug. 3, 1865, Reed Papers; Thompson to Bradford, June 15, 1866, Ainsworth Papers; Lewiston *North-Idaho Radiator*, March 4, 1865; *Walla Walla Statesman*, Sept. 6, 1862; Portland *Weekly Oregonian*, June 21, 1862; Hale to Dole, Aug. 25, 1862, Records of the Washington Superintendency of Indian Affairs.

14. Elwood Evans to W. H. Wallace, Sept. 15, 1861, William H. Wallace Papers, UW; to Father, Feb. 2, 1862; Alex S. Abernethy to Evans, Aug. 26; Nov. 1, 1861, all Elwood Evans Papers, WAC; Olympia *Washington Standard*, Aug. 24, 31; Nov. 23; Dec. 14, 1861; Jan. 10, 1863; Port Townsend *North-West*, Sept. 19; Oct. 3, 1861; Steilacoom *Puget Sound Herald*, Sept. 5, 19, 1861; Matthew P. Deady to Nesmith, Dec. 14, 1861, Nesmith Papers; J. W. Goodwin to Kendall, March 27, 1862, Kendall Papers, UW.

15. Steilacoom *Puget Sound Herald*, Oct. 24, 1861; Report, Jan. 2, 1862; Kendall to E. White, Nov. 16, 1861, both Kendall Papers, UW; Charles P. Hutchins to Wallace, Oct. 4, 1861, Wallace Papers; Deady to Nesmith, Dec. 14, 1861, Nesmith Papers.

16. Anson G. Henry to Abraham Lincoln, July 17, 1859, Abraham Lincoln Papers, Library of Congress; to Jno. Edmunds, May 17, 1862; Aug. 20, 1864; Tilton to Commissioner, General Land Office, Sept. 30, 1860, all Letters Received from the Surveyors General of Washington, 1854–1883, RG 49, NA; Steilacoom *Puget Sound Herald*, Feb. 6, 23, 30; July 17, 1862; Olympia *Washington Standard*, Feb. 11, 1865. On Henry's involvement in the Lincoln marriage, see Douglas L. Wilson, *Honor's Voice: The Transformation of Abraham Lincoln* (New York: Alfred A. Knopf, 1998), 239–240.

17. At least two reservation agents supplied Henry with copies of Kendall's official correspondence. Henry to Wallace, Oct. 24, 1861; to Dole, Oct. 28, 1861; to Lincoln, Feb. 3, 1862, all Lincoln Papers; Nov. 16, 1861, Edward R. Geary Papers, OHS; to Edward D. Baker, Oct. 30, 1861; to Kendall, Sept. 29, 1861; Kendall to David Logan, Dec. 7, 1861; to Caleb B. Smith, Feb. 24, 1862, all Kendall Papers, UW; Evans to Father, Feb. 2, 1862, Evans Papers; Olympia *Washington Standard*, Oct. 26; Nov. 16; Dec. 14, 1861; Feb. 22; Oct. 25, 1862; Deady to Nesmith, Dec. 14, 1861, Nesmith Papers; R. B. Boyd to S. D. Howe, Sept. 27, 1862, Tulalip Indian Agency Records, RG 75, FRC.

18. August Kautz to Edward Huggins, March 1, 1862, Edward Huggins Papers, UW; Kendall to Logan, Dec. 7, 1861; Goodwin to Kendall, Jan. 13; March 27, 1862, all Kendall Papers, UW; Wallace to George Barnes, April 13, 1862, Wallace Papers; Steilacoom *Puget Sound Herald*, Feb. 27, 1862; Port Townsend *North-West*, March 22, 1862. For evidence of agent Wilbur's anti-Catholic work, see James Wilbur to T. J. McKenny, Sept. 23, 1867, Records of the Washington Superintendency of Indian Affairs; to J. Q. Smith, April 19, 1877, Correspondence of the Office of Indian Affairs.

19. Transforming the December beating into a case of attempted murder by Kendall, the pro-Henry *Standard* described Howe's cane as a "switch" and claimed that the former superintendent was armed with "one of the latest improved cartridge 'four-shooters,' the most powerful arm of the kind invented." William H. Barnhart to Nesmith, May 12, 1862; Deady to Nesmith, April 7, 1862, both Nesmith Papers; Olympia *Washington Standard*, Dec. 20, 1862; Jan. 3, 10, 1863; Steilacoom *Puget Sound Herald*, Jan. 8, 1863.

20. Portland *Daily Oregonian*, Nov. 4, 1862; July 23, 1863; Watt, "Experiences of a Packer," *WHQ*, 20(Jan. 1929), 40; *Walla Walla Statesman*, Feb. 22; Nov. 1, 8; Dec. 6, 1862; Jan. 17; Oct. 10, 1863; April 7; Dec. 15, 1865; Allan Francis to W. H. Seward, Dec. 27, 1864, Dispatches from United States Consuls in Victoria, 1862–1906, T130, NA.

21. *Walla Walla Statesman*, Nov. 29; Dec. 20, 1862; Jan. 3; Feb. 14, 21; March 7; May 23; July 25; Nov. 28, 1863; Feb. 3; April 7; Dec. 8, 1865; Watt, "Experiences of a Packer," *WHQ*, 19(Oct. 1928), 286; Johansen, "Oregon Steam Navigation Company," 185; Bowles, *Across the Continent*, 194–196; Mills, *Stern-Wheelers Up Columbia*, 81–82, 84–85; Sacramento *Daily Union*, May 14, 1862; Lewiston *North-Idaho Radiator*, March 4, 1865. For efforts in Lewiston to open a combined water-land route to Boise, see Lewiston *Golden Age*, Feb. 5, 1863.

22. *Walla Walla Statesman*, Nov. 29, 1862; Feb. 14, 21; Nov. 28, 1863; July 1; Aug. 19, 1864. On the Walla Walla-Umatilla rivalry, see Meinig, *Great Columbia Plain*, 215.

23. Rector, who operated, according to Judge Matthew Deady, "a crop of common school thieves" out of his Willamette Valley headquarters, was the only one of the commissioners to exhibit anything like genuine sympathy for the plight of the Nez Perce. William H. Rector to Dole, Nov. 12, 1862; Jan. 23, 1863; to Hale, Jan. 3, 1863, Records of the Oregon Superintendency of Indian Affairs; Deady to Nesmith, Jan. 12, 1862; Newell to Nesmith, June 30; Dec. 3, 1862; Jan. 20, 1863, all Nesmith Papers; Steilacoom *Puget Sound Herald*, Feb. 27, 1862; Portland *Weekly Oregonian*, May 24, 1862; Hays to Kendall, April 19, 1862, Kendall Papers, OHS; Olympia *Washington Standard*, Nov. 15, 1862; Stevens to William Craig, April 9, 1856; J. W. Anderson to Hale, Jan. 2, 1863, both Records of the Washington Superintendency of Indian Affairs.

24. Hale announced, incorrectly, that the acreage ceded was open to immediate white settlement. His superiors repudiated the statement, but did nothing about the larger irresponsibility, the effectual purchase of land belonging to one tribal faction from the leaders of another group of bands. Hale to Dole, May 11; June 25, 1863, Correspondence of the Office of Indian Affairs; T. F. McElroy to John J. McGilvra, May 23, 1863, McGilvra Papers; John B. Dimick to Alla Eberhard, April 28; May 30, 1863, John B. Dimick Papers, OHS; James A. Waymire to A. C. Gibbs, May 22, 1863, Addison C. Gibbs Papers, OHS; Memorandum of Nez Perce Treaty of June 9, 1863, Records of the Idaho Superintendency of Indian Affairs, M832, NA; Olympia *Washington Standard*, June 20, 1863; Alvord to Wallace, July 22, 1863, in *The War of the Rebellion: A Compilation of the Official Records of the Union and Confederate Armies*, Series I, Vol. L(Washington, D.C.: Government Printing Office, 1897), Part II, 539–540; Hutchins to Wallace, Nov. 17, 1863, Wallace Papers. Also see the analysis in Alvin M. Josephy, Jr., *The Nez Perce Indians and the Opening of the Northwest* (New Haven: Yale University Press, abridged ed., 1971), 418–421.

25. *Alta California* reprinted in Olympia *Washington Standard*, March 15, 1862. Olympia's attempted governance of the gold regions, said the San Francisco newspaper, was the equivalent of "tying the miners at Pike's Peak to the whalers of New Bedford."

26. Portland *Weekly Oregonian*, June 7, 1862; Olympia *Washington Standard*, March 8; Aug. 23, 1862; *Walla Walla Statesman*, Oct. 11; Dec. 13, 1862; Jan. 24, 31; Feb. 14; March 21; April 25; Nov. 21; Dec. 5, 1863; E. P. Oliphant to Lincoln, Nov. 15, 1862, U.S. State Department, Washington Territorial Papers, NA.

27. Olympia *Washington Standard*, April 5; May 24, 1862.

28. In the course of congressional deliberations, Idaho, incorrectly thought to be an Indian word meaning "Gem of the Mountains," supplanted Montana as the territory's name. Adding to the frustration east of the mountains, the same westside politicians responsible for the boundary took advantage of every opportunity for position and profit in Idaho. William Wallace, the first governor, delayed formal inauguration of territorial government long enough for Sound-based colleagues to make a last visit to the mining country, collecting taxes and soliciting gratuities for the grant of public favors. Ibid., April 5, 1862; *Walla Walla Statesman*, March 21; April 25; June 27, 1863; Feb. 10; Aug. 11, 1865; Carlos A. Schwantes, *In Mountain Shadows: A History of Idaho* (Lincoln: University of Nebraska Press, 1991), 59; H. A. Goldsborough to McElroy, April 27; May 30; June 2, 1863, Thomas F. McElroy Papers, WSL; J. E. Wyche to Lincoln, March 25, 1863, Records relating to the Appointment of Federal Judges and U.S. Attorneys and Marshals, Washington, 1853–1902, M198, NA. Also see "Idaho's Centennial: How Idaho was Created in 1863," *IY*, 7(Spring 1963), 44–58.

29. Idaho was reduced to its present-day limits upon creation of Montana Territory in 1864. To visit the Nez Perce reservation, at least one Boise headquartered official traveled overland to San Francisco and then up the coast and the Columbia and Snake rivers by a succession of steamers. D. W. Ballard to Lewis L. Bogy, Dec. 5, 1866; DeL. Floyd-Jones to E. Parker, May 2, 1870, both Correspondence of the Office of Indian Affairs; *Walla Walla Statesman*, Dec. 9, 1864; Nov. 24, 1865; W. Foster Hidden, "The Northern Idaho Annexation Issue," *WHQ*, 21(July 1930), 210–211.

30. In 1862 and 1863, Washington and Oregon sent locally raised protective corps east on the overland trail to meet and assist the annual migration. M. Maloney to James A. Hardie, Dec. 21, 1860; Jno. C. Card to McGill, Jan. 17, 1861; McGill to E. V. Sumner, June 24, 1861; Frank Matthias to McGill, May 15, 1861; J. H. Van Bokkelen to McGill, May 23, 1861; Henry Miles to McGill, June 15, 1861, all McGill Papers; L. Jay S. Turney to S. Cameron, Sept. 2, 1861, Washington Territorial Papers, UW; Steilacoom *Puget Sound Herald*, Jan. 17, 1861; Port Townsend *North-West*, May 16; June 20, 1861; Olympia *Washington Standard*, July 20; Aug. 10, 1861; Proclamation by the Governor of Washington Territory, May 10, 1861, State Department, Washington Territorial Papers; William Pickering to Alvord, July 18, 1862; to Lyman Trumbull, Dec. 31, 1862, William Pickering Papers, WSL; M. Crawford to Benjamin Stark, June 6, 1862, Benjamin Stark Papers, OHS; Report, Expedition for the Protection of Emigrants, 1863, Medorem Crawford Papers, UO. Also see G. Thomas Edwards, "Holding the Far West for the Union: The Army in 1861," *Civil War History*, 14(Dec. 1968), 316.

31. J. M. Whittlesey to Assistant Adjutant General, Sept. 27, 1861; L. Thomas to Cornelius, et al., Sept. 26, 1861; Thomas Scott to J. Steinberger, Oct. 18, 1861; Steinberger to Drum, March 28, 1862; Alvord to Assistant

Adjutant General, Feb. 10, 1863; to Drum, July 11, 1864; P. Lugenbeel to Drum, July 20, 1863, all Department of the Pacific Records, 1861–1865, NA; Barnhart to Nesmith, Dec. 31, 1861, Nesmith Papers; J. G. Hyatt to McGill, Oct. 20, 1861, McGill Papers; *Walla Walla Statesman*, Feb. 8, 1862; Steilacoom *Puget Sound Herald*, Feb. 27, 1862; Jan. 29; June 25, 1863.

32. The customs service renamed the *Jefferson Davis*, the Puget Sound revenue cutter, the *Joe Lane*, at best a modest improvement, considering that Oregon's Democratic leader had retired from public life rather than renounce pro-slavery views. A nationwide ban on livestock exports, meant to conserve food for Union armies east of the Mississippi, terminated the profitable sale of Northwest beef in Victoria, with no corresponding benefit to distant military campaigns. Henry to Edmunds, Nov. 15, 1861; Jan. 11; March 3; June 13, 18, 21, 1862, Letters Received from the Surveyors General; Edmunds to Henry, Dec. 28, 1861; April 18, 1862, Records of the Bureau of Land Management, RG 49, FRC; Arthur A. Denny to Daniel Bagley, Dec. 8, 1863, Daniel Bagley Papers, UW; Evans to R. W. Taylor, Sept. 15, 1863; March 30, 1865, Washington Territorial Papers, UW; McElroy to Mother, July 19, 1863; July 24, 1864, McElroy Family Papers, UW; Joseph Cushman to Thomas D. Elliott, Dec. 22, 1863, Oregon and Washington Territorial Papers, House File, Records of the House of Representatives, RG 233, NA; Olympia *Washington Standard*, May 3, 1862; Sept. 19, 1863; Aug. 13, 1864; Port Townsend *North-West*, Nov. 30, 1861; Steilacoom *Puget Sound Herald*, June 25, 1863; Pickering to Seward, July 5, 1864, State Department, Washington Territorial Papers.

33. Olympia *Washington Standard*, Feb. 7; July 11, 1863; Jan. 21, 1865; Olympia *Washington Democrat*, March 4, 1865; C. C. Finkboner to Howe, Nov. 21, 1864, Tulalip Indian Agency Records; Pickering to T. S. Bowers, Feb. 10, 1866, U.S. State Department Appointment Papers, RG 59, NA; Henry A. Webster to Hale, July 22, 1863; July 3, 1864; to Dole, July 18, 1864, Records of the Washington Superintendency of Indian Affairs; Henry to Edmunds, Dec. 1, 1863, Letters Received from the Surveyors General; Evans to First Auditor, Treasury Department, July 16, 1864, Washington Territorial Papers, UW.

34. Dole to Hale, Feb. 21, 1863, Calvin H. Hale Correspondence, WSL; O. B. McFadden to Bagley, March 24, 1863, Miller Family Papers, UW; *Walla Walla Statesman*, Jan. 31, 1863; Olympia *Washington Standard*, Jan. 10, 31, 1863; Dec. 10, 24, 31, 1864; Jan. 7, 14, 1865; Evans to Taylor, June 7, 1865, Washington Territorial Papers, UW.

35. McElroy to Mother, Feb. 26, 1861, McElroy Family Papers; J. G. S. Sparks to Wallace, July 12, 1862, Wallace Papers; Olympia *Washington Standard*, June 15, 1861; Oct. 11, 1862; *Walla Walla Statesman*, March 14; Aug. 29, 1863.

36. "We know nothing of this gentleman," a Puget Sound newspaper observed upon learning of Pickering's appointment, "but he is supposed to be another relative of Abraham's, or at least to have slept in the same bed with him at some period in the course of his life." Steilacoom *Puget Sound Herald*, Jan. 23; June 26, 1862; Olympia *Washington Democrat*, May 6, 1865; Pickering to Lincoln, Dec. 19, 1860; March 30, 1861, State Department Appointment Papers; to Trumbull, Dec. 3, 1862; to Alvord, July 18, 1862, Pickering Papers, WSL; to Bates, Nov. 30, 1863, Records relating to the Appointment of Federal Judges; Message to the Legislature, 1863, William Pickering Papers, UW.

37. Denny to Wallace, Dec. 24, 1863; Henry to Wallace, Dec. 6, 1863, both Wallace Papers; Olympia *Washington Standard*, Jan. 11, 1862; Port Townsend *North-West*, Jan. 18, 1862; J. A. Merryman to Salmon P. Chase, May 25, 1862, McGilvra Papers; Chase to L. C. Gunn, March 17, 1864, Letters Sent by Secretary of Treasury to Collectors of Customs at Pacific Ports, M176, NA; John R. McBride to Bates, Jan. 16, 1864, Records relating to the Appointment of Federal Judges.

38. Olympia *Washington Standard*, Aug. 2, 1862; Oct. 21, 1865; Steilacoom *Puget Sound Herald*, Dec. 12, 1861; Jan. 16; Oct. 9, 16, 1862; Port Townsend *North-West*, Aug. 1, 1861; Jan. 11, 18, 25, 1862; Merryman to Chase, May 25, 1862, McGilvra Papers; Pickering to Wright, Aug. 18, 1862, Pickering Papers, WSL. For an argument that Port Angeles was the better of the two harbors, see N. Sargent to W. P. Fessenden, Dec. 30, 1864, Oregon and Washington Territorial Papers.

39. Port Townsend *North-West*, Jan. 11, March 15; May 24; June 14, 1862; Steilacoom *Puget Sound Herald*, Oct. 9, 1862; Pickering to Seward, Feb. 4, 1863, State Department, Washington Territorial Papers; to Frederick A. Wilson, Dec. 21, 1863, Pickering Papers, UW.

40. Pickering and Henry to Lincoln, Dec. 26, 1863; Victor Smith to C. C. Hewitt, Sept. 20, 1863; McBride to Bates, Jan. 16, 1864, all Records relating to the Appointment of Federal Judges; Denny to Hugh McCulloch, Dec. 18, 1865, Arthur A. Denny Papers, WSHS; Henry to Wallace, Dec. 6, 28, 1863, Wallace Papers; Olympia *Washington Standard*, Dec. 26, 1863; May 7, 1864.

41. Turney had served as acting governor from August 1861 until Pickering's assumption of office. The legislative assembly authorized Governor Pickering to use his personal seal, in lieu of the territorial seal, on official documents. Pickering and Henry failed to secure the removal of U.S. attorney John McGilvra and secretary Elwood Evans, officeholders with influential friends in Washington City. Turney to Bagley, Aug. 29, 1861, Bagley Papers; Steilacoom *Puget Sound Herald*, Aug. 22, 1861; Feb. 13, 1862; Denny and Hale to Pickering, Aug. 5, 1862; Henry to Lincoln, Aug. 9, 1861; Pickering to Seward, Jan. 1, 1864; to Lincoln, Dec. 19, 1860; Aug. 5, 1862; Jan. ? 1864, all State Department Appointment Papers; Nov. 30, 1863; to Bates, Nov. 30, 1863, Records relating to the Appointment of Federal Judges; to Steinberger, March 28, 1863, Pickering Papers, WSL; to Wallace, Jan. 5, 1864, Wallace Papers; Olympia *Washington Standard*, Feb. 8, 1862; J. Flinn to McGilvra, June 8, 1863, McGilvra Papers; *Walla Walla Statesman*, Jan. 31, 1863.

42. Steilacoom *Puget Sound Herald*, June 20, 1861; *Seattle Weekly Gazette*, Aug. 13, 1864; Seattle *Washington Gazette*, Aug. 15, 1863.

43. Edmunds to George W. Julian, Feb. 1, 1864, McGilvra Papers; Olympia *Washington Standard*, Feb. 9, 1861; Turney to Bagley, et al., Aug. 29, 1861; to Bates, Sept. 27, 1861, Washington Territorial Papers, UW.

44. Governor Pickering acquired two hundred acres in the Issaquah Valley east of Seattle. Olympia *Washington Standard*, Nov. 1, 1862; Sept. 5, 1863; Charles M. Gates, "Daniel Bagley and the University of Washington Land Grant, 1861–1868," *PNQ*, 52(April 1961), 58–59, 62; Port Townsend *North-West*, May 2, 1861; Steilacoom *Puget Sound Herald*, June 20, 1861; Bagley to Marshall Blinn, May 19; June 26, 1863; Nov. 18, 1864, Bagley Papers; *Seattle Weekly Gazette*, Aug. 13, 1864; Pickering to Bagley, Feb. 2, 1867, Pickering Papers, UW.

45. Charles F. Whittlesey to Eugene Semple, Aug. 22, 1888, Eugene Semple Papers, WSA; Frederick J. Yonce, "Public Land Disposal in Washington" (Ph.D. diss., University of Washington, 1969), 175–179; Pickering to Bagley, Feb. 25, 1868, Pickering Papers, UW; Port Townsend *Weekly Message*, Feb. 6, 13, 1868; Gates, "Bagley and the University of Washington Land Grant," 60–64; McGilvra to James Harlan, Feb. 24, 1864; Edmunds to Julian, Feb. 1, 1864; B. F. Harding to McGilvra, March 11, 1864, all McGilvra Papers; *Walla Walla Statesman*, Feb. 20, 1864. The "fraud" accusation is from a Seattle newspaper quoted in Roy Robbins, "The Federal Land System in an Embryo State," *PHR*, 4(Dec. 1935), 371.

46. Steilacoom *Puget Sound Herald*, July 11, 1861; Olympia *Pacific Tribune*, Jan. 14, 1864; Olympia *Washington Standard*, Feb. 8; July 19; Dec. 27, 1862; Dec. 10, 1864; Wallace to Barnes, April 13, 1862, Wallace Papers.

47. *Vancouver Register*, Aug. 7, 1869; H. H. Bancroft, *History of Washington, Idaho, and Montana, 1845–1889* (San Francisco: The History Company, 1890), 264–265; Olympia *Washington Standard*, June 27, 1863; Sept. 24, 1864; Hewitt to Wallace, Dec. ? 1863; Sparks to Wallace, Dec. 16, 1863, both Wallace Papers; Steilacoom *Puget Sound Herald*, June 25, 1863.

48. Ibid.

49. Olympia *Washington Standard*, May 30; June 27; July 4; Aug. 8, 1863; Steilacoom *Puget Sound Herald*, June 18; July 9; Dec. 12, 1863; *Walla Walla Statesman*, July 11, 1863; Henry to Wallace, Dec. 6, 1863; Hewitt to Wallace, Dec. 7, 1863; Sparks to Wallace, Dec. 16, 1863; Denny to Wallace, Dec. 24, 1863, all Wallace Papers. The Turney vote had no bearing on the outcome. The former territorial secretary was last heard from, politically, attempting to secure the governorship of Alaska in 1867. Turney to Seward, June 19, 1867, State Department Appointment Papers.

50. Seattle *People's Telegram*, Nov. 21, 1864; McElroy to Mother, July 24, 1864, McElroy Family Papers.

51. Olympia *Washington Standard*, Dec. 8, 1860; July 23, 1864.

52. Olympia *Pacific Tribune*, Aug. 20, 1864; Steilacoom *Puget Sound Herald*, June 5, 1862; Olympia *Washington Standard*, July 23, 1864; *Seattle Weekly Gazette*, Aug. 6, 1864. Also see Pickering to Bagley, May 23, 1866, Pickering Papers, UW.

53. Steilacoom *Puget Sound Herald*, April 17; June 5; July 17; Oct. 16; Nov. 6, 20, 27, 1862.

54. *Seattle Weekly Gazette*, Aug. 27; Sept. 3, 1864.

55. Steilacoom *Puget Sound Herald*, Feb. 28, 1861; Olympia *Washington Standard*, March 9, 1861; Olympia *Washington Democrat*, Feb. 23, 1865; *Seattle Weekly Gazette*, Aug. 27, 1864.

56. *Seattle Weekly Gazette*, Sept. 20; Nov. 21, 1864; July 13, 29, 1865; Olympia *Washington Standard*, July 2, 1864; March 18, 1865; Olympia *Washington Democrat*, July 14, 1865.

57. The patronage dispute was sufficiently important to justify Pickering leaving the territory in the midst of the legislation session, with political enemy Elwood Evans in charge as acting governor. Olympia *Washington Standard*, Dec. 24, 1864; Jan. 28; Feb. 11, 1865; Olympia *Washington Democrat*, Jan. 21; May 6, 1865; *Walla Walla Statesman*, Feb. 17, 1865.

58. Pickering to James Speed, July 11, 1865, Records relating to the Appointment of Federal Judges; to Bowers, Feb. 10, 1865, State Department Appointment Papers; to Denny, July 1, 1865, Denny Papers.

59. Pickering to Bowers, Feb. 10, 1866, State Department Appointment Papers.

Notes—Chapter Five
The Tyre of the Pacific

1. Sept. 9, 1865.

2. Seventeen of the three hundred people aboard the *Brother Jonathan* survived the sinking. The other victims included George Wright, the veteran of eastern Washington's Indian wars, and Victor Smith, Henry's former antagonist as customs collector. Olympia *Washington Standard*, May 6; Aug. 5, 19, 1865; Olympia *Pacific Tribune*, Jan. 14; Aug. 12, 1865; Olympia *Washington Democrat*, May 6, 1865; Arthur A. Denny to Daniel Bagley, March 4, 19, 1865, Daniel Bagley Papers, UW.

3. The assumption that Garfielde was paid in 1865 is based upon the fact of his compensation agreement for similar services on behalf of Alvan Flanders in 1867. Pickering to W. H. Seward, n.d., U.S. State Department Appointment Papers, RG 59, NA; Olympia *Washington Democrat*, June 17, 1865; *Walla Walla Statesman*, June 2,

1865; Olympia *Pacific Tribune*, April 8; June 17, 1865; Aug. 18, 1866; Olympia *Washington Standard*, May 13, 1865; May 18, 1867; Selucious Garfielde to Clarence Bagley, March 21, 1870, Clarence Bagley Papers, UW; *Vancouver Register*, May 1, 1869.

4. *Walla Walla Statesman*, Sept. 11, 1868; Garfielde to J. S. Wilson, March 27, 1869, Letters Received from the Surveyors General of Washington, 1854–1883, RG 49, NA; Olympia *Washington Standard*, Jan. 14, 1865; Olympia *Pacific Tribune*, Jan. 14; April 29; June 17, 1865; Seattle *Weekly Intelligencer*, May 2, 1870; Oct. 9, 1871; Olympia *Washington Democrat*, May 13, 1865; *Walla Walla Union*, April 2, 1870.

5. Elwood Evans also toured the territory, as a second string stand-in for Garfielde. Olympia *Pacific Tribune*, May 6, 27; June 17, 1865; Olympia *Washington Democrat*, April 29; May 20, 1865; Olympia *Washington Standard*, May 20, 1865; *Seattle Weekly Gazette*, May 4; June 8, 1865; Elwood Evans to First Auditor, Department of the Treasury, June 9, 1865, Washington Territorial Papers, UW.

6. Insulted by his repudiation, Tilton temporarily left the territory. Denny won all 141 votes cast at Port Gamble, headquarters of the Puget Mill Company. In a further hint of polling irregularities, Tilton received only one vote on Bellingham Bay. Olympia *Washington Standard*, June 10; July 15, 1865; May 18, 1867; Olympia *Pacific Tribune*, June 10, 1865; Election Returns, Kitsap County, William Pickering Papers, WSA; Evans to First Auditor, June 9, 1865, Washington Territorial Papers, UW; *Seattle Weekly Gazette*, Oct. 21, 1865; *Walla Walla Statesman*, Dec. 29, 1865.

7. Denny complained that friends at home "seemed to think that I could do every thing in one day and write each man a letter in the evening telling him that it was done." Olympia *Pacific Tribune*, Nov. 11; Dec. 9, 1865; March 24; May 5; June 16; Aug. 4; Oct. 13; Dec. 29, 1866; Jan. 26, 1867; Denny to D. Bagley, March 20; May 7, 1866, D. Bagley Papers; *Walla Walla Statesman*, Feb. 23; March 2, 9, 16; April 20; May 11, 25; Dec. 14, 1866; March 8; April 12, 1867; March 13, 1868; Garfielde to C. Bagley, Nov. 29, 1869, C. Bagley Papers; Olympia *Washington Standard*, March 11; June 17, 24; Sept. 16, 1865; June 23, 1866; March 23; Aug. 10, 1867; Port Townsend *Weekly Message*, March 5, 1868; Andrew J. Lawrence to Andrew Johnson, Jan. 16, 1867, Records relating to the Appointment of Federal Judges and U.S. Attorneys and Marshals, Washington, 1853–1902, M198, NA; Olympia *Territorial Republican*, Aug. 17, 1868.

8. Cole served in later years as postmaster of Portland and in local office in northeastern Washington. Olympia *Washington Standard*, Jan. 12, 1867; Olympia *Pacific Tribune*, Jan. 12, 1867; *Walla Walla Statesman*, Jan. 25, 1867; Pickering to William Pickering, Jr., Jan. 19, 1867, William Pickering Papers, UW; Chas. A. White to W. W. Miller, Feb. 3, 1867, Miller Family Papers, UW; Marshall F. Moore to Seward, Jan. 6, 1868, State Department, Washington Territorial Papers; Ellensburgh *Kittitas Standard*, Aug. 18, 1883. On Cole's loyalty to the president, see Lawrence to Johnson, Jan. 16, 1867, Records relating to the Appointment of Federal Judges.

9. Flanders had been "one of the most ardent Republicans in California." *Walla Walla Statesman*, April 26; May 3, 24, 31; June 14; July 12, 1867; Olympia *Pacific Tribune*, April 20, 27, 1867; Olympia *Washington Standard*, May 4, 25; Aug. 10, 1867; Port Townsend *Weekly Message*, May 20, 27, 1867; A. J. Cain to Johnson, April 16, 1868, Records relating to the Appointment of Federal Judges.

10. Olympia *Washington Standard*, Aug. 10, 1867; Garfielde to Hamilton Fish, Aug. 5, 1871, Selucious Garfielde Letters, UW; Benj. S. Pardee to William P. Winans, May 19, 1870, William P. Winans Papers, WSU; Miller to O. B. McFadden, Oct. 10, 1872; to J. R. Judson, Oct. 11, 1872; to M. H. Frost, Oct. 18, 1872; to Henry Roeder, Oct. 25, 1872; to James Tilton, Oct. 31, 1872; to S. D. Smith, Nov. 7, 1872, Miller Family Papers; William H. Avery to C. H. Brown, July 27; Aug. 4, 1871, William H. Avery Correspondence, WSL; Seattle *Weekly Intelligencer*, Nov. 6, 1871.

11. *The North-West Coast: A Lecture by Hon. S. Garfielde* (Washington, D.C.: N.p., n.d.), 6; *Report of the Commissioner of the General Land Office, 1868*, 335; *McCormick's Almanac, 1872* (Portland: S. J. McCormick, 1872), 35; A. S. Mercer, *Washington Territory: The Great Northwest, Her Material Resources and Claims to Emigration* (Utica: L. C. Childs, 1865), 17–18; E. P. Ferry to Wilson, Aug. 10, 1870, Letters Received from the Surveyors General.

12. Julian Hawthorne, ed., *History of Washington, The Evergreen State* (New York: American Historical Publishing Co., 2 vols., 1893), 2:215–216; *Report of the Commissioner of the General Land Office, 1867*, 62–63; Garfielde to Jno. Edmunds, July 12, 1866; Ferry to Wilson, Aug. 25, 1870, both Letters Received from the Surveyors General; James E. Defebaugh, *History of the Lumber Industry in America* (Chicago: The American Lumberman, 2 vols., 1906–1907), 1:499–500, 503–505.

13. Most observers believed that Kitsap County property values were substantially under-assessed, from the fact that the sawmills controlled local government. *Walla Walla Statesman*, Jan. 18, 1867; *Ninth Census* (Washington, D.C.: Government Printing Office, 1872), 1:71, 283, 637, 762; 3:612–613; Edmond S. Meany, Jr., "The History of the Lumber Industry in the Pacific Northwest to 1917" (Ph.D. diss., Harvard University, 1935), 125–131; Defebaugh, *History of the Lumber Industry in America*, 1:499–505; Ezra Meeker, *Washington Territory West of the Cascade Mountains* (Olympia: Transcript Office, 1870), 19; *McCormick's Almanac, 1870* (Portland: S. J. McCormick, 1870), 30–34; Mrs. Frances Fuller Victor, *All Over Oregon and Washington* (San Francisco: John H. Carmany & Co., 1872), 249; Olympia *Washington Standard*, Oct. 30, 1869; Port Townsend *Weekly Message*, May 16, 30, 1870; Iva L. Buchanan, "An Economic History of Kitsap County, Washington, to 1889" (Ph.D. diss., University of Washington, 1930), 295.

14. Despite the fortuitous nature of the stumpage fee system, mill owners protested whenever an increased payment was suggested. Frederick J. Yonce, "Lumbering and the Public Timberlands in Washington: The Era of Disposal," *Journal of Forest History*, 20(Jan. 1978), 6–10; Meany, "History of the Lumber Industry," 170–172, 182–185; J. W. Sprague to Frederick K. Billings, Aug. 9, 1871, Northern Pacific Railway Company Land Department Records, MHS; Roy M. Robbins, "The Federal Land System in an Embryo State," *PHR*, 4(Dec. 1935), 374; Eldridge Morse Notebooks, 24:5, BL; *Report of the Commissioner of the General Land Office, 1867,* 79; *1873,* 13; Ivan Doig, "John J. McGilvra and Timber Trespass: Seeking a Puget Sound Timber Policy, 1861–1865," *Forest History*, 13(Jan. 1970), 6–17; Edward Clayson, Sr., *Historical Narratives of Puget Sound: Hoods Canal, 1865–1885* (Seattle: R. L. Davis Printing Co., 1911), 69–71; Olympia *Washington Standard*, Dec. 2, 1865; *Seattle Weekly Gazette*, Nov. 25, 1865; Olympia *Pacific Tribune*, Nov. 4; Dec. 16, 23, 1865; April 14, 1866; Seattle *Puget Sound Semi-Weekly*, April 12, 1866; Iva L. Buchanan, "Lumbering and Logging in the Puget Sound Region in Territorial Days," *PNQ*, 27(Jan. 1936), 43–44.

15. The once vital Shoalwater Bay oystering trade declined in importance, due to overharvesting of the natural beds and shellfish propagation in California waters. Meeker, *Washington Territory West of the Cascade Mountains*, 38; Whatcom *Bellingham Bay Mail*, July 19, 1873; Jan. 30; April 10, 1875; Seattle *Weekly Intelligencer*, Oct. 17, 1870; Seattle *Washington Gazette*, Aug. 15, 1863; Seattle *Puget Sound Daily*, June 15, 1866; Clarence B. Bagley, *History of Seattle: From the Earliest Settlement to the Present Day* (Chicago: The S. J. Clarke Publishing Company, 3 vols., 1916), 1:230; Morse Notebooks, 23:9; Victor, *All Over Oregon and Washington*, 247; J. M. Harrison, *Harrison's Guide and Resources of the Pacific Slope*, Part 1, *Embracing Washington Territory* (San Francisco: C. A. Murdock & Co., 2nd ed., 1876), 19; Carrie Adell Strahorn, *Fifteen Thousand Miles by Stage* (New York: G. P. Putnam's Sons, 1911), 363; S. D. Woods, *Lights and Shadows of Life on the Pacific Coast* (New York: Funk & Wagnalls Company, 1910), 264, 286–287; W. B. Seymore, "Port Orchard Fifty Years Ago," *WHQ*, 8(Oct. 1917), 258.

16. Thomas Condon to Watson C. Squire, Oct. 22, 1884, enclosing Geological Sketch of Washington Territory; George F. Whitworth to Squire, Oct. 31, 1884, both Watson C. Squire Papers, WSA; Olympia *Washington Standard*, Oct. 19, 1867; Ferry to Wilson, Aug. 10, 1870, Letters Received from the Surveyors General; Seattle *Weekly Intelligencer*, Jan. 29, 1872.

17. Olympia *Washington Standard*, Oct. 19, 1867; Ferry to Wilson, Aug. 10, 1870; Garfielde to Edmunds, July 12, 1866, both Letters Received from the Surveyors General; Seattle *Weekly Intelligencer*, Aug. 3; Sept. 21; Oct. 12, 1868; Whatcom *Bellingham Bay Mail*, Aug. 16; Nov. 1, 29, 1873; Jan. 23; June 18, 1875; June 3, 1876; S. Baxter to P. B. Cornwall, Feb. 27; March 16, 1874, Sehome Coal Company Records, Center for Pacific Northwest Studies, Western Washington University.

18. The Black River, Lake Washington's natural outlet and a tributary of the Duwamish, was briefly mined in the mid–1850s. *Seattle Gazette*, Dec. 10, 17, 1863; Olympia *Pacific Tribune*, Dec. 31, 1864; April 14, 1866; Olympia *Washington Standard*, Oct. 19, 1867; Whitworth to Squire, Oct. 31, 1884, Squire Papers; Port Townsend *Weekly Message*, Sept. 5, 1867.

19. *Seattle Gazette*, Feb. 9, 1864; W. McMicken to S. G. Reed, Nov. 22, 1883, enclosing circular on King County Mineral Resources, Simeon G. Reed Papers, Reed College Library; Whitworth to Squire, Oct. 31, 1884, Squire Papers; Seattle *Weekly Intelligencer*, Sept. 2, 30, 1867; Garfielde to C. Bagley, Nov. 24; Dec. 22, 1867, C. Bagley Papers; *Walla Walla Union*, Oct. 28, 1871; Port Townsend *Weekly Message*, Sept. 5, 1867.

20. Denny to D. Bagley, March 20, 1866; Garfielde to D. Bagley, Dec. 15, 1867; Oct. 7, 1869, all D. Bagley Papers; to C. Bagley, March 10, 1870; Whitworth to C. Bagley, Jan. 6, 1870, both C. Bagley Papers; Seattle *Weekly Intelligencer*, March 30; May 4; Sept. 14, 1868; Aug. 2, 1869; Feb. 7, 1870; July 24; Sept. 11, 1871; Jan. 29; June 3; Sept. 23, 1872; Ferry to Wilson, Aug. 10, 1870, Letters Received from the Surveyors General. Production figures are from unidentified newspaper clipping, Daniel H. Gilman Papers, UW.

21. Seattle citizens claimed that the census substantially understated the actual population. Alexander N. MacDonald, "Seattle's Economic Development, 1880–1910" (Ph.d. diss., University of Washington, 1959), 14–18; *Ninth Census*, 1:283; Seattle *Weekly Intelligencer*, May 30; July 25; Aug. 29; Sept. 26, 1870; Sept. 24; Dec. 11, 1871; Aug. 19; Nov. 18; Dec. 30, 1872; Seattle *Puget Sound Daily*, July 28, 1866; Port Townsend *Weekly Message*, Sept. 29, 1869; Olympia *Washington Standard*, Jan. 29, 1870.

22. *Walla Walla Statesman*, June 26; Sept. 18, 1868.

23. Walla Walla's trade with the Oregon mines went by a roundabout route and was both noncompetitive and inconsequential. The Dalles *Daily Mountaineer*, Nov. 15, 1865; Portland *Daily Oregonian*, July 8, 1863; April 8, 1864; Oct. 17; Nov. 20, 1865; *Walla Walla Statesman*, July 14, 1865; Feb. 9; Nov. 2, 9, 30; Dec. 7, 21, 1866; Jan. 18; July 19, 1867; Aug. 21, 1868. Also see Clarence F. McIntosh, "The Chico and Red Bluff Route: Stage Lines from Southern Idaho to the Sacramento Valley, 1865–1867," *IY*, 6(Fall 1962), 12–15, 18–19.

24. Thirty-nine steamers reached Fort Benton, the head of navigation on the Missouri, in 1867. Walla Walla also profited from trade with the Kootenay mines of British Columbia. *Walla Walla Statesman*, Nov. 10, 1865; April 6, 13, 20; May 4; June 22; July 27; Oct. 12, 1866; May 17; Aug. 9, 1867; Aug. 20, 1869; Portland *Daily Oregonian*, Sept. 18, 1862; Jan. 24, 1863; July 12, 1865; Sept. 18, 1866; Lewiston *North-Idaho Radiator*, March 25, 1865; Alexander C. McGregor, "The Economic Impact of the Mullan Road on Walla Walla, 1860–1883," *PNQ*, 65(July 1974), 118, 122, 124–125; The Dalles *Daily Mountaineer*, Nov. 4, 1865; Michael P. Malone, Richard B. Roeder and William L. Lang, *Montana: A History of Two Centuries* (Seattle: University of

Washington Press, rev. ed., 1991), 73. Also see Alton B. Oviatt, "Pacific Coast Competition for the Gold Camp Trade of Montana," *PNQ*, 56(1965), 168–176; and, on the Walla Walla-White Bluffs rivalry, D. W. Meinig, *The Great Columbia Plain: A Historical Geography, 1805–1910* (Seattle: University of Washington Press, 1968), 215–217.

25. *Walla Walla Statesman*, April 27; June 8, 29; July 20; Nov. 30, 1866; June 7, 1867; Report on Washington and Idaho, 1879, Henry Villard Papers, Houghton Library, Harvard University; Ferry to Wilson, Aug. 10, 1870, Letters Received from the Surveyors General; W. Milnor Roberts to Adeline Roberts, July 23, 1869, W. Milnor Roberts Papers, Montana State University Library; R. Bethell Claxton to Jay Cooke, Aug. 4, 1869, Jay Cooke Papers, Historical Society of Pennsylvania; Robert C. Nesbit and Charles M. Gates, "Agriculture in Eastern Washington, 1890–1910," *PNQ*, 37(Oct. 1946), 280–281; The Dalles *Daily Mountaineer*, Dec. 3, 1865; Frank T. Gilbert, *Historic Sketches of Walla Walla, Whitman, Columbia and Garfield Counties, Washington Territory* (Portland: A. G. Walling, 1882), 284; *Walla Walla Union*, June 4, 1870.

26. *Walla Walla Union*, Nov. 12, 19, 1870; June 24, 1871; *Walla Walla Statesman*, June 22; Nov. 30, 1866; Aug. 16, 30, 1867.

27. Despite reduced freight and passenger rates and heavy expenditures on the Cascades and Dalles portage railroads, the O.S.N. paid out $300,000 in dividends in 1873 and 1874. Over its entire history, the company spent $3 million on improvements and distributed $5 million in dividends. *Walla Walla Union*, Sept. 2, 9, 1871; John C. Ainsworth to H. M. Robert, Nov. 23, 1871, Portland District Records, U.S. Army Corps of Engineers, RG 77, FRC; Reed to Charles Tilton, Feb. 9, 1875; to Ainsworth, Feb. ? 1870, Reed Papers; The Dalles *Daily Mountaineer*, Feb. 20; May 6, 1864; *Walla Walla Statesman*, Dec. 8, 1865; Dorothy O. Johansen, "The Oregon Steam Navigation Company: An Example of Capitalism on the Frontier," *PHR*, 10(June 1941), 188.

28. *Walla Walla Statesman*, Feb. 24, 1865; Jan. 26; Feb. 16; March 30, 1866; Winans to "My Dear Friend," Aug. 5, 1865, Winans Papers; *Walla Walla Union*, Nov. 26; Dec. 17, 1870; Seattle *Weekly Intelligencer*, Oct. 24, 1870; G. F. Cramer to N. Michler, March 20, 1875, Portland District Records.

29. *Walla Walla Union*, April 2; Nov. 26, 1870; *Walla Walla Statesman*, Oct. 11, 25, 1867; Sept. 4, 11, 1868; Seattle *Weekly Intelligencer*, Nov. 1, 1873; Lewiston *Idaho Signal*, Aug. 10, 1872.

30. Ainsworth contended that timber shortages on the upper Columbia prevented the O.S.N. from rapidly building new boats. *Walla Walla Statesman*, Nov. 5, 1867; March 27, 1868; *Walla Walla Union*, Nov. 11; Dec. 16, 1871; _____ to R. S. Williamson, Nov. 1, 1871; Ainsworth to Robert, Nov. 23, 1871, both Portland District Records.

31. *Walla Walla Statesman*, March 20, 27; April 3, 10, 17; Sept. 11, 1868; Oct. 18, 1873; *Walla Walla Union*, May 20, 27; Aug. 19, 26; Sept. 2, 23; Oct. 21; Nov. 11, 18, 1871; Reed to Philip Ritz, Oct. 22, 1873, Reed Papers. Also see Carlos A. Schwantes, *Railroad Signatures across the Pacific Northwest* (Seattle: University of Washington Press, 1993), 35; Peter J. Lewty, *To the Columbia Gateway: The Oregon Railway and the Northern Pacific, 1879–1884* (Pullman: Washington State University Press, 1987), 33–35.

32. *Kalama Semi-Weekly Beacon*, June 13, 1871; Winans to "My Dear Friend," Aug. 5, 1865, Winans Papers; *Walla Walla Statesman*, Dec. 15, 1865; Jan. 5; July 7; Oct. 19, 26; Nov. 9, 30, 1866; Aug. 16; Sept. 13, 1867; July 24, 1868; Aug. 27, 1869; *Walla Walla Union*, June 10; Sept. 16, 1871. On the founding of Whitman, see G. Thomas Edwards, *The Triumph of Tradition: The Emergence of Whitman College, 1859–1924* (Walla Walla: Whitman College, 1992), chapt. 1.

33. *Walla Walla Union*, March 25, 1871; *Walla Walla Statesman*, Feb. 8; Nov. 29, 1867; April 10; Sept. 16, 1868; Claxton to Cooke, Aug. 4, 1869, Cooke Papers; Report on Washington and Idaho, 1879, Villard Papers. Also see Meinig, *Great Columbia Plain*, 233.

34. The total 1872 Stevens County tax bill was $983, one-fifteenth the figure for Walla Walla County. Olympia *Washington Standard*, Oct. 19, 1867; Colfax *Palouse Gazette*, Oct. 20, 1877; Pinkney Lugenbeel to County Commissioners, Spokane County, July ? 1861, Winans Papers; Assessment Roll, Stevens County, 1872, Edward S. Salomon Papers, WSA; Olympia *Pacific Tribune*, July 8, 1865; Seattle *Weekly Intelligencer*, Jan. 6, 1873.

35. Dayton *Columbia Chronicle*, Aug. 17, 1878; E. W. Hilgard to Henry Villard, Oct. 28, 1882; Report on Washington and Idaho, 1879, both Villard Papers; Roberts to A. Roberts, July 24, 26, 1869, Roberts Papers; *Walla Walla Statesman*, Aug. 7, 14, 1868; Oct. 15, 1870; *Walla Walla Union*, Sept. 16, 1871.

36. Some contemporary observers, considering several of the tributaries to be independent entities, listed as many as seven distinct valleys in the Yakima drainage. *Yakima Record*, Nov. 11, 1882; Whatcom *Bellingham Bay Mail*, April 6, 1878; Meinig, *Great Columbia Plain*, 6–7; M. H. Shipley and J. Bailey to J. N. Dolph, n.d.; Hilgard to Villard, Oct. 20, 1862, both Villard Papers; Smith & Reeves to T. M. Reed, June 16, 1873, Letters Received from the Surveyors General; Umatilla *Columbia Press*, Sept. 21, 1867.

37. *Walla Walla Union*, March 25; Nov. 11, 1871; Umatilla *Columbia Press*, Sept. 21, 1867.

38. *Yakima Record*, April 17, 1880; Dalles *Weekly Mountaineer*, July 3, 10; Aug. 14, 1868; Olympia *Washington Standard*, Jan. 6, 1866; July 13, 1867; The Dalles *Daily Mountaineer*, Nov. 29, 1865; Umatilla *Columbia Press*, Sept. 21, 1867; Seattle *Weekly Intelligencer*, Sept. 9, 1867; April 13, 1868; *Walla Walla Statesman*, Feb. 22; Oct. 4, 1867; Meinig, *Great Columbia Plain*, 236.

39. W. D. Lyman, *History of the Yakima Valley* (Chicago: S. J. Clarke Publishing Co., 2 vols., 1919), 1:566–569, 574; Seattle *Weekly Intelligencer*, Sept. 9, 1867; May 31, 1869; Oct. 2, 1871; *Yakima Signal*, April 7, 1883; *An Illustrated History of Klickitat, Yakima and Kittitas Counties* (N.p.: Interstate Publishing Company, 1904), 238–239, 243; Dalles *Weekly Mountaineer*, July 3, 1868; Nov. 12, 1870; Olympia *Washington Standard*, Jan. 6, 1866;

Walla Walla Statesman, Dec. 8, 1865; Seattle *Puget Sound Weekly*, Sept. 17, 1866; Reed to Charles B. Reed, et al., Oct. 22, 1873, Reed Papers.

40. Seattle *Puget Sound Weekly*, May 7; Sept. 17, 1866. Also see *Seattle Weekly Gazette*, Oct. 28, 1865.

41. Fallen timber quickly reclosed the Naches Pass road. Olympia *Washington Standard*, July 15; Oct. 21; Nov. 4, 1865; Jan. 6, 1866; Olympia *Pacific Tribune*, May 13; July 8, 15, 1865; Olympia *Washington Democrat*, July 15, 1865; Seattle *Weekly Intelligencer*, Oct. 14, 1867; Aug. 24, 1868; Jan. 4, 1869; *Seattle Weekly Gazette*, Aug. 12; Dec. 2, 1865; Seattle *Puget Sound Daily*, May 5, 1866.

42. Governor Pickering, who owned land on the Snoqualmie Pass route, worked on Seattle's behalf. King County nearly ruined its credit status financing the project. Seattle *Puget Sound Daily*, July 17, 1866; Pickering to D. Bagley, June 11, 1866, Pickering Papers, UW; Olympia *Washington Standard*, Aug. 25, 1866; Olympia *Pacific Tribune*, Aug. 25, 1866; Seattle *Puget Sound Weekly*, Sept. 3, 10, 1866; *Walla Walla Statesman*, Dec. 28, 1866; Seattle *Weekly Intelligencer*, Aug. 5, 19; Sept. 16, 1867; Aug. 3; Sept. 7, 14; Oct. 12; Dec. 7, 1868; Nov. 8, 1869; May 20, 1872.

43. Seattle *Weekly Intelligencer*, Sept. 16, 1867; May 31; June 7, 14; July 19; Aug. 2; Nov. 8, 1869; Port Townsend *Weekly Message*, Aug. 20, 1868; *Walla Walla Statesman*, Oct. 16, 1869.

44. In states, the grant was limited to twenty-mile wide strips. The railroad also received indemnity land in compensation for odd-numbered sections already in private ownership. Miller to Phillips Taber & Co., Dec. 1, 1870, Miller Family Papers; W. H. Wallace to Son, Jan. 19, 1871, William H. Wallace Papers, WSHS; Seattle *Weekly Intelligencer*, Feb. 19, 1872; Frederick J. Yonce, "Public Land Disposal in Washington" (Ph.D. diss., University of Washington, 1969), 201; Ross R. Cotroneo, "The History of the Northern Pacific Land Grant, 1900–1952" (Ph.D. diss., University of Idaho, 1966), 47.

45. Holladay went into railroading after selling his stagecoach interests. Seattle *Weekly Intelligencer*, Aug. 10; Dec. 14, 1868; July 25; Dec. 19, 1870; *Walla Walla Statesman*, Nov. 23, 1866; Aug. 28; Sept. 18, 1868; April 23, 1869; Port Townsend *Weekly Message*, Aug. 1; Sept. 19, 1867; July 9, 23, 1868; March 10, 1869; *Walla Walla Union*, May 14; Nov. 12, 1870; Dalles *Weekly Mountaineer*, March 14, 1868; *Vancouver Register*, July 17; Dec. 11, 1869; Jan. 22; Feb. 12, 26, 1870; Miller to Wm. S. Ladd, May 9, 1870; to J. M. Lucas, May 10, 1870; to Samuel Linkton, May 10, 1870; to Peter Burkey, May 11, 1870, Miller Family Papers; Olympia *Daily Tribune*, Jan. 3, 4, 1868; Olympia *Territorial Republican*, Nov. 23, 1868. Also see Schwantes, *Railroad Signatures*, 53–54; and, for Holladay's Oregon and California Railroad, Donald B. Robertson, *Encyclopedia of Western Railroad History*, Vol. 3, *Oregon-Washington* (Caldwell: The Caxton Printers, Ltd., 1995), 96–101.

46. Port Townsend *Weekly Message*, March 31; June 21, 1869; *Walla Walla Statesman*, Nov. 23, 1866; July 23, 1869; *Walla Walla Union*, May 22, 1869; Pickering to D. Bagley, May 23, 1866, Pickering Papers, UW; Cooke to Ainsworth, March 14, 1873, John C. Ainsworth Papers, UO; Dalles *Weekly Mountaineer*, May 20, 1871; Seattle *Weekly Intelligencer*, April 22, 1872. For details on congressional legislation and internal N.P. developments, see Robin W. Winks, *Frederick Billings: A Life* (New York: Oxford University Press, 1991), 186–189; Lewty, *To the Columbia Gateway*, 2–3.

47. Returning to the Pacific Northwest, James Tilton was in charge of the early railroad survey work. The inhospitable nature of the Bitterroot Mountains prevented use of either the Clearwater or the Salmon River valleys, compelling the N.P. to bypass Walla Walla. Port Townsend *Weekly Message*, Aug. 1, 1867; Seattle *Weekly Intelligencer*, Aug. 5, 12, 1867; Aug. 9, 1869; Aug. 8; Nov. 21, 1870; May 1; Aug. 14, 1871; *Walla Walla Statesman*, May 31; Aug. 2, 1867; *Vancouver Register*, July 30, 1870; *Walla Walla Union*, Aug. 26, 1871; Roberts to the President and Directors of the Northern Pacific R. Road, July ? 1878, Roberts Papers.

48. Malcolm Clark, Jr., ed., *Pharisee among Philistines: The Diary of Judge Matthew P. Deady, 1871–1892* (Portland: Oregon Historical Society, 2 vols., 1975), 1:69; The Dalles *Weekly Mountaineer*, Dec. 14, 1867; *Seattle Weekly Gazette*, Dec. 16, 1865; Port Townsend *Weekly Message*, Aug. 20, 1868; March 4, 1870; Olympia *Territorial Republican*, Sept. 14, 1868; *Vancouver Register*, May 1, 1869; Seattle *Weekly Intelligencer*, Oct. 3, 1870; Jan. 2; July 24, 1871; June 24, 1872; Stevens to Edwin F. Johnson, Dec. 9, 1868, Hazard Stevens Papers, UO. Some eastern Oregon communities shared these views. A Umatilla newspaper, for instance, stressed the "great obstacle" of the Columbia River bar in advising that the town's economic future depended on railroad connections with Puget Sound. Umatilla *Columbia Press*, Aug. 31, 1867.

49. Sprague to Billings, July 30, 1872; A. B. Nettleton to Billings, Sept. 11, 1872, both Northern Pacific Land Department Records; Olympia *Washington Standard*, Feb. 19, 1870; Seattle *Weekly Intelligencer*, Aug. 9; Oct. 25, 1869; Feb. 14; June 20, 1870; Port Townsend *Weekly Message*, Sept. 22, 1869; Feb. 28, 1870.

50. A leading stockholder advised that "care…be taken to have the line longer than we will build on," reserving the maximum number of acres for possible inclusion in the grant. The Dalles *Weekly Mountaineer*, May 20, 1871; Samuel Wilkeson to Cooke, Aug. 19, 1869, Cooke Papers; J. D. Cox to Wilson, Aug. 13, 1870; Sprague to Billings, Dec. 19, 1871, both Northern Pacific Land Department Records; Miller to Wm. Moody, Oct. 26, 1870; to Garfielde, Jan. 1, 1871, Miller Family Papers; Seattle *Weekly Intelligencer*, Feb. 19, 1872. Also see Leslie E. Decker, "The Railroads and the Land Office: Administrative Policy and the Land Grant Controversy, 1864–1896," *Mississippi Valley Historical Review*, 46(March 1960), 679–699.

51. Port Townsend *Weekly Message*, Aug. 29, 1867; April 4, 1871; Albert D. Richardson, *Beyond the Mississippi: From the Great River to the Great Ocean* (Hartford: American Publishing Company, 1867), 413–414; *Walla Walla Statesman*, Jan. 11; Oct. 18, 1867; Strahorn, *Fifteen Thousand Miles by Stage*, 359–360; Ferry to Willis

Drummond, June 24, 1871, Letters Received from the Surveyors General; Wallace to Son, Jan. 19; June 27, 1871, Wallace Papers; Olympia *Pacific Tribune*, July 28, 1866; Seattle *Weekly Intelligencer*, Nov. 11, 1867; Dec. 28, 1868; Olympia *Washington Standard*, Oct. 16, 30, 1869; Huntington & Son to A. Flanders, May 21, 1868, Alvan Flanders Papers, WSA; Giles Ford to E. S. Salomon and J. G. Sparks, Sept. 31, 1870, Salomon Papers.

52. M. M. McCarver to L. M. Starr and James Steel, Aug. 20, 23, 24, 29; Sept. 8, 27, 1868, Thomas W. Prosch Papers, UW; Seattle *Weekly Intelligencer*, May 4; June 1; Nov. 23, 1868; Puget Sound Journal, May 4, 1871, Roberts Papers. Also see Murray Morgan, *Puget's Sound: A Narrative of Early Tacoma and the Southern Sound* (Seattle: University of Washington Press, 1979), 148–153.

53. In a new manifestation of sophisticated affluence, Seattleites had taken to cooling their summertime libations with ice imported from the California Sierra. Seattle *Weekly Intelligencer*, Nov. 20, 1871; Jan. 29; Aug. 19, 1872; Sprague to Billings, April 30, 1872, Northern Pacific Land Department Records; Whatcom *Bellingham Bay Mail*, July 5; Oct. 4, 1873; Port Townsend *Weekly Message*, Oct. 31, 1867; Sept. 8, 1869; Feb. 25; March 11, 1870; April 4, 1871; Port Townsend *Weekly Argus*, April 6, 1871.

54. Garfielde "has done us as much if not more good," Cooke wrote, "than any other man." Garfielde to Wilson, July 27, 1869, Letters Received from the Surveyors General; to Billings, Sept. 11, 14, 1871; J. V. Painter to Jas. G. Dudley, May 22, 1871; Nettleton to Billings, Sept. 21, 1871; Ferry to John S. Loomis, June 9, 1871; Sprague to Billings, June 9, 27; July 11, 1871; March 2, 1872; to Wm. A. Howard, Jan. 22, 1873; Jno. R. Wheat to Billings, Aug. 3, 1872; to Howard, April 14, 1873; C. A. Huntington to Billings, March 9, 1872; Cooke to Billings, March 1, 4, 1872, all Northern Pacific Land Department Records; to Ainsworth, May 1, 1873; J. B. Allen to Ainsworth, April 17, 1877; S. C. Wingard to Ainsworth, April 29; May 26, 1872, all Ainsworth Papers; Samuel Ross to E. S. Parker, Sept. 14, 1869, Correspondence of the Office of Indian Affairs, Letters Received, 1824–1881, M234, NA; Oct. 3, 1869; May 2, 1870; T. J. McKenny to Lewis V. Bogy, Feb. 11, 1867, all Records of the Washington Superintendency of Indian Affairs, 1853–1874, M5, NA; Olympia *Daily Tribune*, Oct. 5, 6, 1869; J. Gregory Smith to Garfielde, April 17, 1870, Garfielde Letters.

55. "Large donations," suggested the N.P. attorney in Olympia, Hazard Stevens, could be obtained through "a judicious appeal to the rivalry between the several towns." Cooke to Ainsworth, Dec. 21, 1872, Ainsworth Papers; Stevens to Johnson, Oct. 11, 1869; Sprague to Stevens, April 24, 1871, both Stevens Papers.

56. Seattle *Weekly Intelligencer*, May 17; Sept. 6, 1869; Sept. 7, 1870; *Kalama Semi-Weekly Beacon*, June 6; July 14, 1871; Miller to Ladd, May 9, 1870, Miller Family Papers.

57. Port Townsend *Weekly Argus*, April 27, 1871; Proposal to the Northern Pacific Railroad Company, April 18, 1871, Miller Family Papers; Sprague to Billings, Nov. 26, 1871, Northern Pacific Land Department Records; *Kalama Semi-Weekly Beacon*, June 9, 1871; McCarver to Starr and Steel, Sept. 17, 1868, Prosch Papers; Whatcom *Bellingham Bay Mail*, July 12, 1873; Port Townsend *Weekly Message*, Oct. 17, 1867.

58. Seattle *Weekly Intelligencer*, Feb. 15, 1869; Oct. 10, 1870; Jan. 9; May 8; Aug. 7, 1871.

59. Cyrus Walker of the Puget Mill Company, the leading Washington lumberman of the day, was the source for the conviction that the most valuable forested land lay north of Seattle. Ibid., Aug. 12, 1867; May 10; July 12; Aug. 9; Sept. 13, 1869; Cooke to Ainsworth, June 1, 1874, Ainsworth Papers; Cyrus Walker to Tilton, Dec. 2, 1872, Northern Pacific Land Department Records; Claxton to Cooke, Aug. 10, 1869; Roberts to Cooke, July 13, 1869, both Cooke Papers; to James B. Eads, July 19, 1869; Puget Sound Journal, May 4, 11, 12, 1871, all Roberts Papers. Also see W. Milnor Roberts, "Special Report of a Reconnoissance of the Route for the Northern Pacific Railroad Between Lake Superior and Puget Sound via the Columbia River," in Misc. Pamphlets, Northwest Collection, UW.

60. Disgusted with the soggy nature of both the land and the water, resident N.P. officials privately contended that the town ought to have been named "Calamity." *Kalama Semi-Weekly Beacon*, May 23, 26, 30; June 6, 13; July 4, 1871; Seattle *Weekly Intelligencer*, Nov. 21, 1870; Feb. 20; March 13; June 26; Sept. 11, 1871; Jan. 22, 1872; *Walla Walla Union*, Oct. 28, 1871; Wheat to Dudley, July 30, 1872; to Billings, Oct. 25, 29, 1873; Sprague to Billings, Nov. 26, 1871; N. P. Jacobs to Howard, Aug. 7, 1873, all Northern Pacific Land Department Records.

61. Despite an eventual G.L.O. ruling in its favor, the N.P. curried favor with officeholders by purchasing the suspiciously timed claims. Sprague to Billings, May 30; Sept. 21, 1871; March 2, 27; April 30; May 31, 1872; to Howard, April 18, 1873; to Loomis, July 8; Aug. 9, 12, 1871; Feb. 15; March 2, 1872; Wheat to Billings, Aug. 26, 1872; to Howard, April 22, 1873; Stevens to Sprague, Sept. 3, 1872; Jacobs to Howard, June 20, 1873; Ainsworth to Geo. W. Cass, April 12, 1873, all Northern Pacific Land Department Records; Seattle *Weekly Intelligencer*, Oct. 23, 1871; Cooke to Ainsworth, May 21; Aug. 23, 1872; Feb. 18; March 14; May 1, 1873, Ainsworth Papers. On the "great anxiety" felt by settlers on the odd-numbered sections, see also Ferry to Drummond, June 16, 1871, Letters Received from the Surveyors General. Puget Sound friends of the N.P. thought that the railroad was too safe an investment to be appealing in speculation-oriented times. See Whatcom *Bellingham Bay Mail*, Aug. 2, 1873.

62. Selucious Garfielde attempted to have Fred Drew of the Puget Mill Company, a timber industry veteran allegedly involved in fraud, appointed federal anti-theft agent on the Sound. Sprague to Billings, May 9; June 9; Aug. 9, 15; Sept. 21, 1871; June 12, 1872; to Loomis, Aug. 15, 1871; Drummond to Register and Receiver, Olympia, May 2, 1872; to Leander Holmes, April 7, 1871; Garfielde to Billings, Sept. 11, 14, 1871; B. F. Tuttle to Sprague, Aug. 26, 1871, all Northern Pacific Land Department Records. Also see Yonce, "Lumbering and the Public Timberlands," 8.

63. The same objective, preservation of the grant's value, caused the N.P. to become one of the earliest Pacific Northwest advocates of anti-forest fire legislation. Sprague to Billings, May 9; June 9, 1871; Jan. 5, 1872; Stevens to Sprague, Aug. 9, 23, 26, 1871; Tuttle to Sprague, Aug. 9, 1871, all Northern Pacific Land Department Records. Also see Robert E. Ficken, *The Forested Land: A History of Lumbering in Western Washington* (Seattle: University of Washington Press, 1987), 45–46; Yonce, "Lumbering and the Public Timberlands," 10–11.

64. Stevens to Sprague, Aug. 9, 23, 1871; Sprague to Billings, March 25, 1872, all Northern Pacific Land Department Records.

65. Sprague to Billings, March 30; July 20, 1872; Stevens to Sprague, July 13, 1872; to Billings, Oct. 7, 1872; to Jacobs, Aug. 9, 1873; J. P. Clarke and Robert G. Stuart to Drummond, July 24, 1872; Wingard to Sprague, Aug. 10, 1873; Wheat to Billings, Aug. 20; Nov. 25, 1872; to Howard, April 18, 1873; to Jacobs, Aug. 5, 20, 1873; Jacobs to Howard, July 11; Aug. 26, 27; Sept. 27; Nov. 25, 1873; Howard to Billings, Dec. 12, 1873, all Ibid.; Tuttle to Jacobs, Sept. 9, 1873, Northern Pacific Railroad Land Department Western District Records, WSHS; Billings to Ainsworth, Nov. 21, 1873, Ainsworth Papers; Whatcom *Bellingham Bay Mail*, Nov. 29, 1873. Stevens still held stumpage money due the railroad in December 1874, a year after his firing. Ainsworth to Stevens, Dec. 4, 1874, Stevens Papers.

66. Sprague to Billings, Nov. 26, 1871; B. F. Wade to Billings, Nov. 27, 1872, both Northern Pacific Land Department Records; Miller to D. L. Phillips, Nov. 19, 1871; to G. L. Smith, Jan. 4, 1872; to Ladd & Tilton, July 18, 1872; to D. B. Finch, April 14; July 21, 1873; to Frank Matthias, June 25, 1873, Miller Family Papers; Olympia *Puget Sound Weekly Courier*, July 13, 1872; Wallace to Son, Jan. 30, 1872, Wallace Papers; Seattle *Weekly Intelligencer*, Dec. 4, 11, 1871; Jan. 8; March 18, 1872; Cass to Stevens, March 31, 1873, Stevens Papers.

67. Wallace to Son, June 25; Sept. 13, 1872; Jan. 31, 1873, Wallace Papers; *Walla Walla Union*, Dec. 16, 1871; Seattle *Weekly Intelligencer*, March 3, 29, 1873; Winks, *Billings*, 203; C. B. Wright to Ainsworth, May 17; June 18, 1873, Ainsworth Papers; Ainsworth to Billings, March 1, 1875, Northern Pacific Land Department Records.

68. Seattle *Weekly Intelligencer*, June 28; July 5, 12, 19, 1873.

69. Ibid., July 19; Aug. 2; Sept. 13, 1873; Miller to Finch, July 21, 1873, Miller Family Papers; Whatcom *Bellingham Bay Mail*, Oct. 4, 1873. Also see Morgan, *Puget's Sound*, 164.

70. See chapter six for Seattle's railroad project. Jacobs to Howard, July 15, 16, 1873, Northern Pacific Land Department Records; Cooke to Ainsworth, June 1, 1874; Wright to Ainsworth, July 12, 1873, both Ainsworth Papers; Seattle *Weekly Intelligencer*, July 19; Aug. 2, 16; Sept. 13; Oct. 25, 1873; Whatcom *Bellingham Bay Mail*, Aug. 2, 1873.

71. Technical difficulties interfered with transfer of Lake Superior and Puget Sound Company holdings to the new Tacoma Land Company, the railroad townsite subsidiary managed by Ainsworth. Under the arrangement finally concluded, the latter secured two-thirds of the property belonging to the former. The Northern Pacific took direct possession of the remainder. Wright to Ainsworth, Jan. 8, 14, 22, 1874; Billings to Ainsworth, Dec. 9, 1873; Cass to Ainsworth, Oct. 23, 1873, all Ainsworth Papers; Ainsworth to Billings, Nov. 4; Dec. 5, 1873; Wheat to Billings, Jan. 8, 1874, all Northern Pacific Land Department Records; Reed to Sprague, Sept. 23, 1873, Reed Papers. For local reaction to Cooke's fall, see Whatcom *Bellingham Bay Mail*, Sept. 20, 1873; Seattle *Weekly Intelligencer*, Sept. 20, 1873.

72. John Leng, *America in 1876: Pencillings during a Tour in the Centennial Year* (Dundee: Dundee Advertiser Office, 1877), 123–124, 126. On anti-N.P. sentiment, see Robbins, "Federal Land System in an Embryo State," 367–368.

73. Dorsey Baker's nomination strategy consisted of passing out "miserable looking cigars" to convention delegates. *Walla Walla Statesman*, April 30; Aug. 20, 1869; Olympia *Washington Standard*, May 22, 29, 1869; Port Townsend *Weekly Message*, June 2, 1869.

74. Port Townsend *Weekly Message*, Nov. 19, 1869; Olympia *Washington Standard*, May 29, 1869; *Walla Walla Statesman*, April 16; May 7, 28; July 30, 1869; *Walla Walla Union*, April 2, 1870; *Vancouver Register*, May 1, 1869.

75. Port Townsend *Weekly Message*, May 5, 26, 1869; March 4, 1870; Seattle *Weekly Intelligencer*, March 7, 1870; *Vancouver Register*, May 1, 22, 1869; Olympia *Washington Standard*, May 29; June 5, 1869; *Walla Walla Statesman*, June 4, 1869.

76. Rufus Leighton to Charles W. Slack, Aug. 18, 1869, "Nomination" Letters from Collectors of Customs, Port Townsend, Washington, to the Secretary of the Treasury, 1865–1910, RG 56, NA; Seattle *Weekly Intelligencer*, July 26, 1869; Port Townsend *Weekly Message*, Nov. 19; Dec. 10, 24, 1869; Jan. 28, 1870; *Vancouver Register*, Oct. 23, 1869; Jan. 29, 1870; Olympia *Washington Standard*, Dec. 11, 1869; *Walla Walla Statesman*, Dec. 11, 1869; Garfielde to D. Bagley, Oct. 7, 1869, D. Bagley Papers; Flanders to the President of the United States, Dec. 29, 1869, State Department, Washington Territorial Papers.

77. "Tell him that you want his support," a Garfielde colleague wrote in stressing the need to counter Blinn's resources by raising money from Ben Holladay, ". . . in fact, *f__k* him all up." Blinn's 147 votes, out of more than six thousand cast, had no impact on the outcome. *Walla Walla Union*, March 12, 19; June 4, 1870; *Vancouver Register*, March 5, 1870; Port Townsend *Weekly Message*, March 25; May 23, 1870; Seattle *Weekly Intelligencer*, May 2; June 27, 1870; Miller to Linkton, May 10, 1870; to Garfielde, May 12, 1870; to Fayette McMullin, May 13, 1870, Miller Family Papers; Ezra Smith to Garfielde, May 11, 1870, Garfielde Letters.

78. F. A. Walker to McKenny, April 18; July 6, 1872, Thomas J. McKenny Correspondence, WSL; Garfielde to Walker, June 25, 1872; E. H. Ludington to Assistant Adjutant General, Aug. 11, 1872, both Correspondence of the Office of Indian Affairs; Winans to Garfielde, July 15, 1872, Winans Papers; John A. Simms to R. H. Milroy, Nov. 20, 1872; to Wm. Vandever, Oct. 23, 1874, John A. Simms Papers, WSU; to J. Q. Smith, Aug. 26, 1876; to E. A. Hayt, Feb. 28, 1878; to R. E. Trowbridge, Aug. 18, 1880, Colville Indian Agency Records, RG 75, FRC.

79. Sprague to Billings, Nov. 26; Dec. 5, 1871; May 4, 1872; Garfielde to Nettleton, Nov. 21, 1871; May 7, 1872; to Cooke, Feb. 14, 1872; Wade to Billings, Jan. 23, 1872; to Nettleton, May 2, 1872; Nettleton to Billings, May 4, 1872; Cooke to Billings, Feb. 16, 1872, all Northern Pacific Land Department Records. Governor Ferry, the leading member of Garfielde's Olympia "ring," had no responsibility over timber matters and was left undisturbed by the railroad. For the delegate's sponsorship of Ferry, see Garfielde to the President, Jan. 25, 1872, Letters of Application and Recommendation during the Administration of Ulysses S. Grant, 1869–1877, M968, NA.

80. Resigning his Oregon position in 1853 to make room for Matthew P. Deady, McFadden accepted appointment in Washington Territory as compensation for this sacrifice in the interest of Democratic party politics. Sprague to Billings, Nov. 11, 1872; McMicken to Billings, Nov. 19, 1872, both Northern Pacific Land Department Records; McFadden to Wm. L. Marcy, Aug. 15, 1853; to Caleb Cushing, May 16, 1854; to J. Black, Nov. 7, 1857; Aaron E. Wait to Robert McClelland, Dec. 23, 1853; Isaac I. Stevens to Black, Feb. 2; March 16, 1858, all Records relating to the Appointment of Federal Judges; Olympia *Puget Sound Weekly Courier*, Oct. 5, 1872; Hill Harmon to Ferry, Oct. 30, 1872, Elisha P. Ferry Papers, UW.

81. Olympia *Puget Sound Weekly Courier*, Oct. 5, 26; Nov. 9, 23, 30, 1872; Miller to Judson, Oct. 11, 1872; to Frost, Oct. 18, 1872; to Roeder, Oct. 25, 1872, Miller Family Papers. For the delegate's role in arranging favorable press coverage, see Garfielde to Ferry, Jan. 4, 1872, Ferry Papers, UW.

82. A recent congressional act had changed the territorial election from June to November. Miller to Smith, Nov. 7, 1872; to Simms, Nov. 19, 1872; Simms to Miller, Oct. 5; Nov. 29, 1872; Jan. 20, 1873, all Miller Family Papers; Seattle *Weekly Intelligencer*, Dec. 2, 1872; Sprague to Billings, Nov. 26, 30, 1872; McMicken to Billings, Dec. 30, 1872, all Northern Pacific Land Department Records; Wm. Windom to McMicken, Dec. 18, 1872, McMicken Family Papers, UW; Cass to Ainsworth, Dec. 20, 1872, Ainsworth Papers.

83. Miller to Simms, Nov. 10, 1872, Miller Family Papers; Whatcom *Bellingham Bay Mail*, Dec. 27, 1873; Jan. 17, 1874; Garfielde to Ainsworth, April 23, 1874, Ainsworth Papers; to D. Bagley, Feb. 3, 1873; Jan. 25, 1875; O. Jacobs to D. Bagley, May 25, 1876, all D. Bagley Papers; Appointment Certificate, Nov. 11, 1874, Elisha P. Ferry Papers, WSA; *Yakima Record*, Sept. 25, 1880; May 12, 1883.

84. The census listed nine out of ten Oregonians and Californians as white. Three-fourths of Idaho's people were white. The two reservations east of the Cascades accounted for most of the total acreage. *Ninth Census*, 1:xvii; *The Statistical History of the United States: From Colonial Times to the Present* (New York: Basic Books, Inc., 1976), 25, 27, 33; McMicken to Squire, Oct. 27, 1884, Squire Papers; Milroy to H. Price, March 27, 1883, Yakima Indian Agency Records, RG 75, FRC; Thomas Odeneal to E. Smith, May 20, 1873, Correspondence of the Office of Indian Affairs.

85. Port Townsend *Weekly Message*, April 8, 1870; James G. Swan to Leighton, July 1, 1869, James G. Swan Papers, University of British Columbia Library; Wm. J. Pollock to Samuel J. Kirkwood, April 7, 1881; R. S. Gardner to Secretary of the Interior, Feb. 23, 1883, both Reports of Inspection of the Field Jurisdictions of the Office of Indian Affairs, 1873–1900, M1070, NA; C. C. Finkboner to Geo. D. Hill, Sept. 28; Nov. 30, 1869; Feb. 28; May 2; Oct. 2, 1870; Jan. 31, 1871; to E. C. Chirouse, May 30, 1871, Tulalip Indian Agency Records, RG 75, FRC; James O'Neill to D. W. Ballard, July 20, 1866, in *Annual Report of the Commissioner of Indian Affairs, 1866*, 193; John B. Monteith to E. Smith, Oct. 5, 1875; to J. Smith, Sept. 15, 1876, Northern Idaho Indian Agency Records, RG 75, FRC; *Walla Walla Union*, Nov. 19, 1870; May 20, 1871.

86. Port Townsend *North-West*, March 1, 29, 1862; Port Townsend *Weekly Message*, July 25, 1867; June 25; Sept. 24, 1868; Oct. 6, 1869; Olympia *Washington Standard*, Nov. 11, 1865; Reminiscences, 1878, James G. Swan Papers, WSHS; Chirouse to Wm. H. Boyle, Jan. 27, 1875; Wm. DeShaw to Edmond Mallet, May 29, 1877, both Correspondence of the Office of Indian Affairs; *Walla Walla Statesman*, March 29; Nov. 15, 1862; March 21, 1863; March 2, 1866; Dec. 6, 1867; Sept. 11, 1868; *Walla Walla Union*, Nov. 19, 1870; March 18, 1871; James G. Swan Diary, Feb. 6, 1861, UW; Port Townsend *Weekly Argus*, Jan. 5, 1871; Steilacoom *Puget Sound Herald*, July 10, 1862; Seattle *People's Telegram*, Nov. 21, 1864; Winans to "Dear Judge," April 3, 1871, Winans Papers; to McKenny, Feb. 5; March 6; June 30, 1871, Records of the Washington Superintendency of Indian Affairs.

87. *Ninth Census*, 1:xvii; Roger Daniels, *Asian America: Chinese and Japanese in the United States since 1850* (Seattle: University of Washington Press, 1988), 9; Reed to John R. Foster, April 26, 1870, Reed Papers; Kate C. McBeth letter fragment, 1879, McBeth-Crawford Collection, Idaho State Historical Society; *Walla Walla Statesman*, April 12, 1867; Aug. 28, 1868.

88. According to an 1861 letter from Orofino, there were "no Chinamen" in the camp at that time. *Walla Walla Statesman*, April 9, 1864; April 7, 1865; Jan. 11, 1867; April 30, 1869; Portland *Daily Oregonian*, April 13; July 12; Dec. 20, 1865; Nov. 21, 1866; Seattle *Weekly Intelligencer*, July 5, 1869; Nov. 1, 1873; Steilacoom *Puget Sound Herald*, Sept. 5, 1861.

89. Seattle *Weekly Intelligencer*, Nov. 7, 1870; Sept. 11, 1871; June 7, 1873; Olympia *Washington Standard*, July 17, 24, 1869; *Walla Walla Union,* Sept. 23, 1871; *Walla Walla Statesman,* Nov. 22, 1862; May 21, 1870; Portland *Daily Oregonian,* May 4, 1865; Port Townsend *Weekly Message,* May 23, 1871.

90. *Seattle Weekly Gazette,* Aug. 27, 1864; Olympia *Washington Standard,* Sept. 9; Nov. 4, 1865; Denny to Hugh McCulloch, n.d., Arthur A. Denny Papers, WSHS; Seattle *Weekly Intelligencer,* June 7, 1869; May 23; July 4, 1870; Sept. 30, 1872; Port Townsend *Weekly Message,* Dec. 5, 1867; *Walla Walla Statesman,* May 28, 1869; *Walla Walla Union,* Feb. 25; March 11, 1871.

91. *Walla Walla Statesman,* Jan. 12; Dec. 14, 1866; Sept. 6; Oct. 4, 1867; March 13; July 31, 1868; May 28; Sept. 25, 1869; *Walla Walla Union,* Feb. 25; March 11; June 17, 1871; Seattle *Weekly Intelligencer,* Feb. 24, 1873; Olympia *Daily Tribune,* Jan. 3, 4, 1868; Port Townsend *Weekly Message,* Dec. 5, 1867; *Olympia Transcript,* Dec. 28, 1867.

92. *Walla Walla Statesman,* Dec. 14, 28, 1866; Aug. 2, 1867; Port Townsend *Weekly Message,* Feb. 17, 1869.

93. Port Townsend *Weekly Message,* Oct. 24; Nov. 21, 1867; Jan. 30, 1868; Olympia *Washington Standard,* Sept. 27, 1862; *Walla Walla Statesman,* Oct. 18, 1862.

Notes—Chapter Six
First Great Want of the People

1. Sept. 19, 1874.

2. "We ought to be helped by Government," Northern Pacific director Frederick Billings complained, "but the Press and Public Opinion are not in our favor." The N.P. collapse stimulated organization, east and west of the Cascades, of the Patrons of Husbandry, an agricultural organization dedicated to reform of transportation abuses. W. W. Miller to D. B. Finch, July 21, 1873; to A. J. Baldwin, Feb. 19, 1874, Miller Family Papers, UW; O. B. McFadden to Frederick Billings, Dec. 3, 1873, Northern Pacific Railway Company Land Department Records, 1870–1876, MHS; Seattle *Puget Sound Dispatch,* March 5, 12, 1874; Seattle *Weekly Intelligencer,* Sept. 13; Oct. 25; Nov. 1, 8, 15, 1873; *Olympia Transcript,* Jan. 31, 1874; Whatcom *Bellingham Bay Mail,* Aug. 29, 1874; *Walla Walla Union,* April 10, 1875; Anna Maria Foxwell James to Brother, Feb. 11, 1875, James Family Papers, UW; Thomas W. Prosch to Clarence Bagley, June 25, 1874. Thomas W. Prosch Papers, UW; Billings to John C. Ainsworth, Nov. 21, 1873, John C. Ainsworth Papers, UO.

3. Ainsworth to Billings, Nov. 4, 1873, Northern Pacific Land Department Records; Minutes, June 1, 1883, Tacoma Land and Improvement Company Papers, Tacoma Public Library; Tacoma *Weekly Pacific Tribune,* April 3; May 15; July 17, 1874; *Olympia Transcript,* Feb. 7, 1874; *Lewiston Teller,* Sept. 3, 1880; J. W. Boddem-Whetham, *Western Wanderings: A Record of Travel in the Evening Land* (London: Richard Bentley and Son, 1874), 282; John Leng, *America in 1876: Pencillings during a Tour in the Centennial Year* (Dundee: Dundee Advertiser Office, 1877), 145–146; J. Murphy, "Summer Ramblings in Washington Territory," *Appleton's Journal,* 3(Nov. 1877), 386; Charles Nordhoff, *Northern California, Oregon, and the Sandwich Islands* (New York: Harper & Brothers, 1874), 221–222.

4. Technically, the Tacoma Land Company succeeded to the charter of the Continental Improvement Company, incorporated in Pennsylvania in 1868. Olympia *Puget Sound Weekly Courier,* Jan. 24, 1874; C. B. Wright to Geo. B. Hibbard, Feb. 26, 1874; Articles of Incorporation; Minutes, June 1, 1883; Annual Report, March 4, 1884, all Tacoma Land and Improvement Company Papers; Tacoma *Weekly Pacific Tribune,* March 20, 1874. Kalama-based N.P. executives complained of being "gobbled up" by the land company. Wm. A. Howard to Billings, Dec. 10, 1873, Northern Pacific Land Department Records.

5. Preceding Olmsted, James Tilton drew the original sketch of the planned city. Wright to Ainsworth, Oct. 3, 18; Dec. 27, 1873; Jan. 8, 14, 29; Feb. 7, 1874, Ainsworth Papers; Tacoma *Weekly Pacific Tribune,* Jan. 2, 1874; Norman J. Johnston, "The Frederick Law Olmsted Plan for Tacoma," *PNQ,* 66(July 1975), 97–104; Murray Morgan, *Puget's Sound: A Narrative of Early Tacoma and the Southern Sound* (Seattle: University of Washington Press, 1979), 169–175; Seattle *Puget Sound Dispatch,* April 2, 1874.

6. Urging Ainsworth on, C. B. Wright vowed to "teach Seattle that we mean what we say about the Terminus being at Tacoma." Ainsworth to Billings, March 1, 1875, Northern Pacific Land Department Records; Wright to Ainsworth, Feb. 7, 1874, Ainsworth Papers; Seattle *Puget Sound Dispatch,* Feb. 26, 1874; *Olympia Transcript,* Feb. 21; April 4, 1874; Tacoma *Weekly Pacific Tribune,* Aug. 21, 1874. For figures on railroad-owned acreage at Tacoma, see Annual Report, March 2, 1880, Tacoma Land and Improvement Company Papers; *Walla Walla Union,* March 27, 1875.

7. Seattle *Weekly Intelligencer,* Sept. 20, 27, 1873; Seattle *Puget Sound Dispatch,* Jan. 8; Feb. 12; March 26; April 2, 1874; *Olympia Transcript,* Jan. 10; Feb. 21; April 4, 1874; Olympia *Puget Sound Weekly Courier,* Feb. 28, 1874.

8. The Northern Pacific originally intended to purchase the Starr boats, a transaction ruined by the railroad's bankruptcy. Seattle *Puget Sound Dispatch,* March 26; July 9, 1874; Ainsworth to Thomas Hosmer, Feb. 2, 1874, Northern Pacific Land Department Western District Records, WSHS; *Olympia Transcript,* April 4, 1874; Tacoma *Weekly Pacific Tribune,* April 3, 10, 24; May 8; July 31, 1874; Wright to Ainsworth, Feb. 7, 1874,

Ainsworth Papers; Billings to Howard, Aug. 28, 1873, Northern Pacific Land Department Records; Malcolm Clark, Jr., ed., *Pharisee among Philistines: The Diary of Judge Matthew P. Deady, 1871–1892* (Portland: Oregon Historical Society, 2 vols., 1975), 1:138; Minutes, Sept. 19, 1873; March 10, 1875, Tacoma Land and Improvement Company Papers.

9. *Olympia Transcript*, Jan. 24, 1874; Wright to Ainsworth, Dec. 27, 1873; Jan. 14; Feb. 7; May 27; June 30, 1874, Ainsworth Papers; Tacoma *Weekly Pacific Tribune*, May 15, 1874; *Walla Walla Union*, April 18; May 23, 1874; McFadden to Billings, Dec. 3, 1873, Northern Pacific Land Department Records; to William McMicken, Dec. 29, 1873, McMicken Family Papers, UW; Seattle *Puget Sound Dispatch*, June 18, 1874; The Dalles *Daily Mountaineer*, July 17, 1875; *Walla Walla Statesman*, Aug. 29, 1875; Seattle *Weekly Intelligencer*, Sept. 4, 1875; *Vancouver Independent*, Sept. 25, 1875. On the N.P. sale, see Robin W. Winks, *Frederick Billings: A Life* (New York: Oxford University Press, 1991), 211–214.

10. Walla Wallans referred to the Portland, Dalles & Salt Lake as "our line." *Walla Walla Union*, Oct. 4; Dec. 13, 1873; Jan. 17, 31; Feb. 21; May 2, 1874; Jan. 2; March 20, 1875; May 5, 1877; Seattle *Weekly Intelligencer*, Jan. 10, 1874; March 25, 1876; Olympia *Puget Sound Weekly Courier*, Jan. 31; May 2, 1874; Seattle *Puget Sound Dispatch*, July 2, 1874; *Walla Walla Statesman*, Dec. 26, 1874; The Dalles *Weekly Mountaineer*, Feb. 21, 1874. Also see Peter J. Lewty, *To the Columbia Gateway: The Oregon Railway and the Northern Pacific, 1879–1884* (Pullman: Washington State University Press, 1987), 82.

11. A fully-loaded narrow gauge train hauled two pounds of paying freight for every pound of dead weight, compared to a one-to-one ratio on a broad gauge system. These differentials translated into savings in the cost of construction and operation. Olympia *Washington Standard*, May 22, 1875; July 21, 1877; Lewty, *To the Columbia Gateway*, 34–35; The Dalles *Weekly Mountaineer*, May 10, 1873; *Walla Walla Union*, March 28; May 16; July 4, 1874; *Walla Walla Statesman*, Jan. 16, 1875; Philip Ritz to Ainsworth, Sept. 7, 1873, Ainsworth Papers; W. F. Kimball to John J. McGilvra, Oct. 3, 1873, John J. McGilvra Papers, UW; S. G. Reed to Ritz, Oct. 22, 1873, Simeon G. Reed Papers, Reed College Library; Olympia *Puget Sound Weekly Courier*, May 2, 1874. Also see D. W. Meinig, *The Great Columbia Plain: A Historical Geography, 1805–1910* (Seattle: University of Washington Press, 1968), 242.

12. *Walla Walla Union*, Jan. 16, 23, 1875; Lewty, *To the Columbia Gateway*, 36; *Walla Walla Statesman*, Sept. 25; Nov. 6, 1875; July 22, 1876; Olympia *Transcript*, Nov. 20, 1875. Also see W. W. Baker, "The Building of the Walla Walla & Columbia River Railroad," *WHQ*, 14(Jan. 1923), 3–13.

13. Although Baker claimed that he made no money from the railroad, most observers considered the line a highly-profitable venture. *Walla Walla Statesman*, Sept. 11, 1875; Feb. 5, 19; March 18; April 22; June 3; Aug. 26, 1876; *Olympia Transcript*, Oct. 28, 1876; *Walla Walla Union*, Sept. 29; Nov. 10, 1877; Astoria *Weekly Astorian*, April 29, 1876; Pendleton *East Oregonian*, Dec. 8, 1877.

14. "There is no use in talking about Olympia," O. B. McFadden privately confided, "unless we can get a Rail Road." J. J. Gilbert, Reminiscences, 3–4, BL; *Olympia Transcript*, Jan. 10, 1874; Olympia *Puget Sound Weekly Courier*, Jan. 3, 10, 17; Feb. 14, 21; May 30, 1874; McFadden to McMicken, Dec. 29, 1873, McMicken Family Papers. *Oregonian* reprinted in Tacoma *Weekly Pacific Tribune*, Jan. 30, 1874.

15. The bond vote, with an overall two-thirds majority required for passage, was 426-48 favorable in Olympia and 85-70 against in rural precincts outside the city. *Olympia Transcript*, Jan. 3, 10, 31; Feb. 7; March 28; April 4, 25; May 9; June 27; July 4, 25; Aug. 15, 1874; Olympia *Puget Sound Weekly Courier*, Jan. 3, 10, 24; Feb. 7, 14; March 14; May 23, 1874; Miller to McFadden, Aug. 26, 1873; Jan. 6, 12; Feb. 4, 10; April 22, 1874, Miller Family Papers; Seattle *Puget Sound Dispatch*, March 19, 1874; Tacoma *Weekly Pacific Tribune*, Feb. 6, 1874. Another old-time Democrat, William Winlock Miller, was one of the few critics of the railroad project. See William L. Lang, *Confederacy of Ambition: William Winlock Miller and the Making of Washington Territory* (Seattle: University of Washington Press, 1996), 227–228. Also see, in general, Winlock Miller, Jr., "The Olympia Narrow Gauge Railroad," *WHQ*, 16(Oct. 1925), 243–250.

16. *Olympia Transcript*, May 9; July 25, 1874; Oct. 28, 1876; Olympia *Puget Sound Weekly Courier*, June 6, 1874; Olympia *Washington Standard*, March 20; April 24; May 22, 1875; May 12, 26, 1877.

17. The new company featured the politician management typical of Olympia business enterprises. John R. Judson, currently a leader of the territorial Democracy, served as president, and Republican Robert H. Milroy as vice president. Olympia *Washington Standard*, May 12; June 9, 16, 23, 30, 1877; Thornton F. McElroy to H. McElroy, Aug. 7, 1878, McElroy Family Papers, UW.

18. In an act of questionable legality, the territorial legislature authorized use of the tideflats between Yesler's mill and the mouth of the Duwamish River. Seattle *Weekly Intelligencer* July 19, 26; Aug. 9, 16; Sept. 6, 27; Oct. 25; Nov. 1, 1873; McGilvra to H. G. Struve, July 21, 1873; Roswell Scott to McGilvra, Aug. 21, 1873, both McGilvra Papers; *Walla Walla Union*, April 18, 1874; The Dalles *Weekly Mountaineer*, July 25, 1874. On the tideland grant, see Bills Presented to Governor for Approval, 1873, Elisha P. Ferry Papers, WSA. The persistent local interest in terminus matters is noted in John R. Finger, "The Seattle Spirit, 1851–1893," *Journal of the West*, 13(July 1974), 35–38. Brief accounts of the railroad venture are found in Murray Morgan, *Skid Road: An Informal Portrait of Seattle* (Seattle: University of Washington Press ed., 1982, 1951), 72–74; Roger Sale, *Seattle, Past to Present* (Seattle: University of Washington Press, 1976), 32–34.

19. Astoria *Weekly Astorian*, Oct. 28, 1876; Seattle *Weekly Pacific Tribune*, Aug. 11; Nov. 24, 1876; Seattle *Weekly Intelligencer*, Jan. 24; Feb. 28; June 6, 1874; Nov. 18, 1876; Olympia *Washington Standard*, June 12, 1875; George F. Whitworth to Watson C. Squire, Oct. 31, 1884, Watson C. Squire Papers, WSA.

20. Morris was also involved in the Olympia-Tenino project. Seattle *Puget Sound Dispatch*, Jan. 1, 15; April 2, 1874; Seattle *Weekly Intelligencer*, March 7; Dec. 9, 1874; *Walla Walla Union*, Feb. 28; Nov. 28, 1874; McMicken to Willis Drummond, Nov. 8, 1873, Letters Received from the Surveyors General of Washington, 1854–1883, RG 49, NA; *Walla Walla Statesman*, March 6, 1875; Selucious Garfielde to McGilvra, April 2, 1875, McGilvra Papers.

21. King and Walla Walla counties were eventually authorized to issue $100,000 worth of bonds apiece. All other counties in the territory received authority to sell between $2,500 and $75,000, the specific amount to be determined according to supposed project benefit. The Dalles *Weekly Mountaineer*, June 27, 1874; Lewiston *Idaho Signal*, Jan. 3, 1874; Lewiston *Northerner*, Dec. 12, 1874; Pendleton *East Oregonian*, April 5, 1879; Seattle *Puget Sound Dispatch*, April 30; Aug. 6; Sept. 10, 1874; Seattle *Weekly Intelligencer*, Sept. 20, 1873; Jan. 3, 17; May 16, 1874; March 6, 1875; *Walla Walla Statesman*, Dec. 26, 1874; *Walla Walla Union*, Oct. 25; Dec. 13, 1873; July 25, 1874; Kimball to McGilvra, Oct. 3; Nov. 4, 1873; W. E. Stubbs to McGilvra, Oct. 19, 1873, all McGilvra Papers; Olympia *Washington Standard*, Nov. 17, 1877; Minutes, Board of Trustees Meeting, Seattle & Walla Walla Railroad, March 8, 1878, Arthur A. Denny Papers, WSHS.

22. Seattle *Puget Sound Dispatch*, April 16, 23; May 7, 14, 21, 1874; McGilvra to G. A. Meiggs, April 14, 1874, McGilvra Papers; Seattle *Weekly Intelligencer*, May 9, 16, 1874.

23. Seattle *Puget Sound Dispatch*, June 4, 11, 1874; Seattle *Weekly Intelligencer*, June 6, 1874; Oct. 2, 1875; *Walla Walla Union*, June 13, 1874; Whatcom *Bellingham Bay Mail*, June 13, 1874. The characterization of Yesler is from Thomas Burke to R. H. McDonald, July 8, 1881, Thomas Burke Papers, UW.

24. Seattle *Weekly Intelligencer*, Aug. 21; Sept. 4; Oct. 2, 1875; Jan. 22; April 1, 8, 15, 22; May 27; Nov. 18, 1876; Seattle *Daily Intelligencer*, June 12, 1876; *Walla Walla Union*, Nov. 7, 1874; Minutes, Board of Trustees Meetings, Jan. 16; May 28, 1879, Denny Papers; Donald B. Robertson, *Encyclopedia of Western Railroad History*, Vol. 3, *Oregon-Washington* (Caldwell: The Caxton Printers, Ltd., 1995), 265.

25. *Walla Walla Union*, Jan. 10, 24; April 4, 11; Aug. 1, 1874; Feb. 6; March 6, 1875; Ainsworth to H. C. Robert, Nov. 23, 1871; N. Michler Annual Report, Improvement of the Upper Columbia and Snake Rivers, 1875; Chas. F. Powell to G. H. Mendell, Jan. 14, 1886, all Portland District Records, U.S. Army Corps of Engineers, RG 77, FRC; to Chief of Engineers, May 30, 1882, in *Annual Report of the Chief of Engineers, 1882*, 2700; Reed to Geo. H. Williams, March 16, 1870, Reed Papers; *Walla Walla Statesman*, Jan. 16; Feb. 13, 1875.

26. Lewiston business interests contended that "a properly constituted" boat could safely use the Snake "the year round, or, at all events, whenever navigation to Wallula is practicable." *Walla Walla Statesman*, Dec. 11, 1875; The Dalles *Weekly Mountaineer*, July 18, 1874; Powell to Mendell, Jan. 14, 1886; Michler Annual Report, 1875; John Gates to J. M. Wilson, Dec. 9, 1877, all Portland District Records; Reed to A. H. Gordon, Sept. 11, 1873; to R. P. Steen, July 27, 1876, Reed Papers; Lewiston *Northerner*, Dec. 5, 1874; *Lewiston Teller*, Oct. 21, 1876. For the *Annie Faxon*, see Randall V. Mills, *Stern-Wheelers Up Columbia: A Century of Steamboating in the Oregon Country* (Palo Alto: Pacific Books, 1947), 118–119.

27. The O.S.N. played an integral part in federal navigation work, transporting laborers free of charge, dropping off supplies at isolated sites and using company steamers to position drilling scows. James Montgomery, a regular O.S.N. and N.P. contractor, secured most of the Army contracts. Reed to Frank T. Dodge, Aug. 12, 1868, Reed Papers; to R. S. Williamson, Nov. 1, 1871; to A. A. Humphreys, Jan. 2; Aug. 15; May 9, 1873; to Ainsworth, Sept. 11, 1872; Ainsworth to Robert, Nov. 23, 1871; Sept. 7, 1872; Eugene F. Coe to H. W. Corbett, Oct. 24, 1872; R. B. Randall to Robert, March 7, 1873; to N. Michler, March 30, 1873; to James Daly, March 5; Nov. 29, 1874; Philip G. Eastwick to G. L. Gillespie, Oct. 8, 1879; Richard M. Tabor to Michler, Nov. 25, 1875; to Gillespie, Nov. 20, 1879; James K. Kelly to Humphreys, Nov. 25, 1875; Robert Grant to Kelly, Nov. 6, 1875; Williamson to Robert, Nov. 8, 1871; Michler to Humphreys, April 23; Sept. 12, 1874; June 7; Sept. 30, 1875, all Portland District Records; *Walla Walla Union*, Nov. 14, 28, 1874; Dec. 13, 1879.

28. Michler to Humphreys, April 23, 1874; April 21, 1875; S. R. Smith to W. A. Jones, Nov. 14, 1888; Randall to Michler, Jan. 14, 1875; to Daly, Feb. 7, 1875; Tabor to Wilson, Jan. 27; March 1, 8, 11, 1876; N. Michler Report of Operations…March 1875; G. F. Cramer to Michler, March 20, 1875; Wilson to Humphreys, March 2, 8, 1876; Coe to Wilson, Dec. 16, 1876, all Portland District Records; *Walla Walla Union*, March 20, 1875; *Walla Walla Statesman*, March 11, 1876.

29. "One competent pilot," the *Walla Walla Union* claimed, ". . . is worth a twenty-one lot full of 'topogwaphical enginears [sic].'" Randall to Michler, Dec. 2, 1874; Jan. 14, 1875; T. W. Symons, Improvement of Upper Columbia and Snake Rivers, Annual Report, 1891, all Portland District Records; *Walla Walla Statesman*, Oct. 2, 1875; *Walla Walla Union*, Dec. 13, 1879. On river logbooks, see Dubuar Scrapbooks, 56:13, UW.

30. Symons Annual Report, 1891, Portland District Records; Reed to Williams, March 16, 1870; to Wright, Aug. 12, 1878; S. G. Reed, "The Columbia River and the O.S.N. Company," Aug. 11, 1878, all Reed Papers; *Walla Walla Union*, Dec. 13, 1873; Jan. 31, 1874; June 12, 1875; *Walla Walla Statesman*, June 12, 1875; The Dalles *Weekly Mountaineer*, March 8, 1873; July 11, 1874; June 19; July 19, 1875; Portland *Oregonian*, April 12, 1878; Colfax *Palouse Gazette*, May 11, 25; June 15, 1878; Dayton *Columbia Chronicle*, May 11, 18, 25, 1878; Lewiston *Northerner*, Oct. 31, 1874; Pendleton *East Oregonian*, March 23, 1878.

31. There being no competition on the upper Columbia in 1874, the O.S.N. maintained prevailing charges above The Dalles. Punishing The Dalles for supporting Moody's challenge, the company altered its schedules so that passengers would have no time to patronize the town's hotels, restaurants and other businesses. *Walla Walla Union*, July 25; Aug. 8, 29; Sept. 26, 1874; March 27, 1875; The Dalles *Weekly Mountaineer*, July 25; Aug. 1,

8, 1874; *Walla Walla Statesman*, Dec. 18, 1875; Lewiston *Idaho Signal*, Aug. 10, 1872; Lewiston *Northerner*, Feb. 27, 1875.

32. Symons Annual Report, 1891, Portland District Records; *Walla Walla Union*, Oct. 18; Dec. 20, 1873; Jan. 10, 1874; Feb. 20, 1875; The Dalles *Weekly Mountaineer*, Nov. 1, 1873; Feb. 21; Sept. 5, 1874; Dec. 18, 1875; Dayton *Columbia Chronicle*, May 31, 1879; *Walla Walla Statesman*, May 8; June 19; Aug. 21; Dec. 18, 1875; *Dayton News*, Jan. 12, 1877; *Lewiston Teller*, Nov. 11, 1876; April 21, 1877.

33. Channing M. Bolton to Wilson, Feb. 3, 1877, Portland District Records; Report of Board of Engineers for the Pacific Coast, San Francisco, Sept. 24, 1877, in *Annual Report of the Chief of Engineers, 1878*, 1343–1344; *Walla Walla Union*, Nov. 21, 1874; The Dalles *Weekly Mountaineer*, Nov. 25, 1875; William F. Willingham, "Engineering the Cascades Canal and Locks," *OHQ*, 88(Fall 1987), 232–233.

34. John G. Parke to Wilson, April 30; May 18; June 8, 1877; Bolton to Wilson, May 31, 1877; B. S. Alexander to Humphreys, Aug. 27, 1877; Ainsworth to J. J. Brazee, March 20, 1877; to Wilson, April 11, 1877; Reed to Wilson, Jan. 1, 7; Feb. 21, 1878; Rufus Mallory to Wilson, Aug. 2, 1878; George H. Elliott to Wilson, Aug. 8, 1878; Humphreys to Wilson, Oct. 24, 1876, all Portland District Records; Willingham, "Engineering the Cascades Canal," 233–253; The Dalles *Weekly Mountaineer*, Nov. 20, 1875; *Walla Walla Statesman*, Aug. 21; Dec. 11, 1875; Aug. 19; Oct. 7, 1876; March 10; July 28, 1877; Reed to Steen, Aug. 21, 1877, Reed Papers; *Walla Walla Union*, July 4, 1874; Nov. 3, 1877.

35. In a graphic demonstration of the decline of the old mining trails, General William Tecumseh Sherman literally had to fight his way down the Mullan Road in the course of an 1877 western tour, sending thirty soldiers ahead to clear timber and other obstructions and taking fifteen days to cover the distance between Missoula and Walla Walla. Eradication of pests helped to increase grain output. A two-cent Walla Walla County bounty resulted in the killing of fifteen thousand squirrels in 1878, saving an estimated thirty thousand acres of wheat. *Walla Walla Union*, June 20, 1874; Jan. 9, 1875; April 7, 14, 21; Sept. 22, 1877; Reed to Chas. B. Reed, et al., Oct. 22, 1873, Reed Papers; *Walla Walla Statesman*, Aug. 29, 1875; June 3, 10; Oct. 28, 1876; May 12; Aug. 4, 25, 1877; April 6, 1878; *Dayton News*, May 19, 1877. On the connection between railroading and wheat, see James F. Shepherd, "The Development of Wheat Production in the Pacific Northwest," *Agricultural History*, 49(Jan. 1975), 263; Robert G. Nesbit and Charles M. Gates, "Agriculture in Eastern Washington, 1890–1910," *PNQ*, 37(Oct. 1946), 281.

36. Arriving settlers pressed the Walla Walla land office for detailed information as to "whether the lands are rolling, broken, level, watered or arid, alkali or alluvial, timber or sage brush, bunch grass or rye grass." *Walla Walla Statesman*, May 5; June 16; Nov. 10, 1877; March 23; April 6, 1878; *Walla Walla Union*, April 10, 1875; May 5; Dec. 29, 1877; Sept. 6, 1879; Wm. Stephens to McMicken, Oct. 23, 1873; McMicken to S. S. Burdett, Oct. 7, 1875; to Commissioner, General Land Office, July 3, 1876, all Letters Received from the Surveyors General; Report on Washington and Idaho, 1879, Henry Villard Papers; Houghton Library, Harvard University; Colfax *Palouse Gazette*, Nov. 1, 1878; Pendleton *East Oregonian*, Oct. 20, 1877; Dayton *Columbia Chronicle*, April 20; Dec. 7, 1878; June 7, 1879; Frank Stevens Diary, July 15, 1880, WSL; *Dayton News*, Jan. 15, 1876; May 19, 1877. Also see Meinig, *Great Columbia Plain*, 242.

37. A. J. Wait, one of the founders of Dayton, had become disenchanted with his earlier nearby settlement, Waitsburg. *Dayton News*, Jan. 15, 1876; *Walla Walla Union*, Feb. 21, 1874; Feb. 6, 1875; *Walla Walla Statesman*, June 12, 1875; Dec. 29, 1877; Lucy A. Ide Diary, Sept. 14, 1878, EWSHS; Dayton *Columbia Chronicle*, April 27; May 4; July 6, 27, 1878; Jan. 25; April 5, 1879; Report on Washington and Idaho, 1879, Villard Papers; Colfax *Palouse Gazette*, Feb. 17, 1877; Pendleton *East Oregonian*, Feb. 17, 1877; Pomeroy *Washington Independent*, Nov. 25, 1880. Also see Meinig, *Great Columbia Plain*, 243.

38. Compensating for the inconvenience imposed upon Snake River shippers, the O.S.N. charged a lower rate than from Wallula on shipments to Portland. *Walla Walla Statesman*, June 12, 1875; March 18; April 22; Sept. 2, 9, 1876; July 28; Sept. 8; Oct. 6, 13, 1877; March 9, 16, 30; April 6, 1878; Report on Washington and Idaho, 1879, Villard Papers; *Dayton News*, March 18, 1876; *Walla Walla Union*, Sept. 27, 1879.

39. The Timber and Stone Act of 1878 allowed sale of 160 acre tracts, but compelled "settlers" to resort to a variety of subterfuges to qualify as purchasers. Dayton *Columbia Chronicle*, June 8, 1878; *Walla Walla Union*, June 16, 1877; Oct. 4, 1879; *Walla Walla Statesman*, Nov. 20, 1880; John Muir to Elijah Smith, July 23, 1884, Oregon Improvement Company Records, UW; McMicken to Burdett, Dec. 13, 1875; to J. A. Williamson, Sept. 3, 1879, Letters Received from the Surveyors General.

40. Governor Ferry wanted to name the new county after Elisha Ping, a member of the territorial council. *Walla Walla Statesman*, July 24; Aug. 7; Nov. 6, 27, 1875; *West Shore*, 1(Dec. 1875), 3; Colfax *Palouse Gazette*, March 9, 1878; Oct. 7, 1881; *Spokan Times*, Aug. 21, 1880; James W. Phillips, *Washington State Place Names* (Seattle: University of Washington Press, 1971), 29.

41. Palouse-bound settlers applied to the Northern Pacific for the right to purchase land once the odd-numbered sections were transferred to the railroad. *Walla Walla Statesman*, Sept. 2, 1876; Jan. 20; Aug. 25, 1877; June 8, 1878; Oct. 23, 1880; *West Shore*, 2(May 1877), 158; J. J. Browne to Anna Stratton Browne, April 28, 1878, J. J. Browne Papers, EWSHS; Colfax *Palouse Gazette*, Nov. 1, 1878; Report on Washington and Idaho, 1879, Villard Papers; *Spokan Times*, Aug. 21, 1880; Samuel A. Black to Geo. Stark, May 27, 1878, Northern Pacific Railway Company Papers, Series C, Settlement and Development, MHS.

42. Dayton *Columbia Chronicle*, Aug. 24, 1878; Browne to A. Browne, Aug. 15, 28, 1878, Browne Papers; Report on Washington and Idaho, 1879, Villard Papers; Colfax *Palouse Gazette*, Sept. 29; Oct. 6, 27; Dec. 8, 1877;

Walla Walla Union, April 14, 1877; *Walla Walla Statesman,* July 28, 1877.

43. Browne to A. Browne, April 17, 1878, Browne Papers; Report on Washington and Idaho, 1879, Villard Papers; Colfax *Palouse Gazette,* Nov. 10, 1877; June 8, 15; July 20, 1878; James M. Nosler Diary, Jan. 12, 1873, UW.

44. Fitz-Hugh Ludlow, "On the Columbia River," *Atlantic Monthly,* 14(Dec. 1864), 711; Edwin Richardson to T. M. Reed, May 21, 1873, Letters Received from the Surveyors General; John Monteith to F. A. Walker, Jan. 23, 1873; T. B. Odeneal to E. P. Smith, May 20, 1873, both Correspondence of the Office of Indian Affairs, Letters Received, 1824–1881, M234, NA; Edwin Eells to T. K. Cree, ? 1873, Edwin Eells Papers, WSHS; R. H. Milroy to James T. Barry, July 18, 1877, R. H. Milroy Letterbook, UW; to H. Price, March 27, 1883, Yakima Indian Agency Records, RG 75, FRC; Wm. Vandever to Commissioner of Indian Affairs, Nov. 2, 1874, Reports of Inspection of the Field Jurisdictions of the Office of Indian Affairs, 1873–1900, M1070, NA; Alfred Meacham to E. S. Parker, March 22, 1870, Records of the Oregon Superintendency of Indian Affairs, 1848–1873, M2, NA. Also see Robert H. Ruby and John A. Brown, *Dreamer-Prophets of the Columbia Plateau: Smohalla and Skolaskin* (Norman: University of Oklahoma Press, 1989), chapt. 3.

45. The off-reservation Nez Perce population was 1,250 and the on-reservation 1,550. Proceedings of a Council with the Nez Perce Indians, June 27, 1867; Geo. C. Hough to N. G. Taylor, June 27, 1867; James O'Neill to Taylor, July 2, 1867; to D. W. Ballard, Jan. 31; Aug. 31, 1867; to Hough, Jan. 4, 1867; D. W. Sells to Parker, April 20, 1870; Odeneal to Commissioner of Indian Affairs, April 4, 1873; Tabular Statement of the improvements and valuation of the same of the Nez Perce Indians on lands outside the Nez Perce Reservation, Aug. 1874; Monteith to Parker, Sept. 18, 1871, all Correspondence of the Office of Indian Affairs; to H. Clay Wood, April 6, 24, 1876, Northern Idaho Indian Agency Records, RG 75, FRC; *Annual Report of the Commissioner of Indian Affairs, 1874,* 55. For a first-hand account of the 1868 Nez Perce mission to Washington City, see Robert Newell Diary, OHS.

46. Arguing that "900 square miles of the best land in Idaho is far more than is needed for the tribe," settlers called for a new reduction of the reservation. Monteith to Parker, Sept. 18, 1871; to E. Smith, Dec. 22, 1873; to Walker, April 25; Aug. 27, 1872, Northern Idaho Indian Agency Records; Aug. 13, 1872; Alonzo Leland to Commissioner of Indian Affairs, enclosing petition, April 30, 1872; Odeneal to Commissioner of Indian Affairs, April 4, 1873; Columbus Delano to Acting Commissioner of Indian Affairs, April 28, 1873,all Correspondence of the Office of Indian Affairs; Lewiston *Idaho Signal,* March 16, 1872; Olympia *Washington Standard,* Nov. 24, 1877, reprinting from *Lewiston Teller.*

47. *Walla Walla Union,* June 13, 1874; *Walla Walla Statesman,* Nov. 11, 1876; The Dalles *Weekly Mountaineer,* July 5, 1873; O. O. Howard endorsement to report on Young Joseph, June 11, 1876; J. Q. Smith to Secretary of the Interior, March 5, 1877; Monteith to J. Smith, Feb. 9, 1877; O. O. Howard to J. C. Kelton, April 24, 1877; to Assistant Adjutant General, May 22, 1877, all Letters Received by the Office of the Adjutant General, 1871–1880, M666, NA; D. H. Jerome, et al. to J. Smith, Dec. 1, 1876, in *Annual Report of the Commissioner of Indian Affairs, 1877,* 213.

48. According to one report, representatives of Chief Joseph purchased guns and ammunition on Puget Sound, paying top dollar prices in gold. Another rumor had the Makah Indians at faraway Cape Flattery preparing to paddle away in their whaling canoes to the assistance of the Nez Perce. Home guard units were formed in such distant-from-the-scene-of-action places as Yakima City and Goldendale in the Klickitat Valley. Governor Ferry was widely-criticized for failing to send territorial arms to those locations. *Walla Walla Statesman,* June 23, 30; July 14; Sept. 29, 1877; Olympia *Washington Standard,* July 14, 1877; H. P. Carr to Elisha P. Ferry, June 30; July 16, 1877; H. Richardson to Ferry, July 2, 1877; J. W. Masters to Ferry, July 5, 1877; E. Richardson to Ferry, July 9, 1877; Yakima City Petition to the Governor, June 20, 1877; S. C. Wingard to Ferry, June 19, 1877, all Ferry Papers, WSA; C. A. Huntington to J. Smith, July 14, 1877, Correspondence of the Office of Indian Affairs; *Walla Walla Union,* June 23, 30; July 7, 14; Aug. 18, 1877; C. M. Holton to Ferry, July 25, 1889, Elisha P. Ferry Papers, UW.

49. Colfax *Palouse Gazette,* April 20, 1878; A. J. Cain to Ferry, July 29, 1877, Ferry Papers, WSA; *Walla Walla Union,* July 14, 1877; *Walla Walla Statesman,* June 23; Aug. 11, 1877. For an example of promotional arguments touting the superiority of eastern Oregon over eastern Washington, see Pendleton *East Oregonian,* May 1, 1880.

50. *Spokan Times,* Aug. 21, 1880; *Yakima Record,* March 27; April 17; Aug. 24, 1880; *Walla Walla Union,* Oct. 17, 1874; May 26, 1877; Rose M. Boening, "History of Irrigation in the State of Washington," *WHQ,* 9(Oct. 1918), 265, 268; The Dalles *Weekly Mountaineer,* Aug. 8, 1874; July 3, 1875.

51. The actual followers of Chief Moses, the *Walla Walla Union* reported, did not "exceed 100 persons, warriors, women, papooses, all told." *Walla Walla Statesman,* March 23; July 13, 1878; Nov. 15, 1879; Henry M. Pierce, *Report of an Expedition from Fort Colville to Puget Sound, Washington Territory* (Washington, D.C.: Government Printing Office, 1883), 11–12; Richardson to Reed, May 21, 1873, Letters Received from the Surveyors General; Irvin McDowell to W. T. Sherman, July 9, 1878, Letters Received by the Adjutant General, 1871–1880; May 18, 1878; B. F. Whitson to Howard, Nov. 11, 1878, both Correspondence of the Office of Indian Affairs; Colfax *Palouse Gazette,* Feb. 2, 1878; *Walla Walla Union,* Jan. 26; March 16, 1878; Dayton *Columbia Chronicle,* June 15, 1878. The standard work on Moses is Robert H. Ruby and John A. Brown, *Half-Sun on the Columbia: A Biography of Chief Moses* (Norman: University of Oklahoma Press, 1965).

52. Colfax *Palouse Gazette,* June 8, 1878; *Walla Walla Statesman,* June 8, 15; July 6, 1878; James Wilbur to E. Hayt, July 16, 1878, Correspondence of the Office of Indian Affairs; Olympia *Washington Standard,* July 13, 1878;

Milroy to Hayt, Aug. 1, 1878; to A. W. Nickerson, Aug. 19, 1878, Milroy Letterbook; McDowell to Sherman, July 9, 10, 12, 16, 20, 30; Aug. 1, 1878, Letters Received by the Adjutant General, 1871–1880.

53. Wilbur to Hayt, Dec. 23, 31, 1878; Jan. 20, 30, 1879, Correspondence of the Office of Indian Affairs; C. Schurz to Ferry, May 17, 1879, Ferry Papers, UW; Robert S. Gardner to Secretary of the Interior, Nov. 19, 1882, Reports of Inspection. On speculator interest in the Moses reservation, see Eugene Canfield to Ferry, Dec. 23, 1882, Ferry Papers, WSA; to N. W. H. Owings, March 5, 1883, William A. Newell Papers, WSA. On the reservation's brief history, see Ruby and Brown, *Half-Sun on the Columbia*, 149–155, 167–213.

54. *Spokan Times*, Aug. 21, 1880.

55. "That portion of the Territory," Seattle attorney Thomas Burke wrote of eastern Washington, "seems to be altogether more prosperous than the western part." *Spokan Times*, Aug. 21, 1880; Colfax *Palouse Gazette*, Oct. 7, 1881; Burke to J. Danziger, Jan. 15, 1880, Burke Papers.

56. Seattle *Weekly Intelligencer*, Aug. 1, 1870; March 25, 1876; Seattle *Weekly Pacific Tribune*, July 28, 1876; Ernest Ingersoll, "From the Fraser to the Columbia—Part II," *Harper's New Monthly Magazine*, 68(May 1884), 882; Nordhoff, *Northern California, Oregon, and the Sandwich Islands*, 222–223; Mrs. Frances Fuller Victor, *All Over Oregon and Washington* (San Francisco: John H. Carmany & Co., 1872), 243–244; Port Townsend *Puget Sound Weekly Argus*, Nov. 9, 1877; Olympia *Puget Sound Weekly Courier*, April 25, 1874.

57. Rather than build a suitable customs house at Port Townsend, the government relied upon a succession of rented shanties, producing "a feeling of shame" among townspeople. Whatcom *Bellingham Bay Mail*, Aug. 23; Sept. 6, 1873; April 25; Aug. 8; Sept. 12; Dec. 19, 1874; April 23; Sept. 25; Dec. 4, 1875; March 4; Dec. 23, 1876; Oct. 13; Dec. 29, 1877; May 18, 1878; LaConner *Puget Sound Mail*, Oct. 18; Nov. 8, 1879; Murphy, "Summer Ramblings in Washington Territory," 395; Snohomish City *Northern Star*, Sept. 9, 1876; Port Townsend *Puget Sound Weekly Argus*, Feb. 2, 1875; Aug. 3, 10, 1877; *Olympia Transcript*, May 16, 1874.

58. John Muir, *Travels in Alaska* (Boston and New York: Houghton Mifflin Company, 1915), 8–9; James Wyatt Oates, "Washington Territory," *Californian*, 1(Feb. 1880), 113; Mrs. A. H. H. Stuart, *Washington Territory: Its Soil, Climate, Productions and General Resources* (Olympia: *Washington Standard*, 1875), 15; C. M. Scammon, "Lumbering in Washington Territory," *Overland Monthly*, 5(July 1870), 55; Henry J. Winser, *The Pacific Northwest* (New York: N.p., 1882), 29; J. Orin Oliphant, ed., *The Territory of Washington in 1879, As Described by an Impartial Pen, in the Hand of Francis H. Cook* (Cheney: State Normal School, 1925), 17.

59. In 1876, Washington exported goods valued at $738,560, importing a relatively modest $79,111. Ferry to J. S. Wilson, Aug. 25, 1870, Letters Received from the Surveyors General; Winser, *Pacific Northwest*, 28, 79; Olympia *Transcript*, Oct. 23, 1875; Seattle *Puget Sound Dispatch*, March 19, 1874; J. M. Harrison, *Harrison's Guide and Resources of the Pacific Slope*, Part 1, *Embracing Washington Territory* (San Francisco: C. A. Murdock & Company, 2nd ed., 1876), 29; Ezra Meeker, *Washington Territory West of the Cascade Mountains* (Olympia: Transcript Office, 1870), 32; Seattle *Weekly Pacific Tribune*, Jan. 5, 1877; *Tenth Census of the United States*, Vol. II, *Report on the Manufactures of the United States* (Washington, D.C.: Government Printing Office, 1883), 186–187; D. H. Stearns, *The Official Gazette and Travelers' and Immigrants' Guide to Oregon and Washington Territory* (Portland: Geo. H. Hines' Printing Establishment, 1877), 18.

60. Washington ranked even lower, at the thirty-first place as of 1880, in the value of its lumber output. Oliphant, ed., *Territory of Washington in 1879*, 18; Seattle *Daily Intelligencer*, June 10, 1876; Henry B. Steer, comp., *Lumber Production in the United States, 1799–1946*, U.S. Department of Agriculture Misc. Pub. No. 669 (Washington, D.C.: Government Printing Office, 1948), 11; Edmond S. Meany, Jr., "The History of the Lumber Industry in the Pacific Northwest to 1917" (Ph.D. diss., Harvard University, 1935), 125–126; *Tenth Census of the United States*, Vol. IX, *Report on the Forests of North America* (Washington, D.C.: Government Printing Office, 1884), 486–487; James E. Defebaugh, *History of the Lumber Industry in America* (Chicago: The American Lumberman, 2 vols., 1906–1907), 1:499–500, 530–534; *Twelfth Census of the United States*, Vol. IX, *Manufactures*, Part III (Washington, D.C.: Government Printing Office, 1902), 874.

61. Federal appointees warned that the territorial capitol building was endangered by fires originating in logging operations near Olympia. Olympia *Puget Sound Weekly Courier*, Jan. 6, 1872; Feb. 7, 1874; Seattle *Weekly Intelligencer*, Sept. 4, 1871; Aug. 21, 1875; Charles Lord Russell of Killowen, *Diary of a Visit to the United States of America in the Year 1883* (New York: The United States Catholic Historical Society, 1910), 99–100, 110; M. A. R., "An Autumn Ramble in Washington Territory," *Overland Monthly*, 7(Jan. 1886), 41; Lemuel Ely Quigg, *New Empires in the Northwest* (New York: The Tribune Association, 1889), 72; Harold K. Steen, "Forestry in Washington to 1925" (Ph.D. diss., University of Washington, 1969), 25–26; J. T. Brown to Thomas H. Brents, May 28, 1880, Manson F. Backus Collection, UW.

62. *Olympia Transcript*, April 11, 1874; Dec. 18, 1875; Jan. 13, 1877; Stuart, *Washington Territory*, 13; Tacoma *Weekly Pacific Tribune*, Jan. 16, 23; April 3, 1874; Whatcom *Bellingham Bay Mail*, Nov. 29, 1873; Seattle *Daily Intelligencer*, Aug. 11, 1877; Seattle *Weekly Intelligencer*, Sept. 18, 1871; April 29, 1876; Port Townsend *Puget Sound Weekly Argus*, Dec. 7, 1877. For a list of the three dozen steamers active on Puget Sound in the mid-1870s, two-thirds of them locally built, see Seattle *Weekly Pacific Tribune*, Nov. 3, 1876.

63. Fish canned on both sides of the river were marketed as Oregon salmon. *West Shore*, 2(June 1877), 173; Carlos A. Schwantes, *The Pacific Northwest: An Interpretive History* (Lincoln: University of Nebraska Press, 1989), 163–164; William G. Robbins, "The World of Columbia River Salmon: Nature, Culture, and the Great River of the West," in Joseph Cone and Sandy Ridlington, eds., *The Northwest Salmon Crisis: A Documentary History* (Corvallis: Oregon State University Press, 1996), 9–10; *Walla Walla Union*, Nov. 1, 1873; *Vancouver*

Independent, Jan. 20, 1877; Olympia *Washington Standard*, July 14, 1877; *Walla Walla Statesman*, July 22, 1876; *Olympia Transcript*, Aug. 1, 1874; Jan. 13, 1877; Seattle *Daily Intelligencer*, Aug. 3, 1877; Tacoma *Weekly Pacific Tribune*, May 15, 1874. Also see, for the overall development of the industry, Gordon B. Dodds, *The Salmon King of Oregon: R. D. Hume and the Pacific Fisheries* (Chapel Hill: University of North Carolina Press, 1959).

64. The canneries were ramshackle structures, costing no more than $5,000 to build and aptly described by salmon magnate R. D. Hume as "wheezy and dilapidated." *Walla Walla Statesman*, July 22, 1876; *West Shore*, 2(June 1877), 173, 180; Seattle *Daily Intelligencer*, Aug. 10, 1877; R. D. Hume, "Salmon of the Pacific Coast," in Cone and Ridlington, eds., *Northwest Salmon Crisis*, 61. On the early employment of Chinese workers, see Chris Friday, *Organizing Asian-American Labor: The Pacific Coast Canned-Salmon Industry, 1870–1942* (Philadelphia: Temple University Press, 1994), 17–21.

65. Olympia *Washington Standard*, May 15, 1875; July 14, 1877; *Vancouver Register*, March 5, 1875; *Olympia Transcript*, Dec. 23, 1876; James G. Swan to Ferry, Nov. 13, 1877, Ferry Papers, WSA; *West Shore*, 2(June 1877), 180. Early studies discovered an additional culprit in pollution from sawmills. Robert Bunting, *The Pacific Raincoast: Environment and Culture in an American Eden, 1778–1900* (Lawrence: University of Kansas Press, 1996), 145–147. On the origin and early work of the Fish Commission, see Arthur F. McEvoy, *The Fisherman's Problem: Ecology and Law in the California Fisheries, 1850–1980* (New York: Cambridge University Press, 1986), 100–108.

66. Olympia *Washington Standard*, July 14; Aug. 25; Sept. 15, 1877; Seattle *Daily Intelligencer*, Aug. 4, 8, 10, 16, 1877; *Tacoma Herald*, July 14, 1877; John O'Keane to Hayt, Sept. 1, 1879, Tulalip Indian Agency Records, RG 75, FRC; Ferry to Wm. Reid, April 12, 1879, Ferry Papers, WSA; Port Townsend *Puget Sound Weekly Argus*, Oct. 19, 1877; Whatcom *Bellingham Bay Mail*, Sept. 1, 1877; Swan to William A. Newell, June 13; Sept. 12, 1881, James G. Swan Papers, University of British Columbia Library.

67. *Olympia Transcript*, Dec. 18, 1875; Seattle *Weekly Intelligencer*, June 10, 1872; Aug. 13, 1877; Port Townsend *Puget Sound Weekly Argus*, Nov. 23; Dec. 28, 1877; Murphy, "Summer Ramblings in Washington Territory," 390; Snohomish City *Northern Star*, April 8; Dec. 23, 1876; Whatcom *Bellingham Bay Mail*, June 6, 1874; Seattle *Daily Intelligencer*, Aug. 13, 1877.

68. The most efficient dikes were three to four feet high, with sufficient width and strength to impede burrowing animals. Seattle *Weekly Intelligencer*, Nov. 28, 1870; Snohomish City *Northern Star*, April 8; Sept. 30, 1876; Henry J. Winser to Henry Villard, Nov. 19, 1881, Villard Papers; LaConner *Puget Sound Mail*, Oct. 11; Nov. 1, 1879; Whatcom *Bellingham Bay Mail*, July 21, 1877.

69. Once the hard part of the work was completed, Congress approved a regular Corps of Engineers snag removal program to keep the streams open. Whatcom *Bellingham Bay Mail*, Dec. 27, 1873; Jan. 3; Sept. 5, 1874; March 4; June 10, 1876; Feb. 24, 1877; Port Townsend *Puget Sound Weekly Argus*, Feb. 2, 1875; Aug. 24; Nov. 23, 1877; *Olympia Transcript*, Oct. 23, 1875; *Annual Report of the Chief of Engineers, 1875*, 791–792; Robert A. Habersham to Gillespie, June 30, 1881; Gillespie to Wright, Nov. 18, 1880, both in Ibid., 1881, 2606, 2612; Seattle *Weekly Pacific Tribune*, Dec. 22, 1876; McMicken to Williamson, Aug. 14, 1877, Letters Received from the Surveyors General; Snohomish City *Northern Star*, April 8; July 1; Dec. 2, 1876; Seattle *Daily Intelligencer*, June 12, 1876; Eldridge Morse Notebooks, 20:8, BL.

70. Seattle *Puget Sound Dispatch*, May 14, 1874; Seattle *Daily Intelligencer*, Aug. 14, 1877; Port Townsend *Puget Sound Weekly Argus*, Nov. 2, 1877; Ezra Meeker to Squire, Oct. 17, 1884, Squire Papers, WSA; *Olympia Transcript*, April 11, 1874; Seattle *Weekly Pacific Tribune*, Sept. 29, 1876; *Walla Walla Statesman*, Nov. 20, 1875.

71. The principal Pacific Mail ports-of-call were Victoria, Tacoma and Olympia, with stops at Seattle and other intermediate points. The *Pacific* victims included the son-in-law of Jefferson Davis and the husband of writer Frances Fuller Victor. *Olympia Transcript*, Nov. 13, 20, 27; Dec. 11, 1875; Whatcom *Bellingham Bay Mail*, Nov. 13, 27; Dec. 4, 1875; Jan. 8, 1876; Seattle *Weekly Intelligencer*, Aug. 14, 1871; Nov. 13, 1875; April 1, 1876; Seattle *Daily Intelligencer*, June 14, 1876; LaConner *Puget Sound Mail*, Nov. 1, 1879.

72. Whatcom *Bellingham Bay Mail*, July 5, 1873; Aug. 7, 1875; June 17, 1876; Olympia *Washington Standard*, May 26, 1877; *Tacoma Herald*, May 26, 1877; Snohomish City *Northern Star*, July 22; Aug. 5, 1876; Seattle *Weekly Pacific Tribune*, Nov. 3, 1876; *Vancouver Independent*, Feb. 23, 1877; LaConner *Puget Sound Mail*, Oct. 25, 1879.

73. Burke and Rasin to R. P. Woodruff, June 4, 1881, Burke Papers; Colfax *Palouse Gazette*, Oct. 7, 1881; Seattle *Weekly Intelligencer*, Sept. 18, 1875; March 4; June 3, 1876; Seattle *Weekly Pacific Tribune*, Aug. 11, 18; Sept. 29; Oct. 6, 20, 1876.

74. *Vancouver Register*, April 30; June 4, 1875; *Walla Walla Union*, June 12, 1875; Seattle *Weekly Pacific Tribune*, July 21, 1876; Cooke to Ainsworth, June 1, 1874; Wright to Ainsworth, May 27; June 11, 30, 1874, all Ainsworth Papers; Ainsworth to Billings, Jan. 1, 1875; Hibbard to Billings, April 13, 1875, both Northern Pacific Land Department Records.

75. *Walla Walla Union*, Sept. 22, 1877; March 16, 1878; Dec. 6, 1879; *Vancouver Independent*, Sept. 25, 1875; Whatcom *Bellingham Bay Mail*, July 7, 1877.

76. *Walla Walla Statesman*, June 16, 1877; March 29; May 31, 1879; *Olympia Transcript*, Dec. 25, 1875; March 25, 1876; Seattle *Weekly Intelligencer*, Jan. 1; March 25, 1876; *Dayton News*, March 31, 1877; Port Townsend *Puget Sound Weekly Argus*, Oct. 12, 1877; *Walla Walla Union*, May 5, 1877; Jan. 5, 1878; Colfax *Palouse Gazette*, Feb. 7, 21; Nov. 28, 1879; Dayton *Columbia Chronicle*, March 1, 1879; McGilvra to J. H. Lutrell, April 25, 1877,

McGilvra Papers; Whatcom *Bellingham Bay Mail*, Jan. 26, 1878; *Tacoma Herald*, May 5, 1877; Jan. 9, 23; March 8, 15, 1878. On the abandoned N.P. policies regarding prices and disputed claims, see Hibbard to Billings, March 20; April 13, 1875, Northern Pacific Land Department Records.

77. Colfax *Palouse Gazette*, Nov. 17, 1877, reprinting from Portland *Oregonian*; Jan. 26; Feb. 13, 1880; Whatcom *Bellingham Bay Mail*, Jan. 20, 1877; *Walla Walla Statesman*, Oct. 23, 1880; *Walla Walla Union*, Dec. 8, 1877; Dayton *Columbia Chronicle*, June 29, 1878; *Tacoma Herald*, April 12, 1878.

78. "The truth is he is not the man to be at the head now—and to lead us forward," Billings, the largest N.P. stockholder, wrote of his decision to supplant Wright. "He was first-rate in the transition period—for he is great on *dickering*—but now we want a man broader, franker, able to inspire confidence." Wright continued to serve as president of the Tacoma Land Company. George Stark to Ainsworth, May 11, 1877; Billings to Ainsworth, Nov. 11, 1878; Oct. 9; Nov. 7, 1879; to Sprague, Aug. 4, 1879, all Ainsworth Papers; *Tacoma Herald*, April 28, 1877; Colfax *Palouse Gazette*, June 20; Dec. 26, 1879. Also see Winks, *Billings*, 216–219.

79. The mine was named for Samuel Wilkeson, an important N.P. stockholder and officer since the time of Jay Cooke. Ainsworth to Billings, Feb. 27; March 1, 1875; Hibbard to Billings, Feb. 24, 27, 1875, all Northern Pacific Land Department Records; Seattle *Weekly Intelligencer*, March 6, 1875; Whitworth to Squire, Oct. 31, 1884, Squire Papers, WSA; M. Fallows to Ainsworth, April 16, 1879; Stark to Ainsworth, May 28; June 13, 1877, all Ainsworth Papers; *Tacoma Herald*, May 26; June 23, 1877; Feb. 23; March 15; April 5, 1878; *Lewiston Teller*, Sept. 3, 1880; Olympia *Washington Standard*, Dec. 8, 1877.

80. New Tacoma was incorporated in 1879. The land company made sure that most of its property remained outside the city limits, reducing present and prospective municipal taxes. Seattle *Weekly Pacific Tribune*, Dec. 1, 1876; Wright to Ainsworth, Feb. 22; March 31, 1875, Ainsworth Papers; *Lewiston Teller*, Sept. 10, 1880; *Tacoma Herald*, July 21, 1877; Minutes, April 3, 1877; Annual Report, March 2, 1880, both Tacoma Land and Improvement Company Papers; Colfax *Palouse Gazette*, Oct. 7, 1881.

81. The House failed in 1878 to act upon a Senate-passed bill extending the time limit. The Justice Department subsequently ruled that revocation of the land grant required congressional action. After construction resumed, Congress approved a seven year extension. The resumption of work also preempted Jay Gould's Utah Northern, currently building into Idaho from the Central Pacific and rumored to be interested in acquiring the O.S.N. as an outlet for the sea. Olympia *Washington Standard*, Dec. 22, 1879; Billings to Ainsworth, Dec. 19, 1878, in Colfax *Palouse Gazette*, Dec. 27, 1878; June 17, 1879, Ainsworth Papers; W. Milnor Roberts to President and Directors of the Northern Pacific R. Road, Jan. ? 1878, W. Milnor Roberts Papers, Montana State University Library; Jno. R. Wheat to Stark, March 28, 1878; Samuel Black to Stark, Feb. 3, 1879, both Northern Pacific Railway Papers, Series C; *Walla Walla Statesman*, June 7, 14; July 5, 1879; Dayton *Columbia Chronicle*, June 28; Aug. 2, 1879; Winks, *Billings*, 218, 230–231.

82. Ainsworth was two miles from the site of the modern city of Pasco. *Spokan Times*, April 24, 1879; Thomas W. Symons, "Report of an Examination of the Upper Columbia River and the Territory in Its Vicinity in September and October, 1881, 11 Ex. Doc. No. 186, 47th Cong., 1st sess., 50–51; *Lewiston Teller*, Sept. 17, 1880; Sprague to James B. Williams, June 1, 1881, Northern Pacific Railway Papers, Series C; Robert Hitchman, *Place Names of Washington* (Tacoma: Washington State Historical Society, 1985), 3.

83. The five hundred Chinese working on the Pend Oreille division at the high point of construction received 85 cents a day in comparison to between $1.75 and $2 for white laborers. Colfax *Palouse Gazette*, Oct. 3, 1879; Feb. 27, 1880; *Walla Walla Union*, Sept. 27, 1879; Aug. 26, 1882; *Walla Walla Statesman*, Nov. 15, 1879; *Lewiston Teller*, Sept. 17; Dec. 3, 24, 1880; *Yakima Record*, June 19, 1880; Jan. 15, 21; May 28, 1881; July 29, 1882; McMicken to J. M. Armstrong, Feb. 20, 1880, Letters Received from the Surveyors General.

84. The bemused query of one arriving railroad passenger—"Where is Ritzville?"—is suggestive of the community's early size. Colfax *Palouse Gazette*, March 19; June 4, 1880; *Spokan Times*, April 1; June 12, 1880; Pomeroy *Washington Independent*, Sept. 30, 1880; *Walla Walla Statesman*, Oct. 16, 1880; Meinig, *Great Columbia Plain*, 265; Robert E. Ficken and Charles P. LeWarne, *Washington: A Centennial History* (Seattle: University of Washington Press, 1988), 61. Also see John Fahey, *The Inland Empire: Unfolding Years, 1879–1929* (Seattle: University of Washington Press, 1986), 12–13.

85. Colfax *Palouse Gazette*, April 6, 1878; Aug. 6, 1880; *Tacoma Herald*, April 19, 1878; Browne to A. Browne, April 20, 21, 1878, Browne Papers; Dayton *Columbia Chronicle*, May 3, 1879; *Spokan Times*, June 19, 1880. On the founding and early history of Spokane, see also *Reminiscences of James N. Glover* (Fairfield: Ye Galleon Press, 1985), 86. Regularly listed among the "town proprietors," Browne quickly became involved in a variety of business ventures and advertised his services as an "able lawyer" willing to "attend to both sides of parties engaged in litigation."

86. Browne to A. Browne, April 20, 1878, Browne Papers; *Walla Walla Statesman*, May 11, 1878; Colfax *Palouse Gazette*, Oct. 25, 1878; March 7; April 18, 1879; March 26, 1880; Oct. 7, 1881; *Walla Walla Union*, Dec. 6, 1879; *Spokan Times*, April 1; May 22; Aug. 21; Sept. 25, 1880; A. E. Keats to Uncle, July 7, 1880, A. E. Keats Letters, EWSHS.

87. *Spokan Times*, April 24; June 19, 1879; June 19, 26; July 31; Sept. 11, 1880; Colfax *Palouse Gazette*, Feb. 9, 1878; July 30, 1880; John A. Simms to Hayt, June 30, 1879, Correspondence of the Office of Indian Affairs; Feb. 3, 1879; H.T. Cowley to Hayt, Jan. 23, 1880; Annual Report of Resident Farmer, Coeur d'Alene, 1880; Sydney Waters to H. Price, April 4, 26, 1884, all Colville Indian Agency Records, RG 75, FRC; Keats to Uncle, July 7, 1880, Keats Letters.

88. *Walla Walla Statesman*, April 12, 1879; R. R. Thompson to Ainsworth, Dec. 29, 1878; Villard to Ainsworth, May 11, 1878, both Ainsworth Papers; Reed to Thompson, Dec. 28, 1877, Reed Papers.

89. Four-fifths of the O.S.N. stock went to the new firm. Villard's operations included the Oregon Central and the Oregon & California railroads and the Oregon Steam Ship Company. The O.I.C. also took over nine thousand acres of timber in the Blue Mountains and a flume running to Dayton. Pendleton *East Oregonian*, June 28, 1879; Colfax *Palouse Gazette*, June 27; Dec. 12, 1879; *Walla Walla Statesman*, July 19, 1879; Nov. 6, 1880; Villard to Ainsworth, May 11, 1878, Ainsworth Papers; Pomeroy *Washington Independent*, Sept. 30, 1880; John L. Howard to Smith, Aug. 23, 1884, Oregon Improvement Company Records; Frank T. Gilbert, *Historic Sketches of Walla Walla, Whitman, Columbia and Garfield Counties, Washington Territory* (Portland: A. G. Walling, 1882), 279.

90. Conceding the leadership role to Villard, Ainsworth and Simeon Reed served on the O.R. & N. board of directors. Carlos A. Schwantes, *Railroad Signatures across the Pacific Northwest* (Seattle: University of Washington Press, 1993), 60–62; Sharp to Ainsworth, June 13, 1877; Billings to Ainsworth, June 17, 1879, both Ainsworth Papers; John C. Ainsworth Reminiscences, 128, OHS; Pendleton *East Oregonian*, Sept. 10, 1880. The standard work remains James B. Hedges, *Henry Villard and the Railways of the Northwest* (New Haven: Yale University Press, 1930).

91. The O.R. & N. had a cost advantage over the N.P., a land grant railroad required by law to patronize American manufacturers. *Walla Walla Union*, Nov. 22, 1879; Jan. 17, 1880; Colfax *Palouse Gazette*, Feb. 6, 1880; Pendleton *East Oregonian*, March 13, 1880; *Walla Walla Statesman*, Jan. 17, 1880; Lewty, *To the Columbia Gateway*, 44–46. Ainsworth had urged that the railroad be built downstream from Wallula, so that wheat could be shipped increasing distances by rail as work progressed. "To build up[river]," he complained, ". . . would make the Rail Road practicaly [sic] of no use till it could be finished to Wallula." Ainsworth to Villard, Dec. 17, 1879, Ainsworth Papers.

92. Baker's scheme entailed the abandonment of Wallula, supposedly the oldest town in the territory (dating to fur-trader times), from continuing use of adobe structures originally erected by the Hudson's Bay Company. *Walla Walla Union,* Sept. 29; Oct. 13; Dec. 8, 1877; March 2, 1878; Nov. 29, 1879; Jan. 10, 1880; *Tacoma Herald*, March 29, 1878; *Walla Walla Statesman*, July 5; Aug. 23, 1879; April 10, 1880; *Yakima Record*, Nov. 27, 1880.

93. Initially acquiring a six-sevenths interest in the Walla Walla & Columbia River, the O.R. & N. purchased the remainder in 1880. As "an act of courtesy," Dorsey Baker was briefly left in charge. Villard also planned to connect Walla Walla and Umatilla with various points in northeastern Oregon. Pendleton *East Oregonian*, July 12, 1879; Sept. 10, 1880; *Walla Walla Statesman*, Jan. 17, 1880; *Walla Walla Union,* Jan. 17, 1880; *Spokan Times*, June 12; Aug. 21; Sept. 11, 25, 1880; Pomeroy *Washington Independent*, Sept. 23; Nov. 25, 1880.

94. Billings to Ainsworth, Nov. 24; Dec. 18, 1879; Feb. 12, 1880, Ainsworth Papers; Wright to Reed, May 12, 1880; Reed to Villard, Feb. 12, 21, 1880; to Wright, Jan. 19, 1880, all Reed Papers; *Walla Walla Statesman*, Jan. 3, 1880; *Spokan Times*, Dec. 4, 1880; Villard to Stockholders of the Oregon Railway & Navigation Company, Jan. 3, 1880, Watson C. Squire Papers, UW; *Walla Walla Union,* Dec. 6, 1879.

95. Officially appointed as a citizen of Illinois, Ferry actually had been in the territory since 1869 and was sometimes considered the first genuine Washington resident to become governor. Under Hill Harmon's direction, the asylum spent three times as much per patient as the prevailing rate in California. Reacting to adverse public opinion, the legislature placed the hospital under direct territorial management in 1875. O. Jacobs to Daniel Bagley, May 25, 1876, Daniel Bagley Papers, UW; Olympia *Washington Standard*, Aug. 14, 1869; July 14, 1877; Mercedes Sprague Gleason, "The Territorial Governors of the State of Washington, 1853–1889" (M.A. thesis, University of Washington, 1955), 74; *Vancouver Register*, Aug. 27, 1870; Whatcom *Bellingham Bay Mail*, July 5, 1873; Jan. 8, 1876; *Vancouver Independent*, Jan. 8, 1876; July 19, 1877; Seattle *Weekly Pacific Tribune*, Dec. 22, 1876; *Spokan Times,* Feb. 5, 1880; Burke to J. Hoover, July 29, 1880, Burke Papers; Miller to S. D. Smith, Nov. 7, 1872, Miller Family Papers; J. F. Farnsworth to the President, Oct. 11, 1871, Letters of Application and Recommendation during the Administration of Ulysses S. Grant, 1869–1877, M968, NA; *Walla Walla Statesman*, Sept. 11; Nov. 20, 1875; June 17, 1876; Oct. 20; Dec. 22, 1877; *Walla Walla Union,* Dec. 27, 1879; *Olympia Transcript*, Nov. 6, 1875; Garfielde to Ferry, Jan. 4, 1872; Wellington Clark to Ferry, Aug. 16, 1889; C. M. Bradshaw to Ferry, June 28, 1878, all Ferry Papers, UW; Port Townsend *Weekly Argus*, Oct. 26, 1877; Seattle *Weekly Intelligencer*, Jan. 23, 1875.

96. A onetime Indiana jurist, Milroy's preference was for an appointment to the territorial supreme court. *Walla Walla Statesman*, July 14, 1877; Milroy to U.S. Grant, May 26, 1869, May 26, 1869; Grant Administration Letters of Application; to Williams, Oct. 5, 1874; to W. T. Otto, Oct. 6, 1874, Records relating to the Appointment of Federal Judges and U.S. Attorneys and Marshals, Washington, 1853–1902, M198, NA; to Simms, Oct. 13, 1874, Colville Indian Agency Records; E. C. Kemble to E. Smith, Oct. 15, 17; Nov. 8, 15, 1873, Reports of Inspection; Ferry to E. Smith, Dec. 11, 1873, Ferry Papers, WSA; Seattle *Puget Sound Dispatch*, Jan. 15; March 5, 1874; *Olympia Transcript*, Feb. 28, 1874; *Walla Walla Union,* Jan. 17, 1874; Seattle *Weekly Intelligencer*, Jan. 10, 1874.

97. *Walla Walla Union,* Aug. 15, 1874; Seattle *Puget Sound Dispatch*, July 30; Sept. 3, 1874; Whatcom *Bellingham Bay Mail*, Sept. 12, 1874; Tacoma *Weekly Pacific Tribune*, July 7, 1874; *Walla Walla Statesman*, July 3, 1875; June 17, 1876; Feb. 10; Oct. 6, 1877; Aug 3; Sept. 28, 1878; Dayton *Columbia Chronicle*, Sept. 28, 1878; Olympia *Puget Sound Weekly Courier*, Feb. 28, 1874; *Olympia Transcript*, Feb. 28, 1874; Struve to Howard, Feb. 4, 1886;

Howard to Smith, Aug. 21; Sept. 28, 1885; Jan. 8, 29; Feb. 6, 10, 15; March 5, 1886, all Oregon Improvement Company Records.

98. Roger S. Greene to C. C. Washburn, May 2, 1870; J. M. Fletcher to George F. Hoar, May, 1874; S. W. Brown to John H. Mitchell, May 12, 1874; Justin Chenoweth to Rutherford B. Hayes, Jan. 9, 1878; Milroy to Charles Devins, May 10, 1878; Jacobs to Brents, Nov. 29, 1882; Struve to Grover Cleveland, Feb. 20, 1885; Evans to J. B. Metcalfe, Feb. 28, 1885; Metcalfe to A. H. Garland, April 15; June 13, 1885; McGilvra to Cleveland, n.d., all Letters relating to the Appointment of Federal Judges; Sprague to Howard, Jan. 22, 1873, Northern Pacific Land Department Records. For evidence of Greene's pro-Northern Pacific legal rulings, see *Olympia Transcript,* Aug. 1, 1874.

99. *Walla Walla Statesman,* March 17, 1877; Seattle *Puget Sound Dispatch,* Jan. 8, 1874; Dayton *Columbia Chronicle,* May 25, 1878; *Yakima Record,* March 13, 1880; *Dayton News,* Jan. 29, 1876; Seattle *Weekly Pacific Tribune,* July 21, 1876.

100. In Congress, Brents was mainly known for a prolonged legal dispute with a Capitol Hill tailor over an ill-fitted $15 suit. He also attempted to have his Walla Walla antagonist, Judge Lewis, removed from the bench. Miller to Friends, July 1, 1875, Miller Family Papers; Olympia *Washington Standard,* June 26; July 3, 1875; Seattle *Weekly Intelligencer,* April 11, 1874; June 26, 1875; Whatcom *Bellingham Bay Mail,* July 3, 1875; Seattle *Puget Sound Dispatch,* April 9; Oct. 1, 1874; *Walla Walla Union,* Sept. 19, 26; Oct. 3, 1874; March 20, 27, 1875; May 26, 1877; *Tacoma Herald,* May 5, 1877; Jan. 26; Feb. 2, 9, 1878; *Walla Walla Statesman,* Oct. 12, 1878; Oct. 23, 1880; Colfax *Palouse Gazette,* Sept. 5, 1879; July 30; Oct. 1, 29, 1880; Pendleton *East Oregonian,* May 10, 1879; June 5, 1880; *Yakima Record,* Oct. 23, 1880; Mitchell to Williams, Dec. 7, 1874; Brents to Mitchell, Feb. 5, 1875; to Hayes, Nov. 25, 1878; N. T. Caton, et al. to Grant, Feb. ? 1875; Lewis B. Noble to Sargent, Nov. 25, 1878; Charles H. Larrabee to Schurz, Nov. 17, 1878, all Letters relating to the Appointment of Federal Judges; Burke to J. B. Allen, May 31, 1880, Burke Papers.

101. Statehood advocates also pointed out that Washington cast a substantially higher total vote in local elections than was the case in better-known territories like Dakota and Montana. Seattle *Weekly Intelligencer,* Nov. 27, 1875; Whatcom *Bellingham Bay Mail,* April 6, 20, 1878; *Vancouver Register,* Sept. 24, 1875; Dayton *Columbia Chronicle,* Sept. 7, 1878; *Walla Walla Statesman,* Jan. 21, 1882.

102. The *Walla Walla Union* observed that Washingtonians "have been as completely ignored as if our country were on the waters of the Amazon, instead of the Columbia." Allegedly resorting to bribery to secure confirmation of his initial slate of nominees to official positions previously filled by the assembly, Governor Ferry generated new outrage among defenders of local control. Olympia *Washington Standard,* Feb. 27; March 6; April 25, 1875; Aug. 18; Oct. 13, 1877; Whatcom *Bellingham Bay Mail,* Nov. 6, 13, 20, 1875; Jan. 8, 15, 1876; *Walla Walla Union,* Nov. 1, 1873; Jan. 10; March 14, 1874; Jan. 30; April 17, 1875; *Olympia Transcript,* Oct. 30; Nov. 6, 13, 20, 1875; Seattle *Weekly Intelligencer,* Feb. 24, 1873; Nov. 6; Dec. 25, 1875; *Walla Walla Statesman,* Jan. 8, 22, 1876; March 2, 1878; *Dayton News,* Jan. 15, 1876; Seattle *Weekly Pacific Tribune,* July 28, 1876; Dayton *Columbia Chronicle,* April 20; Sept. 14, 1878; Colfax *Palouse Gazette,* Oct. 6, 1877; Aug. 30, 1878; Lewiston *Idaho Signal,* Nov. 22, 1872; Robert H. Simmons, "The Transition of the Washington Executive from Territory to Statehood," *PNQ,* 55(April 1964), 78.

103. The 1874 vote for a statehood convention drew a favorable response from less than a fifth of the electorate. *Vancouver Register,* March 19, 1875; *Olympia Transcript,* Oct. 28, 1876; Seattle *Weekly Intelligencer,* Dec. 5, 1874.

104. Whatcom *Bellingham Bay Mail,* June 9, 1877; Olympia *Washington Standard,* June 2; Nov. 3, 1877; *Seattle Morning Dispatch,* May 15, 1877; Colfax *Palouse Gazette,* March 23, 1878.

105. *Walla Walla Statesman,* April 20, 1878; Olympia *Puget Sound Weekly Courier,* March 8, 15; April 19, 1878; Whatcom *Bellingham Bay Mail,* April 13, 1878; Colfax *Palouse Gazette,* June 8, 1878. On Abernethy's connection with N.P. town lot sales in Spokane, see *Spokan Times,* July 31; Sept. 4, 1880. For a complete list of the delegates, see "Washington's First Constitution, 1878," *WHQ,* 9(1918), 130.

106. "Washington's First Constitution," *WHQ,* 9(1918), 132–134, 136–140, 143, 146–150, 221, 305; *Walla Walla Statesman,* Aug. 3, 1878; *Walla Walla Union,* Sept. 22; Nov. 17, 1877; Dec. 7, 1878. On Duniway's convention appearance, see Ruth Barnes Moynihan, *Rebel for Rights: Abigail Scott Duniway* (New Haven: Yale University Press), 182.

107. *Walla Walla Statesman,* July 20, 1878; "Washington's First Constitution," 10(1919), 59–64, 66, 119–120, 123–124.

108. The constitution was victorious in eighteen of the twenty-three counties, with no official tally reported from Stevens County. Whitman County endorsed the constitution by an overwhelming 766-116 margin. Out of the 1,226 Walla Walla Valley voters taking part in the congressional canvass, only 89 endorsed the document. The Pierce County vote presumably reflected the local influence of the Northern Pacific, a corporation able to operate more freely under territorial than under state auspices. Pierce was also one of the three Puget Sound counties to support Walla Walla Democrat N. T. Caton, the railroad's eastern Washington attorney, for Congress. *Walla Walla Union,* Dec. 7, 1878; *Olympia Transcript,* Sept. 30, 1876. For Caton's connection with the railroad, see Caton to Hibbard, April 20, 1875, Northern Pacific Western District Records.

109. *Walla Walla Union,* Feb. 16; Dec. 7, 1878; Colfax *Palouse Gazette,* Dec. 1, 1877; June 27, 1879; Seattle *Weekly Intelligencer,* Nov. 27, 1875; Olympia *Washington Standard,* Sept. 22, 1877; Whatcom *Bellingham Bay Mail,* Oct. 6, 1877; April 6, 20, 1878; *Spokan Times,* Aug. 21, 1880.

Notes—Chapter Seven
Great Auxiliary Meteors

1. Tacoma *Weekly Ledger*, Aug. 4, 1882.
2. An imposing stone and iron truss bridge, costing in excess of $1 million, replaced the ferry in April 1884. *West Shore*, 8(Aug. 1882), 145–146; 10(July 1884), 203; *Walla Walla Union*, June 4, 1881; *Spokan Times*, June 16, 1881; *Walla Walla Statesman*, July 2, 1881; *Lewiston Teller*, March 16, 1882.
3. Another writer called the region "the Sahara of Washington Territory." E. V. Smalley, "Notes of Northwestern Travel," *Northwest*, 1(Aug. 1883), 11; *West Shore*, 7(Sept. 1881), 225; 8(Aug. 1882), 146; Tacoma *Weekly Ledger*, June 3; July 1, 1881; Dayton *Columbia Chronicle*, Oct. 22, 1881; *Walla Walla Statesman*, April 29, 1882.
4. Tacoma *Weekly Ledger*, Sept. 16, 1881; *Lewiston Teller*, May 19, 1881; G. H. Atkinson, "A Winter Trip to the Upper Columbia Basin," *West Shore*, 7(Dec. 1881), 286–287. On Atkinson, see D. W. Meinig, *The Great Columbia Plain: A Historical Geography, 1805–1910* (Seattle: University of Washington Press, 1968), 309–311, 317–318.
5. In addition to twenty-plus miles of track, the Seattle & Walla Walla owned four locomotives, seventy-five cars and six hundred lots on or near the Seattle waterfront. Denny failed to secure assistance in San Francisco, the traditional funding center for regional business. Squire was, by mid-1880, the third-largest individual property owner in Seattle. *Walla Walla Statesman*, Jan. 21, 1882; Seattle *Daily Intelligencer*, July 8; Aug. 14, 1881; *Yakima Record*, Oct. 23, 1880; Geo. C. Bode to A. A. Denny, June 9, 1880, Arthur A. Denny Papers, WSHS; T. R. Tannatt to Henry Villard, July 31; Aug. 6, 1880; Denny to Tannatt, Aug. 12, 1880, all Oregon Improvement Company Records, UW; Roswell Scott to Watson C. Squire, Oct. 11, 1879; Frederick W. Pitkin to Henry M. Teller, March 24, 1884, both Watson C. Squire Papers, UW; *Lewiston Teller*, Oct. 15, 1880. See, for general biographical details, Scott Evan Shapiro, "Watson C. Squire: Senator from Washington, 1889–97" (Honor's thesis, Wesleyan University, 1992).
6. Villard to Stockholders of the Oregon Railway & Navigation Company, Jan. 3, 1880, Squire Papers; F. H. Whitworth to E. W. Hilgard, June 29, 1880; Tannatt to Villard, Aug. 4, 6, 12, 18, 24, 1880, all Oregon Improvement Company Records; *Lewiston Teller*, Oct. 15, 1880.
7. John Leary, one of Denny's railroading associates, recalled that the Villard acquisition had been "obtained by misrepresentation, if not by actual fraud." Squire sued to obtain his commission, but was apparently never paid. Squire to Denny, March 16, 1880; Tannatt to Villard, Oct. 9, 1880, both Oregon Improvement Company Records; Minutes, Board of Trustees Meetings, July 26; Oct. 7, 1880; Articles of Agreement, Oct. 11, 1880, all Denny Papers; Scott to Squire, July 27, 1880; Denny to Squire, Nov. 2, 1880; Squire to Denny, Oct. 29, 1880; to A. Mackintosh, Nov. 9, 1880; Chamberlain, Carter & Hornblower to Squire, Feb. 2; July 11, 1881; June 6, 1882, all Squire Papers; Unident. Newspaper clipping, Oct. 18, 1892, Robert Bridges Scrabooks, 2:n.p., UW; Seattle *Daily Intelligencer*, Aug. 12, 1881; *Lewiston Teller*, Oct. 15, 1880; *Walla Walla Statesman*, Oct. 23, 1880; *Yakima Record*, Oct. 23, 1880; *Spokan Times*, Dec. 16, 1880.
8. "The song of the Oregon Railway and Navigation Co.," Murphy joked, "seems to be a sort of a Sweet Buy and Buy." Olympia *Washington Standard*, June 3, 10, 1881; *Walla Walla Statesman*, Jan. 29; Feb. 26; March 12, 1881; *Spokan Times*, July 14, 1881; Waitsburg *Weekly Times*, May 28, 1881; *Pataha City Spirit*, May 11, 1881.
9. *Walla Walla Union*, Jan. 1, 1881; Robin W. Winks, *Frederick Billings: A Life* (New York: Oxford University Press, 1991), 244–245; Peter J. Lewty, *To the Columbia Gateway: The Oregon Railway and the Northern Pacific, 1879–1884* (Pullman: Washington State University Press, 1987), 65–66; Olympia *Puget Sound Weekly Courier*, Jan. 21; March 18, 1881; Dayton *Columbia Chronicle*, Jan. 15, 1881; *Walla Walla Statesman*, Jan. 17, 1880; Minutes, Feb. 7, 1881, Tacoma Land and Improvement Company Papers, Tacoma Public Library; Frederick Billings to John C. Ainsworth, Oct. 9; Nov. 7, 1879, John C. Ainsworth Papers, UO; Tacoma *Weekly Ledger*, Jan. 14; July 15, 1881; Port Townsend *Puget Sound Weekly Argus*, Feb. 25, 1881.
10. *Walla Walla Union*, Feb. 26, 1881; *Walla Walla Statesman*, April 9, 1881; Tacoma *Weekly Ledger*, April 15, 22, 1881, reprinting, respectively, from *New York Times*, March 24, 1881 and St. Paul *Pioneer Press*, March 29, 1881; *Lewiston Teller*, April 7, 1881; Olympia *Puget Sound Weekly Courier*, March 18, 1881. For full details on Villard's fight for the N.P., see Winks, *Billings*, chapt. 22; Lewty, *To the Columbia Gateway*, chapt. 7.
11. Lewiston *Nez Perce News*, May 26; June 2, 1881; *Spokan Times*, March 10; April 14, 1881; *Walla Walla Union*, March 26; April 9; June 11, 1881; Olympia *Washington Standard*, May 27, 1881; *Lewiston Teller*, April 21; May 12, 26; June 2; July 21, 1881; *Yakima Record*, May 28, 1881; Olympia *Puget Sound Weekly Courier*, March 25; April 1; May 27, 1881; Pendleton *East Oregonian*, April 9; May 27, 1881; Waitsburg *Weekly Times*, April 9, 1881; *Walla Walla Statesman*, July 2, 1881; Seattle *Daily Intelligencer*, July 26, 1881; Tacoma *Weekly Ledger*, March 4, 11, 18; April 1, 8, 15, 22; May 13, 1881.
12. Lacking respect for Billings as the result of earlier dealings, Villard had expected his antagonist to easily capitulate. Olympia *Puget Sound Weekly Courier*, April 15, 1881; *Walla Walla Union*, April 16; May 21; June 11, 1881; *Lewiston Teller*, Oct. 27, 1881; *Walla Walla Statesman*, Sept. 17, 1881; Winks, *Billings*, 249–251; *Pataha City Spirit*, June 1, 1881; Villard to Ainsworth, Jan. 27, 1880, Ainsworth Papers; to S. G. Reed, Feb. 12, 1880; Reed to C. B. Wright, Jan. 29, 1880, both Simeon G. Reed Papers, Reed College Library.
13. *Walla Walla Statesman*, Sept. 17, 1881; June 14, 1882; *Walla Walla Union*, July 2, 1881; Olympia *Washington Standard*, April 7, 1882; Colfax *Palouse Gazette*, April 21, 1882; Oct. 19, 1883; Pendleton *East Oregonian*, May

23; Sept. 22, 1882; Dec. 21, 1883; Tacoma *Weekly Ledger*, Jan. 27; June 30, 1882; *Lewiston Teller*, Nov. 10, 1881. On Survey work in the coal regions near Commencement Bay, see *Tacoma News*, Oct. 11, 1883; *Northwest*, 1(April 1883), 12. For a report on Yakima Valley soil conditions, see Hilgard to Villard, Oct. 20, 1882, Henry Villard Papers, Houghton Library, Harvard University.

14. "We have heard some men say it is bad policy to criticize the public acts of Mr. Villard," Lewiston's Alonzo Leland wrote in late 1881. The N.P., though, was "the peoples [sic] highway…paid for with the people's land" and its president, when transgressing upon the public interest, "should be censured the same as any other public servant." Villard told a Seattle audience in April 1883 that he "read all your papers regularly and know all that is going on here." He also donated money to the University of Oregon. *Yakima Signal*, Feb. 24; March 10; April 14, 28; Aug. 25; Nov. 24, 1883; *West Shore*, 7(Jan. 1881), 3; 10(Feb. 1884), 33; *Walla Walla Statesman*, Sept. 2, 1882; Olympia *Puget Sound Weekly Courier*, June 10, 1881; April 17, 1883; *Seattle Post-Intelligencer*, April 25, 1882; March 23; April 19, 21; Aug. 14, 1883; Colfax *Palouse Gazette*, Oct. 7, 1881; Aug. 4, 1882; May 4, 1883; *Whatcom Reveille*, Nov. 30, 1883; Palouse City *Boomerang*, Sept. 7, 1883; *Olympia Transcript*, Sept. 15, 1883; Port Townsend *Puget Sound Weekly Argus*, Nov. 18, 1881; Olympia *Washington Standard*, Dec. 9, 1881; *Seattle Weekly Chronicle*, Jan. 27, 1883; Tacoma *Weekly Ledger*, Oct. 28, 1881; *Lewiston Teller*, Oct. 27, 1881.

15. *Tacoma Daily Ledger*, Sept. 23, 1883; *Seattle Weekly Chronicle*, Aug. 30, 1883; *Seattle Post-Intelligencer*, Aug. 4; Sept. 12, 1883; *Walla Walla Union*, May 12, 1883; *Walla Walla Statesman*, Jan. 4, 1884.

16. Appearing before the territorial assembly, Villard sat in the house speaker's chair and was introduced by Governor William Newell. *Walla Walla Statesman*, May 5, 1883; *Walla Walla Union*, May 5, 1883; Lovenia Culver to Parents, Sept. 16, 1883, Lovenia Culver Letters, EWSHS; *Seattle Post-Intelligencer*, Aug. 4, 10, 17, 19, 29; Sept. 16, 1883; Olympia *Washington Standard*, Oct. 21, 28, 1881; Aug. 31, 1883.

17. Villard confessed to being "a well pumped dry" on the subject of railroading. The N.P. publicity department supplied newspapers with advance copies of his formal addresses. *Tacoma News*, Oct. 11, 1883; *West Shore*, 7(Oct. 1881), 244; *Walla Walla Statesman*, Oct. 15, 1881; May 5, 1883; *Walla Walla Union*, May 5, 1883; *Seattle Post-Intelligencer*, April 21; Sept. 9, 1883; Pendleton *East Oregonian*, May 1, 1883; *Tacoma Daily Ledger*, April 23, 1883.

18. The feeder network east of the Cascades was constructed under Oregon & Transcontinental financial auspices. Olympia *Puget Sound Weekly Courier*, May 27, 1881; April 24, 1883; *Walla Walla Union*, May 5, 1883; *West Shore*, 8(July 1882), 137; Pendleton *East Oregonian*, Nov. 4, 1881; *Walla Walla Statesman*, Dec. 31, 1881.

19. Port Townsend *Puget Sound Weekly Argus*, April 26, 1883; Tacoma *Weekly Ledger*, Dec. 16, 30, 1881; June 30, 1882; Olympia *Washington Standard*, Oct. 7, 28, 1881; *Seattle Weekly Chronicle*, Dec. 19, 26, 1881; *Lewiston Teller*, Dec. 22, 1881; *Seattle Post-Intelligencer*, July 9, 1882; Pendleton *East Oregonian*, Nov. 4, 1881; *West Shore*, 7(Oct. 1881), 257, 260–261.

20. By the spring of 1883, less than two hundred miles separated east and westbound tracklayers on the Pacific slope of the Montana Rockies. *Walla Walla Union*, May 28; Aug. 27, 1881; *Spokane Falls Chronicle*, June 29, 1881; *Lewiston Teller*, Sept. 22, 1881; Tacoma *Weekly Ledger*, Nov. 1881; *Walla Walla Statesman*, Dec. 10, 1881; April 1, 1882; *Seattle Post-Intelligencer*, June 12, 1883; *West Shore*, 10 (July 1884), 204; Olympia *Washington Standard*, April 7, 1882; June 30, 1883; *Northwest*, 1(March 1883), 4. Also see Atkinson, "Winter Trip to the Upper Columbia Basin," 286.

21. The cost of construction in the Columbia Gorge averaged out to $42,000 per mile. Through trains ran at first only in daylight hours, so that engineers could keep an eye out for landslides and sand. *Lewiston Teller*, Dec. 15, 1881; May 11, 1882; *West Shore*, 7(Sept. 1881), 228; Olympia *Puget Sound Weekly Courier*, June 17, 1881; Feb. 27, 1883; Olympia *Washington Standard*, May 26; June 16, 1882; *Walla Walla Statesman*, Jan. 28; May 27; Oct. 7, 1882; Jan. 27; March 3, 1883; *Seattle Post-Intelligencer*, May 23, 1882; *Walla Walla Union*, May 26, 1883; Randall V. Mills, *Stern-Wheelers Up Columbia: A Century of Steamboating in the Oregon Country* (Palo Alto: Pacific Books, 1947), 131–132.

22. The first standard gauge locomotive entered Walla Walla in May 1881. The narrow gauge equipment was placed in service on the old Cascades portage railroad and at various points on Puget Sound. Steamers occasionally, and with great difficulty, passed upriver from Lewiston as far as Asotin, a new Washington Territory town. A large sawmill at Texas Ferry was supplied by log drives out of the Clearwater River. *West Shore*, 6(Oct. 1880), 256–257; *Spokan Times*, Oct. 25, 1881; Pendleton *East Oregonian*, Nov. 11, 1881; March 17, 1883; *Lewiston Teller*, Sept. 8, 1881; Feb. 3; May 4, 1882; Oct. 18, 25, 1882; Olympia *Puget Sound Weekly Courier*, March 27; April 3, 1883; *Walla Walla Union*, May 7, 1881; Oct. 14, 1882; April 28, 1883.

23. Palouse farmers had dealt with the grade problem by sending wheat down gravity chutes to the riverside landings. Prior to the N.P. takeover, Villard had considered a further extension northward to Cheney on the transcontinental mainline. *Walla Walla Union*, July 16, 1881; April 7; June 16, 1883; *Spokan Times*, Feb. 17, 1881; Colfax *Palouse Gazette*, Feb. 25, 1881; Feb. 24; May 19; June 30, 1882; April 20, 1883; *Walla Walla Statesman*, May 27; June 24, 1882; April 28, 1883; *West Shore*, 8(March 1882), 58; (July 1882), 123; Keith C. Petersen, *River of Life, Channel of Death: Fish and Dams on the Lower Snake* (Lewiston: Confluence Press, 1995), 67–68.

24. Although Kalama itself, the onetime boomtown where "submerged flats" had been "bought and sold…at thousands of dollars per lot," was supposedly "wiped out," fifteen families remained in the community. Tacoma *Weekly Ledger*, Oct. 6, 1882; *Seattle Weekly Chronicle*, Nov. 21, 1881; Aug. 2, 1883; Olympia *Puget Sound Weekly*

Courier, July 3, 1883; *Seattle Post-Intelligencer*, April 29, 1882; Olympia *Washington Standard*, May 27, 1881; *West Shore*, 7(Dec. 1881), 297; 8(July 1882), 123.

25. Burke & Rasin to A. B. Wyckoff, Dec. 20, 1880; to R. P. Woodruff, June 4, 1881, Thomas Burke Papers, UW; Tannatt to Villard, Oct. 19, 1880, Oregon Improvement Company Records; Seattle *Daily Intelligencer*, Aug. 28, 1881.

26. *Olympia Transcript*, Feb. 4, 1882; Port Townsend *Puget Sound Weekly Argus*, Dec. 20, 1883; *Seattle Weekly Chronicle*, Sept. 6; Dec. 13, 1883; Seattle *Daily Intelligencer*, July 27, 1881; Tacoma *Weekly Ledger*, Jan. 14; Dec. 30, 1881; March 10; June 9; July 21, 1882; *Tacoma Daily Ledger*, June 26; Aug. 21, 1883; *Tacoma News*, Dec. 27, 1883.

27. "The respectable and responsible people of Seattle," a subordinate informed Villard, "have unbounded faith in any statement made by you." *Seattle Weekly Chronicle*, Dec. 26, 1881; Nov. 4, 1882; Oct. 11, 1883; *Northwest*, 1(July 1883), 3; Olympia *Washington Standard*, Oct. 7, 1881; *Seattle Post-Intelligencer*, July 9, 1882; *West Shore*, 8(Sept. 1882), 162; Thomas Burke to Jno. R. Wheat, Oct. 26, 1881, Burke Papers; John L. Howard to Villard, Jan. 6, 1883, Oregon Improvement Company Records. Historians have also been misled by Villard's supposed pro-Seattle stance. See, for example, Murray Morgan, *Skid Road: An Informal Portrait of Seattle* (Seattle: University of Washington Press ed., 1982, 1951),74–76.

28. *Seattle Weekly Chronicle*, Dec. 19, 26, 1881; Nov. 8, 1883; Howard to Villard, April 1, 6, 23, 1882; June 4, 1883; to C. H. Prescott, June 20, 1882; to McNaught, April 23, 1883; McNaught to Villard, May 19, 1883, all Oregon Improvement Company Records; *West Shore*, 7(Dec. 1881), 297; Denny to Villard, Nov. 18, 1882, Villard Papers; Burke to F. H. Osgood, Dec. 3, 1883, Burke Papers; *Seattle Post-Intelligencer*, May 29; June 10; July 25, 1883; *Northwest*, 1(July 1883), 3.

29. *Seattle Weekly Chronicle*, March 31, 1882; *Seattle Post-Intelligencer*, April 7, 13, 18; Oct. 1, 1882; Burke to N. T. Caton, Nov. 23, 1882, Burke Papers; *West Shore*, 8(Sept. 1882), 162–163; *Olympia Transcript*, April 1, 1882; Tacoma *Weekly Ledger*, March 31; Sept. 29, 1882. Burke's habitually used title came from service as King County probate judge in the mid-1870s. See Robert C. Nesbit, *"He Built Seattle": A Biography of Judge Thomas Burke* (Seattle: University of Washington Press, 1961), 23–25.

30. Villard allowed P. B. Cornwall to participate in the Columbia & Puget Sound extension to keep that investor from putting money into the cross-mountain project. Howard to A. W. Holmes, April 9, 1884, Oregon Improvement Company Records; *Seattle Weekly Chronicle*, Aug. 25; Nov. 4, 1882; *Seattle Post-Intelligencer*, Oct. 6, 1882; Oct. 18; Nov. 29, 1883; May 9, 1884; *Tacoma Daily Ledger*, Aug. 15, 1883; *Northwest*, 1(July 1883), 15. Also see Port Townsend *Puget Sound Weekly Argus*, April 26, 1883.

31. Arthur Denny privately informed Villard that his Seattle colleagues did not consider the Squak Junction linkage "what they thought they had a right to expect as a connection with the outside world." *Seattle Post-Intelligencer*, Jan. 21; July 12, 1883; *Seattle Weekly Chronicle*, Sept. 6, 1883; *Tacoma Daily Ledger*, Sept. 12, 1883; Jan. 27, 1884; *Tacoma News*, Nov. 22, 1883; Tacoma *Weekly Ledger*, June 2, 1882; *Olympia Transcript*, March 4, 25, 1882; Denny to Villard, Nov. 18, 1882, Villard Papers.

32. *Tacoma Daily Ledger*, Dec. 13, 16, 1883; Carlos A. Schwantes, *Railroad Signatures across the Pacific Northwest* (Seattle: University of Washington Press, 1993), 23–24.

33. *Seattle Post-Intelligencer*, May 8, 1888; *West Shore*, 8(Feb. 1882), 35; *Tacoma Daily Ledger*, Dec. 7, 1883; *Yakima Record*, April 28, 1883; *Olympia Transcript*, March 29, 1884; Eugene Semple to First Auditor of the Treasury, Nov. 28, 1888, Eugene Semple Papers, UW.

34. *Yakima Record*, Jan. 26, 1884; Olympia *Puget Sound Weekly Courier*, Feb. 27, 1883; Jan. 15, 1884; *Olympia Transcript*, Jan. 7, 1882; Olympia *Washington Standard*, March 7, 1882; *Walla Walla Union*, Nov. 14, 1885; *Tacoma Daily Ledger*, May 3, 1883.

35. Dallam condemned the O.R. & N. as "the weakest excuse for railroading that has ever been exhibited in America." *Yakima Signal*, March 10, 1883; *Spokane Falls Review*, Dec. 27, 1884; Jan. 17, 1885; Jan. 28, 1886; Jan. 28, 1888; *Seattle Post-Intelligencer*, Jan. 6, 1885; *Tacoma Daily Ledger*, Jan. 28, 1886; *West Shore*, 11(Jan. 1885), 29. Also see Schwantes, *Railroad Signatures*, 18–22.

36. The bored passengers on one bar-bound ship hired an Astoria band to entertain them during their ordeal. Pendleton *East Oregonian*, July 15, 1884; *Walla Walla Union*, Jan. 20, 1883; Tacoma *Weekly Ledger*, Jan. 13, 1882; Olympia *Puget Sound Weekly Courier*, May 1; Sept. 11, 1883; Olympia *Washington Standard*, Jan. 27, 1882; *Olympia Transcript*, Sept. 16, 1882; *Tacoma Daily Ledger*, Jan. 5, 1884; Jan. 25, 1887; *Seattle Weekly Chronicle*, Feb. 17, 1882; *Tacoma News*, July 30, 1886.

37. *Whatcom Reveille*, Aug. 3, 1883; *Walla Walla Union*, Aug. 12, 1882; *Yakima Signal*, Feb. 17; April 21; Oct. 13; Nov. 17, 1883; *Yakima Record*, March 31, 1883; Ellensburgh *Kittitas Standard*, Aug. 11, 18; Sept. 15; Nov. 3, 17, 24; Dec. 1, 29, 1883; Feb. 2, 1884; Seattle *Daily Times*, May 17, 1886; *Seattle Post-Intelligencer*, Feb. 26, 1884. Also see J. Orin Oliphant, *On the Cattle Ranges of the Oregon Country* (Seattle: University of Washington Press, 1968), 115–128; Meinig, *Great Columbia Plain*, 286–287.

38. Grays Harbor was another possible O.S.L. destination. Completed to the mouth of the Fraser River in 1885, the Canadian Pacific also attracted notice, since feeder lines need only be built north to the border from Seattle and Spokane Falls. *Walla Walla Statesman*, Jan. 27, 1883; *Seattle Post-Intelligencer*, June 16; Sept. 8; Nov. 16, 1882; *Lewiston Teller*, Aug. 24, 1882; Feb. 8; March 15, 1883; *Walla Walla Union*, Oct. 14, 1882; Pendleton *East Oregonian*, Aug. 18; Oct. 6, 1882; March 27, 1883; *Seattle Weekly Chronicle*, Nov. 8, 1883; *Olympia Transcript*, March11, 1882; *Yakima Signal*, Nov. 20, 1883; *Whatcom Reveille*, July 13; Aug. 10, 24, 1883; Palouse

City *Boomerang*, May 30, 1883; Montesano *Chehalis Valley Vidette*, Feb. 15; April 5, 1883. Also see Meinig, *Great Columbia Plain*, 260–261; Schwantes, *Railroad Signatures*, 68; Robert G. Athearn, "The Oregon Short Line," *IY*, 13 (Winter 1969–1970), 2–18.

39. Convinced of monopoly's benefits, Henry Villard informed a Walla Walla audience that "Washington will not suffer by competition between great corporations for some years yet." *Lewiston Teller*, March 1, 1883; Colfax *Palouse Gazette*, March 2, 1883; *Walla Walla Union*, Feb. 24; March 10, 17, 24, 31; May 5, 1883; *Yakima Signal*, Feb. 24; March 3, 1883; Dayton *Columbia Chronicle*, March 3, 1883; Pendleton *East Oregonian*, March 6, 1883; *West Shore*, 9(March 1883), 63; 10(Dec. 1884), 373–374. Also see Lewty, *To the Columbia Gateway*, 135–136.

40. Railroad officials expected "all the trade of the upper Yakima valley" to come to the original twenty-five mile mark depot. They also anticipated that construction "will probably not be extended beyond that point for a year or two, perhaps longer." *Walla Walla Union*, May 19, 1883; March 29, 1884; *Tacoma Daily Ledger*, April 21, 1883; *Yakima Signal*, June 2, 9, 1883; *Seattle Post-Intelligencer*, June 12, 1883; Colfax *Palouse Gazette*, June 15, 1883; Ellensburgh *Kittitas Standard*, June 23, 1883; *Tacoma News*, Oct. 11, 1883; Chas. B. Lamborn to Paul Schulze, Nov. 15, 1883, Northern Pacific Railroad/North Yakima Records, WSHS; *Olympia Transcript*, April 22, 1882.

41. M. H. Shipley and J. Bailey to J. N. Dolph, n.d.; Hilgard to Villard, Dec. 20, 1882, both Villard Papers; Ellensburgh *Kittitas Standard*, June 30, 1883; *Yakima Signal*, March 17; Sept. 15; Oct. 13, 1883.

42. Eighteen freight wagons, each carrying two tons of merchandise, arrived in Yakima City from The Dalles in the course of a fall 1882 week. *Walla Walla Statesman*, April 1, 1882; *Yakima Signal*, Feb. 24; March 31; June 2, 1883; *Yakima Record*, March 18; May 13; Oct. 14; Nov. 25, 1882; April 14; Dec. 22, 1883; The Dalles *Times-Mountaineer*, May 19, 1883.

43. Ellensburg's rise sparked an ultimately successful movement for creation of Kittitas County. Settlers also crossed the intervening divide to plant the first fruit orchards on the Wenatchee River. *Yakima Record*, May 27; Dec. 23, 30, 1882; March 10; April 21; Nov. 24, 1883; *Walla Walla Daily Journal*, Aug. 2, 7, 1883; Yakima Co., 1883, NPRR Bureau of Immigration Forms, Northern Pacific Railway Company Papers, Series C, Settlement and Development, MHS; Rose M. Boening, "History of Irrigation in the State of Washington," *WHQ*, 9(Oct. 1918), 268; Ellensburgh *Kittitas Standard*, July 7, 14, 28; Aug. 18, 25; Sept. 1; Oct. 27; Nov. 10, 1883; *Yakima Signal*, April 14,21; May 19; Sept. 1, 1883; *Walla Walla Union*, Sept. 9, 1882; *Sprague Herald*, Jan. 25, 1884.

44. Spending company funds on such projects as an Indian dialect dictionary and an investigation of crickets, the Transcontinental Survey drew particular attention from Villard's critics. "A corps of entomologists," one writer complained, "swarmed over the country and waged war on every bug and beetle which was encountered." *Spokane Falls Review*, Sept. 17, 1884; *Tacoma Daily Ledger*, Sept. 9, 23, 25; Oct. 4, 1883; *Walla Walla Union*, Oct. 27, 1883; Oct. 11, 1884; *Walla Walla Statesman*, Oct. 6; Dec. 29, 1883; *Olympia Transcript*, Oct. 20, 1883; Jan. 12, 1884; *West Shore*, 8(April 1882), 64; *Lewiston Teller*, Aug. 23, 1883; *Tacoma News*, Sept. 26, 1883; Olympia *Puget Sound Weekly Courier*, Sept. 25, 1883; Pendleton *East Oregonian*, Sept. 25, 1883; Colfax *Palouse Gazette*, Sept. 28, 1883.

45. The ceremony featured the driving, by alternating blows from Villard and his one genuinely heroic guest, Ulysses Grant, of a rusty spike supposedly used, over a decade before, to fasten the first N.P. rail. *Whatcom Reveille*, Nov. 9, 1883; Olympia *Puget Sound Weekly Courier*, Aug. 28; Sept. 11, 1883; *Seattle Post-Intelligencer*, Aug. 25; Sept. 12, 1883; Edward W. Nolan, "'Not without Labor and Expense': The Villard-Northern Pacific Expedition, 1883," *Montana: The Magazine of Western History*, 33 (Summer 1983), 2–11; *Olympia Transcript*, July 21, 1883; Jan. 12, 1884; Smalley, "Notes of Northwestern Travel," 10; Colfax *Palouse Gazette*, Oct. 5, 1883; *Tacoma Daily Ledger*, June 21; Sept. 9, 1883; *Seattle Weekly Chronicle*, Aug. 23, 1883; *Walla Walla Statesman*, Nov. 3, 1883; *Yakima Signal*, Aug. 18; Sept. 8, 1883.

46. Robert Harris, an experienced eastern railroad executive, became the new N.P. president. Elijah Smith, an Atlantic coast-based investor concerned primarily with the O.R. & N. and the Oregon Improvement Company, led a strong minority group, intent upon restoring the bias toward Portland and the Columbia River. *Tacoma Daily Ledger*, Sept. 25, 26, 28; Oct. 4, 7, 14, 20, 21, 24; Nov. 11, 21; Dec. 18, 1883; Jan. 3–5, 18, 29; Feb. 12, 1884; *Tacoma News*, Oct. 4, 11, 1883; *Seattle Post-Intelligencer*, Oct. 7; Dec. 18, 1883; *Seattle Weekly Chronicle*, Oct. 11, 1883; Olympia *Puget Sound Weekly Courier*, Sept. 25, 1883; *Walla Walla Union*, Oct. 27, 1883; *Olympia Transcript*, Dec. 22, 1883; *Walla Walla Statesman*, Dec. 29, 1883; Pendleton *East Oregonian*, Jan. 4, 1884. Observations on the internal N.P. factions are based on voting blocs at the 1885 annual meeting. As a result of Villard's transactions over the years, J. P. Morgan and other New York bankers voted the O. & T. interest. *Northwest*, 3(Oct. 1885), 13.

47. Briefly following Seattle's lead, an Olympia newspaper portrayed Villard's defeat as "almost Napoleonic" and "like the Spartans at Thermoplye [sic]." *Seattle Post-Intelligencer*, Jan. 5; Feb. 27, 1884; *Seattle Weekly Chronicle*, Feb. 7, 1884; Olympia *Puget Sound Weekly Courier*, Jan. 8; Feb. 5, 1884; *Olympia Transcript*, Jan. 12, 1884; *Yakima Signal*, Feb. 9, 1884; *Lewiston Teller*, Oct. 11, 1883; *Tacoma News*, Jan. 10, 17, 24; Feb. 28; April 10; June 19, 1884; *Tacoma Daily Ledger*, Jan. 5, 10, 17, 19, 23, 24, 29; Feb. 2; April 17; May 11, 1884; Pendleton *East Oregonian*, Feb. 1, 1884.

48. *Tacoma Daily Ledger*, Oct. 16; Nov. 7, 1883; Feb. 14, 1884; *Whatcom Reveille*, Nov. 9, 1883; *Yakima Signal*, Nov. 17, 1883; Olympia *Puget Sound Weekly Courier*, March 4, 1884; *Seattle Weekly Chronicle*, Nov. 15, 1883.

49. The Oregon Improvement Company ran the Orphan Road between early July and late August 1884, ceasing operation due to continuing disputes with the N.P. *Seattle Post-Intelligencer*, March 4, 1884; *Tacoma Daily Ledger*, Jan. 30; April 12, 1884; April 2, 1887; *Tacoma News*, April 17, 24; Aug. 14, 1884; Howard to Elijah Smith, July 17, 29; Aug. 8, 1884; to Prescott, Feb. 20, 1884; John Muir to Smith, April 28; May 22; June 3, 30; July 15, 16; Aug. 21; Sept. 5, 6; Dec. 11, 1884; Villard to Board of Directors of the Northern Pacific Railroad Co., April 14, 1884; John Mitchell to Smith, April 7; July 3, 1884, all Oregon Improvement Company Records; Prescott to Schulze, Feb. 14, 1885, Northern Pacific Railroad Land Department Western District Records, WSHS; *Olympia Transcript*, May 10, 1884; *Northwest*, 3(Sept. 1885), 13–14.

50. Burke to Mrs. S. L. Ackerson, Feb. 11; April 26, 1884; to D. H. Gilman, July 6, 1884, Burke Papers; Muir to Holmes, March 7, 13, 21; April 1, 3, 1884; Howard to Smith, June 17, 21, 23, 24, 26, 28; July 2, 9, 23, 26, 29; Aug. 4, 7, 8, 9, 19, 30, 1884, all Oregon Improvement Company Records; *Walla Walla Union*, May 10, 1884; *Seattle Post-Intelligencer*, May 9, 1884.

51. *Spokane Falls Chronicle*, Jan. 10, 1884; *Tacoma Daily Ledger*, Jan. 19, 29; Feb. 10, 1884; *Walla Walla Union*, March 29, 1884; *Lewiston Teller*, Jan. 17, 1884; Olympia *Puget Sound Weekly Courier*, March 4, 1884; Olympia *Washington Standard*, May 2, 1884.

52. *Walla Walla Statesman*, Feb. 10, 1884; *Yakima Signal*, Feb. 2, 1884; Ellensburgh *Kittitas Standard*, Aug. 11, 1883; Olympia *Puget Sound Weekly Courier*, April 24, 1883; March 4, 1884; Tacoma *Weekly Ledger*, Nov. 10, 1882; Murray Morgan, *Puget's Sound: A Narrative of Early Tacoma and the Southern Sound* (Seattle: University of Washington Press, 1979), 195–200.

53. E. V. Smalley, "Completion of the Northern Pacific," *Northwest*, 5(June 1887), 1–3; *Tacoma Daily Ledger*, Feb. 23, 1884; Feb. 25, 1886; *Seattle Post-Intelligencer*, May 9, 1884.

54. *Northwest*, 3(Sept. 1885), 7; 4(July 1886), 27–28; 6(July 1888), 21; *West Shore*, 11(Feb. 1885), 33; *Lewiston Teller*, Sept. 8, 1887; Smalley, "Completion of the Northern Pacific," 3; H. K. Owens to R. W. Mitchell, May 30, 1885, Northern Pacific/North Yakima Records.

55. *West Shore*, 9(June 1883), 141; 11(March 1885), 62; (May 1885), 136; Lamborn to Robert Harris, Jan. 5, 1885; to Schulze, May 23, 1884, Northern Pacific/North Yakima Records; *Northwest*, 3(Feb. 1885), 9.

56. "If the Northern Pacific finds it an easy matter to move Yakima…", the Seattle *P-I* reflected, "no town or city in the Northwest could feel secure, and each one would be liable to be shifted about one or more times, as this or that particular clique…secured the upper hand in the councils of the company." *Northwest*, 3(Jan. 1885), 19; Lamborn to Schulze, Aug. 28; Nov. 25, 1884; to Harris, Jan. 5, 1885; Schulze to Harris, May 20, 1885, all Northern Pacific/North Yakima Records; *Olympia Transcript*, Jan. 17, 1885; Pendleton *East Oregonian*, March 13, 1885; *West Shore*, 11(March 1885), 62; Port Townsend *Puget Sound Weekly Argus*, Oct. 14, 1886; *Seattle Post-Intelligencer*, March 7, 1885.

57. The Northern Pacific reserved for itself the best-located lots in North Yakima. The capital, if removed to North Yakima, was estimated to be worth "from one hundred to one hundred and fifty thousand dollars net" to the N.P. *Olympia Transcript*, Jan. 24, 1885; Lamborn to Schulze, Aug. 28; Nov. 4, 11, 1884; to Harris, Jan. 5, 1885; T. F. Oakes to Harris, Dec. 11, 1884; McNaught to Harris, March 26; May 4, 10, 1885; Schulze to Harris, May 20, 1885, all Northern Pacific/North Yakima Records; *West Shore*, 11(May 1885), 137.

58. *West Shore*, 11(May 1885), 136–137; 13(Oct. 1887), 716–718; *Northwest*, 3(May 1885), 4; Thos. H. Cavanaugh to Schulze, May 28, 1885, Northern Pacific/North Yakima Records.

59. With approaches and snowsheds figured-in, the projected cost mounted to $4.1 million. *Walla Walla Union*, Sept. 26, 1885; *Tacoma Daily Ledger*, Jan. 19, 1886; H. L. Wells, "The Switchback and Tunnel," *West Shore*, 13(Sept. 1887), 653–654.

60. Helen Parker McMicken Diary, Dec. 21, 1887, McMicken Family Papers, UW; Wells, "Switchback and Tunnel," 654–656; *West Shore*, 14(March 1888), 157–158; *Yakima Republic*, June 23, 30, 1887; *Lewiston Teller*, Sept. 8, 1887; *Tacoma Daily Ledger*, Aug. 14, 1887; *Spokane Falls Review*, July 9, 1887; D. H. Dwight to D. D. Dwight, Aug. 28, 1887, Daniel H. Dwight Papers, EWSHS.

61. *Tacoma Daily Ledger*, June 2, 1887; *Yakima Republic*, June 9, 1887.

62. *Tacoma Daily Ledger*, July 4, 5, 1887; Morgan, *Puget's Sound*, 209–210.

63. The Switchback was prone to closure by snowfall. Smalley, "Completion of the Northern Pacific," 3–4; *Northwest*, 4(Oct. 1886), 8; *West Shore*, 14(June 1888), 340; *Walla Walla Union*, Aug. 27, 1887; *Spokane Falls Review*, Feb. 3, 1888. For full details on the tunnel project, see Morgan, *Puget's Sound*, 203–211.

64. In a brief and unsuccessful 1886 strike, workers demanded wage increases. The highest daily pay, $3.50, went to drillers—and an eight-hour day. *West Shore*, 14(March 1888), 148; (June 1888), 340; *Walla Walla Union*, Aug. 27, 1887; *Tacoma News*, July 30, 1886; Smalley, "Completion of the Northern Pacific," 4; Wells, "Switchback and Tunnel," 656–657; *Northwest*, 4(Oct. 1886), 8.

65. The Switchback was maintained in ready-to-use shape in the event of the tunnel being closed by landslide. Morgan, *Puget's Sound*, 211; *West Shore*, 14(Dec. 1888), 676; *Northwest*, 6(June 1888), 27.

66. A new set of fiscal requirements returned the N.P. to Villard's nominal control in 1888. Stating that he was now "a financier and not a railroad man," Villard made no attempt to reassert the forceful management style of his earlier tenure. The Columbia & Puget Sound coal line and the Olympia-Tenino railroad accounted for most of the remaining mileage. In 1888, more miles of railroad were built in Washington than in any other western territory. *Yakima Record*, Jan. 12, 1884; *West Shore*, 14(March 1888), 166; *Northwest*, 5(Nov. 1887), 19; 6(Dec. 1888), 26. For the composition of the N.P. and the O.R. & N. systems, see *Spokane Falls Review*, Dec. 18, 1886.

Notes—Chapter Eight
A Stalwart Young Empire

1. Jan. 29, 1881.
2. Alice Roberts to Family, June 5, 1885, Alice Roberts Letters, EWSHS.
3. In 1880, Washington had only 40 percent of Oregon's population. By 1890, it surpassed Oregon by a substantial margin. Washington was also more densely populated, with 5.3 persons per square mile in 1890 versus a 3.3 Oregonian rate. The population of the United States as a whole increased by 25 percent during the 1880s. *The Statistical History of the United States: From Colonial Times to the Present* (New York: Basic Books, Inc., 1976), 15, 33, 36. Urban population observations are based on unofficial figures compiled by the Northern Pacific. *Ellensburgh Capital,* April 18, 1889.
4. *Seattle Post-Intelligencer,* April 27, 1882; Olympia *Puget Sound Weekly Courier,* March 27; April 17, 1883; Port Townsend *Puget Sound Weekly Argus,* Feb. 25, 1881; *Medical Lake Press,* Dec. 22, 1882; Cheney *North-West Tribune,* Feb. 17, 1882; *Asotin Spirit,* Feb. 1, 1884; *Chehalis Nugget,* Aug. 1, 1885; *Tacoma Daily Ledger,* May 23; June 3, 8, 1883.
5. James B. Hedges, "Promotion of Immigration to the Pacific Northwest by the Railroads," *Mississippi Valley Historical Review,* 15(Sept. 1928), 194–199; D. W. Meinig, *The Great Columbia Plain: A Historical Geography, 1805–1910* (Seattle: University of Washington Press. 1968), 261–264; Colfax *Palouse Gazette,* April 20, 1883; *Seattle Post-Intelligencer,* April 29, 1882; *Seattle Weekly Chronicle,* March 16, 1883; *Olympia Transcript,* March 18, 1882.
6. Tickets carried specific destinations, causing settlement to focus upon areas tributary to communities so designated. "It is not in the interest of towns," complained boosters of settlements unfavored by the railroad, "to inform strangers of the advantages of any other places." Palouse City *Boomerang,* Jan. 10, 1883; *Tacoma Daily Ledger,* June 21, 1883; *Walla Walla Union,* Sept. 19, 1885; Meinig, *Great Columbia Plain,* 266; John Sprague to Anne Sprague, Oct. 15, 1883, John Sprague Letters, EWSHS; Roberts to Sister, April 18, 1884, Roberts Letters; *Spokane Falls Review,* June 3, 1885; Waterville *Big Bend Empire,* April 18, 1889.
7. The Oregon Improvement Company charged $7 to $10 an acre for eastern Washington land. Charles Lamborn to L. R. Kidder, Oct. 10, 1883, Northern Pacific Railway Company Papers, Series C, Settlement and Development, MHS; to Paul Schulze, April 26, 1884; J. D. Laman to Schulze, Nov. 19, 1883, both Northern Pacific Railroad Land Department Western District Records, WSHS; *Yakima Signal,* Jan. 6; Feb. 17, 1883; March 22, 1884; Tacoma *Weekly Ledger,* Jan. 14, 1881; Feb. 13, 1882; Ellensburgh *Kittitas Standard,* June 30, 1883; Colfax *Palouse Gazette,* March 23, 1883; *Walla Walla Union,* March 31; July 28, 1883; March 22; April 19, 1884; *Yakima Record,* May 19, 1883; *West Shore,* 7(Aug. 1881), 220; 9(Feb. 1883), 23; 13(Feb. 1887), 185; Seattle *Daily Intelligencer,* June 9, 1881. Also see Meinig, *Great Columbia Plain,* 296; and, for settler complaints regarding other aspects of railroad land policy, John Fahey, *The Inland Empire: Unfolding Years, 1879–1929* (Seattle: University of Washington Press, 1986), 25–27. Following James J. Hill's dictum that one acre of timberland was worth forty acres of agricultural land, the N.P. withheld forested acreage from sale. Roy E. Appleman, "Timber Empire from the Public Domain," *Mississippi Valley Historical Review,* 26(Sept. 1939), 193; Ross R. Cotroneo, "The History of the Northern Pacific Land Grant, 1900–1952" (Ph.D. diss., University of Idaho, 1966), 246.
8. The homestead and preemption statutes limited purchases to 160 acres. Government timber culture legislation also granted 160 acres, with a requirement that trees be planted. The Desert Land Act offered up to 640 acres at $1.25 an acre. Claiming to have "wore out a half dozen men writing letters," congressional delegate Thomas Brents actively promoted settlement of the public domain in eastern Washington. The Colfax land office was moved to Spokane Falls in 1883. *Walla Walla Union,* June 7, 1884; Dayton *Columbia Chronicle,* March 31, 1883; Colfax *Palouse Gazette,* April 27, 1883; Seattle *Daily Intelligencer,* Aug. 27, 1881; Cheney *North-West Tribune,* Aug. 11, 1882; Port Townsend *Puget Sound Weekly Argus,* Jan. 24, 1884; *Walla Walla Statesman,* Jan. 26, 1884; *West Shore,* 9(July 1883), 165; 15(Jan. 1889), 49; Meinig, *Great Columbia Plain,* 294–295; Fahey, *Inland Empire,* 6.
9. According to a local newspaper, one Walla Walla lawyer processed land office filings "by going in the back way…for other parties who had paid good sums for the dirty work." Another attorney promised to secure approval or denial, as desired, of any claim in return for $100. Pomeroy *Washington Independent,* Jan. 13, 1881; Palouse City *Boomerang,* Oct. 4, 1882; *Walla Walla Daily Journal,* Aug. 13, 1883. For railroad attempts to curb timber theft in eastern Washington, see J. M. Allen to Schulze, Jan. 12; Feb. 17; March 29, 1883; James McNaught to Schulze, April 7, 1883, all Northern Pacific Western District Records. On land fraud, also see Fahey, *Inland Empire,* 6–7; Meinig, *Great Columbia Plain,* 295–296.
10. Lewiston *Nez Perce News,* July 24, 1884; Palouse City *Boomerang,* June 13, 1883; *Northwest,* 4(Feb. 1886), 1; (May 1886), 1; *West Shore,* 9(April 1883), 71; *Spokan Times,* April 21, 1881; Ritzville *Adams County Record,* Nov. 17, 1885; Ellensburgh *Kittitas Standard,* Aug. 18, 1883.
11. Olympia *Washington Standard,* Aug. 1, 1884; Pendleton *East Oregonian,* June 19, 1883; Colfax *Palouse Gazette,* Aug. 3, 1883; *Walla Walla Union,* Jan. 23, 1886; *Spokane Falls Review,* Jan. 12, 1886.
12. According to one visitor, Riparia was little more than a "sand Bank." *Walla Walla Union,* Oct. 1, 1877; Peter J. Lewty, *Across the Columbia Plain: Railroad Expansion in the Interior Northwest, 1885–1893* (Pullman: Washington

State University Press, 1995), 22–26; C. J. Smith to T. W. Symons, June 10, 1890; W. Young to C. F. Powell, March 24, 1886; Frank T. Dodge to W. A. Jones, March 27, 1885, all Portland District Records, U.S. Army Corps of Engineers, RG 77, FRC; Robert J. Skaife Diary, May 16, 1888, WSU. For an account of a Snake River trip to Riparia, see *Lewiston Teller,* July 25, 1888.

13. With Portland warehouses filled at the end of 1883, a hundred rail cars of wheat were stranded at Walla Walla and an even larger number at Wallula. The O.R. & N. planned, but never built, a railroad up the Snake from Riparia to Lewiston. *Lewiston Teller,* Nov. 17; Dec. 1, 8, 15, 1881; March 9, 1882; Sept. 20; Oct. 18, 1883; Nov. 20; Dec. 11, 1884; Oct. 29, 1885; *Walla Walla Union,* Dec. 24, 1881; *West Shore,* 11(Aug. 1885), 227–228; *Walla Walla Statesman,* Dec. 24, 1881; Seattle *Daily Times,* May 27, 1886; Walla Walla *Semi-Weekly Journal,* Nov. 27, 1883; *Seattle Post-Intelligencer,* Aug. 23, 1882.

14. A portion of each cargo, depending upon water levels in the lower Columbia, usually had to be lightered between Portland and Astoria. Sacks also eliminated the danger of bulk cargo shifting. *Walla Walla Union,* June 18, 1881; July 7, 21; Aug. 11, 1883; *West Shore,* 9(Aug. 1883), 171; 15(Feb. 1889), 87–88; Roberts to Dear ones all, Sept. 14, 1888, Roberts Letters; Fahey, *Inland Empire,* 56–57; *Olympia Transcript,* Feb. 25, 1882; *Spokane Falls Review,* July 30; Oct. 20, 1885.

15. *Walla Walla Union,* May 24, 1884; Sept. 26, 1885; *Tacoma Daily Ledger,* Feb. 1, 1884; *West Shore,* 14(March 1888), 115-116.

16. In theory, Walla Walla shippers might have connected with the N.P. at Wallula Junction. O.R. & N. short-haul rates to that point, however, were high enough to render the option cost-prohibitive. *Walla Walla Union,* July 23, 1881; Dec. 6, 20, 1884; Jan. 3; Aug. 22; Sept. 5; Oct. 24, 1885; March 31, 1888; *Lewiston Teller,* Jan. 17, 1884; Nov. 13, 1885; *West Shore,* 15(Jan. 1889), 54; Fahey, *Inland Empire,* 31, 34; Meinig, *Great Columbia Plain,* 273. For details on Hunt, see Lewty, *Across the Columbia Plain,* chapt. 7.

17. Palouse City *Boomerang,* Sept. 20, 1882; April 4; Sept. 14, 1883; *Pullman Herald,* Jan. 29; Feb. 16, 1889; Colfax *Palouse Gazette,* Feb. 20, 1880; *Walla Walla Statesman,* June 3; Nov. 25, 1882; *Moscow Mirror,* Jan. 15, 1886; Ritzville *Adams County Record,* June 8, 1886; *West Shore,* 7(Aug. 1881), 208; E. V. Smalley, "The Fertile Palouse Country," *Northwest,* 5(May 1887), 1–3; *Lewiston Teller,* May 19, 1881; Whitman County Bureau of Immigration Form, 1883, Northern Pacific Railway Papers, Series C; Schedule of Agricultural Products, Whitman County, 1884, Watson C. Squire Papers, WSA.

18. Cheney *North-West Tribune,* May 26, 1882; *Spokane Falls Review,* July 1, 1884; Sept. 8; Oct. 5, 6, 14, 1885; Roberts to Dear Ones at Home, Feb. 24, 1889, Roberts Letters.

19. "The leading roads of the country," N.P. executive Thomas F. Oakes informed the board of directors, "are no longer single lines between terminal points, but systems of lines occupying wide belts of country." The S. & P. actually began at Marshall, seven miles southwest of the Falls on the N.P. mainline. *Spokan Times,* April 28, 1881; *Spokane Falls Review,* Oct. 7, 12–14, 30; Nov. 6, 12, 1885; *Moscow Mirror,* Dec. 25, 1885; *Northwest,* 4(Jan. 1886), 13; (April 1886), 41; *Walla Walla Union,* July 31, 1886. Also see Lewty, *Across the Columbia Plain,* 27–30.

20. *Moscow Mirror,* Nov. 6; Dec. 25, 1885; Jan. 22, 1886; *Spokane Falls Review,* May 16, 1886; Aug. 7, 1887; Jan. 22; April 20; May 8; June 5; July 29; Dec. 6, 1888; *Yakima Republic,* May 12, 1887; *West Shore,* 14(May 1888), 285; (Aug. 1888), 450. Upon completion of the railroad, Moscow growers abandoned their traditional market outlet, Lewiston on the Snake. Lewiston *Nez Perce News,* Sept. 10, 1885; Palouse City *Boomerang,* May 30, 1883. Newspapers on both sides of the Cascades followed the prolonged O.R. & N. lease situation in detail. For full coverage, see Lewty, *Across the Columbia Plain,* 1–19, 30–34.

21. Waterville *Big Bend Empire,* May 20, 1889; *West Shore,* 9(Feb. 1883), 38; (March 1883), 50; 12(June 1886), 177; 14(June 1888), 344; Cheney *North-West Tribune,* June 30, 1882; *Northwest,* 4(Aug. 1886), 11; (Sept. 1886), 7; Henry Victor Journal, ? 1883, WSU; *Spokane Falls Chronicle,* June 27, 1882; *Medical Lake Press,* Oct. 14, 1882. Viewing the Big Bend as "the last great range they now have for their stock," whites of the McIntee stripe opposed conventional settlement. William McMicken to N. C. McFarland, Sept. 27, 1881, Letters Received from the Surveyors General of Washington, 1854–1883, RG 49, NA.

22. The best tracts were "all settled," one visitor advised, and "little houses" were seen "in all directions." McMicken to Commissioner, General Land Office, June 22, 1881; to McFarland, Sept. 27, 1881, Letters Received from the Surveyors General; Cheney *North-West Tribune,* June 30, 1882; *Sprague Herald,* Aug. 26, 1882; Feb. 16; April 20, 1883; Ellensburgh *Kittitas Standard,* Aug. 11, 1883; Sprague to Wife and Children, Nov. 4, 1883, Sprague Letters; *Spokane Falls Chronicle,* June 20, 1882; C. B. Dunning to ?, July 29, 188?; C. B. Dunning Papers, EWSHS.

23. Okanogan City should not be confused with the modern town of Okanogan in the Okanogan Valley. Waterville, the aptly named first viable community west of the Grand Coulee, was founded in 1886. A would-be settler wrote from another part of the Big Bend that he had "seen where they was diging [sic] wells and they had to blast the rock and there was not any water." Homesteaders blazed a wagon road from Waterville to a point opposite the mouth of the Wenatchee River, in the vain expectation of steamer service on the upper Columbia. *Spokane Falls Chronicle,* Dec. 6, 1883; *Walla Walla Union,* June 14, 1884; Walter T. Henne Diary, Jan. 13, 1884, EWSHS; *Northwest,* 4(Sept. 1886), 7; Ritzville *Adams County Record,* Dec. 22, 1885; July 13, 20, 1886; Sprague to Wife and Children, Nov. 4, 1883, Sprague Letters; Jones to Chief of Engineers, n.d., Portland District Records; Francis R. Shunk to Symons, April 16, 1892; J. G. Holcombe to Symons, June 30, 1892, both Seattle District Records, U.S. Army Corps of Engineers, RG 77, FRC; *Ellensburgh Capital,* Dec. 6, 1888;

Walla Walla Statesman, Jan. 27, 1883; Waterville *Big Bend Empire*, Feb. 14, 1889; McMicken to McFarland, Sept. 27, 1881, Letters Received from the Surveyors General.

24. Wheat shipped east for domestic consumption sold at a higher price than in San Francisco. Palouse City *Boomerang*, April 18, 1883; *Walla Walla Union*, June 16; July 21; Sept. 1, 15, 1883; Nov. 14, 1885; Dec. 3, 1887; *Yakima Signal*, Oct. 13, 1883; *Tacoma News*, March 19, 1886; *Spokane Falls Review*, May 13, 1886; Ritzville *Adams County Record*, Dec. 15, 1885.

25. *Walla Walla Union*, Aug. 18, 1883; March 29; April 5; July 5, 1884; Aug. 28, 1886; *Moscow Mirror*, April 22, 1887; Palouse City *Boomerang*, Dec. 20, 1882; Sept. 28, 1883; *Spokane Falls Review*, April 5, 20, 1888.

26. Walla Walla's otherwise decent 31 percent population increase for the decade was well below the territorial pace. Carlos A. Schwantes, *The Pacific Northwest: An Interpretive History* (Lincoln: University of Nebraska Press, 1989), 192; Olympia *Washington Standard*, June 23, 1882; *West Shore*, 7(Sept. 1881), 227; 13(March 1887), 199; *Walla Walla Daily Journal*, Aug. 6, 1883; *Walla Walla Statesman*, Sept. 2, 16, 1882; June 30, 1883.

27. Sprinklers kept Main Street, the principal business thoroughfare, constantly dampened. Olympia *Washington Standard*, June 23, 1882; *Seattle Post-Intelligencer*, May 3, 1882; *Lewiston Teller*, Oct. 25, 1883; Pendleton *East Oregonian*, April 27, 1883; *Walla Walla Statesman*, Dec. 2, 1882; *Walla Walla Union*, April 28; May 5, 12, 1883; Dec. 20, 1884; Feb. 25, 1888; Lewiston *Nez Perce News*, June 25, 1885.

28. Another regular visitor attributed the community's "loathsome decay" to the "narrow, contracted and self-conceited men who hold that a few miserly collected dollars is a safe and sure transportation to the other world." *Walla Walla Union*, June 25; July 2, 1881; *Walla Walla Statesman*, Aug. 5, 12, 1882; *Lewiston Teller*, May 4, 1882; *Northwest*, 3(Sept. 1885), 10; Lewiston *Nez Perce News*, June 11, 1885.

29. *Walla Walla Union*, Sept. 23, 1882; Dec. 8, 1883; March 20, 1886; *Seattle Weekly Chronicle*, Oct. 4, 1883; *Seattle Post-Intelligencer*, May 13, 1882; Olympia *Washington Standard*, Oct. 28, 1881; Chehalis *Lewis County Nugget*, Aug. 4, 1883.

30. Parker claimed that local taxpayers paid a Walla Walla banker twice the actual value for the acreage. Citing "some of the methods adopted" in securing the funding bill, anti-prison advocates west of the Cascades unsuccessfully protested the penitentiary measure. Frank J. Parker to Eugene Semple, April 28, 30; May 1; Dec. 3, 5, 1887; F. W. Paine to Semple, April 28, 1887, all Eugene Semple Papers, UW; *Walla Walla Union*, Dec. 8, 1883; March 20, 1886; Olympia *Washington Standard*, June 27, 1884; March 12, 1886; *Spokane Falls Review*, Feb. 19, 1887; Board of Penitentiary Building Commissioners to Semple, Nov. 21, 1887, Eugene Semple Papers, WSA; *Tacoma News*, March 26, 1886.

31. Frank Parker, intent upon securing a position for himself, kept Governor Semple informed as to the state of affairs at the penitentiary. Two prisoners briefly escaped en route from Seatco to Walla Walla. Semple to Paine, April 25; May 5, 11, 14, 1887; Parker to Semple, April 28, 30; Dec. 5, 1887; Feb. 7, 1888; Paine to Semple, April 28; May 13, 1887, all Semple Papers, UW; Watson C. Squire to Paine, April 9, 1887, Semple Papers, WSA.

32. The $173,000 prison appropriation was seventeen times greater than the amount provided for the University of Washington. *Walla Walla Union*, Feb. 18; April 7, 1888; Board of Penitentiary Building Commissioners to Semple, Nov. 21, 1887; Paine to Semple, Aug. 12; Nov. 30, 1887, all Semple Papers, WSA; Parker to Semple, Dec. 3, 1887, Semple Papers, UW; *West Shore*, 14(March 1888), 163. The first prison scandal, dealing with inadequate food, clothing and exercise, erupted in early 1889. *Pullman Herald*, Feb. 9, 1889.

33. By 1881, most inhabitants agreed that Spokane should be spelled with an "e." *Spokane Falls Chronicle*, June 29; July 9, 1881; *Walla Walla Union*, May 28, 1881; *West Shore*, 8(Aug. 1882), 158; E. V. Smalley, "Notes of Northwestern Travel," *Northwest*, 1(Aug. 1883), 10. The "Falls" was officially dropped from the city's name in 1891. See Katherine G. Morrissey, *Mental Territories: Mapping the Inland Empire* (Ithaca: Cornell University Press, 1997), 60.

34. Spokane County had six times as many school age children in 1881 as the entire white population of 1877. *Spokan Times*, Feb. 24; June 9; Aug. 2, 9; Oct. 25; Dec. 31, 1881; Jan. 28; March 4, 1882; A. E. Keats to Cousin Julia, Sept. 4, 1881; Aug. 14, 1883, A. E. Keats Letters, EWSHS; James M. Nosler Diary, May 27, 1883, UW; Henry J. Winser to Henry Villard, Oct. 26, 1882, Henry Villard Papers, Houghton Library, Harvard University; Spokane Co. Bureau of Immigration Form, 1883, Northern Pacific Railway Papers, Series C; *West Shore*, 8(Feb. 1882), 23; 9(Feb. 1883), 37; 10(April 1884), 118; *Seattle Post-Intelligencer*, July 31; Oct. 14; Nov. 25, 1883; The Dalles *Times-Mountaineer*, May 26, 1883; *Sprague Herald*, Aug. 24, 1883; *Spokane Falls Chronicle*, July 4, 25, 1882; *Spokane Falls Review*, July 18, 20, 28; Aug. 23; Sept. 15; Nov. 15, 1884; *Walla Walla Union*, May 28, 1881; John Fahey, *The Ballyhoo Bonanza: Charles Sweeney and the Idaho Mines* (Seattle: University of Washington Press, 1971), 13–14; J. J. Browne to Anna Stratton Browne, Sept. 9, 1883; J. J. Browne Papers, EWSHS; Cheney *North-West Tribune*, Nov. 24, 1882.

35. *West Shore*, 8(Feb. 1882), 39; 19(Feb. 1884), 60; 13(March 1887), 267; (May 1887), 408; *Spokane Falls Review*, July 29, 1885; E. V. Smalley, "A New Mining District," *Northwest*, 4(Jan. 1886), 1–5; S. L. Alexander Diary, July 31, 1885, EWSHS; *Ellensburgh Capital*, Feb. 14; April 25, 1889; *Walla Walla Union*, May 5, 1888.

36. Colfax *Palouse Gazette*, Sept. 28; Oct. 5, 1883; Browne to A. Browne, Sept. 25, 1883, Browne Papers; *Spokane Falls Chronicle*, Jan. 17, 1884; *Olympia Transcript*, Feb. 2, 1884; *Walla Walla Statesman*, Nov. 10; Dec. 22, 1883; *Walla Walla Union*, Dec. 1, 1883; March 15, 1884; *West Shore*, 10(Feb. 1884), 40; *Whatcom Reveille*, Dec. 28, 1883; Olympia *Puget Sound Weekly Courier*, Feb. 5, 1884; Fahey, *Ballyhoo Bonanza*, 18–20.

37. At high water on the Coeur d'Alene River, steamboats ran to within eight miles of Eagle City. *Olympia Transcript*, Feb. 9; March 1, 1884; Olympia *Puget Sound Weekly Courier*, Feb. 12, 1884; Pendleton *East Oregonian*, Jan. 29, 1884; *West Shore*, 10(Feb. 1884), 40; *Spokane Falls Chronicle*, Feb. 17; July 9, 1884; Browne to A. Browne, Feb. 27, 1884, Browne Papers; John Fahey, *Inland Empire: D. C. Corbin and Spokane* (Seattle: University of Washington Press, 1965), 27. On the connection between Spokane and the mines, see also W. Hudson Kensel, "Inland Empire Mining and the Growth of Spokane, 1883–1905," *PNQ*, 60(April 1969), 84–97.

38. Even Wyatt Earp failed to survive the environmental challenges of the Coeur d'Alene. *West Shore*, 10(May 1884), 128; (Aug. 1884), 227–228; S. B. Pettengill, "The Coeur d'Alene Mines," Ibid., 12(Sept. 1886), 265–266; *Northwest*, 3(April 1885), 5; *Spokane Falls Review*, July 9, 19; Oct. 14; Nov. 29, 1884; Jan. 17; Sept. 5, 1885; *Lewiston Teller*, Aug. 7, 1884.

39. By the spring of 1885, a wagon road linked Murray with the steamer landing at Mission. Corbin leased his Coeur d'Alene Railway & Navigation Company to the Northern Pacific in 1888. In a widening of the Palouse railroad war, the O.R. & N. planned to lay track into the Coeur d'Alene. *Spokane Falls Review*, Oct. 14; Nov. 29, 1884; May 14; July 3; Sept. 6; Oct 2, 16, 1885; Jan. 9; March 16; Oct. 2, 17, 1886; June 7, 1887; April 6, 17; July 14, 1888; Fahey, *Ballyhoo Bonanza*, 21–24, and *Corbin*, chaps. 3, 4; Pettengill, "Coeur d'Alene Mines," 265–266; *Wallace Free Press*, Oct. 22, 1887.

40. When bad weather closed the N.P. west of Spokane, local homes went without heat for lack of imported coal. Relations with the Indians continued to be testy. On a visit to Spokane in 1886, Chief Joseph lost his horse to a thief, with the connivance of police officers. D. H. Dwight to D. D. Dwight, April 28; June 13, 1887; Jan. 20; April 15, 1888; April 20, 1889, Daniel H. Dwight Papers, EWSHS; *Spokane Falls Review*, June 16, 1884; July 28; Aug. 15; Sept. 30, 1885; April 4; June 22; Sept. 19, 1886; Jan. 1; April 24; July 27; Aug. 7, 17, 19, 28; Oct. 25, 1887; Jan. 1, 25; Feb. 4, 8; March 1–3, 16, 18, 20, 22; April 18, 28; May 8, 11; Dec. 8, 1888; *Walla Walla Union*, April 21, 1888; Browne to A. Browne, March 7, 8, 12, 1886, Browne Papers; Fahey, *Corbin*, chaps. 5–6; *Ellensburgh Capital*, Feb. 21; April 18, 1889; *West Shore*, 14(Dec. 1888), 676; 15(Jan. 1889), 51; G. B. Dennis to Cyrus Bradley, July 5, 1889, Cyrus Bradley Papers, WSU; E. K. Pendergast to Sister, Sept. 30, 1889; to Father, March 16, 1890, E. K. Pendergast Correspondence, WSHS.

41. Washington recorded a much higher yield-per-acre, 17.3, compared to 15.9 in Oregon and 9.2 in California. New machinery and expanding markets generated an increase in Inland Empire wheat acreage from 366,000 acres in 1890 to 2.1 million acres in 1910. *Spokane Falls Review*, Oct. 6, 1885; James F. Shepherd, "The Development of Wheat Production in the Pacific Northwest," *Agricultural History*, 49(Jan. 1975), 258–271; Robert C. Nesbit and Charles M. Gates, "Agriculture in Eastern Washington, 1890–1910," *PNQ*, 37(Oct. 1946), 279, 282–286; *Walla Walla Statesman*, Jan. 21; April 8; May 13, 1882; *West Shore*, 13(Jan. 1887), 90; *Seattle Post-Intelligencer*, Aug. 8, 1882; May 30, 1885; *Walla Walla Union*, Feb. 6, 1886.

42. *Tacoma Daily Ledger*, May 1, 1883; *West Shore*, 15(Jan. 1889), 44; S. B. Pettengill, "The Puget Sound of To-day," Ibid., 13(Jan. 1887), 40; James Bryce, *The American Commonwealth* (New York: Macmillan and Co., 2 vols., 3rd ed., 1895), 1:585; F. I. Vassault, "Lumbering in Washington," *Overland Monthly*, 20(July 1892), 24; Septima M. Collins, *A Woman's Trip to Alaska* (New York: Cassell Publishing Company, 1890), 54; Rudyard Kipling, *From Sea to Sea and Other Sketches* (Garden City: Doubleday, Page & Company, 2 vols., 1925, 1899), 2:93; Olympia *Washington Standard*, Aug. 4, 1884; March 13, 1885, the latter reprinting from Portland *Journal of Commerce*.

43. Washington produced less lumber than Oregon in 1880. Ten years later, the infant state's output was three times greater. California production was twice as large as Washington's in 1880. By 1887, the latter exceeded the former by 50 percent. Port Townsend *Puget Sound Weekly Argus*, March 3, 1882; *West Shore*, 7(Nov. 5, 1881), 280; 14(April 1888), 221; *Tacoma Daily Ledger*, April 14, 1887; *Seattle Weekly Chronicle*, July 28, 1882; Olympia *Puget Sound Weekly Courier*, June 17, 1881; *Tacoma News*, Aug. 28, 1884; Olympia *Washington Standard*, Aug. 29, 1884; Robert E. Ficken, *The Forested Land: A History of Lumbering in Western Washington* (Seattle: University of Washington Press, 1987), 55, 75; Edmond S. Meany, Jr., "The History of the Lumber Industry in the Pacific Northwest to 1917" (Ph.D. diss., Harvard University, 1935), 125–126; James N. Tattersall, "The Economic Development of the Pacific Northwest to 1920" (Ph.D. diss., University of Washington, 1960), 179–180.

44. W. H. Ruffner, *A Report on Washington Territory* (New York: Seattle, Lake Shore and Eastern Railway, 1889), 70; *Tacoma Daily Ledger*, Jan. 1, 1886; Jan. 1, 1887; Port Townsend *Puget Sound Weekly Argus*, Jan. 5, 1883; Dec. 31, 1885; *Walla Walla Statesman*, Dec. 10, 1881; A. M. Bash to Squire, Nov. 17, 1884, Squire Papers, WSA.

45. *Northwest*, 1(March 1883), 1–2; Olympia *Puget Sound Weekly Courier*, March 6; April 10, 1883; *Seattle Weekly Chronicle*, June 16, 1882; Port Townsend *Puget Sound Weekly Argus*, Jan. 12, 1883; Feb. 18; March 18; April 22, 1886; John S. Hittell, *The Commerce and Industries of the Pacific Coast* (San Francisco: A. L. Bancroft & Company, 2nd ed., 1882), 588–589, 592–593; Seattle *Daily Intelligencer*, July 3, 1881; *Tacoma News*, June 11, 1885; *West Shore*, 8(Oct. 1882), 182; 13(June 1887), 481; *Seattle Post-Intelligencer*, July 12, 1882; Ficken, *Forested Land*, 69; Richard C. Berner, "The Port Blakely Mill Company, 1876–89," *PNQ*, 57(Oct. 1966), 164, 168; Ruffner, *Report on Washington Territory*, 71–72.

46. Michigan alone supplied 23 percent of U.S. lumber production in 1880, a figure falling to 4 percent by 1909. Over half the remaining virgin timber in the United States was in the Pacific Northwest. Griggs contracted with the Northern Pacific after Frederick Weyerhaeuser, America's best-known timberman, rejected a similar

arrangement. *West Shore*, 11(May 1885), 159; (Sept. 1885), 259; 14(May 1888), 286; Meany, "History of the Lumber Industry," 137–138; Ficken, *Forested Land*, 58–60; Seattle *Daily Intelligencer*, Sept. 2, 1881; *Olympia Transcript*, Dec. 2, 1882; Olympia *Washington Standard*, Sept. 16, 1881; *Tacoma Daily Ledger*, Nov. 27, 1883; Edward G. Jones, *The Oregonian's Handbook of the Pacific Northwest* (Portland: The Oregonian Publishing Company, 1894), 54, 56–57; John E. Defebaugh, *History of the Lumber Industry in America* (Chicago: The American Lumberman, 2 vols., 1906–1907), 1:299–300; Wilson Compton, *The Organization of the Lumber Industry* (Chicago: The American Lumberman, 1916), 26, 117; *Seattle Post-Intelligencer*, April 23; July 8; Nov. 1, 1882; C. B. Wright to Isaac W. Anderson, May 1, 1888, Tacoma Land and Improvement Company Papers, Tacoma Public Library; Murray Morgan, *The Mill on the Boot: The Story of the St. Paul & Tacoma Lumber Company* (Seattle: University of Washington Press, 1982), 48–65; *Walla Walla Union*, April 14, 1888, reprinting from *Minneapolis Lumberman*.

47. The Wishkah, Hoquiam and Humptulips, all important Olympic Peninsula streams, flowed directly into Grays Harbor. *West Shore*, 7(Jan. 1881), 18; 11(March 1885), 80–81; 14(Nov. 1888), 573; Montesano *Chehalis Valley Vidette*, Feb. 1, 15, 22; March 8; Sept. 6, 1883; Chehalis *Lewis County Bee*, June 13, 1884; *Chehalis Nugget*, June 17, 1887; Olympia *Washington Standard*, Aug. 4, 1882; Sept. 5, 1884; Shelton *Mason County Journal*, April 8; June 17, 1887; Chehalis County Bureau of Immigration Form, 1883, Northern Pacific Railway Company Papers, Series C; Robert A. Habersham to Powell, Nov. 2, 14, 1881, in *Annual Report of the Chief of Engineers, 1882*, 2689, 2723; Powell to Chief of Engineers, Jan. 25, 27, 1882, Portland District Records; *Aberdeen Herald*, Nov. 3, 1886.

48. The original local rail project, the Puget Sound & Grays Harbor Railroad, failed when Olympia merchants, concerned over the impact of the terminus location on property values in the capital, withheld support. The North Western company assumed control of existing Simpson plants on Shoalwater Bay and at Knapton near the mouth of the Columbia. *West Shore*, 14(Aug. 1888), 452; (Nov. 1888), 573–575, 602–603; *Olympia Transcript*, Feb. 11; March 11; April 1, 1882; Aug. 16, 1883; Montesano *Chehalis Valley Vidette*, Feb. 1; March 22, 29; April 12; Aug. 9, 1883; Herbert Hunt and Floyd C. Kaylor, *Washington West of the Cascades* (Chicago: S. J. Clarke Publishing Company, 2 vols., 1917), 2:60–64, 92–95, 262–266, 278–279; Wallace J. Miller, *South-western Washington* (Olympia: Pacific Publishing Company, 1890), 112, 173, 175, 179, 188–193; Jones, *Oregonian's Handbook*, 329–334; Samuel Benn Reminiscences, 2, BL; Louise Schafer, "Report from Aberdeen," *PNQ*, 47(Jan. 1956), 10, 14; Shelton *Mason County Journal*, Dec. 9, 1887; Jan. 13, 1888; Julian Hawthorne, ed., *History of Washington, The Evergreen State* (New York: American Historical Publishing Co., 2 vols., 1893), 2:194, 196; Washington Pioneer Project, *Told by the Pioneers: Reminiscences of Pioneer Life in Washington* (Olympia: W.P.A., 3 vols., 1937–1939), 2:27; Mrs. Frances Fuller Victor, *All Over Oregon and Washington* (San Francisco: John H. Carmany & Co., 1872), 264–265; Olympia *Washington Standard*, June 17, 1881; Sept. 7, 1883; Olympia *Puget Sound Weekly Courier*, Sept. 4, 11, 18, 1883; *Tacoma Daily Ledger*, April 29, 1883; *Seattle Post-Intelligencer*, Oct. 21, 1882.

49. By 1900, nearly three hundred donkey engines were in use by Washington loggers, compared to three dozen in Oregon. The first Washington logging railroads tended to be primitive affairs, with oxen pulling cars on wooden rails. In one of the earliest documented usages of locomotive power, the Olympia-Tenino railroad converted to the hauling of logs. C. M. Scammon, "Lumbering in Washington Territory," *Overland Monthly*, 5(July 1870), 57–58; *West Shore*, 8(July 1882), 136; (Oct. 1882), 182; Eldridge Morse Notebooks, 23:20–26, BL; Seattle *Daily Intelligencer*, July 24, 1881; *Olympia Transcript*, Feb. 4, 1882; Olympia *Puget Sound Weekly Courier*, Jan. 15, 1884; Olympia *Washington Standard*, June 9, 1882; June 11, 1886; Port Townsend *Puget Sound Weekly Argus*, Dec. 9, 1886; *Tenth Census of the United States*, Vol. IX, *Report on the Forests of North America* (Washington, D.C.: Government Printing Office, 1884), 574; Meany, "History of the Lumber Industry," 246–247, 260; Seattle *Weekly Chronicle*, June 9, 1882; *Tacoma News*, Dec. 10, 1886; *Seattle Post-Intelligencer*, Jan. 26, 1887; Ficken, *Forested Land*, 59. For Henry Yesler's logging recollections, see Clarence B. Bagley, *History of Seattle: From the Earliest Settlement to the Present Time* (Chicago: S. J. Clarke Publishing Company, 3 vols., 1916), 1:224. On steam donkeys, see the discussions in Richard White, *Land Use, Environment, and Social Change: The Shaping of Island County, Washington* (Seattle: University of Washington Press, 1980), 96–97, 105–106; William G. Robbins, *Landscapes of Promise: The Oregon Story, 1800–1940* (Seattle: University of Washington Press, 1997), 213–215.

50. Mason County was connected to the outside world by a steamer to Olympia. Olympia *Puget Sound Weekly Courier*, June 26; Sept. 11, 1883; Shelton *Mason County Journal*, Dec. 31, 1886; Jan. 7, 21, 28; April 15; May 27; Dec. 23, 1887; *West Shore*, 11(June 1885), 189; 13(June 1887), 483; *Seattle Post-Intelligencer*, Dec. 10, 1882; Miller, *South-western Washington*, 110; Jones, *Oregonian's Handbook*, 340; Berner, "Port Blakely Mill Company," 161–163; Robert E. Ficken, *Lumber and Politics: The Career of Mark E. Reed* (Seattle: University of Washington Press, 1979), 12–14. In 1891, federal work began on navigation channels and on jetties at the mouth of Grays Harbor.

51. The only noteworthy coal production east of the Cascades was at Roslyn, where an N.P.-operated mine supplied the railroad and customers as far east as Spokane. *Seattle Post-Intelligencer*, Jan. 7, 1885; Feb. 20; May 20, 1886; Feb. 17, 1887; *Tacoma Daily Ledger*, Sept. 13, 1883; Jan. 1, 1887; *West Shore*, 13(May 1887), 404; 14(Jan. 1888), 51; H. C. Lytle to A. G. Postlethwaite, Jan. 16, 1889; to John Haugley, June 15, 1889, Northern Pacific Coal Company Records, WSHS.

52. San Francisco Bay ferries relied entirely upon Tacoma coal. The Carbonado mine was sold to the Central Pacific Railroad in 1882 for $750,000. The C.P., which also owned mining properties on Vancouver Island, antagonized other Washington producers by lobbying for removal of the tariff on imported coal. In spite of his modest official title, Howard was responsible for all aspects of the coal trade, the most important of the several O.I.C. business endeavors. George F. Whitworth to Squire, Oct. 31, 1884, Squire Papers, WSA; Tacoma *Weekly Ledger*, July 15, 1881; March 31, 1882; *Tacoma News*, Oct. 11, 1883; Jan. 3, 1884; Jan. 29, 1885; March 5, 1886; Jan. 7, 1887; *Seattle Weekly Chronicle*, Dec. 26, 1881; Oct. 4, 1883; *Tacoma Daily Ledger*, April 29; Dec. 20, 27, 1883; April 13, 1887; Seattle *Daily Intelligencer*, June 23; Sept. 2–4, 1881; *Walla Walla Statesman*, Jan. 14, 1882; *West Shore*, 8(Sept. 1882), 162; 11(March 1885), 71; John L. Howard to Elijah Smith, Nov. 7, 1884; to Villard, Jan. 17; Feb. 6; Dec. 22, 1881; April 1, 1882; to Horace White, May 14, 1881, Oregon Improvement Company Records, UW; Colfax *Palouse Gazette*, April 7, 1882; *Seattle Post-Intelligencer*, Nov. 7, 1882.

53. Howard dealt with the waste problem, in part, by using inferior coal in the rail line roadbed. Putting the "Pennsylvania of the Pacific" designation in perspective, Washington Territory produced only one-sixtieth of the coal output credited to Pennsylvania. Howard to Smith, Feb. 26; Aug. 19, 21, 30; Oct. 11; Nov. 11, 1884; Jan. 15, 25; April 14; May 20; June 2, 1885; Sept. 26, 1886; Nov. 21, 1887; to Villard, March 12, 1881; March 1; April 1, 23, 1882; to C. H. Prescott, Jan. 16, 1884, Oregon Improvement Company Records; Thomas Burke to Thomas H. Brents, Oct. 27, 1882, Thomas Burke Papers, UW; *West Shore*, 14(April 1888), 176–179; Daniel H. Gilman to Jones, May 29, 1884, Daniel H. Gilman Papers, UW; Seattle *Daily Intelligencer*, June 16, 1881; Seattle *Post-Intelligencer*, Sept. 25, 1883; Jan. 1, 1886; Feb. 17, 1887; *Seattle Weekly Chronicle*, Oct. 25, 1883; *Tacoma News*, Dec. 4, 1884. In a related development, the Irondale plant, opened near Port Townsend in 1881, made Washington a pioneer of Pacific coast iron manufacturing. See Diane F. Britton, *The Iron and Steel Industry in the Far West: Irondale*, Washington (Niwot: University Press of Colorado, 1991).

54. In return for financing, boat operators customarily turned a third of their catch over to the canneries. A fixed price, set at the beginning of each season, was paid for the remainder. The average boat earned $24 a day in 1882. *West Shore*, 9(Aug. 1883), 192; 10(May 1884), 157; 11(Feb. 1885), 32; 14(Aug. 1888), 451; (Oct. 1888), 527–528, 530–531; Seattle *Daily Intelligencer*, Sept. 4, 1881; Montesano *Chehalis Valley Vidette*, April 26, 1883; *Olympia Transcript*, Sept. 2, 1882; July 14, 1883; Semple to Sheriff of Skamania County, Aug. 13, 22, 1887; to Sheriff of Wahkiakum County, March 17, 1888, Semple Papers, UW; *Northwest*, 3(Dec. 1885), 5; Tacoma *Weekly Ledger*, June 9, 1882; *Seattle Post-Intelligencer*, July 21, 1883.

55. Because Columbia River fish sold for a higher price in San Francisco—$1.20 per dozen cans versus $1.05— Puget Sound canneries often marketed their output as "Columbia River Salmon." The falloff on the Columbia, plus increasing demand, had an impact elsewhere on the coast. British Columbia producers sold over a million dollars worth of salmon a year. Alaska production mounted by a factor of ten between 1883 and 1888. The nineteen canneries operating on the Sound in 1899 turned out 919, 000 cases. A modest shellfish industry also developed during the 1880s. The half-dozen active firms, some harvesting their own beds and others purchasing from Indian suppliers, shipped $50,000 worth of Olympia oysters to San Francisco over a fifteen month period in 1881 and 1882. *Seattle Post-Intelligencer*, Aug. 9, 1887; *West Shore*, 9(July 1883), 152; 13(May 1887), 406; 14(Jan. 1888), 48; 15(April 1889), 221; *Tacoma News*, Oct. 4, 1883; Sept. 18, 1885; Seattle *Daily Intelligencer*, Aug. 21, 1881; Daniel L. Boxberger, *To Fish in Common: The Ethnohistory of Lummi Indian Salmon Fishing* (Lincoln: University of Nebraska Press, 1989), 38–39; *Walla Walla Union*, April 23, 1881; *Olympia Transcript*, March 4, 1882; Jan. 19, 1884; Olympia *Washington Standard*, Feb. 3, 1882.

56. *Tacoma Daily Ledger*, May 12; Nov. 25; Dec. 9, 12, 1883; Feb. 15, 1884; Jan. 3, 7, 9, 1886; April 20; July 15, 1887; David Starr Jordan, *The Days of a Man* (Yonkers: World Book Company, 2 vols., 1922), 1:223; Schwantes, *Pacific Northwest*, 192; Kipling, *From Sea to Sea*, 2:90–93, 102; Collins, *Woman's Trip to Alaska*, 34–38; *Tacoma News*, March 13, 1884; Dec. 11, 1885; David Newsom to *Pacific Christian Advocate*, Sept. 8, 1881, in *David Newsom: The Western Observer, 1805–1882* (Portland: Oregon Historical Society, 1972), 254; William M. Thayer, *Marvels of the New West* (Norwich: The Henry Bill Publishing Company, 1887), 337–341; Lemuel Ely Quigg, *New Empires in the Northwest* (New York: The Tribune Association, 1889), 75.

57. *Walla Walla Statesman*, Feb. 2, 1884; *Walla Walla Union*, July 9, 1887; Aug. 11, 1888; *West Shore*, 14(Feb. 1888), 109; *Northwest*, 2(Oct. 1884), 3–4; 5(June 1887), 24; *Spokane Falls Review*, July 9, 1887; *Tacoma News*, Dec. 13, 1883; June 26; July 3, 1884; Sept. 18, 1885; Nov. 12, 1886; Jan. 14, 1887; *Tacoma Daily Ledger*, June 5; Aug. 30, 1883; Jan. 22, 1884; Jan. 20, 1885; Jan. 8, 18, 27; Aug. 4, 1887; Annual Report, March 4, 1884; Anderson to Wright, March 10, 1888, both Tacoma Land and Improvement Company Papers; Murray Morgan, *Puget's Sound: A Narrative of Early Tacoma and the Southern Sound* (Seattle: University of Washington Press, 1979), 253254; Powell to Chief of Engineers, Nov. 3, 1884, in *Annual Report of the Chief of Engineers 1885*, 2419.

58. "Without the backing of the railroad," a visitor exclaimed, "Tacoma would be simply nothing." *Seattle Post-Intelligencer*, June 9, 1883; *Tacoma News*, July 24, 31, 1884; Sept. 25; Oct. 2, 1885; Sept. 24, 1886; Jan. 14, 1887; *Tacoma Daily Ledger*, June 30; July 1, 3, 4, 31; Aug. 30; Dec. 6, 11, 1883; Jan. 4; May 9, 1884; Jan. 8; March 6, 7, 1886; Sept. 4, 1887; Howard to Smith, Sept. 27, 1884, Oregon Improvement Company Records; Morgan, *Puget's Sound*, 181–182; Minutes, Feb. 20; Nov. 11, 1882; April 11, 1883; May 27, 1885, Tacoma Land and Improvement Company Papers; *Spokane Falls Review*, July 9, 1887.

59. According to a visitor from Walla Walla, Seattle was "situated on more Hills than old Rome when in the height of its world won glory." An eastern writer described Seattle as "rising like a well-filled ampitheatre, and looking

out upon a magnificent waterfront populous with commerce." Capturing the dynamism, James Bryce wrote of finding "business in full swing at seven o'clock A.M.: the shops open, the streets full of people." *West Shore*, 9(March 1883), 49; 12(March 1886), 72; 13(Aug. 1887), 639; 14 (April 1888), 169–170; H. H. D., "The City of Seattle," *Northwest*, 1(Feb. 1883), 4; *Walla Walla Statesman*, Feb. 9, 1884; Ernest Ingersoll, "From the Fraser to the Columbia—Part II," *Harper's New Monthly Magazine*, 68(May 1884), 870; Charles Lord Russell of Killowen, *Diary of a visit to the United States of America in the Year 1883* (New York: The United States Catholic Historical Society, 1910), 107; *Seattle Post-Intelligencer*, Nov. 19, 25, 1882; Feb. 7; March 4; June 27; Nov. 21, 1883; Dec. 19, 1884; Olympia *Washington Standard*, Oct. 19, 1883; Dec. 19, 1884; *Walla Walla Union*, July 19, 1884; Aug. 20, 1887; Burke to Hanson Rasin, Oct. 25, 1889; to Gilman, Sept. 28, 1888, Burke Papers; *Seattle Weekly Chronicle*, May 31, 1883; Schwantes, *Pacific Northwest*, 192; Bryce, *American Commonwealth*, 2:830–831.

60. In order, the four richest individuals were Henry Yesler, Arthur Denny, Watson Squire and David Denny. The Columbia & Puget Sound coal mine railroad was the only corporation listed in the top ten. The irascible Yesler prospered "in spite of himself," wrote Thomas Burke, "for the general advancement of the city forces Yesler along with it." *Seattle Post-Intelligencer*, Sept. 16, 1882; Jan. 21; May 10, 23, 1883; Jan. 27, 1884; March 25; Sept. 28; Oct. 21, 1888; Burke & Rasin to John E. McLain, Sept. 28, 1881; Burke to Louise Ackerson, Nov. 27, 1888; to W. M. York, Dec. 15, 1881, all Burke Papers; *Seattle Weekly Chronicle*, Feb. 24; July 21, 1882; Nov. 22, 1883; Olympia Puget Sound *Weekly Chronicle*, April 24, 1883; Seattle *Daily Intelligencer*, July 6, 1881; *Seattle Times*, May 16, 30, 1889; *Tacoma Daily Ledger*, Aug. 4, 1883.

61. Special Message of William A. Newell, Nov. 4, 1881, U.S. Interior Department, Washington Territorial Papers, 1854–1902, NA; Port Townsend *Puget Sound Weekly Argus*, Nov. 18, 1881; Olympia *Washington Standard*, Dec. 9, 1881; *Seattle Weekly Chronicle*, Jan. 27; Nov. 8, 1883; *Seattle Post-Intelligencer*, May 7, 1882; Aug. 14, 17, 1883; June 13, 1885; Jan. 3, 1886; *Olympia Transcript*, Oct. 13, 1883; Tacoma *Weekly Ledger*, Nov. 11, 1881; *Tacoma News*, Nov. 22, 1883; Olympia *Puget Sound Weekly Courier*, Oct. 23, 1883; *Walla Walla Statesman*, Aug. 12, 1882; Dayton *Columbia Chronicle*, Oct. 21, 1882; *Tacoma Daily Ledger*, Oct. 12, 1883; Jan. 19, 1886; Charles F. Whittlesey to Semple, Aug. 22, 1888, Semple Papers, WSA; *Walla Walla Union*, Aug. 6, 1881; Semple to J. B. Metcalfe, March 2, 24; April 26, 1888; to Board of Regents, Nov. 30, 1888; Metcalfe to Semple, March 23; April 5; May 10, 1888, all Semple Papers, UW.

62. *Seattle Post-Intelligencer*, Sept. 20, 1883; March 29; Oct. 27, 1885; March 19, 1886; *Northwest*, 3(Sept. 1885), 13–14; Howard to Smith, May 19, 1885; March 22, 1886; John Muir to Smith, Sept. 6, 1884, all Oregon Improvement Company Records.

63. Gilman and Burke expected to profit also from land investments along the route and from the construction firm established to build the railroad. Gilman to Jones, Dec. 8, 10, 1883; Jan. 13, 1884; July 30; Aug. 14, 1886; F. H. Whitworth to Gilman, Dec. 1, 1883, all Gilman Papers; *Whatcom Reveille*, Oct. 26, 1883; Howard to Smith, July 29, 1884; Sept. 21; Oct. 13, 1886; Feb. 26, 1889, Oregon Improvement Company Records; Burke to Gilman, April 22, 24; Oct. 3, 1888; to Ackerson, June 5, 1888; to J. D. Smith, April 13, 1889, Burke Papers; *Seattle Post-Intelligencer*, Dec. 28, 1886; Aug. 21; Oct. 2, 1887; March 18, 28; April 21, 29, 1888. For full details on the road, see Robert C. Nesbit, *"He Built Seattle": A Biography of Judge Thomas Burke* (Seattle: University of Washington Press, 1961), chapt. 6. Also see *West Shore*, 11(June 1885), 190; 12(Aug. 1886), 258; 13(Jan. 1887),90.

64. Currently in brief service as territorial chief justice, Burke compared the raising of new capital to having "sixty cases…to hear and decide in about twenty-two days." *Seattle Post-Intelligencer*, June 1, 1888; Gilman to Jones, Feb. 9; May 15, 1887, Gilman Papers; Burke to Gilman, April 18, 1886; May 7, 21, 27; Oct. 3, 1888; to Henry Crawford, Jan. 6, 1887; to J. A. Jameson, March 22, 1888; to Jones, April 4; Oct. 15, 1888; Jan. 4, 1889; to "Dear Captain," Dec. 30, 1888; to L.S. J. Hunt, Jan. 4, 1889; to Browne, Nov. 26, 1888; to T. M. Logan, Sept. 4, 1888; G. M. Haller to Don Carlos Corbett, April 19, 1889, all Burke Papers; *West Shore*, 13(Aug. 1887), 639–640; 14(Dec. 1888), 673–674; Dwight to D. Dwight, April 8, 22, 1888, Dwight Papers; Robert E. Ficken, *Rufus Woods, the Columbia River, and the Building of Modern Washington* (Pullman: Washington State University Press, 1995); Donald B. Robertson, *Encyclopedia of Western Railroad History*, Vol. 3, *Oregon-Washington* (Caldwell: The Caxton Printers, Ltd., 1995), 265–267. Construction money apparently also came from James J. Hill. See Michael P. Malone, *James J. Hill: Empire Builder of the Northwest* (Norman: University of Oklahoma Press, 1996), 142.

65. One in three King County residents was foreign-born, compared to one in six in Walla Walla County. *Walla Walla Statesman*, Feb. 12, 1881; Oct. 27, 1883; Tacoma *Weekly Ledger*, June 10, 1881; *Walla Walla Union*, July 9, 1881; Olympia *Washington Standard*, Sept. 14, 1883; Cheney *North-West Tribune*, Feb. 16, 1883; *Spokane Falls Review*, May 28, 1886; *Seattle Post-Intelligencer*, Jan. 27, 1883.

66. *Seattle Times*, May 29–31, 1889; *Tacoma Daily Ledger*, May 18, 1883; *Seattle Post-Intelligencer*, Aug. 8, 1883; July 17, 1887; O. Jacobs to Brents, Nov. 29, 1882; John J. McGilvra to Grover Cleveland, n.d., both Records relating to the Appointment of Federal Judges and U.S. Attorneys and Marshals, Washington, 1853–1902, M198, NA; Port Townsend *Puget Sound Weekly Argus*, Jan. 20; April 14, 1882; *Spokane Falls Review*, Sept. 13, 1884; Olympia *Washington Standard*, Nov. 9, 1883. For details on a Colfax lynching, see Ibid., Aug. 22, 1884.

67. Olympia's "old, shabby, [and] ill ventilated" high school was "at least 25 years behind the times." Cheney *North-West Tribune*, July 7, 1882; *Walla Walla Union*, Jan. 23, 1875; March 31, 1883; Colfax *Palouse Gazette*, Nov.

10, 1877; *Spokane Falls Chronicle*, Aug. 24, 1881; July 4, 1882; *Seattle Weekly Chronicle*, Feb. 17, 1882; Ritzville *Adams County Record*, May 18, 1886; Olympia *Puget Sound Weekly Courier*, Sept. 25, 1883.

68. Olympia *Washington Standard*, Aug. 4, 18, 1882; Sept. 14, 1883; Jan. 23, 1885; Olympia *Puget Sound Weekly Courier*, Sept. 11, 25; Oct. 16; Nov. 6, 1883; Feb. 5, 1884; *Spokane Falls Chronicle*, Sept. 7, 1881; Tacoma *Weekly Ledger*, June 16, 1882; *Tacoma News*, May 14, 1886; *Tacoma Daily Ledger*, March 9, 1884.

69. In 1855, Washington pioneers narrowly rejected—the vote was 564 for and 650 against—a territorial alcohol ban. Local jurisdictions also imposed license fees on saloons. Pomeroy *Washington Independent*, Sept. 16, 1880; *Asotin Spirit*, Feb. 1, 1884; Port Townsend *Puget Sound Weekly Argus*, Jan. 28, 1886; *Spokane Falls Review*, July 1, 1886; *Tacoma Daily Ledger*, Aug. 2, 1883; Jan. 21, 1886; *Walla Walla Daily Journal*, Aug. 9, 1883; *Walla Walla Union*, June 21, 1884; March 27; Sept. 11, 1886; *Walla Walla Statesman*, Nov. 24, 1877; *Yakima Republic*, March 17, 1887; *Whatcom Reveille*, Nov. 16, 1883; Norman H. Clark, *The Dry Years: Prohibition and Social Change in Washington* (Seattle: University of Washington Press, rev. ed., 1988, 1965), chapt. 2.

70. The somewhat complicated procedure provided for separate votes in municipalities and in unincorporated county precincts. Clark, *Dry Years*, 36; *Walla Walla Union*, March 27; April 3; June 26, 1886; *Spokane Falls Review*, June 9, 20, 29, 1886; Port Townsend *Puget Sound Weekly Argus*, March 18, 1886.

71. Prohibition triumphed in Colfax by a margin of twenty-six votes out of more than nine hundred cast. Olympia *Washington Standard*, July 2, 9, 1886; *Seattle Post-Intelligencer*, June 29, 1886; *Walla Walla Union*, July 3, 1886; *Northwest*, 4(Aug. 1886), 11; *Tacoma News*, July 2, 1886.

72. *Pataha City Spirit*, Aug. 20, 1881; *Walla Walla Union*, June 23; July 14, 1883; *Tacoma News*, Oct. 25; Nov. 22, 1883; Olympia *Washington Standard*, Nov. 4, 1881; Nov. 16, 1883; *Spokane Falls Review*, Jan. 15, 1888; *Whatcom Reveille*, Nov. 9, 1883; Burke, et al. to Semple, Jan. 16, 1888, Semple Papers, UW; *Spokane Falls Chronicle*, June 29, 1881.

73. Women already voted in local school elections. The assembly was influenced by the ambitions of male politicians. Governor William Newell, a prime suffrage supporter, had vainly attempted, in an equal rights variant of nepotism, to appoint his daughter territorial librarian. The Reverend Daniel Bagley intended to organize female voters behind his curiously ironic campaign to reform Republican party politics. Judge Roger Greene, the "wet-nurse of woman suffrage," planned to impanel juries of upper and middle class patrons as a means of closing gambling dens and houses of prostitution. Conservative property owners from both sides of the Cascades favored the reform as the first step toward a fundamental electoral realignment and disenfranchisement of nontaxpayers. T. A. Larson, "The Woman Suffrage Movement in Washington," *PNQ*, 67(April 1976), 52–54; Olympia *Washington Standard*, Nov. 11, 18; Dec. 2, 9, 1881; Aug. 11, 1882; Sept. 14, 1883; *Olympia Transcript*, March 29, 1884; Metcalfe to A. H. Garland, April 15, 1885; Asahel Bush to Garland, April 24, 1885, both Records relating to the Appointment of Federal Judges; *Walla Walla Union*, June 23; July 14; Sept. 8, 1883; June 21, 1884; Nov. 26, 1887; Port Townsend *Puget Sound Weekly Argus*, March 13, 1884; *Tacoma Daily Ledger*, Dec. 12, 1883; *Tacoma News*, Dec. 11, 1884; *Spokane Falls Review*, Oct. 9, 1885; *Northwest*, 4(Aug. 1886), 11, 15; Chauncey Barbour to Semple, Jan. 17, 1887; H. N. Belt to Semple, Jan. 18, 1888, both Semple Papers, UW.

74. Ritzville *Adams County Record*, Dec. 8, 1885; Olympia *Washington Standard*, Dec. 26, 1884; Elwood Evans to Metcalfe, Feb. 28, 1885, Records relating to the Appointment of Federal Judges; Port Townsend *Puget Sound Weekly Argus*, March 6, 1884; Olympia *Puget Sound Weekly Courier*, Feb. 26, 1884; *Tacoma Daily Ledger*, March 13, 1884.

75. The court issued its initial ruling in a case, ironically argued by suffrage advocate Elwood Evans, challenging the right of women to serve on juries. Larson, "Woman Suffrage Movement," 54–55; *Seattle Post-Intelligencer*, Feb. 4, 5, 1887; Aug. 15, 1888; *Tacoma Daily Ledger*, Feb. 5, 9, 1887; *Tacoma News*, Feb. 11, 18, 1887; Beriah Brown, Jr. to Semple, Jan. 16, 1888; A. H. Clarke to Semple, Jan. 17, 1888; C. P. Masterson to Semple, Jan. 17, 1888; J. W. Sprague to Semple, Jan. 18, 1888, all Semple Papers, UW; *Spokane Falls Review*, Jan. 10, 13, 17, 1888.

76. The published federal census listed both Chinese and Indians as "colored." *Walla Walla Union*, Feb. 12, 1881; Cheney *North-West Tribune*, July 7, 1882; Tacoma *Weekly Ledger*, March 31, 1882; Colfax *Palouse Gazette*, Feb. 27; Nov. 19, 1880; April 28, 1882; *Walla Walla Statesman*, Dec. 10, 1881; Olympia *Washington Standard*, June 16, 1882; Olympia *Puget Sound Weekly Courier*, June 17, 1881; *Yakima Signal*, March 31, 1883; Shelton *Mason County Journal*, April 22, 1887.

77. *Whatcom Reveille*, July 20, 1883; *Seattle Post-Intelligencer*, Nov. 21, 1883; Olympia *Puget Sound Weekly Courier*, Jan. 2; June 26, 1883; Anacortes *Northwest Enterprise*, June 28, 1884; C. L. Hooper to Squire, Oct. 15, 1884, Squire Papers, WSA; *Tacoma News*, Sept. 11; Oct. 16, 1885; Port Townsend *Puget Sound Weekly Argus*, July 26; Aug. 2, 1883; *Tacoma Daily Ledger*, Aug. 11, 1883; *Olympia Transcript*, Nov. 3, 1883; Shelton *Mason County Journal*, Oct. 28, 1887.

78. Cheney *North-West Tribune*, April 28, 1882; Tacoma *Weekly Ledger*, April 28, 1882; *Walla Walla Union*, Feb. 21, 1874; Dec. 16, 1882; Jan. 26, 1884; *Walla Walla Statesman*, June 7, 1879; Olympia *Puget Sound Weekly Courier*, March 11, 1884; Seattle Daily Herald, Aug. 1, 1882; *Seattle Weekly Chronicle*, Aug. 9, 16, 23, 1882; *Seattle Post-Intelligencer*, Nov. 2, 1882.

79. *Walla Walla Union*, Jan. 17, 1880; *Walla Walla Statesman*, June 14, 1879; Olympia *Puget Sound Weekly Courier*, March 25, 1884; *Spokan Times*, Aug. 2, 1881; *Tacoma News*, March 19, 1885; *Tacoma Daily Ledger*, Feb. 12, 1886; Olympia *Washington Standard*, Feb. 20, 1885.

80. Unlike other immigrants, most of the Chinese expected to someday return home in possession of at least relative wealth. In late 1883, a Puget Sound newspaper reported the departure, via San Francisco, of a thousand Chinese, carrying $750,000. The general view of the Chinese as willing low-wage workers was occasionally incorrect. In 1880, for instance, Asian laborers went on strike over pay at one of the coal mines, only to be fired and replaced by whites. Howard to Smith, April 29; Sept. 25, 28, 1885, Oregon Improvement Company Records; *Seattle Post-Intelligencer*, Sept. 30, 1885; *Walla Walla Statesman*, April 8, 1882; *Tacoma Daily Ledger*, Nov. 22, 1883; *Spokan Times*, Dec. 23, 1880.

81. A half dozen coal miners died in accidents in a three-month period of 1887. Ficken, *Forested Land*, 72; Quarterly Report, Inspector of Mines, Nov. 1887, Semple Papers, WSA; *Seattle Daily Intelligencer*, June 16, 1881; Olympia *Puget Sound Weekly Courier*, March 4, 1884; Carlos A. Schwantes, *Radical Heritage: Labor, Socialism and Reform in Washington and British Columbia, 1885–1917* (Seattle: University of Washington Press, 1979), 25–27.

82. Shelton *Mason County Journal*, June 24, 1887; *Seattle Times*, May 12, 14; July 20, 1886; *Spokane Falls Review*, March 21, 1886; Haller to Frank W. Hastings, Feb. 23, 1886, Burke Papers; *Tacoma Daily Ledger*, April 25; July 21, 1883.

83. In Tacoma, the anti-Chinese movement merged with, and energized, popular opposition to the Northern Pacific. The voters elected Jacob Weisbach to the mayoralty in 1884, succeeding, in symbolic change-of-the-guard fashion, John Sprague, the longtime N.P. executive and the community's first elected mayor. Three actual Knights of Labor members eventually won places on the city council. *Tacoma News*, Sept. 25; Oct. 23; Nov. 27, 1885; Pendleton *East Oregonian*, Feb. 3, 1885; *Tacoma Daily Ledger*, May 6, 1884; Jan. 6, 1886; Jan. 19, 1887; Morgan, *Puget's Sound*, 218–220.

84. *Seattle Post-Intelligencer*, Sept. 8, 1885; *Northwest*, 3(Oct. 1885), 12; Pendleton *East Oregonian*, Oct. 2, 1885; Howard to Smith, Sept. 25, 1888, Oregon Improvement Company Records. Walker quoted in Ficken, *Forested Land*, 73. Also see *Tacoma News*, Oct. 9, 1885.

85. Chinese pickers hired by another Issaquah grower were turned back by angry white and Indian residents. John Howard was one of the few observers expecting the killers to go free from the beginning. "In the present state of public sentiment," he wrote in late September, "the average mixed jury can hardly be expected to punish." The Chinese government hired former governor Elisha Ferry and other leading members of the bar to assist in the prosecution. J. T. Ronald to Squire, May 17; July 22, 1886, Watson C. Squire Papers, UW; Squire to L. Q. Lamar, Oct. 12, 1885, Washington Territorial Papers; Olympia *Washington Standard*, Sept. 11, 1885; *Spokane Falls Review*, Nov. 26, 1885; *Seattle Post-Intelligencer*, Sept. 11, 1885; Howard to Smith, Sept. 25, 1885, Oregon Improvement Company Records.

86. Muir to Holmes, March 22, 1884; Howard to Smith, Aug. 25; Sept. 15, 25, 28, 1885, all Oregon Improvement Company Records; Squire to Lamar, Oct. 12, 1885, Washington Territorial Papers; *Seattle Post-Intelligencer*, Sept. 23; Oct. 6, 1885; *Tacoma News*, Oct. 2, 1885; Murray Morgan, *Skid Road: An Informal Portrait of Seattle* (Seattle: University of Washington Press ed., 1982, 1951), 88–89.

87. When a falling tree killed a dozen Chinese railroad workers in early 1887, a Spokane newspaper commented that "the elements appear to be as merciless toward Chinamen as the people of Tacoma." A demand for compensation from the Chinese government was rejected, locally, as an insult to the fair name of Tacoma. *Tacoma News*, Oct. 16, 30; Nov. 6, 13, 20, 27; Dec. 11, 18, 1885; Jan. 1; Feb. 19; June 25, 1886; F. Campbell to Squire, June 10, 1886; Proclamation, Nov. 4, 1885, both Squire Papers, UW; Squire to Lamar, Nov. 4, 7, 1885, Washington Territorial Papers; *Seattle Post-Intelligencer*, Nov. 5, 1885; Gilman to Jones, Nov. 15, 1885, Gilman Papers; Morgan, *Puget's Sound*, 237–244; Pettengill, "Puget Sound of Today," 49; *Tacoma Daily Ledger*, Feb. 17, 1886; *Spokane Falls Review*, Feb. 1, 1887. Also see Jules A. Karlin, "The Anti-Chinese Outbreak in Tacoma, 1885," *PNQ*, 39(April 1948), 103–130.

88. The Army stationed 1,273 of its total 25,499 soldiers in Washington Territory, presumably for use in labor disputes. Pointing out that "it has been impossible to find guilty men when they have fouly murdered Chinamen," the *Tacoma News* predicted that "not one juryman in ten thousand" would find the local persons arrested "guilty of any crime." The charges were dropped in 1887. Olympia *Washington Standard*, Nov. 20, 1885; *Spokane Falls Review*, Dec. 9, 1885; Squire to Lamar, Nov. 7, 17, 1885; Proclamation by the President of the United States, Nov. 7, 1885, all Washington Territorial Papers; James N. Allison to Squire, Nov. 7, 1885, Squire Papers, UW; Morgan, *Puget's Sound*, 246–251; *Seattle Post-Intelligencer*, Nov. 8, 10, 15, 1885; April 2, 1886; *Tacoma News*, Nov. 13, 1885.

89. *Seattle Post-Intelligencer*, Jan. 23; Feb. 9–14, 16, 17, 1886; Burke to J. F. Ellis, Feb. 17, 1886; to Charles Voorhees, Feb. 18, 1886; to Ackerson, Feb. 21, 1886; to Bailey Gatzert, March 3, 1886, Burke Papers; Henry L. Yesler to Squire, Feb. 7, 1886; Squire to John Gibbon, Feb. 7, 1886; to Lamar, Feb. 8, 1886; to Cleveland, Feb. 8, 1886 (three wires of this date); Proclamation, Feb. 8, 1886; General Orders 1–3, 5, 9, 12; Secretary of War to Squire, Feb. 13, 1886; Gibbon to Squire, Feb. 12, 1886; A. E. Alden to Squire, Feb. 18, 20, 22, 1886; List of Persons Arrested by the Provost Marshal under Martial Law, Feb. 23, 1886, all Squire Papers, UW. For a detailed account of all developments, see Morgan, *Skid Road*, 95–102. For contemporary coverage, see, in addition to the *P-I* cited above, *West Shore*, 12(March 1886), 76–78. Among those serving in the Home Guard was young newspaper staffer Edmond Meany, later the founder of Washington historiography. See George A. Frykman, *Seattle's Historian and Promoter: The Life of Edmond Stephen Meany* (Pullman: Washington State University Press, 1998), 14–15.

90. Elsewhere in Washington Territory, firm local resolve resulted in rejection of the expulsion movement. "Law abiding citizens" prevented assault upon the Chinese residents of Olympia. Port Townsend voted to "leave the question entirely in the hands of the Government." An anti-Chinese meeting in North Yakima adjourned with no action taken. The closest thing to violence in Spokane was a threatening letter delivered to an Asian merchant. Gibbon to Squire, Feb. 12, 1886; Squire to J. D. DeRussy, May 14, 1887; to W. C. Endicott, Feb. 13, 1886; Warner Miller to Squire, Dec. 29, 1885; Benjamin H. Bristow to Squire, Feb. 19, 1887; clipping from *Frank Leslie's Illustrated Magazine*, Feb. 20, 1886; A. H. Chambers to Squire, Feb. 9, 1886; Henry Landes to Squire, Feb. 10; March 9, 1886, all Squire Papers, UW; Port Townsend *Puget Sound Weekly Argus*, Feb. 10, 1887; W. H. White, et al. To the President, Feb. 23, 1886, Burke Papers; *Yakima Republic*, April 14, 1887; *Spokane Falls Review*, March 30, 1886; Oct. 21, 1887; *Walla Walla Union*, Oct. 10; Nov. 14, 1885.

91. *Seattle Post-Intelligencer*, May 16; June 27, 30; July 3, 9, 10, 12, 1886; July 12, 14, 1887; Olympia *Washington Standard*, Aug. 13, 1886; Ficken, *Forested Land*, 73–75; *Seattle Daily Press*, May 6, 19; June 12, 1886; *Tacoma News*, July 30, 1886; *Seattle Times*, May 7, 8, 12, 17, 19, 21; June 30; July 12, 13, 19, 1886; *Tacoma Daily Ledger*, April 30; May 1, 4, 1887; Howard to Smith, Feb. 23, 27; March 4, 13, 16, 29; April 1, 16, 20; May 4, 21, 1886; April 19; May 17, 1887; Feb. 28; March 13, 28; May 30; Aug. 14, 27, 29; Sept. 1, 14, 28; Oct. 15; Dec. 12, 1888, Oregon Improvement Company Records; Schwantes, *Radical Heritage*, 29–32; *West Shore*, 14(March 1888), 165.

92. Howard to Smith, May 30; Aug. 14, 27, 29; Sept. 14, 28, 1888, Oregon Improvement Company Records; William Cochrane to Semple, Jan. 31, 1889; T. J. Hamilton to Semple, Jan. 30, 1889, Semple Papers, UW; Haines to Semple, Jan. 8, 1889, Semple Papers, WSA; Lytle to J. M. Hoagland, April 26, 1889, Northern Pacific Coal Company Records. On the willingness of lumber companies to "voluntarily" institute labor reforms, see Ficken, *Forested Land*, 74.

93. Although no friend of the Chinese—he walked out of a Port Angeles restaurant upon learning that the establishment employed an Asian cook—Semple took firm preemptive action when a new Seattle anti-Chinese outbreak was rumored in the spring of 1887. Semple to G. H. Mendell, Sept. 1, 1888, Semple Papers, WSA; to ?, May 3, 1887, Washington Territorial Papers; to Secretary of the Interior, Aug. 31, 1887; to John F. King, Feb. 5; March 11, 1886; to Metcalfe, Aug. 21, 1888; to S. T. Packwood, Aug. 27, 1888; Jan. 25, 1889; to Code Commissioners, Sept. 3, 1888; to W. H. Galvani, Sept. 6, 1888; to H. J. Snively, Sept. 26, 1888; to H. W. McNeill, Jan. 24, 1889; to U.S. Attorney General, Feb. 11, 1889; to Frank R. Croasthwaite, April 9, 1889; to Miles C. Moore, March 23, 1889; Cochrane to Semple, Jan. 31, 1889, all Semple Papers, UW; Alan Hynding, *The Public Life of Eugene Semple: Promoter and Politician of the Pacific Northwest* (Seattle: University of Washington Press, 1973), 44–45, 62–66, 89–91, 97–113; Howard to Smith, Jan. 3, 1885, Oregon Improvement Company Records; *Wallace Free Press*, Aug. 27, 1887.

94. McGilvra to the President, Dec. 16, 1886; Jno. T. Morgan to Garland, July 20, 1885; J. F. Banks to Morgan, Dec. 9, 1885; Richard A. Hutchinson to Cleveland, Aug. 1, 1885; J. F. Parker to Garland, Dec. 24, 1885, all Records relating to the Appointment of Federal Judges; *Whatcom Reveille*, June 29; Nov. 2, 1883; *Spokane Falls Review*, Aug. 30, 1884; Nov. 4, 1888; *Seattle Post-Intelligencer*, Jan. 29, 1884; March 1, 1885; *Tacoma News*, Nov. 1, 1883; *Kelso Courier*, Dec. 21, 1888. Woman suffrage advocates damned Turner for casting the decisive tally declaring the female voting law unconstitutional. *Tacoma Daily Ledger*, Feb. 5, 9, 1887.

95. Confirming his reputation as a victim of the "office-seeking disease," Newell secured an inspector's position with the Office of Indian Affairs after leaving the governorship and later ran as an independent candidate for congressional delegate. Moore, who nearly lost his feet to frostbite in the early prospecting days, liked to refer to himself as "the old settler" and a "sturdy self-reliant pioneer." *Spokane Falls Chronicle*, Jan. 24, 1884; *Spokane Falls Review*, June 17, 1884; *Tacoma News*, Jan. 17, 1884; *Yakima Record*, Jan. 26, 1884; Mercedes Sprague Gleason, "The Territorial Governors of the State of Washington—1853–1889" (Master of Librarianship Thesis, University of Washington, 1955), 79; E. P. Ferry to Chester A. Arthur, March 27, 1884; Thomas W. Knox to William E. Chandler, April 17, 1884; Frederick W. Pitkin to H. M. Teller, March 24, 1884; Titus Sheard, et al. to the President, n.d., all Squire Papers, UW; Shelton *Mason County Journal*, April 15, 1887; *Ellensburgh Capital*, March 28, 1889; Waterville *Big Bend Empire*, April 4, 1889; Port Townsend *Puget Sound Weekly Argus*, July 22, 1886; *Seattle Post-Intelligencer*, May 31, 1885; Miles C. Moore Autobiography, 11–12, UW; Charles M. Gates, ed., *Messages of the Governors of the Territory of Washington to the Legislative Assembly, 1854–1889* (Seattle: University of Washington Press, 1940), 278–279. For Semple's pre-gubernatorial career, see Hynding, *Public Life of Eugene Semple*, chaps. 1–4.

96. The Seattle newspaper considered the surveyor generalship the most desirable appointment, "for the reason that there is more money in that than in any of the other places." *Seattle Post-Intelligencer*, March 3, 1883; Ronald to Semple, Jan. 14, 1888, Semple Papers, WSA; L. B. Nash to Garland, Aug. 26, 1888; Wm. H. Upton to Garland, Oct. 1, 1885; Haller to A. P. Gorman, Nov. 11, 1886; C. H. Hanford to Gorman, Nov. 6, 1886; Memorandum, n.d., all Records relating to the Appointment of Federal Judges; Burke to Jones, Jan. 4, 1889; to Nash, Feb. 22, 1889; to Erasmus W. Hills, Feb. 17, 1889; to Benjamin Harrison, Sept. 16, 1889, Burke Papers; Olympia *Washington Standard*, Nov. 19, 1886.

97. At the time of his appointment, Burke's legal practice alone generated an annual income of $27,000. Burke to N. T. Caton, Nov. 23, 1882; to Voorhees, March 20, 1885; to John J. Burke, Dec. 17, 1888; Jan. 5, 1889; to Jones, Dec. 21, 1888; to Ackerson, Dec. 23, 1888, Burke Papers; *Kelso Courier*, Dec. 28, 1888. On Burke's supreme court service, see Nesbit, *"He Built Seattle,"* 291–296.

98. Colfax *Palouse Gazette*, July 14, 1882; *Walla Walla Statesman*, Aug. 19, 1882; Olympia *Washington Standard*, July 21, 1882; *Olympia Transcript*, July 15, 1882; Port Townsend *Puget Sound Weekly Argus*, Aug. 11; Sept. 15; Oct. 6; Dec. 5, 1882; *Seattle Post-Intelligencer*, May 14; Aug. 18, 1882; *Yakima Record*, Aug. 26, 1882; Burke to J. E. Willis, Aug. 31, 1886, Burke Papers; *Walla Walla Union*, Nov. 1, 1884.

99. *Seattle Post-Intelligencer*, Nov. 2, 1882; Port Townsend *Puget Sound Weekly Argus*, Aug. 12, 1886; *Yakima Record*, Nov. 18, 1882; Olympia *Washington Standard*, July 29, 1881; Brents to Clarence B. Bagley, July 17, 1880, Clarence B. Bagley Papers, UW; to the President, Dec. 21, 1882; John B. Allen to Charles Devens, May 13, 1880, both Records relating to the Appointment of Federal Judges; Wellington Clark to Ferry, Aug. 16, 1889, Elisha P. Ferry Papers, UW; Greene to N. H. Owings, Dec. 23, 1880, N. H. Owings Papers, UW; C. H. Bradshaw to Owings, Nov. 2, 1882, William A. Newell Papers, WSA.

100. Territorial politicians rarely addressed the tariff, civil service reform or other national issues. *Seattle Post-Intelligencer*, Oct. 25; Nov. 9, 1882; July 26, 1883; Feb. 28; March 1, 2; May 7, 8, 18, 21, 22, 25, 1884; *Walla Walla Statesman*, June 24; July 29; Aug. 5, 1882; *Walla Walla Union,* Sept. 23; Oct. 21; Nov. 4, 18, 1882; April 5, 12, 19; May 17; Oct. 11, 1884; *Spokane Falls Review*, Oct. 1; Nov. 17, 1886; Nov. 23, 1887; Olympia *Washington Standard*, Sept. 22, 29; Oct. 6, 13, 20; Nov. 10, 1882; Feb. 22; May 2, 1884; Port Townsend *Puget Sound Weekly Argus*, Oct. 27; Nov. 24, 1882; Cheney *North-West Tribune*, March 3, 1882; March 28, 1884; Ellensburgh *Kittitas Standard*, Oct. 6, 1883; Olympia *Puget Sound Weekly Courier*, Jan. 21, 1881; Feb. 5, 1884; Tacoma *Weekly Ledger*, Feb. 17, 24; June 16, 1882; *West Shore*, 8(April 1882), 62; Howard to Smith, Oct. 18, 1884, Oregon Improvement Company Records; Burke to Alfred N. Marion, April 16, 1884, Burke Papers; *Spokane Falls Chronicle*, Feb. 14, 1884; *Tacoma Daily Ledger*, Jan. 27, 31; Feb. 21, 22; March 2, 9; April 10, 15; May 4, 1884; *Tacoma News*, Feb. 21; March 6, 1884.

101. Voorhees privately admitted to having "spent several months in Washington Territory." Brother James Voorhees was a veteran Shakespearian stage performer. On the stump, Voorhees called one N.P. executive a "venal, subservient Dutch tramp" and another railroad official "a dirty, lying son of a bitch." Armstrong won three-quarters of the vote in Northern Pacific-dominated Pierce County. *Tacoma Daily Ledger*, March 10; May 20, 1887; *Walla Walla Union,* July 14, 1883; Oct. 4, 1884; Olympia *Washington Standard*, Oct. 17; Dec. 5, 1884; Sept. 10, 1886; Ritzville *Adams County Record*, Sept. 14, 1886; *Seattle Post-Intelligencer*, Jan. 13, 1885; *Seattle Times*, Sept. 20, 1886; Voorhees to Garland, Nov. 25, 1885, Records relating to the Appointment of Federal Judges; *Olympia Transcript*, Sept. 13, 1884; *Spokane Falls Review*, Aug. 23, 1884; Dayton *Columbia Chronicle*, Dec. 16, 1882.

102. *Tacoma Daily Ledger*, Jan. 23, 1885; Jan. 9, 1886; *Walla Walla Union,* June 27; Sept. 5, 19, 1885; Feb. 27; July 31; Aug. 14; Sept. 25; Oct. 9, 1886; *Northwest*, 4(Aug. 1886), 11; *Seattle Post-Intelligencer*, June 17, 1886; Jan. 20; Feb. 18, 1887; *Spokane Falls Review*, July 17, 1885; April 13; Sept. 23; Oct. 7, 1886; *Tacoma News*, June 18; July 30, 1886; Port Townsend *Puget Sound Weekly Argus*, Feb. 11; Aug. 26; Oct. 21, 1886; Olympia *Washington Standard*, Oct. 2, 23; Nov. 20; Dec. 4, 1885; Jan. 1, 1886; March 18, 1887; Burke to J. P. Judson, Feb. 17, 1885; to Voorhees. Feb. 20, 1885; to N. Ostrander, Feb. 22, 1885; to Marion, Feb. 22, 1885; to C. H. Warren, March 16, 1885, Burke Papers.

103. Former governor William Newell received five percent of the vote in 1886 as a third party candidate. Fifteen counties shifted to Allen from the 1886 Voorhees column. Overall, Allen won thirty of the thirty-two counties, with one even. *Olympia Transcript*, Sept. 13, 1884; Port Townsend *Puget Sound Weekly Argus*, Nov. 4, 17, 1886; *Seattle Times*, Aug. 20; Sept. 14, 1886; *Spokane Falls Review*, Aug. 12; Sept. 12, 14, 28, 1886; *Seattle Post-Intelligencer*, June 5, 16, 1886; *Tacoma News*, Dec. 3, 1886; *Walla Walla Union,* Dec. 8, 1888.

104. Burke to Gilman, July 18, 1884, Burke Papers; *Pullman Herald*, Dec. 1, 1888; *Kelso Courier*, Sept. 28; Nov. 2, 1888; *Ellensburgh Capital*, Feb. 7, 1889.

105. *Seattle Post-Intelligencer*, May 8, 1888; Port Townsend *Puget Sound Weekly Argus*, May 13, 1881; Olympia *Washington Standard*, Oct. 7, 1881; *Tacoma Daily Ledger*, Dec. 7, 1883; Olympia *Puget Sound Weekly Courier*, Jan. 1, 1884; *Walla Walla Statesman*, Dec. 8, 1883; *Walla Walla Union,* Sept. 20, 1884.

Notes—Chapter Nine
Through Years Added to Years

1. *Walla Walla Union*, Nov. 23, 1889.
2. *Seattle Post-Intelligencer*, June 23, 1889; *Seattle Times*, June 10, 11, 1889; Murray Morgan, *Skid Road: An Informal Portrait of Seattle* (Seattle: University of Washington Press ed., 1982, 1951), 107–113; Clarence B. Bagley, *History of Seattle: From the Earliest Settlement to the Present Time* (Chicago: The S. J. Clarke Publishing Company, 3 vols., 1916), 1:230–231; Frederick James Grant, ed., *History of Seattle, Washington* (New York: American Publishing and Engraving Co., 1891), 260; John L. Howard to Elijah Smith, June 8, 1889, Oregon Improvement Company Records, UW; Thomas Burke to Mrs. S. Louise Ackerson, July 1, 1889, Thomas Burke Papers, UW.
3. *Seattle Post-Intelligencer*, July 29, 1887; May 9, 1888; June 20, 1889; Burke to Ackerson, July 1, 1889, Burke Papers; *Seattle Times*, June 11, 12, 1889; Robert E. Ficken, *The Forested Land: A History of Lumbering in West-*

ern Washington (Seattle: University of Washington Press, 1988), 60. Also see Morgan, *Skid Road*, 113–115; John R. Finger, "The Seattle Spirit, 1851–1893," *Journal of the West*, 13(July 1974), 28–45.

4. Municipal authorities attempted to limit reconstruction of houses of prostitution and Chinese laundries, but rejected a proposed three month closure of the city's hundred-some saloons as an infringement on private property rights. *Seattle Times*, June 10, 11, 13, 15, 17, 18, 26, 28; July 1; Aug. 10, 1889; *Seattle Post-Intelligencer*, June 19–21, 23, 26, 30; July 1, 1889; Ficken, *Forested Land*, 60.

5. *Seattle Times*, May 24; Aug. 5, 1889; Robert E. Ficken and Charles P. LeWarne, *Washington: A Centennial History* (Seattle: University of Washington Press, 1988), xix; Seattle *Daily Intelligencer*, June 25, 1881; Olympia *Puget Sound Weekly Courier*, April 3, 1883; *Olympia Transcript*, May 20, 1882; Olympia *Washington Standard*, May 26, 1882; *Spokane Falls Chronicle*, July 27, 1881; July 25, 1882; *Spokane Falls Review*, Aug. 30; Sept. 15, 1884; *Yakima Signal*, Feb. 17, 1883.

6. Other eastern Washington towns had similar experiences. A wind-accentuated blaze destroyed fifty-eight buildings in Colfax on July 14, 1882, leaving only five structures standing in the town center. A fire originating in a Chinese laundry devastated the Sprague business district in December 1882. Cheney burned in February 1883. A May 1888 conflagration ruined Palouse City, where the citizenry had taken no action to protect against or fight fires. Founded in 1882, Pullman lost its commercial district to fire three times by 1889. The one eastside blaze not considered a disaster was the April 1884 destruction of Ainsworth. *Spokan Times*, Aug. 7, 1880; *Spokane Falls Chronicle*, June 29; July 27, 1881; July 18, 25, 1882; *Sprague Herald*, July 22; Dec. 15, 1882; Jan. 26, 1883; *Spokane Falls Review*, Aug. 20; Nov. 8; Dec. 23, 1884; March 16, 1886; Sept. 18, 1888; D. H. Dwight to D. D. Dwight, May 18, 1887, Daniel H. Dwight Papers, EWSHS; Colfax *Palouse Gazette*, July 21, 1882; Cheney *North-West Tribune*, July 21, 1882; Feb. 9, 1883; *Walla Walla Union*, April 5, 1884; May 26, 1888; *Pullman Herald*, Jan. 29, 1889.

7. The inconvenience caused by destruction of the invaluable land office records produced a campaign in Olympia to ban smoking in public buildings. The fire phenomenon was not limited to Washington Territory. In June 1886, for instance, the new Canadian Pacific terminal city, Vancouver, B.C., was destroyed. *Olympia Transcript*, May 20, 27, 1882; Sept. 1, 15, 1883; Olympia *Washington Standard*, May 26, 1882; Sept. 14, 21, 1883; Aug. 8, 1884; June 18, 1886; Olympia *Puget Sound Weekly Courier*, Sept. 18, 25, 1883; William McMicken to Commissioner, General Land Office, Sept. 13, 1883, Letters Received from the Surveyors General of Washington, 1854–1883, RG 49, NA; *Tacoma Daily Ledger*, April 13, 15, 1884; *Tacoma News*, Jan. 29, 1885; L. Harrison to McMicken, April 16, 1884, Vol. 2, Series 88, Records of the Bureau of Land Management, RG 49, FRC.

8. By 1889, the traditional "h" was often dropped from Ellensburgh's name. *Ellensburgh Capital*, July 8, 1889; Katherine G. Morrissey, *Mental Territories: Mapping the Inland Empire* (Ithaca: Cornell University Press, 1997), 43–57; John Fahey, *Inland Empire: D. C. Corbin and Spokane* (Seattle: University of Washington Press, 1965), 83–84; and *The Inland Empire: Unfolding Years, 1879–1929* (Seattle: University of Washington Press, 1986), 215–216; *Seattle Times*, Aug. 6, 1889.

9. Washington, one writer quipped, "would make three Nevada's." Port Townsend *Puget Sound Weekly Argus*, Nov. 24, 1882; *Seattle Post-Intelligencer*, Aug. 22, 1883; *Spokane Fall Chronicle*, Jan. 4, 1883; *Tacoma Daily Ledger*, Jan. 8, 1885; Jan. 1, 1887; *Olympia Transcript*, Jan. 14, 1882; *Spokane Falls Review*, July 19, 1884; *Whatcom Reveille*, June 29, 1883.

10. *Olympia Transcript*, Jan. 21, 1882; Olympia *Puget Sound Weekly Courier*, Feb. 18; April 1, 1881; *Seattle Post-Intelligencer*, July 19, 1882; Aug. 31, 1883; *Walla Walla Union*, Nov. 19, 1881; Jan. 28; Feb. 18; Aug. 26, 1882; March 24; Sept. 1, 1883; Port Townsend *Puget Sound Weekly Argus*, Sept. 16, 1881; *Lewiston Teller*, Dec. 1, 1881; Colfax *Palouse Gazette*, Sept. 1, 1882; Olympia *Washington Standard*, Dec. 16, 1881.

11. Cheney *North-West Tribune*, Jan. 27; July 28, 1882; Colfax *Palouse Gazette*, Nov. 5, 1880; *Yakima Republic*, March 10, 1887; Port Townsend *Puget Sound Weekly Argus*, Sept. 29, 1882; *Seattle Post-Intelligencer*, Nov. 25, 1882; Feb. 25, 1886; March 4, 5, 1887; *Lewiston Teller*, Feb. 9, 16; June 29; July 13; Aug. 31, 1882; *Moscow Mirror*, Oct. 30; Dec. 4, 1885; Feb. 26, 1886; *Wallace Free Press*, Oct. 3; Nov. 5, 12, 1887; *Northwest*, 4(Feb. 1886), 9; Palouse City *Boomerang*, Sept. 20, 1882; *Spokane Falls Review*, Oct. 21, 1887; Jan. 1; July 29, 1888; *Walla Walla Union*, Oct. 7; Nov. 18, 1882; Feb. 20, 1886; Merle W. Wells, "Politics in the Panhandle: Opposition to the Admission of Washington and North Idaho, 1886–1888," *PNQ*, 46(July 1955), 79–89.

12. "Rainier," the obvious alternative to "Tacoma," was rejected for patriotic reasons. "It would be absurd," noted one critic, "to alienate the name of the Father of his Country from Washington Territory and bestow upon it that of an English Lord who never saw any part of America." *Seattle Post-Intelligencer*, April 23; Dec. 13, 1882; Jan. 1, 1885; Jan. 18, 1889; Olympia *Washington Standard*, Jan. 13, 1866; Cheney *North-West Tribune*, Dec. 22, 1882; *Spokane Falls Review*, Sept. 29, 1887; March 2, 1888; *Tacoma Daily Ledger*, July 15, 24; Aug. 5, 1887; *Walla Walla Union*, June 23, 1883; March 22, 1884; *Yakima Signal*, Aug. 4, 1883; Anacortes *Northwest Enterprise*, April 5, 1884; *Tacoma News*, Nov. 1, 1883; *Yakima Republic*, April 28, 1887; *Northwest*, 4(Feb. 1886), 10; 5(May 1887), 10; (Dec. 1887), 16; 6(April 1888), 35; Ellensburgh *Kittitas Standard*, Sept. 22, 1883.

13. Twenty-one respondents endorsed such variants on Washington as "Washingtonia," "Washingtona," "George Washington" and "Martha Washington." Nineteen *P-I* readers voted for "Tacoma." *Seattle Post-Intelligencer*, May 13, 1888; *Olympia Transcript*, Oct. 27, 1883; Port Townsend *Puget Sound Weekly Argus*, Jan. 24, 1889; *Kelso Courier*, Feb. 1, 1889.

14. *Spokane Falls Review*, Oct. 27, 1887; Jan. 8, 1888; *West Shore*, 7(Sept. 1881), 240; 11(March 1885), 64; 15(April 1889), 204, 207; Olympia *Puget Sound Weekly Courier*, March 27, 1883; *Olympia Transcript*, June 10, 1882; March 1, 1884; Olympia *Washington Standard*, June 17, 1881; May 25; Aug. 3, 1883; Oct. 15; Nov. 26, 1886.

15. Other communities seeking the capital included Waitsburg, Pasco and Ellensburg. North Yakima's defunct predecessor, Yakima City, had once been promoted for the honor. Spokane did intend to offer itself should northern Idaho be annexed and the boundary line moved to the east. *Spokane Falls Review*, Jan. 5, 6, 12, 14; Dec. 20, 1888; *West Shore*, 13(Sept. 1887), 697–703; (Oct. 1887), 719–720; 14(Nov. 1888), 624; *Yakima Republic*, March 17; Dec. 1, 1887; Ritzville *Adams County Record*, Jan. 26, 1886; *Seattle Post-Intelligencer*, Feb. 4, 1886; *Yakima Record*, July 17, 1880.

16. *Olympia Transcript*, June 24, 1882; *Walla Walla Statesman*, March 3, 1883; *Walla Walla Union,* March 10, 1883; Montesano *Chehalis Valley Vidette*, Feb. 1, 1883; Alex. Montgomery to D. W. Voorhees, March 26, 1886, U.S. Interior Department, Washington Territorial Papers, 1854–1902, NA; *Seattle Weekly Chronicle*, Feb. 23, 1883; *Yakima Signal*, Sept. 1, 1883.

17. Annexation of northern Idaho was written off as a lost cause by 1889. Southern Idaho, appealing to the north through such gestures as placement of the territorial university in Moscow, vowed to fight Washington's admission in the event annexation was pursued. Statehood, the veteran editor John Miller Murphy observed in a postelection commentary, was "the prevailing rage at this time." Dayton *Columbia Chronicle*, March 3, 1883; Olympia *Puget Sound Weekly Courier*, March 6, 1883; Shelton *Mason County Journal*, Nov. 25, 1887; *Seattle Post-Intelligencer*, July 3, 1885; March 20; Nov. 27; Dec. 15, 19, 1888; *Spokane Falls Review*, July 8, 1885; Jan. 26, 30; Feb. 7, 1889; *Tacoma Daily Ledger*, Dec. 2, 1888; *Ellensburgh Capital*, Nov. 15, 22, 29, 1888; *Walla Walla Union*, Nov. 23, 1888; Carlos A. Schwantes, *The Pacific Northwest: An Interpretive History* (Lincoln: University of Nebraska Press, 1989), 211.

18. *Seattle Post-Intelligencer*, Dec. 8, 1888; Jan. 2, 5, 1889; *Tacoma Daily Ledger*, Nov. 21, 28; Dec. 20, 1888; *Ellensburgh Capital*, Dec. 13, 1888; *Spokane Falls Review*, Dec. 21, 1888.

19. *Ellensburgh Capital*, Jan. 3, 10, 1889; *Tacoma News*, Jan. 4, 1889; A Petition to the Congress of the United States, Jan. 3, 1889, Washington Territorial Papers; *Seattle Post-Intelligencer*, Jan. 5, 26, 1889; *Spokane Falls Review*, Jan. 5, 12, 1889.

20. The initial Democratic omnibus plan also included New Mexico Territory. *Seattle Post-Intelligencer*, Dec. 19, 26, 1888; Jan. 26; Feb. 21, 22; March 7, 1889; *Tacoma Daily Ledger*, Dec. 15, 1888; Feb. 23; May 1, 1889; *Spokane Falls Review*, Dec. 21, 1888; *Tacoma News*, Feb. 21, 1889; John B. Allen to Elisha P. Ferry, March 1, 1889, Elisha P. Ferry Papers, UW. Left out of the omnibus act, Idaho secured admission in 1890.

21. The maximum two-out-of-three procedure was known as the "Illinois Plan" from use in the selection of that state's house of representatives. Delegate qualifications were the same as those for the territorial legislature, thus preventing current federal appointees from serving. The most unusual district embraced the small eastern Washington counties of Adams, Garfield, Asotin and Franklin, only two of which had a common boundary. *Tacoma Daily Ledger*, March 5, 19; April 23, 1889; *Walla Walla Union,* March 23; April 20, 1889; *Spokane Falls Review*, March 22, 1889; Eugene Semple to Burke, March 12, 1889; to C. H. Hanford, March 18, 1889, Eugene Semple Papers, UW; *Ellensburgh Capital*, April 25, 1889.

22. *Seattle Post-Intelligencer*, May 15; July 6, 1889; *Spokane Falls Review*, Nov. 4, 1888; June 6, 1889; *Seattle Times*, May 15, 1889. For the official list of winners, see Members of Constitutional Convention, Convened July 4, 1889, Miles C. Moore Papers, WSA. Biographical details are from *Tacoma Daily Ledger*, July 4, 7, 1889; Olympia *Washington Standard*, July 19, 1889; *The Journal of the Washington State Constitutional Convention, 1889,* ed. Beverly Paulik Rosenow (Seattle: Book Publishing Company, 1962), 465–490. A dozen delegates, including five from Scotland, were foreign-born. Only one, Gwin Hicks of Tacoma, was a Washington native by birth. Fourteen individuals had spent substantial time in California before moving to Washington Territory. Two delegates, Edward Eldridge of Whatcom and Francis Henry of Thurston County, had attended the 1878 convention.

23. *Tacoma Daily Ledger*, May 8, 1889; *Tacoma News*, April 13; June 4, 1889; *Pullman Herald*, April 6, 1889; *Spokane Falls Review*, May 3, 1889; Olympia *Washington Standard*, May 10, 1889; Port Townsend *Puget Sound Weekly Argus*, May 16, 1889.

24. Washington surrendered all claims to remaining federal land within its borders. *Tacoma Daily Ledger*, March 27; May 3, 10, 14, 1889; *Seattle Post-Intelligencer*, March 8, 12; May 21; June 2, 1889; Olympia *Washington Standard*, June 28, 1889; *Spokane Falls Review*, May 18, 1889; *Seattle Times*, July 16, 1889; Port Townsend *Puget Sound Weekly Argus*, May 23, 1889.

25. The constitution confirmed titles in the small number of cases where the General Land Office had mistakenly issued patents embracing tidal acreage. *Tacoma News*, Dec. 13, 1883; July 3, 1884; March 29; May 31, 1889; Roy O. Hoover, "The Public Land Policy of Washington State: The Initial Period, 1889–1912" (Ph.D. diss., Washington State University, 1967), 19; Burke to Woodward & Woodward, Nov. 12, 1886; to C. J. Beerstecher, Dec. 18, 1879, Burke Papers; *Seattle Times*, May 16; Aug. 16, 1889; *Tacoma Daily Ledger*, May 16, 1889; *Whatcom Reveille*, Aug. 17, 31; Oct. 26, 1883; Olympia *Washington Standard*, June 7, 1889; *Anacortes Progress*, Aug. 3, 1889; Frederick J. Yonce, "Public Land Disposal in Washington" (Ph.D. diss., University of Washington, 1969), 189192.

26. Judge Thomas Burke experienced great difficulty, for instance, in securing municipal approval for a new Railroad Avenue parallel to the Seattle waterfront, providing the right-of-way for the Lake Shore & Eastern and later for James J. Hill's Great Northern. Howard to C. H. Prescott, Feb. 20, 1884; to Smith, June 23, 1884; July 15; Aug. 4, 1887; June 4; Oct. 5, 1888; Feb. 13, 1889, Oregon Improvement Company Records; Burke & Haller to F. W. James, Feb. 1, 1887; Burke to W. H. Chickering, Feb. 4, 1887; to Henry Crawford, Feb. 13, 1887; to Ackerson, Feb. 15, 1887; to Carrie L. Allen, May 1, 1888, all Burke Papers; *Seattle Post-Intelligencer*, Feb. 22, 1887; Feb. 19, 21; July 13, 14, 1889; *Tacoma Daily Ledger*, Sept. 4, 1887; March 10; May 16, 1889; *Seattle Times*, July 15; Aug. 12, 1889; *Tacoma News*, Sept. 25; Oct. 2, 1885; Sept. 24; Oct. 1, 1886; April 13, 1889; *Whatcom Reveille*, Aug. 17, 1883; *Spokane Falls Review*, March 7, 1889; *Seattle Weekly Chronicle*, March 9, 1883; Olympia *Washington Standard*, June 7, 1889. On the Railroad Avenue imbroglio, see Robert C. Nesbit, *"He Built Seattle": A Biography of Judge Thomas Burke* (Seattle: University of Washington Press, 1961), 116–117, 215–216. Eastern Washington newspapers published some of the best analyses of the tideland question. See, for example, *Walla Walla Union*, April 27, 1889.

27. Howard to Smith, June 23, 1884; June 4; Oct. 5, 1888; Feb. 13, 1889; to C. A. Dolph, May 9, 1889, Oregon Improvement Company Records; *Tacoma Daily Ledger*, March 6, 27; April 25, 1889; *Tacoma News*, April 6, 13, 25; June 22; July 11, 1889; *Seattle Post-Intelligencer*, May 5, 21, 1889.

28. In the aftermath of the disaster, the *P-I* commented, Seattleites had nearly "forgotten" the convention. *Tacoma Daily Ledger*, July 4, 1889; *Walla Walla Union,* July 13, 20, 27; Aug. 3, 10, 1889; *Seattle Post-Intelligencer*, June 22, 1889.

29. *Walla Walla Union,* July 13, 1889; *Tacoma Daily Ledger*, July 4, 5, 1889. Led by Hoyt and based upon the railroad issue, Republican opposition in King County was the main threat to Elisha Ferry's gubernatorial ambitions. W. Lair Hill to Austin Mires, Aug. 26, 1889, Austin Mires Papers, WSU.

30. Delegates came and went according to the dictates of private business. The Ellensburg members, for example, returned home after the time in that city. A dozen delegates were away on an August day devoted to resolution of some major issues. Among the major expenses were staff salaries, ranging from $6 a day for the chief clerk to $1.50 for the chaplain, the $27 daily cost of ice, and the $800 spent to print a thousand copies of the constitution. Convention managers eventually exceeded their congressionally mandated budget by 50 percent, a cost overrun incorporated into the territorial debt assumed by the new state government. The largest committee, state lands, had fifteen members and the smallest, military affairs, had five. *Journal of the Constitutional Convention*, 5, 7–8, 15–16, 19–20, 34–35, 37, 187–188, 438–439; *Walla Walla Union*, July 27; Aug. 3, 10; Oct. 5, 1889; Miles C. Moore to F. R. Gault, July 25, 1889, Miles C. Moore Letterbook, WSL; *Seattle Times*, July 17, 19, 23, 1889; *Spokane Falls Review*, July 26; Aug. 2, 1889; *Tacoma Daily Ledger*, July 13; Aug. 2, 1889; Ferry to J. H. McGraw, Oct. 1, 1892, Ferry Papers.

31. Thomas Reed was the father of Mark Reed, the influential twentieth century lumberman and Republican party leader. Including Reed, five of the seven members of the committee on the state capital hailed from western Washington. Although the voting for the capital location was separate from that on the constitution, the procedure to be used was part of the document, as Article XIV, Section 1. *Journal of the Constitutional Convention*, 48, 64, 120, 137, 224, 251–252, 287–288; T. A. Larson, "The Woman Suffrage Movement in Washington," *PNQ*, 67(April 1976), 55; Norman H. Clark, *The Dry Years: Prohibition and Social Change in Washington* (Seattle: University of Washington Press, rev. ed., 1988, 1965), 43–45; *Seattle Post-Intelligencer*, Aug. 4, 1889.

32. *Journal of the Constitutional Convention*, 99–106, 118–121, 130–144, 308–315; *Seattle Times*, July 18, 20, 27, 1889; *Walla Walla Union*, July 20, 27, 1889; *Seattle Post-Intelligencer*, July 14, 21, 1889.

33. See Article XII, Sections 15, 18, 20 and 22 for anti-corporate rhetoric. The legislature was authorized to sell timber and minerals separate from the land. Article VIII, Section 6 allowed an additional five percent debt for major public improvements like the waterworks contemplated in Seattle. *Journal of the Constitutional Convention*, 38–39, 41–42, 56–57, 60, 69, 71–72, 95, 150–155, 188–189, 202, 204–208, 212, 249–250, 255–256, 259–263; *Seattle Post-Intelligencer*, July 13, 15, 17, 18; Aug. 2, 5, 7, 18, 1889; *Seattle Times*, July 12, 23, 24; Aug. 1, 2, 7, 1889; *Tacoma Daily Ledger*, July 18, 1889; *Walla Walla Union,* July 20; Aug. 3, 10, 1889.

34. Tideland leases were limited to thirty years. *Anacortes Progress*, Aug. 17, 1889; Joseph Simon to Howard, May 10, 17, 1889; Dolph to Smith, April 26, 1889; Howard to Smith, July 25; Aug. 19, 1889; to Simon, May 20, 1889; J. C. Haines to Smith, Aug. 26, 1889, all Oregon Improvement Company Records; *Seattle Post-Intelligencer*, July 11–13, 24; Aug. 8, 9, 19, 1889; *Spokane Falls Review*, July 23, 1889; John Leary, et al. to Shore Owners, July 20, 1889, Ferry Papers; Ficken, *Forested Land*, 76; *Journal of the Constitutional Convention*, 42, 55, 61–62, 72; 85, 316–317, 348–350; 363–364; *Seattle Times*, Aug. 14, 1889. Walkers thoughts and actions regarding tidelands are detailed in his letters to W. H. Talbot of July 12, 15, 21, 24, 31, 1889, Cyrus Walker Letterbooks, Ames Collection, UW. For the details of harbor line designation during the 1890s, see Hoover, "Public Land Policy of Washington State," 119–147.

35. *Anacortes Progress*, Aug. 24, 1889; *Walla Walla Union,* Sept. 28, 1889; *Seattle Post-Intelligencer*, Aug. 23, 1889; *Spokane Falls Review*, Aug. 27, 1889; *Tacoma Daily Ledger*, Aug. 12, 24, 1889.

36. *Spokane Falls Review*, Aug. 25; Sept. 1, 4, 5, 20, 22, 27, 1889; Thomas Ewing to Watson C. Squire, Dec. 23, 1889, Watson C. Squire Papers, UW; *Seattle Times*, Sept. 24, 1889; *Walla Walla Union,* Sept. 21, 28, 1889; *Seattle Post-Intelligencer*, Aug. 14, 1889; *Tacoma News*, Nov. 6, 1885; D. E. Woodruff to Ferry, Sept. 7, 1889, Ferry Papers.

37. Franklin and Skamania cast the smallest number of votes, a total of 243 between the two counties. In a lingering reflection of traditional opposition to statehood, over six thousand persons voting for governor declined to register an opinion on the constitution. *Seattle Post-Intelligencer*, Oct. 23, 1889; *Walla Walla Union*, Nov. 2, 1889; *Tacoma Daily Ledger*, Oct. 23, 1889.

38. Olympia was the choice of eighteen counties, Ellensburg of nine and North Yakima of seven. Olympia was favored by 98 percent of Thurston County voters, North Yakima of 97 percent in Yakima County and Ellensburg of 91 percent in Kittitas County. In excess of a thousand votes were divided among other towns, with Centralia receiving 607, abandoned Yakima City 314 and Pasco 130. *Walla Walla Union*, Nov. 2, 1889; *Seattle Post-Intelligencer*, Oct. 24, 1889; *Spokane Falls Review*, Oct. 3, 1889; *Tacoma Daily Ledger*, Oct. 23, 1889.

39. Washington's legal membership in the Union was dated November 11, 1889, the day President Benjamin Harrison signed the admission act. *Walla Walla Union*, Nov. 23, 1889.

Bibliography

Unpublished Manuscripts and Government Documents

John C. Ainsworth Papers, University of Oregon Library
_____ Reminiscences, Oregon Historical Society
S. L. Alexander Diary, Eastern Washington State Historical Society
James Archer Letters, Maryland Historical Society
William H. Avery Correspondence, Washington State Library
Manson F. Backus Collection, University of Washington Library
Clarence Bagley Collection, University of Washington Library
_____ Papers, University of Washington Library
Daniel Bagley Papers, University of Washington Library
William J. Ballou Reminiscences, Bancroft Library, University of California, Berkeley
H. H. Bancroft Scrapbook, Bancroft Library, University of California, Berkeley
Samuel Benn Reminiscences, Bancroft Library, University of California, Berkeley
Daniel B. Bigelow Diary, Washington State Historical Society
_____ Reminiscences, Washington State Historical Society
Blaine Family Letters, University of Washington Library
George C. Blankenship Diary, University of Washington Library
Cyrus Bradley Papers, Washington State University Library
Robert Bridges Scrapbooks, University of Washington Library
Albert Briggs Reminiscences, Bancroft Library, University of California, Berkeley
Joseph H. Brown Papers, Oregon Historical Society
J. J. Browne Papers, Eastern Washington State Historical Society
Thomas Burke Papers, University of Washington Library
Bureau of Land Management Records, Series 88, RG 49, Federal Records Center, Seattle
Thomas M. Chambers Papers, Washington State Historical Society
Colville Indian Agency Records, RG 75, Federal Records Center, Seattle
Jay Cooke Papers, Historical Society of Pennsylvania
Correspondence of the Office of Exploration and Surveys Concerning Isaac Stevens' Survey of a Northern Route for the Pacific R.R., 1853–61, RG 48, National Archives
Correspondence of the Office of Indian Affairs, Letters Received, 1824–1881, M234, National Archives
Correspondence of the Office of Indian Affairs, Letters Sent, 1824–1881, M21, National Archives
Medorem Crawford Papers, University of Oregon Library
Walter Crockett Letters, University of Washington Library
George L. Curry Letters, Oregon Historical Society
Matthew P. Deady Papers, Oregon Historical Society
Arthur A. Denny Papers, Washington State Historical Society
Department of Oregon Records, U.S. Army Continental Commands, RG 393, National Archives
Department of the Pacific Records, 1861–1865, National Archives
Dispatches from United States Consuls in Victoria, 1862–1906, T130, National Archives
John B. Dimick Papers, Oregon Historical Society
James Doty Journal, University of Washington Library
Sir James Douglas Private Papers, Bancroft Library, University of California, Berkeley
Dubuar Scrapbooks, University of Washington Library
C. B. Dunning Papers, Eastern Washington State Historical Society
Daniel H. Dwight Papers, Eastern Washington State Historical Society
Harriet Carleton Dyer Correspondence, Washington State Historical Society
Winfield S. Ebey Papers, University of Washington Library

Edwin Eells Papers, Washington State Historical Society
Edward Eldridge Reminiscences, Bancroft Library, University of California, Berkeley
Elwood Evans Papers, Western Americana Collection, Yale University
Elisha P. Ferry Papers, University of Washington Library
_____ Washington State Archives
Alvan Flanders Papers, Washington State Archives
Fort Nisqually Journal, University of Washington Library
Robert Frost Reminiscences, University of Washington Library
Guert Gansevoort Letterbook, Library of Congress
Selucious Garfielde Letters, University of Washington Library
Edward R. Geary Papers, Oregon Historical Society
Addison C. Gibbs Papers, Oregon Historical Society
George Gibbs Letters, Western Americana Collection, Yale University
Daniel H. Gilman Papers, University of Washington Library
Richard D. Gholson Papers, Washington State Archives
Calvin H. Hale Correspondence, Washington State Library
Alfred Hall Correspondence, Bancroft Library, University of California, Berkeley
Granville O. Haller Papers, University of Washington Library
Abby J. Hanford Reminiscences, Bancroft Library, University of California, Berkeley
L. B. Hastings Journal, Washington State Historical Society
Walter T. Henne Diary, Eastern Washington State Historical Society
Nathaniel P. Hill Diary, Jefferson County Historical Society
Hudson's Bay Company Account Books at Fort Nisqually, 1833–1850, University of Washington
    Library
James Family Papers, University of Washington Library
August V. Kautz Journal, Library of Congress
A. E. Keats Letters, Eastern Washington State Historical Society
Josiah Keller Papers, Western Americana Collection, Yale University
Benjamin F. Kendall Papers, Oregon Historical Society
_____ University of Washington Library
Joseph Lane Papers, Indiana University Library
_____ Oregon Historical Society
James S. Lawson Reminiscences, Bancroft Library, University of California, Berkeley
Letters and Reports Received by the Secretary of the Treasury from Special Agents, 1854–1861, M177,
    National Archives
Letters of Application and Recommendation during the Administration of Ulysses S. Grant, 1869–
    1877, M968, National Archives
Letters Received by the Office of the Adjutant General, 1822–1860, M567, National Archives
Letters Received by the Office of the Adjutant General, 1871–1880, M666, National Archives
Letters Received from the Surveyors General of Washington, 1854–1883, RG 49, National Archives
Letters Sent by Secretary of Treasury to Collectors of Customs at Pacific Ports, M176, National Archives
Abraham Lincoln Papers, Library of Congress
Michael F. Luark Diary, University of Washington Library
Charles H. Mason Correspondence, Washington State Library
_____ Western Americana Collection, Yale University
McBeth-Crawford Collection, Idaho State Historical Society
George B. McClellan Correspondence, University of Washington Library
McElroy Family Papers, University of Washington Library
Thomas F. McElroy Papers, Washington State Library
Henry McGill Papers, Washington State Library
John J. McGilvra Papers, University of Washington Library
McMicken Family Papers, University of Washington Library
Fayette McMullin Papers, Washington State Library
_____ Washington State Archives
Miller Family Papers, University of Washington Library
William Winlock Miller Collection, University of Washington Library

William Winlock Miller Letterbook, University of Washington Library
R. H. Milroy Letterbook, University of Washington Library
Marshall Moore Papers, Washington State Archives
Miles C. Moore Autobiography, University of Washington Library
_____ Letterbook, Washington State Library
_____ Papers, Washington State Archives
Eldridge Morse Notebooks, Bancroft Library, University of California, Berkeley
Henry C. Mosely Diary, Washington State Historical Society
Mrs. John B. Moyer, comp., Statistics of the First Federal Census of Washington Territory, 1860, type-
     script, University of Washington Library
Mary Mullany Letters, Oregon Historical Society
John Miller Murphy Papers, Washington State Library
James W. Nesmith Papers, Oregon Historical Society
Robert Newell Diary, Oregon Historical Society
William A. Newell Papers, Washington State Archives
"Nomination" Letters from Collectors of Customs, Port Townsend, Washington, to the Secretary of the
     Treasury, 1865–1910, RG 56, National Archives
Northern Idaho Indian Agency Records, RG 75, Federal Records Center, Seattle
Northern Pacific Coal Company Records, Washington State Historical Society
Northern Pacific Railroad Land Department Western District Records, Washington State Historical
     Society
Northern Pacific Railroad/North Yakima Records, Washington State Historical Society
Northern Pacific Railway Company Papers, Series C, Settlement and Development, Minnesota Histori-
     cal Society
Northern Pacific Railway Company Land Department Records, Minnesota Historical Society
James M. Nosler Diary, University of Washington Library
Oregon and Washington Territorial Papers, House File, Records of the House of Representatives, RG
     233, National Archives
Oregon Improvement Company Records, University of Washington Library
N. H. Owings Papers, University of Washington Library
Pacific Coast Office of Military Roads Records, RG 77, National Archives
Pacific Division Records, U.S. Army Continental Commands, RG 393, National Archives
F. W. Pettygrove Letters, Oregon Historical Society
_____ Reminiscences, Bancroft Library, University of California, Berkeley
E. K. Pendergast Correspondence, Washington State Historical Society
William Pickering Papers, University of Washington Library
_____ Washington State Library
Pierce and Buchanan Administration Appointment Files, National Archives
Portland District Records, U.S. Army Corps of Engineers, RG 77, Federal Records Center, Seattle
Thomas W. Prosch Papers, University of Washington Library
Antonio Rabbeson Reminiscences, Bancroft Library, University of California, Berkeley
Records of the Idaho Superintendency of Indian Affairs, M832, National Archives
Records of the Oregon Superintendency of Indian Affairs, 1845–1873, M2, National Archives
Records of the Topographical Engineers, RG 77, National Archives
Records of the Washington Superintendency of Indian Affairs, 1853–1874, M5, National Archives
Records of the Washington Territory Volunteers, Washington State Library
Records relating to the Appointment of Federal Judges and U.S. Attorneys and Marshals, Washington,
     1853–1902, M198, National Archives
Records relating to the First Northwest Boundary Survey Commission, 1853–1869, National Archives
Simeon G. Reed Papers, Reed College Library
Reports of Inspection of the Field Jurisdictions of the Office of Indian Affairs, 1873–1900, M1070,
     National Archives
Alice Roberts Letters, Eastern Washington State Historical Society
W. Milnor Roberts Papers, Montana State University Library
Henry Roeder Reminiscences, Bancroft Library, University of California, Berkeley
Edward S. Salomon Papers, Washington State Archives

Seattle District Records, U.S. Army Corps of Engineers, RG 77, Federal Records Center, Seattle
Sehome Coal Company Records, Center for Pacific Northwest Studies, Western Washington University
    sity
Eugene Semple Papers, University of Washington Library
_____ Washington State Archives
Wesley Shannon Letters, Oregon Historical Society
John A. Simms Papers, Washington State University Library
Robert J. Skaife Diary, Washington State University Library
John Sprague Letters, Eastern Washington State Historical Society
Watson C. Squire Papers, University of Washington Library
_____ Washington State Archives
Benjamin Stark Papers, Oregon Historical Society
Hazard Stevens Correspondence, Washington State Library
_____ Papers, University of Oregon Library
Isaac I. Stevens Papers, University of Washington Library
_____ Western Americana Collection, Yale University
George Suckley Letters, Western Americana Collection, Yale University
James G. Swan Papers, University of British Columbia Library
Tacoma Land and Improvement Company Papers, Tacoma Public Library
Kate D. Taylor Papers, Oregon Historical Society
Samuel R. Thurston Correspondence, Washington State Library
_____ Papers, Oregon Historical Society
William F. Tolmie Papers, University of Washington Library
William Petit Trowbridge Journal, Washington State Historical Society
Tulalip Indian Agency Records, RG 75, Federal Records Center, Seattle
U.S. Interior Department, Washington Territorial Papers, 1854–1902, National Archives
U.S. State Department Appointment Papers, RG 49, National Archives
_____ Washington Territorial Papers, National Archives
Henry Villard Papers, Houghton Library, Harvard University
Cyrus Walker Letterbooks, Ames Collection, University of Washington Library
William H. Wallace Papers, University of Washington Library
Washington Territory, Documents, Washington State Historical Society
_____ Papers, University of Washington Library
Martin Weld Letters, University of Washington Library
William P. Winans Papers, Washington State University Library
John Wool Papers, New York State Library
Yakima Indian Agency Records, RG 75, Federal Records Center, Seattle
Henry L. Yesler Reminiscences, Bancroft Library, University of California, Berkeley

Selected Published Primary Sources

Atkinson, G. H. "A Winter Trip to the Upper Columbia Basin," *West Shore*, 7(Dec. 1881).
Bagley, Clarence B., ed. "Attitude of the Hudson's Bay Company during the Indian War of 1855–1856,"
    Washington Historical Quarterly, 8(Oct. 1917).
Bischoff, William N., S.J. "The Yakima Campaign of 1856," *Mid-America*, 31(July 1949).
Bowles, Samuel. *Across the Continent: A Summer's Journey to the Rocky Mountains, the Mormons, and the*
    Pacific States, with Speaker Colfax. Springfield: Samuel Bowles & Company, 1866.
"Business Broadside of 1853," *Washington Historical Quarterly*, 20(July 1929).
Clayson, Edward, Sr. *Historical Narratives of Puget Sound: Hoods Canal, 1865–1885.* Seattle: R. L. Davis
    Printing Co., 1911.
Collins, Septima. *A Woman's Trip to Alaska.* New York: Cassell Publishing Company, 1890.
"Defending Puget Sound Against the Northern Indians," *Pacific Northwest Quarterly*, 36(Jan. 1945).
Denny, Arthur A. *Pioneer Days on Puget Sound.* Seattle: C. B. Bagley, Printer, 1888.
Farrar, Victor J., ed. "Diary of Colonel and Mrs. I. N. Ebey," *Washington Historical Quarterly*, 7(Oct.
    1916), 8(April 1918).

Gates, Charles M., ed. *Messages of the Governors of the Territory of Washington to the Legislative Assembly, 1854–1889*. Seattle: University of Washington Press, 1940.

"Grievances of the Nez Perce," *Idaho Yesterdays*, 4(Fall 1960).

H. H. D. "The City of Seattle," *Northwest*, 1(Feb. 1883).

Hancock, Samuel. *The Narrative of Samuel Hancock, 1845–1860*. New York: Robert M. McBride & Company, 1927.

Ingersoll, Ernest. "From the Frazier to the Columbia," *Harper's New Monthly Magazine*, 68(April-May 1884).

Judson, Phoebe Goodell. *A Pioneer's Search for an Ideal Home*. Lincoln: University of Nebraska Press, 1984.

Kip, Lawrence. *Army Life on the Pacific: A Journal of the Expedition Against the Northern Indians*. New York: Redfield, 1859.

Kipling, Rudyard. *From Sea to Sea and Other Sketches*. Garden City: Doubleday, Page & Company, 2 vols., 1925.

Leighton, Caroline C. *Life at Puget Sound*. Boston: Lee and Shepard, 1884.

M. A. R. "An Autumn Ramble in Washington Territory." *Overland Monthly*, 7(Jan. 1886).

Meeker, Ezra. *Washington Territory West of the Cascade Mountains*. Olympia: Transcript Office, 1870.

_____. *Pioneer Reminiscences of Puget Sound*. Seattle: Lowman & Hanford, 1905.

Mercer, A. S. *Washington Territory*. Ithaca: L. C. Childs, 1865.

Miller, Wallace J. *South-western Washington*. Olympia: Pacific Publishing Company, 1890.

Muir, John. *Travels in Alaska*. Boston and New York: Houghton Mifflin Company, 1915.

Murphy, J. "Summer Ramblings in Washington Territory," *Appleton's Journal*, 3(Nov. 1877).

Nordhoff, Charles. *Northern California, Oregon, and the Sandwich Islands*. New York: Harper & Brothers, 1874).

Oates, James Wyatt. "Washington Territory," *Californian*, 1(Feb. 1880).

Oliphant, J. Orin, ed. *The Territory of Washington in 1879, As Described by an Impartial Pen, in the Hand of Francis H. Cook*. Cheney: State Normal School, 1925.

Pettengill, S. B. "The Coeur d'Alene Mines," *West Shore*, 12(Sept. 1886).

_____. "The Puget Sound of To-day," *West Shore*, 13(Jan. 1887).

Prosch, Charles. *Reminiscences of Washington Territory*. Seattle: N.p., 1904).

Reminiscences of James N. Glover. Fairfield: Ye Galleon Press, 1985.

Richardson, Albert D. *Beyond the Mississippi: From the Great River to the Great Ocean*. Hartford: American Publishing Company, 1867.

Scammon, C. M. "Lumbering in Washington Territory," *Overland Monthly*, 5(July 1870).

Smalley, E. V. "Notes of Northwestern Travel," *Northwest*, 1(Aug. 1883).

_____. "A New Mining District," *Northwest*, 4(Jan. 1886).

_____. "The Fertile Palouse Country," *Northwest*, 5(May 1887).

Strahorn, Carrie Adell. *Fifteen Thousand Miles by Stage*. New York: G. P. Putnam's Sons, 1911.

Stuart, Mrs. A. H. H. *Washington Territory: Its Soil, Climate, Productions and General Resources*. Olympia: Washington Standard, 1875.

Swan, James G. *The Northwest Coast, or, Three Years' Residence in Washington Territory*. Seattle: University of Washington Press, 1972.

"Edmund Sylvester's Narrative of the Founding of Olympia," *Pacific Northwest Quarterly*, 36(Oct. 1945).

The Journal of the Washington State Constitutional Convention, 1889, ed. Beverly Paulik Rosenow. Seattle: Book Publishing Company, 1962.

Vassault, F. I. "Lumbering in Washington," *Overland Monthly*, 20(July 1892).

Victor, Mrs. Frances Fuller. *All Over Oregon and Washington*. San Francisco: John H. Carmany & Co., 1872.

"Washington's First Constitution," *Washington Historical Quarterly*, 9(1918), 10(1919).

Wells, H. L. "The Switchback and Tunnel," *West Shore*, 13(Sept. 1887).

Winton, Harry N. M., ed. "The Powder River and John Day Mines; Diary of Winfield Scott Ebey," *Pacific Northwest Quarterly*, 34(Jan. 1943).

Newspapers

Aberdeen Herald
Asotin Spirit
Astoria *Weekly Astorian*
Bellingham *American Reveille*
Chehalis *Lewis County Bee*
Chehalis *Lewis County Nugget*
Cheney *North-West Tribune*
Colfax *Palouse Gazette*
Dalles *Daily Mountaineer*
Dalles Times-Mountaineer
Dalles *Weekly Mountaineer*
Dayton *Columbia Chronicle*
Dayton *News*
Ellensburgh Capital
Ellensburgh *Kittitas Standard*
Kalama Semi-Weekly Beacon
Kelso Courier
LaConner *Puget Sound Mail*
Lewiston *Idaho Signal*
Lewiston *Golden Age*
Lewiston *Nez Perce News*
Lewiston *North-Idaho Radiator*
Lewiston Teller
Medical Lake Press
Montesano *Chehalis Valley Vidette*
Moscow Mirror
Olympia *Columbian*
Olympia *Daily Tribune*
Olympia *Pacific Tribune*
Olympia *Pioneer and Democrat*
Olympia *Puget Sound Weekly Courier*
Olympia *Territorial Republican*
Olympia Transcript
Olympia *Washington Democrat*
Olympia *Washington Pioneer*
Olympia *Washington Standard*
Oregon City *Oregon Spectator*
Oregon City *Oregon Statesman*
Palouse City *Boomerang*
Pendleton *East Oregonian*
Pomeroy *Washington Independent*
Port Townsend *North-West*
Port Townsend *Puget Sound Weekly Argus*

Port Townsend Register
Port Townsend *Weekly Message*
Portland *Oregonian*
Pullman Herald
Ritzville *Adams County Record*
Seattle *Daily Herald*
Seattle *Daily Intelligencer*
Seattle *Gazette*
Seattle *People's Telegram*
Seattle *Post-Intelligencer*
Seattle *Puget Sound Daily*
Seattle *Puget Sound Dispatch*
Seattle *Puget Sound Semi-Weekly*
Seattle *Puget Sound Weekly*
Seattle *Times*
Seattle *Weekly Intelligencer*
Seattle *Weekly Pacific Tribune*
Shelton *Mason County Journal*
Snohomish City *Northern Star*
Spokan Times
Spokane Falls Chronicle
Spokane Falls Review
Sprague Herald
Tacoma Herald
Tacoma News
Tacoma *Weekly Ledger*
Tacoma *Weekly Pacific Tribune*
Umatilla *Columbia Press*
Vancouver *Chronicle*
Vancouver Independent
Vancouver Register
Wallace Free Press
Walla Walla Daily Journal
Walla Walla *Semi-Weekly Journal*
Walla Walla Statesman
Walla Walla Union
Waitsburg *Weekly Times*
Waterville *Big Bend Empire*
Whatcom *Bellingham Bay Mail*
Whatcom Reveille
Yakima Record
Yakima Republic
Yakima Signal

Selected Secondary Sources

Books

Armbruster, Kurt E. *Orphan Road: The Railroad Comes to Seattle, 1853–1911.* Pullman: Washington State University Press, 1999.

Asher, Brad. *Beyond the Reservation: Indians, Settlers, and the Law in Washington Territory, 1853–1889.* Norman: University of Oklahoma Press, 1999.

Bancroft, Hubert Howe. *History of Washington, Idaho, and Montana, 1845–1889.* San Francisco: The History Company, 1890.

Britton, Diane F. *The Iron and Steel Industry in the Far West: Irondale, Washington.* Niwot: University Press of Colorado, 1991.

Bunting, Robert. *The Pacific Raincoast: Environment and Culture in an American Eden, 1778–1900.* Lawrence: University of Kansas Press, 1996.

Burns, Robert Ignatius, S.J. *The Jesuits and the Indian Wars of the Northwest.* New Haven: Yale University Press, 1966.

Clark, Norman H. *The Dry Years: Prohibition and Social Control in Washington.* Seattle: University of Washington Press, rev. ed., 1988.

Cox, Thomas R. *Mills and Markets: A History of the Pacific Coast Lumber Industry to 1900.* Seattle: University of Washington Press, 1974.

Dodds, Gordon B. *The Salmon King of Oregon: R. D. Hume and the Pacific Fisheries.* Chapel Hill: University of North Carolina Press, 1959.

Edwards, G. Thomas. *The Triumph of Tradition: The Emergence of Whitman College, 1859–1924.* Walla Walla: Whitman College, 1992.

Fahey, John. *Inland Empire: D. C. Corbin and Spokane.* Seattle: University of Washington Press, 1965.

_____. *The Ballyhoo Bonanza: Charles Sweeney and the Idaho Mines.* Seattle: University of Washington Press, 1971.

_____. *The Inland Empire: Unfolding Years, 1879–1929.* Seattle: University of Washington Press, 1986.

Ficken, Robert E. *The Forested Land: A History of Lumbering in Western Washington.* Seattle: University of Washington Press, 1987.

_____, and Charles P. LeWarne. *Washington: A Centennial History.* Seattle: University of Washington Press, 1988.

Friday, Chris. *Organizing Asian-American Labor: The Pacific Coast Canned Salmon Industry, 1870–1942.* Philadelphia: Temple University Press, 1994.

Harmon, Alexandra. *Indians in the Making: Ethnic Relations and Indian Identities around Puget Sound.* Berkeley: University of California Press, 1998.

Hendrickson, James E. *Joe Lane of Oregon: Machine Politics and the Sectional Crisis, 1849–1861.* New Haven: Yale University Press, 1967.

Hynding, Alan. *The Public Life of Eugene Semple: Promoter and Politician of the Pacific Northwest.* Seattle: University of Washington Press, 1973.

Jackson, W. Turrentine. *Wagon Roads West: A Study of Federal Road Surveys and Construction in the Trans-Mississippi West, 1846–1869.* New Haven: Yale University Press, 1964.

Johannsen, Robert W. *Frontier Politics and the Sectional Conflict: The Pacific Northwest on the Eve of the Civil War.* Seattle: University of Washington Press, 1955.

Josephy, Alvin M., Jr. *The Nez Perce Indians and the Opening of the Northwest.* New Haven: Yale University Press, 1971.

Lang, William L. *Confederacy of Ambition: William Winlock Miller and the Making of Washington Territory.* Seattle: University of Washington Press, 1996.

Lewty, Peter J. *To the Columbia Gateway: The Oregon Railway and the Northern Pacific, 1879–1884.* Pullman: Washington State University Press, 1987.

_____. *Across the Columbia Plain: Railroad Expansion in the Interior Northwest, 1885–1893.* Pullman: Washington State University Press, 1995.

McClelland, John M., Jr. *Cowlitz Corridor: Historical River Highway of the Pacific Northwest.* Longview: Longview Publishing Company, 1953.

Meinig, D. W. *The Great Columbia Plain: A Historical Geography, 1805–1910.* Seattle: University of Washington Press, 1968.

Mills, Randall V. *Stern-Wheelers Up Columbia: A Century of Steamboating in the Oregon Country.* Palo Alto: Pacific Books, 1947.

Morgan, Murray. *Puget's Sound: A Narrative of Early Tacoma and the Southern Sound.* Seattle: University of Washington Press, 1979.

_____. *Skid Road: An Informal Portrait of Seattle.* Seattle: University of Washington Press, 1982.

Morrissey, Katherine G. *Mental Territories: Mapping the Inland Empire.* Ithaca: Cornell University Press, 1997.

Nesbit, Robert C. *"He Built Seattle": A Biography of Judge Thomas Burke*. Seattle: University of Washington Press, 1961.

Oliphant, J. Orin. *On the Cattle Ranges of the Oregon Country*. Seattle: University of Washington Press, 1968.

Petersen, Keith C. *River of Life, Channel of Death: Fish and Dams on the Lower Snake*. Lewiston: Confluence Press, 1995.

Pomeroy, Earl. *The Territories and the United States, 1861–1890: Studies in Colonial Administration*. Seattle: University of Washington Press, 1969.

Richards, Kent D. *Isaac I. Stevens: Young Man in a Hurry*. Provo: Brigham Young University Press, 1979 [Pullman: WSU Press, 1993].

Robbins, William G. *Landscapes of Promise: The Oregon Story, 1800–1940*. Seattle: University of Washington Press, 1997.

Ruby, Robert H., and John A. Brown. *Half-Sun on the Columbia: A Biography of Chief Moses*. Norman: University of Oklahoma Press, 1965.

_____. *Dreamer-Prophets of the Columbia Plateau: Smohalla and Skolaskin*. Norman: University of Oklahoma Press, 1989.

Schwantes, Carlos A. *Radical Heritage: Labor, Socialism, and Reform in Washington and British Columbia, 1885–1917*. Seattle: University of Washington Press, 1979.

_____. *The Pacific Northwest: An Interpretive History*. Lincoln: University of Nebraska Press, 1989.

_____. *Railroad Signatures across the Pacific Northwest*. Seattle: University of Washington Press, 1993.

_____. *Long Day's Journey: The Steamboat & Stagecoach Era in the Northern West*. Seattle: University of Washington Press, 1999.

Taylor, Joseph E., III. *Making Salmon: An Environmental History of the Northwest Fisheries Crisis*. Seattle: University of Washington Press, 1999.

White, Richard. *Land Use, Environment, and Social Change: The Shaping of Island County, Washington*. Seattle: University of Washington Press, 1980.

_____. *The Organic Machine*. New York: Hill and Wang, 1995.

Winks, Robin. *Frederick Billings: A Life*. New York: Oxford University Press, 1991.

Wunder, John R. *Inferior Courts, Superior Justice: A History of the Justices of the Peace on the North-West Frontier, 1853–1889*. Westport: Greenwood Press, 1979.

Articles and Essays

Berner, Richard C. "The Port Blakely Mill Company, 1876–89," *Pacific Northwest Quarterly*, 57(Oct. 1966).

Brown, Richard Maxwell. "Rainfall and History: Perspectives on the Pacific Northwest," in G. Thomas Edwards and Carlos A Schwantes, eds., *Experiences in a Promised Land: Essays in Pacific Northwest History*. Seattle: University of Washington Press, 1986.

Buchanan, Iva L. "Lumbering and Logging in the Puget Sound Region in Territorial Days," *Pacific Northwest Quarterly*, 28(Jan. 1936).

Cole, Terrence. "The *Other* Washington: The Naming of Northern Oregon," *Columbia*, 8(Fall 1994).

DeLorme, Roland L. "Westward the Bureaucrats: Government Officials on the Washington and Arizona Frontier," *Arizona and the West*, 22(Autumn 1980).

Doig, Ivan. "John J. McGilvra and Timber Trespass: Seeking a Puget Sound Timber Policy, 1861–1865," *Forest History*, 13(Jan. 1970).

Edwards, G. Thomas. "Holding the Far West for the Union: The Army in 1861," *Civil War History*, 14(Dec. 1968).

Finger, John R. "A Study of Frontier Enterprise: Seattle's First Sawmill, 1853–1869," *Forest History*, 15(Jan. 1972).

_____. "The Seattle Spirit, 1851–1893," *Journal of the West*, 13(July 1974).

Gates, Charles M. "Daniel Bagley and the University of Washington Land Grant, 1861–1868," *Pacific Northwest Quarterly*, 52(April 1961).

Johansen, Dorothy O. "The Oregon Steam Navigation Company: An Example of Capitalism on the Frontier," *Pacific Historical Review*, 10(June 1941).

Johnston, Norman J. "The Frederick Law Olmsted Plan for Tacoma," *Pacific Northwest Quarterly*, 66(July 1975).

Karlin, Jules A. "The Anti-Chinese Outbreak in Tacoma, 1885," *Pacific Northwest Quarterly*, 39(April 1948).

Katz, W. A. "*The Columbian*: Washington Territory's First Newspaper," *Oregon Historical Quarterly*, 64(March 1963).

Larson, T. A. "The Woman Suffrage Movement in Washington," *Pacific Northwest Quarterly*, 67(April 1976).

Lokken, Roy. "The Martial Law Controversy in Washington Territory, 1856," *Pacific Northwest Quarterly*, 43(April 1952).

McClelland, John, Jr. "Almost Columbia, Triumphantly Washington," in David H. Stratton, ed., *Washington Comes of Age: The State in the National Experience*. Pullman: Washington State University Press, 1992.

McGregor, Alexander C. "The Economic Impact of the Mullan Road on Walla Walla, 1860–1883," *Pacific Northwest Quarterly*, 65(July 1974).

Nesbit, Robert C., and Charles M. Gates. "Agriculture in Eastern Washington, 1890–1910," *Pacific Northwest Quarterly*, 37(Oct. 1946).

Nolan, Edward W. "'Not without Labor and Expense': The Villard-Northern Pacific Expedition, 1883," *Montana; the Magazine of Western History*, 33(Summer 1983).

Owens, Kenneth N. "Pattern and Structure in Western Territorial Politics," *Western Historical Quarterly*, 1(Oct. 1970).

Richards, Kent D. "A Good Servicable Road: The Cowlitz Columbia River to Puget Sound Connection," *Columbia*, 6(Winter 1992–1993).

Robbins, Roy. "The Federal Land System in an Embryo State," *Pacific Historical Review*, 4(Dec. 1935).

Robbins, William G. "The World of Columbia River Salmon: Nature, Culture, and the Great River of the West," in Joseph Cone and Sandy Ridlington, eds., *The Northwest Salmon Crisis: A Documentary History*. Corvallis: Oregon State University Press, 1996.

Simmons, Robert H. "The Transition of the Washington Executive from Territory to Statehood," *Pacific Northwest Quarterly*, 55(April 1964).

Wells, Merle W. "Politics in the Panhandle: Opposition to the Admission of Washington and North Idaho, 1886–1888," *Pacific Northwest Quarterly*, 46(July 1955).

Yonce, Frederick J. "Lumbering and the Public Timberlands in Washington: The Era of Disposal," *Journal of Forest History*, 20(Jan. 1978).

Dissertations

Buchanan, Iva L. "An Economic History of Kitsap County, Washington, to 1889," Ph.D. diss., University of Washington, 1930.

Hoover, Roy O. "The Public Land Policy of Washington State: The Initial Period, 1889–1912," Ph.D. diss., Washington State University, 1967.

MacDonald, Alexander. "Seattle's Economic Development, 1880–1910," Ph.D. diss., University of Washington, 1959.

Meany, Edmond S., Jr. "The History of the Lumber Industry in the Pacific Northwest to 1917," Ph.D. diss., Harvard University, 1935.

Pohl, Thomas W. "Seattle, 1851–1861: A Frontier Community," Ph.D. diss., University of Washington, 1970.

Steen, Harold K. "Forestry in Washington to 1925," Ph.D. diss., University of Washington, 1969.

Yonce, Frederick J. "Public Land Disposal in Washington," Ph.D. diss., University of Washington, 1969.

Index

8·13·1853. Columbia

Cowlitz Navigation !

THE UNDERSIGNED is prepared, at all times, to transport passengers and freight up and down the Cowlitz river.
The mail canoe leaves the Cowlitz Landing every Thursday morning, at 7 o'clock, for Rainier, and leaves Rainier every Tuesday morning at 6 o'clock for the Landing.
For freight or passage at Monticello or Rainier, apply to Henry Winsor or R. C. Smith.
                                F. A. CLARKE.
Cowlitz Landing, July 2, 1853. 43tf